Understanding Medical Coding:
A Comprehensive Guide

SECOND EDITION

Sandra L. Johnson, CMA, CPC

Connie McHugh, LPN, CPC, CPC-H, PMCC

DELMAR
CENGAGE Learning™

Australia • Brazil • Japan • Korea • Mexico • Singapore • Spain • United Kingdom • United States

DELMAR
CENGAGE Learning

Understanding Medical Coding: A Comprehensive Guide, Second Edition
Sandra Johnson, Connie McHugh

Vice President, Health Care Business Unit: William Brottmiller

Editorial Director: Matthew Kane

Acquisitions Editor: Rhonda Dearborn

Product Manager: Sarah Duncan

Editorial Assistant: Debra Gorgos

Marketing Director: Jennifer McAvey

Marketing Coordinator: Kimberly Duffy

Technology Director: Laurie K. Davis

Technology Project Manager: Mary Colleen Liburdi

Technology Project Coordinator: Carolyn Fox

Production Director: Carolyn Miller

Production Manager: Barbara A. Bullock

Content Project Manager: James Zayicek

For product information and technology assistance, contact us at
Cengage Learning Customer & Sales Support, 1-800-354-9706

For permission to use material from this text or product,
submit all requests online at **www.cengage.com/permissions**
Further permissions questions can be emailed to
permissionrequest@cengage.com

Library of Congress Control Number: 2006003055

ISBN-13: 978-1-4180-1044-7

ISBN-10: 1-4180-1044-8

Delmar
Executive Woods
5 Maxwell Drive
Clifton Park, NY 12065
USA

Cengage Learning is a leading provider of customized learning solutions with office locations around the globe, including Singapore, the United Kingdom, Australia, Mexico, Brazil, and Japan. Locate your local office at **international.cengage.com/region**

Cengage Learning products are represented in Canada by Nelson Education, Ltd.

For your course and learning solutions, visit **delmar.cengage.com**

Visit our corporate website at **www.cengage.com**

Notice to the Reader

Publisher does not warrant or guarantee any of the products described herein or perform any independent analysis in connection with any of the product information contained herein. Publisher does not assume, and expressly disclaims, any obligation to obtain and include information other than that provided to it by the manufacturer. The reader is expressly warned to consider and adopt all safety precautions that might be indicated by the activities described herein and to avoid all potential hazards. By following the instructions contained herein, the reader willingly assumes all risks in connection with such instructions. The publisher makes no representations or warranties of any kind, including but not limited to, the warranties of fitness for particular purpose or merchantability, nor are any such representations implied with respect to the material set forth herein, and the publisher takes no responsibility with respect to such material. The publisher shall not be liable for any special, consequential, or exemplary damages resulting, in whole or part, from the readers' use of, or reliance upon, this material.

Printed in the United States of America
5 6 7 11

Contributors

Sandra Johnson, BS, CMA, CPC
Indiana University Southeast
Lecturer of Biology/Allied Health
New Albany, IN
Chapter 1, Introduction to Coding
Chapter 2, ICD-9-CM and ICD-10-CM
Chapter 6, Anesthesia/General Surgery
Chapter 8, Orthopedics
Chapter 11, Radiology, Pathology, and Laboratory
Chapter 13, Billing and Collections
Chapter 14, Filing the Claim Form

Connie McHugh, LPN, CPC, CPC-H, PMCC
President, Healthcare Consulting Firm
Practice Advisors Corporation
Traverse City, MI
Chapter 3, HCPCS Level II
Chapter 4, Current Procedural Terminology (CPT) Basics
Chapter 5, Evaluation and Management
Chapter 7, Integumentary System
Chapter 9, Cardiology and the Cardiovascular System
Chapter 10, OB/GYN
Chapter 12, Medicine
Chapter 15, Payment for Professional Health Care Services, Auditing, and Appeals

Lynette M. Williamson, MBA, RHIA, CCS, CPC
Program Director, Health Information Technology
Camden County College
Camden, NJ
Chapter 16, Inpatient Coding

Contents

CHAPTER 3   HCPCS LEVEL II   85

CHAPTER 4   CURRENT PROCEDURAL TERMINOLOGY (CPT) BASICS   103

CHAPTER 8   ORTHOPEDICS   245

CHAPTER 9   CARDIOLOGY AND THE CARDIOVASCULAR SYSTEM   273

CHAPTER 10   OB/GYN   331

CHAPTER 11   RADIOLOGY, PATHOLOGY, AND LABORATORY   385

CHAPTER 12   MEDICINE   409

Preface

Understanding Medical Coding, Second Edition is a practical and relevant guide for the modern health care environment. The demand for qualified coders and billers continues to increase within hospitals, physician offices, ambulatory care centers, and specialty clinics. Codes, along with rules and regulations of insurance programs and carriers, change annually, but basic coding principles remain the same—in how to code, submit claim forms, and bill patients. The second edition of *Understanding Medical Coding: A Comprehensive Guide* contains 16 chapters with objectives to broaden knowledge and increase coding skills by the presentation of specific issues with a particular coding specialty.

KEY FEATURES

Understanding Medical Coding, Second Edition provides an overview of CPT and ICD-9-CM coding, and addresses coding issues within specific coding content areas. This edition provides more code-specific information, concentrating on specialties and levels of coding. The book takes you through all steps necessary to code a claim correctly, link the corrrect codes for reimbursement for insurance carriers and government entities, and explains adjustments and how and when to bill patients. It even provides information on what to do if there is a denial or rejection. This is the product of choice for coding competency.

Each chapter contains the following learning aids to challenge learners:

• **Key Terms.** Important terms are listed alphabetically at the beginning of each module. The key term is bolded when introduced within the context with the definition included.

• **Learning Objectives.** Goals are listed at the beginning of each chapter. These objectives address those concepts the learner should understand, and they allow immediate feedback on progress.

• **Practice Exercises.** Exercises utilizing CPT, ICD-9-CM, and HCPCS codes are included to challenge the learner's knowledge and application of the material presented and to facilitate problem solving.

• **Coding Tips.** Each chapter includes advice to help code complex situations unique to medical specialties.

• **Highlights.** Each chapter features Highlights, which focus on the essential skills and information coders will need to excel on the job.

• **HIPAA alert icons.** Important information relating to the Health Insurance Portability and Accountability Act of 1996 are emphasized by a HIPAA icon to help learners become aware of these important regulations

• **Summary.** Each chapter summarizes content covered and highlights main points.

- **Glossary.** Included at the end of the textbook to give a complete listing of all key terms for a quick and handy reference.

NEW TO THE EDITION

The second edition adds user-friendly improvements for learners, with consistent logic and layout, very detailed sections for the beginner to the advanced coder, and new supplemental products. Some new additions include:

- **Chapter 1, Introduction to Coding,** includes career and certification information.
- **Chapter 4, CPT Basics,** is designed with the beginning coder in mind.
- **Chapter 5, Evaluation and Management,** has been expanded into a complete, thorough chapter with very clear guidelines.
- **Chapter 3, HCPCSII, Chapter 12, Medicine,** and **Chapter 16, Inpatient Coding,** are completely new.
- **HIPAA alert icons** throughout all chapters highlight important privacy issues

LEARNING PACKAGE

StudyWARE

StudyWARE is an interactive software packaged with this book! It includes learning activities and quizzes to help learners study key concepts and test comprehension of the information presented in the book. The activity and quiz content correlate to each chapter of the book. The activities included on the StudyWARE are: Flashcards, Concentration, Hangman, Coding Cases, and Championship Game.

Workbook

The workbook helps learners reinforce the essential skills needed to become a successful coder. The workbook corresponds to each chapter of the book, and includes coding problems, review questions, and American Academy of Professional Coders (AAPC) style coding certificate questions.

Workbook ISBN 1-4180-1045-6

Instructor's Manual

The Instructor's Manual is greatly expanded for this edition! It is a teachng tool to help instructors plan a course and implement coding activities. It includes the answers to all exercises in the book and workbook, as well as:

- Sample course outlines for both basic and advanced coding courses
- Suggested grading rubric
- Teaching tips
- ICD-9-CM: Fun Coding exercises
- Cumulative exam with AAPC style certification questions

Instructor's Manual ISBN 1-4180-1046-4

Electronic Classroom Manager

This CD-ROM product provides support in the classroom, to help instructors prepare for class, create lesson plans, and deliver effective presentations.

The Electronic Classroom Manager CD-ROM includes:
- PowerPoint lecture presentations for each chapter
- A computerized test bank
- Championship Coding game
- Crossover grid from the first edition of *Understanding Medical Coding* to the second edition

Electronic Classroom Manager, ISBN 1-4180-1047-2

Web Tutor Advantage

Designed to complement the book, Web Tutor is an online course management tool that takes the course beyond the boundaries of the classroom wall. Web Tutor is available on both the WebCT and Blackboard platforms, and includes great instructor features such as a White Board, Threaded Discussion, and Email. Content specifically tied to the book chapters includes: highlights, objectives, FAQs, quizzes, coding cases, key terms, and web links. A mid term exam and final exam are also included.

Web Tutor Advantage on Blackboard, ISBN 1-4180-1049-9
Web Tutor Advantage on WebCT, ISBN 1-4180-1048-0
Text bundled with Web Tutor Advantage on Blackboard, ISBN 1-4180-4298-6
Text bundled with Web Tutor Advantage on WebCT, ISBN 1-4180-4300-1

ACKNOWLEDGMENTS

The second edition of the book could not have been so greatly improved without the help of many individuals.

The comments and suggestions of the reviewers helped to finalize chapters into text material. All are to be commended for their hard work, diligence, and dedication to this project. Reviewers include:

George Fakhoury, MD, DORCP, CMA
Academic Program Manager-
Healthcare
Heald College, Central
Administrative Office
San Francisco, CA

Marsha Lalley, BSM, MSM
Instructor, Medical Administrative
Assisting
Minneapolis Community and
Technical College
Minneapolis, MN

Paula Murphy, MA
Reimbursement Manager
Ortho Neuro
Westerville, OH

Linda Pretre, RHIA, CCS
Health Information Program Director
Sanford-Brown College
St. Louis, MO

Heather Skow, CPC, CHCT, CCP,
CMBS, RHE
Medical Deptartment Faculty
Member/Chief Compliance Officer
Spencerian College
Louisville, KY

Margaret Stackhouse, CPC, RHIA,
MCSE
Compliance Auditor
Children's Hospital of Pittsburgh and
Children's Community Pediatrics
Adjunct Instructor
Pittsburgh Technical Institute
Pittsburgh, PA

The publishers and authors would like to acknowledge the following educators and practitioners who contributed to the first edition of this textbook:

Gay Boughton-Barnes, CPC, MPC
Coding and Reimbursement Manager
Oklahoma Heart Institute
Tulsa, OK

Kathryn Cianciolo, MA, RRA, CCS,
CCS-P
Consultant
Waukesha, WI

Linda French, CMA-C
Instructor
Simi Adult School and Career
Institute
Simi Valley, CA

Nancy Heldt, CCS
Coding Supervisor
Florida Hospital
Winter Park Tech
Winter Park, FL

Sandra L. Johnson, CMA
Lecturer of Biology/Allied Health
Indiana University Southeast
New Albany, IN

Marie A. Moisio, MA, RRA
Assistant Professor
Northern Michigan University
Marquette, MI

Amy C. Morgan, RRA
Consultant
Asheville, NC

Julie Orloff, RMA, CMA, CPT
Program Coordinator
Medical Assisting/Medical Coding
Specialist
National School of Technology
North Miami Beach, FL

Eugene Richard, RRA, CCS, CCS-P
Vice President
Health Systems Management
Network
Belen, NM

Lois M. Smith, RN, CMA
Department Chair
Medical Assisting and Allied Health
Arapahoe Community College
Littleton, CO

Karen S. Scott, MEd, RRA
Assistant Professor
Health Information Management
University of Tennessee, Memphis
Memphis, TN

Acknowledgments from Author Sandra L. Johnson

Because writing a textbook involves many people, I wish to personally acknowledge some special individuals.

Thanks to Rhonda Dearborn, acquisitions editor, for her continued support in this textbook and its supplemental tools.

Thanks to Sarah Duncan, product manager, whose role included mentoring, cheerleading, and mothering. I really appreciated her guidance and patience.

A special thanks goes to my students. Students are definitely not the only learners in this project. I learn as much from my students as they learn from me. I have been blessed with great students who have made me proud of their accomplishments and achievements in their allied health careers. I wish I could thank each one of you individually, but you know who you are!

Special recognition must be given to my husband, Bruce, for his patience and understanding when the textbook prevailed over him. His support and encouragement kept me going when my plate got too full.

Sandra Johnson

Acknowledgments from Author Connie McHugh

As I tackle projects, it never ceases to amaze me of the loving family support from my daughters, grand-daughters (including twin baby girls), phenomenal parents and sisters. Allocating precious time becomes an ever increasing challenge in my life, often stealing from those that I love the most.

There are those long-term friends always willing to listen when I simply had to bounce an idea or obtain an opinion, a much needed moment to relax or the occasional nudge into action. Donna DeSoto, Katharine Mikula, CPC, and Susie Mann are friends that are consistently supportive. Louis Zako, M.D., a true friend of mine for many years, has been an inspiration for me with his extensive experience in the healthcare business, his leadership and fantastic command of the English language.

Two fine coders assisted by reviewing and offering their recommendations, in the most expeditious of timetables are Bea Olsen, CPC and Linda Farrington, CPC. I can't thank you enough for evaluating specific details.

Without the Rhonda Dearborn, Sara Prime and the copyeditors at Carlisle Publishing, this project never would have been completed. Thank you for the opportunity, and every guidance toward accuracy, with the many consoling words.

I encourage each medical coding student to learn constantly. Each day I truly learn something new and remain open to interpretations, backed by research and data. I love coding education and encourage others to enter into this unique profession.

Connie McHugh

About the Authors

Sandra L. Johnson, CMA, CPC, has worked twenty-five years in the health care field, with nineteen years teaching experience in medical assisting, medical coding, and transcription courses. She is an active member of the American Association of Medical Assistants and the American Academy of Professional Coders. She was awarded the Indiana Medical Assistant of the year in 1993, has been a multiple nominee for Who's Who Among America's Teachers, and the recipient of the Glenn W. Sample Award for Instructional Excellence 1996 and 2004 from Ivy Tech State College. She is a coding and transcription instructor at Indiana University Southeast, and is pursuing a master's degree in Human Resource Development with a specialization in health and safety management from Indiana State University.

Connie McHugh, LPN, CPC, CPC-H, PMCC, first began coding in 1986, manages Coding Hotlines and has been teaching coding nationally since 1991. Her extensive healthcare background includes clinical experiences of ICU/CCU, to Hospital Administration, founded a healthcare consulting firm and has served on board of directors for various organizations including American Academy Professional Coders and Arizona Medical Group Management Association. She is currently the Associate Vice President for Membership and Accreditation for the Arizona Medical Association.

With her vast knowledge, she continues to instruct coding frequently encouraging students to request examples during the sessions. This style enhances training and provides specific examples. She has presented to thousands of students from physicians to those entering the field while successfully preparing many to sit for their national certification examinations.

Chapter 1
Introduction to Coding

LEARNING OBJECTIVES

Upon successful completion of this chapter, you should be able to:

1. Define coding and its purpose in health care.
2. Differentiate between insurance abuse and insurance fraud and list examples of each.
3. Recognize professional associations and credentials offered by each.
4. Identify the legal implications and ramifications of incorrect coding and the rules to follow for compliance and protection.
5. Name the resources available for coders.
6. List the types of codes used in health care and define each one.

INTRODUCTION

Coding is defined as the translation of diagnoses, procedures, services, and supplies into numeric and/or alphanumeric components for statistical reporting and reimbursement purposes. Coding occurs when a medical term is cross-referenced into a three-, four-, or five-digit alphanumeric or numeric code. Coders abstract information from a patient record to assign the correct code(s).

Knowledge of medical terminology is required to describe accurately the patient's reason for the encounter, which is the diagnosis, symptom, or complaint. Specific terms are also required to describe accurately surgical procedures, diagnostic tests, and medical services provided to the patient. With the passage of the Medicare Catastrophic Coverage Act of 1988, the Health Care Financing Administration (HCFA), now the **Centers for Medicare & Medicaid Services (CMS),** mandated the use of ICD-9-CM codes to report diagnoses and the treatment and HCPCS codes for services and supplies provided relative to those diagnoses.

Centers for Medicare & Medicaid Services (CMS)
An administrative agency within the Department of Health and Human Services (DHHS) that oversees Medicare, Medicaid, and other government programs. Formerly known as the Health Care Financing Administration (HCFA).

A CAREER AS A MEDICAL CODER

The term "coder" actually describes many aspects of the coding/insurance specialist:

- Billers and/or coders who are employed in physician practices, immediate or urgent care centers, and other ambulatory providers of medical care.
- Coders in Health Information Administration departments of hospitals and skilled nursing facilities.
- Claims processors for government agencies and commercial insurance carriers.
- Educators in coding and insurance programs of allied health and vocational schools, community colleges, and universities.
- Self-employed consultants who work with medical practices assisting with billing, coding, auditing, and compliance issues.
- Writers and editors of informational and continuing education articles in professional journals and newsletters, and medical billing and insurance coding textbooks.

The U.S. Department of Labor, Bureau of Labor Statistics projects careers in health insurance areas as noted in the previous list will increase through the year 2012.

WHAT SKILLS ARE REQUIRED IN MEDICAL CODING?

While many medical coders have been trained on-the-job, formal training provided by allied health/vocational schools, community colleges, and universities is necessary. Such courses as medical terminology, anatomy and physiology, and basic coding as well as advanced instruction to include both the inpatient and outpatient coding essentials provide a good background for employment opportunities and the education necessary for certification. A certificate or degree in medical coding offered by educational institutions prepares an individual for both certification and employment.

Computer skills are required for electronic claims processing and electronic data interchange (EDI) to share information between the provider and the insurance carrier. Internet knowledge is needed to explore the numerous web sites available to coders. Professional organizations, insurance companies, and government agencies such as Medicare and Medicaid, provide professional journals, newsletters, and bulletins via the Internet. Professional organizations also offer continuing education opportunities to their members online. Coding tools are available and listed later in this chapter.

A credential in coding is recommended, and required by many health care facilities, as certification provides validation of the knowledge and skills necessary to earn respect and recognition in the profession. Recertification is required to maintain the credential and certification status by meeting continuing education requirements established by each association. Membership in a professional association is a benefit to a coder. Publications such as journals and newsletters as well as web sites for members-only provide continuing education, networking with other coding professionals, and employment and professional development opportunities.

The **American Academy of Professional Coders (AAPC)** is an organization with national certification in four areas:

American Academy of Professional Coders (AAPC) The professional association for medical coders providing ongoing education, certification, networking and recognition, with certifications for coders in physicians' offices and hospital outpatient facilities.

- Certified Professional Coder Apprentice—CPC-A. This certification allows applicants who have not met the medical experience requirement in the outpatient setting the opportunity to become certified.

- Certified Professional Coder—CPC. This certification is for coders with work experience and for the CPC-A who meet this requirement.
- Certified Professional Coder—CPC-H. This certification is for hospital-based coders.
- Certified Professional Coder Apprentice—CPC-HA. This certification allows hospital-based coders to become certified while working in coding to gain the experience required for the CPC-H credential.

The AAPC can be contacted at www.aapc.com or at 800-626-8699.

American Health Information Management Association (AHIMA)
One of the four cooperating parties for ICD-9-CM. Professional association for over 38,000 Health Information Management Professionals throughout the country.

The **American Health Information Management Association (AHIMA)** provides certification in three areas for health information management professionals:

- Certified Coding Associate—CCA. This is certification for entry-level coders.
- Certified Coding Specialist—CCS. This is a certification based on ICD-9-CM and CPT surgical coding performed in the hospital setting.
- Certified Coding Specialist/Physician Based—CCS-P. This is certification for coders based on ICD-9-CM, multispecialty CPT coding, and HCPCS for physician practices.

The AHIMA can be contacted at www.ahima.org or 312-233-1100.

Board of Advanced Medical Coding (BAMC)
An organization of coders, clinicians, and compliance professionals dedicated to the evaluation, recognition, and career advancement of professional medical coders within physician practices, facility and post-acute settings.

The **Board of Advanced Medical Coding (BAMC)** provides specialty certification in the following areas:

- Anesthesia/Pain Management
- Cardiology
- Dermatology
- Facility Outpatient/Ambulatory Surgical Center
- Family Practice/Pediatrics
- Gastroenterology
- General Surgery
- Obstetrics/Gynecology
- Ophthalmology
- Orthopedics
- Radiology
- Urology

The BAMC can be contacted at www.advancedmedicalcoding.com or 800-897-4509.

EXERCISE 1–1

Visit the web site for the American Academy for Professional Coders www.aapc.com. Click on the Certification tab to read about the credentials available to coders in physician practices or other outpatient areas. Click on the Education tab to learn more about continuing education and recertification. Search the site for AAPC chapters in your state and local area, and workshops and seminars offered for recertification.

WHAT IS FRAUD AND ABUSE?

Health Insurance Portability and Accountability Act (HIPAA)
Mandates regulations that govern privacy, security, and electronic transactions standards for health care information.

To accurately assign codes, there must be an understanding of fraud and abuse and the rules of confidentiality. The **Health Insurance Portability and Accountability Act (HIPAA)** of 1996 defines **insurance fraud** as "knowingly and willfully executing, or attempting to execute, a scheme or artifact: 1) to defraud any health-care benefit program; or, 2) to obtain, by false or fraudulent pretenses, representing, or promising, any of the money or property owned by or under the custody or control of a health care benefit program." Statistics compiled by the **Health Insurance Association of America (HIAA)** identify the following major categories of health care fraud:

insurance fraud
Intentional, deliberate misrepresentation of information for profit or to gain some unfair or dishonest advantage.

- Misrepresented diagnosis—43%
- Billing for services not performed—34%
- Waiver of patient deductibles—21%
- Other—2%

Health Insurance Association of America (HIAA)
An agency providing statistics and resources for public health information which includes diseases, pregnancies, aging, and mortality.

Some examples of fraudulent activities are: Lying

- Upcoding to a higher level of service to increase revenue.
- Submitting claims for services not medically necessary.
- Kickbacks or receiving rebates or any type of compensation for referrals.
- Misrepresenting a diagnosis to justify payment.
- Unbundling or billing separately for laboratory tests performed together in order to receive higher reimbursement.
- Billing Medicare patients a higher fee than non-Medicare patients.
- Billing for services, equipment, supplies, or procedures that were never provided.

insurance abuse
Inconsistent activities considered unacceptable business practice.

Insurance abuse is not to be confused with fraud. Insurance abuse is defined as activities that are inconsistent with accepted business practices. Some examples of abuse are:

- overcharging for services, equipment, or procedures.
- violating participating provider agreements with insurance companies, such as routinely not collecting co-pays or unnecessary referrals to other providers. In some instances, routinely waiving a patient's co-pay could be considered a fraudulent activity as it is a violation of the insurance contract.
- improper billing practices.

While fraud must be proven in a court of law as an intentional, deliberate act, coders and physicians must pay scrupulous attention to details when documenting medical information, coding, and submitting claims. Medical records documentation must be complete, legible, and accurate to appropriately assign Evaluation and Management codes; diagnosis codes must be correctly linked to the CPT codes to provide medical necessity for the service or procedure provided. If an abusive practice is ignored or continued without correction, an investigation as a potential fraudulent act could occur.

 The Health Insurance Portability and Accountability Act of 1996 establishes a formal link between government programs and the private insurance companies in an effort to provide recognition and penalties for submission of fraudulent claims. Penalties include a $10,000 fine per claim form when an individual knowingly and willfully misrepresents information submitted to result in greater payment or benefits, plus three times the fraudulent claim amount.

There are also civil penalties for fraudulent claims and coding errors contained in the **Omnibus Budget Reconciliation Act (OBRA)** of 1987. OBRA penalizes the health-care provider for errors made by coders in the amount of $2,000 fine per violation (a single coding error), an assessment in lieu of damages of up to twice the amount of the error submitted on the claim, and exclusion from Medicare and Medicaid programs for up to five years.

To avoid legal implications and ramifications, follow these rules:

- Keep current with coding and billing practices. Purchase new code books annually. Update encounter forms, charge tickets, and computer programs yearly as well.

- Know and understand coding rules and use them correctly.

- Code only what is documented in the medical record. If there is a question or confusion, ask for clarification.

- Respond to Explanation of Benefits (EOBs) and other correspondence from insurance companies. Failure to do so can be considered "reckless disregard."

- Develop and follow a coding compliance program. This includes educating everyone in the practice of the importance of billing and coding policies, and these policies should be in a written format. The compliance plan should include provider credentialing, documentation standards for medical records, and training and education, as well as continuing education and professional development. A compliance officer or officers should be appointed to identify any noncompliant issues and make the necessary corrections. An internal audit system ensures that precertification authorizations have been completed and documented, and that codes assigned to procedures and services are relevant to the documentation in the medical record to provide medical necessity.

TOOLS OF THE TRADE

When it comes to coding and billing, the proper tools are essential for optimal reimbursement. Be sure the following resources are available in the workplace:

- current ICD-9-CM manual (issued every October)
- current CPT manual (issued every January)
- current HCPCS manual (issued every January)
- medical dictionary, including supplemental resources for medical abbreviations and acronyms
- carrier bulletins, newsletters, and Web sites

Recommended Resources for Coders

American Academy for Professional Coders—www.aapc.com
American Health Information Management Association—www.ahima.org
Board of Advanced Medical Coding—www.advancedmedicalcoding.com
Code Correct—www.codecorrect.com
CPT Assistant—A monthly newsletter published by the American Medical Association (AMA), available by calling the AMA's Unified Service Center at 800-621-8335.
Decision Coder—www.decisionhealth.com
Medicare Part B News—www.partbnews.com
National Correct Coding Initiative—www.cms.hhs.gov/physicians/cciedits

EXERCISE 1–2

Visit the web site for the American Health Information Management Association (AHIMA) at www.ahima.org. Click on About AHIMA to learn about the health information management profession, credentialing, and certification. Click on the HIM Resources to read more about ICD-10-CM.

TYPES OF CODING

Healthcare Common Procedure Coding System (HCPCS)
Coding system that consists of CPT and national codes (level II), used to identify procedures, supplies, medications (except vaccines), and equipment.

In 1983, Medicare created the **Healthcare Common Procedure Coding System (HCPCS)** (pronounced "hick picks"). HCPCS codes are required when reporting services and procedures provided to Medicare and Medicaid beneficiaries. HCPCS is a three-level coding system:

Level I—CPT
Level II—National Codes
Level III—Local Codes—Deleted 12/31/03

ICD 9-CM Volume I & II
ICD 9-CM Volume III

Level I—CPT Codes

Physicians' Current Procedural Terminology (CPT)
Numeric codes and descriptors for services and procedures performed by providers, published by the American Medical Association.

Used in all facilities

The **Physicians' Current Procedural Terminology (CPT),** published by the American Medical Association, is a listing of descriptive terms with codes for reporting medical services and procedures performed by health care providers. CPT provides uniformity in accurately describing medical, surgical, and diagnostic services for effective communication among physicians, patients, and third-party payers. CPT was introduced in 1966, and has undergone editing and modification to the current revision. The greatest change in CPT, having a major impact on coders, occurred in 1992 when "evaluation and management" services were created. This CPT section requires practitioners to make a decision as to level of service for offices, hospitals, nursing home services, etc.

Because CPT codes are updated annually, Appendix B of the CPT book summarizes the changes since the previous edition, including additions and deletions essential for updating computer programs and/or encounter forms used in the facility.

The CPT Manual is referred to today as a volume reflecting the year of publication (for example, CPT-2005.) This textbook will refer to this procedural coding manual as CPT.

Modifiers

Appendix A of the CPT book contains a complete list of modifiers. A modifier is a two-digit code added to the main CPT code indicating the procedure has been altered by a specific circumstance.

CPT example: Procedure: Biopsy of right breast, needle core
CPT code: 19100

The code 19100 indicates a unilateral procedure. To indicate a bilateral procedure, the modifier -50 would be added to the CPT code. Example: 19100-50.

Level II—National Codes (referred to as HCPCS)

[handwritten margin note: Durable medical equipment, Ambulance Services, Supplies/medication, Blue Cross Blue Shield Codes]

Level II consists of alphanumeric "national codes" supplied by the federal government. These codes supplement CPT codes enabling providers to report non-physician services such as durable medical equipment, ambulance services, supplies and medications, particularly injectable drugs. When billing Medicare and Medicaid for supplies and medications, avoid using CPT code 99070 (supplies and materials provided by the physician over and above those usually included with the office visit or other services). Level II codes list supplies and medications, especially injectable drugs, in more detail.

Examples of Level II codes:
Injection, dimenhydrinate, up to 50 mg J1240
Elastic bandage (Ace) A4460

Modifiers

Level II also contains modifiers that are either alphanumeric or letters that can be used with all levels of HCPCS codes.

EXAMPLES:

-LT—used to identify procedures performed on the left side of the body

-RR—used to identify durable medical equipment to be rented

A listing of HCPCS Level II codes is available for purchase as an individual publication updated annually.

Level III—Local Codes

Level III codes called "local codes" were deleted 12/31/03 under HIPAA regulations. Many local code concepts were moved to Level II.

EXERCISE 1–3

Visit the Medicare Part B web site at www.partbnews.com. This site provides a free List-serv™ to receive e-mail updates and allow access to related articles about reimbursement, coding, and current information relating to Medicare for both providers and beneficiaries.

ICD-9-CM Codes

International Classification of Diseases, 9th Revision, Clinical Modification (ICD-9-CM)
Coding system used to report diagnoses, diseases, and symptoms and reason for encounters for insurance claims.

The **International Classification of Diseases, 9th Revision, Clinical Modification (ICD-9-CM)** is a modification of ICD-9, which was created by the World Health Organization (WHO) based in Geneva, Switzerland. Since 1979, ICD-9-CM has provided a diagnostic coding system for the compilation and reporting of morbidity and mortality statistics for reimbursement purposes in the United States. It allows for the reporting of conditions, injuries, and traumas along with complications and circumstances occurring with the illness or injury. It also provides the reason for patient care.

The ICD-9-CM contains three volumes. All health care facilities utilize Volume 1 (Tabular List of Diseases) and Volume 2 (Alphabetic Index to Diseases) to report diagnoses. Hospitals use Volume 3 to report inpatient procedures (CPT is used to report procedures performed in physician offices, ambulatory care centers, and hospital outpatient departments).

ICD-9-CM requires assignment of the most specific code to represent the problem being treated by the provider. This means the primary diagnosis should be the one for the condition indicated within the medical record as the primary reason the patient sought medical care in an outpatient or office setting, or the principal diagnosis in an inpatient setting.

ICD-9-CM serves three major functions for insurance purposes:

1. It justifies procedures and services rendered by the physician.
2. It assists in establishing medical necessity for services and procedures performed by the physician.
3. It serves as an indicator in measuring the quality of health care delivered by the physician provider.

ICD-10-CM

ICD-10-CM is still being modified for implementation in the near future. While changes and training will be necessary, the basic guidelines will remain the same as ICD-9-CM. Anatomy is the foundation for ICD-10-CM, and criteria to select and assign a diagnostic code will be based on etiology, site, or morphology.

The format will remain in three volumes:

> Volume 1—Tabular List
> Volume 2—Instruction Manual
> Volume 3—Alphabetic List

ICD-10-PCS will replace Volume 3 of the current ICD-9-CM publication.

The greatest difference between ICD-9-CM and ICD-10-CM is the revised codes are alphanumeric with more detailed descriptions.

Early planning is the key element for a smooth transition to ICD-10-CM. Cost will be a key player in the implementation as technology changes will need to be made. Also, there must be a plan on how business will be conducted during the transition phase. Chapter 2 will discuss format and implementation of ICD-10-CM.

SUMMARY

The ultimate goal in coding is to present a clear picture of medical procedures and services performed (CPT codes), linking the diagnosis, symptom, complaint, or condition (ICD-9-CM codes), thus establishing the medical necessity required for third-party reimbursement.

Continuing education is a must for medical billers and coders. Staying current and up to date on all billing and coding regulations is mandatory.

One example is CMS's enforcement of Evaluation and Management Documentation Guidelines, developed jointly by CMS and the American Medical Association (AMA). These guidelines clearly outline documentation required in a patient's medical record for the CPT code submitted on the claim form, giving requirements for specific levels of service. The goal is to provide consistency and uniformity in medical record documentation for evaluation and management services. Many delays have occurred as the AMA and CMS continue to review and test the new guidelines. Billers and coders must keep abreast of these changes for final approval of these guidelines and their enforcement.

As we move closer to replacing ICD-9-CM with ICD-10-CM, coders well-versed in ICD-9-CM will find the transition to ICD-10-CM relatively straightforward as the format and many of the coding conventions remain the same. Training will be conducted for all persons involved in the coding and billing process. Chapter 2 of this text presents an overview of ICD-10.

REFERENCES

American Academy for Professional Coders (AAPC). www.aapc.com.

American Health Information Management Association (AHIMA). www.ahima.org.

Board of Advanced Medical Coding (BAMC) www.advancedmedicalcoding.com.

Fordney, M., & French, L. (2003). *Medical insurance billing and coding: an essentials worktext.* Philadelphia: Elsevier.

Green, M., & Rowell, J. (2006). *Understanding health insurance: A guide to professional billing and reimbursement* (8th ed.). Clifton Park, NY: Thomson Delmar Learning.

Chapter 2
ICD-9-CM

KEY TERMS

alphabetic index
American Hospital Association (AHA)
category
cooperating parties
DRG
eponym
etiology

ICD-10-CM
ICD-10-PCS
main term
National Center for Health
   Statistics (NCHS)
primary (first) diagnosis
principal diagnosis

sequencing
subcategory
subclassification
tabular list
transient

All Official Coding Guidelines listed in this chapter are reprinted from Coding Clinic for ICD-9-CM with permission from the American Hospital Association.

LEARNING OBJECTIVES

Upon successful completion of this chapter, you should be able to:

1. Follow ICD-9-CM rules and regulations and code accurately.
2. Utilize *Coding Clinic for ICD-9-CM* and other resources appropriately.
3. Identify the correct principal and primary diagnoses.
4. Select instances in which V codes and E codes are appropriate and assign the correct codes in those circumstances.
5. Utilize resources including books, the Internet, and available organizations to increase coding accuracy.
6. Describe the ICD-10-CM coding system.

INTRODUCTION

The best way to use this chapter is to have the ICD-9-CM code book out while reviewing the material. Work through the examples as the information is discussed to have a thorough understanding of the material as it is presented.

X is used in this chapter to show that varying fourth and fifth digits may be used, depending on the specific diagnosis. For example, 250.XX shows that the diabetes category of 250 is used with appropriate fourth and fifth digits to further identify the type (fourth digit) and manifestations (fifth digit) of the disease.

HISTORY AND USAGE OF ICD-9-CM

ICD-9-CM stands for *International Classification of Diseases, Ninth Revision, Clinical Modification.* It is used for coding and classifying diagnoses and procedures by a numerical system. Classifying diseases by their cause has been done in various forms for many years, even as far back as the Greek civilization.

The ICD system has been around for many years and as the "ninth revision" implies, it has been updated many times to reflect changes in medicine. The ICD-9 classification was developed and is updated by the World Health Organization (WHO). It was modified by the United States in the 1970s to provide greater specificity for use in classifying both diseases and procedures for hospital and physician usage. This modification is called ICD-9-CM.

ICD-9-CM was not developed for use as a reimbursement system, even though it is now the basis for hospital reimbursement within the **DRG** system. It was designed for statistical collection. It is a classification system, which means diagnoses and procedures are grouped together into various classes.

The ICD-9-CM code book is updated every year with changes effective October 1 of that year. It is essential that code books and coding software be updated yearly with the revisions. Many code books come in a loose-leaf version with updates provided at an extra charge.

DRG
Diagnosis Related Groups, method of prospective payment used by Medicare and other third-party payers for hospital inpatients.

The Cooperating Parties

cooperating parties
Four agencies who share responsibility for maintaining and updating ICD-9-CM.

There are four agencies known as the **cooperating parties** that have the responsibility for maintaining and updating ICD-9-CM. These are the **American Hospital Association (AHA),** the **National Center for Health Statistics (NCHS),** the Centers for Medicare & Medicaid Services (CMS) and the American Health Information Management Association (AHIMA). Each agency has varying responsibilities as shown in Table 2–1.

The ICD-9-CM Coordination and Maintenance Committee, made up of various federal ICD-9-CM users, serves as an advisory committee to the cooperating parties.

American Hospital Association (AHA)
American Hospital Association, one of the four cooperating parties for ICD-9-CM.

National Center for Health Statistics (NCHS)
National Center for Health Statistics, one of the four cooperating parties for ICD-9-CM.

Coding Clinic for ICD-9-CM

The *Coding Clinic for ICD-9-CM* is a quarterly publication published by the AHA. It is considered to be the official publication for ICD-9-CM coding guidelines and advice from the four cooperating parties. The advice given is to be followed by coders in all settings, including physician office, clinic, outpatient, and hospital inpatient coding. Coders should regularly review this publication for information regarding ICD-9-CM coding. Many publishers have included references to specific official coding guidelines in their coding publications. Several sections of this module include guidelines reprinted from *Coding Clinic* to further illustrate concepts.

Sequencing Diagnosis Codes

sequencing
Arranging codes in the proper order according to the definitions of principal or primary diagnosis.

Several of the official coding guidelines in this module refer to sequencing guidelines. **Sequencing** refers to the selection of the appropriate first diagnosis for the

TABLE 2–1	Responsibilities of the Cooperating Parties for ICD-9-CM.
NCHS	Maintains and updates the diagnosis portion of ICD-9-CM
CMS	Maintains and updates the procedure portion (Volume 3)
AHA	Maintains the Central Office on ICD-9-CM to answer questions from coders and produces the *Coding Clinic for ICD-9-CM,* the official guidelines for ICD-9-CM usage
AHIMA	Provides training and certification for coding professionals

patient's encounter. In the hospital inpatient setting, this is known as the **principal diagnosis.** The principal diagnosis is the condition, after study, that brought the patient to the hospital for care. For example, if after the patient was admitted for chest pain it was found that the chest pain was caused by an acute myocardial infarction, the infarction would be the principal diagnosis.

In the outpatient or physician's office setting, the first diagnosis is known as the **first-listed diagnosis (primary).** It is the main reason that caused the patient to seek treatment for that visit. This may be a symptom such as vomiting, chronic illness, or acute disease, such as gastroenteritis or laceration.

principal diagnosis
The reason, after study, which caused the patient to be admitted to the hospital.

first-listed diagnosis
In the outpatient setting, the primary diagnosis is the main reason for the visit. It is usually the diagnosis taking the majority of resources for the visit.

HOW TO LOOK UP A TERM

ICD-9-CM consists of three volumes: Volume One includes a tabular numerical listing of diagnosis codes, Volume Two contains the alphabetic listing of diagnoses, and Volume Three includes a tabular and alphabetic listing of procedures primarily used in the hospital patient setting. The first step in coding is to locate the diagnostic term in the alphabetic index in Volume Two of ICD-9-CM. It is the Alphabetic Index to Disease and Injuries.

Step One: Locating the Main Term

The first step to looking up a term in the ICD-9-CM book is to look in the alphabetic index of Volume Two under the **main term.** The main term is printed in bold type at the left margin, and is the main "thing" (disease, injury, etc.) wrong with the patient. Examples of main terms are fracture, pneumonia, disease, injury, and enlarged. Anatomic terms such as kidney, shoulder, etc., are *never* main terms in ICD-9-CM. If a coder tries to look up a code by the anatomic site, an instructional note to "See condition" will be found. This means the coder should look up the main condition that is wrong with the patient. This does not mean to look under the main term "condition." For example, if the patient comes to the physician's office for a sore throat, and the coder looked up the term "throat," there is a note that says *see condition.* (The throat is not what is wrong with the patient; the soreness is the main thing wrong, or the main condition.) The coder should look under the main term of *sore* to get a code of 462.

The **alphabetic index** is cross-referenced extremely well to allow the coder to locate the correct code using several different terms. For example, the diagnosis "Congestive heart failure" can be found under the main term "failure" as well as "congestive". By looking up this diagnosis either way, the coder is led to the correct code of 428.0.

main term
The patient's illness or disease. In ICD-9-CM the main term is the primary way to locate the disease in the alphabetic index. Main terms are printed in boldface type, even with the left margin on each page.

alphabetic index
Volume 2 of ICD-9-CM, the alphabetic listing of diagnoses.

EXERCISE 2–1

Underline the main term in each example.

1. Senile cataract

2. Carcinoma of the breast

3. Mitral valve prolapse

4. Urinary cystitis

5. Hypertensive cardiovascular disease
   OR

6. Sudden infant death syndrome

7. Nontoxic thyroid goiter

8. Sickle cell anemia

9. Acute situational depression

10. Upper respiratory tract infection

11. Sore throat

12. Migraine headache

13. Chronic lower back pain

14. Rectal mass

15. Left ureteral calculus

Step 2: Identify Subterms

etiology
Cause of the disease or illness.

Below the main terms are indented subterms that further describe the condition. They may describe different sites of the illness, **etiology** (cause), or type of illness. Look in your ICD-9-CM book for the following main term in the alphabetic index.

> **Bronchiolitis** (acute) (infectious) (subacute) 466.19
> with influenza, flu, or grippe 487.1
> chemical 506.0

In the above example, Bronchiolitis was the main term. "With" and "chemical" are indented equally under the main term, so both are considered subterms. "Influenza, flu, or grippe" are subterms under the subterm "with" only. When a main term is located with many subterms, the coder may need to use a ruler to ensure correct usage.

 *Highlight*

eponym
A disease, disorder, or procedure named after the person who researched, identified, or developed a particular procedure, disease, or disorder.

Eponyms are diseases, disorders, and procedures named after the person who researched, identified, or developed a particular procedure, disease, or disorder. In addition to locating the code under the main term, it can also be located by the name. For example, Bell's palsy can be located under both "Bell" and "palsy."

Carryover Lines

Carryover lines are lines indented two more spaces further than subterms and are used to show the relationship between the information on both lines. They are used when there is too much information to fit on one line in the code book. For example:

> **Hypoplasia**
> leg (*see also* Absence, limb, congenital,
>   lower) 755.30

In this case, the note in parentheses should be read as "(*see also* Absence, limb, congenital, lower)."

Nonessential Modifiers

Nonessential modifiers are terms in parentheses following main terms. These are modifiers or terms describing the main term whose presence or absence in the diagnostic statement does not change the code assignment. For example:

> **Intussusception** (colon) (enteric) (intestine)
>   (rectum) 560.0
>   appendix 543.9

Intussusception is the main term. "Colon," "enteric," "intestine," and "rectum" are nonessential modifiers. So if the coder's diagnostic statement said Intussusception only and did not mention the colon, the coder is still correct in using the 560.0 code.

Step 3
Verify codes in tabular and assign 4ᵗʰ/5ᵗʰ digits if required.

TABULAR LIST

tabular list
Volume One of ICD-9-CM is a tabular listing (numerical order) of diseases.

Volume One, the "Classification of Diseases and Injuries," is the **tabular listing** of diagnoses. Once a coder has identified a code in the alphabetic index, it must be verified in the tabular list. In the tabular list, codes are arranged numerically in 17 chapters and are grouped according to their cause (etiology), such as fractures, or body system, such as digestive system.

Chapter Title	Code Categories
1. Infectious and Parasitic Diseases	001–139
2. Neoplasms	140–239
3. Endocrine, Nutritional, and Metabolic Diseases and Immunity Disorders	240–279
4. Diseases of the Blood and Blood-Forming Organs	280–289
5. Mental Disorders	290–319
6. Diseases of the Nervous System and Sense Organs	320–389
7. Diseases of the Circulatory System	390–459
8. Diseases of the Respiratory System	460–519
9. Diseases of the Digestive System	520–579
10. Diseases of the Genitourinary System	580–629
11. Complications of Pregnancy, Childbirth, and the Puerperium	630–679
12. Diseases of the Skin and Subcutaneous Tissue	680–709
13. Diseases of the Musculoskeletal System and Connective Tissue	710–739
14. Congenital Anomalies	740–759
15. Certain Conditions Originating in the Perinatal Period	760–779
16. Symptoms, Signs, and Ill-Defined Conditions	780–799
17. Injury and Poisoning	800–999

V CODES AND E CODES

Besides the numerical listing of diseases in the tabular list, three alphanumeric classifications are included in ICD-9-CM. These are V codes, E codes and M codes.

V Codes

V codes can be used to describe the main reason for the patient's visit in cases where the patient is not "sick," or used as a secondary diagnosis to provide further information about the patient's medical condition. One example would be a patient who is not sick and comes in to receive a TB skin test. There is a V code, V74.1, Screening for pulmonary tuberculosis, that is used if a diagnosis is not identified for the patient.

V 70.0   Routine physical

V 72.31   Routine OBGYN

V 54.11   Fracture aftercare

V 45.4   Surgical Status

S/P = Status post

E Codes

E codes are external causes of injury and poisoning. While E codes are optional by some carriers, many state statutes require the assignment of an E code to a claim form. E codes are used as secondary diagnoses to show the cause of injury, such as a fall or automobile accident, if it is known. An example of an injury E code is E828.2, Accident involving animal being ridden, rider of animal. E codes will be covered in more detail later in this chapter.

category
Categories are three-digit representations of a single disease or group of similar conditions, such as category 250, Diabetes Mellitus. Many categories are divided further into subcategories and subclassifications.

M CODES

M (morphology) codes, located in the alphabetic index, are used to further identify the behavior and cell type of a neoplasm and are used in conjunction with neoplasm codes from the main classification. M codes are used primarily by cancer registries and are not assigned when submitting a claim to a carrier by the physician's office.

 *Highlight*

When researching oat cell carcinoma, refer to the alphabetic index of ICD-9-CM under the main term carcinoma, further researching the subterm oat cell. The code M8042/3 is found, indicating the behavior and cell type of a neoplasm typically located in the bronchogenic area.

subcategory
Four-digit subcategories are subdivisions of categories to provide greater specificity regarding etiology, site, or manifestations.

subclassification
Fifth-digit subclassifications are subdivisions of subcategories to provide even greater specificity regarding etiology, site, or manifestation of the illness or disease.

CATEGORIES, SUBCATEGORIES, AND SUBCLASSIFICATIONS

The Tabular (Numerical) List of ICD-9-CM is set up in categories, subcategories, and fifth-digit subclassifications. **Categories** are groups of three-digit codes made up of similar diseases or a single disease. An example of a category is 715, Osteoarthrosis and Allied Disorders. **Subcategories** consist of four digits and provide more information such as site of the illness, cause, or other characteristics of the disease. One of the fourth-digit subcategories is 715.0, Osteoarthrosis, generalized. Fifth-digit **subclassifications** are available in many categories to provide even greater specificity. The fifth digits for category 715 show specific sites of the osteoarthrosis, such as fifth digit 5 specifying the site of the pelvic region and thigh. Even though the coder will find both codes 715 and 715.0 in the code book, neither of these codes can be used because there is a fifth-digit subclassification that must be used. The coder must always code to the greatest level of specificity. In other words, *if there is a fifth-digit subclassification available, it must be used.*

Fifth digits may be found in various sections of the code book, so great care must be taken to make sure the correct code is being used. Many of the fifth digits are not shown in the alphabetic index, so the coder must take the time to review and verify the code in the tabular list. For example, with the diagnosis of Threatened labor, the coder would look under the main term of "threatened" and the subterm of "labor." The code given is 644.1. There is no note in the alphabetic index to indicate the need for a fifth digit, but upon verifying the code in the tabular section, it is obvious to the coder that a fifth digit is needed to show the current episode of care (delivered, antepartum, etc.). Many of the code books have been modified by the use of color coding or symbols to indicate the need to use a fifth digit. The coder should become familiar with the symbols/colors used in his or her book.

■ *Highlight*

> *Remember: Category code = 3 digits*
> *Subcategory code = 4 digits*
> *Subclassification code = 5 digits*

> *Example: 389.10*
> *389 = category code*
> *1 = subcategory code*
> *0 = subclassification code*

Residual Subcategories

ICD-9-CM allows for coding of all possible diagnoses and procedures. When the coder has a limited amount of information, a "residual" subcategory may be used. These include "other" and "unspecified" categories. These generally end in digits .8 for other and .9 for unspecified. For example, code 343.8 is for Other specified infantile cerebral palsy. There is a note following this code that says to "use this code when the diagnosis is specified as a certain type of 'infantile cerebral palsy,' but is not listed above" (343.0–343.4). Code 343.9 is Infantile cerebral palsy, unspecified. If the code found ends in a .8 or .9, this should serve as a flag for the coder. While these residual codes are used appropriately in many cases, it may mean that a more specific code can be found for the diagnosis in question. Insurance companies are reviewing payment for codes that they consider "nonspecific," so the coder should be sure to check the medical record and the code book for further clarification prior to assigning a code ending with a .8 or a .9.

Trusting the Alphabetic Index

Due to space constraints, sometimes a term listed in the alphabetic index will not be repeated in the tabular list. In these cases, the coder must trust the alphabetic index and use the code listed.

For example, if the patient's diagnosis was "Horner's syndrome," the alphabetic index gives the code 337.9. When verifying this code in the tabular list, the description given for 337.9 is Unspecified disorder of autonomic nervous system and there is no mention of Horner's syndrome. The coder would still use code 337.9 to properly code this diagnosis.

CODING CONVENTIONS

ICD-9-CM uses several terms, abbreviations, punctuations, and symbols to lead the coder to the correct codes. These should be studied carefully and must be followed whenever present in the code book.

Braces ({ }) are used in the tabular list to reduce repetitive wording by connecting a series of terms on the left with a statement on the right.

> 461 Acute Sinusitis
> Includes:
>   abscess
>   empyema } acute, of sinus
>   infection

This means that if the patient has an acute *abscess* of the sinus or acute *empyema* of the sinus or acute *infection* of the sinus that these diagnoses are all coded properly to code 461.

Brackets ([ ]) are used in the tabular list to enclose synonyms, alternative wordings, and explanatory phrases such as:

> 460 Acute Nasopharyngitis [common cold]

The common cold is just another name for acute nasopharyngitis.

Slanted square brackets (*[ ]*) are used only in the alphabetic index to enclose a second code number that must be used with the first, and is always sequenced second. The first code (the one not in italicized brackets) represents the underlying condition. The second code represents the manifestation or what resulted from the underlying condition.

Official Coding Guidelines

Codes in brackets in the alphabetic index can never be sequenced as principal diagnosis. Coding directives require that the codes in brackets be sequenced in the order as they appear in the Alphabetic Index.

For example, with the diagnosis of Diabetic Retinitis, the coder is given two codes, 250.5 [362.01]. Since 362.01 is listed second and is enclosed in slanted square brackets, the coder is directed to code both the 250.5x as the principal or first diagnosis and to code 362.01 as a secondary diagnosis to fully describe the condition.

Section marks (§) indicate a footnote that normally means that a fifth digit is needed in that category. Some code books use other symbols besides the section mark to indicate the need for fifth digits.

> § 660.0 Obstruction caused by malposition of fetus

Look up code 660.0 in the tabular list. In most books, a section mark or other symbol will be located next to the code to indicate that a fifth digit must be used with this code. Some books do not use the section mark. The coder should become familiar with the symbols used in his/her individual code book to designate footnotes.

Cross-Reference Terms

There are several cross-reference terms used in the alphabetic index of ICD-9-CM that lead the coder to other categories or to use a second code.

See, See Also

"See" is a cross-reference that requires the coder to look up a different term. The "See also" cross-reference directs the coder to look under another main term if there is not enough information under the first term to identify the proper code. Look in the alphabetic index to locate the main term "laceration." The coder will note that there are few subterms listed under the main term laceration, and the following instruction is given:

> Laceration—see also wound, open, by site

For example, if the patient had a laceration of the hand, there is not a subterm under "laceration for hand." The coder would then look under the main term "wound, open" and see if there is a subterm for "hand." The correct code for this diagnosis is 882.0.

Includes and Excludes Notes

Includes notes provide further examples or defines the category. For example, in the tabular list under code 785.4, Gangrene, the code book gives examples of diagnoses that can be coded using this code, such as Gangrene: Not otherwise specified, and Gangrenous cellulitis.

Excludes notes are easier to spot, as "Excludes" is printed in italics and in a box. If a condition is found under the excludes box, it means the condition must be coded elsewhere or needs further codes to complete the description. Under the code 382.3, Unspecified chronic suppurative otitis media, the following excludes note is found:

> | *Excludes:* | *tuberculous otitis media (017.4)*

This note tells the coder that if the diagnosis is tuberculous otitis media, 382.3 is not the correct code to use. Instead, the coder should use 017.4 to correctly code the diagnosis.

There are times when the "Excludes" instruction can be confusing. When looking for the correct code for the diagnosis of arteriosclerotic cardiovascular disease, the coder is led to 429.2, Cardiovascular Disease, Unspecified. A note below this code directs the coder to "use additional code, if desired, to identify presence of arteriosclerosis." A secondary code of 440.9 is needed to show both the cardiovascular disease and the arteriosclerosis. When the coder verifies the appropriateness of 440.9, there is an exclusion note that reads:

> | *Excludes:* | *arteriosclerotic cardiovascular disease /ASCVD/ (429.2)*

This note is to let the coder know that both codes are necessary to fully describe the patient's condition.

Notes

Notes appear in both the tabular list and alphabetic index to provide further instructions or give definitions. For example, under the main term "Injury" in the alphabetic index, there is a note that says *"Note—for abrasion, insect bite (non-venomous), blister, or scratch, see Injury, superficial."*

Code Also

Code also means the coder must use a second code to fully describe the condition. Sometimes the code book will instruct the coder to "use additional code, if desired." The words "if desired" should be ignored. The coder should use an additional code if the documentation supports the code assignment. Code 599.0, *Urinary tract infection, site not specified* has a note that reads "Use additional code to identify organism, such as Escherichia coli, [E. coli] (041.4)." This note means that if the coder has documentation to identify the E. coli or other bacteria, a second code should be used.

Multiple Coding

Official Coding Guidelines

Multiple coding is required for certain conditions not subject to the rules for combination codes. Instructions for conditions that require multiple coding appear in the alphabetic index and the tabular list:

A. *Alphabetic Index: Codes for both etiology and manifestation of a disease appear following the subentry term, with the second code italicized and in slanted brackets. Assign both codes in the same sequence in which they appear in the alphabetic index.*

An example of etiology and manifestation codes is the term diabetic neuropathy. When the coder looks up the main term of neuropathy, subterm diabetic, two codes are given, 250.6 *[357.2]*. This indicates that both codes must be used to fully describe the patient's condition, with the code for diabetes (etiology), 250.6X, sequenced first and 357.2 for neuropathy (manifestation) sequenced second.

B. *Tabular List: Instructional terms, such as "Code also . . . ," "Use additional code for any . . . ," and "Note . . . ," indicate when to use more than one code.*

"Code also underlying disease"—Assign the codes for both the manifestation and the underlying cause. The codes for manifestations that are printed in italics cannot be used (designated) as principal diagnosis.

"Use additional code, if desired, to identify manifestation as . . . ,"—Assign also the code that identifies the manifestation, such as, but not limited to, the examples listed. The codes for manifestations that appear in italicized print cannot be used (designated) as principal diagnosis.

C. *Apply multiple coding instructions throughout the classification where appropriate, whether or not multiple coding directions appear in the alphabetic index or the tabular list. Avoid indiscriminate multiple coding of irrelevant information, such as symptoms or signs characteristic of the diagnosis.*

The code book does not always give hints, such as "use additional code" or "code also" to let the coder know that more than one code is necessary. It is important that the coder use additional codes until all component parts of the diagnosis are fully described.

Abbreviations NEC (Not Elsewhere Classified) and NOS (Not Otherwise Specified)

NEC is an abbreviation that means Not Elsewhere Classified. This means that a more specific category is not available in ICD-9-CM. In the diagnosis Sudden sensorineural deafness, if the coder looks up the main term "deafness," there is a subterm of "sudden, NEC," code 388.2. If the coder continues to search the list of subterms, sensorineural is also found, code 389.10. Since sudden is followed by NEC, it is less specific than sensorineural, so code 389.10 should be selected.

> ### *Official Coding Guidelines*
>
> *Codes labeled "other specified" (NEC—not elsewhere classified) or "unspecified" (NOS—not otherwise specified) are used only when neither the diagnostic statement nor a thorough review of the medical record provides adequate information to permit assignment of a more specific code.*
>
> *Use the code assignment for "other" or NEC when the information at hand specifies a condition but no separate code for the condition is provided.*

NOS stands for Not Otherwise Specified. It should be interpreted as "unspecified" and is used when the coder has no further information available in the medical record to fully define the condition. Under code 780.99, other generalized symptoms, one of the examples given is Chill(s), not otherwise specified. If the coder had more information regarding the chills, such as cause, a more specific code could be appropriately used. If the documentation in the chart only stated "chills," then 780.99 would be the correct code assignment.

> ### *Official Coding Guidelines*
>
> *Use "unspecified" (NOS) when the information at hand does not permit either a more specific or "other" code assignment.*

Combination Codes

> ### *Official Coding Guidelines*
>
> *A single code used to classify two diagnoses or a diagnosis with an associated secondary process (manifestation) or an associated complication is called a combination code. Combination codes are identified by referring to subterm*

> *entries in the alphabetic index and by reading the inclusion and exclusion notes in the tabular list.*
>
> *A. Assign only the combination code when that code fully identifies the diagnostic conditions involved or when the alphabetic index so directs. Multiple coding should not be used when the classification provides a combination code that clearly identifies all of the elements documented in the diagnosis. When the combination code lacks necessary specificity in describing the manifestation or complication, an additional code may be used as a secondary code.*

At times, the code book provides a combination code that identifies the entire diagnostic statement. For example, in the diagnosis Pneumonia with influenza, when the coder looks up the main term *"pneumonia,"* there is a subterm for "with influenza." Code 487.0 is all that is needed to code both conditions.

Some coders like to use a cheat sheet that lists many of the common diagnoses and procedures used in their facility or physician practices. While this may save time in coding some diagnoses, it can also lead to many coding errors. ICD-9-CM does provide many combination codes that are to be used when two diagnoses are both present. If a coder is simply reading the code from a cheat sheet, the instructions to use combination codes will not be located. This is also true in the case of a physician simply checking off diagnoses from a fee ticket, superbill, or other standardized coding form. A common mistake is that of a patient with congestive heart failure (428.0) due to hypertension (401.9). ICD-9-CM provides a combination code to describe both conditions. If the coder looks in the hypertension table at hypertension, the subterm "with, heart involvement (conditions classifiable to 429.0–429.3, 429.8, 429.9 due to hypertension) (see also hypertension, heart)" is provided. When the coder then looks at hypertension, heart, subterm "with heart failure, congestive," the correct code is 402.91 (unspecified).

There is not a magic number of codes that can be used per diagnosis. Remember that coding is similar to putting a puzzle together. The coder has to solve each part of the puzzle before obtaining the entire picture.

✳ REVIEW OF THE BASIC STEPS IN CODING ✳

To illustrate the steps in coding, the diagnostic statement of "cholelithiasis with acute cholecystitis" is coded as follows:

1. **Identify the main term(s) of the condition(s) to be coded.**

   The main term is *cholelithiasis. Cholecystitis* can be a main term also.

2. **Locate the main terms in the alphabetic index.**

   Using the alphabetic index, locate the main term "Cholelithiasis."

3. **Refer to any subterms indented under the main term.** This may be an extensive list, so it is important that the coder uses care in searching the listing. Also refer to any nonessential modifiers, instructional terms, or notes to select the most likely code.

   Next to the main term cholelithiasis there are two nonessential modifiers in parentheses, (impacted) (multiple). There is also a note that instructs the coder on the usage of fifth digits for this code category. The terms look as follows:

Cholelithiasis (impacted)(multiple) 574.2
  with
    cholecystitis 574.1
      acute 574.0
      chronic 574.1

Following ICD-9-CM coding rules, the coder would use the subterms "with, cholecystitis, acute" and the note listing the fifth digits to find the most likely code of 574.00.

4. **Verify the code(s) in the tabular list.**

   The coder would go to the tabular list in numerical order to locate the code 574.00. The fourth-digit subcategory of 574.0 has a description of "Calculus of gallbladder with acute cholecystitis."

5. **Check all instructional terms in the Tabular List and be sure to assign all codes to their highest degree of specificity.**

   The coder is also instructed by the symbols in the code book that code 574.0 must have a fifth digit. Since there is no mention of obstruction, the proper fifth digit is 0.

6. **Continue coding the diagnostic statement until all of the elements are identified completely.**

   All parts of the diagnostic statement are identified by using this one (combination) code.

✳ EXERCISE 2–2

Assign ICD-9-CM codes to the following diagnoses.

1. Migraine headache 346.90

2. Congestive heart failure 428.0

3. Type I diabetes mellitus, uncontrolled 250.03

4. Acute myocardial infarction, anterior wall, initial episode 410.11

5. Fracture of hip 820.8

6. Acute gastroenteritis 558.9

7. Esophageal ulcer 530.20

8. Coronary insufficiency 411.89

9. Bell's palsy 351.0

10. Hypothyroidism 244.9

11. Urinary retention 788.20

12. Alzheimer's disease 331.0

13. AIDS 042

14. Syncope 780.2

15. Tension headache 307.81

16. Tonsillitis   463
17. Pain left great toe   429.5
18. Epistaxis   784.7
19. Generalized anxiety disorder   300.02
20. Dermatomyositis   710.3

PROCEDURAL CODING WITH ICD-9-CM

ICD-9-CM classifies procedures in Volume Three, which includes the alphabetic index and tabular list for procedures. The procedures are grouped by system, and use numerical codes only. The process for coding procedures is the same as that followed in coding diagnoses, i.e., locate the main term in the alphabetic index and verify it in the tabular list. The main term for procedures is the name of the procedure itself; for example, cardiac catheterization would appear under "catheterization," subterm "cardiac." Volume Three of the ICD-9-CM code book is not used in the physician's office/clinic setting. Procedures in these settings are coded using another coding system called *Current Procedural Terminology (CPT)*. This is discussed in Chapter 4 of this text.

Subterms

Many subterms classify the procedure as to site and/or surgical technique. It is very important to search the subterms carefully to ensure use of the proper code.

Canceled Procedure

If a procedure was canceled, the coder should code it as far as it proceeded. For example, if a laparoscopically assisted cholecystectomy was planned, and after making the laparotomy incision the patient went into cardiac arrest, the laparotomy and not the cholecystectomy would be coded. (There are V codes available to code the diagnosis of surgery canceled.)

Code Also

The instructional term "code also" is used in the tabular list for procedures to mean "code also if another procedure was performed." The note under code 36.1 states "Code also cardiopulmonary bypass [extracorporeal circulation] [heart-lung machine] (39.61)." The cardiopulmonary bypass is generally a part of any heart bypass procedure (codes 36.10–36.19), as well as other heart procedures, but must be coded in addition to the bypass code.

Omit Code

Another common instructional term in coding procedures is "omit code." At times, a procedure may be done solely as an approach to be able to perform another procedure. It is at this time that the coder may see the instructional term "omit code," which means that the coder does not code this separately if it was performed as an operative approach. For example, if the patient had a laparotomy with a partial hepatectomy, the coder would only use 50.22 to code the hepatectomy.

EXERCISE 2–3

✳ Code the following procedures using ICD-9-CM Volume Three:

1. Cholecystectomy ~~51.04~~ → 51.22
2. Esophagogastroduodenoscopy (EGD) 45.13
3. Suture of laceration of skin of hand ~~82.45~~ 86.59
4. Laparotomy with herniorrhaphy, bilateral direct inguinal hernia with graft ~~17.11~~ 53.14 or 53.11
5. Excision, lesion, breast 85.21
6. Needle biopsy liver 50.11
7. Transuretheral resection of prostate 60.29
8. EKG 89.52
9. Unilateral thyroid lobectomy 06.2   *p1251*
10. Laparoscopic cholecystectomy ~~51.22~~ 51.23

How to Code an Operative Report

The operative reports included here are representative of those that coders in both hospitals and clinics may have to code. To code an operative report the coder should first read through the entire report and make notes (or underline) any possible diagnoses or abnormalities noted and any procedures performed. This is an important step because sometimes the coder will find other diagnoses and procedures performed that the physician failed to list at the top of the report. The coder should then review the physician's list of diagnoses and procedures to see if these match. If the coder should locate a potential diagnosis or procedure not listed by the physician he or she should bring this to the physician's attention to see if it is significant enough to code. If preoperative and postoperative diagnoses are different, the coder should use the postoperative diagnosis, which was determined following the surgery.

The coder should also review the pathology report if specimens were sent to pathology, to verify the diagnosis. If there is a discrepancy between the pathologist's and surgeon's diagnoses, this matter should be discussed with the surgeon.

EXERCISE 2–4

Using all volumes of the ICD-9-CM code book, code all diagnoses and procedures in the three operative reports that follow. If more information is needed from the physician, list questions on the line provided.

---

1.   **Operative Report**

SURGEON:

OPERATION: 1. Total Abdominal Hysterectomy

                      2. Right Ovarian Cystectomy

PREOPERATIVE DIAGNOSIS: Symptomatic fibroids

POSTOPERATIVE DIAGNOSIS: 1. Symptomatic fibroids. 2. Endometriosis, ovary

ANESTHESIA: General endotracheal

COMPLICATIONS: None

ESTIMATED BLOOD LOSS: 200 cc

FINDINGS: Diffusely enlarged uterus with normal left ovary. Right ovary had a simple cyst, 2×2 cm, as well as endometriosis. Specimens sent to pathology.

PROCEDURE: The risks, benefits, indications, and alternatives of the procedure were reviewed with the patient and informed consent was obtained. The patient was taken to the operating room with IV running. The patient was placed in the supine position and given general anesthesia and was prepared and draped in the usual sterile fashion. A vertical incision was made approximately at the level of the umbilicus and incised down to the symphysis pubis and extended sharply to the rectus fascia. The rectus muscles were then separated to obtain good visualization. The muscles of the anterior abdominal wall were separated in the midline by sharp and blunt dissection. The peritoneum was grasped between two pick-ups, elevated and entered sharply with the scalpel. The pelvis was examined with the findings as noted above. An O'Connor O'Sullivan retractor was placed in the incision and the bowel was packed away with moist laparotomy sponges. The uterus was clamped with a traumatic clamp for better visualization. The round ligaments on both sides were clamped, transected, and sutured with 0 Vicryl. The anterior leaf of the broad ligament was incised along the bladder reflection to the midline from both sides. The bladder was then gently dissected off the lower uterine segment of the cervix with a sponge stick. The utero-ovarian ligament, on both sides was then doubly clamped, transected, and sutured with 0 Vicryl. Hemostasis was visualized. The uterine arteries were skeletonized bilaterally, clamped with Heaney clamps, transected, and suture ligated with 0 Vicryl. Again hemostasis was assured. The cervix and uterus were amputated with a scalpel. The vaginal cuff angles were closed with figure-of-eight stitches of 0 Vicryl and were then transfixed to the ipsilateral, cardinal, and uterosacral ligaments. The remainder of the vaginal cuff was closed with a series of interrupted 0 Vicryl figure-of-eight sutures. Hemostasis was assured. Both right ovarian cysts were incised with scalpel and sacs were removed with blunt dissection. A 25-gauge needle was placed in the endometrioma to assure cystic nature. The cysts were closed with 3-0 Vicryl in a running suture. The pelvis was copiously irrigated with warm, normal saline, and all laparotomy sponges and instruments were removed from the abdomen. The fascia was closed with a running PDS and hemostasis was assured. The skin was closed with staples. Sponge, lap, needle, and instrument counts were correct times two. The patient was taken to the recovery room in stable condition. Specimens included the right ovarian cyst wall and uterus.

Diagnoses: _218.9, 617.1_____

Procedures: _68.49, 65.29_____

Question for Physician: _____

---

2.   **Operative Report**

SURGEON:

OPERATION:

PREOPERATIVE DIAGNOSIS: Ruptured disc, L-4 central

POSTOPERATIVE DIAGNOSIS: Same

ANESTHESIA: General endotracheal

COMPLICATIONS: None

ESTIMATED BLOOD LOSS: 150 cc

PROCEDURE: Bilateral subtotal hemilaminectomy and foraminotomy with
removal of the lower one-third of the fourth lumbar spinous process and
exploration of L-4 right and central. Under general anesthesia, after prep-
ping and draping in the usual manner, a linear incision was made over
L-4 and L-5. Removal of the lower one-third of L-4 spinous processes and
bilateral subtotal hemilaminectomy and foraminotomy were performed
at L-4 decompressing the canal stenosis bilaterally. The ligamental flava
was removed with Kerrison rongeurs mainly on the right side and the
dura was retracted medially and the above findings were present. The ball
probe passed easily in the foramen after decompression. The bleeding
was minimal. The incision was closed using 1 Chromic on the muscle and
fascia, 2-0 Chromic on the subcutaneous tissue, and mattress 4-0 Nylon
and skin clips on the skin.

FINDINGS: There was a canal stenosis secondary to hypertrophy of the facet
and ligament. The disc was firm and flat. There was a small osteoarthritic
spur present underneath the nerve root.

The patient was taken to the recovery room in satisfactory condition.

Diagnoses: _722.10_____

Procedures: _80.51 , 03.09_____

Question for Physician: _____

---

3.   **Operative Report**

SURGEON: Ben Davis, MD

OPERATION: Attempted Laparoscopic Cholecystectomy Followed by Open
Cholecystectomy

PREOPERATIVE DIAGNOSIS: Acute Cholecystitis

continues

POSTOPERATIVE DIAGNOSIS: Acute Cholecystitis

ANESTHESIA: General endotracheal

COMPLICATIONS: None

ESTIMATED BLOOD LOSS: Approximately 200 cc

FINDINGS:

INDICATIONS: The patient is a 25-year-old white female who notes a several day history of increasing right upper quadrant pain associated with nausea, vomiting, and fever. The patient had an ultrasound performed, which showed significant pericholecystic fluid with cholelithiasis consistent with acute cholecystitis. Risks and benefits were discussed with the patient, and she elected to proceed with the cholecystectomy.

PROCEDURE: The patient was placed in the supine position on the table. General endotracheal anesthesia was administered and the abdomen prepped and draped in the usual sterile fashion, using Betadine solution. Initially, a supraumbilical incision was made due to the patient's prior history of a laparoscopic tubal ligation as well as a cesarean section with a lower midline. The supraumbilical incision was carried down to the level of the fascia. Using sharp dissection, the fascia was incised linearly. The lateral borders of the fascia were grasped with stay sutures of heavy Vicryl. An incision was made into the posterior sheath. There were significant adhesions encountered at this level, and an inadvertent enterotomy was made, which was noted immediately. The enterotomy was closed with running 3-0 Chromic suture followed by imbricating 3-0 GI silks. Excellent closure was noted of the small intestine, which was then returned to the abdominal cavity. Adhesions were sharply taken down to allow for direct placement of a Hasson type trocar into the abdominal cavity. Capnoperitoneum was then introduced to 15 mm mercury pressure.

Upon examining the abdomen, the gallbladder was incredibly distended with focal gangrenous changes. There was a significant amount of edema and adhesions of the omentum to this area with a moderate amount of free greenish fluid in the abdomen and along the right gutter. A 10 mm trocar was then placed under direct vision in the subxiphoid area and two 5 mm trocars placed in the anterior axillary line of the right upper and right lower quadrants. All this was done with direct vision. The gallbladder was then attempted to be grasped, however, due to its significant distention required decompression through percutaneous aspiration. The gallbladder was then grasped and the liver retracted superiorly, and dissection was then carried out along the gallbladder, taking down the omental adhesions inferiorly. There was a significant amount of edema and adhesions noted. As dissection proceeded more proximally, the tissue was very friable, and it was felt that with the exposure and due to the significant edema, that laparoscopic cholecystectomy would be impossible. Therefore, the laparoscopic procedure was abandoned, and other trocars all removed and capnoperitoneum released and the camera removed.

An incision was made subcostally, connecting the two superior trocar sites and carried down through to the level of the muscular fascia, using Bovie electrocautery. The muscular layers were then divided, exposing the peritoneum, which was then divided throughout the length of the incision. Retractors were placed to facilitate exposure. Dissection was then carried out from distally to proximally, initially scoring the peritoneum over the gallbladder and dissecting circumferentially around the gallbladder bed. Dissection was then carried proximally where the cystic artery was identified and a significant amount of edematous doubly ligated proximally and stapled with a surgical clip distally. The artery was then divided, and careful dissection was then carried out proximally where the cystic duct was identified and divided between heavy silk ligatures. Careful dissection was then carried out along the infundibulum, and the gallbladder was removed from the gallbladder bed and sent for permanent specimen. Again, there was a significant amount of focal necrosis noted throughout the walls of the gallbladder, and several small stones were noted within the gallbladder itself. Hemostasis was then achieved with Bovie electrocautery.

The wound was irrigated with a significant amount of sterile saline solution. The pelvis was then irrigated with saline solution and aspirated. Due to the significant edema and the fluid noted in the gallbladder bed on initial placement of the trocar, a 10 flat Jackson-Pratt drain was placed in the hole. When hemostasis was deemed adequate, the subcostal incision was closed in muscular layers, using heavy PDS suture. The wound was then irrigated, and figure-of-eight fashion was used to close the fascia at the umbilicus. A separate suture was used to secure the Jackson-Pratt drain at the skin. The patient tolerated the procedure well, and needle and sponge counts were correct at the conclusion of the case. The patient was extubated and transferred to the recovery room in stable condition.

Diagnoses: _____

Procedures: _____

Question for Physician: _____

Coding Signs and Symptoms

In many circumstances, the physician may initially not know what the patient's diagnosis is, so the coder may only be able to code the patient's signs and symptoms. It is important to understand the difference between signs and symptoms.

- A sign is visible evidence that the physician can determine objectively (e.g., overactive bowel sounds, laceration to the skin).

- A symptom is a subjective, descriptive term, usually in the patient's own words, e.g., "My head hurts."

EXERCISE 2–5

In the following statements, identify each as a sign or a symptom.

1. Diaper rash _objective = sign_

2. Chest pressure _symptom_

3. Laceration of forehead _sign_

4. Fever _Symptom / Sign_
5. Strep throat _~~Symptom~~ Sign_
6. Swelling of right hand _Sign_
7. Muscle cramping _Symptom_
8. Tachycardia _Sign_
9. Abdominal pain _Symptom_
10. Elevated blood pressure _Sign_

Official Coding Guidelines

Conditions That Are an Integral Part of a Disease Process

Conditions that are integral to the disease process should not be assigned as additional codes.

Coding Tip   *Signs and symptoms must be coded with care. If a sign or symptom is a common occurrence with a particular diagnosis, then it is not coded once the diagnosis has been made. For example, chest congestion is a sign of pneumonia. Only the pneumonia would be coded.*

Conditions That Are Not an Integral Part of a Disease Process

Additional conditions that may not be associated routinely with a disease process should be coded when present.

If a sign or symptom occurs that is not a part of the usual disease process, then that condition is coded. For example, if the patient had a rash on the skin (782.1) with gastroenteritis (558.9), both diagnoses would be coded.

In the emergency room setting, the physician may not be able to make an exact diagnosis, and will recommend that the patient follow up with his or her primary care physician. In these cases, the documentation only substantiates coding of the patient's signs and symptoms. For example, if the patient is seen in the emergency department with dizziness, the ER physician will try to determine the etiology, but may not be able to find a definitive cause. He may refer the patient to an ear, nose, and throat specialist to see if there is an inner ear problem.

Uncertain Diagnosis

If the diagnosis documented at the time of discharge is qualified as "probable," "suspected," "likely," "questionable," "possible," or "rule out," code the condition as if it existed or was established.

In hospital inpatient coding, conditions listed as "suspected," "rule out," or "possible" are coded as if the condition exists. In these cases, sometimes the physician will also want the signs and symptoms coded for use in further study.

Official Coding Guidelines—Outpatient Services

Do not code outpatient diagnoses documented as "probable," "suspected," "questionable," "rule out." Rather, code the condition(s) to the highest degree of certainty for that encounter/visit, such as symptoms, signs, abnormal test results, or other reason for visit.

Please note: This is contrary to the coding practices used by hospitals and medical records departments for coding the diagnosis of hospital inpatients.

In those instances where the physician or other health care practitioner does not document (identify) a definite condition or problem at the conclusion of a patient care encounter/visit, the coder should select the documented chief complaint(s) as the reason for the encounter/visit.

With physician's office and outpatient/emergency room coding, the coder may only assign codes to the highest degree of certainty. In these situations, do not code suspected, ruled out, or possible conditions.

To illustrate, if the patient had the diagnosis of "wheezing, rule out pneumonia," and was seen in the physician's office, the coder would only code the wheezing, 786.02. In the inpatient setting, the coder would code both the 786.02 and the 486 for the pneumonia.

Abnormal Positive Findings

Abnormal positive findings (laboratory, x-ray, pathologic, and other diagnostic results) are not coded and reported unless the physician indicates their clinical significance. If the findings are outside the normal range and the physician has ordered other tests to evaluate the condition or prescribed treatment, it is appropriate to ask the physician whether the diagnosis should be added.

Lab reports usually show "normal" values, and when searching through the patient's record, the coder may find a value that is not within normal range. If the patient's potassium level was a bit high, he or she might possibly have Hyperkalemia (276.7). But the results may not be enough out of the normal limit range to really be significant. It is up to the physician to make this determination. The coder should ask the physician if this is truly hyperkalemia and should not code it without clarification from the physician. Abnormal findings in the chart are coded only if the physician indicates that these findings have a clinical significance.

EXERCISE 2–6

Based on coding rules for outpatient/physician billing, code the following statements.

1. Abnormal EKG, R/O sick sinus syndrome ___794.31___

2. Chest pain/R/O myocardial infarction ___786.50___

3. Fever of unknown origin _780.60_

4. Positive tuberculin skin test _795.5_

5. Weight loss of undetermined etiology _783.21_

6. Abnormal pulmonary function studies _794.2_

7. Positive serology for HIV ~~795.71~~ _V08_

8. Pap smear with abnormal findings ~~795.00~~ _795.1_

9. Abnormal glucose tolerance test, R/O diabetes _790.29_

10. Positive throat culture, R/O strep _795.39_

INFECTIONS

> ### Official Coding Guidelines
>
> **Septicemia and Septic Shock**
>
> *When the diagnosis of septicemia with shock or the diagnosis of general sepsis with septic shock is documented, code and list the septicemia first and report the septic shock code as a secondary condition. The septicemia code assignment should identify the type of bacteria if it is known.*
>
> *Sepsis and septic shock associated with abortion, ectopic pregnancy, and molar pregnancy are classified to category codes in Chapter 11 (630–639).*
>
> *Negative or inconclusive blood cultures do not preclude a diagnosis of septicemia in patients with clinical evidence of the condition.*

Septicemia/sepsis is a severe infection due to bacteria in the blood and is marked by high fever, chills, and can lead to shock and death. Usually, blood cultures (placing a sample of blood in a specially treated dish and watching the sample over a period of time to see if microorganisms grow from the specimen) are taken to determine the type of bacteria causing the severe infection.

Coding Tip *Bacteremia is the presence of bacteria in the blood, and is coded to 790.7. It can lead to sepsis/septicemia, but is not necessarily the same thing.*

How to Locate the Code for a Microorganism

If a specific organism causing a patient condition is identified, and the code book directs the coder to "Use additional code, if desired, to identify organism," at times the code book does not give any hints as to where to look to find the code for the organism. The coder can look under the main term "infection" to locate the code for the organism, such as 041.4, *Escherichia coli* [*E. coli*].

For example, if the patient has the diagnosis of urinary tract infection, 599.0, there is a note following the description for code 599.0 in the tabular list of the code book that says, "Use additional code to identify organism, such as *Escherichia coli*, [*E. coli*] (041.4)."

HIV INFECTIONS

Official Coding Guidelines

Code Only Confirmed Cases of HIV Infection/Illness

This is an exception to the guideline that states "If the diagnosis documented at the time of discharge is qualified as 'probable,' 'suspect,' 'likely,' 'questionable,' or 'still to be ruled out,' code the condition as if it existed or was established . . ." In this context, "confirmation" does not require documentation of positive serology or culture for HIV; the physician's diagnostic statement that the patient is HIV positive, or has an HIV-related illness, is sufficient.

■ *Highlight*

Whenever dealing with a possible diagnosis of HIV or AIDS, the coder should take extreme care to verify the accuracy of the diagnosis. The coder should always remember the patient behind the codes and must realize that a wrong code placed on a patient's chart can affect the patient's insurance coverage, employment, and life.

Selection of HIV Code

042 Human Immunodeficiency Virus [HIV] Disease

Patients with an HIV-related illness should be coded to 042, Human immunodeficiency virus [HIV] disease.

V08 Asymptomatic Human Immunodeficiency Virus (HIV) Infection

Patients with physician-documented asymptomatic HIV infections who have never had an HIV-related illness should be coded to V08, Asymptomatic human immunodeficiency virus [HIV] infection.

795.71 Nonspecific Serologic Evidence of Human Immunodeficiency Virus [HIV]

Code 795.71, Nonspecific serologic evidence of human immunodeficiency virus [HIV] should be used for patients (including infants) with inconclusive HIV test results.

Previously Diagnosed HIV-Related Illness

Patients with any known prior diagnosis of an HIV-related illness should be coded to 042. Once a patient has developed an HIV-related illness, the patient should always be assigned code 042 on every subsequent admission. Patients previously diagnosed with any HIV illness (042) should never be assigned with 795.71 or V08.

Sequencing

The circumstances of admission govern the selection of principal diagnosis for patients with HIV-related illnesses. In other words, "that condition established after study to be chiefly responsible for occasioning the admission of the patient to the hospital for care."

Patients who are admitted for an HIV-related illness should be assigned a minimum of two codes: first assign code 042 to identify the HIV disease and then sequence additional codes to identify the other diagnoses.

If a patient is admitted for an HIV-related condition, the principal diagnosis should be 042, followed by additional diagnosis codes for all reported HIV-related conditions.

If a patient with HIV disease is admitted for an unrelated condition (such as a traumatic injury), the code for the unrelated condition (e.g., the nature of injury code) should be the principal diagnosis. Other diagnoses would be 042 followed by additional diagnosis codes for all reported HIV-related conditions.

Whether the patient is newly diagnosed or has had previous admissions for HIV conditions (or has expired) is irrelevant to the sequencing decision.

HIV Infections in Pregnancy, Childbirth, and Puerperium

During pregnancy, childbirth, or the puerperium, a patient admitted because of an HIV-related illness should receive a principal diagnosis of 647.8X, other specified infectious and parasitic disease in the mother classifiable elsewhere, but complicating the pregnancy, childbirth, or the puerperium, followed by 042 and the code(s) for the HIV-related illness(es). This is an exception to the sequencing rule stated in the previous HIV code information.

Patients with asymptomatic HIV infection status admitted during pregnancy, childbirth, or the puerperium should receive codes of 647.8X and V08.

Asymptomatic HIV Infection

V08 Asymptomatic human immunodeficiency virus (HIV) infection, is to be applied when the patient without any documentation of symptoms is listed as being HIV positive, known HIV, HIV test positive, or similar terminology. Do not use this code if the term AIDS is used or if the patient is treated for any HIV-related illness or is described as having any condition(s) resulting from his/her HIV positive status; use code 042 in these cases.

Nonspecific Laboratory Test for HIV

795.71 Nonspecific serologic evidence of human immunodeficiency virus (HIV)

Patients with inconclusive HIV serology, but no definitive diagnosis or manifestations of the illness may be assigned code 795.71.

Testing for HIV

If the patient is asymptomatic but wishes to know his/her HIV status, use code V73.89, Screening for other specified viral disease. Use code V69.8, Other problems related to lifestyle, as a secondary code if an asymptomatic patient is in a known high-risk group for HIV. Should a patient with signs or symptoms or illness, or a confirmed HIV-related diagnosis be tested for HIV, code the signs and symptoms or the diagnosis. An additional counseling code, V65.44, may be used if counseling is provided during the encounter for the test.

When the patient returns to be informed of his/her HIV test results, use code V65.44, HIV counseling, if the results of the test are negative. If the results are positive but the patient is asymptomatic, use code V08, Asymptomatic HIV infection. If the results are positive and the patient is symptomatic, use code 042, HIV infection, with codes for the HIV-related symptoms or diagnosis. The HIV counseling code may also be used if counseling is provided for patients with positive test results.

CIRCULATORY SYSTEM CODING

Chapter 9 of this text covers cardiology in detail. Please refer to that chapter for more information on coding cardiovascular diseases and procedures.

There are many instructional notes used in the circulatory chapter of ICD-9-CM. The coder should review these notes and assign these codes with care.

Hypertension

Official Coding Guidelines

Hypertension, Essential, or NOS

Assign hypertension (arterial) (essential) (primary) (systemic) (NOS) to category code 401 with the appropriate fourth digit to indicate malignant (.0), benign (.1), or unspecified (.9). Do not use either .0 malignant or .1 benign unless medical record documentation supports such a designation.

The hypertension table, located under the main term "hypertension" in the alphabetic index of the code book, is very extensive concerning the coding of all conditions due to or associated with hypertension (see Figure 2–1). Three columns are listed—malignant, benign, and unspecified. Benign hypertension is considered to be mild and usually under control with medication. Malignant hypertension is a life-threatening, severe form of hypertension. The coder cannot assume that the hypertension is either malignant or benign unless specified by the physician. Otherwise, the coder must use the unspecified codes as listed.

If the patient has essential hypertension, the coder must use 401.9, unspecified.

Official Coding Guidelines

Hypertension with Heart Disease

Certain heart conditions (429.0–429.3, 429.8, 429.9) are assigned to a code from category 402 when a causal relationship is stated (due to hypertension) or implied (hypertensive). Use only the code from category 402. The same heart conditions (429.0–429.3, 429.8, 429.9) with hypertension, but without a stated causal relationship, are coded separately. Sequence according to the circumstances of the admission.

	Malignant	Benign	Unspecified
Hypertension, hypertensive (arterial) (arteriolar) (crisis) (degeneration) (disease) (essential) (fluctuating) (idiopathic) (intermittent) (labile) (low renin) (orthostatic) (paroxysmal) (primary) (systemic) (uncontrolled) (vascular)	401.0	401.1	401.9
with			
heart involvement ▶ (conditions classifiable to 429.0-429.3, 429.8, 429.9 due to hypertension) ◀ (see also Hypertension, heart..	402.00	402.10	402.90
with kidney involvement — see Hypertension, cardiorenal			
renal involvement (only conditions classifiable to 585, 586, 587) (excludes conditions classifiable to 584) (see also Hypertension, kidney..................................	403.00	403.10	403.90
renal sclerosis or failure....................................	403.00	403.10	403.90
with heart involvement — see Hypertension, cardiorenal			
failure (and sclerosis) (see also Hypertension, kidney)...........	403.01	403.11	403.91
sclerosis without failure (see also Hypertension, kidney).......	403.00	403.10	403.90
accelerated — (see also Hypertension, by type, malignant).............	401.0	———	———
antepartum — see Hypertension, complicating pregnancy, childbirth, or the puerperium			
cardiorenal (disease)..	404.00	404.10	404.90
with			
heart failure..	404.01	404.11	404.91
and renal failure.................................	404.03	404.13	404.93
renal failure...	404.02	404.12	404.92
and heart failure................................	404.03	404.13	404.93
cardiovascular disease (arteriosclerotic) (sclerotic).........................	402.00	402.10	402.90
with			
heart failure..	402.01	402.11	402.91
renal involvement (conditions classifiable to 403) (see also Hypertension, cardiorenal).............................	404.00	404.10	404.90

Figure 2–1 ICD-9-CM Hypertension table (partial). From *ICD-9-CM for Hospitals—Volumes 1, 2, 3, 2005 Professional.* Reprinted with permission of Ingenix.

Coding Tip *ICD-9-CM makes a distinction between diagnoses "with hypertension" and "due to hypertension." Hypertensive should be interpreted as "due to hypertension" and coded appropriately.*

If the patient has CHF (congestive heart failure) due to hypertensive heart disease, the correct code is 402.91, hypertensive heart disease with congestive heart failure, since the causal relationship is specified by the words "due to." Congestive heart failure, with hypertension, on the other hand, would be coded 428.0 and 401.9 since no causal relationship is stated.

Hypertensive Renal Disease with Chronic Renal Failure

Assign codes from category 403, hypertensive renal disease, when conditions classified to categories 585–587 are present. Unlike hypertension with heart disease, ICD-9-CM presumes a cause-and-effect relationship and classifies chronic renal failure with hypertension as hypertensive renal disease. Acute renal failure is not included in this cause-and-effect relationship.

If the patient's diagnosis is renal sclerosis with hypertension, the coder goes to the main term "sclerosis," subterm "renal" "with hypertension (see also hypertension, kidney)" and assigns 403.90. No causal relationship must be stated to use this combination code.

Hypertensive Heart and Renal Disease

Assign codes from combination category 404, hypertensive heart and renal disease, when both hypertensive renal disease and hypertensive heart disease are stated in the diagnosis. Assume a relationship between the hypertension and the renal disease, whether or not the condition is so designated.

Coding Tip

If the patient has both hypertensive heart disease and renal disease, the coder would begin under the main term "disease, heart" and will locate the subterm "with, kidney disease—see hypertension, cardiorenal." The coder will then turn to the hypertension table and will select code 404.90, hypertensive heart and renal disease, unspecified, without mention of congestive heart failure or renal failure.

Hypertensive Retinopathy

Two codes are necessary to identify the condition. First assign code 362.11, hypertensive retinopathy, then the appropriate code from categories 401–405 to indicate the type of hypertension.

Hypertension, Secondary

Two codes are required. One identifies the underlying condition and one from category 405 to identify the hypertension. Sequencing of codes is determined by the reason for admission to the hospital.

Secondary hypertension is different from essential hypertension. Secondary hypertension is due to a disease, such as primary renal disease (405.x1), or other (405.x9). (The x in the fourth-digit location is to indicate that the fourth digit will vary dependent on whether the hypertension is benign, malignant, or unspecified.) Therefore, both the disease causing the hypertension, as well as the secondary hypertension, must be coded.

Hypertension, Transient

Assign code 796.2, Elevated blood pressure reading without diagnosis of hypertension, unless patient has an established diagnosis of hypertension. Assign code 642.3X for transient hypertension of pregnancy.

transient
Short-term or disappearing after a short amount of time.

Transient means the condition existed only temporarily. If the coder refers to the Hypertension table, the last entry is for transient, and gives the code of 796.2. Transient hypertension with a subterm "of pregnancy" is to be coded as 642.3x.

Hypertension, Controlled

Assign appropriate code from categories 401–405. This diagnostic statement usually refers to an existing state of hypertension under control by therapy.

Just because the hypertension is under control does not mean it is benign or not significant enough to be coded. If the patient is currently taking medication or receiving treatment for the hypertension, it should be coded.

Hypertension, Uncontrolled

Uncontrolled hypertension may refer to untreated hypertension or hypertension not responding to current therapeutic regimen. In either case, assign the appropriate code from categories 401–405 to designate the state and type of hypertension. Code to the type of hypertension.

Uncontrolled is a nonessential modifier for all diagnoses of hypertension, which means its presence or absence does not affect the code assignment. In other words, assign the code for the type of hypertension (such as hypertensive heart disease), and whether the hypertension is malignant, benign, or unspecified.

Elevated Blood Pressure

For a statement of elevated blood pressure without further specificity, assign code 796.2, Elevated blood pressure reading without diagnosis of hypertension, rather than a code from category 401 (essential hypertension).

Sometimes circumstances such as a trauma cause a patient's blood pressure to go up. If the patient has a high blood pressure reading without being diagnosed as having hypertension, coders should assign code 796.2, Elevated blood pressure reading without diagnosis of hypertension.

Myocardial Infarctions

Myocardial infarctions are coded according to site of the damage to the heart, with a fifth digit included to show episode of care.

0 Episode of Care Unspecified

Use this fifth digit when the source document does not contain sufficient information for the assignment of fifth digit 1 or 2.

1 Initial Episode of Care

Use fifth digit 1 to designate the first episode of care (regardless of facility site) for a newly diagnosed myocardial infarction. The fifth digit 1 is assigned regardless of the number of times a patient may be transferred during the initial episode of care.

2 Subsequent Episode of Care

Use fifth digit 2 to designate an episode of care following the initial episode when the patient is admitted for further observation, evaluation, or treatment, for a myocardial infarction that has received initial treatment but is still less than 8 weeks old.

A myocardial infarction (MI) is considered to be in the acute phase during the first eight weeks following the infarction. The fifth digits of 1 and 2 are used to distinguish the episode of care during that acute period. Fifth digit 0 should never be used on an inpatient chart, because there should be substantial documentation to specify the episode of care. If there is not sufficient documentation, the coder should ask the physician to provide the required information.

The physician should specify the site of the MI for proper code assignment. A code of "myocardial infarction, unspecified" may be rejected by the carrier as a nonspecific principal diagnosis. The coder can look at the EKG reports to see if the location is documented in the report, but the site must be verified with the physician.

Another test to look for in documenting an MI is the serum enzyme lab tests (CK, CK-MB, LD). These tests rise and fall at predictable intervals following an MI, and will be ordered and done at specific intervals according to the approximate age of the MI. They may be negative if the patient waits to seek treatment. Elevation of the cardiac enzymes may be indicative of an MI.

A previous myocardial infarction is coded to 412 when the physician states history of or old myocardial infarction presenting no symptoms during the current treatment. If the chart states "history of myocardial infarction," it is always considered relevant and should be coded to 412.

If the patient has a previous MI and presents with symptoms, the correct code is 414.8, Other Specified Forms of Chronic Ischemic Heart Disease. The included note under code 414.8 states: "Any condition classifiable to 410 specified as chronic, or presenting with symptoms after 8 weeks from date of infarction."

■ *Highlight*

The acute myocardial infarction (410) must be specified as past the acute stage and is now chronic. Also, symptoms occurring after eight weeks must be attributable to the MI and not any new, acute condition.

Angina

Angina pectoris is chest pain with cardiac origin. All chest pains should not be coded to the angina category. Unstable angina should be coded only when documented by the physician, and is also known as "pre-infarct angina." This diagnosis should not be coded with documented evidence of myocardial infarction.

Congestive Heart Failure

Congestive heart failure (CHF) is the condition where the heart cannot pump the required amount of blood, causing fluid buildup in the lungs and other areas, including the lower extremities. One common medication for patients with CHF is Lasix, a diuretic that helps the body rid itself of excessive fluid.

■ *Highlight*

When the coder is searching through the patient's chart for documentation to substantiate the CHF diagnosis, the coder can look for Lasix or other diuretics on the patient's medication sheets. Commonly, a patient presenting with severe edema of the extremities will be weighed on admission, given the diuretic, and weighed again in the morning. A patient with CHF can lose 10–15 pounds literally overnight.

Cerebrovascular Disease

Cerebrovascular disease is coded according to the type of condition, including hemorrhage, occlusion, and other cerebrovascular disease. Category 436, Acute, but ill-defined cerebrovascular disease, is used only when the diagnosis is stated as cerebrovascular accident (CVA) without further mention of cause.

If the physician lists the diagnosis as CVA, the coder should check the chart for further information as to the cause of the CVA (stroke). A cerebrovascular accident may be caused by many problems, including the following:

1. Subarachnoid hemorrhage—A hemorrhage into the subarachnoid space
2. Intracerebral hemorrhage—A hemorrhage within the brain
3. Subdural hematoma—A localized collection of hemorrhaged blood in the subdural space
4. Occlusion—Decreased blood flow of the arteries that supply the brain tissues
5. Cerebral thrombosis—An abnormal collection of blood causing an obstruction in the arteries supplying the brain with blood
6. Cerebral embolism—Obstruction of the arteries that supply the brain caused by a blood clot coming from elsewhere in the body

The coder should review the chart for documentation of the cause of a CVA before using code 436. Code 436 is considered to be a nonspecific diagnosis and should not be used when a more specific cause can be identified. According to the exclusion note under code 436, it is also not to be used in conjunction with codes from categories 430–435.

| Excludes: | *any condition classifiable to categories 430–435* |

Coding Tip *The codes in category 435 are for transient cerebral ischemia, temporary decreased blood flow to the brain. The symptoms for a TIA are the same as for a CVA, except that the symptoms disappear after about 24 hours. The codes for TIA and CVA should not be used together in a single hospital episode, unless there are two distinct episodes. (For example, the patient had a TIA with symptoms clearing, then 4 days later had a full-blown CVA.) The coder should be alerted to check with the physician prior to coding both codes.*

Coding Clinic Note: Late Effect of Cerebrovascular Disease

Category 438 is used to indicate conditions classifiable to categories 430–437 as the causes of late effects (neurologic deficits). The "late effects" include neurologic deficits that persist after initial onset of conditions classifiable to 430–437.

> *Unlike other late effects, the neurologic deficits caused by cerebrovascular disease are present from the onset rather than arising months later.*
>
> *Codes from category 438 may be assigned as additional diagnoses when a patient is admitted with a current diagnosis classifiable to the 430–437 categories.*

Codes in category 438 include the type of residuals (current condition) within the code. A code such as 438.41 is for Late effects of cerebrovascular disease, monoplegia of lower limb affecting dominant side.

> *Assign code V12.59, Personal history of disease (and not code 438) as an additional code for history of cerebrovascular disease when no neurologic deficits are present.*

Cardiovascular Procedures

Hospital coders use ICD-9-CM to code cardiovascular procedures.

Cardiac catheterization has become a very common method of diagnosing cardiac conditions. The physician uses a catheter inserted through an artery or vein to the heart guided to the heart chambers for diagnosing lesions, and blockage, and can be used in conjunction with other tools to open blocked vessels. These catheters are inserted through the femoral or antecubital vein for a right heart catheterization, and through the brachial or femoral artery for a left cardiac catheterization. ICD-9-CM provides codes for right, left, and combined left and right cardiac catheterizations, so the coder should study the documentation carefully prior to coding these procedures.

CABG, or coronary artery bypass graft, is where a vessel is taken from another location and anastomosed onto the blocked area to bypass the blockage. The procedure codes are based on the type of bypass and the number of vessels that are involved. For example, an aortocoronary bypass of three coronary vessels is coded to 36.13. If the mammary artery is used, it is coded to either 36.15, Single internal mammary-coronary artery bypass, or 36.16, Double internal mammary-coronary artery bypass.

Balloon angioplasty, or percutaneous transluminal coronary angioplasty (PTCA) is often done in conjunction with the cardiac catheterization. In many cases, this is attempted prior to putting the patient through a CABG procedure. A catheter is placed in the blocked area and a balloon that is on the tip of the catheter is inflated to try to rid the vessel of the blocked material.

EXERCISE 2–7

Using the ICD-9-CM code book, assign the correct diagnosis and procedure code(s) to the six scenarios that follow. If more information is needed from the physician, list questions on the line provided.

1. The patient was in the hospital with hemiplegia and aphasia due to acute CVA caused by subarachnoid hemorrhage as noted on CT scan of brain

done on admission. On discharge, the aphasia had cleared, but the hemiplegia is present and will require home care.

Diagnoses: _430_ 342.90 _____

Question(s) for Physician: _____

2. The patient was admitted with a two-day history of intolerable abdominal pain. The diagnosis of acute cholecystitis with cholelithiasis was made. The patient is on medication for hypertension, chronic rheumatoid arthritis, and is a non–insulin-dependent diabetic. She also had a heart bypass procedure last April. Treatment was laparoscopically assisted cholecystectomy. Patient was discharged two days post-op to be followed by the surgeon in two weeks.

Diagnoses: 574.00, 401.0, 714.0, 250.00, V45.81 _____

Question(s) for Physician: _____

3. Mr. Jones came to the clinic today because he was feeling weak and has seen a decrease in urine output over the last two days and has not been able to keep any food down. He is HIV-positive, but has been asymptomatic until now. Lab results indicate dehydration and gastroenteritis. I am going to send him over to the hospital to be admitted for IV treatment of the dehydration.

Diagnoses: 042 276.51   558.9 _____

Question(s) for Physician: _____

4. Note to Home Health Nurse: Ms. Swanson is ready to be discharged from the hospital to go home. We have treated her in the hospital for pneumo-coccal pneumonia due to her AIDS and this is better but not completely resolved yet, but she insists on going home. She also has Kaposi's sarcoma of the skin due to AIDS.

Diagnoses: 042, 481, 176.0 _____

Question(s) for Physician: _____

---

5. ## Discharge Summary

History of Present Illness:

The patient is a 54-year-old black male with a five-day history of feeling ill. When his daughter went by his house today to check on him, she found him clammy with a fever and very disoriented. Lab results in the

---

ER showed UTI, probable sepsis, renal insufficiency. BUN, creatinine elevated. WBC was 23,000. The patient was admitted for treatment of probable urinary sepsis.

(handwritten: 2nd above UTI; 1st beside probable)

Findings While in Hospital:

WBCs fell during hospitalization to 9,000. Urine culture grew E. coli, blood cultures also grew out E. coli. No other abnormalities noted.

Hospital Course:

The patient was started on IV fluid rehydration; electrolytes improved throughout stay. He was started on IV antibiotics and was switched to oral antibiotics the day of discharge. The patient was discharged to his daughter's care at her home until he gets back on his feet again.

Diagnoses: _____ (599.0) (038.42) 041.4

(handwritten: 2nd above 599.0; 1st above 038.42)

Question(s) for Physician: Renal insufficiency; coded?

---

6.   **Discharge Summary**

History of Present Illness:

The patient, a 53-year-old Caucasian male, was admitted through the emergency room with unstable angina pectoris, diaphoresis, and pain radiating to the left arm. The patient had a previous MI three years ago.

Hospital Course:

Cardiac enzymes were done at 12, 24, and 36 hours and were elevated. Serial EKGs were performed, which confirmed the diagnosis of AMI, Inferolateral wall. A left cardiac catheterization was performed on the first day of hospitalization with findings of the LAD blocked at 95% and second artery blocked at 100%. We then scheduled the patient for bypass. On the second hospital day he had an aortocoronary bypass, two coronary arteries performed successfully. After two days in CCU, the patient was transferred to a regular hospital bed. The patient was discharged after uneventful recovery period on the sixth day of hospitalization.

(handwritten margin note: 2nd (old MCI) history, status)

(handwritten: 1st above diagnosis of AMI)

Diagnoses: 410.21, 412

Question(s) for Physician: _____

DIABETES MELLITUS

Diabetes mellitus is one of the most common diseases of the endocrine system and one that coders have many problems coding.

Fifth digits are required on all diabetes mellitus codes to show if the patient is insulin dependent or non–insulin-dependent, and whether the diabetes is controlled or uncontrolled.

Fifth digits are as follows:

    0 Type II or unspecified type, not stated as uncontrolled
      Fifth digit 0 is for use for Type II patients, even if the patient requires insulin
    1 Type I (juvenile type), not stated as uncontrolled
    2 Type II or unspecified type, uncontrolled
      Fifth digit 2 is for use for Type II patients, even if the patient requires insulin
    3 Type I (juvenile type), uncontrolled

Coding Tip *Fifth digits 0 and 2 are used for Type II, adult-onset diabetic patients, even if the patient requires insulin.*

Type I or Juvenile type, is when the patient's body does not produce insulin, thus making the patient dependent on insulin on a regular basis to survive.

Type II is usually controlled by diet and oral medications. The NIDDM patient sometimes must be given injections of insulin, but is not dependent on the insulin to survive.

Fifth digits 2 and 3 show whether the diabetes is stated to be uncontrolled. This is not a judgment that should be made by the coder, and if the documentation in the chart does not specifically state uncontrolled, the coder must use the fifth digit (0 or 1) that shows the diabetes as "not stated to be uncontrolled."

Many diabetic patients will develop further complications caused by the diabetes. In these cases, there are usually two codes needed to fully identify the condition. The diabetes code should be listed first and the complication of the diabetes listed next, such as 250.1x followed by 362.01 for diabetic retinopathy.

If a diabetic patient develops hypoglycemia, code 250.8x should be used, diabetes with other specified complications. Code 251.2, Hypoglycemia, unspecified, is not to be used if the patient has diabetes.

EXERCISE 2–8

Using the ICD-9-CM code book, assign code(s) to the following statements. (Number of lines indicate number of codes required.)

1. Type II diabetic gangrene _250.70_ _785.4_

2. Type II diabetes, uncontrolled with skin ulcer _250.82_ _707.9_

3. Type II diabetes mellitus with Kimmelstiel-Wilson disease _250.40_
   _581.81_

4. Uncontrolled type I diabetes with cataracts _250.53_ _366.41_

5. Type I diabetes mellitus with diabetic nephrosis _250.41_ _581.81_

6. Retinal hemorrhage in patient with insulin dependent diabetes _250.51_
   _362.01_

7. Type I diabetes mellitus with ketoacidosis _250.11_

8. Gestational diabetes in otherwise nondiabetic woman _648.80_

9. Diabetes in patient 6-months pregnant _250.00_ _648.00_

10. Hypoglycemia coma in patient without diabetes _251.0_

USING V CODES

V codes include factors influencing health status and contact with health services, and can be used as principal and secondary diagnoses. V codes are used when a person who is not currently sick uses health care services, such as need for a vaccination, or check-up, or when a problem affects the patient's current illness, such as a history of carcinoma, or status post-coronary artery bypass graft. Sometimes it is difficult to locate a needed V code because of the main terms used in ICD-9-CM. Many common main terms to locate V codes are as follows:

> Admission for, Attention to, Examination, Follow up, History of, Observation for, Screening, Status post, Supervision, Testing

If the patient uses medical facilities and does not have a medical diagnosis, the V code can be used as the principal or primary diagnosis. For example, a mother comes in for a six-week check-up following delivery and has no problems. Code V24.2, Routine postpartum follow-up is assigned.

V64.4 is used when a laparoscopic surgical procedure was converted to an open procedure. The coder can locate this code in the Alphabetic Index of Diseases by looking under the main term "laparoscopic" or "conversion."

To code a patient's encounter for a screening mammogram, use either code V76.12, Special screening for malignant neoplasm, breast, other screening mammogram, or V76.11, Screening mammogram for high-risk patient. The physician should be queried to determine which of these two codes is most appropriate for the patient. Any abnormality found on the screening mammogram, such as a lump, should be listed as a secondary diagnosis.

V codes are diagnosis codes, not procedure codes. If a patient is admitted for a service, such as the patient's encounter for screening mammogram, the coder will also need to code a procedure code for the screening mammogram itself (87.37).

Code a patient encounter for a preoperative examination using V72.8x as the first diagnosis. The reason for the surgery should be assigned as an additional diagnosis.

▬ *Highlight*

> *Check with local carriers as to individual preferences for diagnosis coding of preadmission testing or preoperative examinations, as these may vary per insurance carrier.*

If a past condition may affect the current treatment, the V code can be used as a secondary diagnosis, such as V45.81, status post CABG (heart bypass surgery).

Codes V72.5, Radiological examination, NEC and V72.6, Laboratory examination, are not to be used if any sign, symptom, or reason for a test is documented.

V codes are used to distinguish a patient's *exposure* to a disease or condition, and to indicate the disease or condition itself has not been diagnosed. For example, a patient is seen and tested for exposure to HIV. The patient at this point is not diagnosed with HIV, but rather the exposure to the disease. The main term to research in the ICD-9-CM code is "exposure."

Official Coding Guidelines

Codes from the V71.0–V71.9 Series, Observation and Evaluation for Suspected Conditions

Codes from the V71.0–V71.9 series are assigned as principal diagnoses for encounters or admissions to evaluate the patient's condition when there is some evidence to suggest the existence of an abnormal condition or following an accident or other incident that ordinarily results in a health problem, and where no supporting evidence for the suspected condition is found and no treatment is currently required. The fact that the patient may be scheduled for continuing observation in the office/clinic setting following discharge does not limit the use of this category.

Official Outpatient Coding Guidelines

K. For patients receiving diagnostic services only during an encounter/ visit, sequence first the diagnosis, condition, problem, or other reason for encounter/visit shown in the medical record to be chiefly responsible for the outpatient services provided during the encounter/visit. Codes for other diagnoses (e.g., chronic conditions) may be sequenced as additional diagnoses.

L. For patients receiving therapeutic services only during an encounter/ visit, sequence first the diagnosis, condition, problem, or other reason for encounter/visit shown in the medical record to be chiefly responsible for the outpatient services provided during the encounter/visit. Codes for other diagnoses (e.g., chronic conditions) may be sequenced as additional diagnoses.

The only exception to this rule is that patients receiving chemotherapy, radiation therapy, or rehabilitation, the appropriate V code for the service is listed first, and the diagnosis or problem for which the service is being performed listed second.

There are certain V codes that, according to *Coding Clinic for ICD-9-CM*, are considered to be nonspecific, used only as principal/primary diagnosis, or are only to be used secondary to other ICD-9-CM codes. In *Coding Clinic for ICD-9-CM*, Fourth Quarter, 1996, pp. 58–62, a list is provided to help the coder know appropriate usage of V codes.

Nonspecific V Codes

According to *Coding Clinic for ICD-9-CM*, Fourth Quarter, 1996, pp. 58–62, "Certain V codes are so nonspecific, or potentially redundant with other codes in the classification, that there can be little justification for their use in the inpatient setting. Their use in the outpatient setting should be limited to those instances when there is no further documentation to permit more precise coding. Otherwise, any sign or symptom or any other reason for the visit that is captured in another code should be used." These categories/codes are:

> V11, V13.4, V13.6, V15.7, V23.2, V40, V41, V47, V48, V49
>
> (Exceptions: V49.6 and V49.7), V51, V58.2, V58.9, V72.5, V72.6)
>
> "Codes V72.5 and V72.6 are not to be used if any sign, symptom, or reason for a test is documented. See sections K and L of the outpatient guidelines."

First Listed

The following are V codes/categories/subcategories that are only acceptable as first listed. This means they should only be listed as first (primary or principal) diagnoses, never as secondary diagnoses.

> V22.0, V22.1, V58.0, V58.1 (V58.0 and V58.1 may be used together on a record with either one being sequenced first, when a patient receives both chemotherapy and radiation therapy during the same encounter.), V58.3, V58.5, V20, V24, V29, V30–39, V59, V66 (except V66.7, Palliative care), V67, V68, V70, V71, V72 (except V72.5 and V72.6)

Additional Only

There are certain V code categories/subcategories that may only be used as additional codes, and never should be used as first (primary or principal) diagnoses. These are as follows:

> V22.2, V66.7, V09, V10, V12, V13 (except V13.4 and V13.6), V14, V15 (Except V15.7), V16–V19, V21, V27, V42, V43, V44, V45, V46, V49.6x, V49.7x, V60, V62, V63, V64

EXERCISE 2–9

Assign the V code from ICD-9-CM to the following statements.

1. Physical exam required for nursing school V70.3

2. Family history of colon cancer V16.0

3. Exposure to SARS V01.82

4. Diaphragm fitting V25.02

5. Family history of ischemic heart disease V17.3

6. Personal history of allergy to penicillin V14.0

7. Normal pregnancy without complications V22.2

8. Annual pelvic exam including Pap smear   V72.31
9. Influenza vaccination   V04.81
10. Six-month well-baby check   V20.2
11. Screening for osteoporosis   V82.81
12. Contact with anthrax   V01.81
13. Marriage counseling   V61.10
14. Exposure to blood-tainted emesis   V15.85
15. Blood-alcohol testing   V70.4

OBSTETRICAL CODING

Obstetric (OB) coding seems to be the section that gives coders the most trouble. See Chapter 10, "Obstetrics and Gynecology," for more information on coding these diagnoses and procedures.

Many conditions that are normally coded in different chapters are considered complications of pregnancy, so are reclassified to the pregnancy chapter when the patient is pregnant. Conditions that complicate or are associated with pregnancy are normally listed under the main terms: pregnancy, labor, delivery, puerperium.

Nearly all pregnancy codes require a fifth digit. The following fifth-digit sub-classification is for use with categories 640–648, and 651–676 to denote the current episode of care:

> 0 Unspecified as to Episode of Care or Not Applicable
> 1 Delivered, With or Without Mention of Antepartum Condition
> 2 Delivered, With Mention of Postpartum Complication
> 3 Antepartum Condition or Complication
> 4 Postpartum Condition or Complication

When determining the correct fifth digit to use, the coder should review the patient's medical record to determine if the patient delivered during this episode of care. If the patient did deliver during this admission, the correct fifth digit choices would be limited to either 1 or 2 only. The coder should also review the fifth digits listed in brackets below each code in the pregnancy chapter. Certain codes limit the choices of fifth digits. For example, with code 644.0, Threatened premature labor, the correct fifth digits can only be 0 (unspecified as to episode of care or not applicable), or 3 (antepartum condition or complication).

Official Coding Guidelines

Complication of Pregnancy

When a patient is admitted because of a condition that is either a complication of pregnancy or that is complicating the pregnancy, the code for the ob-

stetric complication is the principal diagnosis. An additional code may be assigned as needed to provide specificity.

For example, if the patient is an insulin-dependent diabetic and is pregnant, the coder would begin under the main term "pregnancy," subterm "complicated by," "diabetes (mellitus) (conditions classifiable to 250). The principal or first diagnosis listed would be 648.0x, Other current conditions in the mother classifiable elsewhere, but complicating pregnancy, childbirth, or the puerperium; Diabetes mellitus. There is a note following category 648 that reminds the coder to "Use additional code(s) to identify the condition." This means that both codes are needed to fully identify the patient's condition. The coder would assign code 250.01 as a secondary diagnosis to indicate that the patient was an insulin-dependent diabetic.

Coding Non-Obstetric Conditions

If a woman is pregnant, the treatment decisions for a non obstetrical condition may be different because of the pregnancy. To locate these conditions, the coder should look in the alphabetic section under "Pregnancy, complicated by." If the specific condition cannot be found, there is code 646.8, Other specified complications of pregnancy, that should be used in conjunction with the non-obstetrical condition. If a physician treating the non-obstetric condition uses the appropriate codes from the pregnancy chapter, and provides sufficient documentation in the patient's chart, it will indicate that the patient's condition was complicated by the pregnancy. This complication increases the amount of effort, and could increase the number of treatment options for the patient, therefore providing justification to use a higher level of office visit code in CPT.

Code 650

Code 650 is for delivery in a completely normal case, and cannot be used in conjunction with any other code in the pregnancy chapter. This code can only be used when the following criteria are met:

1. Liveborn
2. Term (37 completed weeks but less than 42)
3. Single birth
4. No complications
5. No instrumentation except episiotomy or artificial rupture of membranes
6. Cephalic or vertex presentation
7. No fetal manipulation (turning or version of the fetus)

If the delivery meets all of these criteria, use code 650. If not, use a code for every factor in the case that does not meet the criteria. For example, the patient delivers a single liveborn infant at 38 weeks gestation with cephalic (head) presentation. A small episiotomy was performed. Using the previous list, the coder can determine that all criteria are met, so code 650 is used for the delivery. If the patient delivered liveborn twins at 36 weeks by cesarean section, this case does not meet criteria numbers 2, 3, and 5. The coder would code three diagnoses codes; one for each criteria not met (651.01, Twin pregnancy, delivered; 644.21, early onset of delivery; 669.71, cesarean delivery, without mention of indication).

Selection of Principal Diagnosis

When a delivery occurs, the principal diagnosis should correspond to the main circumstances or complication of the delivery. In cases of cesarean deliveries, the principal diagnosis should correspond to the reason the cesarean was performed, unless the reason for admission was unrelated to the condition resulting in the cesarean delivery.

Many hospitals use V27 codes as secondary codes to identify outcome of delivery on the mother's chart. These codes specify if the baby was liveborn, single, twin, stillborn, and so on, and are not used on the baby's chart. V27.0, for example, would be used for a single liveborn outcome of delivery.

Codes V22.0, Supervision of normal first pregnancy, and V22.1, Supervision of other normal pregnancy, are used for routine prenatal or postpartum care. These codes should not be used in conjunction with any other code from the pregnancy chapter.

Procedures having to do with labor or delivery are commonly located under the main term of "delivery." All deliveries should be coded with a procedure code. If the 650 code is used to show a totally normal delivery, then the most appropriate procedure code is 73.59, Assisted spontaneous delivery.

Official Coding Guidelines

Fetal Conditions Affecting the Management of the Mother

Codes from category 655, "Known or suspected fetal abnormality affecting management of the mother," and category 656, "Other fetal and placental problems affecting the management of the mother," are assigned only when the fetal condition is actually responsible for modifying the management of the mother, i.e., by requiring diagnostic studies, additional observation, special care, or termination of pregnancy. The fact that the fetal condition exists does not justify assigning a code from this series to the mother's record.

If the fetus was known to have spina bifida, for example, this would require additional studies and additional observation and probable cesarean delivery to prevent trauma to the fetus. In this case, it would be appropriate to use code 655.03 on visits prior to the delivery, then 655.01 as one of the delivery diagnoses.

It should be noted that there are many codes to be used on the baby's chart noting problems with the mother that affected the baby. These should not be confused with pregnancy codes, and are usually codes in the 740–779 category range. For example, in the alphabetic index under the main term "pregnancy, twin," there is a subterm for "affecting fetus or newborn 761.5." This code is only to be used on the baby's chart, and only if the twin pregnancy somehow affected the newborn.

Abortion is any loss of the fetus prior to 22 completed weeks of gestation, whether it be spontaneous (miscarriage) or induced. There are several fifth digits needed in the abortion categories, and these do change according to the code, so the coder should pay careful attention to the required fifth digits. The diagnosis of abortion, spontaneous, with excessive hemorrhage, incomplete, for example, would be coded 634.11.

Delivery of Infants and Congenital Anomalies

The V codes for newborns (which is the newborn's principal diagnosis) are included in the V30–V39 codes. These codes are not for use on the mother's chart.

> ### *Use of Codes V30–V39*
>
> *When coding the birth of an infant, assign a code from categories V30–V39, according to the type of birth. A code from this series is assigned as a principal diagnosis, and assigned only once to a newborn at the time of birth.*
>
> ### *Newborn Transfers*
>
> *If the newborn is transferred to another institution, the V30 series is not used [by the receiving facility].*

When coding the newborn's medical stay, the principal diagnosis is always a code from V30–V39 to show that the baby was born during this episode of care. Any complicating factors or anomalies would be coded secondarily. These codes are only used on the original chart, and are not used by a secondary hospital where the newborn was transferred.

> ### *Official Coding Guidelines*
>
> ### *Newborn Guidelines*
>
> *The newborn period is defined as beginning at birth and lasting through the 28th day following birth.*
>
> *The following guidelines are provided for reporting purposes. Hospitals may record other diagnoses as needed for internal data use.*
>
> *All clinically significant conditions noted on routine newborn examination should be coded. A condition is clinically significant if it requires:*
>
> - *clinical evaluation*
> - *therapeutic treatment*
> - *diagnostic procedures*
> - *extended length of hospital stay*
> - *increased nursing care and/or monitoring*
> - *has implications for future health care needs*
>
> *Note: The newborn guidelines listed above are the same as the general coding guidelines for "other diagnoses," except for the final bullet regarding implications for future health care needs. Whether a condition is clinically significant can be determined only by the physician.*

For example, the infant is a term liveborn, born in this hospital by vaginal delivery, in fetal distress, first noted during labor. The principal diagnosis is V30.00, with a secondary diagnosis of 768.3 for Fetal distress, first noted during labor, in liveborn infant.

Use of Category V29

A. Assign a code from V29, "Observation and evaluation of newborns and infants for suspected conditions not found," to identify those instances when a healthy newborn is evaluated for a suspected condition that is determined after study not to be present. Do not use a code from category V29 when the patient has identified signs or symptoms of a suspected problem; in such case, code the sign or symptom.

B. A V29 code is to be used as a secondary code after the V30, Liveborn Infants According to the Type of Birth, code. It may also be assigned as a principal code for readmissions or encounters when the V30 code no longer applies. It is for use only for healthy newborns and infants for which no condition after study is found to be present.

The note following category V29 reads as follows: "Note: This category is to be used for newborns, within the neonatal period (the first 28 days of life), who are suspected of having an abnormal condition resulting from exposure from the mother or the birth process, but without signs or symptoms, and, which after examination and observation, is found not to exist."

For example, there is a diagnosis of term birth living child, born at another hospital and transferred here to observe for the possibility of meconium aspiration. After observation, the baby was found to be healthy. Code V29.2 would be used for this diagnosis. The coder would not assign code V30.00 because the infant was not born at this hospital.

Maternal Causes of Perinatal Morbidity

Codes from categories 760–763, Maternal causes of perinatal morbidity and mortality, are assigned only when the maternal condition has actually affected the fetus or newborn. The fact that the mother has an associated medical condition or experiences some complication of pregnancy, labor, or delivery does not justify the routine assignment of codes from these categories to the newborn record.

The note following category 760 reads "Includes: The listed maternal conditions only when specified as a cause of mortality or morbidity of the fetus or newborn." If the mother is malnourished and this has affected the fetus, the coder would assign code 760.4, Fetus or newborn affected by maternal conditions which may be unrelated to present pregnancy, maternal nutritional disorders, as a secondary diagnosis.

Congenital Anomalies

Assign an appropriate code from categories 740–759, Congenital Anomalies, when a specific abnormality is diagnosed for an infant. Such abnormalities may occur as a set of symptoms or multiple malformations. A code should be assigned for each presenting manifestation of the syndrome if the syndrome is not specifically indexed in ICD-9-CM.

Coding of Other (Additional) Diagnoses

A. *Assign codes for conditions that require treatment or further investigation, prolong the length of stay, or require resource utilization.*

B. *Assign codes for conditions that have been specified by the physician as having implications for future health care needs. Note: This guideline should not be used for adult patients.*

C. *Assign a code for newborn conditions originating in the perinatal period (categories 760–779), as well as complications arising during the current episode of care classified in other chapters, only if the diagnoses have been documented by the responsible physician at the time of transfer or discharge as having affected the fetus or newborn.*

D. *Insignificant conditions or signs or symptoms that resolve without treatment are not coded.*

Spina bifida, a defective closure of the vertebral column, is categorized according to the level of severity, and should be coded to the highest degree of severity that is known. It is further subdivided to show the presence/absence of hydrocephalus, abnormal accumulation of fluid in the brain. Procedures include closure of the defect (03.5x categories), and in many cases, a shunt is implanted to allow for drainage of fluid build-up.

■ *Highlight*

Congenital heart conditions can be extensive and should be coded with great care. They are divided between cyanotic and acyanotic defects. Cyanotic defects occur when the defect allows for mixing of oxygenated and deoxygenated blood within the heart. Two of the most common cardiac defects are:

Ventricular septal defect *(an opening in the ventricular septum allowing the blood to go from the left to right ventricle). The appropriate code is 745.4. The repair code should be found within the 35.xx category.*

Patent ductus arteriosus *is a condition where the fetal blood vessel connecting the aorta and pulmonary artery that allows blood to bypass the fetal lungs remains open (patent). This should close within the first few hours after birth. If it remains open, heart failure and pulmonary congestion result, and surgical repair is almost always needed. The code for the patent ductus arteriosus is 747.0; the procedure to be coded is 38.85, Other surgical occlusion of vessels.*

Prematurity and Fetal Growth Retardation

Codes from categories 764 and 765 should not be assigned based on recorded birthweight or estimated gestational age, but upon the attending physician's clinical assessment of maturity of infant.

Note: Since physicians may utilize different criteria in determining prematurity, do not code the diagnosis of prematurity unless the physician documents this condition.

Categories 764 and 765 show slow fetal growth and low birthweight. They include fifth digits to show the weight of the newborn, and are in grams. If the baby's weight is recorded in pounds, the coder will need to use a conversion chart for appropriate coding. (500 grams is equivalent to approximately one pound, one and two-thirds ounces.)

EXERCISE 2–10

Using the ICD-9-CM code book, code the following diagnoses. If more information is needed from the physician, list questions on the line provided.

1. Thirty-three-year-old white female with history of multiple miscarriages, now at 27 weeks gestation and is put on bedrest by physician for remainder of gestation. Home care to see patient on weekly basis to monitor mother and child.

   Diagnoses: _V23.23_____

   Question(s) for Physician: _____

2. This 27-day-old infant was followed today in the clinic for jaundice. Radiology report shows congenital obstruction of the bile duct. We are going to refer the parents to the pediatric surgery clinic for surgical evaluation. ~~774.5~~

   Diagnoses: _~~751.61~~, 751.61, 774.5_____

   Question(s) for Physician: _____

3. Progress Note: This baby was born prematurely this morning at 36 weeks gestation at home and is admitted for observation. Weight is 2456 grams.

   Birthdate → V30.1

   Diagnoses: _765.28, 765.18_____

   Question(s) for Physician: _____

4. Final diagnoses: Uterine pregnancy, term. Spontaneous delivery of single liveborn infant, cephalic presentation. Postpartum hemorrhage, onset 32 hours following delivery.

   Diagnoses: _V27.0, 666.22_____

   Question(s) for Physician: _____

NEOPLASMS

The term "neoplasm" literally means "new growth." A common error made by many people is to think that all neoplasms are malignant, or cancerous. It is important that the correct code assignment be made, especially in dealing with a disease such as cancer, and the coder must be sure of the correct diagnosis. An incorrect malignancy coded on a patient's chart can cause long-term problems, such as the loss of insurance, denial of life insurance policies, and increased rates. The final coding of a suspect mass or tumor should not be completed until after review of the pathology report.

The Neoplasm Table

ICD-9-CM has provided an extensive table that is used to code most neoplasms. Figure 2–2 shows a partial sample of this table. It is located in the alphabetic index under the main term Neoplasm. The table is divided into site, then codes to show the neoplasm's behavior.

Within the Malignant section there are three available choices:

Primary is the site where the neoplasm originated.

Secondary is the site to which the primary site has spread, either by metastasis (movement to another body location), direct extension to an adjacent organ, or invasion into the blood or lymph system.

In situ is where the cells are malignant, but have not spread (invaded) the basement membrane of the structure.

	Malignant					
	Primary	Secondary	Ca in situ	Benign	Uncertain Behavior	Unspecified
Neoplasm, neoplastic	199.1	199.1	234.9	229.9	238.9	239.9

Notes — 1. The list below gives the code numbers for neoplasms by anatomical site. For each site there are six possible code numbers according to whether the neoplasm in question is malignant, benign, in situ, of uncertain behavior, or of unspecified nature. The description of the neoplasm will often indicate which of the six columns is appropriate; e.g., malignant melanoma of skin, benign fibroadenoma of breast, carcinaoma in situ of cervix uteri.

Where such descriptors are not present, the remainder of the Index should be consulted where guidance is given to the appropriate column for each morphological (histologic) variety listed; e.g., Mesonephroma — see Neoplasm, malignant; Embryoma — see also Neoplasm, uncertain behavior; Disease, Bowen's — see Neoplasm, skin, in situ. However, the guidance in the Index can be overridden if one of the descriptors mentioned above is present; e.g., malignant adenoma of colon is coded to 153.9 and not to 211.3 as the adjective "malignant" overrides the Index entry "Adenoma — see also Neoplasm, benign."

*2. Sites marked with the sign * (e.g., face NEC*) should be classified to malignant neoplasm of skin of these sites if the variety of neoplasm is a squamous cell carcinoma or an epidermoid carcinoma, and to benign neoplasm of skin of these sites if the variety of neoplasm is a papilloma (any type).*

abdomen, abdominal	195.2	198.89	234.8	229.8	238.8	239.8
cavity	195.2	198.89	234.8	229.8	238.8	239.8
organ	195.2	198.89	234.8	229.8	238.8	239.8
viscera	195.2	198.89	234.8	229.8	238.8	239.8
wall	173.5	198.2	232.5	216.5	238.2	239.2
connective tissue	171.5	198.89	—	215.5	238.1	239.2
abdominopelvic	195.8	198.89	234.8	229.8	238.8	239.8
accessory sinus — see Neoplasm, sinus						
acoustic nerve	192.0	198.4	—	225.1	237.9	239.7
acromion (process)	170.4	198.5	—	213.4	238.0	239.2

Figure 2–2 ICD-9-CM table (partial). *From ICD-9-CM for Hospitals—Volumes 1, 2, &3, 2005 Professional.* Reprinted with permission of Ingenix.

Benign is when the tumor is not spreading or invasive into other sites.

Uncertain behavior diagnosis is when the pathologist is unable to determine whether the neoplasm is malignant or benign.

Unspecified nature can be used when the documentation does not support a more specific code. This may be used when the patient is transferred to another facility or is discharged without further workup done on the neoplasm.

How to Code a Neoplasm

Step 1: The coder should first go to the alphabetic index to look for the main term of the histological type, such as carcinoma, adenoma, leiomyoma, etc. There the coder will find an "M" (morphology) code, which identifies the histological type, behavior, and site. These M codes are used as secondary codes and are optional, used primarily by cancer registries.

Step 2: Look for a subterm that describes the site found in the diagnostic statement. If a code is located, that is as far as the coder must search to describe the condition. For example, if the patient has Leiomyoma of the uterus, the coder would look under the main term "leiomyoma," subterm "uterus" to locate the code 218.9.

Step 3: If the site is not listed, under the main term for the histological type there should be an instruction to "See also Neoplasm, by site, behavior" (such as benign, malignant, etc.).

Step 4: The coder should then turn to the neoplasm table and locate the appropriate code. The neoplasm table is located in the Alphabetic Index under the main term "Neoplasm."

For example, if the patient had a diagnosis of Liposarcoma, shoulder, the coder would begin under the main term liposarcoma. There is no subterm for shoulder, but a note located next to the main term tells the coder to "*see also* Neoplasm, connective tissue, malignant." This note directs the coder to go to the Neoplasm table to locate the correct code of 171.2.

Coding Tip | *A mistake made by many coders is to first check the table of Neoplasms and not begin by looking up the histological site. This is a common coding error, and should be avoided by the trained coder.*

■ *Highlight*

Neoplasm coding tips:

- *If a malignant neoplasm has been removed, but has recurred at the primary site, code the recurrence as a primary site.*

- *Be careful of the word "metastatic." It can be used to describe both a primary and secondary site. Metastatic from the breast means the breast is the primary site. Malignancy, breast metastatic to the liver, for example, means the breast is the primary site and the liver is the secondary site.*

- *If the primary or secondary site is unknown, ICD-9-CM provides 199.1 and 199.0, unknown site, to fully describe the patient's condition.*

- *If the patient has had a malignancy removed and is still in the initial stage of treatment, such as chemotherapy or radiation therapy, the cancer should be coded as if it was still present.*

- *If the patient has had a malignancy removed and is back for follow-up to look for further signs of cancer, and there is none, then a "history of malignant neoplasm" code is used from the V10 section.*

- *If the patient is undergoing testing because a family member has or previously had cancer, a V16 code can be used to show "family history of malignant neoplasm."*

Principal Diagnosis

Neoplasms often cause problems to the coder when trying to determine the correct principal diagnosis. The following official coding guidelines provide sequencing guidance:

Official Coding Guidelines

Neoplasms

A. *If the treatment is directed at the malignancy, designate the malignancy as the principal diagnosis, except when the purpose of the encounter or hospital admission is for radiotherapy session(s), V58.0, or for chemotherapy session(s), V58.1, in which instance the malignancy is coded and sequenced second.*

B. *When a patient is admitted for the purpose of radiotherapy or chemotherapy and develops complications, such as uncontrolled nausea and vomiting or dehydration, the principal diagnosis is Encounter for radiotherapy, V58.0, or Encounter for chemotherapy, V58.1.*

C. *When an episode of inpatient care involves surgical removal of a primary site or secondary site malignancy followed by adjunct chemotherapy or radiotherapy, code the malignancy as the principal diagnosis, using codes in the 140–198 series, or, where appropriate, in the 200–203 series.*

D. *When the reason for admission is to determine the extent of the malignancy, or for a procedure such as paracentesis or thoracentesis, the primary malignancy or appropriate metastatic site is designated as the principal diagnosis, even though chemotherapy or radiotherapy is administered.*

E. *When the primary malignancy has been previously excised or eradicated from its site and there is no adjunct treatment directed to the site and no evidence of any remaining malignancy at the primary site, use the appropriate code from the V10 series to indicate the former site of primary malignancy. Any mention of extension, invasion, or metastasis to a nearby structure or organ or to a distant site is coded as a secondary malignant neoplasm to the site and may be the principal diagnosis in the absence of the primary site.*

F. *When a patient is admitted because of a primary neoplasm with metastasis and treatment is directed toward the secondary site only, the secondary neoplasm is designated as the principal diagnosis even though the primary malignancy is still present.*

G. *Symptoms, signs, and ill-defined conditions listed in Chapter 16 of the ICD-9-CM Code Book characteristic of, or associated with, an existing primary or secondary site malignancy cannot be used to replace the malignancy as principal diagnosis, regardless of the number of admissions or encounters for treatment and care of the neoplasm.*

H. Coding and sequencing of complications associated with the malignancy neoplasm or with the therapy thereof are subject to the following guidelines:

When admission is for management of an anemia associated with the malignancy, and the treatment is only for anemia, the anemia is designated as the principal diagnosis and is followed by the appropriate code(s) for the malignancy.

When admission is for management of an anemia associated with chemotherapy or radiotherapy and the only treatment is for the anemia, the anemia is designated as the principal diagnosis followed by the appropriate code(s) for the malignancy.

When the admission is for management of dehydration due to the malignancy of the therapy, or a combination of both, and only the dehydration is being treated (intravenous rehydration), the dehydration is designated as the principal diagnosis, followed by the code(s) for the malignancy.

When the admission is for treatment of a complication resulting from a surgical procedure such as a colon resection, performed for the treatment of a malignancy, designate the complication as the principal diagnosis if the treatment is directed at resolving the complication.

EXERCISE 2–11

Using all volumes of ICD-9-CM, code the following diagnoses and procedures.

1. Malignant carcinoma of appendix with appendectomy and resection of cecum

   Diagnoses 153.5

   Procedures 47.09 45.72

2. Metastatic carcinoma to pelvic bone from prostate / secondary

   Diagnoses 185   198.5

3. Hodgkin's disease with cervical lymph node biopsy

   Diagnoses 201.90

   Procedures 40.11

4. Recurrent of papillary carcinoma of bladder, low-grade transitional cell

   Diagnoses 188.9

5. Carcinoma of the brain metastatic from the lungs 2nd

   Diagnoses 162.9 198.3

6. Carcinoma in situ of the cervix uteri

   Diagnoses 233.1

7. Carcinoma of the right breast, lower-outer quadrant with metastasis to the lung

   Diagnoses **174.5   197.0**

8. Benign neoplasm of tongue

   Diagnoses **210.1**

9. Malignant neoplasm of tongue

   Diagnoses **141.9**

10. Carcinoma of anterior bladder wall metastatic to rectum and colon

    Diagnoses **188.3   197.5**

11. Carcinoma of the right breast with metastatis to the axillary lymph nodes

    Diagnoses **174.9   196.3**

12. Carcinoma of the axillary lymph nodes and lungs, metastatic from the breast

    Diagnoses **174.9   196.3   197.0**

13. Kaposi's sarcoma

    Diagnoses **176.9**

14. Benign carcinoma of the turbinate bone

    Diagnoses **213.0**

15. Basal cell carcinoma of the chin

    Diagnoses **173.3**

---

16. **Report of Operation**

ATTENDING SURGEON: John Thomas, MD

OPERATION: Left modified radical mastectomy

PREOPERATIVE DIAGNOSIS: Carcinoma of the left breast

POSTOPERATIVE DIAGNOSIS: Carcinoma of the left breast

ANESTHESIA:

COMPLICATIONS:

ESTIMATED BLOOD LOSS:

FLUIDS:

FINDINGS:

PROCEDURE: The patient was adequately anesthetized. The left breast was adequately prepped and draped in a sterile fashion. With a skin marker, the portion of skin and breast tissue to be removed was delineated with the skin marker and then, at this point, incisions were made and with

continues

sharp dissection the superior and inferior flaps were fashioned. At this point, the entire breast and anterior pectoral fascia was excised en bloc into the axillary tissues and with very careful dissection a left axillary dissection was performed. The long thoracic and thoracodorsal nerves were both ligated with 3-0 silk sutures. After the breast and axillary contents had been excised en bloc, thorough antibiotic irrigation was performed. Adequate hemostasis was obtained. Two Hemovac drains were appropriately placed and sutured to the skin at their exit site with 2-0 silk suture. The wound was then closed with staples. A sterile dressing was applied. The patient tolerated the procedure well, was awakened, and taken to the recovery room in satisfactory condition.

Diagnoses: _____

Procedures: _____

Question(s) for physician: _____

E CODING

External causes of injury codes are used as secondary codes to show the cause of the injury whenever it is known, such as a fall or automobile accident. Most E codes are not mandatory, but it is recommended that they be used wherever possible to fully describe the patient's condition. There is a separate alphabetic E code index (in the alphabetic index section of the code book located behind the table of drugs and chemicals) to facilitate locating the appropriate E code. They include type of injury (fall, MVA), place of accident, specific person involved (pedestrian, driver of car), and E codes for late effects. Some states are now beginning to mandate the use of all E codes, or E codes for certain conditions. The use of the E codes helps to tell the whole story behind what happened to the patient. If an accident or injury code is used, such as those from codes 800–995, payment on a claim may be delayed prior to investigation of the facts surrounding the injury. By using the E code to tell the cause of the injury, the carrier then has all of the information needed to pay the claim.

> **EXAMPLE**
>
> A man injured his left thumb while trying to dislodge an object from a garbage disposal at home. The wound lacerated the thumb with tendon involvement.
>
> First, code the wound of the thumb 883.2.
>
> Second, code the location of the accident, which is in his home, E849.0.
>
> Third, code the appliance/implement that caused the accident, E920.2.
>
> Note: The location is important to verify where the accident happened in relation to work, home, or other area.

There are definitions for types of accidents, such as railway accident and motor vehicle traffic accident, as well as definitions for types of vehicles and persons injured, such as off-road vehicle, pedal cyclist, and pedestrian. These definitions are located on the first page of the E code tabular list, which is located just past the V code tabular list in the ICD-9-CM book.

For example, if a patient had a closed fracture of the shaft of the femur due to crashing the snowmobile he was driving into a tree, the coder would first code the fracture, 821.01. To show the cause of the fracture, code E820.0. The coder would locate the correct E code by checking the E code alphabetic index under the main term "crash," subterm "motor vehicle." The code book gives the instruction to "*see also* Accident, motor vehicle." Under the main term "Accident, motor vehicle," the subterm "nontraffic, not on public highway–*see* categories E820–E825." The coder could also look under the main term "Accident," subterm "snow vehicle, motor driven (not on public highway)" to find the code E820. When the coder verifies this code in the E code tabular list, we find that the fourth digit of 0 is needed to indicate that the injured person was the driver of the snowmobile (Driver of motor vehicle other than motorcycle).

■ *Highlight*

> *The coder should review the facility's policy on the use of E codes and follow it consistently. E codes are* never *assigned as principal or primary diagnoses.*

Official Coding Guidelines

Place of Occurrence Guideline

Use an additional code from category E849 to indicate the Place of Occurrence for injuries and poisonings. The Place of Occurrence describes the place where the event occurred and not the patient's activity at the time of the event.
Do not use E849.9 if the place of occurrence is not stated.

While these E codes are not required, they do provide further information about the cause of the patient's injury. In other words, if the patient was injured on the job in a factory, the coder could use code E849.3, Industrial place and premises. This would most likely be a Worker's Compensation case.

Multiple Cause E Code Coding Guidelines

If two or more events cause separate injuries, an E code should be assigned for each cause.
E codes for child and adult abuse take priority over all other E codes.

Fourth digits in the category E967, Child and adult battering and other maltreatment, show the specific person who has abused the patient, such as E967.2 By mother or stepmother, and E967.8 By non-related caregiver.

E codes for cataclysmic events take priority over all other E codes except child and adult abuse.

Cataclysmic events are those such as hurricanes, E908.0; tornadoes, E908.1; earthquakes, E909.0; etc.

E codes for transport accidents take priority over all other E codes except cataclysmic events and child and adult abuse.

According to the ICD-9-CM book, a transport accident, E800–E848, is defined as "any accident involving a device designed primarily for, or being used at the time primarily for, conveying persons or goods from one place to another." Examples of transport accidents are those in airplanes, cars, trains, and boats. These are defined at the beginning of the E code tabular list, which can be found following the V code tabular list.

The first listed E code should correspond to the cause of the most serious diagnosis due to an assault, accident, or self-harm, following the order of hierarchy listed in the previous section.

Child and Adult Abuse Guidelines

When the cause of an injury or neglect is intentional child or adult abuse (995.50–995.59, 995.80–995.85), the first listed E code should be assigned from categories E960–E968, Homicide and injury purposely inflicted by other persons (except category E967). An E code from category E967, Child and adult battering and other maltreatment should be added as an additional E code to identify the perpetrator, if known.

For example, if a child was abused by her stepfather by attempted drowning, 994.1, Drowning and other nonfatal submersion, would be listed first, then code E964, Assault by submersion [drowning], followed by code E967.0, Child and adult battering and other maltreatment by father or stepfather.

In cases of neglect when the intent is determined to be accidental, E code E904.0, Abandonment or neglect of infant and helpless person, should be the first listed E code.

Unknown or Suspected Intent Guidelines

If the intent (accident, self-harm, assault) of the cause of an injury or poisoning is unknown or unspecified, code the intent as undetermined E980–E989.

If the intent (accident, self-harm, assault) of the cause of an injury or poisoning is questionable, probable or suspected, code the intent as undetermined E980–E989.

This section of the E code tabular list is titled "Injury Undetermined Whether Accidentally or Purposely Inflicted (E980–E989)" and includes the following note: "Categories E980–E989 are for use when it is unspecified or it cannot be determined whether the injuries are accidental (unintentional), suicide (attempted), or assault."

For example, code E980.8 is for Poisoning by solid or liquid substances, undetermined whether accidentally or purposely inflicted, arsenic and its compounds.

Undetermined Cause

When the intent of an injury or poisoning is known, but the cause is unknown, use codes E928.9, Unspecified accident, E958.9, Suicide and self-inflicted injury by unspecified means, and E968.9, Assault by unspecified means.

These E codes should rarely be used as the documentation in the medical record, in both the inpatient and outpatient settings, should normally provide sufficient detail to determine the cause of the injury.

INJURIES

Many injuries are classified according to the general type of injury, such as wound, injury, internal, or injury, superficial.

It is important to follow all instructional terms to "see" and "see also" to obtain the correct code.

Official Coding Guidelines

Multiple Injuries

When multiple injuries exist, the code for the most severe injury, as determined by the attending physician, is sequenced first.

Coding for Multiple Injuries

When coding multiple injuries such as fracture of tibia and fibula, assign separate codes for each injury unless a combination code is provided, in which case the combination code is assigned. Multiple injury codes are provided in ICD-9-CM, but should not be assigned unless information for a more specific code is not available.

A. The code for the most serious injury, as determined by the physician, is sequenced first.

B. Superficial injuries such as abrasions or contusions are not coded when associated with more severe injuries of the same site.

C. When a primary injury results in minor damage to peripheral nerves or blood vessels, the primary injury is sequenced first with additional code(s) from categories 950–957, Injury to nerves and spinal cord, and/or 900–904, Injury to blood vessels. When the primary injury is to the blood vessels or nerves, that injury should be sequenced first.

EXERCISE 2–12

Assign ICD-9-CM codes to the following, including E codes.

1. Concussion sustained from motor vehicle accident to driver, single car involved

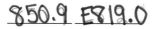
850.9 E819.0

2. Struck by falling tree limb during severe thunderstorm, lacerating right eyebrow
   wound

   ~~873.42~~ ~~E884.9~~ E908.8
   E916

3. Puncture wound to left index finger due to accidental stick with hypodermic needle

   ~~883.0~~ E920.5

E code last

FRACTURES

Fractures are classified according to whether they are open or closed. A closed fracture is one where there is no open wound into the skin. An open fracture is a fracture where there is an open wound into the skin. If the diagnostic statement does not identify whether the fracture is open or closed, it is coded as closed. ICD-9-CM provides notes in the alphabetic index to indicate types of fractures and whether they are commonly considered open or closed. The coder should review these carefully. Examples of closed fractures are comminuted, greenstick, simple, and impacted. Examples of open fractures are compound, infected, puncture, and with foreign body. Refer to Chapter 8 of this text for more information on orthopedics.

Official Coding Guidelines

Multiple Fractures

The principle of multiple coding of injuries should be followed in coding multiple fractures. Multiple fractures of specified sites are coded individually by site in accordance with both the provisions within categories 800–829 (fractures) and the level of detail furnished by medical record content. Combination categories for multiple fractures are provided for use when there is insufficient detail in the medical record (such as trauma cases transferred to another hospital); when the reporting form limits the number of codes that can be used in reporting pertinent clinical data; or when there is insufficient specificity at the fourth-digit or fifth-digit level. More specific guidelines are as follows:

A. _Multiple fractures of the same limb classifiable to the same three-digit or four-digit category are coded to that category._

B. _Multiple unilateral or bilateral fractures of same bone(s) but classified to different fourth-digit subdivisions (bone part) within the same three-digit category are coded individually by site._

C. _Multiple fracture categories 819 and 828 classify bilateral fractures of both upper limbs (819) and both lower limbs (828), but without any detail at the fourth-digit level other than open and closed type of fracture._

D. _Multiple fractures are sequenced in accordance with the severity of the fracture and the physician should be asked to list the fracture diagnoses in the order of severity._

Pathological fractures occur due to a disease rather than a trauma. If the fracture is stated to be "pathological," "spontaneous," or "due to disease," it is coded as a pathological fracture, with a fifth digit indicating the site of the fracture. It is necessary to also code the disease as the underlying cause of the fracture. For example, the patient has a fracture of the hip due to osteoporosis. Under the main term fracture, the coder would find the subterm "pathologic," subterm "hip" with the appropriate code assignment of 733.14, Pathologic fracture of neck of femur. The coder should also code the osteoporosis, 733.00, to show the underlying cause of the fracture.

EXERCISE 2–13

Assign ICD-9-CM codes to the following statements.

1. Greenstick fracture, third toe, right foot _826.0_

2. Multiple compression fractures of vertebrae due to senile osteoporosis _733.13_ _733.01_ ← came in for this
   treating →
3. Fracture of left ilium in patient with Type II diabetes _808.41_ _250.00_

4. Multiple fractures, distal end, right femur _821.29_

5. Open fracture maxilla _802.5_

   on the road
6. Motor vehicle accident to passenger in car. Examination revealed fracture of the shaft of the right radius and ulna and laceration of the forehead.

   _813.23_ _873.42_ _E819.1_ _E849.5_

BURNS

A burn is classified according to first, second, or third degree. For two degrees of burn in the same location, the coder should only code to the highest degree. For example, if the patient has second- and third-degree burns of the back, the coder would only assign code 942.34, Third-degree burn, back. Codes in category 948 are based on the "rule of nines" as shown in Figure 2–3. These codes indicate the extent of the body affected by the burn and the percentage of the body surface that is third degree. This category is to be used as a primary or principal diagnosis when the site of the burn is unspecified, or as a secondary diagnosis used in conjunction with the burn site code if known. The fourth digit indicates the percent of *body surface* burned and the fifth digit indicates the percent of body surface with *third-degree burns*. For example, if a patient had 40% of the body burned and 15% of the body surface has third-degree burns, the code used would be 948.41.

> ### Official Coding Guidelines
>
> ### Current Burns and Encounters for Late Effects of Burns
>
> *Current burns (940–948) are classified by depth, extent, and, if desired, by agent (E code). By depth burns are classified as first degree (erythema), second degree (blistering), and third degree (full-thickness involvement).*
>
> *continues*

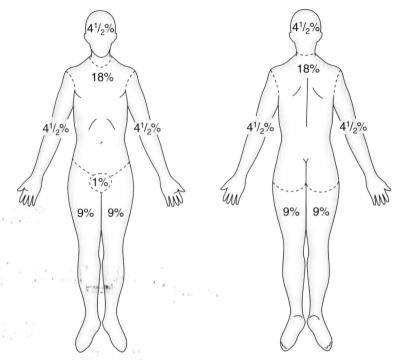

Figure 2–3 The rule of nines.

Multiple Burns

Sequence first the code that reflects the highest degree of burn when more than one burn is present.

A. *All burns are coded with the highest degree of burn sequenced first.*

B. *Classify burns of the same local site (three-digit category level, 940–947) but of different degrees to the subcategory identifying the highest degree recorded in the diagnosis.*

C. *Nonhealing burns are coded as acute burns. Necrosis of burned skin should be coded as a nonhealed burn.*

D. *Assign code 958.3, Posttraumatic wound infection, not elsewhere classified, as an additional code for any documented infected burn site.*

E. *When coding multiple burns, assign separate codes for each burn site. Category 946, Burns of multiple specified sites, should only be used if the location of the burns are not documented. Category 946, Burns of multiple specified sites, should only be used if the location of the burns are not documented. Category 949, Burn, unspecified, is extremely vague and should rarely be used.*

F. *Assign codes from category 948, Burns, classified according to extent of body surface involved, when the site of the burn is not specified or when there is a need for additional data. It is advisable to use category 948 as additional coding when needed to provide data for evaluating burn mortality, such as that needed by burn units. It is also advisable to use category 948 as an additional code for reporting purposes when there is mention of third-degree burn involving 20 percent or more of the body surface.*

continues

In assigning a code from category 948:

- *Fourth-digit codes are used to identify the percentage of total body surface involved in a burn (all degrees).*
- *Fifth-digits are assigned to identify the percentage of body surface involved in a third-degree burn.*
- *Fifth-digit zero (0) is assigned when less than 10 percent or when no body surface is involved in a third-degree burn.*

Category 948 is based on the classic "rule of nines" in estimating body surface involved; head and neck are assigned 9 percent, each arm 9 percent, each leg 18 percent, and genitalia 1 percent. Physicians may change these percentage assignments when necessary to accommodate infants and children who have proportionately larger heads than adults and patients who have large buttocks, thighs, or abdomen that involve burns.

G. *Encounters for the treatment of the late effects of burns (i.e., scars or joint contractures) should be coded to the residual condition (sequelae) by the appropriate late effect code (906.5–906.9). A late effect E code may also be used, if desired.*

H. *When appropriate, both a sequelae with a late effect code, and current burn code may be assigned on the same record.*

Debridement of Wounds, Infection, or Burn

A. *For coding purposes, excisional debridement, 86.22 from Volume 3, is assigned only when the procedure is performed by a physician in the hospital inpatient setting.*

B. *For coding purposes, nonexcisional debridement performed by the physician or nonphysician health care professional is assigned to 86.28 from Volume 3. Any "excisional" type procedure performed by a nonphysician is assigned to 86.28 in the hospital inpatient setting. Also refer to Chapter 7 of this text for more information on coding burns.*

EXERCISE 2–14

Assign ICD-9-CM codes to the following statements.

1. Second degree burn of right hand, first degree burn of left hand while preparing french fries at a local fast-food restaurant 944.20 944.10 E924.0

2. Chemical burn of mouth, pharynx, and esophagus 947.0 947.2 E924.1

3. Severe sunburn of face, arms, and shoulders 692.71

4. Burn to right upper leg due to cigarette 945.06 E898.1

5. First degree burns of face and both eyes, involving cornea, eyelids, nose, cheeks, and lips 941.12

POISONING VERSUS ADVERSE EFFECTS

The Table of Drugs and Chemicals is located following the Alphabetic Index to Diseases and is used to code poisonings and adverse reactions.

Poisoning

A poisoning is a condition caused by drugs, medicines, and biological substances when taken improperly or not in accordance with the physician's orders. Examples of poisonings are:

- Wrong dosage given in error.
- Wrong medication given or taken by patient.
- Overdose.
- Prescription drugs taken in conjunction with alcohol.
- Prescription drugs taken with over-the-counter medications not prescribed by the physician.

Official Coding Guidelines

When coding a poisoning or reaction to the improper use of a medication (e.g., wrong dose, wrong substance, wrong route of administration) the poisoning code is sequenced first, followed by a code for the manifestation. If there is also a diagnosis of drug abuse or dependence to the substance, the abuse or dependence is coded as an additional code.

For poisoning when an error was made in drug prescription or in the administration of the drug by a physician, nurse, patient or other person, use the appropriate code from the 960–979 series. If an overdose of a drug was intentionally taken or administered and resulted in drug toxicity it would be coded as a poisoning (960–979 series). If a nonprescription drug or medicinal agent was taken in combination with a correctly prescribed and properly administered drug, any drug toxicity or other reaction resulting from the interaction of the two drugs would be classified as a poisoning.

How to Code Poisonings

Poisonings are coded by looking in the Table of Drugs and Chemicals (see Figure 2–4) for the drug or causative agent. Assign the code from the poisoning column as the primary/principal diagnosis. Code the specific effect of the poisoning—such as nausea or coma. Code the external cause of the poisoning from the appropriate column of the table. Unless the medical record provides documentation otherwise, the cause should be listed as accidental. A poisoning code is never used in conjunction with an E code from the Therapeutic Use column. Many coders find it helpful to highlight the Therapeutic Use E code column to emphasize that this code can never be used with any other type of code in the Table of Drugs and Chemicals. An example of a poisoning is a child brought to the ER in a coma after ingesting his mother's Thorazine. The coder would go to the Table of Drugs and Chemicals and find the poisoning code for Thorazine, 969.1. The correct E code is E853.0, Accidental. Then the coder would select the appropriate code for the coma, 780.01.

never used with another code

Substance	Poisoning	External Cause (E Code)				
		Accident	Therapeutic Use	Suicide Attempt	Assault	Undetermined
1-propanol	980.3	E860.4	—	E950.9	E962.1	E980.9
2-propanol	980.2	E860.3	—	E950.9	E962.1	E980.9
2, 4-D (dichlorophenoxyacetic acid)	989.4	E863.5	—	E950.6	E962.1	E980.7
2, 4-toluene diisocyanate	983.0	E864.0	—	E950.7	E962.1	E980.6
2, 4, 5-T (trichlorophenoxyacetic acid)	989.2	E863.5	—	E950.6	E962.1	E980.7
14-hydroxydihydromorphinone	965.09	E850.2	E935.2	E950.0	E962.0	E980.0
A						
ABOB	961.7	E857	E931.7	E950.4	E962.0	E980.4
Abrus (seed)	988.2	E865.3	—	E950.9	E962.1	E980.9
Absinthe	980.0	E860.0	—	E950.9	E962.1	E980.9
beverage	980.0	E860.0	E934.2	E950.4	E962.0	E980.4
Acenocoumarin, acenocoumarol	964.2	E858.2	E934.2	E950.4	E962.0	E980.3
Acepromazine	969.1	E853.0	E939.1	E950.3	E962.0	E980.3
Acetal	982.8	E862.4	—	E950.9	E962.1	E980.9
Acetaldehyde (vapor)	987.8	E869.8		E952.8	E962.2	E982.8
liquid	989.89	E866.8	—	E950.9	E962.1	E980.9
Acetaminophen	965.4	E850.4	E935.4	E950.0	E962.0	E980.0
Acetaminosalol	965.1	E850.3	E935.3	E950.0	E962.0	E980.0
Acetanilid(e)	965.4	E850.4	E935.4	E950.0	E962.0	E980.0
Acetarsol, acetarsone	961.1	E857	E931.1	E950.4	E962.0	E980.4
Acetazolamide	974.2	E858.5	E944.2	E950.4	E962.0	E980.4
Acetic						
aoid	083.1	E861.1	—	E950.7	E962.1	E980.6
with sodium acetate (ointment)	976.3	E858.7	E946.3	E950.4	E962.0	E980.4
irrigating solution	974.5	E858.5	E944.5	E950.4	E962.0	E980.4
lotion	976.2	E858.7	E946.2	E950.4	E962.0	E980.4
anhydride	983.1	E864.1	—	E950.7	E962.1	E980.6
ether						

Figure 2–4 ICD-9-CM Table of Drugs and Chemicals (partial). From *ICD-9-CM for Hospitals—Volumes 1, 2, & 3, 2005 Professional*. Reprinted with permission of Ingenix.

EXERCISE 2–15

Assign ICD-9-CM codes to the following statements.

1. Ingestion of Clorox by 18-month-old child _983.9_ _E864.3_

2. Hemorrhaging due to accidental overdose of prescribed Coumadin
_459.0 E964.2 E858.2_

3. A patient is seen in the ER complaining of dizziness. The patient had recently started a prescription of Zoloft and this evening had three vodka tonics. The patient had been cautioned by both the physician and the pharmacist against drinking alcohol while taking medication. The Zoloft had been taken as prescribed. _969.09 780.4 E854.0_

Zoloft antidepressant

Adverse Effects

Adverse effects of drugs are when the patient is given or takes the medication properly, but has a side effect due to the medication, such as anaphylactic shock due to penicillin.

> ### Official Coding Guidelines
>
> #### Adverse Effect
>
> *When the drug was correctly prescribed and properly administered, code the reaction plus the appropriate code from the E930–E949 series. Adverse effects of therapeutic substances correctly prescribed and properly administered (toxicity, synergistic reaction, side effect, and idiosyncratic reaction) may be due to (1) differences among patients, such as age, sex, disease, and genetic factors, and (2) drug-related factors, such as type of drug, route of administration, duration of therapy, dosage, and bioavailability. Codes for the E930–E949 series must be used to identify the causative substance for an adverse effect of drug, medicinal, and biological substances, correctly prescribed and properly administered. The effect, such as tachycardia, delirium, gastrointestinal, hemorrhaging, vomiting, hypocalcemia, hepatitis, renal failure, or respiratory failure, is coded and followed by the appropriate code from the E930–E949 series.*

How to Code Adverse Effects

To code an adverse effect, first code the effect itself, such as shock, tachycardia, etc. Then locate the drug in the Table of Drugs and Chemicals and select the E code from the Therapeutic Use column. This E code usage is mandatory. A poisoning code is never used when using a code from the Therapeutic Use column. Sequencing of these codes is very important. If a patient had vomiting and diarrhea due to prescribed Erythromycin, the coder would first code the vomiting and diarrhea, 787.03, 787.91, and then should use the E code E930.3 to show the adverse effect caused by the medication.

■ *Highlight*

> *The coder should always check the documentation in the record very carefully, and should not use any assault or attempted suicide codes unless the physician specifically states the cause as such.*

EXERCISE 2–16

Assign ICD-9-CM codes for the following statements.

1. Hypokalemia resulting from reaction to increased dosage of Diuril prescribed by the physician 276.8   E994.3

2. Urticaria secondary to allergy to Tetracycline prescribed p.o. 708.0
   E930.4

3. Excessive drowsiness due to side effects of Chlor-Trimeton __780.09__
__E923.0__

4. Tachycardia due to h.s. OTC antihistamines __785.0__ __E933.0__

5. Anaphylactic shock after IM injection of penicillin __995.0__ __E930.0__

COMPLICATIONS

Sometimes a condition will result as a complication from an implanted device or surgical procedure. ICD-9-CM distinguishes between two types of complications, medical complications, such as infection due to a procedure or device, and mechanical complications, such as failure of an implanted pacemaker. If a patient has a complication, such as rejection of an implanted device, this is not considered a mechanical complication, but a medical complication. In other words, the device did not fail, the patient's body rejected it. Code 996.0 lists examples of mechanical complications such as breakdown, displacement, leakage, perforation, and protrusion. Code 996.6 is assigned for infections and inflammatory reactions due to internal prosthetic device, implant, and graft classifiable to 996.0–996.5.

Code 996.7 is used to code other complications of internal devices, such as embolism, hemorrhage, or stenosis, due to the presence of any device, implant or graft classifiable to 996.0–996.5. Category 997 codes complications affecting specified body systems, not elsewhere classified, such as nervous system, cardiac, and digestive system complications. This category also instructs the coder to "use additional code to identify complication" to provide specific information regarding the type of complication, such as heart failure or brain damage.

Official Coding Guidelines

Complications of Surgery and Other Medical Care

When the admission is for treatment of a complication resulting from surgery or other medical care, the complication code is sequenced as the principal diagnosis. If the complication is classified to the 996–999 series (complications), an additional code for the specific complication may be assigned.

How to Code Complications

To code a complication, first look under the main term for the condition and see if there is a complication code, such as colitis, due to radiation therapy. If there is not, check the main term "complication" to locate an appropriate complication code.

If the appropriate code cannot be found, ICD-9-CM has provided a few general complication codes, such as 999.9, Complication of medical care NEC, which can be used in conjunction with the code identifying the specific complication.

If the patient's reason for admission was treatment of the complication, the complication is listed first.

EXERCISE 2–17

Assign ICD-9-CM codes to the following statements, including E codes if indicated.

1. The patient's chief complaint was itching and redness around the pacemaker site implanted two months ago. After examination, diagnosis was made of inflammation of the pacemaker site. The patient was started on antibiotics and is to be rechecked in one week. _996.61_

2. The patient is seen in the ER after two days of diarrhea and abdominal cramping. She has been undergoing radiation therapy for carcinoma of the colon. The diagnosis in the ER today is colitis due to radiation therapy.
   _558.1_ _153.1_ _E879.2_
   colitis   cancer   radiation

   787.91   789.00

   causing

   558.1

LATE EFFECTS

A late effect is a condition or problem resulting from a previous illness or injury causing a long-lasting residual or side effect that may not show up for a period of time. The late effect is often identified in the documentation by such statements as "residual of," "sequela of," "due to previous illness," etc. There is no time limit on when a residual can occur, but is considered a residual if the initial (acute) illness or injury has resolved or healed. For example, a patient can be diagnosed with a cerebrovascular accident (CVA) that can result in symptoms that occur months or years later.

Official Coding Guidelines

A late effect is the residual effect (condition produced) after the acute phase of an illness or injury has terminated. There is no time limit on when a late effect code can be used. The residual may be apparent early or it may occur months or years later, such as that due to a previous injury. Coding of late effects requires two codes:

> *The residual condition or nature of the late effect.*
> *The cause of the late effect.*

The residual condition or nature of the late effect is sequenced first, followed by the cause of the late effect, except in those few instances where the cause for late effect is followed by a manifestation code identified in the tabular list as an italicized code and title.
The code for the acute phase of an illness or injury that leads to the late effect is never used with a code for the cause of the late effect.

Residual Condition or Nature of the Late Effect

The residual condition or nature of the late effect is sequenced first, followed by the late effect code for the cause of the residual condition, except in a few instances where the alphabetic index directs otherwise.

Some conditions that can produce late effects are:

- Adverse or toxic reactions to drugs
- Bacterial and viral infections
- Burns
- Cerebrovascular disease
- Childbirth
- Fractures
- Lacerations

How to Code Late Effects

There are only a limited number of late effect codes for use in ICD-9-CM, and these can be located under the main term "late." This main term also directs the coder to "*see also* condition" because some common late effects have been included under the "condition" main term.

Two codes are commonly used to completely code the late effect:

1. The residual (current condition affecting the patient).
2. The original cause, illness, or injury that is no longer present in acute form.

Another example of coding a late effect is scar on the face due to a previous burn. The scar, or residual, would be coded to 709.2. The code 906.5 would be used to code late effect, burn, face, head, and neck.

Coding Tip	*Late effects of a cerebrovascular accident are coded differently. The 438 category is expanded to include different residuals. For example, if the patient has the diagnosis of hemiplegia affecting the dominant side due to previous cerebrovascular accident, code 438.21 would be used. A note following code 438 reads:*

> **Note**
> This category is to be used to indicate conditions in 430–437 as the cause of late effects. The "late effects" include conditions specified as such, or as sequelae, which may occur at any time after the onset of the causal condition.

EXERCISE 2–18

Assign ICD-9-CM codes to the following statements.

1. Residuals of poliomyelitis 138.90

2. Cerebrovascular accident (CVA) two years ago with residual hemiplegia of the dominant side 438.21

3. Traumatic arthritis, right ankle, following fracture of ankle 716.17

905.4

4. Neural deafness resulting from childhood measles 10 years ago _389.10_
   _139.8_

5. Brain damage following cerebral abscess seven months ago _348.9_
   _324.0_

OFFICIAL CODING GUIDELINES

Many official guidelines from the AHA's *Coding Clinic* have been cited throughout this module. The following are general guidelines that pertain to all sections of the ICD-9-CM code book.

All diagnoses that affect the current encounter must be coded. In the hospital inpatient setting, the principal diagnosis, which by definition is "the condition established after study to be chiefly responsible for occasioning the admission of the patient to the hospital for care," must be listed first. The circumstances of the admission to the facility always determine the order of diagnoses.

In the outpatient, physician's office, or clinic setting, the primary, or first diagnosis should be the main reason for the visit that day. For example, if the patient has hypertension and was seen in the clinic today for shortness of breath, the shortness of breath would be the primary, or first, listed diagnosis. The hypertension would also be coded if it was still being treated.

Official Inpatient *Coding Guidelines*

Two or More Interrelated Conditions, Each Potentially Meeting the Definition for Principal Diagnosis:

When there are two or more interrelated conditions (such as disease in the same ICD-9-CM chapter or manifestation characteristically associated with a certain disease) potentially meeting the definition of principal diagnosis, either condition may be sequenced first, unless the circumstances of the admission, the therapy provided, the tabular list, or the alphabetic index indicate otherwise.

Two or More Diagnoses That Equally Meet the Definition for Principal Diagnosis:

In the unusual instance when two or more diagnoses equally meet the criteria for principal diagnosis as determined by the circumstances of admission, diagnostic workup and/or therapy provided, and the alphabetic index, tabular list, or another coding guideline does not provide sequencing direction, any one of the diagnoses may be sequenced first.

Two or More Comparative or Contrasting Conditions

In those rare instances when two or more contrasting or comparative diagnoses are documented as "either/or" (or similar terminology), they are coded as if the diagnoses were confirmed and the diagnoses are sequenced according to the circumstances of the admission. If no further determination can be made as to which diagnosis should be principal, either diagnosis may be sequenced first.

A Symptom Followed by Contrasting/Comparative Diagnoses

When a symptom(s) is followed by contrasting/comparative diagnoses, the symptom code is sequenced first. All the contrasting/comparative diagnoses should be coded as suspected conditions.

Original Treatment Plan Not Carried Out

Sequence as the principal diagnosis the condition, which, after study, occasioned the admission to the hospital, even though treatment may not have been carried out due to unforeseen circumstances.

Official Coding Guidelines

If the same condition is described as both acute (subacute) and chronic and separate subentries exist in the alphabetic index at the same indentation level, code both and sequence the acute (subacute) condition first.

Previous or history of illnesses or injuries should not be coded unless they affect the patient's current treatment.

Official Coding Guidelines

Impending or Threatened Conditions

Code any condition described at the time of discharge as "impending" or "threatened" as follows:
   If it did occur, code as confirmed diagnosis.
   If it did not occur, reference the alphabetic index to determine if the condition has a subentry term for "impending" or "threatened" and also reference main term entries for Impending and for Threatened.

   If the subterms are listed, assign the given code.

   If the subterms are not listed, code the existing forerunner condition(s) and not the condition described as impending or threatened.

Reporting Additional Diagnoses

"Other diagnoses" are defined as "all conditions that coexist at the time of admission, that develop subsequently, or that affect the treatment received and/or the length of stay. Diagnoses that relate to an earlier episode which have no bearing on the current hospital stay are to be excluded."

Previous Conditions

If the physician has included a diagnosis in the final diagnostic statement, such as the discharge summary or the face sheet, it should ordinarily be coded. Some physicians include in the diagnostic statement resolved conditions or diagnoses and status-post procedures from a previous admission that have no bearing on the current stay. Such conditions are not to be reported and are coded only if required by hospital policy.

However, history codes V10–V19 may be used as secondary codes if the historical condition or family history has an impact on current care or influences treatment.

Diagnoses Not Listed in the Final Diagnostic Statement

When the physician has documented what appears to be a current diagnosis in the body of the record, but has not included the diagnosis in the final diagnostic statement, the physician should be asked whether the diagnosis should be added.

Diagnostic Coding and Reporting Guidelines for Outpatient Services (Hospital-Based and Physician Office)

Revised October 1, 2003

The terms "encounter" and "visit" are often used interchangeably in describing outpatient service contacts and, therefore, appear together in these guidelines without distinguishing one from the other.

Coding guidelines for outpatient and physician reporting of diagnoses will vary in a number of instances from those for inpatient diagnoses, recognizing that:

The Uniform Hospital Discharge Data Set (UHDDS) definition of principal diagnosis applies only to inpatients in acute, short-term, general hospitals.

Coding guidelines for inconclusive diagnoses (probable, suspected, rule out, etc.) were developed for inpatient reporting and do not apply to outpatients.

Diagnoses often are not established at the time of the initial encounter/visit. It may take two or more visits before the diagnosis is confirmed.

The most critical rule involves beginning the search for the correct code assignment through the alphabetic index. Never begin searching initially in the tabular list as this will lead to coding errors.

BASIC CODING GUIDELINES FOR OUTPATIENT SERVICES

A. The appropriate code or codes from 001.0 through V82.9 must be used to identify diagnoses, symptoms, conditions, problems, complaints, or other reason(s) for the encounter/visit.

B. For accurate reporting of ICD-9-CM diagnosis codes, the documentation should describe the patient's condition, using terminology which includes specific diagnoses as well as symptoms, problems, or reasons for the encounter. There are ICD-9-CM codes to describe all of these.

C. The selection of codes 001.0 through 999.9 will frequently be used to describe the reason for the encounter. These codes are from the section of ICD-9-CM for the classification of diseases and injuries (e.g., infectious and parasitic diseases; neoplasms; symptoms, signs, and ill-defined conditions, etc.).

D. Codes that describe symptoms and signs, as opposed to diagnoses, are acceptable for reporting purposes when an established diagnosis has not been diagnosed (confirmed) by the physician. Chapter 16 of ICD-9-CM, "Symptoms, Signs, and Ill-Defined Conditions (codes 780.0 – 799.9)" contains many, but not all codes for symptoms.

E. ICD-9-CM provides codes to deal with encounters for circumstances other than a disease or injury. The Supplementary Classification of Factors Influencing Health Status and Contact with Health Services (V01.0– V82.9) is provided to deal with occasions when circumstances other than a disease or injury are recorded as diagnosis or problems.

F. ICD-9-CM is composed of codes with either 3, 4, or 5 digits. Codes with 3 digits are included in ICD-9-CM as the heading of a category of codes that may be further subdivided by the use of fourth and/or fifth digits, which provide greater specificity.

A three-digit code is to be used only if it is not further subdivided. Where fourth-digit subcategories and/or fifth-digit subclassifications are provided, they must be assigned. A code is invalid if it has not been coded to the full number of digits required for that code.

G. List first the ICD-9-CM code for the diagnosis, condition, problem or other reason for encounter/visit shown in the medical record to be chiefly responsible for the services provided. List additional codes that describe any coexisting conditions.

H. Do not code diagnoses documented as "probable," "suspected," "questionable," "rule out," or "working diagnosis." Rather, code the condition(s) to the highest degree of certainty for that encounter/visit, such as symptoms, signs, abnormal test results, or other reason for visit.

Please note: This is contrary to the coding practices used by hospitals and medical records departments for coding the diagnosis of hospital inpatients.

I. Chronic diseases treated on an ongoing basis may be coded and reported as many times as the patient is receiving treatment and care for the condition(s).

J. Code all documented conditions that coexist at the time of the encounter/visit, and that require or affect patient care treatment or management. Do not code conditions previously treated that no longer exist. However, history codes (V10–V19) may be used as secondary codes if the historical condition or family history has an impact on current care or influences treatment.

K. For patients receiving diagnostic services only during an encounter/visit, sequence first the diagnosis, condition, problem, or other reason for encounter/visit shown in the medical record to be chiefly responsible for the outpatient services provided during the encounter/visit. Codes for other diagnoses (e.g., chronic conditions) may be sequenced as additional diagnoses.

L. For patients receiving therapeutic services only during an encounter/visit, sequence first the diagnosis, condition, problem, or other reason for encounter/visit shown in the medical record to be chiefly responsible for the outpatient services provided during the encounter/visit. Codes for other diagnoses (e.g., chronic conditions) may be sequenced as additional diagnoses.

The only exception to this rule is that patients receiving chemotherapy, radiation therapy, or rehabilitation, the appropriate V code for the service is listed first, and the diagnosis or problem for which the service is being performed listed second.

M. For patients receiving preoperative evaluations only, sequence a code from category V72.8, Other specified examinations, to describe the pre-op consultations. Assign a code for the condition to describe the reason for the surgery as an additional diagnosis. Code also any findings related to the pre-op evaluation.

> *N. For ambulatory surgery, code the diagnosis for which the surgery was performed. If the postoperative diagnosis is known to be different from the preoperative diagnosis, select the postoperative diagnosis for coding, since it is the most definitive.*

ICD-10-CM

ICD-10-CM
International Classification of Diseases, 10th Revision, Clinical Modification.

The beginning of this chapter gives a history of ICD-9-CM. Coders have been anticipating the revision and changes that will bring diagnosis coding to a new format, **ICD-10-CM.** As medicine and technology advance, there is a need for a system to precisely compare data for clinical research, correct statistical information, and payment purposes. With the implementation of the Health Insurance and Portability and Accountability Act of 1996 (HIPAA), the need for revision and flexibility of code sets was obvious. ICD-10-CM allows more complete descriptions designed to collect data in any health care encounter—inpatient, outpatient, home health, etc. This will improve the quality of data input into clinical databases and allow projection for future health care needs and trends. ICD-10-CM will also meet HIPAA criteria with the structure of the alphanumeric system to provide more specific information for ambulatory and managed care, expand injury coding, and describe the clinical picture of the patient more precisely than with ICD-9-CM.

Codes are important in the health care environment today in the following areas identified by the American Health Information Management Association (AHIMA):

- Measuring the quality, safety, and efficacy of health care
- Designing payment systems and processing claims for reimbursement
- Conducting research, epidemiological studies, and clinical trials
- Setting health policy
- Designing health care delivery systems
- Monitoring resource utilization
- Identifying fraudulent practices
- Managing care and disease processes
- Tracking public health and risks
- Providing data to consumers concerning costs and outcomes of treatment options

ICD-10-PCS
International Classification of Diseases, 10th Revision, Procedure Classification System.

Anatomy is the foundation of ICD-10-CM. ICD-10-CM will contain diagnostic codes for inpatient and outpatient reporting, with **ICD-10-PCS** to replace Volume 3 of ICD-9-CM for inpatient procedure coding. ICD-10-CM will remain three volumes as follows:

Volume 1—Tabular List
This is a tabular list of the alphanumeric disease codes. As in ICD-9-CM, the first three digits have common traits, with each digit after three to add specificity.

Volume 2—Instruction Manual
The instruction manual contains descriptions, coding rules, and guidelines for mortality and morbidity coding.

Volume 3—Alphabetic List
This is an alphabetic index to codes classified in the tabular list in Volume 1. This is organized as diseases, entities, and other conditions

relating to etiology, anatomy, or severity. The Table of Drugs and Chemicals is also found in Volume 3.

Code selection will be based on axes or criteria such as etiology, site, or morphology. Format and conventions will remain the same. The biggest difference between ICD-9-CM and ICD-10-CM is that the codes in the new revision are alphanumeric, with more detailed descriptions. There are 21 chapters in ICD-10-CM, as illustrated in Table 2–2.

TABLE 2–2   ICD-10-CM Contents.

Chapter 1	(A00–B99)	Certain infectious and parasitic diseases
Chapter 2	(C00–D48)	Neoplasms
Chapter 3	(D50–D89)	Diseases of the blood and blood-forming organs and certain disorders involving the immune mechanism
Chapter 4	(E00–E90)	Endocrine, nutritional, and metabolic diseases
Chapter 5	(F01–F99)	Mental and behavioral disorders
Chapter 6	(G00–G99)	Diseases of the nervous system
Chapter 7	(H00–H95)	Diseases of the eye and adnexa
Chapter 8	(H60–H95)	Diseases of the ear and mastoid process
Chapter 9	(I00–I97)	Diseases of the circulatory system
Chapter 10	(J00–J99)	Diseases of the respiratory system
Chapter 11	(K00–K93)	Diseases of the digestive system
Chapter 12	(L00–L99)	Diseases of the skin and subcutaneous tissues
Chapter 13	(M00–M99)	Diseases of the musculoskeletal system and connective tissue
Chapter 14	(N00–N99)	Diseases of the genitourinary system
Chapter 15	(O00–O99)	Pregnancy, childbirth, and the puerperium
Chapter 16	(P04–P94)	Certain conditions originating in the newborn (perinatal period)
Chapter 17	(Q00–Q94)	Congenital malformations, deformations, and chromosomal abnormalities
Chapter 18	(R00–R99)	Symptoms, signs, and abnormal clinical and laboratory findings, not elsewhere classified
Chapter 19	(S00–T98)	Injury, poisoning, and certain other consequences of external causes
Chapter 20	(V01–Y97)	External causes of morbidity
Chapter 21	(Z00–Z99)	Factors influencing health status and contact with health service

■ *Highlight*

The Official Coding and Reporting Guidelines of ICD-10-CM can be found at www.cdc.gov/nchs/icd9.htm).

PROCEDURES IN ICD-10-CM

ICD-10-CM does not contain a procedure index. The Centers for Medicare and Medicaid Services (CMS) funded a project with 3M Health Information Systems to develop a replacement for Volume 3 of ICD-9-CM, known as the *International Classification of Disease, 10th Revision Procedure Classification System,* or *ICD-10-PCS.* The following general guidelines were followed in the development of ICD-10-PCS:

- Diagnostic information is not included in the description. Any description of the disease of disorder is in the diagnosis code, not the procedure code.
- The elimination of the Not Otherwise Specified option requires a minimum level of specificity to achieve the code assignment, making the option unnecessary.
- Not Elsewhere Classified is limited, as all possible components of a procedure are included.
- The combination of the seven alphanumeric characters allows all possible procedures to be defined, resulting in greater specificity in coding.

The goal of ICD-10-PCS is the same as that of ICD-10-CM: to improve accuracy and efficiency in coding and allow the capability for expansion of new codes. Characteristics include:

- Completeness—All substantially different procedures will have a unique code.
- Expandability—Adding new medical procedures with new codes will be easier with the increase in the number of code characters.
- Standardized Terminology—Each character has a standard meaning that will contribute to the accuracy of the code assigned.
- Multiaxial—Use of seven characters with a standard meaning within and across all procedure sections will result in more accuracy and precision when assigning a procedure code.

Each character has up to 34 different values. The ten digits 0–9 and the 24 letters A–H, J–N, and P–Z comprise each character. Procedures are divided into sections that relate to the general type of procedure (e.g., medical and surgical, imaging, etc.). The first character of the procedure code always specifies the section. The second through seventh characters have a standard meaning within each section but may have different meanings across sections. In most sections, one of the characters specifies the precise type of procedure being performed (e.g., excision, revision, etc.), while the other characters specify additional information such as the body part on which the procedure is being performed. Codes can be located in an alphabetic index based on the type of procedure being performed. In medical and surgical procedures, the seven characters are as follows:

1 Section
2 Body system
3 Root operation
4 Body part

> 5 Method or approach
> 6 Device
> 7 Qualifier

The index for ICD-10-PCS provides the first three characters of the code. The coder is then referred to the tabular list to locate the remaining four characters needed. The index contains an alphabetical list of primary entries of root operations and composite terms, which are multiple aspects of a procedure. The secondary entries are specific to the root operation and may include body parts, devices used, or a root operation for revision.

For example, code 095HBYZ is the ICD-10-PCS code for the Dilation eustachian tube, right, with Device, NEC, transorifice intraluminal. Following the meanings listed above, the seven digits show:

> 0 means the code falls in the Medical Surgical section
> 9 refers to the body system of ear, nose, sinus
> 5 shows the procedure is a dilation
> H is the eustachian tube, right
> B is the transorifice intraluminal approach
> Y means this is a device NEC (not elsewhere classified)
> Z means there is no qualifier

Another example is code 021OOZ4, Bypass, one coronary artery to right internal mammary artery, open.

> 0 means the code falls in the Medical Surgical section
> 2 refers to the body system, heart and great vessels
> 1 is the root operation of bypass
> O is the body part, the coronary artery
> O is the approach, which is open
> Z indicates that no device was used
> 4 is a qualifier for right internal mammary artery

IMPLEMENTATION OF ICD-10-CM

Implementation date of ICD-10-CM has been delayed many times. Much of that concern is due to the overwhelming task of the transition of ICD-9-CM to ICD-10-CM. The financial aspect is critical, too. Computer software programs will need to be updated as well as charge slips, superbills, and fee tickets to reflect the revised coding system. Education and training will be required. It is important to realize that all levels of the practice or organization are affected by this change, so all personnel must be trained, especially to allow for smooth transition. Experts advise early planning is the key for a smooth transition and successful implementation by doing the following:

- *Create a task force.* Assign each participating individual (e.g., software vendors and suppliers, training for coders, physicians, other key personnel) an area to research.

- *Involve the entire organization.* Communication is key, especially for planning and budgeting.

- *Review documentation and coding policies within the practice or facility.* ICD-10-CM coding requires specific terminology, so the physician needs to be a participant in all phases of implementation.

- *Begin budgeting.* How much will training cost? Will training be internal or external? What kinds of technology changes will need to be made? How will business be conducted during the transition to avoid financial loss?
- *Expect problems.* Any change will have issues to be resolved during the transition and implementation. If timelines are established and the task force is prepared, problems will be minimal.

■ *Highlight*

To receive updated information as to the changes in ICD-10-CM implementation dates, monitor the following web sites:

National Center for Health Statistics (NCHS)
www.cdc.gov/nchs/about/otheract/icd9/abticd10/htm
World Health Organization (WHO) www.who.int/aboutwho/en/mission.html

Coders should stay current with the latest developments on these revisions. No date has been determined yet for implementation of ICD-10-CM. Once the final notice has been published in the *Federal Register,* there will be a two-year time frame for implementation of the revised system.

WEB SITES RELATED TO ICD-10-CM

The following web sites contain information on ICD-10-CM and ICD-10-PCS and maintain updates as to the progress of this revision.

3M Health Information Systems. www.3Mhis.com
American Health Information Management Association (AHIMA). www.ahima.org
Centers for Medicare and Medicaid Services (CMS). www.cms.gov
National Center for Health Statistics (NCHS). www.cdc.gov/nchs
Official Coding and Reporting Guidelines of ICD-10-CM. www.cdc.gov/nchs/icd9.htm
World Health Organization (WHO). www.who.int/en

SUMMARY

ICD-9-CM is the *International Classification of Diseases, 9th Revision, Clinical Modification,* and is used to uniformly classify diagnoses and procedures. CMS (Medicare) requires the usage of ICD-9-CM diagnoses for billing of patients in the inpatient, outpatient, clinic, and physician office setting. The procedure section of ICD-9-CM is not used in the clinic/physician office setting at this time. Official coding guidelines for all users of ICD-9-CM are published in *The Coding Clinic for ICD-9-CM* by the American Hospital Association.

The basic steps in coding are:

a. Identify the main term(s) of the condition to be coded.

b. Locate the main term in the alphabetic index.

c. Refer to any subterms indented under the main term. Refer to any nonessential modifiers, instructional terms, or notes to select the most likely code.

    d. Verify the code(s) in the tabular list. Never code directly from the alphabetic index.

    e. Check all instructional terms in the tabular list and be sure to assign all codes to their highest degree of specificity.

    f. Continue coding the diagnostic statement until all of the elements are identified completely.

In the inpatient setting, diagnoses referred to as "probable," "suspected," "questionable," "possible," or "rule out" are coded as if the condition existed or was established. In all other settings, the coder should only code to the highest degree of specificity known, even if that is a sign or symptom.

V codes can be used as primary or principal diagnoses to indicate the reason for visit if no sign or symptom is present, or as secondary diagnoses to provide further information regarding the patient's visit or health.

Coders should be familiar with tools available, such as books and publications, organizations, the Internet, etc., that can help to increase knowledge and awareness of coding rules, guidelines, new medical techniques, and changes to the coding systems.

ICD-10-CM (diagnoses) and ICD-10-PCS (procedures) are the replacements for ICD-9-CM and are designed as a complete alphanumeric coding system. When an implementation date is decided, it will be published in the *Federal Register*.

REFERENCES

Bowman, E. (1996). Coding and classification systems. In *Health information: Management of a strategic resource*. Philadelphia: Saunders.

Brown, F. (2004). *ICD-9-CM coding handbook, with answers*. Chicago: American Hospital Association, 1997.

Graham, L. *Advanced clinical topics for ICD-9-CM*. 1996. Chicago: American Health Information Management Association.

Green M. & Rowell, J. (2005). *Understanding health insurance: A guide to professional billing and reimbursement* (8th ed.) Clifton Park, NY: Thomson Delmar Learning.

Grider, D. J. (2005). *Principles of ICD-9-CM coding*. Chicago: AMA Press.

Nicholas, T. (1998). *Basic ICD-9-CM coding*. Chicago: American Health Information Management Association.

Prophet, S. (1998). "OIG releases compliance program guidance for hospitals," *Journal of the American Health Information Management Association. 69*(4).

Puckett, C. D. (1997). *The 1998 annual hospital version the educational annotation of ICD-9-CM*, (5th Ed.) Reno, NV: Channel Publishing, Ltd.

Steigerwald, J. (1994). *Advanced ICD-9-CM coding*. Birmingham, AL: Southern Medical Association.

Chapter 3

HCPCS Level II

LEARNING OBJECTIVES

Upon successful completion of this chapter, you should be able to:

1. Select HCPCSII codes to identify procedures, supplies, medications, and equipment items.

2. Identify the structure of HCPCSII codes.

3. Understand the placement position of the HCPCSII codes and modifiers on the claim.

4. Blend the use of CPT codes and HCPCSII for accurate description of the care.

INTRODUCTION

Healthcare Common Procedure Coding System Level II (HCPCSII)
The second level of the coding system created by CMS for reporting of procedures, supplies, medications, equipment, and items.

Since the **Healthcare Common Porcedure Coding System Level II (HCPCSII)** codes are newer to the industry, many physician practices are not as familiar with the codes, structure, and the development processes. The HCPCSII codes are updated frequently, either adding codes or deleting codes throughout the year. This chapter will introduce the coder to the importance of the codes and the modifiers. It is a common fallacy that HCPCSII codes are optional, as some of the codes' payment rates are extremely small (may be under $1.00). HCPSCII codes are required for all health insurance plans since the inception of HIPAA, and the practice may risk enforcement if the HCPC-SII codes are *not* on the electronic claim. The claim is required to accurately reflect the services. Federally funded claims (e.g., CMS, Medicaid, Railroad Retirement, federal employees, TRICARE/CHAMPVA) are rejected if the HCPCSII codes and modifiers are not properly reported.

HISTORY

Healthcare Common Procedure Coding System (HCPCS) is a three-level coding system, created in 1983 (see Table 3–1). HCPCSII codes are required for all health insurance plans since the inception of HIPAA. The practice may risk enforcement if choosing not to accurately describe the services by

TABLE 3–1   Code Level Descriptions per CMS.

Level	Definition
HCPCS I	American Medical Association Current Procedural Terminology
HCPCS II	National Codes ■ The American Dental Association has the copyright for the D code chapter. ■ BCBS contributes to the S code chapter. CMS works with other insurance plans for the remainder of the code chapters.
HCPCS III	CMS local codes were deleted December 31, 2003, under the HIPAA rules. Many of the local code concepts were moved to HCPCSII.

selecting a HCPCSII code and reporting on the electronic claim. HCPCS levels I and II are active, whereas HCPCS Level III local CMS codes became inactive and are no longer HIPAA compliant. The HCPCS level I is synonymous with the American Medical Association CPT codes. Chapter 3 of Understanding Medical Coding will focus on the proper selection of the HCPCS level II codes.

The HCPSCII codes are created to identify procedures, supplies, medications (except vaccines), equipment, and items, a system of coding now maintained by Centers for Medicare and Medicaid Services (CMS). The original goal in introducing HCPSCII was to replace the various local carrier codes that were used by Medicare carriers, each state's Medicaid, BlueCross BlueShield (BCBS), and other insurance companies, and start using national HCPCS codes. In reality, the code system has broadened to include code sets for Dental and Transportation. Further, the HCPCS system assists in tracking various policies set forth by Congress, such as the screening and vaccine services that were authorized under the 1997 Balanced Budget Act.

Coding Tip *The HCPCSII codes are frequently created to assist CMS in tracking, reporting, and implementing policies that were created under the Social Security Act. When Congress introduces health care policies, CMS often creates HCPSCII codes upon the policies' implementation.*

The HCPCSII codes are used by the following health care professionals, as well as by others:

> physicians
> therapists
> home health
> outpatient departments
> ambulance
> dentists
> durable medical goods companies

At the time of this publication, not all insurance plans have adopted the HCPCSII codes. Small commercial insurance plans received an extension to the HIPAA rules for standardized transaction and data sets, allowing them additional time to transition into the use of HCPCSII.

Workers' Compensation and auto insurance plans do not typically use HCPCSII codes. When a coder has determined that the HCPCSII codes are not applicable, the coder may use the CPT code 99070 for all supplies, medications, equipment, and items that are not typically part of the office visit. A copy of the invoice must be sent in with the claim to obtain reimbursement.

FORMAT

The code format layout is relatively simple. The first digit is an alpha character (A through V), followed by four numeric digits, for example A4770. Each chapter of the HCPCSII code book has a description paragraph to guide the coder in selecting the appropriate code. There are now more than 5,000 codes, and additional codes are anticipated in the future. Some HCPCSII code publications include tips and appendices with many of the payment rules conveniently associated to codes. The tips do not include all of the policies, nor are tips prepared for all codes. The tips include such topics as Medicare Carriers Manual, Hospital Outpatient Prospective Payment System, Coverage Issues Manual, Physician Fee Schedule, and the Ambulatory Surgical Center rules. Research is often required to determine the coverage policies per HCPSCII code.

Coding Tip *Many payers have established quantity limitations per code. If the allowable quantity is exceeded, the physician practice is required to properly prepare the Advanced Beneficiary Notice (ABN). The ABN advises the patient a particular service, medication, device or item is not covered by the patient's health benefit plan.*

Familiarity with the HCPCSII codebook and the various symbols will greatly assist coders in accurate code selection, and typically improves the profitability of a health care practice. Examples of medication codes and common dosages and their potential reimbursements will be covered later in this chapter.

Fact versus Fiction

One of the most frequent compliance risks seen in health care practices is the choice to not use HCPCSII codes. The second most common compliance risk is the use of outdated HCPCSII codes. All federally funded providers (e.g., Medicare, Railroad Retirement, Medicaid, federal employees) require HCPCSII codes for all health insurance claim forms that are submitted electronically. This code set is not optional for reimbursement purposes; it is mandatory for accurate claim submission, regardless of the amount of reimbursement anticipated.

HCPCSII modifiers clarify the code use in many ways. The modifiers may describe anatomical sites, more specificity for the service, item or device or other government indicators as implemented. Usually HCPCSII modifiers are two alpha characters.

The unlisted codes are selected as the last option. First investigate the medication, package insert and perhaps the package box to determine the exact medication (item) that is in use. There may be a code that is located in an area of the code book that you are less familiar with. If there is no code for the item, service or medication in the book, the unlisted code is selected nearest to the similar item, service or medication.

The National Correct Coding Initiative (NCCI) manual describes few details for the selection of the HCPCSII codes. The NCCI does not publish the mutually exclusive nor the column1/column2 edits. The HCPCSII edits may or may not be published in the CMS policies. Edits may be published in the future, released with the NCCI quarterly updates.

HCPCSII HIERARCHY

When the documentation reflects duplicate descriptions, how does a coder know whether it is appropriate to select an HCPCSII or a CPT code?

There is less duplication of HCPCSII and CPT codes today than there used to be; however, the possibility for duplication may still occur. The hierarchy for selecting codes is as follows:

- If the descriptions match exactly between the HCPCSII code and the CPT code, use the CPT code.
- If the descriptions do not match exactly between the HCPCSII code and the CPT code, check with the insurance plan prior to reporting the code. The policies may identify distinguishing criteria exceptions for each code.

The principles for selecting the code are:

1. Read the documentation to determine the service, item, or supply
2. Look in the index first.

    Table of Drugs
    The listing of alphabetical generic and brand name medications with the associated dose, common route, and the code.

    a) If the index does not determine the code, the table of contents or the **Table of Drugs** will provide further guidance for you.
    b) Keep in mind that the descriptions relate less to medical terminology than to insurance terms.
    c) "Examination" is a common term describing many services.
    d) "Screening" is another common term describing many services.
3. Locate the code in the HCPCSII code book chapter. Read the guidelines of the chapter first. This will especially be helpful if coding for supplies that are rendered at various facility locations, such as a physician office vs. an ambulatory surgical center.
4. Double-check the details, symbols, and small print. This is probably the single most important skill for coding HCPCSII. If sufficient details are not available, more information must be sought from the physician, and documentation obtained prior to selecting the code.
5. Check the payment rules for the code.
6. Review the modifiers for possible use.
7. Select the code for the claim.

Most HCPCSII codes will need a medical diagnosis to be linked to the code. It is important that the medical record documents the medical necessity of the claim.

CODE REVISIONS

Requests for code changes for most of the HCPCSII code book are first determined by CMS and a committee of the Veterans Administration, Medicaid state agencies, and a CMS committee, SADMERC. This committee then recommends to the

HCPCSII national panel where a unanimous vote is required, prior to implementation. For the D chapter, requests are first sent to the American Dental Association (ADA). For the S chapter, requests are sent to BlueCross/BlueShield.

All of these requirements must be met to add a code:

- FDA authorization has been given (if applicable)
- A medication, device, or supply *must be* on the market for at least 6 months
- 3% or more of the outpatient use is for this product within USA

To change a code description, the medical details and manufacturer information must be submitted.

To delete a code, the specific reason why a code should be deleted must be submitted.

INDEX

The index located in the front of the HCPCSII code book states a combination of medical terminology and insurance or lay person terms. Many medications and some equipment items are listed by both brand name and generic (or chemical) name in the index. However, the Table of Drugs, located in the appendix, is more helpful than the index for drug code selection.

EXERCISE 3-1

This exercise focuses on the development of skills to use the index, table of contents, and Table of Drugs.

1. Select from the index various options to consider for pediatric wheelchair, folding style.

    Index topic _E1232, E1234, E1236 E1238_

    First individual code _wheelchair_

    Series of actual code options _____

2. Select the code range for a leg bag for urine collection sent home with the patient.

    Leg bag _A5112_

3. For birth control purpose, Depo Provera 200 mg is given. _J1055 x2_

HCPCSII CHAPTER DETAILS

The HCPCSII code book is organized by chapters, A0000 through V5364. For each of the chapters in the HCPCSII code book, the paragraphs located at the beginning of each chapter and prior to a group of codes usually outline the accurate selection of the codes per section.

Chapter A0000–A0999 Transportation Services Including Ambulance

The A0000 begins the series of codes for the emergency and nonemergency transportation services (ambulance and patient transport) and their related fees. Unique to this chapter, ICD-9-CM codes are not required, according to the HIPAA standard code sets; however, some insurance plans may still require them. Therefore, it is highly recommended that the medical necessity be documented. This information may further assist claims and benefit clarifications. Special single-digit modifiers are located within this chapter. The first digit of the modifier describes the origin, the second digit modifier describes the destination. The X modifier can be used only in the second position. The local CMS carrier determines the policies for codes in this chapter, for the federally funded programs.

In other areas of the code book are a few special circumstances which are:

Q3019 or Q3020
S0215 (BCBS)
T chapter and T modifiers (Medicaid likely)

Medical and Surgical Supplies Paragraph Guideline

The next section of the A0000 series is the Medical Surgical Supplies codes. It includes "everything but the kitchen sink." In selecting a code, it is important to distinguish the supplies, device, and components of the device, from the maintenance and professional services for use of the device. It is likely the A ____ codes will be used with an additional J ___ medication code and the CPT codes for the professional services.

Claims for HCPCSII codes may or may not be sent to the Medicare Part B carrier. Some of the codes are submitted and paid as part of another division, and are sent to the Durable Medical Equipment Regional Carrier (DMERC). In order to send a claim into the DMERC carrier, a separate enrollment and a simple practice assessment is to be expected.

Coding Tip *Prior to implementing a new process in your practice, it is always a good idea to investigate the process fully and determine the potential for return on the investment. Sales information is not always accurate for code selection nor for anticipated reimbursements.*

Miscellaneous Supplies Paragraph Guideline

For Medicare: Codes A4206–A4306 are *not* selected if performed during a physician office visit service. A4206–A4306 codes are selected when items are sent home with the patient.

Coding Tip *As commercial insurance plans implement the use of HCPCSII codes, selection of the A4206–A4306 code may be more frequent than the use by Medicare. Obtain the policy for each insurance plan prior to choosing not to code the supply items. If the plan does not accept HCPCSII codes, report 99070 for all supplies beyond the typical physician visit.*

Incontinence, External Urinary, Ostomy A4310–A4434 Paragraph Guideline

Permanent, indefinite, and long-term incontinence items are automatically covered by Medicare. Commercial plans might have alternative coverage policies. Local carriers will determine supply payment policies of temporary incontinence items that are provided at the physician's office.

> **Coding Tip**
>
> *An A4550 Surgical tray is commonly used at the physician office place of service. CPT surgical guidelines state that when the supply tray is beyond the typical, additional codes are to be selected. Some insurance plans will accept the CPT code 99070 for this purpose, whereas the Medicare code is A4550 (unless NCCI edits bundle). If the surgical tray includes a specific item that is listed in the HCPCSII code book, select the more specific codes. Otherwise, the A4550 may be the only option. If no surgical tray is provided, select other miscellaneous codes in the HCPCSII per detailed area (see A9999).*

Dressings A6000–A7527 Paragraph Guideline

Medicare requests that when providing a dressing for an Implanted device, the claim is sent to the local carrier. If the dressing is not for an implanted device, the claim is sent to the DMERC (durable medical equipment regional carrier), not the local carrier.

Medical records will often describe a brand name for a dressing, rather than the specific description. The physician should be queried for appropriate details.

Chapter B4034–B9999 Enteral and Parenteral Therapy

enteral
The patient receives feeding or medication into the intestine.

parenteral
The patient receives feeding or medication into the alimentary canal.

Enteral therapy is the intestine, and **parenteral** therapy is within the alimentary canal. Enteral therapy, for example, is provided through the G-tube; parenteral is through a feeding tube typically inserted into one side of the nares. The feeding may be for temporary or long-term use. Feeding may also be supplied via IV therapy.

The codes in this area are used to report tube feedings and other nutritional items. The documentation may indicate a brand name, yet may not be clearly identified for the code descriptions. The physician should be queried so the coder may determine the matching code description per the formula that is rendered.

The dose must be calculated accurately, and the quantity per code selected. Some code descriptions include the administration set, where other codes do not. If the code description does not state an administration set, an additional code must be selected when it is supplied by the physician. Part of the reason there are separate codes is because the administration set may be reused for feedings and might not always be ordered with each feeding tube.

Additional J ____ codes for medications that might be given via the tube or parenteral method are often required. Additional CPT codes for the professional services to place the tube or access are often required.

Chapter C1079–C9722 Outpatient Prospective Payment System

This chapter is CMS-specific and is rarely used by any commercial plans. Even though their intent is for temporary use, many C codes have been in place since 2001.

The codes are selected for items beyond the typical surgical room set-up at an outpatient or ambulatory surgical center (ASC). The C series of codes are surgical facility items, not physician office place of service items. The supplies in this chapter are payable only if the service for placement of the device is medically necessary, as documented in the medical record. Items are paid at a reduced rate, not the purchase price. Items are added to this listing based upon very specialized criteria.

EXAMPLE

For example, C9433 Thiotepa 15 mg is a medication that is instilled into the bladder for treatment of bladder tumors. When Thiotepa is provided on the surgical tray at the Ambulatory Surgical Center (ASC) or outpatient center, the claim for the facility may report the ASC room fee and the C9433 ×1 for the Thiotepa 15 mg that is rendered during the cystoscopy with biopsy physician professional service. The J9340 is not reported, as this dose of medication is rendered during the surgical procedure. The patient is discharged with the indwelling Foley catheter.

Forty-eight hours later, the patient is seen at the physician office and the Thiotepa 15 mg is again instilled via Foley catheter. The physician claim will indicate the instillation service and the J9340 ×1 for the Thiotepa at this location.

CMS provides frequent notification when policy coverage is revised and when codes in this chapter are inactivated. Policies must be checked at least quarterly to identify potential changes, especially if coding for an ASC facility.

Chapter D0000–D9999 Dental Procedures

The HCPCSII codes are selected for dental services, often correlating to the dental insurance benefits and coverage. The place of service and the service the professional performed inform the code selection.

The D0000 code series is the Current Dental Terminology (CDT), which is created, maintained, and modified by the American Dental Association. The national panel for HCPCSII does not oversee the D codes. The U.S. Department of Health and Human Services, the agency overseeing CMS, agrees to include the CDT.

Many of the codes listed in the CDT are duplicated in the CPT codebook. It is usually necessary to contact the insurance plan to verify the correct code required for the care. For example, a physician may perform a surgical procedure that is covered under the patient's dental insurance, rather than the patient's health insurance. The dental insurance plan may accept the CDT code rather than the CPT code for the surgical procedures.

Most of the services in the D chapter are not a covered benefit for the federally funded programs. Since the services are not a covered benefit, the Advanced Beneficiary Notice is not a requirement. Informing the patient prior to the care being rendered if the patient does not have coverage would constitute good customer service.

Depending upon the publication of the HCPCSII code book, there may be a tip beneath the code, guiding to the correlative CPT option. D0210, for example, is similar to 70320 in the CPT codebook.

Chapter E0100–E9999 Durable Medical Equipment

Durable Medical Equipment identifies items and medical equipment. The E codes are very detailed specific descriptions of various equipment items. Many of the codes have multiple coverage rules for Medicare and other insurance plans.

Within this chapter, there are very few unlisted or unspecified options. The description must be matched exactly for accurate code selection. These cannot be approximated.

■ *Highlight*

It is considered a high compliance risk for fraud to select a code that is "close" for equipment items. Accuracy for equipment coding is just as important as CPT or ICD-9-CM code selection.

Chapter G0000–G9999 Procedures/Professional Services (Temporary)

This chapter is frequently used for many physician services. Although described as temporary, some have been active for many years. Policies surrounding the codes change frequently.

Procedures/Professional Services Temporary Guidelines

CMS creates the G codes and their descriptions. The codes may be used in addition to various CPT codes, or in some cases, in lieu of CPT codes. It is especially important to frequently review the policies associated with the use of G codes.

As has been discussed previously, the HCPCSII codes, including the G code chapter, may or may not be used by commercial insurance plans. Determining the insurance benefits, the medical necessity, and then choosing the correlative codes will assist in accurate claims.

The NCCI's National Correct Coding Manual states the G0101 may be selected in addition to unrelated Evaluation and Management (E/M) services at the same encounter. Modifier 25 is added to the E/M code for this example. In the *Understanding Medical Coding* OB/Gyn chapter, however, an example of a claim is prepared to assist in understanding the application of the codes. Per NCCI, G0102 may *not* be selected in addition to an E/M service at the same encounter. Modifier 25 is not applicable per NCCI. This logic is not consistent with CPT.

EXERCISE 3–2

Occult blood examination is performed in the office, with a positive result.

Select only the HCPCSII Code __G0328__

> **Coding Tip**
>
> *If you look up occult blood, you will not find the code. The documentation does not give you the details for ease in locating the code, such as "the examination is performed on fecal material, or stool."*
> - *If you look up the term "fecal," you will be guided to the code.*
> - *Looking up examination will not guide you effectively.*
> - *If you look up "screening," you would have to also know the test is a colorectal cancer-screening test, which in the index gives a range of codes.*

EXAMPLE

A preventive examination is performed for prostate cancer, and a blood sample is obtained by the physician and sent to the lab for PSA test.

What insurance plan does the patient have? What was the exact date of the previous tests? Has the patient experienced any symptoms since the previous date? These questions will guide the coder to the coverage of the benefits and the code selection.

If the patient is a BlueCross BlueShield patient, the coder must verify with the insurance plan the possible use of S0612 Annual digital rectal examination (DRE). It is possible that additional CPT codes will be required along with the S0612, depending upon the documentation and actual care that is provided.

If the patient is a Medicare patient, G0102 Prostate cancer screening, digital rectal examination is selected. The physician practice would not indicate the G0103 for the PSA, since this code reports the laboratory services but not the services for obtaining the sample. The physician would report 36415 for obtaining the sample. It is possible additional CPT codes will be required along with the G0102, depending upon the documentation and actual care that is provided.

When performing the Welcome to Medicare, Initial preventive examination, and also the DRE, both the G0344 and the G0102 codes are selected.

Selecting the proper CPT, G and Q codes, and linking to the ICD-9-CM as described in the medical record is one of the most tedious aspects of coding. As the policies create portions of coverage, the complexity of the coding is growing, creating challenges for physicians and coders.

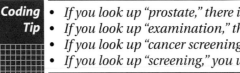

Coding Tip
- *If you look up "prostate," there is no option for this service.*
- *If you look up "examination," there is no option for this service.*
- *If you look up "cancer screening," you are guided to the range of codes.*
- *If you look up "screening," you will find "Prostate, digital rectal" as an option.*

Chapter H0001–H2037 Alcohol and Drug Abuse Treatment Services

This chapter is for specific use by Medicaid agencies. Most other insurance payers do not activate the codes in this chapter.

Alcohol and Drug Abuse Treatment Services Guidelines

The descriptions are very site-specific, often reported by health care professionals to describe mental health care. There are no miscellaneous or unlisted code options.

Chapter J0000–J9999 Drugs Administered Other than Oral Method

This is one of the most important chapters in the code book, requiring your special attention for accuracy.

The heading of the chapter is no longer quite accurate. The oral immunosuppressive drugs are now assigned J codes. As drugs are approved by FDA, they are assigned a J code by CMS. Therefore, "other than oral method" of administration is no longer totally accurate.

Another important detail is that the vaccines and immunizations are reported using CPT codes. The vaccine and immunization medication codes are not found in the HCPCSII code book. Coders who memorize this fact locate codes more readily.

Codes are selected when the physician practice has purchased the medication, representing a cost to the physician practice. If the physician practice has not yet purchased the medication, report only the administration codes (either HCPCSII or CPT, as proper). Some county governments, for example, may choose to distribute a vaccine for all physicians to administer to patients. Only the administration service is submitted as a fee on the claim. When reporting a code for the vaccine a fee representing a cost to the physician should not be listed unless one was actually incurred.

Drugs Administered Paragraph Guideline

Administered drugs are only those that cannot ordinarily be self-administered. There are exceptions and specific policies for insulin and diabetes, but most others have limitations. A drug with limitations, for example, is epinephrine jet injections, for allergic reactions.

Listed as drugs are:

chemotherapy
immunosuppressive
inhalation solutions
other drugs and solutions

The drugs may have an associated policy, limiting the quantity or units that are covered benefits. Most drugs have a quantity limitation, although the associated policy may not be published for each drug code. Determining the correct quantity may require a trial and error process for some insurance plans.

The dose may be described in various terms. Selecting the specific code and also the exact amount of medication that was given requires extreme caution. Units, mg, mcg "per" vs. "up to" are all details of importance. It is often necessary to query the physician and check with the back office staff prior to reporting the code.

Coding Tip

At least every 6 months, obtain a listing of all medications that are stored in the back office of the practice, including the refrigerator. Copy the package insert or box. Then, create a manual of each drug listing by generic and by brand name, with the correlative HCPCSII or CPT code. The back office may choose to purchase a more concentrated dose, a different combination medication, a new medication, or an item that is "on sale" that does not match the J codes that have been listed on the usual encounter capture forms/processes.

EXERCISE 3–3

A Rocephin injection given. What documentation is necessary in order to select the code?

a) Documentation required is <u>amount rendered, why is it taken?</u> *who administered   Route administration*

b) Select the HCPCSII code(s) <u>J0696</u>

■ *Highlight*

The main index of the HCPCSII code book includes many medications, but is not as thorough as the Table of Drugs (see the appendix).

- *Look up Rocephin and you are quickly guided to J0696.*
- *Look up the generic for this medication, Ceftriaxone sodium, and note how similar this is to another medication. Be very cautious to select the codes based upon the exact generic terms. Frequently, you will see terms with the addition of "acetate"; this is not the same substance. Do not select a code that is similar—they must match exactly.*
- *Now look up the Table of Drugs. Rocephin or Ceftriaxone sodium is commonly (not required) to be rendered either IM or IV, listed as 250 mg. The table guides you to J0696.*

- *J0696 Rocephin quantity 1 is for 250 mg. Medicare fee schedule pays $23.99 for 250 mg. If you give 1 gm, this equals 1000 mg; therefore quantity 4 is to be indicated. $23.99 × 4 = $95.96. A charge of $95.96 will be reimbursed by Medicare if medical necessity diagnosis code is a covered benefit.*

EXAMPLE

Depo-Medrol is given. Look at J0120, J0130, and J0140. Determine what dose was given and the exact concentration of the medication. Depo-Medrol is manufactured as Depo, Depo 40, or Depo 80 mg. One might give Depo 80 1/2 cc or Depo 40 1 cc for example.

Within the J chapter, there are multiple options for unlisted, not otherwise classified drugs and solutions. Not every medication that is manufactured and listed in the *Physician Desk Reference* or *Red Book* (two popular medical resources) has an HCPCSII code listed. Consider all unlisted options in the specific area of the chapter, or possibly a CPT code, prior to final selection of the code.

J3490 Unclassified drug
J3590 Unclassified biologic
J8999 Prescription drug oral chemotherapeutic not otherwise specified
J9999 Antineoplastic drug not otherwise classified

EXERCISE 3–4

Select the HCPCSII code(s) and indicate the quantity.

1. Adenosine injection for <u>treatment</u>. 10 mg given J0150 x 2
2. Adenosine injection for <u>diagnostic</u>, 30 mg given J0152
3. IM injection octreotide depot, 180 mg J2353 x 180
4. IM Keflin, 1 gm given J1890

Chapter K0000–K9999 Temporary Codes

This chapter is created for the policies of the durable medical equipment carrier of Medicare, commonly known as the DMERC. They are not commonly used by physician offices. Although the HCPCSII states the codes are temporary, most have been in place for quite some time.

Review the policies prior to selecting the codes in this chapter. Medical necessity documentation in the medical record is required.

Chapter L0000–L4999 Orthotic Procedures

The L0000 series codes describe various items, devices, and procedures, listed by anatomical sites. Most physician practices do not use these codes.

Use the Abbreviations and Acronyms appendix in the HCPCSII code book, if included. If your publication does not contain a special appendix, look for the abbreviations in the front of the book. Most abbreviations included in the HCPCSII are standard.

Prosthetic Procedures Paragraph Guideline

The items listed from L5000 through L5600 are primary "base" codes. Use the codes with the headings of "Additions" for each as provided and appropriate, after the primary code from L5000–5600 areas. Plan on multiple codes for this chapter.

Chapter M0000–M0301 Medical Services

Medical Services are physician office services that are not listed elsewhere. In reality, the codes are mostly obsolete services, with the exception of M0064 Brief office visit for changing of mental psychoneurotic and personality disorder drug prescription. The documentation will guide for the accurate code selection of these uncommon services.

Per NCCI, do not select M0064 and also psychiatric medicine codes in CPT codes for the same service.

Chapter P0000–P9999 Pathology and Laboratory Services

The use of these codes is for the laboratory processing the studies. A commonly used code is P3000, Screening Papanicolaou smear, by technician under physician supervision. The lab would indicate this code for the performance and report of the test. The P9603 and P9604 may be indicated by any practice when documented to depict special travel for specimen collection. P9612 and P9615 are now reported with CPT codes.

Chapter Q0000–Q9999 Temporary Codes

The codes in this chapter were intended as temporary; however, they have been in place for many years. Q codes describe many types of services, medications, and items that have not been authorized within other chapters of the HCPCSII code book.

Commonly used codes for many physician practices are:

- Q0091 Screening Pap smear; obtaining, preparing, and conveying of cervical or vaginal smear to the lab. The code may be reported in addition to various G codes and/or CPT codes as described in the documentation.
- Q0111 Wet mounts, including preparation of vaginal, cervical, or skin specimens
- Q0112 KOH preparations, all potassium hydroxide preps

Per NCCI, Q0091 may be selected in addition to Evaluation and Management services when significant, separately identifiable care is provided at the same encounter. Modifier 25 is added to the E/M code for this example.

Chapter R0000–R59999 Diagnostic Radiology Services

The three codes in this chapter are used for transporting equipment from one place to another, when medically required.

Chapter S0000–S9999 Temporary National Codes

While the heading for this chapter indicates temporary national codes, the intent is to allow insurance plans other than Medicare to standardize systems by adopting a national code structure.

The S codes and their descriptions are created by the BCBS and HIAA for implementation by local insurance plans. BCBS then implement the codes locally. The State Medicaid offices are also now selectively implementing the S codes. Other insurance plans may choose whether or not to implement. The S chapter is used for BCBS, HIAA, and Medicaid, as activated by the local corporations. Policies must be obtained for each insurance plan, for accurate code selection, as these are not universally implemented nationally. S codes are used for medications, services, and items.

Commonly used codes for many physician practices are:

- S0610 Annual gynecological examination; new patient
- S0612 Annual gynecological examination; established patient.

The documentation requirements, the ICD-9-CM linking diagnoses, and the addition of Q0091 or Evaluation and Management services are determined by the insurance plan. For example, the documentation for the annual gynecological examination is not equal to the published Medicare criteria for the G0101 Examination, nor equal to the preventive examination per CPT. Whether or not the Q0091 is accepted in addition to the S0610 or S0612 will also be determined per insurance plan. The documentation requirements and details for HCPCSII are frequently not the same as for CMS or CPT.

Chapter T1000–T9999 National Codes Established for State Medicaid Agencies

These codes are mostly tracking codes created at the request of various Medicaid programs, and may also be used by other insurance plans. They are not applicable for Medicare.

Chapter V0000–V2999 Vision Services

The codes up to V2999 are for vision purposes, usually for eyeglass sales departments. The use of multiple codes is likely for these services.

Reading the descriptions carefully will be required. The hierarchy for these codes is:

- V code instead of a CPT code
- CPT code instead of a V code
- S code instead of a V or CPT code, if BCBS

Chapter V5000–V5999 Hearing Services

The V5000–V5999 are for hearing services, speech tests, and supplies. It is important to check the policies, as many screening hearing services are considered bundled into another examination or noncovered benefits.

Appendix 1—Modifiers

The HCPCSII modifiers are two digit, either alphanumeric or alpha/alpha. Quarterly, the modifiers are activated or deactivated by the local Medicare carrier level for the Medicare claims. AMA/CPT announces annually the modifiers that are nationally accepted for all claims, while other insurance plans create their own policies for activating the remaining modifiers. Just because a modifier is listed in the code book does not necessarily authorize standardized use of the modifier on the claim.

Appendix 2—Abbreviations and Acronyms

This listing may assist in understanding the dosage of medications and the various abbreviations that occur in documentation.

Appendix 3—Table of Drugs

This is one of the most useful areas of the HCPCSII code book. It lists medications alphabetically by generic and brand name, along with the associated dose, common route, and the code.

The Route of Administration column lists the *most common* routes, not necessarily the only routes that are acceptable. Orally administered medications are typically not listed, as these are usually considered to be self-administered, according to the payment policies. If the medication is administered in a method other than listed on this chart, additional investigation is warranted. Read the description of the code, and the policies (if listed) to determine if there are special circumstances for the code. Then, obtain the package insert with the medication, to review if the medication was rendered in accordance with proper medical protocol. It is possible the code would be selected and reported on the claim, however not in every circumstance.

The abbreviations for the route of administration are also provided in this area of the code book.

EXERCISE 3–5

Match the abbreviation with the proper route of administration:

~~IA~~	Variously, into joint, cavity tissue or topical	VAR
~~IV~~	Into catheter or suppositories	OTH
~~IM~~	Subcutaneous	SC
~~IT~~	Orally per drops	ORAL
~~SC~~	Injection not otherwise specified	INJ
~~INH~~	Intramuscular	IM
~~INJ~~	Intra-arterial	IA
~~VAR~~	Intravenous	IV
~~OTH~~	Intrathecal	IT
~~ORAL~~	Inhaled solution via IPPB	INH

Three common types of IV administration are:

IV Gravity
IV Infusion
IV Push

intra-arterial (IA)
The patient receives through the artery system.

intravenous (IV)
The patient receives through the venous system.

intramuscular (IM)
The patient receives an injection into the muscular system. This is the most common method of administration.

intrathecal (IT)
The patient receives through the membrane.

subcutaneous (SC)
The patient receives an injection into the subcutaneous tissue.

inhaled solution (INH)
The patient inhales the medication, may use respiratory equipment commonly known as the Intermittent Positive Pressure Breathing treatment.

injection not otherwise specified (INJ)
The patient receives an injection other than the options listed, such as intradermal or an injection directly into anatomy.

various (VAR)
The patient receives the medication using various, often multiple means.

other (OTH)
The patient receives any other method not listed.

orally (ORAL)
The patient receives medication through the mouth (orally).

Appendix 4—Medicare Policies

Not every publication includes the Medicare policies that are frequently associated with HCPCSII codes. Even when they are included, it is important to check regularly for updates.

Appendix 5—Tables of CPT to HCPCS

This lists the common hierarchy of HCPCSII codes and CPT. The policies are updated frequently and may not be completely identified in this area.

Appendix 6—Revisions to the Code Book

This is an at-a-glance look at the code revisions for the year. No descriptions are listed, so it is necessary to review each code for potential description changes.

Appendix 7—National Average Payment

This lists the HCPCSII codes with a commercial and Medicare average payment fee. Unfortunately, the commercial data is lacking for many codes. The commercial fee was averaged at a 50th percentile factor. The Medicare fee is without the geographic indicator amounts.

ACCURACY TIPS

It is continuously challenging for a health care practice to stay on top of the actual medications and supplies that are rendered for patient care. Frequent and effective communication between the professional staff and the coding department will be necessary in order for accurate HCPCSII code selection to be accomplished.

✳HCPCSII MEDICATION FLOW CHART

1. The physician orders the medication.
   - Is the medication medically necessary? If nonmedically necessary, the medication is probably not covered. Offer Advanced Beneficiary Notice (ABN).
   - Is the medication ordered for an unusual purpose, dose, route, or frequency? It is possibly noncovered. Investigate and offer an ABN.

- Is the medication for cosmetic, contraception, or possible non–FDA-approved purpose? If so, obtain the insurance policies and procedures prior to purchasing the medication, and probably offer the ABN for the patient to assume the financial obligation.

2. Investigate the coverage per top insurance plans.

3. Purchase the medication.

   - Is the brand name or generic purchased?
   - What concentration is purchased?

4. Obtain an ABN signed per date of service, if necessary.

5. Medication is rendered, chart states who gave, place of service, route of administration, and dose. The physician notation and signature are required per date of service.

6. The encounter form completely matches the medication that was given and the documentation of the service.

7. The HCPCSII code is selected and reported on the claim or collected from the patient at the time of the service.

SUMMARY

It is important to make an accurate selection of medication HCPCSII code and quantity. Be familiar with the multiple chapters and appendix options in the HCPCSII code book. Rank the codes based upon the hierarchy, if required. Understand the importance of the HCPCSII codes and modifiers.

REFERENCES

Updatable expert HCPSC level II (16th ed.) (2005). Salt Lake City, UT: Ingenix.

Chapter 4

Current Procedural Terminology (CPT) Basics

LEARNING OBJECTIVES

Upon successful completion of this chapter, you should be able to:

1. Identify the layout of the CPT code book.
2. Recite the symbols, the descriptions, and their purpose.
3. Understand the proper steps for the selection of a CPT code and use of modifiers.

INTRODUCTION

Current Procedural Terminology, referred to as CPT, is published by the American Medical Association. It identifies in detail, specific medical services and procedures performed by physicians and other health care providers. The descriptions of specific medical, surgical, and diagnostic services translate into a numerical five-digit primary code and a four-digit numerical code followed with one alpha (Category II or Category III), with additional two-digit **modifiers.**

The CPT is a uniform reporting system for reliable nationwide communication between health care professionals, patients, and third parties, such as insurance plans. It is now serving to capture statistical data for research and development, particularly the Category II codes (for example, patient safety, smoking cessation, etc.).

The codes are reflective of services performed in the care of patients in the United States and are therefore updated frequently. Each provider is to obtain the most current edition for selecting codes for billing or other reporting purposes. Later in this chapter, how to obtain the semiannual release of information will be discussed.

The CPT was introduced in 1966, standardizing a variety of previously regional systems, and is now updated semi-annually. Some of the milestone changes that have occurred include the implementation of the evaluation and management system in 1992 and the addition of **Category III** codes in 2002. Category III codes describe emerging technology, which were previously indicated with unlisted codes. Another update occurred in 2004, when the appendix listing **Category II** codes was introduced for data

modifier
A two-digit number placed after the usual procedure number, separated by a hyphen, which represents a particular explanation to further describe the procedure or circumstances involved with the procedure.

Category III
Required alphanumeric codes for emerging technology instead of unlisted codes.

Category II
Optional alphanumeric codes for statistical data research and development purposes.

research. Category II codes are selected for tracking of performance measurements. They are optional at this time but likely to become more popular in the health care industry in the near future.

The key to understanding CPT is to keep in mind that the codes are selected to communicate what professional service or procedure a practitioner has performed. The goal is to be as descriptive and inclusive as possible using the code system. Multiple codes may be selected to accomplish this goal, and there are instances when the use of an additional modifier will complete the explanation of the circumstances for the services that are performed. Specific details are essential in determining an appropriate code. The details are found in the documented account of the care, located in the patient's medical record. Certain criteria are required for the selection of a code that help to explain the medical procedure performed.

AMA/CPT CODE BOOK

The CPT code book is available in a standard and a professional edition. The professional edition includes more color illustrations than the standard edition, plus correlating per code references of the *CPT assistant* or CPT *Changes: An Insider's View.* The CPT code book begins with helpful information located inside the front and back covers. The front cover includes a quick-glance, abbreviated listing of the symbols, modifiers, and HCPCSII national codes. In 2005 the place-of-service codes that are updated quarterly by the Centers for Medicare and Medicaid Services (CMS) were listed for convenience.

On the back cover is a listing of common abbreviations that may be found in the CPT or other AMA publications. This listing may be streamlined in the future, as the Joint Commission for Hospital Accreditation is creating standards for acceptable abbreviations that may be used for hospital medical records.

Foreword

Annually, the executive vice president for the AMA issues an explanation regarding what distinguishes the current edition from previous editions. For example, in 2000 HIPAA designated the CPT code set as *the national standard* for reporting physician and other health care professionals' services and procedures. This includes the use of modifiers and descriptions that are published in the CPT.

CPT Editorial Panel and Advisory Committee

When coders and physicians have concerns regarding the description for CPT, taking a moment to write a note helps to improve the system. The AMA panels review information for the annual update of CPT. Anyone may write to the AMA/CPT outlining thoughts, to the addresses listed in the front of the book. The revisions take time for review and discussion. It is advised when communicating concerns that copies of the correspondence be sent to:

> AMA CPT Editorial Panel Chair and Secretary
> AMA CPT Advisory Committee Member for the specialty
> National and State correlative specialty society
> State Medical Association

CPT Code Book Introduction

CPT codes are comprised of different formats of:

Five digits (numbers) for the basic service or procedure
Additional two-digit modifiers that are selected to indicate special circumstances
Category II are four digits followed by one alpha character

The national HCPCSII modifiers are not created by AMA/CPT; however the agreed-upon standard national modifiers are included in the CPT code book.

> **Coding Tip**
>
> *A principal rule (found in the Introduction of CPT) for professional coders is that the selection of a CPT code does not imply insurance payment or reimbursement. CPT codes are for the identification of the accurate service, procedure, medication, or supply as supported by the medical documentation and not a guarantee that payment will be received.*

AMA distributes the most current CPT edition prior to the January 1 implementation date annually. The Category II and Category III codes are updated and distributed on the AMA web site each January 1 and July 1.

The evaluation and management (E/M) codes are selected for services performed by physicians of all specialties. For convenience, CPT places this popular E/M chapter at the front of the code book. Following the E/M chapter, the chapters are sequenced according to numeric value. Both the standard and professional editions have tabbed sections for easy reference, and the professional edition is color coded. Refer to Table 4–1 for an at-a-glance listing of the CPT chapter titles and sections.

In general the CPT code book provides instructions for selecting the accurate CPT code. The instructions consist of the guidelines prior to the section, paragraphs prior to the main terms, references to AMA publications beneath a specific code or parenthetical tips located before or after the codes. The documentation of the performed professional service must be accurately associated to the code selection. The CPT code book specifically cautions against selecting approximate or 'close match' codes.

> **Coding Tip**
>
> *According to the* AMA Principles of CPT Coding, *select the code <u>exactly</u> as described. Modifiers, unlisted codes, or Category III codes may be selected to indicate special circumstances. Do not select a code that is "close."*

CPT also guides physicians of any specialty to select from any area of the CPT code book, to indicate the exact services that are performed. Although it would be rare for every chapter of codes to be selected to describe professional services of one physician, the Anesthesia codes are most likely to be performed by anesthesiologists rather than Family Practice physicians, for example. The CPT code could be selected by any qualified physician or qualified health care professional performing the services. Although the CPT was created for the purpose of identifying physician services, the health care industry has now expanded such that

TABLE 4–1 **CPT Chapter Sections.**

Tab for Section	Series of Codes
Evaluation and Management	99201
Anesthesia	00100
Surgery Guidelines	Prior to surgery chapters
Integumentary	10021
Musculoskeletal	20000
Respiratory	30000
Cardiovascular	33010
Digestive	40490
Urinary	50010
Male/Female and Endocrine	54000
Nervous	61000
Eye and Ocular	65091
Radiology	70010
Pathology and Laboratory	80048
Medicine	90281
Category II	0500F
Category III	0003T
Appendix	Modifiers and other information
Index	Instructions for use of index

other qualified health care personnel may provide the same services. The CPT code may be selected only if the person who performed the service is clearly qualified. The definition of a qualified physician or health care professional directly correlates to licensure and scope of practice for each geographic area per state. Some procedure codes specifically state that the service is performed by a specific level of service, either physician or perhaps therapist. The paragraph prior to the CPT code or the code description will guide for proper selection throughout the book.

EXERCISE 4–1

True or False: It is proper to select the CPT code that almost (but not quite) describes the service or procedure that was documented.

SYMBOLS

Semicolon ;

Certainly one of the more important rules for CPT is saving space; thus the purpose of the semicolon punctuation. Ignoring the semicolon will cause inappropriate and improper code selection. The words in the description prior to a semicolon are the beginning of the description for all codes indented beneath the primary code.

EXAMPLE

The entire description and meaning for 00142 is Anesthesia for procedures on eye; lens surgery. In the code book, next to 00142, only the words "lens surgery" are printed. The description begins with the primary code above 00142, inclusive of all words prior to the semicolon. In this case, the primary code is 00140; with the shared description "Anesthesia for procedures on eye."

Plus sign +

Plus signs indicate add-on codes. The + symbol indicates the particular CPT code is a supplemental service to another performed by the same physician. The description of the code may or may not include terms such as "each additional" or "list separately in addition to__." The add-on codes require another code to be selected along with the + code. The CPT code book often guides to the partnered code (buddy code) that is expected to be selected with the add-on + code. Not every + code is linked with the neighboring codes as the primary codes. Some + codes may be applied to many CPT codes throughout the book. Modifier 51 which indicates multiple procedure concepts, may not be used with + codes. Add-on (+) codes are modifier 51 exempt by CPT concept or rule. A practice should expect 100 percent payment from insurance plans when the + code is submitted on the claim.

Revised ▲

To assist in alerting to changes annually, the code book places the triangular alert prior to the CPT code. Upon receipt of the new code book, review each of the triangles to identify the effect for coding. In the professional edition, the triangle is blue; in the standard edition, all symbols are black.

New code •

The new code dot signifies an entirely new code and description for the book. The dot is red in the professional edition, and black in the standard edition. Some years, new codes are more numerous than revised codes; other years, there are more revisions than new codes.

► New or Revised wording ◄

The sideway triangles alert to a wording or content change. These are frequently seen in the **guidelines,** which are the paragraphs prior to a series of codes. The

guidelines
Within the CPT code book, the guidelines are the pages or paragraphs prior to sections of codes. There are also 1995 or 1997 E/M guidelines that were separately distributed by CMS.

impact can be great, depending upon the details that are stated. The words are in color and usually italicized in a unique font.

Reference to CPT publications ➜

In the professional edition, an additional symbol guides to various references that AMA has published, correlating to the specific CPT code. This symbol, often overlooked entirely, alerts to any changes that have been recently published in other books or newsletters.

Exemptions to use of modifier -51 ⊘

CPT exempts the use of modifier 51 with the symbol or with a rule. The modifier 51 exempt symbol clearly identifies if it is not indicated. Appendix E lists all codes with this exemption.

Example: 90281 Immune globulin human, for intramuscular use

The modifier 51 is also exempt by rule or concept. The + add-codes are automatically exempt from modifier 51 use.

Conscious sedation ⊙

The white circle surrounding a black dot indicates that conscious sedation service is included in the performance of the procedure. An additional conscious sedation CPT code is not additionally selected. This symbol was added to the 2005 CPT code book.

EXERCISE 4–2

List eight CPT symbols and their definitions. Then, list at least one code per each of the symbols.

1.

2.

3.

4.

5.

6.

7.

8.

UNLISTED CODES

Health care is impacted by rapidly progressing technology, and the implementation of new techniques influences the code selection. For this reason, it is important to obtain the latest Category III codes from AMA (updated two times a year, not annually). In the absence of a Category III code to describe a service that is not listed in the CPT code book, an unlisted code is selected. There is at least one in every chapter, and some areas have multiple unlisted codes.

SENDING COPIES OF NOTES

Some services will require additional information to be sent to the insurance plan or other agencies. When sending copies of notes, the CPT guideline states the *pertinent* components of documentation should include:

- Adequate description of the nature, extent, and need for the procedure
- Time, effort, and equipment necessary
- Complexity of symptoms
- Final diagnosis
- Physical findings
- Diagnostic and therapeutic procedures
- Concurrent findings
- Anticipated follow-up care

ILLUSTRATIONS

The CPT professional edition includes handy surgical terminology tips and anatomy and physiology illustrations to assist in the code selection. This section can be very valuable for most coders.

ANESTHESIA

Chapter 6, Anesthesia/General Surgery, discusses the Anesthesia code selection and its rather unique concepts in detail. The guidelines prior to the codes describe the code selection criteria and unique modifier usage. An important fact to note is that anesthesia is often coded with an alternative, specialty-specific coding system published by the American Society of Anesthesiologists (ASA) in lieu of the CPT codes.

CPT SURGICAL GUIDELINES

The surgical guidelines are located between the Anesthesia series of codes and the Integumentary codes. The surgical guidelines are unique to procedures (rather than professional services) and apply to every code from 10000 through to the first Radiology code, 70000. It is important to understand the surgical guidelines, and to stay alert to the detailed and frequent revisions in this area of the code book. The guidelines and their coding concepts extensively effect reimbursement.

incision
Cut into.

It is helpful to first review the history of the definitions per AMA/CPT before getting into the surgical guidelines, as outlined in the CPT Assistant Newsletter. The June 1996 issue of *CPT Assistant* defined surgery as **incision,** excision, amputation, introduction, endoscopy, repair, destruction, suture, and manipulation. As technology advances, additional services are provided in the care of patients, and this concept of surgery may not equal the definition of insurance plans.

Surgical Package

CPT surgical package rules are intended for application with the codes from 10000 through 69990. The CPT defines the surgical package as the following descriptions included within a surgical code:

- local infiltration, metacarpal/metatarsal/digital block or topical anesthesia (commonly lidocaine injection or jelly)
- subsequent to the decision for surgery, one related E/M encounter on the date immediately prior to *or* on the same date as the procedure (including history and physical). (If the decision for surgery is documented for surgical services performed on the same date, the modifier 57 is added to the E/M code.)
- immediate postoperative care, including dictating operative notes, and talking with the family and other physicians
- writing orders
- evaluating the patient in recovery area
- typical postoperative follow-up care (not quantified by days per CPT—this is listed by the insurance benefits)

 Highlight

The variation between CPT and the National Correct Coding Initiative (NCCI) manual for the surgical package topical anesthesia is expanded. NCCI does not allow the selection of the anesthesia code when the anesthesia is a regional block, whereas CPT guides to select the regional block code in addition to the surgical code, when performed by the same physician.

Follow-Up Care for Surgical Procedures

Only the "usual" follow-up care is included in the surgical procedure. Whenever an unusual circumstance, complication, exacerbation, recurrence, or other illness service is provided (and documented) additional CPT codes are selected. These circumstances may require additional modifiers such as modifier -24, -76 or -79, depending upon the scenario. Moreover, all will require proper ICD-9-CM codes describing the complication or specific details.

Multiple Procedures

The use of modifier -51 is frequently reported when multiple procedures are performed on the same date. Occasionally, modifier -59 for distinct procedural service (separate lesion) will be selected. The use of modifier 51 is not yet implemented by all insurance plans, even though the CPT code set standard, per HIPAA, includes this modifier use.

 Coding Tip *Do not use modifier -51 with the + codes throughout the CPT. The + codes are modifier 51 exempt and if reported may further decrease your reimbursement.*

Materials and Supplies

CPT guides you to select 99070 for any supplies "over and above" usually included with the procedure. Insurance plans may have various interpretations for the coding for materials and supplies with the physician services.

Select HCPCSII codes for supplies whenever describing items used during procedures beyond the typical care. Xylocaine/lidocaine is not coded when used as topical anesthetic, because topical anesthesia is included in the CPT surgical package definition. However, other medications are reported. If xylocaine/lidocaine is used for other than topical anesthesia, it is possible that an unlisted HCPCSII code would be selected.

CPT New Symbol for 2005

CPT added a conscious sedation symbol (see code 19298 as an example), which indicates that the conscious sedation service is included in the surgical CPT code, and therefore an additional conscious sedation code is *not* selected.

■ *Highlight*

Conscious sedation rules vary per insurance plan. NCCI states that the conscious sedation service must be performed by another physician (not the surgeon) or a Certified Registered Nurse Anesthetist (CRNA). The physician's RN assistant who is not a CRNA may not serve in this role. CPT states that an "independent trained observer" may assist in the conscious sedation for the surgeon.

Destruction

Surgical destruction is selected if it is separate from the standard management of the problem. CPT lists destruction codes that may be applicable. Cryosurgery, ablation, electrosurgery, laser, and chemical (silver nitrate) are all common forms of destruction. These codes are not used for excision and do not involve closure services (suturing).

EXERCISE 4–3

Where in the CPT code book are the surgical package components described?

_____

_____

RADIOLOGY AND PATHOLOGY GUIDELINES

Chapter 11, Radiology, Pathology, and Laboratory, discusses these coding guidelines in detail. An interesting concept is that both the radiology and the pathology include CPT codes for diagnostic as well as therapeutic services.

CATEGORY II CODES

The most important point is that Category II codes are optional and are not selected in place of the Category I (typical) CPT codes. These are for performance tracking purposes, to decrease chart audits for quality review. The services are to have an evidence base contributing to quality care. The codes are four digits followed by the alpha F, currently ranging from 0001F to 4011F. It is anticipated this range will increase, with the semiannual update from AMA/CPT at www.ama-assn.org.

Two commonly selected Category II codes, in addition to the Preventive examination services, are 4000F Tobacco use cessation intervention, counseling, or 4001F, Tobacco cessation intervention, pharmacologic therapy.

CATEGORY III CODES

Unlike Category II codes, the Category III codes are mandatory and are considered of utmost importance for the process of policies. The codes in this series are selected to describe the service as described, often in lieu of an unlisted code. They were created to describe emerging technology. A particular emerging technology may have a Category III code assigned prior to FDA approval.

The Category III codes are four digits followed by an alpha T. The codes are active for five years and are considered for permanent Category I CPT code assignment, although they may not be assigned as a regular code. The updates are distributed in January and June, at www.ama-assn.org. The list rapidly increases, so it is definitely recommended to obtain the listing each January and June. After the new CPT book is published annually each fall, the list will likely increase by the upcoming January.

Within the Category I regular chapters of the CPT, some of the Category III codes are listed as a parenthetical example, reminding the coder to consider the alternative code. All of the Category III codes are not listed within all areas of the CPT.

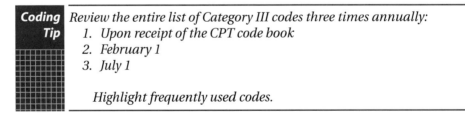

Coding Tip

Review the entire list of Category III codes three times annually:
1. *Upon receipt of the CPT code book*
2. *February 1*
3. *July 1*

Highlight frequently used codes.

Online Medical Evaluation

The 2005 CPT code book introduced the Online E/M Category III code 0074T. The code has specific requirements:

- Response to an *established* patient's online inquiry
- Provided by a qualified health care professional (per scope of practice in a given state)
- Involves the physician's personal timely response
- Must have permanent storage of the entire encounter
- The inquiry is not regarding pre- or post-E/M services
- The inquiry includes all related telephone calls, Rx, or diagnostic testing orders for the problem

- Needs to be using secure HIPAA
- No examination is performed
- Not for every e-mail communication

CPT ERRATA

Each year, AMA/CPT publishes an errata identifying any corrections that are necessary after the annual code book is distributed. This information is distributed via the AMA web site and depending upon the potential correction, may affect the code selection dramatically. Coders are highly advised to obtain the errata and enter the entire list in his or her code book as early as possible each year. An example that has occurred in the past was the erroneous placement of the semicolon, which could have affected procedures for the erroneous code selection for the remainder of the year.

APPENDIX A MODIFIERS

The modifiers are essential, as they reflect a "mirror image" of the procedures or services that are provided. Modifiers are selected to indicate special circumstances, and are necessary to alert the variance from the description of the base code. The two-digit modifiers are placed after the base code, commonly on Category I codes.

■ *Highlight*

The National Correct Coding Initiative manual (NCCI) includes a portion of the AMA/CPT modifiers. The modifiers and many rules for their proper use are listed in the NCCI Manual, which is published and distributed annually in October. The active NCCI modifiers are:

-22, -25, -58, -59, -78, -79, and -91
E1–E4, FA, F1–F9, LC, LD, LT, RC, TA, and T1–T9

Some of the modifiers' descriptions state "Service," guiding to correlate with E/M or other encounter type of care, while other modifier descriptions state "Procedure," guiding the correlation to surgical or other procedural types of care. A modifier may be used for both types of care, if covered in the description.

The CPT code set includes the listing of modifiers and also their descriptions and applications. Upon the implementation of HIPAA, the insurance plans are expected to abide by CPT logic for modifier use.

> **-21 Prolonged E/M Service:** Modifier -21 is placed on the highest level E/M service per category when the documentation indicates "greater than usually required" services are provided. A common example is when the care is not quite critical care management of an organ failure, yet exceeds the 99215 History, exam and medical decision making. If the documentation were present, the coding would be 99215-21. Another example is documentation of the extended counseling and coordination of care rule, beyond the time descriptions for the code. If the documentation is present, the coordination of care of 65 minutes at the unit level, coding might be 99233-21. Figure 4–1 indicates the modifier -21 placement on the claim.

PLEASE
DO NOT
STAPLE
IN THIS
AREA

HEALTH INSURANCE CLAIM FORM

| | PICA | | | | | | PICA | |

1. MEDICARE (Medicare #)   **MEDICAID** (Medicaid #)   **CHAMPUS** (Sponsor's SSN)   **CHAMPVA** (VA File #)   **GROUP HEALTH PLAN** (SSN or ID)   **FECA BLK LUNG** (SSN)   **OTHER** (ID)

1a. INSURED'S I.D. NUMBER   (FOR PROGRAM IN ITEM 1)

2. PATIENT'S NAME (Last Name, First Name, Middle Initial)

3. PATIENT'S BIRTH DATE   MM   DD   YY   **SEX**   M   F

4. INSURED'S NAME (Last Name, First Name, Middle Initial)

5. PATIENT'S ADDRESS (No., Street)

6. PATIENT RELATIONSHIP TO INSURED   Self   Spouse   Child   Other

7. INSURED'S ADDRESS (No., Street)

CITY   **STATE**

8. PATIENT STATUS   Single   Married   Other

CITY   **STATE**

ZIP CODE   **TELEPHONE** (Include Area Code)   (   )

Employed   Full-Time Student   Part-Time Student

ZIP CODE   **TELEPHONE** (INCLUDE AREA CODE)   (   )

9. OTHER INSURED'S NAME (Last Name, First Name, Middle Initial)

10. IS PATIENT'S CONDITION RELATED TO:

11. INSURED'S POLICY GROUP OR FECA NUMBER

a. OTHER INSURED'S POLICY OR GROUP NUMBER

a. EMPLOYMENT? (CURRENT OR PREVIOUS)   YES   NO

a. INSURED'S DATE OF BIRTH   MM   DD   YY   **SEX**   M   F

b. OTHER INSURED'S DATE OF BIRTH   MM   DD   YY   **SEX**   M   F

b. AUTO ACCIDENT?   **PLACE** (State)   YES   NO

b. EMPLOYER'S NAME OR SCHOOL NAME

c. EMPLOYER'S NAME OR SCHOOL NAME

c. OTHER ACCIDENT?   YES   NO

c. INSURANCE PLAN NAME OR PROGRAM NAME

d. INSURANCE PLAN NAME OR PROGRAM NAME

10d. RESERVED FOR LOCAL USE

d. IS THERE ANOTHER HEALTH BENEFIT PLAN?   YES   NO   *If yes*, return to and complete item 9 a-d.

READ BACK OF FORM BEFORE COMPLETING & SIGNING THIS FORM.

12. PATIENT'S OR AUTHORIZED PERSON'S SIGNATURE I authorize the release of any medical or other information necessary to process this claim. I also request payment of government benefits either to myself or to the party who accepts assignment below.

SIGNED _____   DATE _____

13. INSURED'S OR AUTHORIZED PERSON'S SIGNATURE I authorize payment of medical benefits to the undersigned physician or supplier for services described below.

SIGNED _____

14. DATE OF CURRENT: MM   DD   YY   ILLNESS (First symptom) OR INJURY (Accident) OR PREGNANCY(LMP)

15. IF PATIENT HAS HAD SAME OR SIMILAR ILLNESS. GIVE FIRST DATE   MM   DD   YY

16. DATES PATIENT UNABLE TO WORK IN CURRENT OCCUPATION   MM   DD   YY   FROM   TO   MM   DD   YY

17. NAME OF REFERRING PHYSICIAN OR OTHER SOURCE

17a. I.D. NUMBER OF REFERRING PHYSICIAN

18. HOSPITALIZATION DATES RELATED TO CURRENT SERVICES   MM   DD   YY   FROM   TO   MM   DD   YY

19. RESERVED FOR LOCAL USE

20. OUTSIDE LAB?   YES   NO   **$ CHARGES**

21. DIAGNOSIS OR NATURE OF ILLNESS OR INJURY. (RELATE ITEMS 1,2,3 OR 4 TO ITEM 24E BY LINE)

1. |___.___| 3. |___.___|
2. |___.___| 4. |___.___|

22. MEDICAID RESUBMISSION CODE   ORIGINAL REF. NO.

23. PRIOR AUTHORIZATION NUMBER

24. A DATE(S) OF SERVICE						B Place of Service	C Type of Service	D PROCEDURES, SERVICES, OR SUPPLIES (Explain Unusual Circumstances) CPT/HCPCS MODIFIER	E DIAGNOSIS CODE	F $ CHARGES	G DAYS OR UNITS	H EPSDT Family Plan	I EMG	J COB	K RESERVED FOR LOCAL USE
From MM	DD	YY	To MM	DD	YY										
1								99215 | 21							
2															
3															
4															
5															
6															

25. FEDERAL TAX I.D. NUMBER   SSN   EIN

26. PATIENT'S ACCOUNT NO.

27. ACCEPT ASSIGNMENT? (For govt. claims, see back)   YES   NO

28. TOTAL CHARGE $

29. AMOUNT PAID $

30. BALANCE DUE $

31. SIGNATURE OF PHYSICIAN OR SUPPLIER INCLUDING DEGREES OR CREDENTIALS (I certify that the statements on the reverse apply to this bill and are made a part thereof.)

SIGNED _____   DATE _____

32. NAME AND ADDRESS OF FACILITY WHERE SERVICES WERE RENDERED (If other than home or office)

33. PHYSICIAN'S, SUPPLIER'S BILLING NAME, ADDRESS, ZIP CODE & PHONE #

PIN#   GRP#

(APPROVED BY AMA COUNCIL ON MEDICAL SERVICE 8/88)   *PLEASE PRINT OR TYPE*   APPROVED OMB-0938-0008 FORM CMS-1500 (12/90), FORM RRB-1500   APPROVED OMB-1215-0055 FORM OWCP-1500, APPROVED OMB-0720-0001 (CHAMPUS)

Figure 4-1 Placement of modifier -21 on claim form.

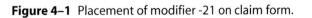

-22 Unusual Procedural Service: Modifier -22 is placed with either the service or the procedure codes, to indicate greater than usual per the code description. Earlier in this chapter, the special report requirements were outlined. It is suggested the special report be submitted when the modifier 22 is selected with the main/base code. As an example, 59409-22 Vaginal delivery only with forceps and extensive difficulty, the physician has documented the complex nature of the care and the total time, including the final outcome of the care.

-23 Unusual Anesthesia: Modifier -23 is placed with a surgical procedure code that does not usually require anesthesia. This modifier is only for general anesthesia, not local, regional, or conscious sedation. An example, Colposcopy with biopsy 56821-23 due to recent cervical bleeding, patient is combative with senile dementia.

-24 Unrelated E/M Service by the Same Physician During a Postoperative Period: Modifier -24 is placed with an E/M *service* depicting that the encounter is unrelated to the previous *procedure* and is provided during a postoperative period. An example is 99213-24 patient with the flu, within 3 weeks of the fracture care of the LT arm, both services by Dr. Jones, Sports Medicine Family Practice.

Modifier -24 is the first of the current modifiers to still have the possible use of the five-digit modifier instead of the more popular two-digit modifier. Workers' Compensation and auto insurance plans may have systems and policies to not use the two-digit modifiers, and will require the five-digit modifiers. The descriptions for the five digit modifiers vary slightly. Figure 4–2 indicates the five-digit modifier placement on the claim in lieu of using the two-digit modifier.

-25 Significant, Separately Identifiable E/M by the Same Physician on the Same Day of the Procedure or Other Service: Modifier -25 is placed with the service, on the E/M codes (technically any E/M within the chapter). Modifier -25 indicates that the patient's condition (may be prompted by a symptom or condition) required a significant, separately identifiable E/M above and

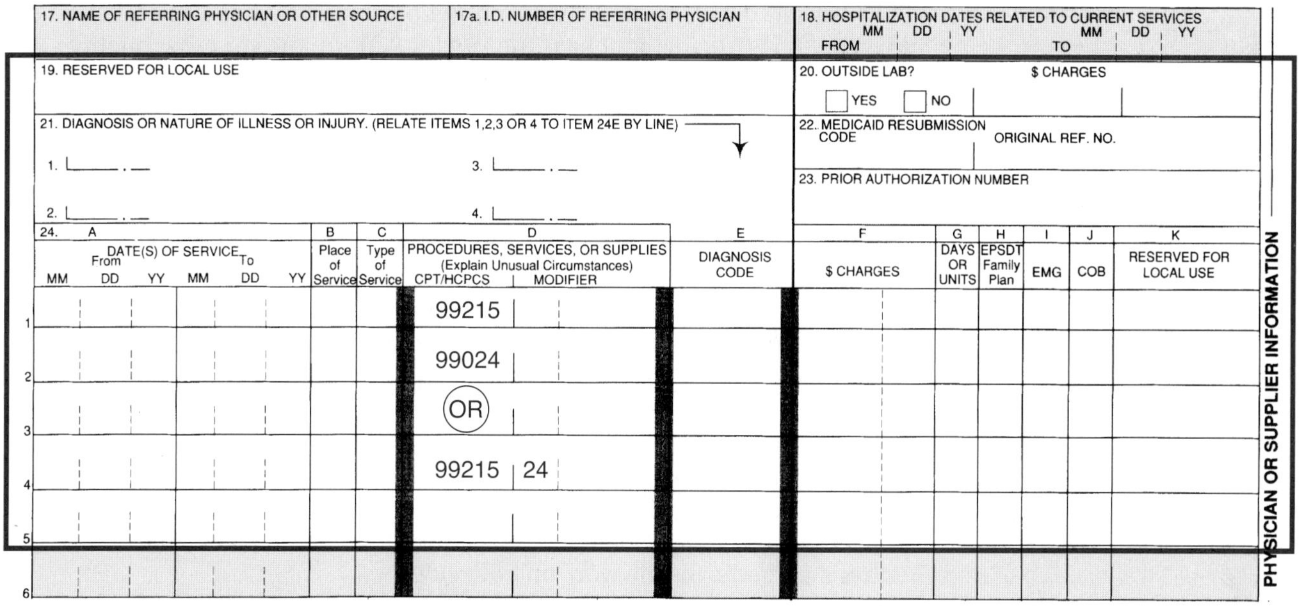

Figure 4–2 Placement of five-digit codes on claim form.

beyond the other service. It also indicates beyond the usual preoperative or postoperative care. Most commonly, -25 is placed with the Office Visit codes, 99201–99215 series. A separate diagnosis is not required in order to select the modifier -25. The Additional history, examination and medical decision making should be documented to signify the separately identifiable care along with the patient's condition that causes the E/M encounter on the same date. As an example, in the morning, the patient has a benign skin lesion destruction (removal). That afternoon, the patient is seen again for an injury to the RT foot. The second, afternoon encounter code is 99213-25.

■ *Highlight*

Many of the E/M codes listed in the NCCI are bundled into surgical codes, when complication visits are performed after the surgical procedure session has ended. The NCCI interpretation varies from AMA/CPT, in that the NCCI requires the patient to have the complication cared for with a return trip to the operating room, with modifier 78. Otherwise, the complication service is included in the post operative component and not additionally coded. Modifier 25 may be selected with CPT codes that have the "XXX" category, which is listed on the Physician Fee Schedule. Modifier 25 may be used when a significant and separately identifiable E/M service on the same date of another service, and the same diagnosis may be used. The inherent work of the initial procedure, supervision of others, or interpretation time is not considered significant or separately identifiable.

-26 Professional Component: Modifier -26 is placed with certain procedures to indicate that only the physician component is performed. The most common procedures that have both the technical and professional components of care are located in the Pathology or Radiology chapters or the Medicine, Cardiology areas of CPT. The modifier -26 is not to be applied to other CPT codes, such as services. As an example, at the hospital, the physician performed the fluoroscopy during the procedure, dictating a report on the medical record, code 73000-26. The equipment, technician, and licensure are owned and managed by the hospital, where a second claim may be sent to the insurance plan with 73000-TC to indicate the other component of care.

-32 Mandated Services: Modifier -32 is placed with Services codes when a peer review organization, payer, or other person mandates a consultation or service. It is anticipated that as the Pay for Performance or other quality indications are developed, this modifier will become more frequently selected. As an example, the insurance plan requires a local physician consultation by a gastroenterologist prior to the performance of the surgical procedure. Code 99241-32 for the gastroenterologist consultation care.

-47 Anesthesia by Surgeon: Modifier -47 is placed on the basic service. Technically, the modifier -47 can be placed on either a procedure or a service code, yet most often is used with procedures. The description states regional or general anesthesia when performed by the same physician or surgeon. It is not used for conscious sedation or local anesthesia purposes.

-50 Bilateral Procedure: -50 is placed on Procedure codes, not on services. The modifier indicates the bilateral procedure is performed during the same session. Modifier -50 would not be selected if the care were at two different sessions on the same date. When the CPT code describes the procedure is bilaterally performed, the modifier -50 does not need to be selected. It is selected if the CPT code describes the procedure unilaterally and the physician performs the work on both sides.

-51 Multiple Procedures: Modifier -51 multiple procedures is probably the most frequently selected modifier. When a primary procedure is performed, often additional procedures are also performed during the same session, requiring the modifier -51 to be placed on the additional procedure codes. The procedures may or may not be through the same incision or anatomical site. There are two main exceptions where modifier 51 is not selected:

- E/M services codes
- Add-on codes

Modifier -51 Exempt: If the modifier -59 is selected, it is not necessary to also add the modifier -51 indicating the additional multiple procedure. Both modifiers are not required.

-52 Reduced Services: The first important concept for the modifier -52 is to understand the basic service or procedure code documentation is described, yet performed in less than complete. In simple terms, do not select a code greater than the documentation has depicted. Modifier -52 is selected when:

- part of the procedure is performed
- the service or procedure is eliminated at the physician's discretion

-53 Discontinued Procedure: Modifier -53 states procedure, and this modifier is not to be selected for services. It is placed with either surgical or diagnostic procedures to describe the special circumstances. The key words for this modifier associate to the care that is *threatening the well-being* of the patient.

-54 Surgical Care Only: Modifier -54 is selected to indicate surgical procedure components are shared between two physicians. When the care is performed, the continuity of care is transferred between the two physicians. Modifier -54 is placed on the primary surgical procedure code.

-55 Postoperative Management Only: Modifier -55 is selected to indicate only that the postoperative care is being performed, and the physician did not perform the preoperative care or the surgical component. Modifier -55 is placed on the surgical procedure code the original surgeon performed. The physicians communicate regarding the transition of the care and the surgical CPT codes.

-56 Preoperative Management Only: Modifier -56 is selected to indicate only that the preoperative care is being performed, and the physician did not perform the postoperative care or the surgical component. Modifier -56 is placed on the primary surgical CPT code.

-58 Staged or Related Procedure or Service by the Same Physician during the Postoperative Period: Modifier -58 is selected to indicate a variety of circumstances. Modifier -58 is not selected for return to the operating room services, and is often used for physician office (or other sites) location care. It is used:

- During the original procedure, the medical plan calls for a portion of the care to be performed again within the postoperative time frame (e.g., pedicle flap care).
- During the postoperative time frame, more extensive care is provided (e.g., complication requiring additional procedure).
- During the postoperative time frame of a diagnostic procedure, therapy is provided.

-59 Distinct Procedural Service: In the CPT code book, the last sentence for this modifier states: "However, when another already established modifier is appropriate it should be used rather than the modifier -59. Only if no more descriptive modifier is available, and the use of modifier -59 best explains the circumstances, should modifier -59 be used." Modifier -59 is typically placed on the second or additional procedures that are indicated on the claim. Modifier -59 indicates an alert that two procedures or services that are not normally coded together are properly coded for a particular circumstance.

It is proper to select modifier -59 for the following purposes:

- Two sessions were performed on the same date; therefore the second procedure or service code is selected.
- On the same date, a different procedure or surgery is performed.
- On the same date, a procedure or service is performed on a separate site.
- On the same date, a procedure or service is performed on a separate organ system (see the E/M guidelines for the listing of organ systems per AMA/CPT).
- On the same date, a separate incision or excision is performed.
- On the same date, a separate lesion care is performed.
- On the same date, a separate unusual injury or area of injury is performed.

The AMA/CPT provides a hint that the modifier -59 may be required, with the description in the procedure codes that state "separate procedure." The separate procedure description is an alert, suggesting that the procedure is often included as part of another procedure performed on the same date during the same session. If the separate procedure is performed for the one of modifier -59 purposes, it would also be selected and modifier -59 placed on the code.

If applicable, the use of the additional anatomical HCPCSII national modifiers are placed after the modifier -59.

▬ *Highlight*

According to NCCI, modifier -59 has the potential for inappropriate use. The NCCI states that modifier -59 cannot be selected for E/M services or for radiation treatment 77427. Modifier -59 often bypasses or overrides the code pair edits listed in the NCCI. Per the NCCI, an indicator of "0" means that no modifiers are to be used, the indicator of "1" allows the NCCI modifiers when appropriate per circumstance, and "9" indicates that there was a past policy.

In 2005, the NCCI added a statement, "if two corresponding procedures are performed at the same patient encounter and in contiguous structures, generally modifiers should not be indicated." This limits many procedures that CPT logic would otherwise guide to select the modifier -59.

Another interesting classification within NCCI, different from AMA/CPT logic, is the Family of Codes. NCCI defines a family as component services, when performed during the same session. This concept guides to select the most comprehensive code and not to select separate, less comprehensive codes.

⟮EXERCISE 4–4⟯

What does the term *separate procedure* mean according to CPT?

_____

_____

-62 Two Surgeons: Modifier -62, commonly known as Co-Surgeons, is used when two surgeons work together for one or more procedures. Each surgeon dictates a report of his or her professional services. Modifier -62 is applied to each of the CPT code that both physicians worked together; both physicians report the same code with modifier -62.

Surgeons may also choose to assist one another during the case, selecting modifier -80 rather than the modifier -62.

In general, the surgeons need to communicate their intentions, and documentation will be necessary to properly describe the co-surgery vs. assistant surgeon per each procedure code during the session. Typically, this is discussed prior to the inception of the operative session.

-63 Procedure Performed on Infants Less Than 4 kg: Modifier -63 is placed on procedure codes for neonates and infants. The present (current) body weight of 4 kg rather than the age determines the modifier selection. This modifier may not be applied to all CPT codes and is not to be placed with:

- E/M services
- Anesthesia
- Radiology
- Pathology/Laboratory
- Medicine

-66 Surgical Team: Modifier -66 is selected when multiple surgeons perform their professional services at the same time during the surgical session. The surgeons each select the CPT code for the work they personally performed, then add modifier -66 to indicate multiple surgeons were active during the session.

A common use for this modifier is the trauma team or a cosmetic team. The surgeons may also provide either co-surgery for one CPT code or assist one another during the case. More often than not, there is a variety of modifiers indicated per these complex cases.

-76 Repeat Procedure by Same Physician: Modifier -76 is selected when a CPT procedure or service is repeated. Most often it is selected when procedures are repeated, within the usual postoperative time period; however, the modifier is not limited to this use. The same CPT code is key.

-77 Repeat Procedure by Another Physician: Modifier -77 is selected when a CPT procedure or service is repeated by another physician, regardless of whether it is the same practice or not. If the procedure or service is repeated by someone other than the original surgeon, modifier -77 is placed on the CPT code. The same CPT code is key.

-78 Return to the Operating Room for a Related Procedure during the Postoperative Period: Modifier -78 is placed on the different CPT code, yet is related to the initial CPT procedure code, and is performed within the postoperative period. The interpretation of "related" will vary between insurance plans. Certainly, if the code were indented in the same series of codes in the CPT code book, it would usually be classified as related.

-79 Unrelated Procedure or Service by the Same Physician during the Postoperative Period: Modifier -79 is selected when the same physician provides an unrelated procedure *or* service during the postoperative period. Again, the insurance plan definition of unrelated or postoperative period can vary.

-80 Assistant Surgeon: Modifier -80 is selected by the assistant surgeon. The assistant communicates with the surgeon to find out the CPT code that was performed, then adds modifier -80 and submits the claim. The assistant surgeon submits a claim, separate from the surgeon. The surgeon dictates the operative report.

-81 Minimum Assistant Surgeon: When a minimum assistant surgeon provides care, modifier -81 is placed on the CPT code selected by the surgeon.

-82 Assistant Surgeon (When Qualified Resident Surgeon Not Available): Modifier -82 is not applicable at all facilities. If the facility typically performs the assistant surgery role with resident surgeons, and the resident is not available, then modifier -82 is selected for the CPT code per assistant surgeon.

-90 Reference (Outside) Laboratory: Some laboratory procedures may be performed at reference labs, rather than performed by the treating physicians. Modifier -90 is placed on laboratory procedure codes.

-91 Repeat Clinical Diagnostic Laboratory Test: Modifier -91 is placed on lab test code, when repeated on the same date. It is not selected when repeating studies are necessary to confirm results, specimen, or equipment problems (including inadequate specimen obtaining, improper prep, reagent problems, or equipment failures). It is also not necessary to select if the test description includes multiple studies.

-99 Multiple Modifiers: Modifier -99 is placed in the first modifier position on the claim, when multiple modifiers are required. This modifier is not accepted by all insurance plans, and the use is not standard.

Anesthesia Physical Status Modifiers

The physical status modifiers are placed only with the Anesthesia codes, in the 00100 series. The P modifier is first, followed by any additional modifiers. The American Society of Anesthesiology assists in policies clarifying each description and the use of the P modifiers.

Ambulatory Surgery Center/Outpatient Modifiers

The modifiers in this area of the CPT code book are limited to the place of service of Ambulatory Surgery Center (ASC) or Outpatient and are reported on the facility claim (not the physician professional service). Many of the modifiers from the general modifier listing are applicable at the ASC, in addition to the following few listed.

-73 Discontinued Outpatient Hospital/Ambulatory Surgery Center Procedure Prior to the Administration of Anesthesia: Modifier -73 is placed on the intended CPT code that is prepared for but is cancelled due to extenuating circumstances of the patient. The patient has received his or her preoperative medication and been taken to the procedure room, yet the anesthesia has not been rendered.

-74 Discontinued Outpatient Hospital/Ambulatory Surgery Center (ASC) Procedure After Administration of Anesthesia: Modifier -74 is similar to the previous modifier; however the patient received the anesthesia or the case began.

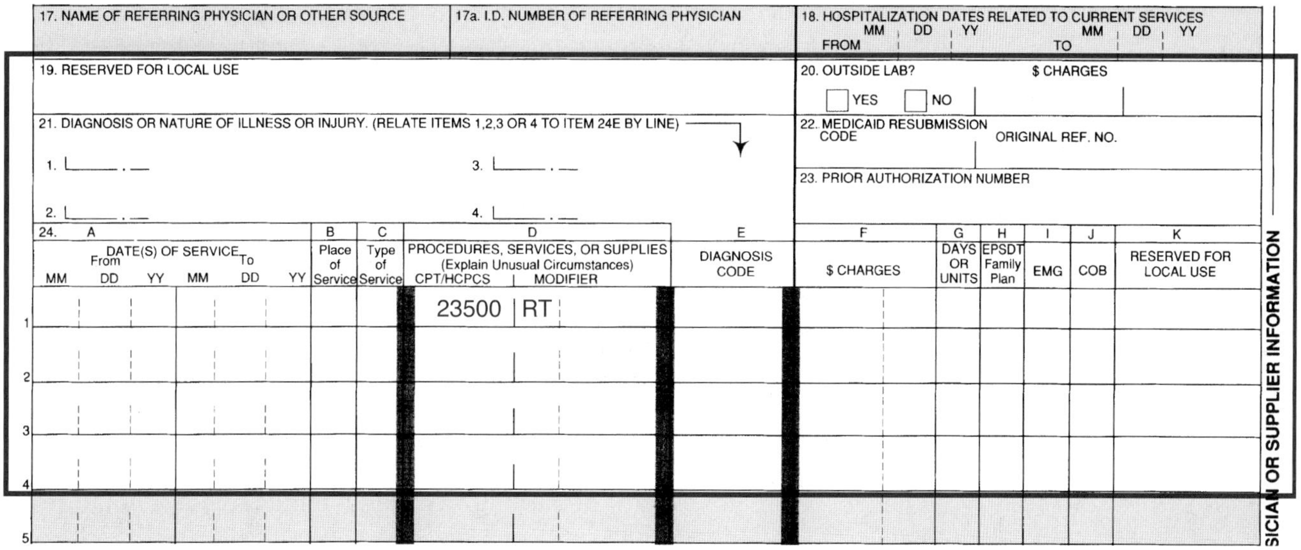

Figure 4–3 CPC code on claim form indicates closed treatment of right clavicular fracture; without manipulation.

Level II HCPCS National Modifiers

The Level II HCPCS modifiers are discussed in detail in Chapter 3. In general, prior to the implementation of ICD-10-CM, the anatomical HCPCSII modifiers are very important to delineate the procedure per site. Once ICD 10 CM is activated, it is anticipated that these modifiers will no longer be required or will become much less frequently reported. Figure 4–3 indicates closed treatment of right clavicular fracture; without manipulation.

EXERCISE 4–5

1. When is a modifier selected?

2. Where are modifiers placed on the claim?

APPENDIX B

This area of the CPT code book offers a great at-a-glance review of the changes for the year. Many coders go straight to Appendix B when they receive the new CPT code book because it clarifies revisions from the previous year of coding.

APPENDIX C—CLINICAL EXAMPLES

Most importantly, the clinical examples contained in Appendix C are not a description of proper documentation. The examples do not list the history, exam, and medical decision-making criteria. They assist in guiding for code selection based upon brief descriptions, per many specialty-specific options, per E/M services.

Often overlooked is the example for the removal of sutures, placed by another surgeon, without anesthesia, which is described in the appendix, guiding to select the E/M based upon the complexity of the suture removals.

A key fact for the clinical examples appendix is that only a portion of the E/M services have clinical examples listed. Codes that do not have a listing may have clarifications located in other AMA publications such as the *CPT Assistant* or the *AMA Principles of CPT Coding.*

APPENDIX D

Appendix D contains a listing of the add-on codes. It reminds coders not to select modifier -51 with these codes.

APPENDIX E

Appendix E lists modifier -51 exempt codes other than the add-on codes.

APPENDIX F

Appendix F lists codes exempt from modifier -63.

APPENDIX G

Appendix G was added in the 2005 CPT code book, listing the conscious sedation codes. The codes listed include the professional service for providing conscious sedation.

APPENDIX H

Appendix H is the Alphabetical Index of Performance Measures by Clinical Topic. This listing correlates to the Category II chapter, with additional details of information. Quality indicators are listed in brief.

APPENDIX I

Appendix I shows genetic testing modifiers placed with molecular laboratory procedure codes.

INDEX

The alphabetic index is designed to guide the user to the correct main text of the CPT code. When selecting a code for services, the index should be the first point of search. Familiarity with the CPT index and the concepts for use will encourage accurate coding and expedite the code selection. The index is streamlined and does not offer multiple, redundant options for each procedure and service.

The index is based on certain concepts to simplify the search process. The main terms are:

- Procedure or Service
- Organ or Other Anatomical Site
- Condition
- Synonyms, Eponyms and Abbreviations

Beneath the main term, three indentation options may be listed. These indented options are modifying terms used to select the code.

The codes will be stated either with a comma or with a hyphen, depending upon the sequence. It is important to review all of the codes in the listed area prior to making the final code selection.

EXERCISE 4–6

Using the index, find the listing for Vaginal cyst biopsies. Find the code in the chapter and recite the description for the code that is selected.

_____

_____

_____

TIPS FOR SELECTING A CPT CODE

1. Read the documentation for the care that was provided. Circle the professional services that you believe were rendered, the medications and supplies given, and tests performed at the encounter/session.
2. Using the CPT index find the possible code(s) to be considered.
3. Review the entire description of the code(s).
4. Read all of the little print before and after the code. Review the chapter guidelines of CPT if necessary, then the guidelines for the main term, the paragraph guidelines close to the code, and the parenthetical examples.
5. Determine if any modifiers are required, including national HCPCSII anatomical modifiers.
6. If necessary, seek additional resources for guidance regarding the selection of the code (AMA CPT Assistant, Changes).

7. If necessary, confirm or query the physician prior to selecting the code.

8. Once the CPT code is selected, review the payer rules for the individual patient prior to placing the code on the claim.

EXERCISE 4–7

1. Recite the entire description for code 38572.

2. Where are the codes located in the CPT for physician visit services?

SUMMARY

Familiarity with the CPT code book symbols, concepts, guidelines, parenthetical tips, and other details will assist accurate code selection. Each service is rendered at a specific location. The code descriptions and selection may vary based upon the site for the care. The actuality of the care that is performed and documented in the medical record supports the code selection. In the absence of documentation, it is improper to select the CPT code.

REFERENCES

AMA current procedural terminology 2005 professional edition. (2004). Chicago: American Medical Association.

AMA principles of CPT coding. (2004). Chicago: American Medical Association.

Centers for Medicare and Medicaid Services. *National correct coding edits,* Version 10.3 (October 2004). Retrieved August 30, 2005, from http://www.cms.hhs.gov/physicians/cciedits.

Chapter 5
Evaluation and Management

LEARNING OBJECTIVES

Upon successful completion of this chapter, you should be able to:

1. Discuss the relevance of evaluation and management (E/M) codes.
2. Identify the criteria for code selecting from the logic of AMA/CPT, Centers for Medicare & Medicaid Services (CMS) 1995 E/M Guidelines or the CMS 1997 E/M Guidelines.
3. Correct selection of E/M codes to match documentation.
4. Locate the E/M criteria for visits/encounters in the CPT code book.
5. Recite the criteria for consultation.

INTRODUCTION

evaluation and management section codes (E/M)
The first section of the CPT coding manual that describes office visits, hospital visits, nursing facility visits, and consultations.

The **evaluation and management section codes (E/M)** identify encounters or visits provided at various locations, under many circumstances. The E/M codes are relevant for describing visits provided by health care professionals for the care of patients. Each time a physician provides a visit, the physician has the option to select from one of three documentation and code selection logics of the AMA/CPT, the CMS 1995 E/M Guidelines, or the 1997 E/M Guidelines. The criteria for each of these options will be outlined in detail seeking to identify the similarities and the variations between the three options.

EXAMPLE

For the federally funded programs (e.g., Medicare, Medicaid, Railroad, TRICARE, Federal Employees Plan) the physician may choose a 1995 or 1997 E/M guideline per encounter. For a 9 A.M. office visit for Mrs. Jones, the physician may have decided to document using 1995 guidelines, while the 10 A.M. office visit for Mr. Smith may be documented using 1997 guidelines.

The code level may be affected by the choice of 1995 vs. 1997 guidelines; either a higher or a lower CPT code may be properly documented. Knowing the areas of variation is an important skill.

The E/M codes are located in the front of the CPT codebook, anticipating frequent use by physicians of all specialties. The series of codes begin with 99201 and end with 99499.

AMA/CPT EVALUATION AND MANAGEMENT (E/M) GUIDELINES

The guidelines are located just prior to the first code, 99201. AMA/CPT has also published a few scenarios. These scenarios do not represent proper documentation, yet are helpful for guiding to the code selection.

E/M services are defined as midnight to midnight. This concept does not always blend clearly with all places of service. For example, a 23-hour stay description by the hospital does not describe the physician services that occur from 11 P.M. of the first date to 1 A.M. of the second date.

The E/M codes are grouped by location or type of care and may have further subdivisions, such as new patient and established patient visits. The layout of the code criteria is consistent beginning with clarifications in a paragraph, the CPT code with description, the components required, counseling and coordination of care information and the assigned time factors.

New Patient Definition

The AMA/CPT new patient definition has been revised within the past few years. Because revisions must always be anticipated, coders need to review this definition whenever a new code book is annually published.

The AMA/CPT E/M guidelines considers a new patient "one who has not received any professional services from the physician or another physician of the same specialty who belongs to the same group practice, within the past three years."

The definition does not state "professional services that have been billed." In other words, if a physician renders care to a patient at the hospital yet does not submit a claim for the service, and a second physician sees the patient at the office one year later, the patient is considered established. Although there is no chart on file at the office, no previous billing record or information filed, if the patient received care from a partner, the patient is an established patient of the practice.

For the E/M services under all three logics, there are documentation requirements and documentation contributing factors. Most of this chapter will discuss the documentation requirements, as these are extensive. In order to select a E/M CPT code, the documentation requirements must be met. The three key components are history, examination, and medical decision making, regardless of the logic selected (AMA/CPT, 1995 or 1997). Additional, contributory factors are counseling, coordination of care, and nature of presenting problem, and yet another component is time. Along with the time component, the counseling and coordination of care are covered later in the chapter with an exception to the three key component requirements for documentation.

One of the contributory factors is the nature of presenting problem, defined as a disease, condition, illness, symptom, sign, finding, complaint, or other reason for the encounter with or without a diagnosis at the time of the encounter. This varies from the chief complaint, which was stated in the patient's own words.

The nature of the presenting problem is the description of the reason for the encounter according to the physician, rather than the patient. Nature of presenting problem has five levels:

Minimal
- Physician supervision without physician present at the encounter

Minor
- Good prognosis with treatment plan compliance
- Transient problem not likely to permanently alter health and the treatment is a definite path

Low severity
- Little or no risk of mortality without treatment
- Full recovery is expected
- Risk of morbidity without treatment is low

Moderate severity
- Increased probability of prolonged impairment
- Uncertain prognosis
- Risk of morbidity without treatment is moderate

High severity
- High probability of severe, prolonged, functional impairment
- Moderate to high risk of mortality without treatment
- Risk of morbidity without treatment is high to extreme

Coding Tip The nature of the presenting problem is not a key component for documentation and does not affect the CPT code selection for the E/M Service. *While physicians often choose to document the nature of presenting problem within their notes, guiding to the treatment plan, the encounter diagnoses and the medical decision-making documentation requirements must be met in order for the E/M CPT code to be selected, rather than the nature of presenting problem note.*

The three key components—history, examination and medical decision making—are required for the selection of the New Patient Outpatient code series. The E/M criteria for new patient code selection and documentation is greater than for established patients.

Established Patient Definition

The AMA CPT E/M guidelines consider an established patient "one who has received professional services from the physician or another physician of the same specialty who belongs to the same group practice, within the past three years."

For a few places of service categories, a special advantage for the established patient definition exists when selecting codes with the decreased, fewer key component requirements. Only two of the three key components are required to be documented in order to select the outpatient services for the established patient. It is optional as to which of the three are documented:

- History and exam
- History and medical decision making
- Exam and medical decision making

The physician may partially document the third component, or have no documentation at all.

EXERCISE 5–1

1. Look in the CPT code book at 99212. Notice the descriptive paragraph states "which requires at least two of three key components." Not every place of service has the "two of three" words throughout the chapter. Only two key components must be met in order to select the code.

2. Look in the CPT code book at 99202. Notice the descriptive paragraph states "which requires at least three of three key components." All three must be met in order to select the code.

3. Look in the CPT code book at 99219. First note the heading states New *or* Established Patients. Notice the descriptive paragraph states "which requires at least three of three key components." All three must be met for both the new and the established patient in order to select the code.

When a physician cares for patients while on call services for another physician, the on-call physician codes are selected as if the absent physician had been providing the care. In other words, if the patient is an established patient for the absent physician, then the patient status is considered established for the on-call physician. The situation can be challenging for the on-call physician who may not have access to the absent physician medical records or all of the medical **history** information; however, if the on-call physician chooses to provide additional service and charting, the additional time typically spent to become better acquainted with the case does not increase the code selection.

history
A record of past events; a systematic account of the medical, emotional, and psychosocial occurrences in a patient's life and of factors in the family, ancestors, and environment that may have a bearing on the patient's condition.

CRITERIA OF DOCUMENTATION AND E/M CODE SELECTION PER AMA/CPT

This section describes the illness, disease-related or "sick" visit. Later in this chapter, preventive or screening **examinations** are described.

examination
A critical inspection and investigation, usually following a particular method, performed for diagnostic or investigational purposes.

History

The history is the narrative, inquiry, and communication component. This is not the area for documenting the findings, examination, or visibly determined aspects of the encounter. The history should depict the "detective work," setting the stage

TABLE 5–1   Criteria for History Component of E/M.

CC	HPI	ROS	PFSH	Type of History Level (must meet all columns)
Documented problem	Brief	N/A	N/A	Problem focused
Documented problem	Brief	Problem pertinent	N/A	Expanded problem focused
Documented problem	Extended	Problem pertinent + limited (per AMA/CPT) additional systems	Problem pertinent	Detailed
Documented problem	Extended	Complete	Complete	Comprehensive

medical decision making
The complexity of establishing a diagnosis and/or selecting a management option.

for the level of the examination and **medical decision making** that may be necessary for the care of the patient today (see Table 5–1). The history component is not for the examination findings during the course of the visit, that is separate and will be covered later in this chapter.

Chief Complaint (CC)

chief complaint (CC)
A subjective statement made by a patient describing his or her most significant or serious symptoms or signs of illness or dysfunction.

The **chief complaint** (CC) must be stated in the medical record. This is the "kick-off" for the remainder of the service, and begins the inquiry and investigation discussions with the patient. The chief complaint is usually in the patient's own words, describing his or her symptoms, problems, condition, diagnosis (if known), or other reason for the visit.

It is inappropriate for the chief complaint documentation to translate the patient's own words into medical terminology.

If the chief complaint is revised (such as the patient scheduled the appointment for athlete's foot and actually wants to request an Rx for Viagra), the medical record documentation must reflect this revision.

If the chief complaint is augmented (such as when the physician enters the room, a long list of items are identified and the physician intends to care for these today), the medical record must reflect this. A problem listing should be converted into the actual chief complaint the patient is describing for care or that the physician has deemed necessary to address today.

A statement such as "follow-up" without the medical illness or disease is too brief and a statement such as "monthly check" describes only the time period and not the reason for the visit. Both of these chief complaints would not be accepted by an auditor, and risk the entire history component be determined lacking.

History of Present Illness (HPI)

history of present illness (HPI)
Inquiry from the first sign or symptom through today of the patient's experiences that associate to the chief complaint and reason for the visit. Specific documentation is required for the HPI.

The **history of present illness** (HPI) continues the investigation, or "detective work" associating to the chief complaint and reason for today's visit to state the current correlative recent details. A good opening inquiry is, "From the first symptom through today, what have you experienced regarding _____?" and document:

- Location
- Quality
- Severity

- Timing
- Context
- Modifying factors
- Associated significant signs and symptoms

The HPI should state pertinent information, correlating to the reason for the visit. The HPI guides the physician to determine the next series of questions, how the chief complaint illness has been affecting the specific body systems.

Review of Systems (ROS)

review of symptoms (ROS)
Inquiry of the signs or symptoms that define the problem, affecting the body systems. Specific documentation is required for the ROS.

The history patient intake form is often used to list the signs and/or symptoms per body system, and should state the body systems that are affected by the chief complaint. For example, "Have you experienced or are you now noticing a problem with _____ affecting your breathing?" This **review of systems (ROS)** with the patient response serves as the baseline data, assisting the physician to begin the provisional diagnosis or definitive diagnosis and additional actions that may need to take place during this visit today. The ROS purpose is to define the problem, clarify the differential diagnoses, and identify testing of baseline data that might affect management options.

The ROS criteria are:

- Constitutional (fever, malaise, weight loss, pallor)
- Eyes
- Ears, nose, mouth, throat
- Cardiovascular
- Respiratory
- Gastrointestinal
- Genitourinary
- Musculoskeletal
- Integumentary (skin and/or breast)
- Neurological
- Psychiatric
- Endocrine
- Hematologic/lymphatic
- Allergic/immunologic

Past History, Family and Social History

past family and social history (PFSH)
Pertinent inquiry of the patient's history of the illness, family history and social history with specific documentation required.

The next area of information gathered during the inquiry, is discussion of the pertinent **past, family, and social history (PFSH)**. Again the term "pertinent" is described in the guidelines, suggesting the importance of the questions correlating to the chief complaint for the care today.

Past History. The past history criteria are for the pertinent information to be documented:

- Past major illnesses and injuries
- Prior operations
- Prior hospitalizations

- Current medications
- Allergies
- Age-appropriate immunization status
- Age-appropriate feeding/dietary status

Family History. The family history criteria are for the pertinent information to be documented:

- Health status or morbidity of parents, siblings, and children
- Specific diseases related to problems identified in the chief complaint, HPI, or ROS
- Diseases of family or hereditary that may place the patient at risk

Social History. The social history criteria are for the pertinent information to be documented, for age-appropriate past and current activities:

- Marital status and/or living arrangements
- Current employment
- Occupational history
- Use of drugs, alcohol, and tobacco
- Level of education
- Sexual history
- Other relevant social factors

The four history criteria components are the chief complaint, HPI, ROS, and PFSH. There are four history level options per E/M code: problem focused, expanded problem focused, detailed and comprehensive. All four criteria must be met or exceeded in order to select one of the history levels. See Table 5–1 to assist in this selection.

AMA/CPT does not publish a number to describe the terms brief, expanded, or complete history levels. They are described as:

- Brief is the CC and brief HPI
- Expanded problem focused is CC, brief HPI, and problem-specific ROS
- Detailed is CC, extended HPI, problem-specific ROS, and pertinent to CC PFSH
- Comprehensive is CC, extended HPI, problem-specific ROS, and the review of all other body systems, *plus* the complete PFSH details

Examination

The examination is the "hands-on" component of the E/M encounter, yet the examination does not require the physician to physically touch the patient for the assessment of each area and/or system. For example, the physician may note jaundice or icteric sclera appearance or the gait and station from simple visual observance of the patient. Additional history criteria may be obtained by the physician during the examination service.

The physician determines the type and extent of the examination to perform. It is important to understand that the physician may choose to examine a body area and/or organ system during a visit. The body areas are:

- Head, including the face
- Neck

- Chest, including breasts and axilla
- Abdomen
- Genitalia, groin, buttocks
- Back
- Each extremity

The organ systems are:

- Eyes
- Ears, nose, mouth, and throat
- Cardiovascular
- Respiratory
- Gastrointestinal
- Genitourinary
- Musculoskeletal
- Skin
- Neurologic
- Psychiatric
- Hematologic/lymphatic/immunologic

The examination level criteria are:

- Problem focused is a limited examination of the affected body area or organ system.
- Expanded problem focused is a limited examination of the affected body area or organ system *and* other symptomatic or related organ system (must have one organ system documented).
- Detailed is an extended examination of the affected body area(s) *and* other symptomatic or related organ system(s) (must have at least one organ system documented).
- Comprehensive is a general multisystem examination (head to toe) or a complete examination of a single organ system (tip: as though a specialist performed the single organ system examination).

Again, note that AMA/CPT has not identified a specific number per exam. Select the level based upon the documented examination level criteria. See Table 5–2 for a simple comparison view of the examination criteria per AMA/CPT.

TABLE 5–2   Examination Criteria for AMA/CPT.

Body Area or Organ System	Other Symptomatic or Related Organ System	Type of Examination
Limited exam of affected	N/A	Problem Focused
Limited exam of affected	Limited exam of other symptomatic or related organ system	Expanded Problem Focused
Extended exam of affected	Extended exam of other symptomatic or related organ system	Detailed
General multisystem or specialty exam		Comprehensive

Medical Decision Making

This component identifies the complexity necessary for the physician to establish the diagnosis for the encounter today. It is often the component that lacks documentation, although the thought processes were used by the physician. For code selection, the criteria must be documented. The criteria must correlate or be pertinent to the chief complaint for the visit.

Medical decision-making criteria:

- Number of possible diagnoses and management options that must be considered
- The amount and/or complexity of medical records, diagnostic tests, and/or other information that must be obtained, reviewed or analyzed
- The risk of significant complications, morbidity and/or mortality, as well as co-morbidities associated with the patient's presenting problem(s), the diagnostic procedure(s) and/or the possible management options.

When selecting the medical decision-making level, two of the three criteria must match. Table 5–3 helps make this selection at a glance. For example, if the documentation reflects a limited number of management options during the encounter (criteria 1), a moderate amount of data has been reviewed (criteria 2), and moderate risk of complications (criteria 3), the level for the type of decision making is moderate, indicating two criteria met the moderate level.

MORE DETAILS

counseling
The act of providing advice and guidance to a patient and his or her family.

coordination of care
The arrangement and/or organization of patient care to include all health care providers.

Additional components for E/M are **counseling, coordination of care,** and nature of presenting problem. Counseling and coordination of care and time will later be addressed in detail.

The nature of presenting problem does not affect the documentation requirements and does not directly affect code selection processes. The nature of the presenting problem simply guides to closure a match for selecting the specific code and may be beneficial documentation for care or other reasons. It is considered contributory to the professional service and not required criteria.

Procedures performed are not included in the E/M services codes. Additional codes are selected for procedures or tests that are performed or professionally interpreted by the physician. The review of the results when documented is captured within the medical decision-making amount and complexity of data to be reviewed, as previously discussed.

TABLE 5–3   Medical Decision Making.

Number of Diagnoses or Management Options	Amount and/or Complexity of Data to be Reviewed	Risk of Complications and/or Morbidity or Mortality	Type of Decision-Making Level
Minimal	Minimal or none	Minimal	Straightforward
Limited	Limited	Low	Low complexity
Multiple	Moderate	Moderate	Moderate complexity
Extensive	Extensive	High	High complexity

TIME

In the real world, not every encounter "fits" into the history, examination and medical decision-making service. Therefore, understanding two additional options, counseling and coordination of care rule, and other criteria, can be helpful.

Counseling and Coordination of Care Rule

An example sets the stage for further discussion of the rule and requirements.

EXAMPLE

The test results of the biopsy have been returned to the physician. The biopsy is positive for malignant adenocarcinoma. The physician asks the patient to come into the office for the results. At this appointment the physician informs the patient of the results, and then discusses the options for treatment to include a referral to a surgeon, a hematologist/oncologist, and a radiation/oncologist. The patient asks his spouse to join in the decisions. They decide to defer the surgical option, and initiate the care with the oncology and radiation oncologist. The physician refers the patient for this care plan, and requests the patient to return in one month for a follow-up appointment.

The required documentation for this example does not include any history, exam, or medical decision making. The entire encounter is surrounding Counseling and Coordination of Care for the adenocarcinoma. The documentation required states the extent of the counseling and/or coordination of care and the time spent. Two styles of acceptable documentation for this rule are:

1. "Time entering room 9:20 A.M. Established patient is informed of biopsy results, counseled regarding treatment options and mortality, morbidity risks. The spouse enters for additional discussion and care is coordinated. Time exiting room is 10:00 A.M."
2. "Established patient is informed of biopsy results, counseled regarding treatment options and mortality, morbidity risks. The spouse enters for additional discussion and care is coordinated. Total time spent is 40 minutes."

The CPT code is then selected without regard to the history, exam, or medical decision-making key components. Look up CPT code 99215. Notice the paragraphs below the medical decision-making component that describe the counseling and coordination of care service, and then the next paragraph states, "Usually, the presenting problem(s) are of moderate to high severity. Physicians typically spend 40 minutes face to face with the patient and/or family." The code selected for the above example is 99215.

Here are tips for applying Counseling and Coordination of Care concepts:

- Counseling and Coordination of Care concepts apply for the treatment and management of an illness or disease. The rule does not apply for risk management, prevention, or other health improvement concepts, as the 99401 series are for these purposes.
- Often the encounter may begin with a history and possibly part of an examination, and then converts to a counseling session. The documentation needs to clearly reflect that counseling and coordination of care dominate at least 50% of the encounter, with a statement and the time when this instance occurs.
- Counseling and Coordination of Care concepts are not for insight-oriented, behavior-modifying and/or supportive psychotherapy sessions. See 90804 series for these purposes.

- Counseling and Coordination of Care at the outpatient locations must capture the time based upon face-to-face with the patient. Inpatient or nursing facility locations that are eligible must capture the time based upon the floor/unit total time, and does include time with parties who have assumed responsibility for care or decision making. The time the physician is located on the unit and at the bedside rendering care for that particular patient is included. Also included is the time spent reviewing the data, writing orders, and communicating with other professionals and the family while on the unit. It does not include time spent by other personnel assisting the physician. The time away from the unit in other areas of the facility is not captured.

- The rule is not for telephone discussion counseling.

- If the patient is not present on the same date as the coordination of care is provided, the code option is the Case Management 99361 series.

- The Counseling and Coordination of Care rule is limited as to the locations that are eligible. Look up 99281 Emergency department visit and notice that the description in the paragraph does not include any time options. The code is not eligible for the counseling rule.

- Counseling and Coordination of Care time does not include time with staff members. Only time with the physician or other health care professional managing the encounter is eligible.

- Preparation or postvisit time is not included in the selection of the code.

When the E/M code is based upon time, such as critical care, or prolonged services, the documentation should state the physician time beginning and ending.

HOW TO SELECT THE E/M CODE FOR THE MOST COMMON ENCOUNTERS

First, review the medical record:

1. How: Determine whether the documentation reflects the key components for illness/disease, meets with the Counseling or Coordination of Care concepts, or other criteria.

Key Components	Counseling or Coordination of Care Rule	Other Criteria
Illness or Disease Care with:	More than 50% of the time	Pediatric Critical Transport
History	The extent of the care is documented	Critical Care
Exam		Prolonged Services/Standby
Medical decision making		Case Management
		Care Plan Oversight
		Preventive Medicine
		Newborn Care
		Special E/M

2. What: Determine the type of service that was rendered (illness/disease management of chronic illness, preventive care, counseling or coordination of care, other criteria service).

3. Where: Determine the place of service the care was rendered.

4. Who: New patient or established patient or perhaps the age for certain services.

Then, review the CPT code book.

1. First, determine the category of service that is likely. Usually this is the place of service or the type of care (outpatient, hospital or critical care, preventive). Table 1 Categories and Subcategories of Service, toward the front of the CPT code book may be of assistance for this step.

2. Next, review the guidelines that are located just prior to the codes in that category for any special circumstances that correlate to the case.

3. Determine the key component requirements (three of three or two of three) for each of the codes in the category. *Compare to the medical record* documentation for code selection.

4. For many visits, the code is now selected. However, if no history, exam, or medical decision making is documented, the service may be eligible for the Counseling and/or Coordination of Care rule.

CMS 1995 EVALUATION AND MANAGEMENT GUIDELINES

The 1995 E/M guidelines are very similar to the AMA/CPT guidelines. The E/M guidelines can be found at www.cms.hhs.gov, then choose Medlearn and Evaluation & Management. The guidelines describe the importance of the documentation purpose:

- Evaluate the plan of treatment and monitor over time
- Communicate with continuity of care
- Accurate and timely claims payment
- Appropriate utilization review and quality of care
- Collection of data for research and education

Notice that only one purpose is regarding payment, while many purposes are for the care of the patient.

Coding Tip

General Principles of Documentation
1. *The medical record shall be complete and legible.*
2. *The documentation of each patient encounter should include:*
   - *Reason for the encounter and relevant history, exam findings, and prior test results*
   - *Assessment, clinical impression or diagnosis*
   - *Plan for care*
   - *Date and legible identity of the observer (everyone who contributes information)*
3. *Document the rationale for ordering diagnostic services.*
4. *Past and present diagnoses should be accessible to the treating and/or consulting physician.*
5. *Appropriate health risk factors should be identified.*
6. *The patient's progress, response to and changes in treatment, and revision of diagnosis should be documented.*
7. *The CPT and ICD-9-CM codes on the claim shall (or must) be supported by the documentation.*

Documentation for E/M

History, examination, and medical decision making are the key components, equal to the CPT guidelines. The Counseling and Coordination of Care rules are also very similar.

History

The definitions of the chief complaint and each of the history components are very similar to the CPT, with a few differences that are described for you. The 1995 guidelines count factors for selecting the level of the key components.

> **HPI:** The 1995 E/M guidelines add one more option to the HPI listing. "Duration" is added, along with location, quality, severity, timing, context, modifying factors, and associated significant signs and symptoms. Table 5–4 is helpful regarding the HPI selection, however notice there are more specific counting definitions for each of the levels to consider than the previous AMA/CPT options.
>
> **ROS.** The systems listed for the ROS are the same as the AMA/CPT; however, there are specific counting definitions for each of the levels. The ROS defines the problem, clarifies the differential diagnoses, and identifies testing of baseline data that might affect management options.
>
> Problem pertinent 1 ROS = positive responses and pertinent negative responses for the specific system
> Extended 2–9 ROS = positive responses and pertinent negative responses for two to nine systems
> Complete 10 ROS = At least 10 organ systems must be reviewed, documenting the positive responses and pertinent negative responses. For systems without a positive response or pertinent negative, add a notation *"all other systems are negative."*

TABLE 5–4   Selecting the History Level for 1995 Guidelines.

CC	HPI	ROS	PFSH	Type of History Level (must meet all columns)
Documented problem	Brief 1–3	N/A	N/A	Problem Focused
Documented problem	Brief 1–3	Problem pertinent	N/A	Expanded Problem Focused
Documented problem	Extended 4+ or associated comorbidities	Extended	Problem pertinent	Detailed
Documented problem	Extended 4+ or associated comorbidities	Complete	Complete	Comprehensive

PFSH: The same information as CPT; however, there are specific counting definitions.

Pertinent 1 = one question response from each of the PFSH
Complete 2 of 3 = Established patient = two of three areas PFSH question responses
Complete 3 of 3 = New patient 3 of 3= three of three areas PFSH question responses

Throughout the 1995 E/M Guidelines are documentation guidelines or DGs. These descriptions further clarify the interpretations and suggestions for use of the E/M guides. Some of the DGs are restrictive in nature, whereas others indicate allowances. Regardless, the DGs are part of the guidelines and need to be understood, implemented, and considered for code selection.
History code selection DG interpretations are:

- Chief complaint, ROS, and PFSH may be included in the HPI or listed.
- ROS and/or PFSH located within the chart must be reviewed and updated by the physician by:
  - describing new information or noting no changes
  - or by noting the date and where in the chart the prior ROS or PFSH are written
- The physician must note supplementation or confirm information that is charted/written by staff, patient, or others contributing to the history.
- If not able to obtain the history, describe the patient's condition or why not able to obtain.

Examination

The examination criteria for the 1995 E/M guidelines are almost identical to the AMA/CPT with the few exceptions of the examination of the:

Body area of back (states that it includes the spine)
Organ systems allow for constitutional

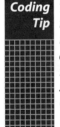

Coding Tip *The physician may choose what type of examination to perform: general multisystem (head to toe examination concept) or specialty (single organ system). In simple terms, any physician may choose to perform any specialty examination, at any encounter, as long as the examination criteria are performed and properly documented. For example, a family physician may choose to provide a comprehensive single organ system ears, nose, mouth and throat specialty examination, if desired. Or an otolaryngologist may choose to provide a general multisystem examination. The physician chooses the type of examination to perform per patient.*

As with the previous history component, the 1995 guidelines add interpretative documentation guidelines and a count definition, which affect the code selection. These are:

- "Abnormal" of the affected area must be elaborated, with positive or negative findings.
- Unexpected findings of asymptomatic areas should be documented.

- "Negative" or "normal" may be stated for asymptomatic areas.
- General multisystem examination must document findings for eight of twelve organ systems.

The final area varies from CPT, in that the examination of an affected body area now also requires eight examination findings from the organ systems. See Table 5–5 for examination selection at a glance.

Medical Decision Making (MDM)

The medical decision making three criteria categories are the same as AMA/CPT logic option; however, the 1995 guidelines augmented the MDM criteria by including a specific chart for the Risk of Complications and/or Morbidity or Mortality.

Criteria 1: Number of diagnoses or management options

Number of diagnoses or management options clarified in the documentation guidelines:

- Established diagnosis = must state improved, well controlled, resolving or worsening, inadequately controlled, or failing to respond
- Not yet diagnosed (provisional diagnosis, symptoms only) = *may state possible, probably, or rule out diagnoses.*
- Initiation of treatment, changes in treatment plan = must state including educational
- Referrals, consultations requested = must state who and where

In the outpatient office setting it is common for the physician to gather information that may occur over multiple visits/encounters prior to determining the definitive, final diagnosis. During each of these encounters, the medical

TABLE 5–5   **Examination Selection Criteria 1995 Guidelines.**

Body Area or Organ System (Back area, includes spine and constitutional organ system)	*Other Symptomatic or Related Organ System (Back area, includes spine and constitutional organ system)*	*Type of Examination*
Limited exam of affected	N/A	Problem Focused
Limited exam of affected	Limited exam of other symptomatic or related organ system	Expanded Problem Focused
Extended exam of affected	Extended exam of other symptomatic or related organ system	Detailed
General multisystem of 8–12 organ systems or Specialty Exam		Comprehensive

record may reflect "rule out," and if documented as above, is captured for the MDM criteria of the CPT code.

When the chart states "rule out diabetes," this statement is counted for the MDM component of the E/M CPT code selection as one diagnosis/management option documented. Rule out terms should be stated on the medical record, supporting the medical necessity for the care. This is especially true for outpatient services.

Criteria 2: Amount and/or complexity of data

Amount and/or complexity of data to be reviewed is clarified by:

- Diagnostic ordered, planned/scheduled, performed = must state
- Review of results = initial and date report or in chart, may state "white blood count (WBC) unremarkable"
- Necessity to obtain old records or additional history from others = must state
- Review of old records or no additional information derived from others = must include elaboration of the findings from the old medical record. "Medical records reviewed" does not count, nor is captured for the MDM criteria.
- Professional conference regarding results = must state
- Direct visualization of radiology films, images, or specimens that were interpreted by another physician = must document that this service has been performed (e.g., IVP films by a urologist).

Criteria 3: Risk of significant complications, morbidity, and/or mortality

Risk of significant complications, morbidity, and/or mortality is clarified by a risk chart. The criteria is clarified with:

- Risk of complications, morbidity, or mortality = must state
- Surgery or invasive procedures ordered, planned, or scheduled = state type of procedure
- Surgery or invasive procedure performed = must state
- Referral or decision for urgent surgery = must state

The risk chart is selected by the *highest level risk on the Table of Risk* (Table 5–6). For example, if the documentation states, "Patient is scheduled for PTCA next week," the risk selection is moderate. Next refer to Table 5–7 Medical Decision Making selection for helpful at-a-glance review of the levels.

How to Select the E/M Code for Most Visits Using the 1995 E/M Guidelines

The selection of the E/M code using the 1995 E/M Guidelines is very similar to the AMA/CPT method. Refer to the previous How to Select the E/M Code for the most common encounters. In reviewing the medical record each of the key components will be counted for the 1995 Guideline code selection.

The 1995 guidelines and AMA/CPT are almost identical for the Counseling and Coordination of Care concept. When 50 percent of the visit is for illness/disease counseling, document and select the code based upon time.

The counseling clarification provided states that the total length of time for the encounter (face to face or floor time, as appropriate) should be documented and the record should describe the counseling and/or activities to coordinate care.

TABLE 5–6   Table of Risk.

Level of Risk	Presenting Problem(s)	Diagnostic Procedures Ordered	Management Options Selected
Minimal	One self-limited or minor problem, e.g., cold, insect bite, tinea corporis	Laboratory tests requiring venipuncture Chest x-rays EKG/EEG Urinalysis Ultrasound, e.g., echocardiography KOH prep	Rest Gargle Elastic bandages Superficial dressings
Low	Two or more self-limited or minor problems One stable chronic illness, e.g., well-controlled hypertension or non-insulin-dependent diabetes, cataract, BPH Acute uncomplicated illness or injury, e.g., cystitis, allergic rhinitis, simple sprain	Physiologic tests not under stress, e.g., pulmonary function tests Noncardiovascular imaging studies with contrast, e.g., barium enema Superficial needle biopsies Clinical laboratory tests requiring arterial puncture Skin biopsies	Over-the-counter drugs Minor surgery with no identified risk factors Physical therapy IV fluids without additives
Moderate	One or more chronic illnesses with mild exacerbation, progression, or side effects of treatment Two or more stable chronic illnesses Undiagnosed new problem with uncertain prognosis, e.g., lump in breast Acute illness with systemic symptoms, e.g., pyelonephritis, pneumonitis, colitis Acute complicated injury, e.g., head injury with brief loss of consciousness	Physiologic tests under stress, e.g., cardiac stress test, fetal contraction stress test Diagnostic endoscopies with no identified risk factors Deep needle or incisional biopsy Cardiovascular imaging studies with contrast and no identified risk factors, e.g., arteriogram, cardiac catheterization Obtain fluid from body cavity, e.g., lumbar puncture, thoracentesis, culdocentesis	Minor surgery with identified risk factors Elective major surgery (open, percutaneous, or endoscopic) with no identified risk factors Prescription drug management Therapeutic nuclear medicine IV fluids with additives Closed treatment of fracture or dislocation without manipulation
High	One or more chronic illnesses with severe exacerbation, progression, or side effects of treatment Acute or chronic illnesses or injuries that pose a threat to life or bodily function, e.g., multiple trauma, acute MI, pulmonary embolus, severe respiratory distress, progressive severe rheumatoid arthritis, psychiatric illness with potential threat to self or others, peritonitis, acute renal failure An abrupt change in neurologic status, e.g., seizure, TIA, weakness, or sensory loss	Cardiovascular imaging studies with contrast with identified risk factors Cardiac electrophysiological tests Diagnostic endoscopies with identified risk factors Discography	Elective major surgery (open, percutaneous or endoscopic) with identified risk factors Emergency major surgery (open, percutaneous or endoscopic) Parenteral controlled substances Drug therapy requiring intensive monitoring for toxicity Decision not to resuscitate or to deescalate care because of poor prognosis

TABLE 5–7   Medical Decision Making (two of the three columns must exceed or match).

Number of Diagnoses or Management Options	Amount and/or Complexity of Data to Be Reviewed	Risk of Complications and/or Morbidity or Mortality	Type of Decision-Making Level
Minimal	Minimal or none	Minimal	Straightforward
Limited	Limited	Low	Low complexity
Multiple	Moderate	Moderate	Moderate complexity
Extensive	Extensive	High	High complexity

CMS 1997 EVALUATION AND MANAGEMENT GUIDELINES

While many aspects of both 1995 and 1997 of the guidelines are identical, the 1997 E/M Guideline examination components are much more detailed and specific. At this point, the variances will be covered.

History

The 1997 guidelines for the HPI add one more option, the status of at least three chronic or inactive conditions to the listing of duration, location, quality, severity, timing, context, modifying factors, and associated significant signs and symptoms. The new option depicts the important area of variation between the 1995 and the 1997 guidelines and is noticed with the Extended HPI. The criterion is:

- The medical record should describe at least four elements of the HPI, *or the status of at least three chronic or inactive conditions.*

This description of the Extended HPI assists the physician to consider selecting the 1997 rather than the 1995 guidelines, to capture credit for the ongoing management of the chief complaint for chronic illnesses. As an example, "follow up for diabetes, CHF, and glaucoma" lists the chief complaint for three chronic illnesses. Upon selecting 1997, however, the physician must complete all of the key component history, exam, and MDM criteria for 1997, and cannot hop between the component for the 1995 or 1997. The history, exam and medical decision making of the 1997 guidelines are all to be documented if the physician selects this guideline. It would be inappropriate to provide and document the 1997 history, 1995 exam, and 1995 MDM.

EXERCISE 5–2

Answer using AMA/CPT logic, 1995 Guidelines, or 1997 Guidelines. ICD-9-CM codes are not required for this exercise.

1. What is the definition of a new patient?

2. What is the definition of an established patient?

3. List the key components in selecting the proper level of evaluation & management service.

4. What are the contributory components?

5. In documenting, what information is typically contained in the chief complaint?

6. What is the term for the chronological description of the patient's present illness from the first sign and/or symptoms to today?

7. List each of the components for HPI.

8. If the patient describes HPI for symptoms that are insignificant and not associated to the chief complaint, does this information contribute to the code selection?

9. What does ROS stand for?

10. What is the purpose of the ROS data?

11. If you provided a problem focused history, what are the components according to CPT?

12. If you provided an EPF history, what are the components?

13. A patient presents with lower back pain, subsequent to a recent urinary tract infection. The location of the pain is over the flank on the right side and is spontaneous. Pain does not seem to improve with Tylenol or with any motion and does not seem to be improving with rest. Patient also relates having a fever for the past day. On the new patient history form, the patient states fever and weakness for two days, recent UTI with history of one or two a year, and has some history of nocturia. What level history is this?

14. A patient presents with lower back pain subsequent to a recent urinary tract infection. The location of the pain is over the flank on the right side, is spontaneous, does not seem to improve with Tylenol or with any motion, and does not seem to be improving with rest. Patient also relates having a fever for the past day. On the new patient history form, the patient states fever and weakness for two days, recent UTI with history of one or two a year, has some history of nocturia, no cardiac history according to the patient, and no respiratory illnesses. Patient indicates prior history of kidney stone treated with lithotripsy in 1994, allergic to sulfa, no current medications, drinks "a lot" of milk/day, and is a nonsmoker. What level history is this?

15. A patient presents with lower back pain subsequent to a recent urinary tract infection. The location of the pain is over the flank on the right side, is spontaneous, does not seem to improve with Tylenol or with any motion, and does not seem to be improving with rest. Patient also relates having a fever for the past day. On the new patient history form, the patient states fever and weakness for two days, recent UTI with history of one or two a year, has some history of nocturia, no cardiac history according to the patient, no respiratory illnesses, no eye problems, no ENT symptoms, no GI problems, no present back injuries or strains, no skin problems, no neurological problems noted, no psychiatric problems, no diabetes or endocrine symptoms, no hematologic symptoms, and is allergic to sulfa. Patient indicates prior history of kidney stone treated with lithotripsy in 1994, no current medications, drinks "a lot" of

milk/day, and is a non-smoker. According to the patient, the back pain is not affecting the remaining systems listed on the form. What level history is this according to CPT?

Examination

The greatest variations between the 1997 and the previous AMA/CPT or 1995 Guidelines are in the examination criteria. The types of examinations for the single organ examinations are dramatically detailed, indicating exactly what anatomy is examined and how to document findings. The body areas and the anatomical examinations are not standard and allow for the physician to choose examination options.

In order to select the same four levels of the examination (problem focused, expanded problem focused, detailed, comprehensive), each examination depicts exactly how the documentation correlates to the exam level selection. This criteria is found on the last page of each of the specific specialty examinations, and each varies. Use caution in determining the components for specialty exams. The Table 5–8, Listing of Examination Options for 1997, will assist in only a portion of the selection process.

TABLE 5–8   Listing of Examination Options for 1997.

General Multisystem Examination	or Specialty Examinations Cardiovascular, Ear, Nose and Throat, Genitourinary, Hematologic/Lymphatic/ Immunologic, Musculoskeletal, Neurological, Respiratory, Skin	or Eye Examination, Psychiatric	Type of Examination
Exam elements criteria of one to five	Exam elements criteria of one to five	Exam elements criteria of one to five	Problem focused
Exam elements criteria of at least six	Exam elements criteria of at least six	Exam elements criteria of at least six	Expanded problem focused
Exam of at least two from six body areas OR at least twelve of two or more body areas	Exam elements of at least twelve	Exam elements of at least nine	Detailed
Exam all elements in nine area and document two of nine areas	Exam all elements in the shaded boxes and document at least one in each unshaded border box	Exam all elements in the shaded boxes and document at least one in each unshaded border box	Comprehensive

Source: CMS 1997 E/M Guidelines

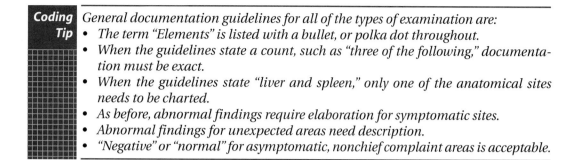

General documentation guidelines for all of the types of examination are:
- *The term "Elements" is listed with a bullet, or polka dot throughout.*
- *When the guidelines state a count, such as "three of the following," documentation must be exact.*
- *When the guidelines state "liver and spleen," only one of the anatomical sites needs to be charted.*
- *As before, abnormal findings require elaboration for symptomatic sites.*
- *Abnormal findings for unexpected areas need description.*
- *"Negative" or "normal" for asymptomatic, nonchief complaint areas is acceptable.*

General Multisystem Examination

Table 5–9 demonstrates the content and documentation requirements for the General Multisystem Examination guide to selecting the examination level. For the detailed exam, it is more common to have documentation of two elements from six areas, rather than 12 elements from only two body areas. Note that the comprehensive level requires two elements from nine areas to be documented.

TABLE 5–9   General Multisystem Content and Documentation Requirements.

System/Body Area	Elements of Examination
Constitutional	■ Measurement of **any three of the following seven** vital signs: 1) sitting or standing blood pressure, 2) supine blood pressure, 3) pulse rate and regularity, 4) respiration, 5) temperature, 6) height, 7) weight (May be measured and recorded by ancillary staff) ■ General appearance of patient (eg, development, nutrition, body habitus, deformities, attention to grooming)
Eyes	■ Inspection of conjunctivae and lids ■ Examination of pupils and irises (eg, reaction to light and accommodation, size and symmetry) ■ Ophthalmoscopic examination of optic discs (eg, size, C/D ratio, appearance) and posterior segments (eg, vessel changes, exudates, hemorrhages)
Ears, Nose, Mouth and Throat	■ External inspection of ears and nose (eg, overall appearance, scars, lesions, masses) ■ Otoscopic examination of external auditory canals and tympanic membranes ■ Assessment of hearing (eg, whispered voice, finger rug, tuning fork) ■ Inspection of nasal mucosa, septum and turbinates ■ Inspection of lips, teeth and gums ■ Examination of oropharynx: oral mucosa, salivary glands, hard and soft palates, tongue, tonsils and posterior pharynx
Neck	■ Examination of neck (eg, masses, overall appearance, symmetry, tracheal position, crepitus) ■ Examination of thyroid (eg, enlargement, tenderness, mass)

continues

TABLE 5–9   **General Multisystem Content and Documentation Requirements** continued

System/Body Area	Elements of Examination
Respiratory	■ Assessment of respiratory effort (eg, intercostal retractions, use of accessory muscles, diaphragmatic movement) ■ Percussion of chest (eg, dullness, flatness, hyperresonance) ■ Palpation of chest (eg, tactile fremitus) ■ Auscultation of lungs (eg, breath sounds, adventitious sounds, rubs)
Cardiovascular	■ Palpation of heart (eg, location, size, thrills) ■ Auscultation of heart with notation of abnormal sounds and murmurs Examination of: ■ carotid arteries (eg, pulse amplitude, bruits) ■ abdominal aorta (eg, size, bruits) ■ femoral arteries (eg, pulse amplitude, bruits) ■ pedal pulses (eg, pulse amplitude) ■ extremities for edema and/or varicosities
Chest (Breasts)	■ Inspection of breasts (eg, symmetry, nipple discharge) ■ Palpation of breasts and axillae (eg, masses or lumps, tenderness)
Gastrointestinal (Abdomen)	■ Examination of abdomen with notation of presence of masses or tenderness ■ Examination of liver and spleen ■ Examination for presence or absence of hernia ■ Examination (when indicated) of anus, perineum and rectum, including sphincter tone, presence of hemorrhoids, rectal masses ■ Obtain stool sample for occult blood test when indicated
Genitourinary	MALE: ■ Examination of the scrotal contents (eg, hydrocele, spermatocele, tenderness of cord, testicular mass) ■ Examination of the penis ■ Digital rectal examination of prostate gland (eg, size, symmetry, nodularity, tenderness) FEMALE: Pelvic examination (with or without specimen collection for smears and cultures), including ■ Examination of external genitalia (eg, general appearance, hair distribution, lesions) and vagina (eg, general appearance, estrogen effect, discharge, lesions, pelvic support, cystocele, rectocele) ■ Examination of urethra (eg, masses, tenderness, scarring) ■ Examination of bladder (eg, fullness, masses, tenderness) ■ Cervix (eg, general appearance, lesions, discharge) ■ Uterus (eg, size, contour, position, mobility, tenderness, consistency, descent or support) ■ Adnexa/parametria (eg, masses, tenderness, organomegaly, nodularity)

continues

TABLE 5–9   **General Multisystem Content and Documentation Requirements** continued

System/Body Area	Elements of Examination
Lymphatic	Palpation of lymph nodes in **two or more** areas: ■ Neck ■ Axillae ■ Groin ■ Other
Musculoskeletal	■ Examination of gait and station ■ Inspection and/or palpation of digits and nails (eg, clubbing, cyanosis, inflammatory conditions, petechiae, ischemia, infections, nodes) Examination of joints, bones and muscles of **one or more of the following six** areas: 1) head and neck; 2) spine, ribs and pelvis; 3) right upper extremity; 4) left upper extremity; 5) right lower extremity; and 6) left lower extremity. The examination of a given area includes: ■ Inspection and/or palpation with notation of presence of any misalignment, asymmetry, crepitation, defects, tenderness, masses, effusions ■ Assessment of range of motion with notation of any pain, crepitation or contracture ■ Assessment of stability with notation of any dislocation (luxation), subluxation or laxity ■ Assessment of muscle strength and tone (eg, flaccid, cog wheel, spastic) with notation of any atrophy or abnormal movements
Skin	■ Inspection of skin and subcutaneous tissue (eg, rashes, lesions, ulcers) ■ Palpation of skin and subcutaneous tissue (eg, induration, subcutaneous nodules, tightening)
Neurologic	■ Test cranial nerves with notation of any deficits ■ Examination of deep tendon reflexes with notation of pathological reflexes (eg, Babinski) ■ Examination of sensation (eg, by touch, pin, vibration, proprioception)
Psychiatric	■ Description of patient's judgement and insight Brief assessment of mental status including: ■ orientation to time, place and person ■ recent and remote memory ■ mood and affect (eg, depression, anxiety, agitation)

Cardiovascular Examination

Table 5–10 shows the content and documentation requirements for the Cardiovascular Examination guide to selecting the examination level. For the detailed exam, any twelve elements meets the criteria. Note how this varies from the previous general multisystem examination. The comprehensive level requires all elements from the shaded boxes of constitutional, respiratory, cardiovascular, gastrointestinal, and neurological plus at least one element from the eyes, ears, nose and throat, neck, musculoskeletal, extremities, and skin areas.

TABLE 5–10   Cardiovascular Examination Content and Documentation Requirements.

System/Body Area	Elements of Examination
Constitutional	■ Measurement of **any three of the following seven** vital signs: 1) sitting or standing blood pressure, 2) supine blood pressure, 3) pulse rate and regularity, 4) respiration, 5) temperature, 6) height, 7) weight (May be measured and recorded by ancillary staff) ■ General appearance of patient (eg, development, nutrition, body habitus, deformities, attention to grooming)
Eyes	■ Inspection of conjunctivae and lids (eg, xanthelasma)
Ears, Nose, Mouth and Throat	■ Inspection of teeth, gums and palate ■ Inspection of oral mucosa with notation of presence of pallor or cyanosis
Neck	■ Examination of jugular veins (eg, distension; a, v or cannon a waves) ■ Examination of thyroid (eg, enlargement, tenderness, mass)
Respiratory	■ Assessment of respiratory effort (eg, intercostal retractions, use of accessory muscles, diaphragmatic movement) ■ Auscultation of lungs (eg, breath sounds, adventitious sounds, rubs)
Cardiovascular	■ Palpation of heart (eg, location, size and forcefulness of the point of maximal impact; thrills, lifts; palpable S3 or S4) ■ Auscultation of heart including sounds, abnormal sounds and murmurs ■ Measurement of blood pressure in two or more extremities when indicated (eg, aortic dissection, coarctation) Examination of: ■ Carotid arteries (eg, waveform, pulse amplitude, bruits, apical-carotid delay) ■ Abdominal aorta (eg, size, bruits) ■ Femoral arteries (eg, pulse amplitude, bruits) ■ Pedal pulses (eg, pulse amplitude) ■ Extremities for peripheral edema and/or varicosities
Gastrointestinal (Abdomen)	■ Examination of abdomen with notation of presence of masses or tenderness ■ Examination of liver and spleen ■ Obtain stool sample for occult blood from patients who are being considered for thrombolytic or anticoagulant therapy
Musculoskeletal	■ Examination of the back with notation of kyphosis or scoliosis ■ Examination of gait with notation of ability to undergo exercise testing and/or participation in exercise programs ■ Assessment of muscle strength and tone (eg, flaccid, cog wheel, spastic) with notation of any atrophy and abnormal movements

continues

TABLE 5–10 **Cardiovascular Examination Content and Documentation Requirements** continued

System/Body Area	Elements of Examination
Extremities	■ Inspection and palpation of digits and nails (eg, clubbing, cyanosis, inflammation, petechiae, ischemia, infections, Osler's nodes)
Skin	■ Inspection and/or palpation of skin and subcutaneous tissue (eg, stasis dermatitis, ulcers, scars, xanthomas)
Neurological/Psychiatric	Brief assessment of mental status including ■ Orientation to time, place and person, ■ Mood and affect (eg, depression, anxiety, agitation)

Ear, Nose, and Throat Examination

Table 5–11 depicts the content and documentation requirements for the Ear, Nose, and Throat Examination guide to selecting the examination level. For the detailed exam, any twelve elements meets the criteria. The comprehensive level requires all elements from the shaded boxes of constitutional, head and face, ears, nose,

TABLE 5–11 **Ear, Nose, and Throat Content and Documentation Requirements.**

System/Body Area	Elements of Examination
Constitutional	■ Measurement of **any three of the following seven** vital signs: 1) sitting or standing blood pressure, 2) supine blood pressure, 3) pulse rate and regularity, 4) respiration, 5) temperature, 6) height, 7) weight (May be measured and recorded by ancillary staff) ■ General appearance of patient (eg, development, nutrition, body habitus, deformities, attention to grooming) ■ Assessment of ability to communicate (eg, use of sign language or other communication aids) and quality of voice
Head and Face	■ Inspection of head and face (eg, overall appearance, scars, lesions and masses) ■ Palpation and/or percussion of face with notation of presence or absence of sinus tenderness ■ Examination of salivary glands ■ Assessment of facial strength
Eyes	■ Test ocular motility including primary gaze alignment

continues

TABLE 5–11 **Ear, Nose, and Throat Content and Documentation Requirements** continued

System/Body Area	Elements of Examination
Ears, Nose, Mouth and Throat	■ Otoscopic examination of external auditory canals and tympanic membranes including pneumo-otoscopy with notation of mobility of membranes ■ Assessment of hearing with tuning forks and clinical speech reception thresholds (eg, whispered voice, finger rub) ■ External inspection of ears and nose (eg, overall appearance, scars, lesions and masses) ■ Inspection of nasal mucosa, septum and turbinates ■ Inspection of lips, teeth and gums ■ Examination of oropharynx: oral mucosa, hard and soft palates, tongue, tonsils and posterior pharynx (eg, asymmetry, lesions, hydration of mucosal surfaces) ■ Inspection of pharyngeal walls and pyriform sinuses (eg, pooling of saliva, asymmetry, lesions) ■ Examination by mirror of larynx including the condition of the epiglottis, false vocal cords, true vocal cords and mobility of larynx (Use of mirror not required in children) ■ Examination by mirror of nasopharynx including appearance of the mucosa, adenoids, posterior choanae and eustachian tubes (Use of mirror not required in children)
Neck	■ Examination of neck (eg, masses, overall appearance, symmetry, tracheal position, crepitus) ■ Examination of thyroid (eg, enlargement, tenderness, mass)
Respiratory	■ Inspection of chest including symmetry, expansion and/or assessment of respiratory effort (eg, intercostal retractions, use of accessory muscles, diaphragmatic movement) ■ Auscultation of lungs (eg, breath sounds, adventitious sounds, rubs)
Cardiovascular	■ Auscultation of heart with notation of abnormal sounds and murmurs ■ Examination of peripheral vascular system by observation (eg, swelling, varicosities) and palpation (eg, pulses, temperature, edema, tenderness)
Lymphatic	■ Palpation of lymph nodes in neck, axillae, groin and/or other location
Neurological/Psychiatric	■ Test cranial nerves with notation of any deficits Brief assessment of mental status including ■ Orientation to time, place and person, ■ Mood and affect (eg, depression, anxiety, agitation)

mouth and throat, and neck, plus at least one element examined from the eyes, respiratory, cardiovascular, lymphatic, and neuro/psych areas. The body areas and elements are defined differently from other levels of exams.

Eye Examination

Table 5–12 shows the content and documentation requirements for the Eye Examination guide to selecting the examination level. For the detailed exam, any nine

TABLE 5–12   Eye Examination Content and Documentation Requirements.

System/Body Area	Elements of Examination
Eyes	■ Test visual acuity (Does not include determination of refractive error) ■ Gross visual field testing by confrontation ■ Test ocular motility including primary gaze alignment ■ Inspection of bulbar and palpebral conjunctivae ■ Examination of ocular adnexae including lids (eg, ptosis or lagophthalmos), lacrimal glands, lacrimal drainage, orbits and preauricular lymph nodes ■ Examination of pupils and irises including shape, direct and consensual reaction (afferent pupil), size (eg, anisocoria) and morphology ■ Slit lamp examination of the corneas including epithelium, stroma, endothelium, and tear film ■ Slit lamp examination of the anterior chambers including depth, cells, and flare ■ Slit lamp examination of the lenses including clarity, anterior and posterior capsule, cortex and nucleus ■ Measurement of intraocular pressures (except in children and patients with trauma or infectious disease) Ophthalmoscopic examination through dilated pupils (unless contraindicates) of ■ Optic discs including size, C/D ratio, appearance (eg, atrophy, cupping, tumor elevation) and nerve fiber layer ■ Posterior segments including retina and vessels (eg, exudates and hemorrhages)
Neurological/Psychiatric	Brief assessment of mental status including ■ Orientation to time, place and person ■ Mood and affect (eg, depression, anxiety, agitation)

elements meets the criteria. The comprehensive level requires all elements from the shaded boxes of eyes only, plus one from the neurological.

Genitourinary Examination

Table 5–13 shows the content and documentation requirements for the Genitourinary Examination guide to selecting the examination level. For the detailed exam, any twelve elements meets the criteria. The comprehensive level requires all elements from the shaded boxes of constitutional, gastrointestinal, genitourinary (male/female), plus at least one element from neck, respiratory, cardiovascular, lymphatic, skin, and neuro/psychiatric areas.

Coding Tip *The Male exam defines the criteria for the digital rectal examination, for the screening code G0102. The Female exam defines the criteria identifying the seven of the eleven areas that must be documented for the screening code G0101.*

TABLE 5–13   Genitourinary Examination Content and Documentation Requirements.

System/Body Area	Elements of Examination
Constitutional	■ Measurement of **any three of the following seven** vital signs: 1) sitting or standing blood pressure, 2) supine blood pressure, 3) pulse rate and regularity, 4) respiration, 5) temperature, 6) height, 7) weight (May be measured and recorded by ancillary staff) ■ General appearance of patient (eg, development, nutrition, body habitus, deformities, attention to grooming)
Neck	■ Examination of neck (eg, masses, overall appearance, symmetry, tracheal position, crepitus) ■ Examination of thyroid (eg, enlargement, tenderness, mass)
Respiratory	■ Assessment of respiratory effort (eg, intercostal retractions, use of accessory muscles, diaphragmatic movement) ■ Auscultation of lungs (eg, breath sounds, adventitious sounds, rubs)
Cardiovascular	■ Auscultation of heart with notation of abnormal sounds and murmurs ■ Examination of peripheral vascular system by observation (eg, swelling, varicosities) and palpation (eg, pulses, temperature, edema, tenderness)
Chest (Breasts)	[See genitourinary (female)]
Gastrointestinal (Abdomen)	■ Examination of abdomen with notation of presence of masses or tenderness ■ Examination for presence or absence of hernia ■ Examination of liver and spleen ■ Obtain stool sample for occult blood test when indicated
Genitourinary	MALE: ■ Inspection of anus and perineum Examination (with or without specimen collection for smears and cultures) of genitalia including: ■ Scrotum (eg, lesions, cysts, rashes) ■ Epididymides (eg, size, symmetry, masses) ■ Testes (eg, size, symmetry, masses) ■ Urethral meatus (eg, size, location, lesions, discharge) ■ Penis (eg, lesions, presence or absence of foreskin, foreskin retractability, plaque, masses, scarring, deformities) Digital rectal examination including: ■ Prostate gland (eg, size, symmetry, nodularity, tenderness) ■ Seminal vesicles (eg, symmetry, tenderness, masses, enlargement) ■ Sphincter tone, presence of hemorrhoids, rectal masses

continues

TABLE 5–13   Genitourinary Examination Content and Documentation Requirements continued

System/Body Area	Elements of Examination
Genitourinary	FEMALE: Includes **at least seven of the following eleven** elements identified by bullets: ■ Inspection and palpation of breasts (eg, masses or lumps, tenderness, symmetry, nipple discharge) ■ Digital rectal examination including sphincter tone, presence of hemorrhoids, rectal masses Pelvic examination (with or without specimen collection for smears and cultures) including: ■ External genitalia (eg, general appearance, hair distribution, lesions) ■ Urethral meatus (eg, size, location, lesions, prolapse) ■ Urethra (eg, masses, tenderness, scarring) ■ Bladder (eg, fullness, masses, tenderness) ■ Vagina (eg, general appearance, estrogen effect, discharge, lesions, pelvic support, cystocele, rectocele) ■ Cervix (eg, general appearance, lesions, discharge) ■ Uterus (eg, size, contour, position, mobility, tenderness, consistence, descent or support) ■ Adnexa/parametria (eg, masses, tenderness, organomegaly, nodularity) ■ Anus and perineum
Lymphatic	■ Palpation of lymph nodes in neck, axillae, groin and/or other location
Skin	■ Inspection and/or palpation of skin and subcutaneous tissue (eg, rashes, lesions, ulcers)
Neurological/Psychiatric	Brief assessment of mental status including ■ Orientation (eg, time, place and person) ■ Mood and affect (eg, depression, anxiety, agitation)

Hematologic/Lymphatic/Immunologic Examination

Table 5–14 shows the content and documentation requirements for the Hematologic/Lymphatic/Immunologic Examination guide to selecting the examination level. For the detailed exam, any twelve elements meets the criteria. The comprehensive level requires all elements from the shaded boxes of constitutional, ears, nose, mouth, and throat, respiratory, cardiovascular, gastrointestinal, plus head and face, eyes, neck, lymphatic, extremities, skin, and neuro/psychiatric areas.

Musculoskeletal Examination

Table 5–15 shows the content and documentation requirements for the Musculoskeletal Examination guide to selecting the examination level. For the detailed exam, any twelve elements meets the criteria. The comprehensive level requires all elements from the shaded boxes of constitutional, musculoskeletal, skin, neurological/psychiatric, plus one from cardiovascular, and lymphatic.

TABLE 5–14   **Hematologic/Lymphatic/Immunologic Examination Content and Documentation Requirements.**

System/Body Area	Elements of Examination
Constitutional	■ Measurement of **any three of the following seven** vital signs: 1) sitting or standing blood pressure, 2) supine blood pressure, 3) pulse rate and regularity, 4) respiration, 5) temperature, 6) height, 7) weight (May be measured and recorded by ancillary staff) ■ General appearance of patient (eg, development, nutrition, body habitus, deformities, attention to grooming)
Head and Face	■ Palpation and/or percussion of face with notation of presence or absence of sinus tenderness
Eyes	■ Inspection of conjunctivae and lids
Ears, Nose, Mouth and Throat	■ Otoscopic examination of external auditory canals and tympanic membranes ■ Inspection of nasal mucosa, septum and turbinates ■ Inspection of teeth and gums ■ Examination of oropharynx (eg, oral mucosa, hard and soft palates, tongue, tonsils, posterior pharynx)
Neck	■ Examination of neck (eg, masses, overall appearance, symmetry, tracheal position, crepitus) ■ Examination of thyroid (eg, enlargement, tenderness, mass)
Respiratory	■ Assessment of respiratory effort (eg, intercostal retractions, use of accessory muscles, diaphragmatic movement) ■ Auscultation of lungs (eg, breath sounds, adventitious sounds, rubs)
Cardiovascular	■ Auscultation of heart with notation of abnormal sounds and murmurs ■ Examination of peripheral vascular system by observation (eg, swelling, varicosities) and palpation (eg, pulses, temperature, edema, tenderness)
Gastrointestinal (Abdomen)	■ Examination of abdomen with notation of presence of masses or tenderness ■ Examination of liver and spleen
Lymphatic	■ Palpation of lymph nodes in neck, axillae, groin, and/or other location
Extremities	■ Inspection and palpation of digits and nails (eg, clubbing, cyanosis, inflammation, petechiae, ischemia, infections, nodes)
Skin	■ Inspection and/or palpation of skin and subcutaneous tissue (eg, rashes, lesions, ulcers, ecchymoses, bruises)
Neurological/ Psychiatric	Brief assessment of mental status including ■ Orientation to time, place and person ■ Mood and affect (eg, depression, anxiety, agitation)

Coding Tip *While much of the musculoskeletal examination includes counting with exact documentation required, it is very simple to count beyond twelve elements. Each anatomical site is counted for each examination per area. For example, if inspection, range of motion, muscle strength is documented for bilaterally for arms, this would be counted as three examinations of two body areas, or a total of six.*

TABLE 5–15 **Musculoskeletal Examination Content and Documentation Requirements.**

System/Body Area	Elements of Examination
Constitutional	■ Measurement of **any three of the following seven** vital signs: 1) sitting or standing blood pressure, 2) supine blood pressure, 3) pulse rate and regularity, 4) respiration, 5) temperature, 6) height, 7) weight (May be measured and recorded by ancillary staff) ■ General appearance of patient (eg, development, nutrition, body habitus, deformities, attention to grooming)
Cardiovascular	■ Examination of peripheral vascular system by observation (eg, swelling, varicosities) and palpation (eg, pulses, temperature, edema, tenderness)
Lymphatic	■ Palpation of lymph nodes in neck, axillae, groin and/or other location
Musculoskeletal	■ Examination of gait and station Examination of joint(s), bone(s) and muscle(s)/tendon(s) of **four of the following six** areas: 1) head and neck; 2) spine, ribs, and pelvis; 3) right upper extremity; 4) left upper extremity; 5) right lower extremity; and 6) left lower extremity. The examination of a given area includes: ■ Inspection, percussion and/or palpation with notation of any misalignment, asymmetry, crepitation, defects, tenderness, masses or effusions ■ Assessment of range of motion with notation of any pain (eg, straight leg raising), crepitation or contracture ■ Assessment of stability with notation of any dislocation (luxation), subluxation or laxity ■ Assessment of muscle strength and tone (eg, flaccid, cog wheel, spastic) with notation of any atrophy or abnormal movements NOTE: For the comprehensive level of examination, all four of the elements identified by a bullet must be performed and documented for each of four anatomic areas. For the three lower levels of examination, each element is counted separately for each body area. For example, assessing range of motion in two extremities constitutes two elements.
Extremities	[See musculoskeletal and skin]
Skin	■ Inspection and/or palpation of skin and subcutaneous tissue (eg, scars, rashes, lesions, cafe-au-lait spots, ulcers) in **four of the following six** areas: 1) head and neck; 2) trunk; 3) right upper extremity; 4) left upper extremity; 5) right lower extremity; and 6) left lower extremity. NOTE: For the comprehensive level, the examination of all four anatomic areas must be performed and documented. For the three lower levels of examination, each body area is counted separately. For example, inspection and/or palpation of the skin and subcutaneous tissue of two extremities constitutes two elements.
Neurological/ Psychiatric	■ Test coordination (eg, finger/nose, heel/knee/shin, rapid alternating movements in the upper and lower extremities, evaluation of fine motor coordination in young children) ■ Examination of deep tendon reflexes and/or nerve stretch test with notation of pathological reflexes (eg, Babinski) ■ Examination of sensation (eg, by touch, pin, vibration, proprioception) Brief assessment of mental status including ■ Orientation to time, place and person ■ Mood and affect (eg, depression, anxiety, agitation)

Neurological Examination

Table 5–16 shows the content and documentation requirements for the Neurological Examination guide to selecting the examination level. For the detailed exam, any twelve elements meets the criteria. The comprehensive level requires all elements from the shaded boxes of constitutional, eyes, musculoskeletal, and neurological, plus one element from the cardiovascular area.

TABLE 5–16   Neurological Examination Content and Documentation Requirements.

System/Body Area	Elements of Examination
Constitutional	■ Measurement of **any three of the following seven** vital signs: 1) sitting or standing blood pressure, 2) supine blood pressure, 3) pulse rate and regularity, 4) respiration, 5) temperature, 6) height, 7) weight (May be measured and recorded by ancillary staff) ■ General appearance of patient (eg, development, nutrition, body habitus, deformities, attention to grooming)
Eyes	■ Ophthalmoscopic examination of optic discs (eg, size, C/D ratio, appearance) and posterior segments (eg, vessel changes, exudates, hemorrhages)
Cardiovascular	■ Examination of carotid arteries (eg, pulse amplitude, bruits) ■ Auscultation of heart with notation of abnormal sounds and murmurs ■ Examination of peripheral vascular system by observation (eg, swelling, varicosities) and palpation (eg, pulses, temperature, edema, tenderness)
Musculoskeletal	■ Examination of gait and station Assessment of motor function including: ■ Muscle strength in upper and lower extremities ■ Muscle tone in upper and lower extremities (eg, flaccid, cog wheel, spastic) with notation of any atrophy or abnormal movements (eg, fasciculation, tardive dyskinesia)
Extremities	[See musculoskeletal]
Neurological	Evaluation of higher integrative functions including: ■ Orientation to time, place and person ■ Recent and remote memory ■ Attention span and concentration ■ Language (eg, naming objects, repeating phrases, spontaneous speech) ■ Fund of knowledge (eg, awareness of current events, past history, vocabulary) Test the following cranial nerves: ■ 2nd cranial nerve (eg, visual acuity, visual fields, fundi) ■ 3rd, 4th and 6th cranial nerves (eg, pupils, eye movements) ■ 5th cranial nerve (eg, facial sensation, corneal reflexes) ■ 7th cranial nerve (eg, facial symmetry, strength) ■ 8th cranial nerve (eg, hearing with tuning fork, whispered voice and/or finger rub) ■ 9th cranial nerve (eg, spontaneous or reflex palate movement) ■ 11th cranial nerve (eg, shoulder shrug strength)

continues

TABLE 5–16   Neurological Examination Content and Documentation Requirements continued

System/Body Area	Elements of Examination
Neurological	■ 12th cranial nerve (eg, tongue protrusion) ■ Examination of sensation (eg, by touch, pin, vibration, proprioception) ■ Examination of deep tendon reflexes in upper and lower extremities with notation of pathological reflexes (eg, Babinski) ■ Test coordination (eg, finger/nose, heel/knee/shin, rapid alternating movements in the upper and lower extremities, evaluation of fine motor coordination in young children)

Psychiatric Examination

Table 5–17 shows the content and documentation requirements for the Psychiatric Examination guide to selecting the examination level. For the detailed exam, any twelve elements meets the criteria. The comprehensive level requires all elements from the shaded boxes of constitutional, and psychiatric, plus one element from musculoskeletal area.

TABLE 5–17   Psychiatric Examination Content and Documentation Requirements.

System/Body Area	Elements of Examination
Constitutional	■ Measurement of **any three of the following seven** vital signs: 1) sitting or standing blood pressure, 2) supine blood pressure, 3) pulse rate and regularity, 4) respiration, 5) temperature, 6) height, 7) weight (May be measured and recorded by ancillary staff) ■ General appearance of patient (eg, development, nutrition, body habitus, deformities, attention to grooming)
Musculoskeletal	■ Assessment of muscle strength and tone (eg, flaccid, cog wheel, spastic) with notation of any atrophy and abnormal movements ■ Examination of gait and station
Psychiatric	■ Description of speech including: rate; volume; articulation; coherence; and spontaneity with notation of abnormalities (eg, perseveration, paucity of language) ■ Description of thought processes including: rate of thoughts; content of thoughts (eg, logical vs. illogical, tangential); abstract reasoning; and computation ■ Description of associations (eg, loose, tangential, circumstantial, intact) ■ Description of abnormal or psychotic thoughts including: hallucinations; delusions; preoccupation with violence; homicidal or suicidal ideation; and obsessions ■ Description of the patient's judgment (eg, concerning everyday activities and social situations) and insight (eg, concerning psychiatric condition) Complete mental status examination including: ■ Orientation to time, place and person ■ Recent and remote memory ■ Attention span and concentration ■ Language (eg, naming objects, repeating phrases) ■ Fund of knowledge (eg, awareness of current events, past history, vocabulary) ■ Mood and affect (eg, depression, anxiety, agitation, hypomania, lability)

Respiratory Examination

Table 5–18 shows the content and documentation requirements for the Respiratory Examination guide to selecting the examination level. For the detailed exam, any twelve elements meets the criteria. The comprehensive level requires all elements from the shaded boxes of constitutional, ears, nose, mouth and throat, neck, respiratory, cardiovascular, and gastrointestinal, plus one element from lymphatic, musculoskeletal, extremities, skin and neuro/psychiatric areas.

TABLE 5–18 Respiratory Examination Content and Documentation Requirements.

System/Body Area	Elements of Examination
Constitutional	■ Measurement of **any three of the following seven** vital signs: 1) sitting or standing blood pressure, 2) supine blood pressure, 3) pulse rate and regularity, 4) respiration, 5) temperature, 6) height, 7) weight (May be measured and recorded by ancillary staff) ■ General appearance of patient (eg, development, nutrition, body habitus, deformities, attention to grooming)
Ears, Nose, Mouth and Throat	■ Inspection of nasal mucosa, septum and turbinates ■ Inspection of teeth and gums ■ Examination of oropharynx (eg, oral mucosa, hard and soft palates, tongue, tonsils and posterior pharynx)
Neck	■ Examination of neck (eg, masses, overall appearance, symmetry, tracheal position, crepitus) ■ Examination of thyroid (eg, enlargement, tenderness, mass) ■ Examination of jugular veins (eg, distension; a, v or cannon a waves)
Respiratory	■ Inspection of chest with notation of symmetry and expansion ■ Assessment of respiratory effort (eg, intercostal retractions, use of accessory muscles, diaphragmatic movement) ■ Percussion of chest (eg, dullness, flatness, hyperresonance) ■ Palpation of chest (eg, tactile fremitus) ■ Auscultation of lungs (eg, breath sounds, adventitious sounds, rubs)
Cardiovascular	■ Auscultation of heart including sounds, abnormal sounds and murmurs ■ Examination of peripheral vascular system by observation (eg, swelling, varicosities) and palpation (eg, pulses, temperature, edema, tenderness)
Gastrointestinal (Abdomen)	■ Examination of abdomen with notation of presence of masses or tenderness ■ Examination of liver and spleen
Lymphatic	■ Palpation of lymph nodes in neck, axillae, groin and/or other location
Musculoskeletal	■ Assessment of muscle strength and tone (eg, flaccid, cog wheel, spastic) with notation of any atrophy and abnormal movements ■ Examination of gait and station
Extremities	■ Inspection and palpation of digits and nails (eg, clubbing, cyanosis, inflammation, petechiae, ischemia, infections, nodes)

continues

TABLE 5–18   Respiratory Examination Content and Documentation Requirements continued

System/Body Area	Elements of Examination
Skin	■ Inspection and/or palpation of skin and subcutaneous tissue (eg, rashes, lesions, ulcers)
Neurological/Psychiatric	Brief assessment of mental status including ■ Orientation to time, place and person ■ Mood and affect (eg, depression, anxiety, agitation)

Skin Examination

Table 5–19 shows the content and documentation requirements for the Skin Examination guide to selecting the examination level. For the detailed exam, any twelve elements meets the criteria. The comprehensive level requires all elements from the shaded boxes of constitutional, ears, nose, mouth and throat, skin, plus one element from neck, cardiovascular, gastrointestinal, lymphatic, extremities, and neuro/psychiatric areas.

TABLE 5–19   Skin Examination Content and Documentation Requirements.

System/Body Area	Elements of Examination
Constitutional	■ Measurement of **any three of the following seven** vital signs: 1) sitting or standing blood pressure, 2) supine blood pressure, 3) pulse rate and regularity, 4) respiration, 5) temperature, 6) height, 7) weight (May be measured and recorded by ancillary staff) ■ General appearance of patient (eg, development, nutrition, body habitus, deformities, attention to grooming)
Eyes	■ Inspection of conjunctivae and lids
Ears, Nose, Mouth and Throat	■ Inspection of lips, teeth and gums ■ Examination of oropharynx (eg, oral mucosa, hard and soft palates, tongue, tonsils, posterior pharynx)
Neck	■ Examination of thyroid (eg, enlargement, tenderness, mass)
Cardiovascular (Abdomen)	■ Examination of peripheral vascular system by observation (eg, swelling, varicosities) and palpation (eg, pulses, temperature, edema, tenderness)
Gastrointestinal (abdomen)	■ Examination of liver and spleen ■ Examination of anus for condyloma and other lesions
Lymphatic	■ Palpation of lymph nodes in neck, axillae, groin and/or other location
Extremities	■ Inspection and palpation of digits and nails (eg, clubbing, cyanosis, inflammation, petechiae, ischemia, infections, nodes)

continues

TABLE 5–19   **Skin Examination Content and Documentation Requirements** continued

System/Body Area	Elements of Examination
Skin	■ Palpation of scalp and inspection of hair of scalp, eyebrow, face, chest, pubic area (when indicated) and extremities ■ Inspection and/or palpation of skin and subcutaneous tissue (eg, rashes, lesions, ulcers, susceptibility to and presence of photo damage) in **eight of the following ten** areas: ■ Head, including the face and ■ Neck ■ Chest, including breasts and axillae ■ Abdomen ■ Genitalia, groin, buttocks ■ Back ■ Right upper extremity ■ Left upper extremity ■ Right lower extremity ■ Left lower extremity NOTE: For the comprehensive level, the examination of at least eight anatomic areas must be performed and documented. For the three lower levels of examination, each body area is counted separately. For example, inspection and/or palpation of the skin and subcutaneous tissue of the right upper extremity and the left upper extremity constitutes two elements. ■ Inspection of eccrine and apocrine glands of skin and subcutaneous tissue with identification and location of any hyperhidrosis, chromhidroses or bromhidrosis
Neurological/Psychiatric	Brief assessment of mental status including ■ Orientation to time, place and person ■ Mood and affect (eg, depression, anxiety, agitation)

EXERCISE 5–3

1. A patient arrives with a sore throat for past two days. The throat is reddened and streaked to the palate, the tonsils and adenoids are enlarged, the lymph are swollen in the front of the neck, normal in the back of the neck. The lungs are clear. What level of exam is this?

2. A patient arrives with a sore throat for past two days. The throat is reddened and streaked to the palate, the tonsils and adenoids are enlarged, tympanic clear, canals red and tenderness upon exam noted, the lymph are swollen in the front neck, normal in the back of the neck. The lungs are clear. Cardiac sounds are normal, regular pulse rate. Mother states of slight rash on the chest yesterday. Temperature 102. What level of exam is this?

3. A patient arrives with a sore throat for past two days. The throat is reddened and streaked to the palate, the tonsils and adenoids are enlarged, nares clear, tympanic clear, canals red and tenderness upon exam noted, sinuses stuffy, conjunctivae of eyelids red and crusty, the lymph are swollen in the

front neck, normal in the back of the neck. The lungs are clear. Cardiac sounds are normal, regular pulse rate. Mother states of slight rash on the chest yesterday, no rash visible today. Temperature 102. (Gastrointestinal, genitourinary, musculoskeletal, neurological, psychiatric are noncontributory today.) What level of exam is this?

Medical Decision Making

The 1997 MDM criteria is equal to the 1995 E/M Guidelines. Refer to Table 5–3 for a quick review of the MDM levels.

Counseling and Coordination of Care Rule

The 1997 E/M Guidelines are equal to the 1995 E/M Guidelines for counseling and coordination of care. When documented, select the code based upon the counseling rule criteria, rather than the history, exam, and MDM.

EXERCISE 5–4

1. What are the three selection components for decision making?

2. If a patient is gravely ill, does this automatically qualify for high complexity decision making?

3. The established patient was recently diagnosed with cancer of the breast and the physician spends 25 minutes counseling her to determine the plan and has further discussions with the patient and her husband at the physician's office.

   a. What components are used to select the code?

   b. Select the code.

   99214

CPT CODE BOOK

Office or Outpatient Services

The codes in the 99201 series in the CPT code book are selected for the typical physician office place of service and are also for various outpatient locations. A patient is classified as an inpatient by the hospital upon admission. When a patient is admitted as an inpatient, do not select codes from the outpatient 99201 series.

There are two options for the code selection, based upon whether the patient is a new patient or an established patient. The criteria is simpler for an established patient, requiring only two of the three key components.

EXERCISE 5–5

Select the appropriate CPT code.
New patient office visit:

1. Comprehensive history, straightforward medical decision, problem focused exam

   CPT(s) _99202_

2. Comprehensive history, detailed exam, low medical decision

   CPT(s) _99203_

3. Comprehensive history, detailed exam, straightforward medical decision making.

   CPT(s) _99202_

Established patient in the office:

4. Expanded problem history, detailed exam, moderate decision making

   CPT(s) _99214_

■ Highlight

Per CCI, the E/M services include cleansing of wounds, closure of wounds with adhesive strips (Band-Aids), basic dressings, counseling, and instructions associated to the illness/problem.

Observation Care

The observation codes are not sequential in the codebook. The discharge from observation is in the code book first, followed by the admission or the combination code options.

Codes for observation should be selected when the patient is designated as observation status, regardless of the physical space where the patient is located. For example, the patient may be in the Obstetrics Department, with monitoring device recordings. The status is observation status, yet the patient is located in the OB department.

The 99217 observation discharge describes the final examination of the patient, the home instructions, and the documentation *that occurs on a different date than the admission to the observation care.* The midnight-to-midnight concept applies for this code. Discharging the patient to another place in the hospital is not coded.

The initial observation care series of codes does not offer the same breakdown that was available with the outpatient codes, regarding new and established patients. The criteria for the codes are all three of three key components. Also note, the components provide "detailed or comprehensive," "straightforward or low," for the 99218 code. No counseling or coordination of care time factors have been assigned for the observation codes.

The initial observation service is the supervising physician, overseeing the care and admitting the patient to observation. If the physician is not the attending physician, the 99201–215, or consultation codes, may be applicable, depending upon the situation.

When the physician sees the patient in the observation status at 2 A.M., then admits the patient to the hospital at 3 A.M., all of the history, exam, and decision making are grouped together for the same date of service, to select one hospital admission code. If the two services are performed on separate dates, a code is selected for both the observation and the hospital admission service.

> **Coding Tip** *Observation services that extend to include a "middle date" do not have a coding option for selection. The proper code is 99499, according to the* AMA Principles of CPT Coding *reference.*

With similar logic, if the patient is first seen at the physician office for a related illness, and later on the same date is admitted to observation, all of the E/M services are grouped together for the same date of service, selecting one code for the observation care.

▬ *Highlight*

> *The CCI manual states that the E/M are not usually reported with multiple codes and only one code per date per physician is to be selected. This is not equal to the AMA/CPT concepts.*

⊙**EXERCISE 5–6**

Sᴜb, same day

Expanded problem focused

1. The physician visits a patient in step-down room for (note: new or established) observation at 5 A.M. and then visits the patient again at 11 A.M. First visit was EPF history, EPF exam, straightforward medical decision. Second visit was augmented to detailed history, detailed exam, straightforward medical decision.

   CPT(s) __99231__

2. The physician writes an order to keep the patient in observation for the second date and visits the patient; Detailed history, Detailed exam and Low medical decision making is documented.

   CPT(s) __99499__

3. The physician admits a patient to the observation area at 5 A.M., Detailed History, Detailed Exam, Low medical decision making is documented. At 3 P.M. the patient is discharged home.

   CPT(s) __99234__   99239

Inpatient Hospital Care

The codes in the 99221 series are to be selected when the physician provides care for the inpatient status, or partial hospital. Both the new or established patient require three of three components for these codes.

The Inpatient Hospital codes do have two breakdown areas to consider: initial care and all other care, known as subsequent care. The initial care is for new patients and established patients.

The initial care codes are selected for the admitting physician's first encounter at the hospital, caring for the patient. The initial care includes all related E/M care provided to the patient on the same date, from all other sites. The E/M components are grouped together to select one code, from the initial care series.

If the physician is not the admitting physician, do not select the initial care codes. The nonattending/admitting physician selects from either subsequent hospital care or consultation (if the criteria is met).

Occasionally, a patient is admitted and discharged on the same date (midnight to midnight). When this occurs, select from the combination codes in the 99234 series, rather than this initial care area of codes.

The Counseling and Coordination of Care rule does apply for the initial care codes, while the physician is on the unit at the hospital. The times that are appropriate are indicated beneath each code. The physician may provide counseling to the caregiver or decision maker if guiding for the care of the patient, and documentation reflects this point. Counseling and coordination of care away from the hospital unit/floor is not captured, and does not meet the criteria.

Notice there are no levels for the key components of the problem focused or expanded problem focused history, or exam. The physician is expected to document to the higher levels of the key components for the initial hospital inpatient care.

EXERCISE 5–7

Select the appropriate CPT code.
1. Initial hospital visit, new patient:

   Detailed history, Detailed exam, Straightforward Medical decision

   CPT(s) _99221_

2. Initial hospital of established patient:

   Expanded PF history and exam, moderate Medical decision.

   CPT(s) _99222_

3. Initial hospital of established patient:

   Comprehensive history, Comp exam, Low Medical decision

   CPT(s) _____

Established patient, second-day hospital visit

4. Expanded PF history, Problem focused exam, Low Medical decision

CPT(s) 99231

Subsequent Hospital Care

The codes in the 99231 series are selected for inpatient care, after the admission service date. These are also selected by other physicians who see the patient yet do not meet the consultation criteria. The codes are selected one per date per physician, excepting the on-call concepts.

Notice that these have lower levels of the three key components. Rarely, the service may be documented beyond the detailed history, detailed exam for 99233. If this occurs, perhaps modifier -21 will be applicable, or the use of other codes for the specific services may be required (critical care or prolonged care).

Combination Admission and Discharge on the Same Date

The codes in the 99234 series are selected when the patient is admitted and discharged on the same date, midnight to midnight, from either the observation area or as an inpatient in the hospital. The same concepts apply as discussed earlier, in that all related E/M services are grouped together to select the code from this area of codes.

If the admit occurs on a different date, other noncombination codes are selected.

The codes in this series require the higher levels of the three key components for new or established patients. The counseling and coordination of care concepts do not have time allocations for these codes.

Discharge

One of the most important facts surrounding the code selection for discharging the patient from the inpatient hospital is that the code descriptions are categorized according to 30 minutes or less, or more than 30 minutes. This time factor is to be documented on the medical record and must be known in order to select the code. In the absence of the information, query the physician prior to selecting the codes.

The codes indicate the total time for the exam, discussion, home instructions for all persons involved, and reports, prescriptions, and referral forms. The physician may provide this service in multiple visits on the same date, and select the code based upon the total time for the date.

The hospital discharge codes are not selected for discharging a patient from a nursing facility, or for discharging a newborn, as there are separate codes for these examples.

Consultations

Consultation encounters (whether provided at the physician office or other locations) have very detailed criteria for documentation and code selection. It is important to understand that these criteria have been established by the AMA for optimal patient care purposes.

The **consultation** is defined as advice provided by a physician regarding the evaluation and/or management of a specific illness. The consulting physician is requested to advise the requesting physician how to evaluate or manage a specific illness. The requesting physician may have medical information regarding the patient, often with the long-term relationship with the patient and family, yet may need assistance for a specific illness to manage toward optimal care. The consultant advising physician may not have the opportunity to evaluate all medical aspects of the patient, and typically will focus his or her attention to the specific illness consultation as requested.

The consultation criteria is:

consultation
A type of service provided by a physician (usually a specialist) whose opinion or advice regarding evaluation and management of a specific problem is requested by another physician or other appropriate source.

- An opinion or advice *regarding a specific problem* is requested by another physician or professional.

  Incorrect: "Medical or Surgical consult" or "ENT consult" is not satisfactory, the specific illness/disease or symptom needs to be in the request.

  Correct: Statement for this criteria would be "Consultation of the endocrinologist regarding diabetes"

- Must be requested by another physician or appropriate source.

  Incorrect: "RN requested consultation regarding management of diabetes."

  Correct: "Physician requested consultation regarding management of diabetes."

- A consultant may initiate diagnostic treatment at the encounter.

  Incorrect: "I'll schedule the patient for PTA" indicates the consultant has assumed the care without the treatment transition authorized by the sending/requesting physician, and is not correct criteria.

  Correct: "I recommend the patient be scheduled for PTA as the treatment choice. Please let me know if you would like me to proceed in scheduling this procedure."

- A consultant provides a written report to the requesting physician so that the physician may manage the care for the specific problem.

  Incorrect: "The surgery was performed with complications of ____."

  Correct: "For diabetes, my recommendations for you are to obtain FBS for 3 consecutive weeks, and schedule nutritional counseling and group diabetic educator sessions. I do not recommend medication treatment at this juncture. Let me know if I can further assist you with the care of this patient."

- A consultant does not assume the management of the condition.

  Incorrect: "I'll see the patient again in 3 days" does not meet the criteria, and suggests that the consultant has assumed partial transfer of care for this illness.

  Correct: "After you have implemented the course of treatment outlined, please let me know if I can further assist in the care of this _____ [problem] and patient."

The true consultation cannot be requested by nonprofessionals, family, or patients. The consultation criteria concepts outline that the advice will be shared and the requesting person will implement the care. The professionals are licensed per state, and the services or procedures may have limitations that vary from state to state. In general, the requesting provider should be qualified and licensed to perform the advice or recommendations that are in the written report from the consultant physician. It is also rare that a nonphysician is legally authorized to provide a consultation advice to a physician. It is expected any physician would not have the necessity to request advice from a nonphysician for the management of an illness or disease.

Procedures that are performed at the time of the consultation encounter require additional codes. These additional services are often diagnostic testing or procedures.

The requesting physician may review the advice provided by the advising consulting physician and may decide to relinquish the management of the disease to the consultant. This process of partial transfer of care may occur rapidly, during a phone call, or at any time throughout the treatment cycle. The documentation should reflect this transfer of care for the specific medical problem, when the requesting physician is no longer managing the care.

The requesting physician may choose to ask for a second consultation regarding a new problem, or may choose to ask for additional guidance regarding the similar or related problem. Additional consultations at the hospital location, known as follow-up consultation codes, are selected when the consultant has been requested to provide additional advice regarding the management of a specific illness. Follow-up visits that are initiated by the consultant at the office location are coded with 99211 series. Follow-up visits that are initiated by the consultant at the hospital location are coded with 99231 series.

Office Consultations and Other Sites

Three key components are required for the new or the established patient and the codes in the 99241 series. The Counseling and Coordination of Care rules are applicable.

Inpatient Consultations for Hospital, Nursing Facilities, and Partial Hospital Sites

A key statement in the CPT codebook, just prior to the code 99251, indicates that only one initial consultation per admission is appropriate.

The codes in this series are for new or established patients, and require three of three components. Inpatient consultations are eligible for the Counseling and Coordination of Care rules and the time factors are stated. All levels of codes are available for selection.

Follow-Up Inpatient Consultations

Occasionally, a requesting physician may need assistance to manage the care of a problem the second time or the consultant must complete the previous work. The purpose of the follow-up consult is only to:

- Monitor progress
- Recommend treatment modifications
- Recommend a new treatment plan due to the change in the patient's status (critical)

If the consultant who provided the initial consultation makes the decision to see that patient again without a request from another physician, the codes are selected from the subsequent hospital visit series and not considered a follow-up consultation.

Follow-up consults are for inpatient hospital and nursing facility locations only. The codes require two of three components as established patients and are eligible for the Counseling and Coordination of Care rules.

EXERCISE 5–8

Select the appropriate CPT code.
office consultations

1. What is the criteria for consultations?

    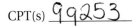 p 66

2. Comprehensive history, comprehensive exam, low medical decision

    CPT(s) 99243

Inpatient (note: new or established) consult

3. Comprehensive history, comprehensive exam, low medical decision

    CPT(s) 99253

Confirmatory Consultations

The confirmatory consultation 99271 series are selected for any locations, for new or established patients, and require three of three components. The confirmatory consultations are not eligible for the Counseling and Coordination of Care rules. The codes in this series are selected for second opinions that may be sought by the patient or others. In providing this service, the physician does not assume the care.

In the future, it is anticipated that more encounters of this nature will be requested by health plans for quality of care issues, or medical staff peer review. When the service is performed for these administrative purposes, the modifier -32 is added to the codes.

Emergency Department Care

The 99281 series of codes is for new and established patients, require three of three components, do not have Counseling and Coordination of Care factors, and allow all levels of selection. The codes are selected when an encounter is provided in the hospital Emergency Department (ED). The facility must be open 24 hours.

Coding Tip *Insurance plans have various interpretations and policies surrounding the definitions for the codes in this series. Some require only that the ER physician use these codes, and any other physician who sees a patient in the ER would select from the 99201–99215 series. This logic is not the CPT standard.*

When critical care services are provided in the ED, additional codes are selected. Procedures may also be performed in the ED (setting a fracture, for example).

EXERCISE 5–9

New patient met at the ER for convenience, patient has been seen by the ER physician:

1. Detailed history, expanded problem exam, low medical decision making

   CPT(s) _99282_

Established patient met at the ER for convenience, patient already saw the ER physician. Select the code for the primary care physician who went to see the patient in the ER:

2. Detailed history, expanded problem exam, low medical decision

   CPT(s) _99282_

Other Emergency Services

Occasionally, two-way radio management of care with ambulance personnel may be provided. The code for this unusual service is 99288.

Pediatric Critical Transport

The physician may attend to a patient between locations for a critical care pediatric patient. The time in and the time out must be documented, indicating the physician personal face-to-face patient time. Under 30 minutes is not reported with the codes in the 99289 series; however, other codes may apply depending upon the circumstances and documentation. The transport care provided by the physician includes:

- Routine monitoring
- Interpretation of cardiac output
- Chest x-ray
- Pulse oximetry
- Blood gases and data stored
- Gastric intubation
- Temporary transcutaneous pacing
- Ventilation management
- Vascular access procedures
- All other procedures that are performed, such as laryngoscopy, are coded.

Physician-involved transportation of noncritical illness does not meet with the criteria for these codes. Critical illness is an acute impairment of one or more vital organ systems (see E/M guidelines for the organ systems) with a high likelihood of life-threatening condition. The physician works to prevent the deterioration of the patient's condition.

The codes are selected:

- 99289 quantity one per date of service (after first 30 minutes up to the first 74 minutes)
- 99290 each additional 30 minutes as applicable per date of service

Any additional E/M codes are also reported, such as the ED, admission to the hospital, and critical care codes.

Critical Care

The codes in the 99291 series are selected for the management of the critical care episode, regardless of the location. This is a constant area of confusion, as the codes are not selected based upon the patient being placed in the ICU or other unit. The location of the patient is not the criteria for the code selection at all. If the patient is located in the ICU and is stable, the regular subsequent hospital visit codes are usually selected.

Critical care is management of the patient with acutely impaired vital organ systems, with life-threatening condition. The high complexity decision making must be documented. Any of the organ systems may be involved in the treatment. The E/M guidelines in the CPT code book list the organ systems under the examination criteria.

The critical care 99291 code series is selected for the neonate or pediatric patient if provided at the outpatient place of service, or physician office, unless the physician continues to provide critical care on the same date at the hospital. For this circumstance, group all of the care into the inpatient pediatric critical care codes.

Critical care is the direct care of the critically ill, managing the vital organ system failure. High complexity decision making needs to be documented, along with the time in and time out per episode. The total critical care time (unit/floor time) for the date, midnight to midnight, is then added together and the code is selected.

Critical care codes are *not* selected based upon the location of the service, and may be provided at any site. Management of noncritical care and no vital organ system deterioration is reported with the E/M codes, and not with the time for critical care.

Critical care codes 99291–99292 are selected based upon 30-minute increments after the first 30 minutes. If under 30 minutes, use the subsequent hospital codes. For example, 105 minutes on one date is coded as:

> 99291 × 1 unit
> 99292 × 2 units
> 99223 × 1 unit
> 31500 intubation, emergency

The time includes the unit and floor time related to managing the patient's life. This includes nursing station, reviewing tests, discussing with other professionals, and documentation time.

Key fact: If the patient is not able to participate in the discussions, the time with the family or decision-makers obtaining the history, condition, prognosis, and treatment options are all coded as critical care time *if this time directly correlates to the care of the patient.* If the discussions occur away from the unit/floor, this criterion is not met. If the discussions do not bear on the care of the patient, the time does not count for the critical care time; however, it may be applicable with another code.

Time necessary to perform procedures is subtracted, or indicated as time out. For example, if the physician is managing a respiratory failure episode, and inserts the laryngoscope, the charting should reflect:

Time in 8:01 A.M. Respiratory failure managed and gases read
Time out 8:04 A.M. Laryngoscope inserted with ease
Time in 8:07 A.M. Respiratory failure episode continues connected to ventilator settings
Time out 8:55 A.M.
Total critical care time thus far for this date is 3 minutes + 48 = 51 minutes. If the physician provides additional critical care on the same date, it would be added to the initial time prior to selecting the codes.

If the diagnosis codes vary per line, link them appropriately for the actual services rendered.

Pediatric, infants, and neonatal critical care have some specific guidelines for the first 28 days of life. When coding for other than the adult, read the guidelines in the CPT book for details.

If critical care codes are selected and reported on the claim in addition to any other E/M services provided by the same physician, modifier -25 may be required. Any additional surgical or other procedure codes may also be reported with the exception of this list of included services:

93561–62 Interpretation of cardiac output measurements
71010, 71015, 71020 Chest x-rays
94760, 94761, 94762 Pulse Oximetry
Blood gases
99000 Diagnostic data stored in computers (EKG, BP)
43752, 91105 Gastric intubation
92953 Temporary transcutaneous pacing
36000, 36410, 36415, 36540, 36600 Vascular access procedures

■ Highlight

- *For the emergency placement of endotracheal tube by laryngoscopy, select only the code for the endotracheal tube placement. The reason for the placement must be documented.*
- *Management and direction of CPR as a nonattending physician code selection is 92950. The time for this service is not included in the critical care time.*
- *Routine monitoring is part of critical care services; do not select additional monitoring codes. If significant review and monitoring is required, document the time specifically required for the service.*
- *Ventilation management and continuous positive airway pressure (CPAP) are included in critical care services.*

Physician transportation with a critically ill patient, other than the pediatric age, uses the critical care codes.

EXERCISE 5-10

The physician indicates on the hospital card that she performed CPR for a 32-year-old patient on the regular floor. Time in 12:10 P.M. She managed the code, performing cardiac output measurements, review of EKG strips, put in the IV and pushed meds, stabilized the patient for transport to ICU. She admitted the patient to ICU. Time out: 1:20 P.M. Time in: 7:30 P.M. Later in the day, she revised the IV orders, reviewed data. Time out: 8:15 P.M. Total time spent for this day was 1 hr 55 min. Code this encounter for the physician services.

CPT(s) _99291×1   99292×2   99231_

Inpatient Neonatal and Pediatric Critical Care

The 99293 code series are specifically for the younger patient and the inpatient setting. The term critical care continues with the definition of management of the organ failure, life-threatening episode.

The codes in this area are selected one time per date of service, rather than the hours that are documented. The neonatal or pediatric critical care codes are selected in addition to other E/M services provided on the same date, or other medically necessary procedures (such as presence at delivery, resuscitation, or endotracheal intubation).

A neonate is defined as through the first 28 days of life. After the critical care service is completed, the codes are either intensive birth weight codes or the subsequent hospital visit codes if the patient is not a low-birth-weight baby.

The infant or young child is defined as 29 days through 24 months. If the child is over 24 months of age, select the codes from the adult critical care and document/capture the time. Again, after the critical care episode, the intensive birth weight codes could be selected when applicable, or the subsequent hospital visit codes.

If the critical care is provided at other than the inpatient setting, select the adult critical care codes. This series of codes is specifically for the inpatient setting only. However, if the critical care is provided at both the outpatient and the inpatient setting on the same date, group all of the services together and select only the inpatient pediatric critical care code for the date of service. Included in the pediatric critical care services are the management, monitoring, and treatment of the patient for:

- Respiratory
- Pharmacologic control of circulatory system
- Enteral and parenteral nutrition
- Metabolic and hematologic care
- Parent/family counseling
- Case management
- Person direct supervision of the health team

Procedures that are included in the pediatric critical care are more than the adult and are:

- Umbilical venous and arterial catheterization
- Central or peripheral cath
- Arterial cath
- Oral or nasogastric (N/G) placement

- Endotracheal intubation
- Lumbar puncture
- Suprapubic cath
- Bladder cath
- Initiation and management of vent
- Continuous positive airway pressure (CPAP)
- Surfactant administration, IV
- Blood transfusion
- Vascular punctures
- Invasive or noninvasive electronic monitoring of vitals
- Pulmonary function testing (PFT) at bedside
- Blood gases reports

This covers many procedures that might be performed on the infant in the critical care episode, yet if the physician does perform additional services, the codes would be selected for any not listed above.

Very Low Birth Weight Services

The codes in the 99298 series are selected for the care of low-birth-weight infants that are not facing life-threatening situations. The codes do not provide for the admission, as these are selected for subsequent to the admission service or after the critical episode has passed, yet require ongoing monitoring. The codes are selected one time per date of service.

The very low birth weight (VLBW) is defined as less than 1500 grams; the low birth weight is 1500–2500 grams. The same management services and the included procedures as listed for the pediatric critical care codes are included for the VLBW services too.

Nursing Facility Care

Nursing facilities now include skilled nursing facilities, intermediate care facilities and long-term care facilities, and psychiatric residential treatment centers. It is anticipated that additional definitions for care facilities would also be included here.

The codes have a much different description than other E/M services. Read carefully for the service per code prior to selection. All of the codes are for the new or the established patient, yet the key components are determined by whether the encounter is a comprehensive assessment or a subsequent encounter.

Nursing facility (NF) care includes the physician completing a resident assessment instrument, with a minimum data set of information.

When the patient is admitted to the NF, all other related E/M services are grouped together selecting the NF code. *However,* hospital, observation, or other facility discharge services additional codes are selected. This is very different from most of the other areas within the code book.

The codes are very specific based upon the services performed. The first is annual comprehensive assessment, the second is an assessment, and the third is an admission or re-admission assessment.

The Counseling and Coordination of Care time factor is delineated.

Subsequent Nursing Facility

The key factor for selecting the 99311 series of codes is the phrase "who do not require a comprehensive assessment and/or do not have a major or permanent change in status" per CPT 2005. If the patient is seen today for a minor treatment, or change in the treatment plan that is not comprehensive, select the 99311 series of codes based upon the PF, EPF, or detailed levels. There is no comprehensive level, as this service would guide to the completion of the assessment, using the previous series of codes.

Nursing Discharge

The codes in the 99315 series are selected based upon documented time for the examination of the patient, discussion of the stay, instructions, preparation of records, prescriptions, and referral forms. The code would be reported for a death as well.

Domiciliary, Rest Home, Custodial Care

Domiciliary, rest home, and custodial care is commonly known as adult foster care or companion care. This type of location does not provide medical care. The physician may provide a visit at the location; the codes are selected from the 99321 series. There are separate codes for the new patient and the established patient, and no counseling times are defined. The levels of the exams are less than other areas of the E/M, assuming the comprehensive care is not likely to be rendered at this location. If additional services were provided, modifier -24 or other codes could be reported as appropriate.

Home Visits

The codes in the 99341 series are for private residence, whether homes owned by the patient or not. Any facility that is considered a residence qualifies as home care per AMA/CPT. The levels for selection are available, there are new patient and established patient options, and the Counseling and Coordination of Care time factors are present.

Prolonged Care Face-to-Face

Prolonged services are divided into sections. The first is when the direct patient contact (face-to-face) occurs. The 99354 series of codes is also likely to be selected when unique situations occur at various locations, or when documentation reflects the additional time for management of the history, exam, or medical decision making beyond the usual care. This series of codes is not reported for the Counseling or Coordination of Care concepts that may also be present. Again, the time in and time out need to be documented. The code selection process is similar to the critical care, in that all time is added together on the same date (midnight to midnight) to select the code. However, unlike critical care services, for prolonged services all additional services and procedures would also be coded and reported on the claim. The typical claim lists the E/M visit code on the first line, with a prolonged code on the second line, properly linking the ICD-9-CM codes.

The codes are selected in segments, after the first 30 minutes of documented prolonged service, selecting a second code for the final full 15 minutes, if applicable. The code is selected based upon the time factor and also the location of the service (outpatient description vs. inpatient).

105 minutes is coded as:
99354 × 1
99355 × 2
99213 (no modifiers are used) × 1
36000 vascular access

Most insurance plans will pay for prolonged with face-to-face care if the record reflects the medical necessity and ICD9-CM codes.

■ *Highlight*

Per CCI, prolonged codes may be used for some of the E/M codes. If the code is based upon time, the prolonged codes cannot be additionally selected (prolonged cannot be added to critical care).

Prolonged Physician Service without Direct Care

The second section for prolonged service code begins with the 99358 series and is selected when the physician provides time beyond the usual care at any location. The codes in this area are not specific to the location, and are selected for outpatient or inpatient settings.

The codes are selected in addition to the E/M care, and the total time for the same date is added together to select the code. Again, the time is captured in segments, after the first full hour, selecting a second code for the final full 15 minutes, if applicable.

The services that may be provided by the physician (if documented with the additional time) are extensive records and tests reviewed, communication with other professionals, and communication with the patient and family. Telephone calls are not to be coded with this prolonged code.

One challenge facing the use of the prolonged codes is documenting the medical necessity or the ICD-9-CM that demonstrates the need for the prolonged service. The insurance plans do not typically pay for the prolonged without direct care codes, or the insurance plan may have deemed the care not a benefit. The advance beneficiary notice may be required, depending upon the insurance plan policies.

Per HIPAA, the prolonged without face-to-face care codes are standard active codes, when the documentation reflects the service. The activation of the codes under HIPAA does not indicate that insurance benefits will pay for the care, however.

Physician Standby Services

The standby concept is simply defined as another physician requested physician attendance without the patient contact. Examples of common use for the 99360 are for surgery standby, frozen section, or OB delivery. The Table 5–20 guides to the options for some scenarios. The consultation request is not necessary, and at the time, the skill of another physician may or may not be required for the care of the patient.

TABLE 5–20   Newborn Services Options.

Newborn Services	Standby
99431 H&P normal newborn, tests, records in birthing room	Select along with 99360
99440 Newborn resuscitation	
99436 Attendance at delivery requested by delivery physician, and stabilization of the newborn	Do not also select 99360; standby is included in the 99436 service

The standby physician may not perform care for any other patient during this time. Therefore, the documentation again requires time in and time out depiction. The time is per date of service, per 30-minute segments after the first 30 minutes.

If the standby physician does progress to perform a surgical or medical procedure, the standby code is not selected. This preoperative time is bundled into the procedure, including OB care. The standby codes are not selected for proctoring or other teaching care, or for hospital mandated on-call care.

Case Management Care

The 99361 series is selected for team conferences and telephone calls that are beyond the usual care. Case management is the physician oversight of care for other professionals, extending the coordination of care concepts. The codes are selected in addition to other E/M codes or CPT services on the same date.

Codes 99361–62 are selected for the health team conferences when the patient is not present, and the series 99371–73 is selected for the telephone call to a patient or others for care based upon the time documented.

The case management codes may not be accepted by insurance plans, and are often not reimbursed. The advance beneficiary notice may be required. Per HIPAA, the codes are a part of the standard of CPT, yet the insurance plans may not have a medical benefit for payment of the care. This is particularly true for Medicare and federally funded programs. Years ago and still active, CMS published a rather firm rule that the physician may not submit a claim indicating the telephone call 99371 codes. Research is required prior to submitting the claim with team conference or telephone call codes.

Workers' compensation or auto insurance policies may accept and encourage the use of the codes.

EXERCISE 5–11

The physician returned four phone calls to the patient, answering questions regarding a recent diagnosis of diabetes.

CPT(s) _99441_

Care Plan Oversight Services

The 99374 series of codes is selected in addition to other E/M or CPT services on the same date, when the intensity of the care is warranted and documented. The care plan oversight (CPO) services are defined as at least 15 minutes over 30 days of care, per agency or type of care. The codes are selected by the supervising physician, assuming the responsibility for the care of the patient, and multiple physicians selecting the CPO codes are not accepted.

The CPO services are often nursing orders and completing forms for Certificate of Medical Necessity, while the patient resides at home, hospice, or nursing facility.

CMS states that the physician who signs the Certificate of Medical Necessity forms assumes all responsibility for accuracy of the information on the form. In other words, the physician should exercise professional judgment prior to signing the form, verifying the medical need for the details listed, or the physician is risking fraud investigation.

Preventive Medicine Services

Preventive medicine services is a very extensive area of learning for the E/M chapter. The first criterion of definitive importance is the documentation of the chief complaint, which identifies that the encounter/visit is for the purpose of prevention, screening, or fitness. This is one of the reasons, as stated earlier, that the definition of the chief complaint is usually stated in the patient's own words. If the patient has not stated the encounter as screening or prevention, the physician should clarify this prior to progressing with the performance of the examination.

Management of chronic illness is not preventive care. If the patient has a stable, chronic illness being treated by the physician today (perhaps with an ongoing treatment plan or regime), the illness E/M codes are selected instead of the preventive care codes.

The Preventive Code 99381 series is selected based upon the age of the patient. The infant age is any time under 1 year. A separate well baby code may also be considered for newborn care. The highest category is any age over 64 years.

The specific criteria for the examination is not delineated and is not equal to the previous components for E/M. No levels for the examination and no key components exist per CPT. The examination should be age and gender appropriate. Some of the specialty societies may have guidelines for a specialty-specific screening service; otherwise, it is the physician's choice as to what needs to be examined and the history obtained. The Preventive Care codes are to include the risk factor reduction interventions, guidance, and education for the patient. The counseling regarding risk factors is included in the 99381 codes, and there are no additional codes for counseling regarding health. Counseling regarding illness may be considered in a separate way.

Multiple codes are anticipated on the claim. Many of the additional services, procedures, and care provided at the preventive examination are reported separately. For example, the vision examination is coded with 99173, the tympanometry is 92567, the dipstick urinalysis is 81002, and the EKG is 93000. If immunizations or medications are rendered, the administration service 90465 series and the medication are coded in addition to the preventive service.

Now for the tricky part. Combination services are abundantly performed in this area, lending to challenging code selection.

1. If an insignificant problem or abnormality is found during the preventive examination that does not require more work of an *additional* history,

examination and decision making, the care of the problem or abnormality is included in the Preventive Care code. No additional codes are reported for this service. (An example will follow in a moment.)

2. If a problem or abnormality is found during the preventive examination that does require an *additional* history, examination, and decision making, the care is additionally coded with a 99201-15 with modifier -25 as well as the Preventive Care code, and any additional testing or medication administration services.

EXAMPLE

New Patient. The 55-year-old patient requests a fitness physical prior to joining the health club. The history intake form reflects family history for cardiac illness. Exam: T 98.8, P 86, R 16, B/P 134/80, RA Sitting. Cardiac sounds regular, lungs clear, no edema extremities, ROM bilaterally equal, DTR normal, Abd soft, nontender, no hernia. Genital exam deferred. Pt requests a prescription for HTN medication, that was given by previous physician. Rx given. 99386 with V70.0 and HTN Rx.

If the physician progressed to order and perform the 12 lead EKG with interpretation, add the 93000.

If the EKG reflects ST changes, possible heart block, causing the physician to progress and perform an *additional* history, exam and decision making surrounding the new chief complaint of possible heart block, add a 9920x-25 for the additional E/M care.

CMS adds another level to the services, the HCPCSII level of care.

Female: The G0101 Cervical or vaginal cancer screening; pelvic and clinical breast exam. This defines only the examination of the seven of eleven body areas. The G0101 does not include a preventive history, nor any risk factor reduction, nor any other body area examinations. If the physician provides these additional services, the Preventive Services or E/M illness CPT codes with modifier 25 are required in addition to the G0101. The G0101 has frequency limitations, as well as high-risk or low-risk diagnosis purposes. The ABN is required prior to the service being performed, for the G0101 aspect of the care, outlining any reasons for nonpayment for the patient. The ABN is not required for the preventive care history or risk factor reduction, because this service is not a covered benefit for Medicare patients.

The Q0091 Screening pap smear; obtaining, prep and conveyance to lab is additionally coded, along with the G0101 when applicable. Again, the high-risk or low-risk diagnosis and the frequency limitations (one time per 3 years basis) are to be considered. Offer the ABN if necessary for this service.

Another area of HCPCSII is the S series of codes that may be required for BCBS or some Medicaid patients. The policies may vary per plan, so it is necessary to determine the local policy prior to selecting the codes from this area. The S code may or may not include the 99386 services. S0605 is digital rectal exam, male annual; S0610 is Annual GYN exam new patient, S0162 is Annual GYN exam established patient.

Male: G0102 DRE examination has frequency limitations and high-risk determinations. The ABN should be properly completed, informing the patient prior to the care. G0102 may not be selected in addition to an E/M service for the same date. If performed at a noncovered encounter, use modifier 25 with distinct documentation, as this should occur rarely.

Female/Male: G0344 Welcome to Medicare Examination includes certain services. The EKG is coded when performed with this examination. The additional tests, may require a HCPCSII code rather than the CPT code. Examples of additional tests are the occult blood service, sigmoidoscopy or colonoscopy, and mammography services.

It is highly recommended that preventive care services be provided on separate dates from the illness E/M services, unless it is medically of utmost necessity for the physician to complete the "old-fashioned" combination service concepts.

If the patient has requested a preventive examination, the service is to be rendered. Revising this chief complaint without strong justification may be considered fraud, and certainly increases the risk for investigation. Unfortunately, many insurance benefits are not covering preventive care services, and the patient is financially obligated for the encounter. "Calling it a sick visit" is against federal laws, with enormous penalties and sanctions possible.

EXERCISE 5–12

1. The established 45-year-old patient requests an annual exam at the time of the appointment. Upon seeing the patient, the physician refills prescriptions and orders a chest X-ray for preventive purposes only.

   CPT(s) _99396_

2. An established patient, 45 years old, requests an annual exam. Upon examining the patient, the physician notes lower lobe sounds of the lungs are not clear on auscultation with personal history of breast cancer. The physician completes the preventive exam and then provides an additional detailed level history, expanded level exam, and low decision.

   CPT(s) _99213 – 25_

Counseling and/or Risk Factor Reduction Care

The codes in the 99401 series are selected when counseling for prevention is performed (diet, exercise, smoking cessation), but no history or exam is provided. The codes are time specific; therefore the exact time needs to be documented, and the codes are in two sections, either individual or groups.

Do not select the 99401 series codes if the physician is treating an illness and counseling regarding that care (diabetes, cancer, etc.). Established illness counseling is coded using the E/M 50 percent rule concepts that were previously discussed.

The new Category II tracking codes may be additionally coded, such as smoking cessation treatment. More is discussed regarding the selection of the Category II codes in Chapter 4, CPT Basics. The codes are located in the back of the CPT code book, just prior to the Modifier Appendix.

There is also a risk assessment form code, 99420, in this area, which is rarely selected.

Newborn Care

The 99431 series of codes is selected based upon the specific type of care and the location of the service, whether in the birthing room or not.

The discharge codes from the 99238 series are applicable if the discharge occurs on a separate date from the admission. The combination admission and discharge of the newborn for the same date is 99435, and this is very commonly performed.

The series also includes the newborn resuscitation code, occasionally selected in addition to other services.

Special Evaluation and Management Services

The 99450 series codes are selected for life and disability insurance policy examinations, typically when the patient purchases an insurance policy. The examinations may be performed at various settings (home, physician office, or other sites) and are not site specific. The series is not defined by new or established patient, and no Counseling or Coordination of Care rules apply.

The 99450 series codes are also selected for the insurance physical. If the physician provides significant, additional history, exam, and decision making or other care, select additional E/M codes.

New Horizons

The Category III codes located in the back of the CPT code book, just prior to the Modifiers Appendix, list the online E/M response to an established patient's request. This is a prime example of a new code option to select for care that is rendered yet may not yet be reimbursed by insurance plan benefits. The advance beneficiary notice is required for most plans and is to be properly completed prior to the care.

SUMMARY

E/M codes are commonly performed by most specialties of physicians. E/M codes are commonly audited by insurance plans. Learning the details of E/M is of utmost importance. The criteria (key components) must be accurately followed for the selection of the E/M codes. Time is a controlling factor for specific codes that include time in the description or for the 50 percent Counseling and Coordination of Care rule.

REFERENCES

AMA CPT assistant. (2004). Chicago: American Medical Association.
AMA current procedural terminology 2005 professional edition. (2004). Chicago: American Medical Association.
AMA principles of CPT coding. (2004). Chicago: American Medical Association.
CMS 1995 Evaluation and Management Guidelines. Retrieved August 15, 2005, from http://www.cms.hhs.gov/medlearn/1995dg.pdf
CMS 1997 Evaluation and Management Guidelines. Retrieved October 18, 2005, from http://www.cms.hhs.gov/medlearn/master1.pdf
ICD-9-CM expert for physicians Volumes 1 & 2 (6th ed). (2004). Salt Lake City, UT: Ingenix.
Updateable expert HCPSC Level II (16th ed.) (2005). Salt Lake City, UT: Ingenix.

Chapter 6
Anesthesia/General Surgery

KEY TERMS

achalasia	conscious sedation	general anesthesia
anesthesia	endoscopy	local anesthesia
anesthesiologist	epidural	physical status modifier
aphakia	fissure	regional anesthesia
catheter	fistula	sphincter

LEARNING OBJECTIVES

Upon successful completion of this chapter, you should be able to:

1. Identify how and when anesthesia codes are used.
2. Identify the physical status modifiers and know how they apply.
3. Identify the organs upon which general surgery is performed.
4. Identify the major procedures performed within general surgery.

INTRODUCTION

anesthesia
The pharmacological suppression of nerve function.

anesthesiologist
A physician specializing in the evaluation and preparation of a patient for surgery, the introduction of the anesthesia for the procedure, the maintenance phase and the emergence and postoperative phase.

This chapter reviews the codes used by physicians performing **anesthesia** for surgeries performed by another physician, and the codes used by surgeons describing general surgical procedures.

An **anesthesiologist** is a physician specializing in the evaluation and preparation of a patient for surgery. Preoperative care includes meeting the patient prior to surgery to get a medical history in order to plan the anesthesia that is right for the patient. During the surgical procedure, there are three phases of anesthesia. First, the induction or introduction of the anesthetic. Second is the maintenance phase. During this phase, the anesthesiologist monitors blood pressure, heart rate, breathing, level of consciousness, and adjustments to control pain. The emergence phase is bringing the patient out of the anesthetic and providing postoperative care while the patient is in the recovery room.

ANESTHESIA

Anesthesia is defined as pharmacological suppression of nerve function that can be administered by general, regional, or local method. The CPT codes for anesthesia are used to report the administration of anesthesia by

181

or under the responsible supervision of a physician. They are reported only by the physician who is administering the anesthesia, and only if that physician is not performing the surgery. If a physician provided anesthesia for a surgery that he performed, the appropriate codes from the surgery section would be applied with a modifier of -47, anesthesia by surgeon, except in the case of conscious sedation (see Sedation With or Without Analgesia [Conscious Sedation] section of the Medicine chapter). **General, regional, local anesthesia** and other supportive services are included in the anesthesia codes.

TYPES OF ANESTHESIA

general anesthesia
A state of unconsciousness, produced by anesthetic agents, with absence of pain sensation over the entire body.

regional anesthesia
The production of insensibility of a part by interrupting the sensory nerve conductivity from that region of the body.

local anesthesia
Anesthesia confined to one part of the body.

General anesthesia provides an unconscious state during a procedure. Usual means of administration are inhalation, intramuscular, rectal, or intravenous. Inhalation anesthesia is introduced through the respiratory system by way of nose and trachea. Rectal anesthesia is administered in the form of a retention enema. Intramuscular anesthesia is given as an injection directly into the muscle. Intravenous anesthetics are introduced into the vein and are generally used as a light anesthetic, sometimes prior to an inhalant being administered. Endotracheal anesthesia is used by administering a gaseous drug by inserting a tube into the mouth or nose.

Regional anesthetics provide insensitivity to pain or a field or nerve block in a particular area of the body. These can be administered by injection or a topical application to the skin or mucous membranes. A nerve block is when an anesthetic is injected directly into or in close proximity to the nerve to desensitize or numb the surrounding tissue. Field block is administered by injecting the area around the surgical site with a local anesthetic. Caudal anesthesia used in childbirth is dripped through a needle inserted into the spinal canal at the sacrum. The needle is left in place during delivery so the anesthetic can drip in gradually. Epidural anesthesia is administered by injection of the anesthetic into the spaces between the vertebrae (also known as spinal and subarachnoid). Local anesthesia desensitizes a particular area undergoing a procedure by injecting the anesthetic subcutaneously. A local anesthetic can also be topically applied directly to the body surface to provide desensitization.

moderate (conscious) sedation
A decreased level of consciousness during a procedure without being put completely to sleep. The patient is able to respond to verbal instructions and stimulation.

Moderate (conscious) sedation provides a decreased level of consciousness without being put completely to sleep. This enables the patient to breathe without assistance. The patient is also able to respond to verbal instructions and stimulation. The physician performing the procedure can provide conscious sedation as long as there is a nurse or other health care professional to observe the patient. If a physician performs a procedure and provides anesthesia for the procedure, codes are assigned from the Medicine Section of CPT (codes 99143–99150). Most often, this type of anesthesia is used for outpatient procedures with the patient released home after the procedure.

ANESTHESIA CODING

Preoperative and postoperative visits by the anesthesiologist, care during the procedure, monitoring of vital signs, and any fluid administration are also included in the anesthesia codes. There are unusual forms of monitoring that may be required from the anesthesiologist (such as central venous monitoring or Swan-Ganz), which should be reported separately as they are not normally part of the anesthesia services. The anesthesia codes may be accessed in the index under the key word anesthesia, and then by body site upon which the surgery is performed.

Anesthesia codes are applied based upon the body site being operated on, and are not based on the type of anesthesia administered. In the Anesthesia chapter of CPT the subheadings are the different body sites that could be operated upon. Select the appropriate code under the subheading that represents the surgery being performed on that body site. Keep in mind that codes from this chapter are applied only for the anesthesia that is being performed for surgery in that area. The surgeon would assign codes from the surgery chapter to represent his or her work.

EXERCISE 6–1

Match the term in column A with the definition in column B.

Column A

_____ 1. Caudal anesthesia

_____ 2. Epidural anesthesia

_____ 3. Nerve block

_____ 4. Topical anesthetic

_____ 5. Field block

_____ 6. Endotracheal anesthetic

Column B

A. Injected into area around surgical site

B. Used in childbirth via drip into spinal canal at sacrum

C. Injected into or close proximity to the nerve to numb surrounding tissue

D. Gaseous drug inserted via oral or nasal tube

E. Injection into spaces between vertebrae

F. Injected subcutaneously or topically

EXERCISE 6–2

Assign the CPT code and moderate (conscious) sedation codes performed by the same physician.

1. A 10-year-old patient received 30 minutes of moderate sedation for a tonsillectomy. _____ _____

2. A 29-year-old patient received 45 minutes of moderate sedation for treatment of a dislocated shoulder. _____ _____ _____

3. A 61-year-old patient undergoes a colonoscopy for bleeding control using bipolar cautery, 30 minutes of moderate sedation. _____ _____

4. A 3-year-old received 1 hour of moderate sedation for closed treatment of a Bennett fracture of the left thumb. _____ _____ _____

P1—A normal healthy patient

P2—A patient with mild systemic disease

P3—A patient with severe systemic disease

P4—A patient with severe systemic disease that is a constant threat to life

P5—A moribund patient who is not expected to survive without the operation

P6—A declared brain-dead patient whose organs are being removed for donation

Figure 6–1 Physical status modifiers.

physical status modifier
A two-digit amendment to the anesthesia CPT codes that describes the physical status of the patient who is receiving anesthesia.

All anesthesia services require the use of the five-digit CPT code plus an additional two-digit modifier to indicate the physical status of the patient. The **physical status modifiers** are consistent with the American Society of Anesthesiologists (ASA) ranking of a patient's physical status. The anesthesiologist provides the ASA ranking, or physical status of the patient. This can usually be found on the anesthesia graph. These modifiers consist of the letter "P" followed by a single digit from 1 to 6 as outlined in Figure 6–1.

For example, an anesthesiologist who provides general anesthesia for a patient who is undergoing a corneal transplant would select the 5-digit code 00144, Anesthesia for procedures on eye: corneal transplant. Included in that code is a preoperative evaluation during which the anesthesiologist discovers that the patient has a severe systemic disease. The 5-digit code of 00144 should be appended with the modifier P3 to indicate the physical status of the patient.

■ *Highlight*

Sometimes anesthesia may be provided under particularly difficult circumstances. These circumstances may be the condition of the patient, notable operative conditions, or unusual risk factors. It would be appropriate to add a code from 99100 to 99140 to indicate these qualifying circumstances. These codes are never to be used alone, but in association with the code for the anesthesia procedure or service. Patients of extreme age (under one year or over seventy), and emergency conditions, are examples of unusual risk factors.

EXERCISE 6–3

Assign the CPT code that an anesthesiologist would report for the following. Code the physical status modifier, if indicated.

1. General anesthesia provided for a patient with mild systemic disease who is undergoing a ventral hernia repair.

   _____

2. Anesthesia for patient, 51 years old, for closed treatment of femoral fracture, in good health.

   _____

3. Anesthesia for 6-month-old infant, for repair of cleft palate.

   _____

4. Anesthesia vaginal hysterectomy, age 42, with benign essential hypertension.

_____

5. Anesthesia for diagnostic arthroscopy of right shoulder, patient is Type 2 diabetic, well-controlled with medication.

_____

GENERAL SURGERY

General surgery refers to operations performed on the following body systems: respiratory, cardiovascular, hemic and lymphatic, mediastinum and diaphragm, digestive, urinary, male genital, female reproductive, endocrine, nervous, eye and ocular adnexa, and auditory. The female reproductive system will be covered separately in Chapter 10 of this text. Subsections within each system list the specific organ followed by the procedure performed on each of these organs.

Modifiers are used extensively in the surgical section. A modifier describes a specific circumstance or an unusual event that alters the definition of the procedure. Unilateral surgery performed upon organs that have a definite right and left side are reported with either the -LT (left side) or -RT (right side) modifier. Surgery performed on eyelids, fingers, and toes should be modified from the list shown in Table 6–1 to

TABLE 6–1   HCPCS Level II Modifiers.

-E1 Upper left, eyelid	-TA Left foot, great toe
-E2 Lower left, eyelid	-T1 Left foot, second digit
-E3 Upper right, eyelid	-T2 Left foot, third digit
-E4 Lower right, eyelid	-T3 Left foot, fourth digit
-FA Left hand, thumb	-T4 Left foot, fifth digit
-F1 Left hand, second digit	-T5 Right foot, great toe
-F2 Left hand, third digit	-T6 Right foot, second digit
-F3 Left hand, fourth digit	-T7 Right foot, third digit
-F4 Left hand, fifth digit	-T8 Right foot, fourth digit
-F5 Right hand, thumb	-T9 Right foot, fifth digit
-F6 Right hand, second digit	
-F7 Right hand, third digit	
-F8 Right hand, fourth digit	
-F9 Right hand, fifth digit	

prevent erroneous denials when duplicate HCPCS codes are billed reporting separate procedures performed on different anatomical sites or different sides of the body.

THE RESPIRATORY SYSTEM

The respiratory system is divided into upper and lower tracts. The organs of the upper tract include the nose, nasal cavity, nasopharynx, oropharynx, laryngopharynx, and larynx. The lower tract (see Figure 6–2) includes the trachea, the bronchi, bronchioles, and alveoli that comprise the lungs. The respiratory section in the CPT code book is subdivided into the following categories: nose, accessory sinuses, larynx, trachea and bronchi, and lungs and pleura.

Nasal Polyps

An excision of nasal polyps, simple, means that there was just one polyp on one side of the nasal cavity. An extensive procedure involves the excision of multiple nasal polyps on one side. Use the bilateral modifier (-50) to report the excision of nasal polyps from both sides of the nasal cavity only if the same degree of excision is performed on both sides.

General Sinus Surgery

For repair codes on the Nasal sinus (30400–30630), primary repair refers to the first repair of any structure. Secondary repair is a repair performed subsequent to a primary repair. Minor revision rhinoplasty, or plastic surgery of the nose, involves only nasal cartilage. Intermediate revision rhinoplasty involves an osteotomy or the cutting of bone. Major revision rhinoplasty includes both cartilage (work on the nasal tip) and an osteotomy.

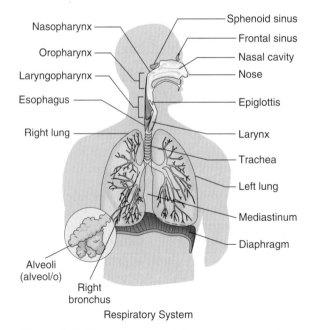

Figure 6–2 The structures of the respiratory system.

Code 30520 is reported for a Septoplasty or submucous resection, with or without cartilage scoring, contouring, or replacement with graft. This is the only code assigned if the cartilage used for the graft is obtained from the immediate surgical area. If, however, the physician must go outside of the septum to obtain enough cartilage for the graft, it would be appropriate to add the code 20912, Cartilage graft, nasal septum.

In order to correctly code the control of nasal hemorrhage, the following questions must be answered:

1. Was the hemorrhage anterior (the forward or front part of the body or body part) or posterior (the back part of the body or body part)?
2. If it was anterior, was the hemorrhage simple or complex?
3. If it was posterior, was the control an initial or a subsequent procedure?

The physician should document in the medical record if the procedure was simple or complex.

Paranasal sinuses are spaces that contain air and are lined with mucous membranes. The four sinus cavities on each side of the face are:

1. frontal, on each side of the forehead, above each eye medially
2. maxillary (also called antrum), located in the cheekbones below each eye
3. sphenoid, located behind the nasal cavity
4. ethmoid, located between the nose and the eye

Laryngoscopy

Laryngoscopy codes are subdivided into diagnostic and surgical. Diagnostic involves viewing only, while surgical involves any excision, destruction, repair, or biopsy. A surgical laryngoscopy always includes a diagnostic laryngoscopy, so the two codes would not be assigned together. A direct laryngoscopy involves passing a rigid or fiberoptic endoscope through the mouth and pharynx to allow for direct visualization of the larynx. An indirect laryngoscopy uses a light source and two mirrors, one positioned at the back of the throat, and the other held in front of the mouth. The tongue is grasped and held out as far as possible and the larynx is observed.

Bronchoscopy

A surgical bronchoscopy includes a diagnostic bronchoscopy. If a biopsy is taken, a foreign body removed, or a tumor or blockage is destroyed, it is considered a surgical bronchoscopy and the appropriate code applied. It would be inappropriate to assign 31622, Bronchoscopy, diagnostic, in addition to the surgical bronchoscopy.

EXERCISE 6–4

Assign the appropriate CPT code for the following statements.

1. Control by packing of anterior nasal hemorrhage, simple

2. Extensive cauterization of nasal hemorrhage

_____

3. Simple excision of nasal polyps, bilateral

_____

4. Nasal/sinus endoscopy, surgical, to control hemorrhage

_____

5. Laryngoscopy, direct, operative with biopsy

_____

6. Bronchoscopy, flexible, diagnostic

_____

7. Thoracentesis for pneumothorax with insertion of tube

_____

8. Unilateral sinusotomy of the frontal, maxillary, and ethmoid paranasal sinuses

_____

9. Laryngoscopy, direct, operative to remove foreign body

_____

10. Pneumocentesis for aspiration

_____

THE CARDIOVASCULAR SYSTEM

The cardiovascular system involves the heart and blood vessels. Some heart surgery requires the use of cardiopulmonary bypass (heart lung machine). A pericardiectomy without the use of cardiopulmonary bypass would be coded 33030, whereas the use of cardiopulmonary bypass during a pericardiectomy would be coded 33031 because the use of cardiopulmonary bypass is stated within the code. The same holds true with the Repair of wounds of the heart and great vessels (33300–33335).

■ Highlight

Assign the code that fully describes all procedures performed.

Pacemakers

A pacemaker system includes a pulse generator and one or more electrodes (leads) inserted through a vein (transvenous) or on the surface of the heart (epicardial). A single chamber device includes the generator and one electrode inserted into either the atrium or ventricle of the heart. A dual chamber device includes the generator and electrodes inserted into *both* the atrium and the ventricle of the heart. The changing of a battery is actually the replacement of a generator. This procedure requires the code for the removal of the old generator and a second code for the insertion of the new generator. Any repositioning or replacement within the first 14 days after initial insertion of the pacemaker is included in the code assignment. Insertion of a temporary pacemaker (33211) is a separate procedure and therefore would not be assigned if the reason for the temporary pacer was for the performance of other heart surgery. Often the temporary pacemaker is inserted to ensure the steady rhythm of the heart while other surgery is being performed. In this case, the temporary pacemaker is inherent in the major procedure and would not be coded separately. There is a specific code for the upgrade of a single chamber system to a dual chamber system (33214). This code includes the removal of the previously placed generator, the testing of the existing lead, the insertion of a new lead, and the insertion of a new pulse generator.

Coronary Artery Bypass Graft

Veins and/or arteries can be used for the performance of coronary artery bypass graft (CABG) surgery (see Figure 6–3). There are separate code ranges for the use of veins, arteries, or a combination of veins and arteries for the graft. If only the veins are used, a code from 33510–33516 must be applied. If only arteries are used, a code from 33533–33545 is applied. When a combination of both veins and arteries are used, it is necessary to report two codes: 1) the appropriate combined Arterial-venous graft code (33517–33523); and 2) the appropriate Arterial graft code (33533–33536). The procurement of the saphenous vein for grafting is included in the description of the code for the venous grafting.

Catheters

catheter
A tubular, flexible instrument for withdrawal of fluids from, or introduction of fluids into, a body cavity.

A **catheter** is defined as a flexible, tubelike instrument used to pass through body channels for withdrawal of fluids from a body cavity or to introduce fluids into a body cavity. The insertion of catheters into the venous system can be especially difficult to code because there are many types and uses of catheters. Codes are assigned as to the location of the area where inserted and the technique, not by brand name of the catheter. These sites include catheters inserted in the jugular, femoral, cephalic, subclavian, or umbilical vein.

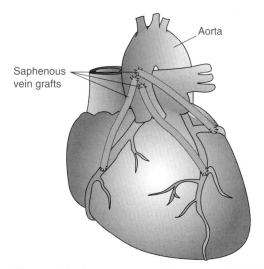

Figure 6–3 Coronary artery bypass graft (CABG) with a saphenous vein.

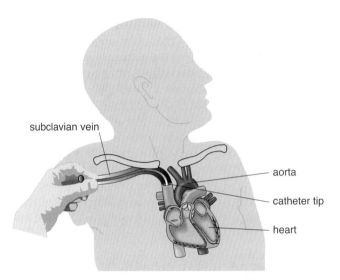

Figure 6–4 Insertion of a central venous catheter.

Central Venous Catheter

Central venous catheters (CVCs) are placed in a large vein, such as the jugular, femoral, or subclavian, with a needle and syringe (see Figure 6–4). The catheter is left in place for blood draws for analysis, or IV fluids, medication, or chemotherapy substances can be directly administered into the vein. Peripherally inserted central catheters (PICC) are inserted into superficial veins, usually in the arms, legs, or feet. Percutaneous catheters are placed through the skin. Cutdown catheter is made by an incision into the side of the vein in order to access the vein in the arm or upper leg. The most common types of CVCs (codes 36555–36556, 36568–36569, 36580, 36584) are:

Broviac
Hickman
Hydrocath
Groshong
dual lumen
triple lumen

Coding Tip *There is no CPT code used to report the removal of a catheter when it requires only the removal of the skin suture holding it in place. To report a simple removal of a catheter, refer to the appropriate Evaluation and Management code. If a catheter becomes embedded and must be removed, assign code 37799 (unlisted vascular procedure) and provide supporting documentation.*

Vascular Access Devices

Vascular access devices (VADs) are devices that provide prolonged vascular access for chemotherapy, IV fluids, medications, and the withdrawal of blood for sampling. VADs are designed to provide long-term access to the vascular system without the necessity and trauma of repeated needle sticks. VADs are surgically implanted creating a subcutaneous pocket to house the portal. A simple venous catheter does not contain a portal, therefore a subcutaneous pocket is not created. One CPT codes describe the Insertion of an implantable venous access port (36557–36561, 36565–36566, 36570–36571). Some of the common types are:

Infuse-a-Port
Medi Port
Dual Port
Groshong Port
Port-a-Cath
Q-Port
Perm-a-Cath

The removal of a vascular access device is code 36589. The removal of an old vascular access device and the insertion of a new device is considered a revision and is coded to 36575–36578, 36581–36583, or 36585.

THE HEMIC AND LYMPHATIC SYSTEMS

The hemic system consists of the spleen and the bone marrow. The harvesting of bone marrow or peripheral stem cells is reported using 38205, 38206, or 38230. The Transplantation of these cells is reported using 38240, or 38241, depending on if the bone marrow or stem cells are allogenic (donated) or autologous (from the patient). Bone marrow aspiration for biopsy purposes would be coded using 38220.

The lymphatic system contains the lymph nodes and the lymphatic channels. The Biopsy or excision of a single or random lymph nodes is coded to 38500–38555. A Radical lymphadenectomy (38700–38780) is the removal of all or most of the lymph nodes in a certain area. The code for the excision of internal mammary nodes (38530) is a separate procedure, meaning it is not to be assigned if it is commonly carried out as an integral component of another procedure. For example, it is common to excise some internal mammary nodes during a breast biopsy or mastectomy. In this case, the code 38530 would not be applied separately. This code may be applied if it is carried out independently or is considered to be unrelated or distinct from other procedures provided at that time.

THE MEDIASTINUM AND DIAPHRAGM

Procedures on the Mediastinum and diaphragm are reported using codes 39000–39599. Diaphragmatic hernias are repaired by transthoracic approach or by abdominal approach. Code selection depends upon the approach used to repair the hernia. In the event that a physician repairs the hernia by some other method (endoscopic repair), the unlisted code for procedures on the Diaphragm (39599) would be assigned.

THE DIGESTIVE SYSTEM

The digestive system is composed of the following organs and structures: the mouth, pharynx, esophagus, stomach, large intestine, and small intestine. Accessory organs of the digestive system include the teeth, salivary glands, liver, gallbladder and pancreas (see Figure 6–5). The main functions of the digestive

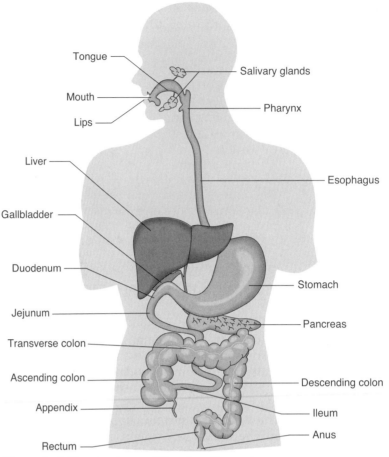

Figure 6–5 The structures of the digestive system.

system are the digestion, absorption, and elimination of food. Physicians who specialize in the diagnosis and treatment of disorders of this body system are called gastroenterologists. Gastro is the root word meaning stomach.

Similar to the other body system areas of CPT, the digestive system subsection is organized by body site and includes codes for the abdomen, peritoneum, and the omentum (a double fold of the peritoneum that hangs down over the small intestine and lies between the liver and the lesser curvature of the stomach). Codes for hernias and **endoscopy** are also included in this subsection.

endoscopy
Inspection of organs or cavities by use of a tube through a natural body opening or through a small incision.

For procedures done on the Lips (40490–40761), the vermillion refers to the part of the lip between the outer skin and the moist oral mucosa of the mouth. It is sometimes referred to as the "lipstick area." The vestibule of the mouth (codes 40800–40845) refers to the oral cavity, not including the dentoalveolar structures.

A uvulopalatopharyngoplasty (UPPP) is the removal of mucosa and muscle from the pharyngeal walls, uvula, and soft palate. What is left is a permanent, noncollapsing, oropharyngeal airway that attempts to correct sleep apnea of the obstructive type. The correct code assignment for UPPP is 42145. The same procedure done by Laser or thermal, cryotherapy, or chemicals is coded to 42160. This procedure is often completed in the physician office since it is minimally invasive and has been referred to as the snore-cure.

Tonsillectomy

A tonsillectomy is coded in conjunction with an adenoidectomy when appropriate.

Coding Tip *It is essential to know the age of the patient receiving the tonsillectomy and/or adenoidectomy. The surgery performed on children under the age of 12 is assigned one set of codes, while the procedure performed on a patient age 12 and over is coded with a different set of codes.*

Endoscopy

A surgical endoscopy always includes a diagnostic endoscopy. Diagnostic refers to viewing only. Once surgery is performed during an endoscopy procedure, it would not be appropriate to use the diagnostic code, as viewing is part of the surgery. Code the diagnostic endoscopy only if a surgical procedure was not performed.

An upper endoscopy is a scope passed through the mouth into the esophagus and in some cases into the stomach and even into the duodenum.

An esophagoscopy is limited to the study of the esophagus. An esophagogastroscopy is when the endoscope passes the diaphragm. An esophagogastroduodenoscopy (EGD) is when the endoscope traverses the pyloric channel. An ileoscopy passes the third part of the duodenum. It is essential to read the operative report to determine how far the scope was passed in order to assign the correct code.

When coding a surgical endoscopy, the following rules must be considered:

1. If a single lesion is biopsied but not excised, use only the biopsy code.
2. If a biopsy of a lesion is obtained and the remaining portion of the same lesion is then excised, code only the excision.
3. If multiple biopsies are obtained (from the same or different lesions) and none of the lesions are excised, use only the biopsy code once.
4. If a biopsy of a lesion is performed and a different lesion is excised during the same procedure, code both the excision and biopsy, if the code for the excision does not include the statement "with or without biopsy." If this statement is included, use a separate biopsy code.

Several methods can be applied for removal of lesions by endoscopy that must be understood for correct assignment of the CPT code (see Table 6–2).

TABLE 6–2   Methods for the Removal of Lesions by Endoscopy.

Hot biopsy	Forceps use an electrical current that excises and fulgurates the polyp simultaneously. Forceps may be passed through a scope to remove tissue for biopsy.
Ablation	Involves the elimination or control of a hemorrhage of a tumor or mucosal lesion.
Electrocautery	Destroys the remaining tissue after a specimen is obtained.
Snare	A loop is slipped out of a long plastic tube and closed down around the lesion to remove it.
Bipolar cautery	Electrosurgery using a pair of electrodes. The tissue that lies between the electrodes is coagulated using a flow of current from one electrode to another.
Cold biopsy	The same method as hot biopsy except that it is not hooked up to the fulgurator and used for smaller specimens.

Bleeding can be controlled using several different methods but all are reported using one single code.

achalasia
The inability of muscles to relax.

Strictures and **achalasia** of the esophagus, or the inability of muscles to relax, can be treated using esophageal dilation. Using an instrument, the orifice is expanded or enlarged to relieve the obstruction.

■ *Highlight*

There are several factors that need to be considered for proper coding of esophageal dilation. These factors involve the type of endoscopy involved, the method of dilation, and direct or indirect visualization. Direct visualization implies an endoscopic procedure. It is important to read the operative report to determine if the esophagus alone was examined, or if the scope was inserted all the way to the duodenum. Types of dilators that can be used include balloon, guide wires, bougie, or retrograde dilators.

Patients that cannot get enough nutrition by mouth can have a percutaneous endoscopic gastrostomy (PEG) tube placed. This is a procedure in which the endoscope is passed into the stomach, and a gastrostomy tube is placed percutaneously through the wall of the stomach as the endoscopist visualizes the insertion from inside. The code assignment for a PEG is 43246.

Endoscopic Retrograde Cholangiopancreatography

Endoscopic retrograde cholangiopancreatography (ERCP) is the injection of contrast medium into the papilla to visualize the pancreatic and common bile ducts by radiographic examination. As implied by the name, this is an endoscopic procedure, meaning that a scope is passed through the patient's mouth and into the duodenum where dye is instilled and then X-rays are taken. Before the endoscope is removed, many other procedures can be performed. A diagnostic ERCP includes the taking of specimens by brushing or washing. If a biopsy is obtained by other methods, the correct code would be 43261. If the ERCP is done and a sphincterotomy (incision of the

sphincter
Muscles that constrict an orifice.

sphincter) is performed, use code 43262. Pressure measurements can be made of the sphincter of Oddi and would be coded to 46263. Stones are often removed with such devices as a basket or balloon and code 43264 should be applied. If the stones are too large for simple removal, a device known as a lithotriptor can be passed through the endoscope and into the bile duct to crush the stones. The use of the lithotriptor necessitates the use of 43265. A drainage tube may be left in place to allow these crushed stones to pass and code 43267 should be applied. If indicated, a stent may be placed. A stent is an indwelling device that is left in position for long-term drainage. Stents are coded to 43268. A replacement of a stent is code 43269. When it is necessary to do a dilation of the bile or pancreatic duct, code 43271 would be applied (see Table 6–3).

It is considered unbundling to assign the code for ERCP, diagnostic when any of the above procedures are done at the same operative episode.

Endoscopic Procedures

Proctosigmoidoscopy *is the examination of the rectum and sigmoid colon.*
Sigmoidoscopy *is the examination of the entire rectum, sigmoid colon, and may include a portion of the descending colon.*
Colonoscopy *is the examination of the entire colon, from the rectum to the cecum, and may include the terminal ileum.*

TABLE 6–3   Procedures That Can Be Performed in Conjunction with ERCP, Using One CPT Code.

ERCP	43260
ERCP with biopsy	43261
ERCP with sphincterotomy/papillotomy	43262
ERCP with pressure measurement	43263
ERCP with removal of stones	43264
ERCP with lithotripsy	43265
ERCP with insertion of drainage tube	43267
ERCP with stent insertion	43268
ERCP with removal of foreign body	43269
ERCP with balloon dilation	43271
ERCP with ablation of lesion	43272

Hemorrhoidectomy

fistula
An abnormal tubelike passage from a normal cavity to another cavity or surface.

fissure
A groove, split, or natural division.

A hemorrhoid is a mass of dilated vascular tissue in the anorectum. A hemorrhoid could be either internal, proximal to the anorectal line, or external, distal to the anorectal line. A hemorrhoidectomy is considered simple unless a plastic procedure is needed in association with the hemorrhoidectomy, in which case it is a complex or extensive hemorrhoidectomy. If a **fistula** or **fissure** is present, and treated at the same time as a hemorrhoidectomy, the use of the combination code (hemorrhoidectomy with fistulectomy or fissurectomy) is necessary. Use the code for subcutaneous fistulectomy if the procedure does not involve the muscle. A submuscular fistulectomy involves the division of muscle. A fistulectomy is considered complex if multiple fistulas are excised.

■ *Highlight*

Note the difference between fissure and fistula.

Fissure—*a sore, crack, or groove in the skin or mucous membrane, such as an anal fissure.*
Fistula—*an abnormal passageway between two tubular organs (e.g., rectum and vagina) or from an organ to the body surface.*

Liver Biopsy

A percutaneous or needle biopsy of the liver is a closed procedure done percutaneously through the skin. A liver biopsy is considered to be open if it is an excisional biopsy or a wedge biopsy. A closed liver biopsy can be accomplished, even during an open abdominal procedure. If, during another procedure in which the abdomen is open, the operative report indicates that a needle or trochar is used to obtain liver tissue, it is considered to be a closed liver biopsy. If the operative report indicates that a wedge of liver tissue was excised, it is considered an open biopsy. Normally, an open biopsy of the liver requires the use of a suture after the removal of the tissue. A fine needle aspiration of the liver is coded from the Laboratory and Pathology chapter of the CPT book (see codes 10021 and 10022).

Cholecystectomy

A cholecystectomy is the surgical removal of the gallbladder. Use codes 10021–47620 if the procedure is open. For laparoscopic procedures, see codes 47560–47579.

Hernia Repair

A hernia is the projection or protrusion of an organ through the wall of the cavity that normally contains it. Reducible hernias can be corrected by manipulation. Nonreducible hernias cannot be reduced by manipulation, but are fixed in the hernial sac, allowing for no mobility of the hernia. An incarcerated hernia is one that is constricted, confined, or imprisoned in the hernia sac, and thus is nonreducible. Strangulation is the most serious complication of a hernia. When the hernia strangulates (or cuts off the blood supply to the herniated part), the result is tissue ischemia or death. A recurrent hernia is one that has been surgically treated prior to the current treatment.

Hernias are classified based on the location (see Figure 6–6). An inguinal hernia is the most common form of hernia, and is a protrusion of the abdominal contents

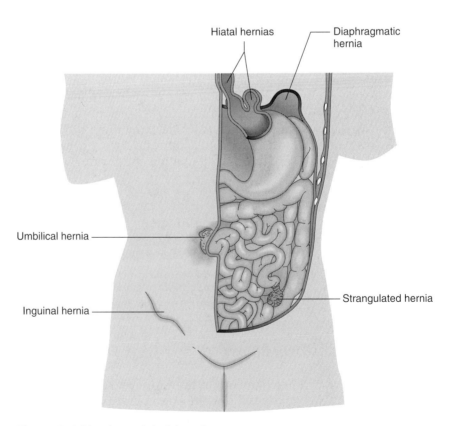

Figure 6–6 Hernias and their locations.

through the inguinal canal, or groin area. A lipoma of the spermatic cord is frequently excised during a hernia. A separate code for the lipoma excision is not applied when an inguinal hernia is repaired, as it is considered a normal part of the procedure.

A femoral hernia is the protrusion of intestine through the femoral canal, next to the femoral vessels. An umbilical hernia is a protrusion of part of the intestine at the umbilicus. An epigastric hernia is the protrusion of fat or peritoneal sac between the umbilicus and the bottom of the sternum. The sac may be empty or contain an incarcerated viscus.

An incisional hernia occurs at the incision site from previous surgery. A hernia may develop at the site of an incision when the wound is new, recent, or even if it is an old wound. Ventral hernias are coded as incisional.

Often the repair of the hernia includes the implantation of mesh or other prosthetic material to hold the surrounding tissue in place. The only time that an additional code is used to indicate the use of mesh (49568) is when an incisional or ventral hernia is repaired. The other types of hernia repairs do not require an additional code to indicate the use of mesh or other prostheses.

If repair or excision is completed to the strangulated organs or structures from a hernia, an appropriate code for the excision or repair should be applied in addition to the hernia repair. For example, if a portion of the sigmoid colon needs to be removed because it is strangulated into the hernia sac, the code for the sigmoid resection would be applied in addition to the hernia repair.

■ *Highlight*

The key elements in the coding of hernia repair are as follows:

> *The age of the patient*
> *The kind of hernia being repaired*
> *The stage of the hernia (initial or recurrent)*
> *The clinical presentation (reducible or incarcerated/strangulated)*
> *The method of repair (open or laparoscopic)*

Codes for bilateral hernia repairs do not exist, so the use of the modifier -50 "bilateral procedure" is imperative when a hernia is repaired on both sides.

EXERCISE 6–5

Assign CPT codes to the following statements.

1. Flexible colonoscopy with biopsy _____

2. Tonsillectomy with adenoidectomy, age 18 _____

3. Hemorrhoidectomy by rubber band procedure _____

4. Esophageal dilation, balloon method, retrograde _____

5. Right inguinal hernia repair, initial, age 56, using Marlex mesh _____

6. Laparoscopic cholecystectomy _____

7. Cholecystectomy with cholangiography _____

8. Appendectomy with generalized peritonitis _____

9. Flexible colonoscopy to remove polyps by snare technique _____

10. ERCP with pressure measurement of sphincter of Oddi _____

THE URINARY SYSTEM

Urinary system coding includes procedures performed on the kidney, ureter, bladder and urethra. Included in this section are also procedures on the prostate that are performed by the transurethral method. Open procedures on the prostate are in the male genital system section. Identify the parts of the urinary system shown in Figure 6–7.

A nephrostomy is the creation of an artificial fistula into the renal pelvis. If the nephrostomy is completed with a nephrotomy (incision into the kidney), assign code 50040. If the procedure is a percutaneous nephrostomy, use code 50395. A nephrolithotomy (50060–50075) is the surgical removal of stones from the kidney through an incision in the body of the kidney. A nephrostolithotomy is a percutaneous procedure used to establish a passageway from the kidney through which stones can be extracted. The code assignment is based on the size of the stone. If

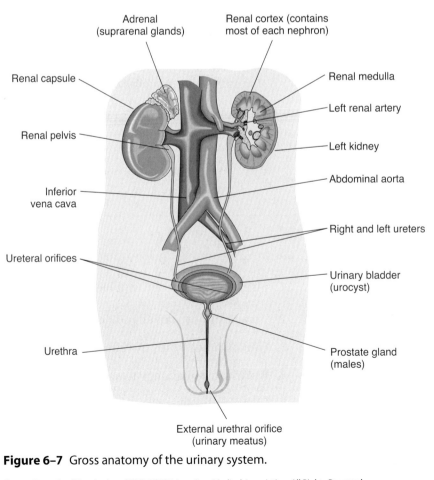

Figure 6–7 Gross anatomy of the urinary system.

a stone that is two centimeters or less is extracted through a nephrostolithotomy, assign code 50080. If the stone extracted through the nephrostolithotomy is over two centimeters, assign code 50081. Sometimes the passageway for removing stones already exists from a previous procedure (nephrostomy or pyelostomy) and a physician will remove a stone through it (see Figure 6–8). In this case assign code 50561 because a new nephrostomy has not been created in this operative episode.

There are many codes in this section that state "exclusive of radiological service." Several procedures on the urinary system are done in conjunction with a radiological procedure to further visualize the organs being examined. The codes in this section do not include the taking of the radiological images. An additional code from the radiology section of the CPT code book must be assigned in order to classify the radiological service performed.

For the surgical removal of stones from the ureter through a direct incision into the ureter, use codes 50610–50630, depending upon what portion of the ureter was incised, the upper one-third, the middle one-third, or the lower one-third.

Indwelling ureteral catheters are inserted into the renal pelvis through the ureter to allow drainage from the renal pelvis when something is impinging the ureters. The most common types of ureteral stents are Gibbons and double-J stents. The approach for the insertion of the catheters determines the code assignment. Insertion of indwelling ureteral catheters through established nephrostomy is code 50553 while those through established ureterostomy is code 50953.

An ileal conduit is a method of diverting the urinary flow by making a conduit with the ureter through a segment of the ileum and out the abdominal wall. A special receptacle collects the urine. This procedure is usually performed when a bladder carcinoma or pelvic tumor is obstructing the ureter making the patient unable to pass urine.

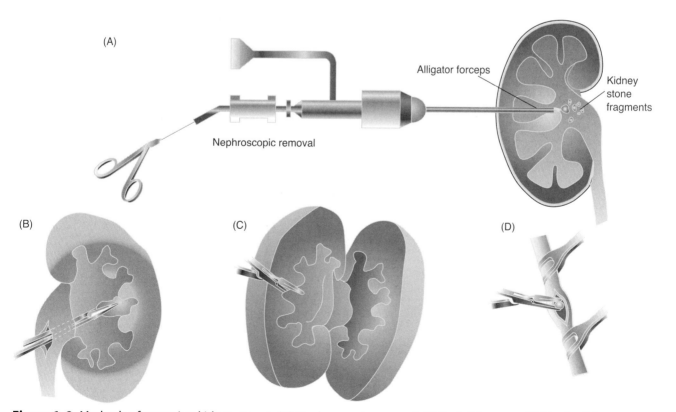

Figure 6–8 Methods of removing kidney stones. (A) Nephroscopic removal. (B) Pyelolithotomy. (C) Nephrolithotomy. (D) Ureterolithotomy.

The insertion of temporary stents during diagnostic or therapeutic cysto-urethroscopic interventions is included in 52320–52334 and should not be reported separately. Use code 52332 in addition to the primary procedure and add modifier -51 multiple procedures when the stents are self-retained and indwelling, not just temporary during the time of the procedure. Because code 52332 is considered a unilateral procedure, assign the modifier -50 bilateral procedure if the procedure was performed on both ureters. The removal of indwelling ureteral stents is coded to 52310 (simple procedure) or 52315 (complicated procedure) with the modifier -58 staged or related procedure or service by the same physician during the postoperative period. The operative report should substantiate the use of the complicated removal of ureteral stents.

All minor procedures done concurrently with endoscopic or transurethral surgeries are included in the main procedure and are not to be coded separately (see instructional notes under Endoscopy-Cystoscopy, Urethroscopy, Cysto-urethroscopy in the CPT book).

THE MALE GENITAL SYSTEM

The male genital system contains the penis, testes, epididymis, tunica vaginalis, vas deferens, scrotum, spermatic cord, seminal vesicles, and prostate (Figure 6–9).

Codes 54050–54065 are used for the destruction for condylomas, papillomas, molluscum contagiosums, and herpetic vesicle lesions. All other lesions of the penis are coded in the integumentary system of CPT. Simple destruction of the

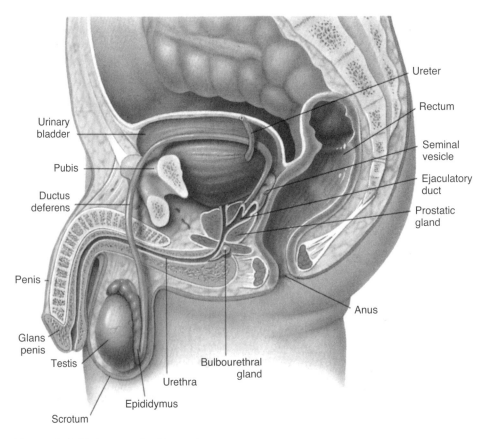

Figure 6–9 Male reproductive system.

lesion of the penis is coded based on the method of the destruction (electrodesiccation, cryosurgery, laser surgery or surgical excision). If the physician states that the procedure was extensive, assign code 54065, regardless of the method used.

The excision of a hydrocele from the tunical vaginalis is code 55040 and the excision of a hydrocele from the spermatic cord is code 55500. For a hydrocelectomy that is performed with an inguinal hernia repair, see codes 49505 or 49507 and 54840 or 55040.

Vasectomies are reported using code 55250. The code description states unilateral or bilateral, therefore the modifier -50, bilateral procedure, would be inappropriate for use with this code. Note that included in this code is any postoperative semen examination(s), no matter how many are performed.

Prostate biopsies are codes 55700–55705. The code assignment is based on the type of biopsy performed (needle or punch, or incisional). The description of the code indicates that any approach used is included in the code assignment. For fine needle aspiration of the prostate, refer to code 88170.

LAPAROSCOPY/HYSTEROSCOPY

More and more procedures are being performed by laparoscopy upon a variety of organ systems in the abdominal and peritoneal region. This less-invasive method greatly reduces the risk to the patient and less recovery time is needed than with open procedures. Procedures that are performed by laparoscopy or hysteroscopy, the inspection of the uterus with a special endoscope, must be reported using codes 58545–58579 (see Figure 6–10).

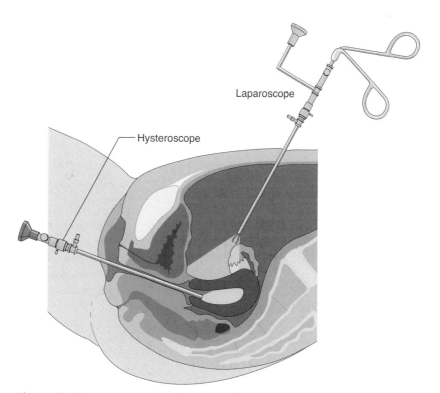

Figure 6–10 Laparoscopy performed with hysteroscopy.

THE NERVOUS SYSTEM

The central nervous system (CNS) includes the brain and spinal cord. The peripheral nervous system (PNS) includes the cranial nerves, the spinal nerves, and the autonomic nervous system. The autonomic nervous system is the portion of the nervous system concerned with regulation of the activity of cardiac muscle, smooth muscle, and glands. Twist drill, Burr Holes, and Trephine all refer to the making of small openings into the bone of the skull.

Surgery on the Base of the Skull

Several surgeons are often required for the surgical management of lesions involving the base of the skull (base of anterior, middle, and posterior cranial fossae). These physicians from different specialties work together or in tandem (one after the other) during the operative session. These operations are usually not staged because it is necessary to close the dura, subcutaneous tissues, and skin in a definitive way in order to avoid serious infections. These procedures are categorized according to:

1) the approach or anatomical area involved
2) the definitive procedure, biopsy, excision, resection, or treatment of lesions
3) repair/reconstruction of defect—reported separately if extensive dural grafting, cranioplasty, pedicle flaps, extensive skin grafts

The *2005 Physicians' Current Procedural Terminology* book states that "When a surgeon performs the approach procedure, another surgeon performs the definitive procedure, and another surgeon performs the repair/reconstruction procedure, each surgeon reports only the code for the specific procedure performed."

Use of Operative Microscope

Code 69990 is assigned for use of the surgical or operative microscope during a microsurgical procedure when anatomic structure or pathology is too small for adequate visualization otherwise. It is an add-on code used in addition to the code for the primary procedure performed. Do not add 69990 when the operating or surgical microscope is included in the procedure.

Lumbar Puncture

In a lumbar puncture, an anesthetic is first injected, then a spinal needle is inserted between the spinous processes of the vertebrae (usually between the third and fourth lumbar vertebrae). The stylet is removed from the needle, and cerebral spinal fluid (CSF) drips from the needle. The CSF pressure is measured and recorded. The physician also evaluates the appearance of the CSF. After the specimen has been collected, a final pressure reading is taken, and the needle is removed.

epidural
Located over or upon the dural.

A blood patch is performed if the spinal fluid continues to leak after the patient has had a spinal puncture or **epidural** anesthesia. The leakage causes the patient to suffer from headaches. The blood patch involves injecting the patient's blood into the site where the spinal puncture catheter originally was inserted. This injection of blood forms a patch, and as a result, stops the leakage of the spinal fluid.

Catheter Implantations

Codes 62350, 62351, and 62355 are not percutaneous procedures. Percutaneous procedures are coded to 62270–62273, 62280–62284, and 62310–62319. Report two codes when a spinal reservoir or pump is implanted or replaced. Assign a code for the catheter implantation and a code for the reservoir or pump. The refilling of implantable pumps is reported with code 96530 in the Medicine chapter of CPT.

Laminotomy/Laminectomy/Decompression

These codes are determined based on the surgical approach, the exact anatomic location within the spine, and the actual procedure performed. For a laminotomy (hemilaminectomy), note that the codes are based on one interspace in a specific area of the spine. If the procedure is performed on more than one interspace, then additional codes should be applied.

THE EYE AND OCULAR ADNEXA

The Eyeball

Evisceration refers to a partial enucleation wherein the white of the eye, the scleral shell is left intact but the intraocular contents are removed. Exenteration is a radical procedure that is performed for malignant, invasive orbital tumors. The procedure involves the removal of the eye, the orbital contents, the extraocular muscles, the orbital fat, and lids.

Secondary Implants

Secondary implants into the eye are inserted subsequent to initial surgery of eyeball removal. If the implant is put in at the same time as the initial removal, it is reported with a combination code (65093, 65103, or 65105). Ocular implants are placed inside the muscular cone. Orbital implants are placed outside the muscular cone. Note that these are not intraocular lens implants for cataracts and refer to codes 66983–66986.

Removal of Foreign Body

It is important to determine if the slit lamp (an operative lamp used in the operative field) is used on patients with removal of foreign body from the cornea, as it affects the code assignment (see codes 65220 and 65222). Equally important is to determine if a magnet is used to remove a foreign body from the posterior segment of the eye as the codes specifically state "magnetic extraction," or "nonmagnetic extraction"(see codes 65260 and 65265).

Anterior Segment of the Eye

The anterior segment of the eye involves the cornea, the anterior chamber, the anterior sclera, the iris, and the lens itself. Keratoplasty is a corneal transplant. If the transplant is involving the outer layer of the cornea only, it is coded as lamellar, code 65710. If the transplant includes all layers of the cornea, it is considered penetrating. If the keratoplasty is penetrating, be sure to identify if aphakia or pseudophakia are present, as it affects the code assignment (see codes 65730–65755). The operative report should state if aphakia or pseudophakia was encountered. If no mention is made, assume that neither is present.

Glaucoma is a condition in which the aqueous humor is unable to drain correctly through the trabecular meshwork. The fluid stays in the eyeball and causes pressure within the eye. In goniotomy the surgeon uses a gonioknife to release the pressure from glaucoma. In trabeculotomy ab externo the surgeon uses a trabeculotome to release the aqueous from outside the eye (ab externo). A trabeculoplasty by laser surgery does not use an incision technique. This procedure is done in a series of single treatment sessions and evaluation is done in between sessions to determine the effect of the treatment. This code is applied only once for the treatment series. Each session would not be coded separately. See the instructional note in the CPT book about the establishment of a new treatment series and the use of a modifier.

Codes 66150–66172 are used for Glaucoma filtering surgery. Sometimes medication and laser treatment fail to adequately control the glaucoma. In these cases, a tiny opening can be made into the sclera, which establishes a new pathway for the fluids in the eye. Use code 66170 for a trabeculectomy upon an eye that has not had previous surgery. Use code 66172 when a trabeculectomy is performed on an eye that has scarring from previous surgery or injury. Examples of previous surgery are history of failed trabeculectomy, history of cataract surgery, history of strabismus surgery, history of penetrating trauma to the eyeball, and conjunctival lacerations.

Iris and Ciliary Body

An iridectomy is the penetrating of the iris, usually for excision of lesions beyond the iris. A cyclectomy goes deeper, going through the iris into the ciliary body.

Lens

aphakia
Absence of the crystalline lens of the eye.

A cataract is the opacity of the lens of the eye. To correct this abnormality, the lens of the eye is removed and an artificial one is implanted. This is known as intraocular lens or IOL. When a lens is removed, the patient is said to have **aphakia**, the absence of the lens. When a new lens is inserted, the patient is said to have pseudophakia, an artificial lens. There are two basic types of cataract extractions, intracapsular cataract extraction (ICCE), and extracapsular cataract extraction (ECCE). An ICCE is the surgical removal of the entire lens along with the front and back of the lens capsule. An ECCE is the surgical removal of the front portion and the nucleus of the lens, leaving the posterior capsule in place (see Figure 6–11). This is sometimes called an endocapsular cataract extraction. If the physician does not clearly state if an ICCE or an ECCE procedure was performed, carefully review the operative report to determine if the posterior capsule was excised.

Phacofragmentation and phacoemulsification are the two methods used to destroy the lens for removal.

When an intraocular lens is inserted within the same operative episode as a cataract extraction, one code is used to describe both procedures. However, if the insertion of the IOL was subsequent to the initial removal of the cataract, the code assignment would be 66985. Make sure that aphakia is present if you assign the code 66985.

For a list of procedures that are considered part of the cataract surgery, refer to the CPT code book under the cataract subsection.

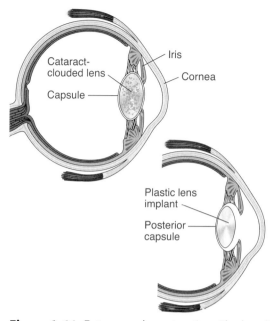

Figure 6–11 Extracapsular extraction. The lens is removed, the posterior lens capsule is left intact and the intraocular lens (IOL) is placed.

When the hospital provides the IOL, they receive the ASC payment, plus a designated amount for the lens. If a physician provides the lens, the appropriate HCPCS code should be reported for proper reimbursement (see codes V2630–V2632).

Posterior Segment

A vitrectomy is the removal of the vitreous humor from the eye. An anterior vitrectomy is performed through the front of the eye. A posterior vitrectomy is performed through the core of the vitreous. Sometimes, during other surgery on the eye, a partial vitrectomy is necessary because the vitreous is in the surgical field, or impedes the operation. When a code exists to describe the primary surgery and the vitrectomy, use only that code. A cataract removal is a good example because it states "with or without vitrectomy." An additional code for the vitrectomy would be inappropriate.

Retinal detachments usually start as a break, hole, or tear in the retina, which is easily repaired by laser or cryoretinopexy. A more extensive procedure is required for retinal detachments in which fluid has accumulated under the retina. The severity of the detachment determines which procedure is used.

A scleral buckling procedure is the suturing of an elastic sponge to the sclera at the site of the detachment. A band can also be placed around the circumference of the eye, depending on the severity of the detachment.

Cryotherapy is the freezing of tissue to destroy abnormal tissue and cause the retina to adhere back to the eye. Diathermy causes the same result, but uses heat to burn through the back of the eye.

Ocular Adnexa

Strabismus surgery is used to correct a misalignment of the eyes. These codes are divided into initial surgery and repeat surgery. The reoperation on strabismus requires more physician effort and skill.

Recession is the lengthening of the muscle and resection is the shortening of the muscle. Strabismus surgery is coded based on the operation being performed on the horizontal muscles or the vertical muscles of the eye. The following chart defines which eye muscles are horizontal and which are vertical:

inferior oblique—vertical
inferior rectus—vertical
lateral rectus—horizontal
medial rectus—horizontal
superior oblique—vertical
superior rectus—vertical

Codes 67320, 67331, 67332, 67334, 67335, and 67340 are add-on codes that are added to the strabismus surgery currently being performed. The add-on codes clarify the specific circumstances and show additional physician work.

Strabismus surgery is considered to be unilateral, so be certain to add the modifier -50 "bilateral procedure."

THE AUDITORY SYSTEM

The auditory system consists of the external, middle, and inner ear (see Figure 6–12).

The External Ear

For surgeries performed on the external ear be certain that the procedure is being done on the external auditory canal and not the skin of the outer ear. Procedures on the skin of the outer ear would be coded from the Integumentary System section.

Code 69220, Debridement, mastoidectomy cavity, simple, is for routine cleaning in patients who have had a mastoidectomy. This type of cleaning usually needs to happen every three to six months. For patients who require extensive cleaning, or cleaning that is more than just routine cleaning, code 69222 would be applied.

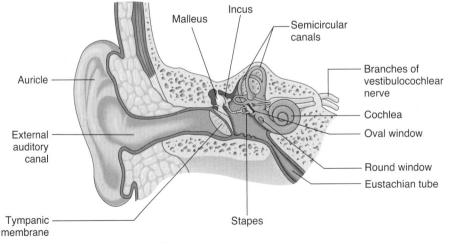

Figure 6–12 The structures of the ear.

The Middle Ear

Code 69400 is the inflation of the eustachian tube by placing a catheter through the nose to force the air into the eustachian tube. Code 69401 is the forcing of air into the eustachian tube through the nose without a catheter. Code 69405 is the catheterization of the eustachian tube through and incision and raising of the eardrum.

A myringotomy is also called a tympanotomy. It is an incision into the eardrum. Notice that code 69424 indicates that it is assigned for the removal of the ventilating tube when they were originally inserted by another physician. The removal of the tubes by the same physician is considered part of the surgical package and would be paid as such. Therefore, when the tubes are removed by the physician who inserted them, a code from this section is not applied.

A tympanostomy is the creation of an artificial opening into the eardrum by the insertion of tubes. Use care in selecting a code for the tympanostomy because the selection of the code is based upon the type of anesthesia used (local or general). This is often done as a bilateral procedure, so be certain to add the modifier -50 "bilateral procedure."

The Inner Ear

Fenestration (69820) creates a new window and sound pathway, bypassing the fixed stapes and oval window.

EXERCISE 6–6

Assign CPT codes for the following statements.

1. Cystoscopy for transperineal needle biopsy of prostate _____

2. Vasectomy including postop semen examination _____

3. Extracapsular cataract removal with insertion of intraocular lens prosthesis, left eye _____

4. Removal of impacted cerumen, bilateral _____

5. Ear piercing _____

6. Myringotomy with eustachian tube inflation _____

7. Orchiectomy, simple, complete _____

8. Lithotripsy of kidney, extracorporeal shock wave _____

9. Stereotactic implantation of depth electrodes into the cerebrum for long-term monitoring of seizure activity _____

10. Hemilaminectomy with decompression of nerve root, including partial facetectomy, foraminotomy, and excision of herniated intervertebral disk, one interspace, lumbar _____

SUMMARY

Anesthesia codes are used to report the administration of anesthesia by or under the responsible supervision of a physician. Anesthesia codes are always followed by a physical status modifier that must come from the physician. When general surgery is performed, the operative report will identify the organ upon which surgery is performed, and the procedure performed. Experience at reading and interpreting operative reports will assist the coder in the correct code assignment. Modifiers are used extensively in the surgery section of CPT to describe a special circumstance or unusual event that alters the definition of the procedure.

REFERENCES

ASC payment groups. Alexandria, VA: St. Anthony.

CPT assistant. (2005). Chicago: American Medical Association.

Dorland's illustrated medical dictionary. Philadelphia: W.B. Saunders.

Jones, B. D. (2003). *Comprehensive medical terminology* (2nd ed.). Clifton Park, NY: Thomson Delmar Learning.

The Merck manual. Rahway, NJ: Merck.

Tamparo, C. D., & M. A. Lewis. (2000). *Diseases of the human body* (3rd ed.). Philadelphia: Davis.

Chapter 7
Integumentary System

abscess	dermis	myocutaneous flap
benign lesion	epidermis	pedicle
biopsy	excision	pedicle flap
burns	fascia	provisional diagnosis
contralateral	fasciocutaneous flap	removal
debridement	malignant lesion	repair
definitive diagnosis	mastectomy	skin tag
dermatitis	muscle flap	ulcer

LEARNING OBJECTIVES

Upon successful completion of this module, you should be able to:

1. Assign ICD-9-CM diagnosis codes to various diseases involving the integumentary system.
2. Assign CPT procedure codes to describe procedures performed on the skin and subcutaneous structures, nails, or breast.
3. Identify common terminology related to disorders of the integumentary and dermatology procedures.
4. Apply official coding guidelines in the assignment of codes.

INTRODUCTION

The integumentary system includes the skin or integument, and its specialized structures including the nails, hair, and sebaceous and sweat glands. The skin is composed of three layers: the epidermis or outer layer, the dermis or middle layer, and the subcutaneous or the inner layer (see Figure 7–1). The epidermis is a layer of squamous epithelial cells. Through keratinization, specialized epithelial or keratinocytes, produce a tough, fibrous protein called keratin. Keratin serves as a barrier repelling bacteria and other substances. The epidermal cells on the palms of the hands or the soles of the feet, for example, contain large concentrations of keratin. The epidermis also contains cells called melanocytes that produce melanin, or the pigment giving skin its color. The dermis is connective tissue made up of collagen and elastic fibers, blood, lymph vessels, nerves, sweat and sebaceous glands, and hair roots. The subcutaneous layer consists of connective and adipose tissue and is where the skin attaches to the muscles and bones. The fascia and muscles are located below the subcutaneous layer.

The skin performs many functions, including protecting internal body organs, regulating body temperature, helping maintain fluid and electrolyte balance, excreting certain body waste, and producing vitamin D.

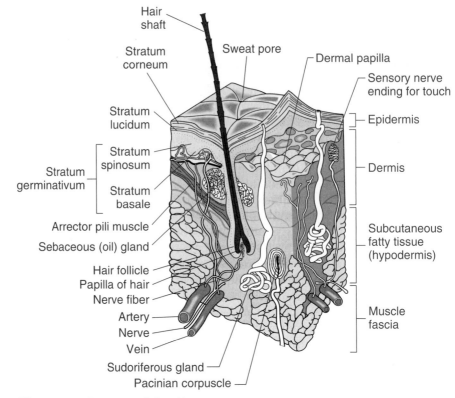

Figure 7–1 Anatomy of the skin.

This module discusses codes used for the procedures performed on the integumentary system, with a focus on CPT. Codes for ICD-9-CM are introduced where appropriate and the exercises incorporate both types of codes.

ICD-9-CM CODE SELECTION

How do you select the code for screening dermatology examinations? How do you select the code by reviewing the final pathology report? How do you select the code if the specimen is not sent for pathology?

These three skills are important for the integumentary (skin) system and will guide you toward accurate claim submission. You will soon learn that the code selection for the integumentary system requires frequent review of the medical record and potentially an addendum documented by the physician.

The HIPAA Administrative Simplification Act identifies ICD-9-CM Volumes 1 & 2 as the standard set of codes to be selected in reporting physician and outpatient care services. On October 1 each year the new codes are published for immediate implementation. No grace period is allowed for health insurance electronic claims. The Official Coding Guidelines for the use of ICD-9-CM list interpretation, sequencing, and proper selection principles for the specific codes; however, the Official Coding Guidelines are not specifically identified within the HIPAA rules.

■ *Highlight*

The medical record must support and substantiate the ICD-9-CM code that is selected and reported on the claim. If the ICD-9-CM code written on the worksheet, order form, or encounter form, however, is not in the medical record, the code is "not medically supported." The insurance plan may audit in the future and likely collect a substantial fine and/or recoup previously paid claims.

benign lesions
A noncancerous injury, wound, or infected patch of skin.

For **benign lesions** or potential cosmetic services (e.g., PUVA light treatments for acne), provide the advance beneficiary notice (ABN) properly completed, for all insurance participating health insurance plans. The participating insurance contract and/or policies published by the plan indicate that the physician practice completed this *before* the service being rendered. Make a listing of the procedures that are likely to require the ABN and discuss the plan to implement the policy within the practice.

The HIPAA rules do not apply for workers' compensation or auto insurance. The rules are for 'Health Insurance'. If the purpose of the visit is for an accident or an injury, it is possible the HIPAA rules, the HIPAA privacy policies and patient release forms are not required. The State laws or specific rules may have adopted the concepts of HIPAA within the workers' compensation or auto insurance, but the plans are not covered by the Federal HIPAA rules. Check with the State laws to determine the privacy policies, electronic claim transmission rules and security rules for workers' compensation and auto insurance benefit claims.

When various types of encounters are performed on the same date of service, the documentation needs to indicate separate medical records based upon the care that is rendered. For example, preventive examinations versus therapeutic treatments, or health insurance benefits versus workers' compensation care.

Official Coding Guidelines

The Official Coding Guidelines for ICD-9-CM are published by the National Center for Health Statistics (NCHS), a division of the Department of Health and Human Services (DHHS). A team made up of the American Hospital Association (AHA), American Health Information Management Association (AHIMA), and Centers for Medicare and Medicaid Services (CMS) creates the guidelines. The DHHS publishes free at www.cdc.gov/nchs/ and "The Coding Clinic" subscription may be purchased from AHA.

It is anticipated that a chapter for skin disease will be created by 2006, and is not available at the current time. Some but not all ICD-9-CM coding publishers include these helpful guidelines in the ICD-9-CM Volumes 1 and 2 code books. An ICD-10-CM alphanumeric system is in use throughout various countries in the world, and is anticipated to be the standard for the United States in the near future. ICD-10-CM provides many more codes for a more accurate reporting of health care services than the ICD-9-CM system.

Screening Rule: Section IV F Encounters for Circumstances Other Than a Disease or Injury

When the chief complaint documented for the office visit is charted as screening for an illness or disease, select V01.0 through V84.8 codes.

INDEX TIP

Screening (for the preventive examination service)
Specific Reason
    Condition
      Malignant Skin

Double check the tiny print in the tabular section for additional codes and/or relationship with the original illness.

EXAMPLE

The chief complaint is preventive examination for skin. The patient is healthy, has no known history of illness and no family history of melanoma; however, her best friend was recently diagnosed. A head-to-toe skin exam reveals no problems, only healthy skin. Patient is advised to continue proper use of sun screening, trained to self-examine, given an educational brochure for skin-care safety, and asked to return every two years in the future unless finding a discoloration or lump.

> V76.85 Other specified examination (may require a second code for any specific screening services performed)
>
> V76.43 Special screening for malignant skin neoplasm (very commonly melanoma)

The documentation of the purpose for the examination is very important. If the examination documented was other than melanoma, the second code might be selected for other skin conditions. V82.0 defines Skin condition screening (use this code for specific nonmalignant diseases). Alternatively, if the patient is suspected to have the melanoma disease, but nothing is found today and the patient will be "followed closely," use V71.1 Observation for suspected malignant neoplasm.

History of Rule: Section IV K Disease. Code All Documented Conditions That Coexist.

There are two important details in this rule. First, the word "documented" means clearly indicated in the medical record. Second, the rule tells us to select codes if *both:*

- the condition coexists at the time of the visit *and*
- treated or affecting treatment or management

The coder will look for the documentation specific details and will review to determine what is treated or managed at this encounter.

INDEX TIP

History of
Personal or Family
Malignant or Other illness
Double check the tiny print in the tabular section for additional codes and/or relationship with the original illness.

■ *Highlight*

Do not select codes for previously treated illness and that no longer exist. This is a common code selection error. For example, last year a malignant neoplasm was excised. Patient returns for examination today and is found to have no further problems. The patient is not taking any medications. It would be erroneous to select the malignant neoplasm code for the preventive visit one year after the care has been rendered because the patient is clear of disease today. The proper coding would be as the previous example depicts (V76.85 with V76.43) and you may choose to add V10.82 for History personal of malignant neoplasm skin. Similarly, you may select V16.8 History family of malignant neoplasm skin.

Rule Out—Rule Section IV I. Probable, Suspected, Questionable, Rule Out or Working Diagnosis

The first area of importance for this rule is that physician coding rule out does not equal the coding principal for hospital facility code selection. We are learning to code for the physician, at any location, not for the hospital facility; therefore, the rule is specific for physician and providers. Next, it is proper to select the code for the sign, symptom, or test results. **Provisional diagnosis** is defined as the physician care that is rendered prior to determining the exact, final diagnosis. Upon the physician reviewing all information, which may be collected over a period of multiple visits or dates, the determination of the **definitive diagnosis** professional opinion occurs. During the provisional diagnosis time, the codes selected are signs and symptoms. At the point of physician documentation of the definitive diagnosis, the disease or illness codes are selected.

provisional diagnosis
Preliminary diagnosis, including the present signs and symptoms

definitive diagnosis
Diagnosis based upon physician findings; the determination of the illness or disease is made by the physician.

EXAMPLE

Patient has a purulent rash extending from the hemicenter of the back to the thighs. Confirmation test is ordered and performed. Possible herpes zoster vs. exposure to nettle plants while hiking Tuesday. See patient again in 48 hours. Code 782.1 for Purulent rash for this first encounter. After the physician reviews the test results and documents a diagnosis, then you may select the code for the definitive diagnosis. In this case, the test results indicate 708.8 Nettles, so for the next encounter, when the patient returns and the documentation indicates nettles diagnosis and treatment, the code 708.8 will be reported.

This same logic is proper for lumps that are excised, with the use of 782.2 Superficial lump (not breast area and not local adiposity and not deep). If the physician excises the lump without submitting a pathology report, this may be the proper code. However, in many circumstances, when the specimen is sent to pathology, in order to properly select the CPT code, it is necessary to await the pathology report. *Do not select an ICD-9-CM code from the Malignant Neoplasm Chart or chapter without the final pathology report to document this finding.*

Coding Tip
- *Use the Neoplasm Chart in the index only when your physician has reviewed and signed off on the pathology report. The surgeon may not always agree with the pathologist and may request a second pathology review prior to determining the definitive or final diagnosis. Do not get caught in the risky trap of coding from a preliminary finding.*
- *If the documentation states malignant with another term, select the code under malignant.*
- *The Neoplasm Chart provides an asterisk (*) to guide to the use of skin codes, then the anatomical site.*

Erroneous ICD-9-CM codes submitted on claims cannot be retracted with ease. In other words, you cannot reverse the harm that you might cause, if you report the patient as positive malignancy, when later the physician determines it to be non-malignant. The patient will already have the erroneous diagnosis listed on his or her database of claim information.

Never select a code based upon whether the claim will be paid. Besides high risk for fraudulent activity, the purpose of utilizing ICD-9-CM codes is for the accurate indication of the illness, disease, or reason for the visit. The patient's insurance benefits may not pay for the **removal** (**excision,** destruction, and cryosurgery) of nonmalignant skin lesions, for example. Do not select malignant ICD-9-CM codes

removal
Removal of lesions can be by excision, destruction, shaving, or ligation. A biopsy only removes a portion of a lesion.

excision
Remove by cutting out.

in order to process the claim as a covered insurance benefit. Use ICD-9-CM codes for signs and symptoms until the diagnosis is determined.

Rule Chronic Disease Section IV J

dermatitis
An inflammation of the upper layers of the skin (eczema). Drugs taken internally can also cause skin reactions, which are considered adverse reactions. Sunburn is classified as dermatitis in ICD-9-CM.

Chronic disease codes are selected when the patient receives treatment for the chronic condition. An example might be chronic eczema 692.9, Unspecified cause eczema. However, once again the details that are documented for today's visit will be required for the code selection. Is this due to contact **dermatitis?** Are there any pustules or seborrheic today? If details are documented, the code selection varies.

> **Coding Tip** *Dermatitis, eczema, and other conditions often consider the cause of the skin affect. Look in the documentation for "due to," "exposure to," or "reaction to." These details guide to the accurate code selection for skin outbreaks.*

If the dermatitis is due to accidental cause (side effect from antibiotic, for example), an additional code is selected to indicate the cause. If multiple medications caused the illness, then use an E code for each medication or substance.

EXAMPLE

Rash due to reaction to properly taken Ampicillin 250 mg.

708.8 Allergic uticaria

E930.0 Penicillin caused allergic or hypersensitivity reaction.

Injury Code Rules

Select the injury code per anatomical site and the type of the injury, based upon the highest level of specificity. A laceration of the left wrist would not add an additional code for the superficial skin injury caused by the laceration, as this would be redundant. Superficial injuries are not coded; instead, select the code for the more complicated or serious injury of the same site. However, if there are multiple injuries treated of different sites, such as left wrist and right cheek, and often different types of care, additional codes may need to be reported.

Fracture

repair
Repair of open wounds or lacerations is classified as simple, intermediate, or complex.

The compound fracture code per anatomical site would include the care for the skin, and therefore a separate code is not necessary. Compound fracture is described as open fracture; tibia alone is coded 823.00, with the additional accidental cause and location E codes if documented. It is not necessary to add an ICD9 code for the **repair** of the skin that is caused by the fracture injury.

burns
A burn is an injury to tissue resulting from heat, chemicals, or electricity. The depth or degree of burns is identified as first degree, second degree, and third degree.

Burns

There are three important required documentation facts that are necessary before selecting an ICD9 code for **burns.** It is also likely that most burn injuries will require the use of the accidental-cause E codes.

1. What is the depth of the burn? (first, second, third, fourth, or fifth)
2. What is the extent of the burn? (Total body surface calculation—rule of nines)
3. What caused the burn? (flame, chemical, sun, etc.)

For the Burn Codes, we are required to sequence the ICD-9-CM codes that are selected. The guidelines instruct us to:

- Select the highest degree of burn (depth question) first.
- If there are multiple burns of the same anatomical site, select the code for the highest degree per anatomical site. For example, first, second, and third degree burn of the right arm, the code is selected for the third degree right arm. Each site is coded, if documented.
- Infected burns are coded as 958.3.

CPT

Integumentary system procedures in CPT are a subsection of the Surgery section and fall in the code range 10021–19499. This range includes procedures on the skin and subcutaneous tissue such as incision and drainage, debridement, paring, biopsy, removal of skin tags, shaving, excision and destruction of lesions, repair of lacerations, Moh's surgery, and skin grafts. Other plastic procedures involve skin grafts, liposuction, cosmetic procedures, treatment of burns, and excision of pressure ulcers. The term plastic surgery refers to procedures that involve tissue transplantation and repositioning. Nail procedures include debridement, excision, and reconstruction of the nail bed. Procedures on the breast include biopsy, mastectomy, and reconstruction.

EVALUATION AND MANAGEMENT SERVICES FOR INTEGUMENTARY/SKIN

The Centers for Medicare and Medicaid Services (CMS) publishes information for the federally funded programs (Medicare, Railroad, Medicaid, TRICARE, and federal employees). The Evaluation and Management (E/M) 1995 and 1997 guidelines were created in partnership with AMA/CPT. The rules state, per encounter or visit, that the physician may choose to perform either the 1995 or the 1997 E/M guidelines. Within each of the guidelines, there is the option to provide the problem focused to comprehensive level general multisystem examination (head-to-toe concept) or integumentary (skin) specialty examination. The AMA/CPT publication is similar to the 1995 guidelines located in the front of CPT in the E/M guidelines pages. The 1997 guideline specialty skin examination elements may be reviewed in Table 7–1. Note the documentation and code selection criteria varies from 1997 General multisystem examination.

Preoperative Component

Per CPT surgical package, when the E/M encounter is performed one day before or the same date as a surgical procedure for the purpose of the decision for surgery, documenting the history, exam, and decision making properly, modifier -57 is attached to the E/M code.

TABLE 7–1   Skin Examination.

Body Area	Examination
Constitutional	■ Measurement of any three of the following: blood pressure, pulse rate and regularity, respiration, temperature, height, weight ■ General appearance of patient
Eyes	■ Inspection of conjunctivae and lids
Ears, Nose, Mouth and Throat	■ Inspection of lips, teeth and gums ■ Examination of oropharynx
Neck	■ Examination of thyroid
Cardiovascular	■ Examination of peripheral vascular system by observation and palpation
Gastrointestinal (Abdomen)	■ Examination of liver and spleen ■ Examination of anus for condyloma and other lesions
Lymphatic	■ Palpation of lymph nodes in neck, axillae, groin and/or other location
Extremities	■ Inspection and palpation of digits and nails
Skin	■ Palpation of scalp and inspection of hard of scalp, eyebrows, face, chest, pubic area and extremities ■ Inspection and/or palpation of skin and subcutaneous tissue in eight of the following areas: head, neck, chest, abdomen, genitalia, back, right upper extremity, left upper extremity, right lower extremity, left lower extremity ■ Inspection of eccrine and apocrine glands of skin and subcutaneous tissue with identification and location of any hyperhidrosis

■ *Highlight*

Modifier -57 has a bit different interpretation from CPT. The National Correct Coding Initiative (NCCI) states the modifier -57 is attached to the E/M for the decision for major *surgery. Although the definition is not specifically listed, the interpretation for major is understood as those CPT services listed with global 90 postoperative days. Many of the CPT services in the integumentary system are not 90 post-op day services.*

For zero or ten-day global postoperative days, the decision for surgery is included in the surgical preoperative component of the surgical code.

Operative Surgical Day Component

Most commonly, the surgical date is considered the date the procedure is rendered, from midnight to midnight. The preoperative date ended at the midnight time, and the postoperative date ends at midnight on the date of the procedure. If the procedure continues after midnight, the operative date progresses to that date. However, not all insurance plans have the same definitions for operative dates.

CPT further guides in Appendix A, to attach modifier -25 to the E/M code, for documentation on the same date of a surgical procedure, of significant, separate, identifiable service beyond the usual preoperative service. What is significant, separate, identifiable? This is documentation of a second history, examination and decision making. This should not be redundant information that correlates to the surgical procedure. In addition, a second diagnosis is not required, although many payers may have the expectation for multiple diagnosis codes.

▬ *Highlight*

The most up-to-date quarterly National Correct Coding Initiative information can be found on the web site of CMS, so it is not necessary to purchase software or other private publications. The address is http://www.cms.hhs.gov/ physicians/cciedits/ if you use the search window of CMS; Enter NCCI then select the link with the most current version. There are three important areas for review per service codes: the mutually exclusive edit quarterly listing, the Column 1/Column 2 edit quarterly listing, and the National Correct Coding Initiative manual (updated October annually) rules. If you choose to purchase a private non-CMS publication, make certain the quarterly effective dates are implemented immediately and accurately for optimal compliance and reimbursement. In the past; for example, the NCCI may have bundled services during the first quarter of the year, and upon implementation of the second quarter NCCI reversed the bundling, paying the physicians for multiple services. Alternatively, if the second quarter bundles services, the physician is required by compliance laws to cease multiple services coding.

The first step for proper compliance is to clearly understand the CPT rules, as HIPAA has identified CPT as the standard for procedure services. This may require researching to determine the logic, cautiously reviewing the principles of CPT, and understanding the terminology.

The second step is to apply the rules for each participating or accepting assignment claim per the patient's insurance plan. Both of these steps are required under HIPAA, prior to submitting the electronic claim. Every insurance plan does not necessarily follow the Correct Coding Initiative edits, as published by CMS. Each insurance plan may have policies and payment rules that may be more or less stringent than CCI. This is especially true for the integumentary system claims.

Postoperative Component

CPT does not list the global postoperative days. Each insurance plan has a listing, which the federally funded programs (Medicare, Railroad, Medicaid, TRICARE, federal employees) publish annually in the *Federal Register* and may update throughout the year. Again, most procedures within the Integumentary area of CPT are either zero or ten global postoperative days.

0 post-op days: E/M service after midnight of the procedure date = no modifier.

Repeat procedure service after midnight of the original procedure date = no modifier.

10 post-op days: E/M service after midnight of the procedure date:

- If the E/M associates to the normal surgical procedure, do not submit the claim for the E/M, as this is included in the typical postoperative service.
- If the E/M is performed for significant, separate, identifiable history, exam, and decision (not associated to the surgical procedure) = modifier -24 and the proper ICD9 indicates the care that is rendered.

0 and 10 post-op days: E/M service before midnight on the same date as the procedure for purpose of complication to the surgical procedure:

- If the E/M is performed for purposes of complications to the surgical procedure = modifier -25, the ICD-9-CM code will reflect the complication

■ *Highlight*

Care for the integumentary system is frequently considered cosmetic or screening services per the insurance benefits and considered noncovered benefits. If the physician is participating or choosing to accept assignment with the insurance plan, it is recommended that the practice effectively determine the patient's benefits with written details of coverage prior to performing the service. Typically, all insurance participation agreements and/or policies require the physician to properly complete the advance beneficiary notice form, no longer a Medicare-only requirement. The form is to be offered and completed prior to the service, outlines the exact CPT code that is planned to be performed today, why it will not be paid by insurance, and the exact fee the patient will be responsible for personal (noninsured) payment.

SURGICAL GUIDELINES FOR INTEGUMENTARY

In Chapter 4, CPT Basics, the surgical guidelines as determined by the AMA are described in detail. Familiarity with the surgical package concepts and the definition for biopsy and destruction will be required for coding the integumentary services.

 HIPAA Administrative Simplification Act identifies that standardized code sets are to be used, per federal law, for all electronic Health insurance claims. Select HCPCSII codes for supplies whenever describing items used during procedures beyond the typical care. The xylocaine/lidocaine is not coded when used as topical anesthetic, as this is included in the CPT surgical definition; however, other medications are reported.

Coding Tip
- *Most supplies for integumentary services are not indicated with a code; they are included with the surgical service. If there is a HCPCSII code, review the policy prior to selecting.*
- *The variance between CPT and CCI for anesthesia is expanded. CCI does not allow the selection of the anesthesia code when the anesthesia is a regional block, whereas CPT guides to select the regional block code in addition to the surgical code, when performed by the same physician.*
- *Conscious sedation rules vary per insurance plan. NCCI states that the conscious sedation service must be performed by another physician (not the surgeon) or a Certified Registered Nurse Anesthetist (CRNA). The physician's RN assistant who is not a CRNA may not serve in this role. CPT states (p. 388) that an "independent trained observer" may assist in the conscious sedation for the surgeon.*

CPT added a conscious sedation symbol (see 19298 as an example), which indicates the conscious sedation service is included in the surgical CPT code, not an additional code. For the integumentary system, this is the only procedure that includes the service.

DESTRUCTION

CPT's definition of destruction is: "Surgical Destruction is selected if it is separate from the standard management of the problem. CPT lists destruction codes that may be applicable. Cryosurgery, ablation, electrosurgery, laser, chemical (silver nitrate) are all common forms of destruction. These codes are not used for excision and do not have closure services (suturing) involved" (AMA/CPT 2005 Surgical Guidelines).

INCISION AND DRAINAGE

Incision and drainage procedure codes (range 10021–19499) are further specified by the terms "simple" and "complicated." The CPT book does not include defined criteria for the use of these terms, and their use is subjective by the physician. However, "complicated" can be substantiated by the difficulty in performing a procedure that may include the presence of infection with an unusual length of time and/or depth.

Terminology is of utmost importance for the accurate code selection. For example, incision, which means to "cut into" differs from other terms, such as excision or destruction. The codes correlate to the type of procedure that is performed: incision, excision, resection, reconstruction, and shaving, to name a few. If you have questions regarding the terms used, research the answer or query the physician prior to selecting codes.

abscess
Skin or cutaneous abscesses are collections of pus caused by a bacterial infection. This is usually caused when a minor skin injury allows skin bacteria to penetrate and cause an infection.

INDEX TIP

Was an incision made (scalpel or other sharp item cut into the site)?

What anatomical site was cut into? Cyst of _____, **abscess** of eyelid

The CPT Index will guide you to the proper chapter and code selection if you begin with these two questions, rather than directly coding from the chapters by habit.

The incision and drainage services include the placement of a drain, wick, or other item that may be left in the opening after the procedure. Incision and drainage services do not include a closure or repair. For most of these codes, it is anticipated that the services do not require a repair, or the wound will not be surgically closed. If a closure is documented and necessary, select the additional repair code.

Coding Tip   *When the procedure performed progresses to excise (or resect, remove, etc.) the site, select the excision code and do not select the incision and drainage codes during the same session. If a separate area is involved, modifier -59 will be reported on the additional services.*

debridement
A procedure where foreign material and contaminated or devitalized tissue are removed from a traumatic or infected lesion or wound until the surrounding healthy tissue is exposed.

DEBRIDEMENT

Debridement is a procedure where foreign material and contaminated or devitalized tissue is removed from a traumatic or infected lesion or wound until the surrounding healthy tissue is exposed. The notes in CPT instruct the coder to another subcategory if the debridement is of the nails or for burn treatment. Some of the codes in this subcategory refer to debridement not only of the skin and subcutaneous tissue, but also the fascia, muscle, and bone (i.e., open fractures).

fascia
The tissue that connects muscles.

> ## INDEX TIP
>
> What is the reason for the debridement?
> What is being debrided? (Through to **fascia** or bone?)
> The CPT index is not very descriptive for the selection; therefore you will have to read the codes for details.

Both codes 11005–78 and 11008 (no modifier -51) would be selected for debridement and mesh removal of LT hernia. Modifier -78 may be required on the 11005, indicating a return to OR, if appropriate. If performed at the physician office, this modifier would not be applied.

Debridement codes are not reported with the wound care codes 97597–97602.

■ *Highlight*

Most of the surgical services in the integumentary system include the debridement at the same session.

PARING OR CUTTING

Paring or cutting involves a superficial removal of a benign hyperkeratotic lesion. These are corns or calluses, described by patients. The cutting or paring may be performed using a razor, shaving, or scissors. These codes are not used if the lesion is removed using destruction methods (see 17000–17004), and are only for the corn or callus purpose.

BIOPSY

biopsy
Tissue or organ removal for study or examination.

Biopsy is the removal of tissue for microscopic review and assists to diagnose the disease. The physician may choose to use a punch, curette, or other instruments to obtain the sample.

> ## INDEX TIP
>
> From what anatomical site is the biopsy being obtained? Many of the areas in the index are detail specific—for example, eyelid biopsy versus conjunctiva, or upper arm versus lower arm. In addition, the index also identifies many internal organ biopsies that are not skin related.

When a lesion is removed in its entirety by an excision, the biopsy service is included and not separately coded. When this is documented do not code it as a biopsy; use the excision of lesion codes (either benign or malignant based upon the pathology report). The surgeon's documentation and the pathology should be equal, both describing that the complete lesion was obtained.

If a biopsy is performed on one anatomical site, while an excision is performed at another separate incision, then both codes are reported. The modifier -59 is used to alert this on the claim, along with the RT/LT modifiers if applicable.

The simple closure is included in the biopsy code. If an intermediate or complex closure were documented, the closure would be additionally reported.

REMOVAL OF SKIN TAGS

skin tag
Small, soft, flesh-colored skin flap that appears mostly on the eyelids, neck, and armpits.

A **skin tag,** or acrochordon, is a small, flesh-colored, benign outgrowth of epidermal and dermal tissue that generally appears on the eyelids, neck, and armpits. A physician may remove a skin tag through a variety of methods, including scissoring, ligature strangulation, electrosurgical destruction, (electrosurgery, cryosurgery, laser or chemical treatment) or a combination of these. The coder should read the patient's medical record carefully to see the number of skin tags removed, since choosing the correct code is based on the number removed.

Shaving of Epidermal or Dermal Lesions

Shaving is topically, horizontally cut, and typically no closure (suturing/stapling) is required. The physician may use a straight razor blade or another instrument. A dressing or butterfly closure is commonly used.

LESION REMOVAL OR DESTRUCTION

Skin lesions are growths that can be either benign or malignant. Lesions may be primary or secondary. Examples of primary lesions include macules, papules, nodules, wheals, and tumors. Secondary lesions generally develop from primary lesions and include ulcers, excoriations, fissures, and scars.

Criteria for Measuring and Proper Documentation for Lesion Size

The lesion size is measured prior to the infusion of the anesthetic. See Figure 7–2 (A, B, and C) for the CPT measurement and documentation criteria. Measure the lesion and the margins together. If irregular, use the greatest width. The measurements are documented in centimeters (Table 7–2).

The anatomical site is documented specifically (note face versus scalp). If during the lesion removal, the incision is extended, the wound is measured for the potential repair code selection.

> **INDEX TIP**
>
> Lesion anatomical site
> Excision—Benign or Malignant?
> Destruction (usually includes laser)

Code Selection for Lesions

When a specimen is submitted for pathology analysis, the report is typically returned in approximately three days. The surgeon reviews the pathology report, findings, and the pathologist final diagnosis, and then either agrees by signing the report or perhaps disagrees. The surgeon may then either contact the

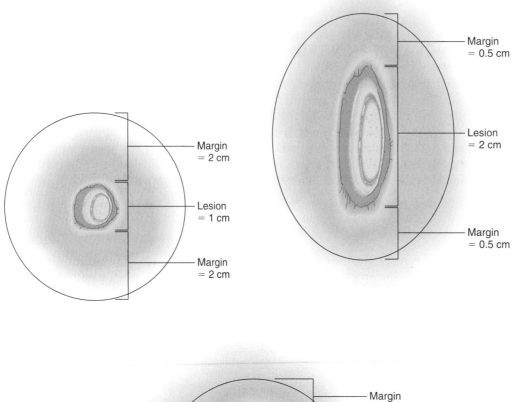

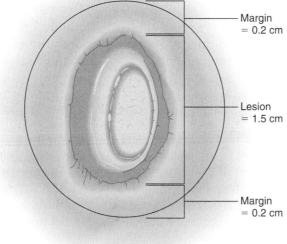

Figure 7–2 Examples of measuring and coding the removal of a lesion.

pathologist, review the slides/specimen personally, or may request a second opinion prior to determining the definitive diagnosis of the lesion site. In the absence of a final definitive diagnosis, the ICD-9-CM codes selected are the signs and symptoms only, not benign or malignant. Within CPT, the codes cannot be selected in the absence of a diagnosis. When coding for the surgeon, select the CPT code after the surgeon has documented the definitive diagnosis,

TABLE 7–2   Metric Conversions.

1 mm = 0.1 cm
10 mm = 1 cm
1 inch = 2.54 cm
0.3937 inch = 1 cm
3/16 inch = 0.5 cm

whether benign or malignant. If no specimen is submitted, there is no proof of malignancy. Therefore, if the surgeon does not have proof, the benign codes are selected.

Excision—Benign Lesions (11400 series)

Excision of benign lesions falls within code range 11400–11471. Excision is the full-thickness removal of a lesion, which includes a simple closure. Benign lesions are harmless and nonrecurring. A closure other than simple (i.e., layered) would be coded in addition to the lesion removal. Types of wound closure are discussed later in this chapter. A plastic repair (i.e., skin graft) includes the lesion removal. If lesion excision is performed by other methods (i.e., electrosurgical destruction, laser, cautery), the CPT notes refer the coder to the destruction codes (17000–17999).

The correct code cannot be assigned without verification from the pathology report. This is the only definitive way to determine if a lesion is benign or malignant.

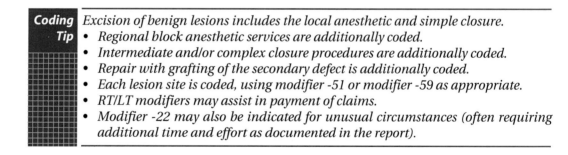

Coding Tip

Excision of benign lesions includes the local anesthetic and simple closure.
- *Regional block anesthetic services are additionally coded.*
- *Intermediate and/or complex closure procedures are additionally coded.*
- *Repair with grafting of the secondary defect is additionally coded.*
- *Each lesion site is coded, using modifier -51 or modifier -59 as appropriate.*
- *RT/LT modifiers may assist in payment of claims.*
- *Modifier -22 may also be indicated for unusual circumstances (often requiring additional time and effort as documented in the report).*

Frequently the benign lesion removals are not covered benefits. Investigate the benefits and properly complete the advance beneficiary notice prior to providing the care. Indicate the GA and GW modifier when applicable.

■ *Highlight*

In most circumstances, excision of a cyst is coded to a benign lesion. However, the CPT book will refer the coder elsewhere for certain sites, such as Cyst of breast (19120), Ganglion cyst of wrist (25111 or 25112), or Mucous cyst of finger (26160).

Excision—Malignant Lesions (11600 series)

malignant lesion
Having the properties of nearby invasive and destructive tumor growth and metastasis; changes in the tissues.

A **malignant lesion** grows worse over time and often resists normal treatment. When a lesion is removed, the physician may not know if it is benign or malignant. If the lesion is malignant, usually further wide excision or resection is done to determine if the lesion has spread to its margins.

Review of Figure 7–2 will guide to the excision that extends to include additional margins of excision. The entire distance that is documented will be calculated for the CPT code selection.

Did the surgeon sign the pathology report? The definitive diagnosis is determined by the surgeon, after reviewing and authorizing the pathology report. Once the physician has determined the definitive diagnosis, the CPT and the ICD9 codes can then be selected accurately.

Coding Tip	• *Excision of malignant lesions includes the local anesthetic and simple closure.* • *Regional block anesthetic services are additionally coded.* • *Intermediate and/or complex closures procedures are additional coded.* • *Repair with grafting of the secondary defect is additionally coded.* • *Each lesion site is coded, using modifier -51 or modifier -59 as appropriate.* • *RT/LT modifiers may assist in payment of claims.* • *Modifier -22 may also be indicated for unusual circumstances (often requiring additional time and effort as documented in the report).* • *Multiple margin excisions during the same session are coded one time for the total margin centimeters. If at another session, use 11600–646 with modifier -58 for re-excision.*

EXERCISE 7–1

Postoperative final diagnosis: Pigmented, ulcerated lesion, face.

Measurement: 6 mm pigmented, ulcerated lesion on the right cheek. Margins of 1 cm × 0.5 cm.

Procedure Performed: Excisional biopsy RT cheek lesion. Lidocaine injected then elliptically excised. The epidermal is closed using 5-0 nylon interrupted sutures.

Pathology Report: Specimen-RT cheek face lesion. Specimen consists of an ellipse of skin measuring 0.9 × 0.6 cm. The epidermal surface shows a 5 mm en-block granular lesion. Diagnosis Actinic keratosis per pathologist, reviewed and signed by the surgeon.

ICD-9-CM Code(s) _____

CPT Code(s) _____

EXERCISE 7–2

Using your CPT and ICD-9-CM coding books, assign the ICD-9-CM code, and CPT procedure code to the following:

Diagnosis: Hydradenitis of the right axilla.

Procedure: The cystic structure in the axilla was excised and skin was sutured.

Pathology: Specimen-skin, right axilla. The specimen shows inflammatory changes consistent with chronic hydradenitis, reviewed and signed by the surgeon.

ICD-9-CM code(s) _____

CPT code(s) _____

NAILS

The 11719 series of codes include procedures on the nail(s) and nailbed. Read the code descriptions carefully, as most describe per individual nail or nailbed.

Biopsy of a nail unit (11755) is only reported once, regardless of the number of biopsies done per individual nail. If procedures are performed on different nails, these can be identified by the HCPCSII anatomical modifiers and/or the number of different nails listed in the units column on the claim.

If a nail injury, the health insurance plan may not cover the care. Review the insurance benefits and provide the advance beneficiary notice for Medicare patients.

Use the HCPCSII modifiers for each anatomical site treated today. These national HCPCSII modifiers are listed in the CPT codebook with the other modifiers and also conveniently found in the HCPCSII book.

F1–F4 FA Left Hand and Thumb
F5–F8 Right Hand
T1–T4 TA Left Foot and Great Toe
T5–T9 Right Foot

 The HIPAA Administrative Simplification Act identifies the HCPCSII modifiers as the standard to report on electronic claims. These anatomical modifiers must be used properly.

 Coding Tip *The documentation of the involvement of the nail plate versus the matrix guides the proper selection of the codes.*

Ask yourself, is the service incision and drainage, debridement, excision, or repair? 11060 is commonly performed.

The Correct Coding Initiative manual states that when performing nail debridement and excision/removal of benign hyperkeratotic lesions on the same anatomical site, select only the debridement code (11720). The anatomical site modifiers must be used for these codes. If performing nail debridement on one site (T5) and excision of lesion on another site (T6), modifier -59 is used to indicate separate anatomical sites.

INTRALESIONAL INJECTIONS AND TISSUE EXPANDERS

Codes in the 11900 series refer to the injection of lesions, tattooing, collagen injection, insertion/replacement/removal of tissue expanders or of contraceptive capsules.

Code 11900 or 11901 is reported for the number of lesions, regardless of the number of injections performed.

Tissue expansion involves creating extra soft tissue and skin for use in reconstruction procedures. In this procedure, a fluid-filled bag is inserted under the skin to which saline is added at intervals to slowly expand the skin. This creates extra skin that may be used for a subsequent skin grafting procedure or a reconstruction. The codes referenced here are for tissue expansion of skin other than the breast.

REPAIR (CLOSURES)

The professional service of closing a wound may be performed using sutures, staples, or tissue adhesives, or in conjunction with adhesive strips (butterfly closure). Figure 7–3 displays a close-up graphic of the types of simple repair closures that

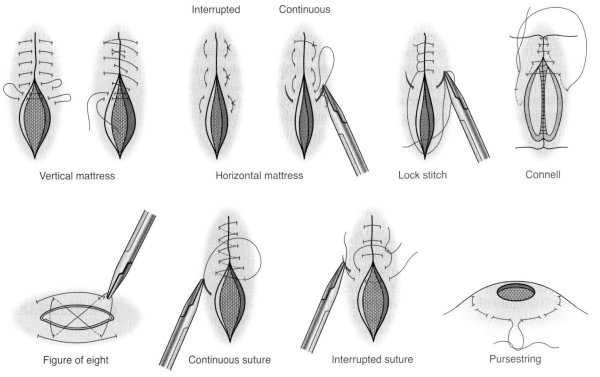

Figure 7–3 Types of wound closure.

may be performed, yet does not depict the intermediate nor complex repairs. If only adhesive strips (Band-Aid, butterfly, etc.) are applied to close the wound, the service is not coded and is included in the typical E/M code services. In other words, use the E/M codes to report the professional physician service of closing a wound *without* the use of suture, staples, or tissue adhesives.

■ *Highlights*

The NCCI rules are equal to CPT for the simple, intermediate, and complex closure concepts. There are many details that directly impact the code selection for closure services.

Simple repair is a one-layer closure and is used to close superficial tissue.

- Includes local anesthesia
- Includes chemical or electrocautery

Intermediate repairs are either

- layered closure of one or more of the deeper layers of subcutaneous and superficial (nonmuscle) fascia, plus the dermal and epidermal layer.
- heavily contaminated opening with extensive cleaning, or removal of matter with single-layer closure.

Complex is more than layered closure, and scar revision, debridement, extensive undermining, stents, or retention sutures.

Coding Tip	
	• *Where the documentation reflects various types of sutures (Vicryl, chromic, Dexon, or gut) it may be an indication the repair is beyond simple closure. Verify the anatomical levels of the skin to determine whether the closure is intermediate or complex, and if necessary query the physician.* • *Physicians and coders frequently overlook complex closure. The surgical package includes normal, uncomplicated closure, not the complex closure that may be provided by the physician. If the repair is measured and the anatomical site documented, the complex codes would also be reported.* • *Excision of a scar is included with the repair code, not an additional code.* • *The term plastic closure does not guide to the level of skin that is closed, nor the type of closure. More documentation is required for the proper selection of the closure CPT code.*

Steps for measurement and proper documentation for repair:

1. Measure and record the length in centimeters. Refer to Table 7–2 for the conversion of inches to centimeters, to assist in the code selection.
2. Record the type of repair (e.g., curved, angular, stellate).
3. State the exact anatomical site for the repair.
4. Group same anatomical sites with the same type of repairs and add the total lengths together, unless the ICD-9-CM diagnoses are not the same for all repairs. This is probably the only area of CPT where a service is added together in selecting a CPT code.
5. Sequence the most complicated repair code first, followed by lesser repair code with modifier -51 as applicable.

6. Prolonged debridement (if documented) is separately coded.

7. Debridement without closure is coded.

8. Repair of nerves, blood vessels (not simple ligation), and tendons *are* coded for complex repairs. Use modifier -51 on each, as applicable.

9. Simple ligation of blood vessels is included in all repair codes.

10. Simple exploration of nerves, blood vessels, or tendons through an open site is not coded.

11. Extensive enlargement, dissection, see 20100–20103 codes. If a separate incision is required with more dissection, then separate codes from other chapters of CPT may apply.

EXERCISE 7–3

Using your CPT and ICD-9-CM coding books, assign the ICD-9-CM code, ICD-9-CM procedure code, and CPT procedure code to the following:

Simple repair of multiple lacerations after playing baseball and falling against a window, which broke. The repairs consist of the left leg, 8.5 cm; left forearm, 5.5 cm; and left hand, 2.5 cm. There was also a superficial abrasion of the left hand which was cleansed and steri-stripped.

ICD-9-CM code(s) _____

CPT code(s) _____

EXERCISE 7–4

Using your CPT and ICD-9-CM coding books, assign the ICD-9-CM code, ICD-9-CM procedure code, and CPT procedure code to the following:

Patient presents to urgent care with a 3 cm laceration on the top of the left mid thigh. Patient accidentally cut it on the tailgate of a truck. The wound extends down to the subcutaneous level, but does not appear to be a deep penetrating laceration. Wound was cleansed with saline and closed with 5-0 Vicryl in the subcutaneous twice and 4-0 Prolene horizontal mattress skin sutures.

ICD-9-CM code(s) _____

CPT code(s) _____

GRAFT CONCEPTS AND TIPS

There are many tips throughout the AMA/CPT code book that guide the proper selection of each of the potential components surrounding the grafting procedures. Review the documentation and highlight the components prior to finalizing the code selection, exercising caution to avoid missing all service codes that have been provided.

> **Preparation Code:** (15000) How was the recipient site prepared?
>
> Debridement
>
> Excision
>
> **Harvest Code:** What type of graft was obtained?
>
> **Graft type:** possibilities with hints:
>
> Adjacent Tissue Transfer or Rearrangement = Peninsula
>
> Split Thickness = Shallow Island
>
> Full Thickness = Deep Island
>
> **Pedicle** = Attached, bridgelike, dependent upon the mainland

pedicle
In skin grafting, it is the stem that attaches to a new growth.

> Bilaminate skin substitute = synthetic, often biologic. Usually described by the brand name of the product
> Autograft = mine, from myself—same person
> Autogenous = my skin is grown in the lab, tissue cultured
> Allograft or homograft = from another of the same species, usually cadaver, however could be a transplant from a living donor
> Xenograft or heterograft = from another species, often porcine (pig) skin
> Bilaminate skin substitute = synthetic skin

How Was the Graft Obtained?

dermis
The middle layer of the integument, or skin.

The most common instrument to obtain and harvest the skin is the Dermatome. The physician may also "mesh" the graft, thereby allowing it to expand to cover more area upon placement to the prepared site. The skin is harvested at different depths of the **dermis,** hence split thickness skin graft (STSG) or full thickness skin graft (FTSG). Watch for details of documentation to identify the type of graft that is being obtained. Refer to Figure 7–1 and Figure 7–4 for important anatomical identifications.

Another common simple procedure is the punch graft. This instrument captures a small, tunnel-like portion of tissue, frequently used for hair transplant or other purposes using the dermal layer.

Pedicle grafts are often performed over a period of time. The surgeon often creates a tube or connects the anatomical site directly, placing vascularity of both the donor site and the recipient site together to heal over time. The area blood vessel, capillary refill, and color help to determine when the two anatomical sites will be surgically separated. The use of modifier -58 is common for these procedures.

Donor Site

How was the donor site cared for? Did the donor site require additional extensive work?

Modifier -58 is frequently used with these procedures, to indicate staged components of the care extending over multiple sessions and dates of service. The

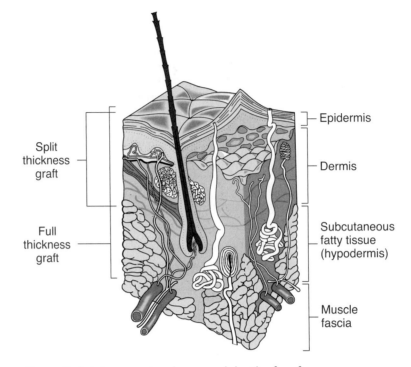

Figure 7–4 Integumentary layers and depth of grafts.

donor component may occur at one session, whereas the placement may occur over multiple sessions, as the recipient site is properly prepared and ready to receive the graft. When placing the graft on the recipient site, you may see terms such as granulation tissue, adequate blood supply or color, and noninfected pertaining to the recipient site in the operative note.

Recipient or Placement Site (Graft)

If the CPT code states microvascular within the description of the code, the microvascular service includes the use of the operating room microscope, and you cannot add 69990.

> **Coding Tip** *The allograft and/or xenograft of the same placement site as any other graft are not additionally coded.*

ADJACENT TISSUE TRANSFER OR REARRANGEMENT

The codes in this range are selected when the tissue (skin) slides over to provide an effective closure. Table 7–3 provides many details of the procedures and terminology that may be encountered while reviewing the operative reports. One additional note to Table 7–3 is that the small autograft may be described as either a pinch or a punch graft. The excision work of the primary lesion with the tissue transfer is included. If an additional lesion were removed, it would be reported with a modifier -59.

If rearranging tissue to repair a laceration, the rearrangement must be medically necessary in order to repair the site, and the documentation needs to reflect the surgeon's work. When the rearrangement is incidentally performed, do not select the codes from this area; instead, use the repair codes only. The adja-

TABLE 7–3   **Examples of Tissue Transfer/Rearrangement.**

Adjacent Tissue Transfer

Types of Tissue Transfer	Description
Advancement flap	Nearby skin is stretched over a wound
Melolabial flap	Flap from the medial cheek used as a rotational flap to repair a defect on the side of the nose
Pedicle flap or double-pedicle flaps	Flaps of the entire skin and subcutaneous tissue transferred to a clean tissue bed
Rotation flap	A semicircular flap of skin that is rotated over the wound site (may also be called transpositional or interpolation flap)
Sliding flaps	Flap that is transferred to a new position using a sliding technique (similar to advancement technique)
V-Y-plasty	An incision is made in the shape of a V, and sutured in the shape of a Y
W-plasty	Similar to a Z-plasty, but used for less linear scar/wound repair
Y-V-plasty	An incision is made in the shape of a Y, and sutured in the shape of a V
Z-plasty	A scar is lengthened, straightened or realigned

Free Skin Grafts

Type of Graft	Description
Allograft	Skin graft is transplanted between two individuals. These are temporary and may be used to cover large burn areas as new skin grows beneath it.
Autograft	Skin graft is transferred from a donor site to a recipient site in the same individual
Full thickness graft	A graft containing an equal and continuous portion of both epidermis and dermis layers
Split graft	A graft containing both epidermis and dermis layers
Xenograft	Skin graft is transplanted between an animal and human. These are temporary grafts used to cover large areas.

cent tissue transfer or rearrangements are commonly performed on anatomical sites that are not flat and may need more tissue for movement (e.g., axilla, elbow) or for nonlinear lacerations. Z-plasty is two incisions of approximately equal length, usually one above and one below the area for repair. W-plasty is a zigzag tissue flap, usually on both sides of the area for repair. V-Y-plasty is the V incision is made, shaping to a Y closure.

Split thickness or full thickness skin graft codes may also be selected when the defect area requires additional coverage grafting.

INDEX TIP

Tissue (Notice the unusual order of the wording in the index.)

Transfer (This term in the index does not correlate to transfer of skin, rather associates with transfer as in transplant.)

Adjacent

Anatomical Site

EXAMPLE

The laceration simple repair may be a covered benefit, yet complex repair or grafting may not be a covered benefit. Verify the insurance benefits before performing the service and properly complete the advance beneficiary notice. Also, workers' compensation carriers may vary upon their policies.

EXERCISE 7–5

Using CPT and ICD-9-CM codebooks, assign the proper codes:

Preoperative Diagnosis: RT ear tumor _____

Postoperative Diagnosis: Malignant carcinoma RT ear _____

Procedure: Excision of RT ear tumor with advancement tissue transfer _____

Measurement: 1.3 cm × 1 cm × 1.5 cm ulcerated lesion located on the helix of the RT auricle _____

The RT ear is prepped and draped and locally anesthetized using 1 percent Xylocaine with epinephrine injection. Initial incision with scalpel is made around the lesion at the helical rim, minimizing the resection of cartilage. It is noted the lesion depth on the anterior lateral side includes a small aspect of the cartilage. A 3 mm margin is then obtained surrounding the lesion site. The specimen is sent for pathological determination. A skin flap is marked 1.5 cm × 2.0 cm and raised in the postauricular region to cover the entire defect nicely. The graft is extended and secured. No cartilage graft is required to fill the minimal cartilage defect. The wound and graft are closed using 5-0 Novofil suture. Antibiotic ointment was applied to the wound, then covered with nonadherent gauze, fluff gauze, and secured with Kerlix. The patient tolerated the procedure well. Estimated blood loss minimal.

Pathology Report: (signed by surgeon accepted)

Specimen A: RT ear tumor

Description: Consists of skin ellipse measuring 2.0 cm × 1.0 cm × 0.3 cm. The ulcerated area is 0.8 cm × 0.5 cm, identified as invasive differentiated squamous cell carcinoma into the tissue. Normal cartilage is seen. The margins are not clear.

Diagnosis: Invasive differentiated squamous Cell carcinoma of RT auricle

ICD-9-CM Code(s) _____

CPT Code(s) _____

FREE SKIN GRAFTS

The codes are selected by the documentation of the defect or recipient placement area and whether split thickness skin graft (STSG) or full thickness skin graft including the dermis (FTSG) is performed.

Usually simple debridement, cleaning of the granulation tissue, or preparation of the area after an injury is included and not additionally coded. If, however, extensive debridement or preparation is documented, 15000 for the debridement or preparation is selected.

Occasionally, a graft is placed in addition to the simple, primary closure for a surgical procedure. The free skin graft code is selected plus the surgical procedure code in this circumstance.

A free skin graft may be required for the Donor site. If the Donor site is repaired with a portion of the harvested tissue, select an additional free skin graft code per anatomical site and depth of the graft that is applied to the donor site. Modifier -59 may be applied or RT/LT as appropriate.

MEASUREMENT TIPS

- Size in square centimeters (Table 7–2 assists in conversion from inches to cm, then a calculation may be necessary to convert to square cm)
- Anatomical site of the defect is to be documented

INDEX TIP

Skins, grafts free are all listed in one area.

Grafts to close surgical wounds are selected from 15000 series of codes, and may be added

---

Per NCCI, the primary code has a limitation of one unit per given area, allowing only one type of skin graft per area. In other words, if the site has a split thickness graft and a full thickness graft, only one code is selected as the primary line item. The secondary line may have multiple units, however modifier -59 will need to be applied.

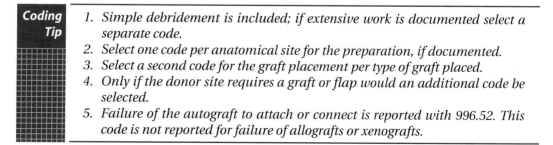

Coding Tip

1. *Simple debridement is included; if extensive work is documented select a separate code.*
2. *Select one code per anatomical site for the preparation, if documented.*
3. *Select a second code for the graft placement per type of graft placed.*
4. *Only if the donor site requires a graft or flap would an additional code be selected.*
5. *Failure of the autograft to attach or connect is reported with 996.52. This code is not reported for failure of allografts or xenografts.*

EXERCISE 7–6

Using CPT and ICD-9-CM coding books, assign the ICD-9-CM code, and CPT Procedure Code to the following:

Diagnosis: Nonhealing wound, tip of nose measuring 3 cm × 2 cm.

Operation: Split thickness skin graft, nose.

Procedure: Borders of granulation tissue are debrided and skin edges freshened. Due to the defect, skin approximation cannot be accomplished. Using a dermatome, a split thickness skin graft is harvested from the right thigh. The graft is placed onto the nose defect and secured with interrupted 5-0 Prolene sutures. The donor site is examined and reveals good hemostasis.

ICD-9-CM code(s) _____

CPT code(s) _____

FLAPS (SKIN AND/OR DEEP TISSUES)

Flaps are usually performed over multiple sessions. Frequently, the first session forms the **pedicle flap,** keeping the blood vessels intact to "feed" the future graft. The first service is usually coded with 15570–76 or the Delay of flap 15600–30. A partial transfer of the pedicle may also be performed to wean the pedicle grafts.

When special devices are placed to secure the flap, the instrumentation or casting services are additional codes. However, simple dressings are included in the flap code.

pedicle flap
A flap of skin that is lifted from a healthy site, a portion of which is grafted to a new site but remains attached to its blood supply.

muscle flap
A layer of muscle is dissected and moved to a new site.

myocutaneous flap
A muscle flap that contains overlying skin.

fasciocutaneous flap
The fasciocutaneous is fibrous tissue beneath the skin; it also encloses muscles and groups of muscles, and separates their several layers or groups. The flap is the placement of portion of tissue or skin and may or not include the fascio. Pedicle, local or distant are all commonly used flap terms.

Pedicle Flap:	A flap of skin is lifted from a healthy site and a portion is immediately grafted to a new site. Part of the graft, or the pedicle, remains temporarily attached to the original site and blood supply.
Muscle Flap:	A layer of muscle is dissected and is moved to a new site.
Myocutaneous Flap:	A muscle flap that contains overlying skin is grafted.
Fasciocutaneous Flap:	A muscle flap that contains overlying skin and connective tissue.

MEASUREMENT TIPS

- Not measured
- The code is selected code per general anatomical *recipient* area region

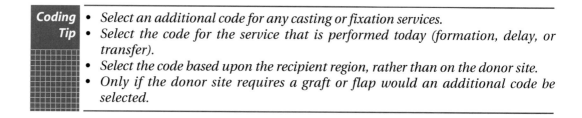

> **INDEX TIP**
>
> Skin Graft and Flap
> Type of Flap (island pedicle, pedicle, etc.)
> Formation, Delay, or Transfer

Coding Tip
- *Select an additional code for any casting or fixation services.*
- *Select the code for the service that is performed today (formation, delay, or transfer).*
- *Select the code based upon the recipient region, rather than on the donor site.*
- *Only if the donor site requires a graft or flap would an additional code be selected.*

Per CCI, if a lesion is excised incidentally at the same site as the flap graft, no additional excision code is selected.

Other Flaps and Grafts

This area of the code book describes complex or combination methods. Read the descriptions carefully and match to the operative notes.

Coding Tip
1. *Many of the codes in the series 15756 include the use of an operating room microscope. Do not also select the 69990 code if the description states microvascular.*
2. *Only if the donor site requires a graft or flap would an additional graft or flap code be selected.*
3. *Composite graft is a combination of tissue and another part of anatomy, cartilage being the most frequent.*
4. *Dermafascia fat grafts combine fat and muscle.*
5. *Punch grafts describe the tool used to obtain the graft, and the code is selected per number of punch grafts performed. Pinch grafts describe a small amount of graft obtained.*

OTHER PROCEDURES

Various Plastic Surgery services are listed in this area of the CPT codebook. Notice that many descriptions state the purpose as well as the procedure. Do not report the procedure code if the description does not match the documentation of the service performed.

Suture removal codes 15850 and 15851 describe removal of sutures under anesthesia by other than the surgeon. A commonly asked coding question is if removing the sutures is not under anesthesia, how is this reported? Suture removal at the physician office provided by the nonsurgeon is coded using E/M codes. This example is described in the Appendix C Clinical Examples of CPT.

Dermabrasion, chemical peels, and blepharoplasty, etc. are likely to be considered cosmetic services. Obtain the insurance benefits in writing prior to performing the service, and properly complete the advance beneficiary notice.

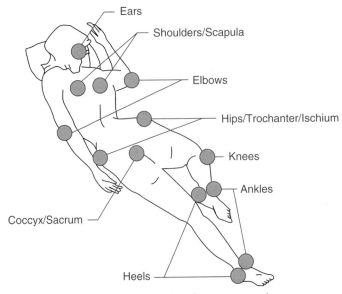

Figure 7–5 Common region sites for pressure ulcers.

PRESSURE ULCERS (DECUBITUS ULCERS)

ulcer
Loss of a portion of the skin, penetrating the dermis. Gangrene can be associated with skin ulcers. These are usually due to a vascular disease, as in diabetes. Decubitus ulcers are also known as bedsores or pressure sore. These result from a lack of blood flow and irritation to the skin over a bony projection. As the name indicates, decubiti occur in bedridden or wheelchair-bound patients or from a cast or splint.

A pressure ulcer is a sore caused by extended pressure on an area of the body that interferes with circulation. Pressure from an appliance, such as a splint, may also cause a pressure ulcer to develop. They may also be called pressure sores, dermal ulcers, decubitus ulcers, or bedsores. Pressure ulcers commonly occur in areas of the body where the bones come close to the surface of the skin, such as the elbows, hips, heels, shoulders, ankles, sacrum, and knees.

Use code range (15920–15999) to code excision of pressure ulcers. Excision of pressure ulcer sites other than of the coccyx, sacrum, ischium, or trochanter are reported with an appropriate code such as debridement, closure or flap, based on the documentation of the procedure performed.

The 15920 series of codes is selected to report the surgical repair service. If additional defect repair (commonly full thickness flaps) are performed, an additional code is selected. The Active wound management 97575 codes are frequently performed prior to the surgical repair services.

Typically the surgeon will excise and debride the **ulcer** site, followed with a graft repair. The graft selected will be determined based upon the depth of the ulcer site, from a STSG to a full delayed pedicle flap. Figure 7–5 lists common terms for the areas pressure ulcers may be found on the patient or described in operative notes.

> ### INDEX TIP
>
> Pressure Ulcer Excision
> Then select the repair of the defect type of graft (split thickness, full thickness, pedicle, etc.)

BURNS, LOCAL TREATMENT

Burns are identified per degree as follows:

epidermis
The outer layer of the integument, or skin.

First Degree	Erythema and redness, affecting the dermis layer
Second Degree	Blistering and oozing, affecting the **epidermis** layer

Third Degree	Full thickness
Deep Third Degree/ Fourth Degree	Deep necrosis of underlying tissues
Deep Third Degree/ Fifth Degree	Bone visibly damaged, probable amputation

To assist in the calculation of the total body surface area (TBSA), use the Rule of Nines. The documentation will be necessary for selection of the CPT and the ICD9 code, with this criteria clearly indicated.

The codes in series 16000 are for the treatment of the burned surface only. If additional bone work or other professional services (critical care visits, IV placement, etc.), select additional codes.

Coding Tip

Total body surface area Rule of Nines
Depth of burn
15000 and 15001 are coded per session
Infants and children are under the age of ten, unless the body habitus is larger

---

Escharotomy is performed to relieve the blood vessels and circulation beneath the burned necrotic binding tissue. This is frequently performed within the first few days of the injury, and may be provided with multiple incisions. Do not use multiple quantities with code 16035; use 16036 for additional quantities. If performed bilaterally, report line item with RT or LT modifiers as applicable.

DESTRUCTION

The Destruction services represent a very common series of codes within the integumentary chapter; for example, common plantar wart removal by laser. Table 7–4 describes various methods that may be used to remove by destruction.

Select 17000 code series for destruction of skin type lesions. See Table 7–5 for common types of lesions that may be removed. If performing on internal or other anatomic sites, select from the other chapters of CPT. *Watch closely for the term "each" in the description of the CPT code.* If the word "each" is in the description, enter the total number on the quantity line on the claim form. Do not select 17000 series codes for skin tags.

Figure 7–6 can assist to understand the linking of the ICD-9-CM per CPT, the quantities, the modifier use, and the necessity to enter line-item details.

TABLE 7–4 **Common Descriptions for Destruction Procedures.**

Destruction	Ablation
	Electrosurgery
	Cryosurgery (cold)
	Laser (any type)
	Chemical

TABLE 7–5   Common Descriptions of Lesion Types.

Common Lesion Types	
	Condylomata
	Papillomata
	Molluscum contagiosum
	Herpetic lesions
	Common wart
	Plantar wart
	Flat wart
	Milia
	Actinic keratosis
	Benign lesions
	Premalignant lesions
	Malignant lesions

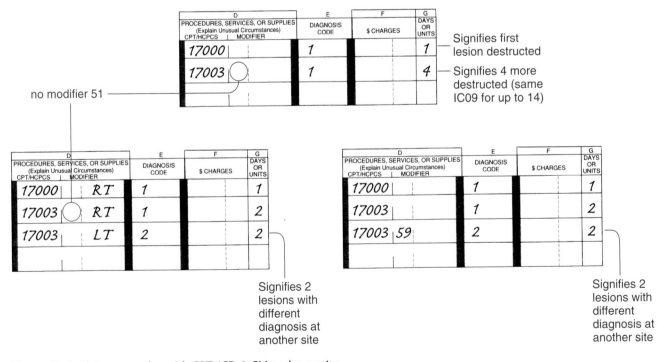

Figure 7–6 Claim examples with CPT, ICD-9-CM and quantity.

Note 17003 is modifier -51 exempt. 100 percent payment should be received by the insurance plan, even if this is an additional service to 17000.

Do not select chemical cauterization if excision of the same lesion is performed (blood vessel cautery would be included in the surgical service).

INDEX TIP

If you look up the various types of destruction, you will be guided to the other chapters for the internal anatomical sites. The quickest method to find the skin service is to begin with the word Destruction.

Destruction

Skin

   (Rather than looking up Lesion)

When performing destruction service with biopsy of a separate anatomical site lesion at the same session, use modifier -59. If of the same anatomical site, only one code is selected and no modifier -59 is reported.

MOH'S MICROGRAPHIC SURGERY

Moh's micrographic surgery (code range 17304–17310) is used for the treatment of complex or ill-defined skin cancer where the physician acts in two integrated, but separate capacities, as the surgeon and pathologist.

If a repair is performed, a separate code is assigned for the repair, flap, or graft codes. These codes are reported by stages and the number of specimens taken. Documentation must be present to support the code assignment.

Documentation describing the surgical and the pathology work are required. This service is typically performed with margin work, then review of microscopic slides, more margin work, etc. Not all physicians are qualified to perform these codes.

Coding Tip

Biopsy of the same site for the initial pathology diagnosis performed on the same date is selected as 11100-59, with 88331 Frozen section.

Select codes based upon the stage
Add total number of specimens
Simple, intermediate, or complex closure codes are selected in addition to the Moh's codes

---

If the surgeon needs to obtain a diagnostic biopsy for the decision for surgery, select the Moh's CPT code and also modifier -58 for staged procedure. Otherwise, the frozen section is not additionally selected, per CCI.

Other Procedures

Codes in range 17340–17999 refer to acne procedures and electrolysis.

BREAST PROCEDURES

It is especially important to use the CPT index for the breast procedure code selection. Fine needle aspiration and stereotactic radiological services are two examples that guide you to other areas throughout the codebook. New technological advances are identified with codes, including the required Category III codes. Category III codes are updated in January and June annually and can be found on the AMA web site.

mastectomy
Excision of the breast.

Surgical procedures such as **mastectomy,** implants, or mammaplasty may be performed on either male or female patients.

Personal identifying information associated with cosmetic or cancer procedures should be held in strict confidentiality. In the office, use caution in discussion of patient care; cover the reports to prohibit "glance" opportunities; minimize computer screens whenever not in use, as examples of extra protections. It is appropriate to discuss care, billing, and operations with professionals; however, it is advised to exercise common privacy techniques.

■ *Highlight*

1. *The codes are selected per lesion.*
2. *When the decision for surgery (excision or resection) is dependent upon the biopsy results during the same session, the biopsy service is also coded with modifier -58. This code and documentation is frequently overlooked.*
3. *All breast excision codes include all levels of repair/closure codes. This is not equal to CPT logic.*

Incision

Per cyst that may be aspirated, the surgeon may choose to use radiology or imaging. When radiology is performed by the surgeon, often using the equipment at an outpatient facility, select 19000 with 76095 and modifier -26 to indicate the professional component for the radiological service.

Excision

Biopsy may be percutaneous (needle core) or open (scalpel) and may or may not use imaging.
Biopsy codes are 19100–19103.

Coding Tip	*Use modifier -50 with the codes in this series* *Additional services that should be coded are for imaging, placement of clips, or markers*

Excisional surgery (removal of cysts, tumors, or lesions per breast) include:

- Certain biopsy procedures
- Surgical treatment of malignancies
- Open excision of lesions is reported with 19110–19126 when no surgical margin work is provided (excision of the lesion and closure only).

Partial mastectomy includes open excisions of breast tissue *with* surgical margin work documentation:

- Lumpectomy
- Tylectomy
- Quadrantectomy
- Segmentectomy

There are specific descriptions for the type of mastectomy that is documented, often with the excision of additional anatomy such as pectoral muscles and lymph nodes. Select the codes carefully and verify within the operative note by reading the entire note.

Chest wall excision describes any lesions (not simply breast invasion) that extend into the bone or mediastinal lymphadenectomy in the operative note. These are involved cases, which may also involve the lungs, typically requiring extensive work.

If a physician performs a breast implant at the time of the mastectomy, additional codes are selected. This implant service is usually a covered medical necessity and paid as a covered benefit by most insurance plans. Indicate the illness as the diagnosis code for the implant.

Introduction

The codes in this series are selected to report needle, wire, or other items used to mark the lesion. All of the codes in this series are per individual lesion, reporting the quantity in the unit area on the claim form. The + codes are linked to specific primary codes. If the physician performs the radiological supervision and interpretation, additional specific codes are selected from the radiology chapter of the CPT code book. If the physician is qualified to provide radiation elements, the additional codes are selected for this service as well.

REPAIR AND/OR RECONSTRUCTION

Use modifier -50 frequently for repair and/or reconstruction codes. These are commonly considered cosmetic surgery codes, when performed for non-medically necessary purposes. For the reduction mammaplasty, often insurance plan benefits will cover a specific weight (or grams) to be removed and proven in the pathology report, with certain preoperative examinations and findings.

■ *Highlight*

Obtain insurance plan preauthorizations in writing with specificity. A general statement of "will cover if medically necessary upon review" does not indicate the policy payment after the procedure has been performed. Properly obtain an advance beneficiary notice for all insurance plans, counseling the patient regarding the potential financial implications.

Cancer and malignant breast excisions may require reconstructive surgery with breast implantation. The reconstruction and implant may be performed at the same time as the initial primary procedure or may be planned, staged or scheduled sometime in the future. The reconstruction and breast implant is usually a covered benefit with most insurance plans.

Code 19364 includes the harvest of the flap, microvascular transfer, closure of the donor site, and inset shaping of the flap. This varies from the previous skin graft logic of coding.

Mastectomy procedures may progress during the same session for additional services, such as reconstruction (implantation of prosthesis, spreader insertion, invasive to other sites). When this occurs, the additional services are coded. Combination services may also have co-surgeons involved, modified with -62 on the codes that are jointly provided. Many procedures may be performed using staged or delayed technique. If the description of the code does not state delayed, the modifier -58 is added to the codes when documented as delayed or staged.

■ *Highlight*

contralateral
The opposite side.

1. *Sentinel node biopsy codes of the same breast are selected in addition to local excision without lymphadenectomy.*
2. **Contralateral** *(opposite side) services are coded with RT or LT per line.*
3. *Also, if there are various pathology diagnoses, each line reflects the proper diagnosis per site. (Excision RT may be malignant, excision LT may be benign.)*

EXERCISE 7-7

Using your CPT and ICD-9-CM, assign the code for the surgeon:

Diagnosis: Primary malignant carcinoma LT breast

Pre-op procedure in Radiology: Mammogram guided wire needle placement

Operation: Open excision LT breast lesion, identified by marker

History: The patient had a stereotactic biopsy of the left breast the week prior, which confirmed the diagnosis of primary malignant carcinoma. Patient is having biopsy to remove any remaining calcifications. The patient was first taken to the Radiology Department for the left breast needle localization.

Procedure 1: Utilizing mammographic guidance, a Kopan's needle is inserted into the upper outer LT breast. After confirmation the needle was within the calcifications, the patient was transported to the surgical suite.

Procedure 2: An elliptical incision was made and carried down through the skin and subcutaneous tissue to the breast tissue. A block of breast tissue was removed to include the need and sent for specimen mammogram. Specimen was then sent to pathology.

ICD-9-CM Code(s) _____

CPT Code(s) _____

SUMMARY

When coding in the integumentary system, document the location specifically. Measure and document size of lesion. Code pathology after the surgeon has reviewed the findings and agrees. Identify the type of repair that is documented as simple, intermediate, complex, or grafting. Determine the surgical package per CPT, then determine the specific insurance plan bundling edits.

REFERENCES

AMA CPT professional 2005 current procedural terminology. Chicago: American Medical Association.

Centers for Medicare and Medicaid Services. *1997 documentation guidelines for evaluation and management services.* Retrieved September 19, 2005, from http://www.cms.hhs.gov/medlearn/emdoc.asp

ICD-9-CM professional for physicians 2005 Volumes 1, 2 & 3. Salt Lake City, UT: Ingenix.

National correct coding policy manual V10.3 October 2004. Retrieved September 19, 2005 from http://www.cmns.hhs.gov/medlearn/

St. Anthony's complete coding tutor: ICD-9-CM, CPT, HCPCS Level II. Salt Lake City, UT: Ingenix.

Chapter 8

Orthopedics

arthropathy
closed fracture
dislocation

internal derangement
myelopathy
open fracture

orthopedics
osteomyelitis
radiculopathy

LEARNING OBJECTIVES

Upon successful completion of this chapter, you should be able to:

1. Explain the proper application of coding rules and conventions in the ICD-9-CM and CPT classification systems as applied to orthopedics and use them to solve any coding problem.

2. Demonstrate clinical knowledge of the normal structure and function of the musculoskeletal tissues by always referencing the proper body system in CPT and ICD-9-CM.

3. Explain the most common diseases, disorders, and injuries of the musculoskeletal system and be able to differentiate between similar conditions with different codes.

4. Accurately and completely classify diagnoses and procedures applicable to orthopedics without overcoding or undercoding the case.

INTRODUCTION

orthopedics
A medical specialty concerned with the prevention, investigation, diagnosis and treatment of diseases, disorders, and injuries of the musculoskeletal system.

Orthopedics (orthopaedics) is a medical specialty concerned with the prevention, investigation, diagnosis, and treatment of diseases, disorders, and injuries of the musculoskeletal system. The orthopedic specialty is a major provider in injuries related to trauma: work-related injuries, motor vehicle accidents, and falls. E codes are necessary to assign to the diagnosis code to describe the reason for the injury and to help determine liability for the charges. Figures 8–1A, 8–1B, and 8–1C presents an overview of the musculoskeletal system. The specialty may employ medical, surgical, physiological, pathological, and other related sciences in the scope of diagnosis and treatment.

This chapter covers the broader concepts and most common themes seen in the field of orthopedics. It is designed to give learners a better understanding of the most common diagnoses and procedures and help them understand classification rules in ICD-9-CM and CPT. Learners will also have the opportunity to see and use some code designations that may be new or unfamiliar to them, learn more about the details of the many diagnoses and procedures available in the classification systems, and gain practical knowledge of how to handle some difficult orthopedic classification issues.

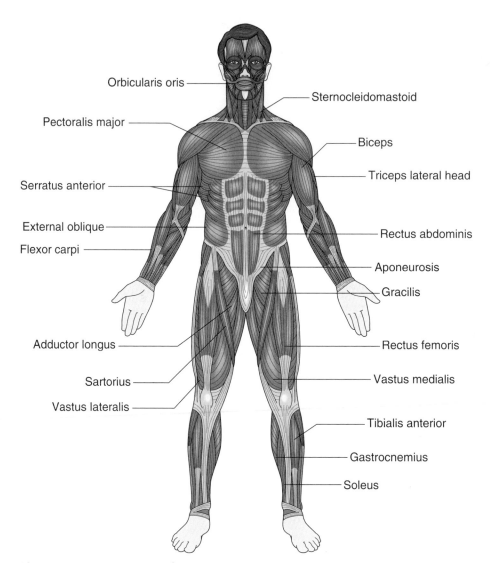

Figure 8–1A An overview of the musculoskeletal system (anterior surface muscles).

Most orthopedic diagnoses will fall into the ICD-9-CM chapters on Diseases of the Musculoskeletal System and Connective Tissue code range 710–739, and Injuries and Poisonings code range 800–999. Some other conditions which are amenable to orthopedic treatment can be found in other chapters, such as malignant neoplasms of bone in the Neoplasms chapter, and musculoskeletal anomalies found in the Congenital Anomalies chapter. Orthopedic procedures are mostly classified between code categories 76–84 in ICD-9-CM Volume Three. CPT classifies most orthopedic procedures within the Musculoskeletal System chapter, code range 20000–29999.

In the next section of this chapter, we will examine the most common conditions and procedures encountered in orthopedics, and review the proper coding and reporting of these in ICD-9-CM and CPT.

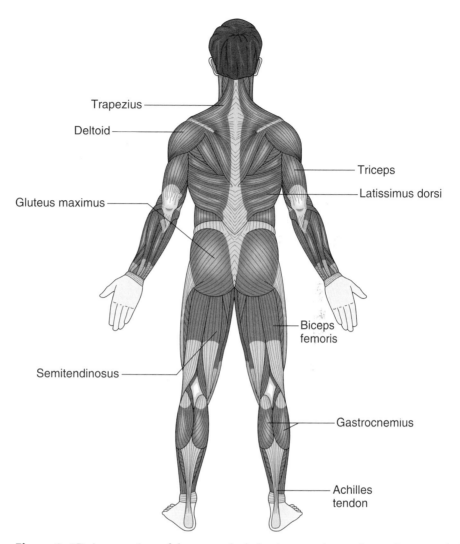

Figure 8–1B An overview of the musculoskeletal system (posterior surface muscles).

FRACTURES

A fracture is a break or disruption in an organ or tissue that accounts for a large number of patients treated in the orthopedic specialty. In orthopedics, fractures of the bone are classified in the ICD-9-CM code category range 800–829 (a few other specific bone fractures are classified elsewhere). They refer to a structural break in the continuity of bone as a result of physical forces exerted beyond its ability to accommodate by resistance, elasticity, or bending. Fractures can occur as a result of direct injury such as being hit in the upper arm with a heavy object, or by indirect injury such as a fracture of the clavicle as a result of falling upon an outstretched hand, where the initial force is transmitted indirectly through one or more joints (Figure 8–2). Muscular contractures, stress, and pathology can also result in fractures.

To properly classify fractures in ICD-9-CM, there are two important pieces of information the coder must have. The first is the site of the fracture and the second is determining whether or not the fracture is open or closed. The site of the fracture is

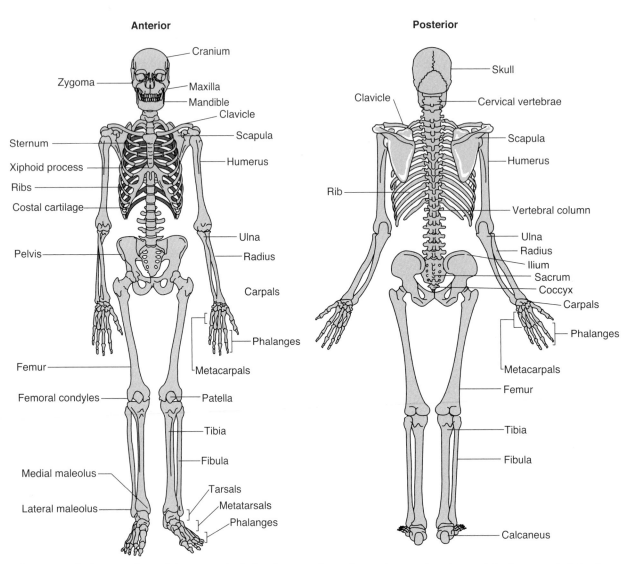

Figure 8–1C An overview of the musculoskeletal system (anterior and posterior views of the human skeleton).

open fracture
One in which the fracture site communicates with the outside environment.

closed fracture
One in which the fracture site does not communicate with the outside environment.

first classified by the name of the fractured bone, and then by the anatomical sub-classification of the region, section, or part of the bone where the fracture occurred. At the beginning of the ICD-9-CM tabular list for fractures code, category range 800–829, the coder will find a list of descriptive terms associated with **open** and **closed fractures** (see Table 8–1).

It is important to remember that some of the terms for closed can sometimes indicate either a closed or an open fracture, depending upon the circumstances, and the terms in the table do not take precedence over the clinical presentation. An open fracture is defined as one in which the fracture site communicates with the outside environment, such as a fracture that punctures the skin and often involves contamination of the wound with foreign materials, such as glass, dirt, or bone fragments. Debridement codes may be needed to remove the foreign material and clean the wound. Codes 11010–11012 are assigned from the integumentary system of CPT and billed with the treatment code for the fracture with modifier -51 to indicate multiple procedures. Thus, it is possible, for example, to have a depressed skull fracture that is classified as an open fracture, if the fracture site has a wound over it that is deep and communicates the fracture site with the outside environment. Open fractures are sometimes graded according to the Gustilo classification in Table 8–2.

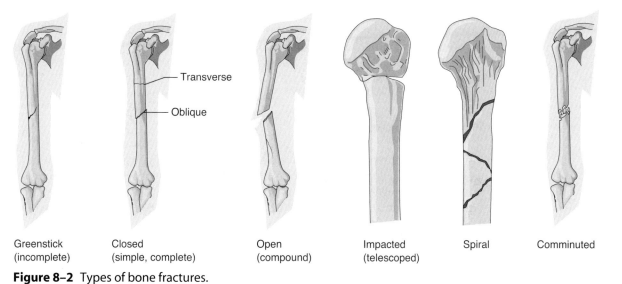

Greenstick
(incomplete)

Closed
(simple, complete)

Transverse

Oblique

Open
(compound)

Impacted
(telescoped)

Spiral

Comminuted

Figure 8–2 Types of bone fractures.

TABLE 8–1   Open and Closed Fracture Terms.

Closed Fracture Terms		*Open Fracture Terms*
comminuted	impacted	compound
depressed	linear	infected
elevated	march	missile
fissured	simple	puncture
fracture, unspecified	slipped epiphysis	with foreign body
greenstick	spiral	

TABLE 8–2   Gustilo Classification of Open Fractures.

Type	Description
Grade I	An open fracture with a wound less than one centimeter in diameter
Grade II	An open fracture with a wound greater than one centimeter and less than 10 centimeters in diameter, but without extensive soft tissue loss or devitalization, and no vascular injury
Grade III	An open fracture with a high-energy wound with extensive soft tissue loss or devitalization, or one in which there has been a major vascular injury
Grade IIIa	A type III injury, but one without extensive periosteal stripping or a vascular injury requiring repair
Grade IIIb	A type III injury accompanied by extensive periosteal stripping or gross contamination
Grade IIIc	A type III injury accompanied by a major vascular injury requiring repair

Note that a grade IIIc open fracture will require additional codes to classify the vascular injury and any subsequent repair. Grade III fractures with extensive soft tissue damage and/or devitalized tissue may require a wound debridement procedure classified to subcategory 79.6, in addition to fracture reduction and fixation in Volume Three of ICD-9-CM.

Pediatric Fractures

Children's fractures differ from those seen in the adult because of the presence of a growth plate called the physis, or cartilago epiphysialis in long bones. Whenever the fracture involves this growth plate, a classification system is used to describe the extent and severity of the fracture, as shown in Table 8–3.

Skull and Facial Fractures

Skull fractures are classified to categories 800–802, 804 and facial fractures are classified to category 802 in ICD-9-CM. Skull fractures require the coder to determine the level of consciousness at the fifth-digit level. Consciousness is a general state of wakefulness and the ability to perceive oneself, one's acts, and one's environment. There are different levels of altered consciousness ranging from slight drowsiness to obtundation to light coma to deep coma. Conditions seen in the awake (conscious) patient that are sometimes confused with a loss of consciousness include inattention, confusion, delirium, hallucinations, and delusions.

Another clinical feature that the coder needs to determine is whether or not the skull fracture is accompanied by an intracranial injury. Contusion, laceration, bleeding, and any other term indicating trauma to the meninges, the brain, or the brain stem affect code selection at the fourth-digit level. Fractures of specified facial bones are classified simply to category 802 by site. Interestingly, ICD-9-CM does not provide a code for facial bone(s) unspecified, so coders must seek additional information when confronted with this unqualified diagnosis.

TABLE 8–3   Salter-Harris Classification.

Type	Description
Type I	The fracture line goes directly through the physis.
Type II	The fracture line is mostly through the physis, but it exits one cortex such that a small fragment of metaphysis is included with the fracture fragment containing the physis and epiphysis.
Type III	The fracture line is mostly through the physis, but it exits one cortex such that a small fragment of epiphysis is included with the fracture fragment containing the metaphysis and diaphysis.
Type IV	The fracture line crossed the physis such that both the fragments contain portions of the metaphysis, physis, and epiphysis.
Type V	In this injury there is no definite fracture line. Like the Type I fracture, it cannot be easily diagnosed radiographically. The injury involves a crush injury to the physis in which the metaphysis and epiphysis are acutely impacted upon one another.

Fractures of the Neck and Trunk

Code categories 805–806 classify fractures of the vertebral column, with code category 807 covering the rib(s), sternum, larynx, and trachea. The pelvis is classified under category 808 and category 809 is reserved for ill-defined fractures of the trunk. Category 805 classifies vertebral fractures not associated with spinal cord injuries. Only subcategories 805.0 and 805.1 for cervical fractures require a fifth digit for specificity. Category 806 classifies fractures of the vertebral column and requires much more detailed information before assigning the proper code. This category is much more specific regarding the site of the fracture, and requires further delineation of the spinal cord injury at the fifth-digit level. Spinal cord injuries generally result in paralytic symptoms and syndromes and are classified at the fifth-digit level.

Category 807 classifies fractures of the ribs, sternum, larynx and trachea. The number of ribs is indicated in subcategory 807.0 and 807.1 at the fifth-digit level. A flail chest is a condition where there is instability of the chest wall, often accompanied by respiratory distress due to massive trauma, and involves a fractured sternum and/or ribs. Note that code 807.4 for flail chest is not assigned with any code from 807.0 or 807.1. Fractures of the larynx and trachea, which include the hyoid and thyroid cartilage, are often accompanied by other significant conditions such as respiratory distress or failure.

Fractures of the Upper and Lower Extremities

Code categories 810–819 classify fractures of the upper extremities, and categories 820–829 classify fractures of the lower extremities. There are two categories that provide codes for certain bone combinations. They are:

813 Fracture of the radius and ulna
823 Fracture of the tibia and fibula

Fifth digits are provided to classify each bone either separately or in combination when the fracture occurs at the same fourth-digit level of specificity. Whenever a fracture occurs to both bones at different fourth-digit levels, it is necessary to assign the codes separately. For example, a closed fracture of the head of the radius and the distal end of the ulna requires two codes, 813.05 and 813.43, because each bone's fracture occurred at a different fourth-digit level site.

Traumatic hip fractures classified to category 820 are very common in the elderly population, and may also involve an impaction type fracture of the acetabulum, codes 808.0 and 808.1. Because of the stresses placed upon this joint and the weakness of the bones in the elderly population, the most common method of treating these fractures is by partial or complete joint replacement. A total hip replacement involves the replacement of both the femoral head and the acetabulum, and a partial hip replacement involves either the acetabulum or the femoral head, although the femoral head is most common. When referencing procedures in ICD-9-CM for total or partial hip replacement, look under index terms such as arthroplasty, reconstruction, and replacement. The elderly are also subject to pathological hip fractures and the classification of these fractures will be discussed later in the chapter.

Multiple Fractures—General Guidelines

The principle of multiple coding of injuries should be followed in coding multiple fractures. Combination categories 819 and 829 should only be used when there is insufficient detail to code each fracture more specifically. Other purposes for categories 819 and 829 are for primary tabulation of data when only one code can be used, and when there is a need for multiple fracture data that has an impact on patient functional status during an episode of care. Use of code categories 819 and 829 is discouraged in the acute care hospital setting.

As illustrated previously, multiple fractures of the same bone(s) classified to different fourth-digit levels require separate codes. ICD-9-CM does not distinguish between unilateral and bilateral fractures in diagnosis classification. Thus, bilateral closed fractures of the ulna shaft, code 813.22, would only require this code to be reported once. However, if the patient sustains two fractures of the ulna classifiable with two distinct ICD-9-CM codes, such as a closed fracture of the ulna shaft left arm and a closed fracture of the ulna olecranon process right arm, the two codes assigned would be 813.22 and 813.01. Procedure coding in ICD-9-CM does allow for multiple reporting of the same procedure code. Two categories allow for coding multiple fractures of the same bone. They are:

815 Fracture of metacarpal bone
816 Fracture of one or more phalanges of hand

A multiple sites fifth digit is available for both categories.

■ *Highlight*

Reporting and sequencing of multiple fractures in acute care hospitals are based upon the Uniform Hospital Discharge Data Set (UHDDS) definitions and generally take into account the severity of the fractures. In the outpatient setting, the UHDDS definitions do not apply and the reason for the outpatient encounter should be based upon the condition chiefly responsible for the outpatient encounter.

Pathological Fractures

Code subcategory 733.1 classifies pathological fractures with fifth digits to further delineate the site of the fracture. Strictly speaking, a pathological fracture is any fracture through diseased bone, but for classification purposes it has been further defined as "without any identifiable trauma or following only minor trauma" (Pickett, 1993). To classify a fracture as pathologic, the qualifying terms of "pathologic" or "spontaneous" should be documented, or the chart should document a cause and effect relationship between the fracture and some underlying pathology. In the latter instance, there should always be a code reported for bone pathology with the pathological fracture code to complete the coding profile.

Fractures not specified as pathologic, spontaneous, or due to an underlying bone disease are classified to the code category range 800–829 as if they were due to injury or trauma. For this reason, when a pathological fracture is implied but not clearly stated in the chart documentation, the responsible physician should be queried as to whether or not this represents a pathological fracture. Situations that imply a pathological fracture include those where the fracture seems out of proportion to the degree of injury or trauma and when there is a disease present that is often associated with pathological fractures, but no cause and effect is documented. Etiologies for pathologic fractures include:

metastatic bone disease
osteoporosis
osteopenia
disuse atrophy

hyperparathyroidism
osteitis deformans
avascular necrosis of bone
osteomyelitis
osteogenesis imperfecta
osteopetrosis
neuromuscular disorders with disuse osteoporosis

osteomyelitis
Infection or inflammation of the bone or bone marrow. It may be acute, subacute, or chronic.

Note that multiple myeloma also causes pathological fractures, but as it is an integral part of the disease process, only the code for multiple myeloma code subcategory 203.0 (with the appropriate fifth digit indicating remission status) is assigned (Richard, 1996). Although virtually all pathologic fractures involve some degree of precipitating trauma or injury, a code from code category range 800–829 is never assigned with a code from subcategory 733.1 for the same fracture.

Fracture Procedures

There are many different ways to treat a fracture. It depends upon the fracture's clinical presentation, which includes its severity, the bones involved, the type and number of fractures, and even related factors such as the age of the patient and underlying bone pathology.

ICD-9-CM

ICD-9-CM classifies most orthopedic procedures within the code category range of 76–84 in Volume Three, with a few related miscellaneous procedures found in code category range 87–99.

Reduction and fixation are the two most common procedures associated with fractures. A reduction of a fracture is a procedure where the physician aligns fractured bones and bone fragments back into their normal anatomical alignment. Except in very rare instances, a reduction will be performed whenever there is a displaced fracture. Non-displaced fractures and fractures where the displacement is minimal and judged to be insignificant do not require reduction. Fixation is a procedure where the fractured bones or bone fragments are secured in their normal anatomical alignment. Fixation may or may not occur following a reduction. Sometimes the fixation is done to stabilize a non-displaced fracture.

The terms "open" and "closed" as they apply to fracture procedures have specific meanings that are unrelated to whether or not the fracture itself is open or closed. Coders must be careful when reviewing chart documentation not to confuse statements relating to the diagnosis with statements relating to the procedure. The fact that a fracture is open or closed has no bearing upon whether or not the procedures to treat the fracture will be open or closed.

A closed reduction is one by which the physician manually, or through the use of traction devices, realigns the bone ends or fragments without surgically exposing the fracture site. In an open reduction, the fracture site is exposed during the reduction procedure, and it is normally performed in an operating room. If the fracture was an open fracture, the operative report may describe the procedure with terms such as "reopening," "debriding," or "exploring" the wound down to the fracture site prior to reduction. In some cases, a closed reduction is followed by an open reduction. In the case of a failed closed reduction, no code is assigned for closed reduction. If the closed reduction was accomplished and later judged to be suboptimal, or if the bones or bone fragments fell out of alignment at a later time, then codes for both the initial closed and the subsequent reduction (which may be open or closed), may be assigned.

Open reduction is indicated when one or more of the following conditions are met:

1. Fractures irreducible by manipulation or closed means.

2. Displaced intra-articular fracture, where the fragments are sufficiently large to allow internal fixation.

3. Certain displaced physical injuries such as displaced Salter III and IV injuries

4. Major avulsion fractures with significant disruption of an important muscle or ligament. These include fractures of the greater tuberosity of the humerus, the greater trochanter, the olecranon, the patella, the intercondylar eminence of the tibia, and the tibial tubercle.

5. Nonunion of a fracture that has received adequate treatment by a closed method.

6. Replantations of extremities or digits. In this case, rigid fixation is necessary to protect the repair of the neurovascular structures. (Crenshaw, 1987)

Internal fixation is the process of directly securing bone ends or fragments together by means of surgical hardware, such as with nails, screws, plates, and rods. In directly securing the bone ends or fragments, some part of the hardware will come in contact with the fracture site, in the same way that a carpenter's nail driven through two wooden boards will come in contact with both boards to directly connect them together. Although Steinmann pins and Kirschner wires are normally associated with external fixation, they can also be used for internal fixation. For this reason, the coder should be careful to review the chart documentation to determine exactly which type of fixation is being performed and not make assumptions based upon a piece of hardware's typical usage. Orthopedic surgeons can be very creative in their use of hardware. For example, intra-articular phalangeal fractures involve the joint surface. If displaced, they are often treated with open reduction and internal fixation using fine Kirschner wire as the fixation hardware.

Internal fixation can be performed without the need for a fracture reduction and is classified to subcategory 78.5. This occurs in two instances. First, the fracture may be in good anatomical alignment so no reduction is necessary. In this case, the internal fixation is performed to stabilize the fracture site. The internal fixation subcategory code 78.5 can also be used to revise or replace a previous internal fixation, such as in the case where the original internal hardware has become displaced or broken. Note that subcategory code 78.5 is assigned only when there has been no reduction of the fracture performed during this episode of care. If a reduction is performed prior to an incision for the internal fixation, this is classified to subcategory 79.1 as a closed reduction with internal fixation.

External fixation is any method of securing the bone ends or fragments in their proper anatomical alignment without directly connecting them with hardware. Simply put, in external fixation the bone ends or fragments are held together without nailing, screwing rodding, plating, or wiring the bone ends or fragments together at the point of fracture. Casts, wraps, splints, and similar immobilization devices are some external fixation devices classified to subcategory 93.5, and should not be confused with the more complex external fixation devices classified to subcategory 78.1. Pins, wires, and screws are used in these external fixation devices (sometimes called minifixators). The key difference is that these pins, wires, and screws are used solely to hold the bone ends or fragments in their normal anatomical position. They do not connect bone (fragment) to bone (fragment) and the fracture site is not touched. Small incisions are normally made near the fracture site to secure them to the adjacent bone. Care must be exercised not to confuse these minor procedures with the surgical procedure of internal fixation. In external fixation, the hardware does not come in contact with or cross the fracture site. When a reduction is performed in addition to an external fixation not classifiable to subcategory 93.5, two codes will be assigned. One is from category 79 to describe the reduction, and one is from subcategory 78.1 for the external fixation. Internal and external fixation should not be coded concurrently for the same fracture during the same operative episode as surgeons will not incorporate both methods of fixation at the same time.

Fourth digits are used to classify the site of fracture reduction in category 79. It is important to note the Excludes note here. The fourth digit of "9" for other specified bone does not include fractures of the following:

facial bones (76.70–76.79)
nasal bones (21.71–21.72)
orbit (76–78–76–79)
skull (02.02)
vertebra (03.53)

The fourth digit of "3" for the carpals and metacarpals covers thirteen different bones. They are shown in Table 8–4 and Figure 8–3.

TABLE 8–4   Carpal and Metacarpal Bones.

Carpals	Metacarpals
Scaphoid (navicular)	First metacarpal
Lunate (semilunar)	Second metacarpal
Triquetral	Third metacarpal
Pisiform	Fourth metacarpal
Trapezoid (lesser multangular)	Fifth metacarpal
Capitate	
Trapezium (greater multangular)	
Hamate	

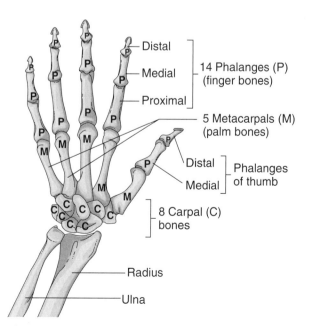

Figure 8–3 Bones of the hand and wrist.

The tarsals and metatarsals are made up of twelve bones as shown in Table 8–5 and Figure 8–4.

The information in Tables 8–4 and 8–5 is also useful for assigning codes in category 78 even though the order and content of the fourth-digit classification is different. Also, be wary of preoperative anesthesia notes, nursing notes, and consent forms when doing chart reviews. Often these forms will routinely refer to any fracture surgery as ORIF (open reduction with internal fixation), when in fact the operative report will describe a different classifiable procedure.

Nonsurgical treatment of fractures include casting, taping, splinting, bandaging, immobilization, and traction. These codes can be found in subcategories 93.4 and 93.5.

CPT

Codes for reporting fracture procedures can be found throughout the CPT chapter on the Musculoskeletal System. As in ICD-9-CM, the codes differentiate between closed or open treatment, but add "percutaneous skeletal fixation" as a third alternative. Closed treatment is used to describe procedures where the fracture site is not surgically opened. It may be used in conjunction with the following methods of

TABLE 8–5   **Tarsal and Metatarsal Bones.**

Tarsals	*Metatarsals*
Talus (astragalus)	First metatarsal
Calcaneus	Second metatarsal
Navicular	Third metatarsal
Cuboid	Fourth metatarsal
Medial cuneiform	Fifth metatarsal
Intermediate cuneiform	
Lateral cuneiform	

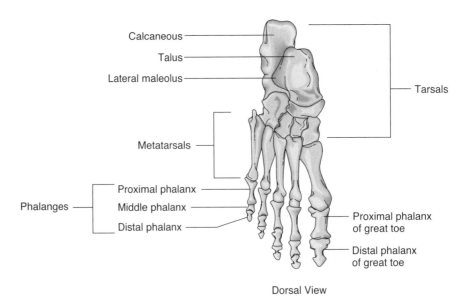

Dorsal View

Figure 8–4 Bones of the ankle and foot.

treating the fracture: with manipulation, without manipulation, or with or without traction. Open treatment is used when the fracture site is surgically opened; the fracture site is visualized and internal fixation may be used. Percutaneous skeletal fixation describes fracture treatment in cases where the fracture is not exposed, but fixation is placed across the fracture site, usually under X-ray imaging.

The term manipulation is used synonymously for reduction in CPT. It is the actual or attempted restoration of a fracture or joint dislocation to its normal anatomical alignment. Note that codes indicating manipulation can be assigned in CPT, even if a fracture reduction is not accomplished. When a closed treatment is done without manipulation, it usually means that no attempt to reduce the fracture has been made, and a cast, splint, bandage, or other traction or immobilization device has been applied. CPT does not classify reductions with open procedures, and the use of internal or external fixation is normally found within the code narrative for the open procedure. When an external fixation is done and it is not listed in the code narrative for the basic fracture or dislocation procedure, select either code 20690 or 20692 as an additional code assignment. If a revision of the external fixation device is performed, code 20693 is assigned.

Some CPT procedure codes for fractures and dislocations use anesthesia as a decision point in determining the correct code. Anesthesia is the pharmacological suppression of nerve function and can be general, regional, or local. It should not be confused with sedation (calming), analgesia (pain reduction), or topical anesthetics (ointments, salves), which are not included in CPT as anesthesia.

Multiple codes can be assigned in CPT for fixation devices and fracture procedures depending upon the number of fractures and the clinical circumstances involved just as in ICD-9-CM. Some important differences do exist however, such as the global services concept for most surgical procedures. For fracture procedures such as subsequent suture removal and casting, strapping, or other immobilization revision or removal, the surgeon performing the service should not bill for these minor procedures at a later date. Certain fracture procedures encourage multiple reporting of the same code by using the terms "each," "single," or "one" in the code narrative. Code 26600 for "Closed treatment of metacarpal fracture, single: without manipulation, each bone," requires the coder to assign this code as many times as necessary to report each metacarpal bone treated in this manner. The bones may be on one or both hands.

CPT surgical package guidelines define the following services always included in addition to the operation:

- local infiltration, metacarpal/metatarsal/digital block, or topical anesthesia
- subsequent to the decision for surgery; one related E/M encounter on the date immediately prior to or on the date of the procedure (including history and physical examination)
- immediate postoperative care, including the dictation of operative notes, discussion with family and/or other physicians
- writing orders
- evaluating the patient in the postanesthesia recovery area
- usual postoperative follow-up care

DISLOCATIONS

dislocation
A disarrangement of two or more bones from their articular processes.

A **dislocation** is a disarrangement of two or more bones from their articular processes. It is synonymous with the term luxation. In a true dislocation, there is a complete loss of congruity between the articular surfaces of a joint. An incomplete dislocation is called a subluxation, but the two terms are sometimes used interchangeably (and incorrectly). ICD-9-CM classifies both dislocations and subluxations with the same codes. When a dislocation is associated with a fracture, only the fracture code is assigned. In a fracture/dislocation, the fracture is located near the joint where the disarticulation took place. It is possible to have a fracture and a dislocation of the same bone, without it being classified as a fracture/dislocation. For example, a patient may have a dislocation of the proximal femur (at the hip joint) and a fracture at the distal femur (at the knee joint). In this case, the fracture and the dislocation have occurred at different sites and two codes can be assigned.

The terminology and coding rules for dislocations are virtually the same as they are for fractures. Dislocations and subluxations are classified to category range 830–839 and the terms open and closed as discussed in the section on fractures have basically the same meaning. Three types of dislocations not classified to this area are:

1. Congenital dislocations (754.0–755.8). These are dislocations that were existing at birth.
2. Pathological dislocations (718.2). Dislocations that may be due to an underlying disease or disorder, and include spontaneous dislocations.
3. Recurrent dislocations (718.3). Dislocations frequently occurring in a major joint such as the shoulder or hip, due to a lack of integrity of the soft tissues of the joint capsule.

Dislocation Procedures

ICD-9-CM Volume 3

Reduction and fixation terminology applies to dislocations as it does to fractures. Closed reductions are classified to subcategory 79.7 and open reductions to subcategory 79.8. The major difference is that subcategory 79.7 includes the application of an external traction device, and subcategory 79.8 includes any internal or external fixation device. A repair of a recurrent dislocation involving soft tissue repair (i.e., arthroplasty) is classified elsewhere, such as code 81.82, Repair of recurrent dislocation of shoulder.

CPT

The terms for open treatment, closed treatment, and percutaneous skeletal fixation have the same meaning for dislocations as they do for fractures. The code ranges classifying different parts of the skeletal system in the Musculoskeletal System chapter of CPT are inconsistent with regard to how dislocations are coded. The terminology of the code ranges may appear in the following five ways:

1. Bones that are part of fixed cartilaginous joint and thus not typically described as a dislocation may be listed with the subtitle "Fracture and/or Dislocation" even though the term dislocation is not present in any of the code descriptions. For example, Fractures of the ribs are classified within the code range 21800–21825. The subtitle of this code range is "Fracture and/or Dislocation" but none of these codes mention the term dislocation, only the fracture.
2. Combination fracture and/or dislocation codes. These codes will describe fractures alone, dislocations alone, or fracture/dislocations. Example: 27217

Open treatment of anterior ring fracture and/or dislocation with internal fixation (includes pubic symphysis and/or rami).

3. Fracture/dislocation codes. These codes specifically classify fractures associated with dislocations. Example: 26665 Open treatment of carpometacarpal fracture dislocation, thumb (Bennett Fracture), with or without internal or external fixation.

4. Dislocation only codes. These codes specifically classify treatment of dislocations alone. Example: 27250 Closed treatment of hip dislocation, traumatic; without anesthesia.

5. Specified clinical types of dislocations. Example: 27265 Closed treatment of post hip arthroplasty dislocation: without anesthesia.

From these varied code narratives, it is easy to see why it is so important to thoroughly read and understand the code narrative before assigning a code.

EXERCISE 8–1

Assign ICD-9-CM codes, first for the diagnosis from Volumes 1 and 2, then the procedure codes from Volume 3, and the CPT procedure codes as indicated.

1. Fracture dislocation of the surgical neck of the humerus, with closed reduction and internal fixation of same.

   ICD-9-CM   _____

   ICD-9-CM Volume 3   _____

   CPT   _____

2. Open reduction without internal fixation of closed navicular and cuboid bone tarsals fractures.

   ICD-9-CM   _____   _____

   ICD-9-CM Volume 3   _____

   CPT   _____   _____

3. Closed fracture of the forearm (Colles type) with percutaneous reduction and mini-fixation.

   ICD-9-CM   _____

   ICD-9-CM Volume 3   _____   _____

   CPT   _____

4. Dislocated patella. Dislocation reduced under intravenous sedation.

   ICD-9-CM   _____

   ICD-9-CM Volume 3   _____

   CPT   _____

5. Fracture of the pelvic ring with slight degree of subluxation, due to advanced osteoporosis. Closed reduction under regional nerve block.

   ICD-9-CM   _____   _____

   ICD-9-CM Volume 3   _____

   CPT   _____

6. Intertrochanteric hip fracture, closed, with femoral head replacement using a Medicon alloy femoral head and Geigger nonmetallic screws with methomethacrylate cement.

   ICD-9-CM   _____

   ICD-9-CM Volume 3   _____

   CPT   _____

ARTHROPATHY

arthropathy
A vague, general term meaning pathology affecting a joint.

Arthropathy is a vague, general term meaning pathology affecting a joint. There are many different descriptive types, which overlap each other, including infective, rheumatoid, degenerative, and internal derangements. This next section will examine the most common types seen by orthopedic physicians.

Infective Arthropathy

Infective arthropathy is any arthritis, arthropathy, polyarthritis, or polyarthropathy associated with an infective agent and is classified to category 711. The agent is most often bacterial, but can also be viral, fungal (mycotic), mycobacterial, parasitic (micro and macroparasites), or helminthic (worms). It should not be confused with infective osteomyelitis, which is an infection of the bone and/or bone marrow classified to category 730. But both infective arthropathy and infective osteomyelitis can occur concurrently.

All of the subcategory codes in category 711 are italicized manifestation subcategories with the exception of 711.0, Pyogenic arthritis, and 711.9, Unspecified infective arthritis. To assign a code from subcategories 711.1–711.8 you must be able to identify the infectious organism by name or type as indicated in the ICD-9-CM index. This will be the first listed diagnosis code, followed by the manifestation code for the arthropathy.

Pyogenic arthritis is arthropathy due to a specific bacterial organism known to produce suppuration. It is important to reference the ICD-9-CM index carefully when coding bacterial arthropathy because certain non-pyogenic bacteria will fall into subcategory 711.4 for "Arthropathy associated with other bacterial disease." Coders should make the effort to first determine from the chart documentation the name of the specific bacteria-caused arthropathy, and then read and be guided by the index entries under the main term Arthritis. When the code assignment is directed to subcategory 711.0, it will always be listed first, followed by the code for the bacterial organism classifiable to subcategories 041.0–041.8. Infective bacterial arthropathy classifiable to subcategory 711.4 will always list the underlying pathogen first as indicated by the index entries. Subcategory 711.9 will classify conditions specified as infective arthropathy, without mention of the type or name of the infectious agent, and thus will not be accompanied by a second code.

Rheumatoid Arthropathy

A distinction needs to be made between arthropathy that falls into the general category of rheumatoid arthritis, and arthropathy associated with acute rheumatic fever. Rheumatic fever is an acute inflammatory disease that attacks the connective tissue in the heart, blood vessels, and joints of children. It is due to infection by group A hemolytic streptococci. Due to the transient nature of the joint lesions and effectiveness of antibiotics, arthropathy associated with rheumatic fever is considered symptomatic and rarely leads to permanent joint pathology. When arthropathy is due to or associated with acute rheumatic fever, only code 390 for Acute rheumatic fever is assigned.

Rheumatoid arthritis as classified to subcategory 714.0 is a chronic, systemic, inflammatory connective tissue disease. It primarily attacks the peripheral joints and surrounding muscles, tendons, ligaments, and blood vessels (see Figure 8–5). The severity and frequency of exacerbations can vary greatly from patient to patient. The etiology of rheumatoid arthritis is unknown. The disease also goes by the names of primary progressive arthritis and proliferative arthritis.

Subcategory code 714.1, Felty's syndrome, is rheumatoid arthritis associated with splenomegaly and leukopenia. Mild anemia and thrombocytopenia may accompany the severe neutropenia, and skin and pulmonary infections are frequent complications. Subcategory code 714.2 classifies rheumatoid arthritis with extra-articular lesions of connective tissue disease in the cardiovascular, reticuloendothelial, digestive, and respiratory systems. Subcategory code 714.3 classifies a number of juvenile chronic polyarthritis diseases, which are rheumatoid-like disorders affecting children, but have a much better prognosis than the adult onset diseases. Subcategory code 714.4 Chronic postrheumatic arthropathy is a form of arthropathy affecting the hands and feet caused by repeated attacks of rheumatic arthritis. Rheumatoid lung code 714.81 is a disease of the lung associated with rheumatoid arthritis. It is sometimes seen in Caplan's Syndrome, a disease that features rheumatoid pneumoconiosis.

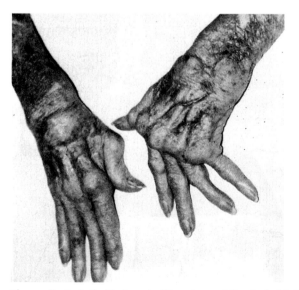

Figure 8–5 Arthritic hands. (Courtesy of the Arthritis Foundation)

As evidenced by the information in the preceding paragraph, rheumatoid arthritis can be associated with a wide variety of concomitant clinical conditions. It can be quite difficult for the coder to determine what concomitant conditions need to be classified separately, and what is integral to the disease processes classifiable to subcategories and subclassifications under category 714. When in doubt, the responsible physician should be consulted before breaking out the variables of rheumatoid arthritis into individual codes.

Degenerative Arthritis

Code category 715 classifies degenerative arthritis, also known as degenerative joint disease, osteoarthritis, senescent arthritis, and hypertrophic arthritis (Figure 8–6). The term arthritis may also be further specified as polyarthritis when more than one joint is involved. Category 721 classifies degenerative arthritis when it involves the bones of the spinal column. This condition is sometimes referred to as spondylosis or spondylarthritis. Categories 715 and 721 should not be considered mutually exclusive for classification purposes. Arthritis of the spine will be discussed later in this chapter under vertebral disorders. Degenerative arthritis is a condition marked by a deterioration of articular cartilage, hypertrophy, and remodeling of the subchondral bone, and secondary inflammation of the synovial membrane.

Within category 715 there are qualifying terms that must be understood to properly assign codes to the fourth-digit level. These terms are:

Generalized: A form of arthritis involving multiple joints that is almost always characterized as a primary osteoarthritis.

Localized: Arthritis restricted or limited to a specific joint. It is possible for arthritis to affect more than one joint and not be classified as generalized. For example, a patient may have a localized arthritis in the right wrist and left elbow, but no indications of arthritis in any other joint. This condition would not be considered generalized.

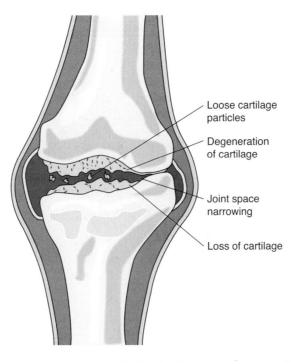

Loose cartilage particles

Degeneration of cartilage

Joint space narrowing

Loss of cartilage

Figure 8–6 Osteoarthritis, also known as degenerative joint disease, in a knee joint.

Primary: Degeneration of the joints without any known preexisting abnormality. It is sometimes referred to as idiopathic.

Secondary: Degeneration of the joints due to an identifiable initiating factor. The factors can include obesity, trauma, congenital malformations, foreign bodies, malalignments of joints, fibrosis and scarring from previous inflammatory disease or infection, metabolic or circulatory bone diseases, and iatrogenic factors such as continuous pressure put on joint surfaces during orthopedic treatment of congenital anomalies (Richard, 1994).

Internal Derangements

internal derangement
A range of injuries of the joint involving the soft tissues such as the synovium, cartilage, and ligaments.

Category code 717 classifies internal derangements of the knee, and category 718 classifies other types of internal derangements involving other joints. It is important to note that conditions of the knee not classified under category 717 may be classified under category 718. For example, a pathological dislocation of the knee is classified 718.26. The square brackets underneath each subcategory code in category 718 will tell you whether or not the code may be used for the knee. Note that some subcategory codes exclude the fifth digit of 6 for lower leg (knee). The term **internal derangement** refers to a range of injuries of the joint involving the soft tissues such as the synovium, cartilage, and ligaments. It is important to differentiate between pathology classified to 717 and 718, and acute injuries classified to sprains, strains, and other acute injuries in the Injury and Poisoning chapter, Chapter 17, of ICD-9-CM. Acute injuries of the joints are always classified to Chapter 17 even if the physician uses the term Internal derangement. The acute phase of the injury is variable depending upon the joint involved and the severity of injury, but typically lasts between two and six weeks. Conditions classifiable to categories 717 and 718 refer to lasting or old internal derangements, and most often with degenerative changes.

Arthropathy Procedures

ICD-9-CM Volume 3

A wide variety of procedures are used to treat arthropathy and many of them are found in categories 80 and 81 in ICD-9-CM Volume Three. The following is a discussion to the most common joint procedures indexed in ICD-9-CM.

Arthrotomy: Incision into a joint. This procedure may be performed to drain a joint of blood, synovial fluid, or purulence. When documented as the approach to further surgery, it should not be coded.

Arthroscopy: The viewing of a joint by means of an endoscope (arthroscope). As with arthrotomy, when the arthroscopy is used to gain entrance to a joint in order to perform further surgery, it is considered an operative approach and not coded.

Biopsy: The removal of a tissue sample for examination. When the entire lesion or tissue is removed, an excision code is used rather than a biopsy code.

Arthrodesis: The process of making a joint immobile by binding it together, usually by grafting bone or bone chips to the joint. The term is used synonymously with fusion.

Arthroplasty: An operation to restore the integrity and function of a joint. An arthroplasty may or may not involve the use of prosthetics and artificial materials.

Replacement: The removal of diseased or deranged joint tissue or bone and replacement with artificial materials, allograft, or autograft tissue.

Revision: Surgery on a joint that has already undergone a primary repair procedure. A revision may make minor repairs to the existing joint, or repeat steps of the primary repair procedure right up to a complete redo of the primary repair procedure.

CPT

CPT organizes all of its procedures in the chapter of the Musculoskeletal System according to the anatomical part, and then by the type of procedure involved. The way that the procedures are listed are fairly consistent throughout the chapter. For example, under the subheading of Forearm and Wrist, the following order of procedures is found:

- Incision
- Excision
- Introduction or Removal
- Repair, Revision, and/or Reconstruction
- Fracture and/or Dislocation
- Arthrodesis
- Amputation
- Other Procedures

Other types of procedures such as Grafts or Replantations may be added to certain anatomical sites whereas some procedure types may be eliminated from others.

It is important to note that Endoscopy/Arthroscopy is found at the end of the chapter in code range 29800–29999. CPT does not follow the same coding rules for arthroscopic procedures as for ICD-9-CM. All CPT arthroscopic procedures will be found at the end of the chapter when the operative approach is documented as arthroscopic (endoscopic). The code assigned will be chosen from this list. When a procedure is converted from endoscopic to an open procedure, the code for the endoscopic procedure may be assigned according to what was done under arthroscopy, and a separate code may be assigned for the open procedure. Some payers will require adding modifier -51 to the arthroscopy procedure to identify it as a multiple procedure performed on the same day.

A common error is that some of the arthroscopic procedures in this chapter, particularly those of the knee, are easy to unbundle (separate). The Correct Coding Initiative (CCI), developed and used by the Centers for Medicare and Medicaid Services, has many edits to prevent unbundling these codes. To begin with, all surgical endoscopies include a diagnostic endoscopy. When assigning more than one knee procedure code for a particular surgery, be sure that the additional codes are not integral parts of the main procedure. For example, code 29880 is for Arthroscopy, knee, surgical; with meniscectomy (medial and lateral) including any meniscal shaving. In reading through the operative report, you may notice mention of any or all of the following:

- Minor synovectomy
- Fat pad resection
- Articular shaving
- Removal of loose bodies
- Evacuation of debris

- Shaving of meniscus or cruciate stump
- Splinting or Casting

All of these procedures are integral parts of an arthroscopic knee meniscectomy and should not be coded and reported separately. They are all found in the CCI billing editing software as well.

EXERCISE 8–2

Assign ICD-9-CM codes, first for the diagnosis from Volumes 1 and 2, then the procedure code from Volume 3, and the CPT procedure code as indicated.

1. Acute pseudomonas infection of the left shoulder and wrist. Incision and drainage of both joints.

   ICD-9-CM _____

   ICD-9-CM Volume 3 _____ _____

   CPT _____ _____

2. Bucket handle tear of lateral meniscus, status port bicycle accident two months ago. Lateral meniscectomy with partial synovectomy and debridement of the patella under endoscopic control.

   ICD-9-CM _____

   ICD-9-CM Volume 3 _____ _____ _____

   CPT _____

3. Arthritis of the left proximal humerus due to multiple myeloma, not currently in remission. Debulking of tumor, proximal humerus.

   ICD-9-CM _____ _____

   ICD-9-CM Volume 3 _____

   CPT _____

4. Degenerative joint disease localized in both knees and hips due to morbid obesity. Bilateral total knee replacement of both knee joints.

   ICD-9-CM _____ _____ _____

   ICD-9-CM Volume 3 _____

   CPT _____

5. Internal derangement of the knee, status post bicycle accident this morning. Incision and drainage of bloody effusion of the left knee.

   ICD-9-CM _____ _____

   ICD-9-CM Volume 3 _____

   CPT _____

VERTEBRAL DISORDERS

ICD-9-CM Volume 1 code categories 720–724 classify disorders of the vertebral column (Figure 8–7) along with some other related pathology of the spinal musculature and the spinal cord and spinal roots. Acute injuries of the vertebral column are not classified here, and should be classified to Chapter 17 through the specific type of injury as referenced in the ICD-9-CM index. The terms spondylosis and spondylitis refer respectively to degeneration and inflammation of the vertebrae. Spondylarthritis is an inflammation of the vertebral articulations.

Important qualifying terms used in the subcategories for spinal arthritis include:

myelopathy
Pathology of the spinal cord due to the arthritic changes of the vertebrae. Paresthesia, loss of sensation, and loss of sphincter control are the most common forms of myelopathy.

Myelopathy: Pathology of the spinal cord due to the arthritic changes of the vertebrae. Paresthesia, loss of sensation, and loss of sphincter control are the most common forms of myelopathy.

Cervical: Referring to the seven cervical vertebrae. The first and second cervical vertebrae are also known as the atlas and axis respectively.

Thoracic: Referring to the twelve thoracic vertebrae.

Lumbar: Referring to the five lumbar vertebrae.

Sacral: Referring to a single fused bone made up of five segments.

Coccyx: Referring to a single fused bone at the end of the spinal column made up of three to five segments.

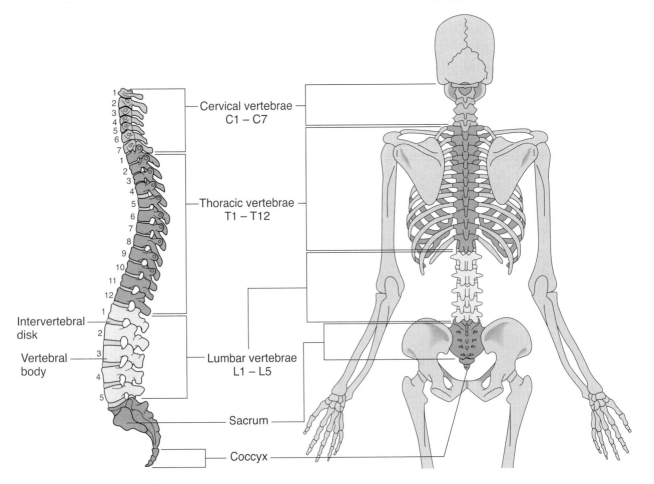

Figure 8–7 Division of a vertebral column.

Lumbosacral: Referring to one or more lumbar vertebrae in conjunction with the sacrum.

Enthesopathy: Pathology occurring at the site where muscle tendons and ligaments attach to bones or joint capsules.

Category 721 classifies degenerative spondylosis and spondylarthritis excluding those inflammatory spondylopathies of the vertebral column classified to category 720. Category 722 classifies intervertebral disk disorders. Both categories 721 and 722 have subcategories that differentiate between conditions "with myelopathy" and "without myelopathy." For coding purposes, myelopathy includes any symptomatic impingement, compression, disruption, or disturbance to the spinal cord or blood supply to the spinal cord, due to spondylosis in category 721 or intervertebral disk disorder in category 722. It is possible for a patient to have concurrently conditions classifiable to both categories 721 and 722.

Sometimes the term radiculitis or radiculopathy is confused with myelopathy in category 722. **Radiculopathy** and radiculitis are diseases and/or inflammation of the spinal nerve roots. The spinal nerves emerge from the spinal cord and can become entrapped, compressed, or irritated by diseased vertebral bodies, or more commonly, displaced intervertebral disks. Radiculopathy manifests itself almost exclusively as sensory symptoms (radicular pain or paresthesia) and/or motor symptoms (painless weakness). Radiculopathy can occur at any level, although involvement of the thoracic vertebrae and coccyx is very rare (Weiderholt, 1988). In all there are thirty-one pairs of spinal nerves; eight cervical, twelve thoracic, five lumbar, five sacral, and one coccygeal.

radiculopathy
Disease of the spinal nerve roots.

Categories 723 and 724 contain many symptomatic conditions that are excluded when used in conjunction with codes from categories 721 and 722. For example, spinal stenosis, codes 723.0 and 724.0X, are often mistakenly assigned as additional codes when the stenosis was caused by spondylosis or by narrowing of the spinal canal due to intervertebral disk displacement. Neuralgia, radiculitis, panniculitis, ankylosis, and compression of the spinal nerve roots are also symptomatic terms found here, that with a more complete review of the chart or better documentation by the physician will almost always refer back to a condition classifiable to categories 721 and 722.

Curvatures and related deformities of the spine can either be congenital (present at birth) or acquired, and ICD-9-CM classifies each type to different chapters. The congenital deformities are found classified to subcategory 756.1 with fifth digits describing the specific type of anomaly. Acquired deformities are classified to all of category 737, and codes 738.4 and 738.5. Acquired deformities may be due to a variety of etiologies including:

- Trauma
- Pathologic weakness of bone
- Degenerative joint disease
- Surgical intervention
- Congenital conditions (e.g., congenital shortness of limb, with acquired compensatory defect)
- Paralytic syndromes
- Poor posture
- Muscle spasms

The subterm "traumatic" listed in the ICD-9-CM index under the main term "Spondylolisthesis" is sometimes misinterpreted by coders. Traumatic spondylolisthesis is a congenital defect due to birth or intrauterine trauma and is classified to code 756.12. Spondylolisthesis due to acute trauma at any time after birth is classified as a current injury in Chapter 17. Spondylolisthesis as a late effect of trauma, such as due to a prior fracture of the vertebrae, is classified as acquired and should also carry the appropriate ICD-9-CM code for late effect—e.g., 905.1 as a secondary code (Richard, 1996).

Vertebral Procedures

ICD-9-CM Volume 3

In ICD-9-CM Volume 3, the three most common procedures for disorders of the vertebra are decompression of the spinal nerve root, vertebral disk excision, and spinal fusion. A decompression of the spinal nerve root is a procedure designed to relieve pressure and irritation of the root that causes radiculopathy. Code 03.09 classifies nerve root decompression without concurrent intervertebral disc excision. The procedure can be a laminotomy or an incision into one or more vertebral laminae; or a laminectomy, which is an excision of vertebral laminae, usually the posterior arch. These procedures can be modified with the prefix "foramen," meaning at the site of the aperture into the vertebral canal bounded by the pedicles of adjacent vertebrae above and below the vertebral bodies anteriorly, and the articular processes posteriorly. In procedures classifiable to 03.09, only a small amount of cartilaginous tissue is removed from around the nerve root—the disc is left essentially intact.

When the spinal root is decompressed by excision of the intervertebral disk, either in part (e.g., hemilaminectomy) or in total, code 80.51 is assigned. Code 03.09 is not assigned with code 80.51 unless a separate nerve root decompression classifiable to 03.09 is performed at a different vertebral level than an excision of intervertebral disk classifiable to 80.51. It is advisable to have the dictated operative report available when coding these procedures, as it can be difficult to differentiate between the two, and preoperative notes and pathology reports can be misleading. Chemical or enzymatic nerve root decompression is classified to code 80.52 and is rarely, if ever, performed in conjunction with procedures classified to codes 03.09 or 80.51. Also note that any facetectomy associated with a laminectomy or hemilaminectomy is not coded as it is considered an incidental part of the main surgical procedure.

Spinal fusion is the process of immobilizing two or more vertebrae by fixation or stiffening. Bones grafts and/or orthopedic hardware may be used to accomplish this task classifiable to subcategory 80.1. Fourth digits are used to identify the region of the vertebra being fused, and the technique used. If hardware is used to do the fusion or bone from a bone bank, no secondary code is necessary, but if an autograft of the patient's bone is used, a secondary code from subcategory 77.7 will be assigned to classify the harvesting of the bone for grafting.

CPT

CPT has many codes to classify spinal nerve decompression and intervertebral disc excision, and they can be found in the code range 63001–63290, Surgery/Nervous System. There are many decision points the coder must be aware of, including:

1. Was the main procedure a laminectomy, laminotomy, or diskectomy?
2. What region (lumbar, thoracic, cervical, sacral) was involved?
3. Was the main procedure accompanied by a facetectomy, foraminotomy, diskectomy, decompression of spinal cord, cauda equina and/or nerve root, myelotomy, cordotomy, or nerve section?

4. Was the procedure a primary or reexploration?

5. How many interspace levels were involved?

6. Was a concurrent arthrodesis performed?

With so many decision points and precise language used in the code narratives, it is imperative to read the descriptions and choose only the one that matches precisely what was done.

Arthrodesis is classified to the code range 22548–22812. These codes classify only the arthrodesis; additional codes are needed if a bone graft was obtained (20930–20938) or if hardware was used (22840–22855). Modifier -51 for multiple procedures are not reported with these codes as they are considered add-on procedure codes. As with ICD-9-CM, CPT classifies arthrodesis by vertebral level and by technique. If a hemidiskectomy was performed with arthrodesis by instrumentation and bone graft, four codes would need to be assigned: one for the hemidiskectomy, one for the arthrodesis, one for the bone graft, and one for the instrumentation. Arthrodesis is also considered a primary procedure if it is performed for a spinal deformity, and these codes are located in the code range 22800–22812. Note that bone grafts and instrumentation are reported in addition to these codes also.

EXERCISE 8-3

Assign ICD-9-CM codes, first for the diagnosis from Volumes 1 and 2, then the procedure code from Volume 3, and the CPT procedure code as indicated.

1. Cervical spondylosis with severe spinal cord compression. Anterior diskectomy at C1-2 with decompression of spinal cord.

   ICD-9-CM   _____

   ICD-9-CM Volume 3   _____

   CPT   _____

2. Spinal stenosis due to herniated nucleus pulposus, L1-2, with radiculitis. Foraminotomy, laminectomy, decompression of spinal nerve root L1-2 with partial resection of bony facet.

   ICD-9-CM   _____

   ICD-9-CM Volume 3   _____

   CPT   _____

3. Degenerative spondylolisthesis. Insertion of Harrington rod, anterolateral technique, dorsolumbar spine spanning four segments.

   ICD-9-CM   _____

   ICD-9-CM Volume 3   _____

   CPT   _____   _____

4. Thoracic and lumbosacral spondylosis with displacement of T10-12. Laminectomy and excision of disk at T10-11, foraminotomy and freeing of spinal nerve root at T11-12. Morcellated bone graft from left hip to posterior T10-11 and T11-12 interspaces for arthrodesis.

ICD-9-CM   _____   _____   _____

ICD-9-CM Volume 3   _____   _____   _____   _____

CPT   _____   _____   _____   _____

SPRAINS AND STRAINS

Sprains and strains of joints and adjacent muscles are classified to code category range 840–848 in ICD-9-CM. A sprain is defined as a severe stretching of a ligament with minor tears and hemorrhage, without subluxation, dislocation, or fracture. A severe sprain can result in occult joint instability. A strain is a less precise term that applies to any soft tissue injury (joint capsule, ligament, muscle, tendon) that occurs from overexertion. Strains and sprains that occur secondarily to any condition classifiable as a fracture, subluxation, or dislocation are incidental and not coded. Sprains and strains usually require only nonoperative procedures such as casting, strapping, splinting, etc., and only when there is joint instability and chronic pain will surgery be indicated.

OTHER CONDITIONS AND PROCEDURES

A few of the other more common orthopedic conditions and procedures are discussed in this section. These include malunion and nonunion of fractures, and bone infections.

Malunion and Nonunion of Fractures

These conditions classifiable to codes 733.81 and 733.82 respectively occur when fractured bones do not heal properly. A distinction needs to be made between malunion and nonunion following a traumatic or pathological fracture, and malunion and nonunion of bone following surgery. When a malunion or nonunion occurs following a fracture, codes 733.81 or 733.82 are assigned. This includes instances where there has been an open or closed reduction and an internal or external fixation. In cases where bone has been grafted for either arthrodesis or to further stabilize and strengthen a fracture site, if the grafted bone does not properly join to the graft site, this is considered a postoperative complication, and a code from the category range 996–999 should be selected such as 996.4 Mechanical complication of internal orthopedic device, implant, or graft.

    When a malunion of a fracture is surgically repaired, the most common method is to perform osteoclasis, code subcategory 78.7, along with an internal fixation with fracture reduction, code subcategories 79.1 (closed reduction) or 79.3 (open reduction) in ICD-9-CM. A small amount of debridement or excision of the bone ends may also be done. A nonunion is more likely to be repaired with an arthrodesis classifiable to subcategory range 81.0–81.2 in ICD-9-CM. As with other arthrodesis procedures, harvesting of bone for grafting should also be reported. In CPT, codes for malunion and nonunion repair are found in each anatomical subsection in the musculoskeletal system chapter under the heading "Repair, Revision, and/or Reconstruction." For example, a repair of a malunion of the tibia without a graft would be coded 27720.

Bone Infections

Acute osteomyelitis, ICD-9-CM subcategory code 730.0, is any acute or subacute infection of the bone or bone marrow. It is usually due to bacteria but can be caused by other infective agents, and is more common among children where the pathogen settles into the metaphyseal bed of the developing long bones. Chronic osteomyelitis code subcategory 730.1 is a persistent or recurring infection of the bone, and is extremely difficult to eradicate completely in the chronic stage. Periostitis is the inflammation of the periosteum, the thick fibrous membrane covering the bone surfaces except at the articular cartilage.

Common ICD-9-CM procedures for these conditions include bone biopsy subcategory code 77.4, local excision of tissue or lesion of bone subcategory code 77.6, sequestrectomy subcategory code 77.0, and bone grafts subcategory codes 78.0 and 77.7. In CPT, most procedures for bone infection will be found in each anatomical subsection in the musculoskeletal chapter under the heading "Excision." Here you will find sequestrectomy codes, as well as various types of excisions with or without grafts. There are two other CPT codes that coders should be aware of. Code 20000 and 20005 classify excisions of superficial or deep soft tissue abscesses, which sometimes accompany osteomyelitis. These codes are at the beginning of the chapter and apply to all sections in the musculoskeletal chapter.

■ *Highlight*

When coding orthopedic conditions, infections, malunion/nonunion of fractures, complications with hardware, scarring, and contractures of joints can affect the healing process of the injury. CPT modifiers -58 and -78 can make the difference between reimbursement or rejection of a claim.

- *-58 Planned staged procedures (i.e., debridements)*
- *-78 Assign to procedures due to complications of the injury*

EXERCISE 8–4

Assign ICD-9-CM codes, first for the diagnosis from Volumes 1 and 2, then the procedure code from Volume 3, and the CPT procedure code as indicated.

1. Nonunion of a bone graft to the lumbosacral fusion performed eight weeks prior to admission. Regrafting of bone fragment from the left iliac crest to the L1-S1 unstable site using posterior interbody technique.

   ICD-9-CM   _____

   ICD-9-CM Volume 3   _____   _____

   CPT   _____   _____

2. Acute osteomyelitis of the radial head due to E. coli. Sequestrectomy of radial head and debridement of surrounding muscle and fascia of the radius.

ICD-9-CM   _____   _____

ICD-9-CM Volume 3   _____   _____

CPT   _____   _____

SUMMARY

Coding for the orthopedic specialty includes fractures and dislocations, sprains and strains, and the disease processes of the musculoskeletal system and connective tissue. The orthopedic specialty is the major medical provider for work-related injuries, motor vehicle accidents, and falls. E-codes are necessary to assign with the ICD-9-CM code to describe the reason for the injury in order to determine liability for the charges. It is important to remember that both the index and the tabular list in each classification system must be referenced for accuracy. In some cases, the correct code may be classified in a different section of the code book, as in the case of congenital deformities in ICD-9-CM.

REFERENCES

American Academy of Orthopaedic Surgeons. (1996). *Complete global services data for orthopaedic surgery*. Park Ridge, IL: American Academy of Orthopaedic Surgeons.

Converse, M. (1986). *Coding clinic for ICD-9-CM*. Chicago: American Hospital Association.

Crenshaw, A. H. (2002). *Campbell's operative orthopedics*. St. Louis, MO: Mosby Year Book.

Mallon, W. J. (1990). *Orthopedics for the house officer*. Baltimore: Williams & Wilkins.

Pickett, D. (1993). *Coding clinic for ICD-9-CM*. Chicago: American Hospital Association.

Richard, E. Fractures: Now's the time to bone up on coding them. *St. Anthony's Clinic Coding and Reimbursement Newsletter*, March 1996, pp. 3–4.

Salter, R. B. (1984). *Textbook of disorders and injuries of the musculoskeletal system*. Baltimore: Williams & Wilkins.

Weiderholt, W. C. (1998). *Neurology for non-neurologists*. Philadelphia: Saunders.

Chapter 9
Cardiology and the Cardiovascular System

KEY TERMS

angioplasty
aorta
bifurcation
cardiogenic shock
cardiomyopathy
cardioversion
circumflex artery
echocardiogram (echo)
heart catheterization

ipsilateral
mitral valve
multiple gated acquisition (MUGA)
nonselective
occlusion
pacemaker
pericardium
plaque
pulmonary artery

pulmonic valve
selective catheterization
semilunar valve
stent
tricuspid valve
vascular families
ventricles

LEARNING OBJECTIVES

Upon successful completion of this module, you should be able to:

1. Recognize cardiovascular anatomy, physiology, and terminology.
2. Identify common diagnostic procedures.
3. Differentiate a diagnostic procedure from a therapeutic service.
4. Recognize nuclear cardiology procedures.

INTRODUCTION

This module introduces the many facets of modern cardiology practice. The two common service areas of care are medical (noninvasive) cardiology versus invasive (therapeutic, or interventional, and nuclear diagnostic) cardiology.

The invasive, therapeutic cardiology services are commonly performed through the percutaneous, or intravascularly, rather than the open cutting surgical procedures as seen in the cardiothoracic, cardiovascular methods.

This chapter will explore various services, procedures, and encounters that are likely to be performed by the cardiology specialty. This chapter also includes discussion of bundling issues, with accurate code selection that are unique and specific for cardiology. Table 9–1 contains common cardiology abbreviation and meanings with which a coder will need to be familiar.

Cardiology physician services often begin with an evaluation and management (E/M) visit or encounter. The services are provided at various locations, depending upon the individual physician choice, skill level, and ownership of equipment. For example, the nuclear cardiologist may

TABLE 9–1   **Common Cardiology Acronyms.**

ACVD	acute cardiovascular disease	**LAD**	left anterior descending
AICD	automatic implantable cardio-verter-defibrillator device	**LBBB**	left bundle branch block
		LV	left ventricle
AMI	acute myocardial infarction	**MVP**	mitral valve prolapse
ASHD	atherosclerotic heart disease	**MUGA**	multiple gated acquisition
BP	blood pressure	**PAD**	peripheral arterial disease
CABG	coronary artery bypass graft	**PT**	prothrombin time
CAD	coronary artery disease	**PTCA**	percutaneous transluminal coronary angioplasty
CHF	congestive heart failure		
CPR	cardiopulmonary resuscitation	**RA**	right atrium
DOE	dyspnea on exertion	**RBBB**	right bundle branch block
DVT	deep vein thrombosis	**RCA**	right coronary artery
HDL	high density lipoprotein	**RV**	right ventricle
HR	heart rate	**SOB**	shortness of breath
HTN	hypertension	**VSD**	ventricular septal defect

pericardium
Sac surrounding the heart.

choose to provide some services at the physician office location, and legally be authorized to do so. Or, due to the lack of equipment availability at the physician office, may choose to perform the same service at the hospital location (either inpatient or outpatient). The place and the level of the service may vary greatly depending upon the documented services that were provided.

During or after the initial encounter, the physician may order and/or personally perform diagnostic services. These services may use conventional radiology or other medical diagnostic testing procedures. The physician may also choose a more invasive diagnostic procedure, by inserting a catheter percutaneously (through the skin) into a vessel (arterial or venous), progressing into the coronary (heart) area, and/or other anatomical organ sites (e.g., renal) and/or peripheral (noncoronary) area. We will discuss the coding combination of each of these procedures.

Many cardiovascular codes are paired or partnered by anatomical sites with the radiological codes. The CPT codes are selected per physician and per service rendered, selecting a 'sister' component radiological code plus the diagnostic procedure code. The cardiology services typically report multiple CPT codes, potentially with multiple pages of claims.

Codes used in cardiology are found in the 30000, 70000, and 90000 series in the CPT code book, as well as the Category III CPT code series. Since cardiology is a high-tech specialty with new devices, advances in procedures, and services continuously presenting in the field, codes are updated more frequently than in other areas of the CPT. Category II tracking codes may also be selected; however, they are not required to be reported on claims at this time. Accurate code selection will require the coder to query the physician, and/or conduct research for detailed information.

Cardiology services claims may be denied if they do not meet the criteria for medical necessity, do not have FDA approval, or they may be restricted by quantity limitations. HIPAA requires that coverage be verified for any service prior to the physician performing the care, for all participating insurance plans or when accepting assignment of electronic claims. The advance beneficiary notice is then properly completed.

CARDIAC AND VASCULAR ANATOMY AND PHYSIOLOGY

The heart is a fist-sized organ that weighs approximately 250 to 350 grams. Pumping in excess of 6,800 liters of blood daily, each heartbeat results in an average expulsion of 145 ml. Its primary purpose is to supply blood to all organs and tissues as well as to furnish a pathway for nutrients, oxygen, hormones, and immunologic substances. An organ that not only delivers, it also furnishes its own clean-up function by removing tissue waste and by-products through venous blood return. The venous blood, depleted of oxygen and full of waste products, is routed through the lungs for fresh oxygenation and the clearing away of waste products.

Muscle Layers

The heart is a muscle that is extremely rich in nerves and vessels and is made up of three major layers. The outermost layer of muscle is called the epicardium. The middle layer, or myocardium, performs the contractile function. The endocardium is the innermost layer, lining the heart's inner chambers.

The Heart Sac

The outside of the heart has a thick and fibrous covering or sac called the **pericardium**. Also in multiple layers, the outer, fibrous pericardium is loose and elastic. The inner layer or serous pericardial layer is also made up of more than one layer of tissue. These are the parietal and the visceral layers. The parietal layer lines the fibrous pericardium while the visceral layers or epicardium adheres to the outside of the heart itself. The pericardial space is located between the visceral and parietal layers. It is filled with a clear fluid that lubricates the heart's surface and prevents friction or rubbing from the sac. Though normal fluid retention in this space is 10–30 ml, up to 300 ml of fluid may accumulate before the heart's contractile function is impaired. Figure 9–1 shows all the major cardiac landmarks as well as the multiple muscle layers discussed previously in this module.

Heart Chambers

Four major chambers are found in the heart. The upper two chambers, or the right and left atrium, and the lower chambers, called right and left **ventricles,** represent the four major chambers. Each is designed with a specific task and process. Figure 9–1 also displays the four distinct heart chambers. The right atrium receives systemic or deoxygenated blood from the extremities through the inferior and superior vena cavae (inferior drains the lower body, and the superior drains the upper regions). The right ventricle is divided into inflow and outflow tracts to account for the progress of the blood through this chamber. In the left atrium, oxygenated blood is returned fresh from the lungs. From here, the blood is expelled into the left ventricle. The left ventricle possesses the thickest and most muscular walls in order to propel fresh blood out into the blood's circulatory pathway throughout the body.

Heart Valves

Two atrioventricular valves and two semilunar valves are found inside the heart's vessels and chambers. The atrioventricular (AV) valves are the **tricuspid,** or three-leafed valve, and the bicuspid (**mitral**) or two-leafed valve. The **semilunar valves** are the **pulmonic valves.** These valves are called semilunar due to their resemblance to the shape of the moon (see Figure 9–2).

ventricles
The two lower chambers of the heart are called the ventricles. The right ventricle is two to three times thinner in muscle tissue than the left ventricle. The greater thickness and muscle mass of the left chamber is necessary to exert enough pressure and force to propel blood into systemic circulation.

tricuspid valve
Diametrically larger and thinner than the mitral valve, three separate leaflets or cusps are found in this critical valve. The anterior, posterior and septal leaflets are competent only if the right ventricle's lateral wall functions correctly. The septal leaflet is attached to the interventricular septum and is in close proximity to the AV node.

mitral valve
A two-leafed or cusped valve shaped like a bishop's miter (head covering), this valve is located between the left atrium and left ventricle. Considered an atrioventricular valve, the mitral opens when the atria contract and sends blood into the ventricles. When the ventricles contract, pressure is exerted on the leaflets causing them to balloon upward toward the atria.

semilunar valve
Named for its resemblance to the shape of the moon, the pulmonic and aortic valves are semilunar in shape.

pulmonic valve
A three-leaflet valve, the pulmonic is another semilunar valve. It is situated between the right ventricle and the pulmonary artery. During heart contractions, internal pressure forces this valve to open. Loss of pressure during diastole (heart relaxation) allows the valve to close.

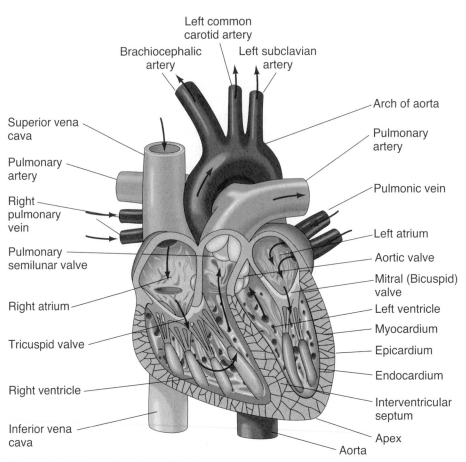

Figure 9–1 Coronal section of the heart.

The Cardiac Cycle

During a cardiac cycle, two phases occur. They are systole and diastole. In diastole, there are two phases. Phase one of diastole occurs when the atria contract and force the AV valves to open. About 70 percent of the blood is expelled from the atria into the relaxed ventricles. Phase two of diastole involves a slowing of blood flow until accelerated atrial contraction forces any remaining blood into the ventricles. In systole, ejection of the blood occurs. Phase one forces the AV valves to snap shut and ventricles begin the contractile phase of the ventricles. When pressure in the ventricles is greater than that in the aorta, the semilunar valves open and blood is expelled into the pulmonary artery and the aorta. As the contraction phase subsides, the muscles of the ventricles relax and intraventricular pressure decreases.

Major Cardiac Vessels

The heart receives its blood supply from the coronary arteries. Major coronary vessels include the right coronary artery, and two major left coronaries: the left anterior descending (LAD) and the **circumflex artery**. **Occlusion** or obstruction of blood flow to any of these vessels due to thrombus or **plaque** deposits can result in a myocardial infarction, or heart attack. Blood circulates throughout the coronary vasculature all during the cardiac cycle but is decreased with systole and increased during diastole. Figure 9–3 shows the position and location of the

circumflex artery
A branch of the LCA (left coronary artery), this artery supplies the left atrium of the heart, the rear surfaces of the left ventricle and the rear portion of the heart's dividing wall or septum.

occlusion
Blockage or obstruction by thrombus or plaque deposits within a blood vessel or passageway.

plaque
Soft deposits of fatty substances that harden with time and produce rocklike obstructions within vessels. Plaque production occurs due to high-fat dietary intake, sedentary lifestyles, and hereditary tendencies in patients with progressive atherosclerosis.

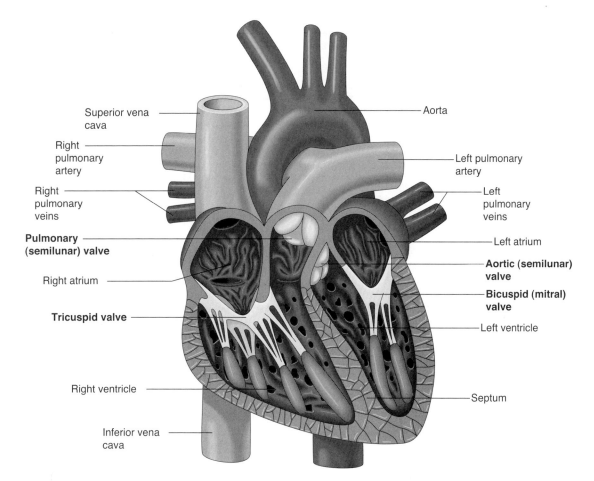

Figure 9–2 Internal view of the heart showing the heart valves, pulmonary arteries and veins.

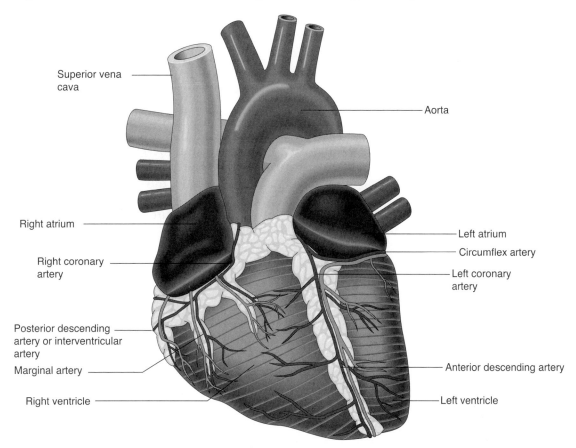

Figure 9–3 Major cardiac vessels of the heart.

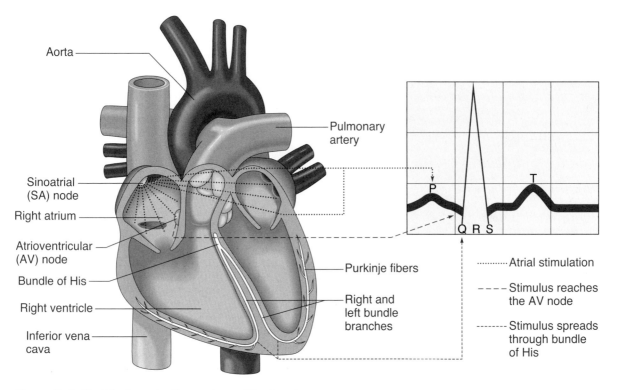

Figure 9–4 Electrical conduction system of the heart.

major vessels previously discussed in this module. Major vessels branching off the aortic arch at the top of the heart are the left common carotid, the left sub-clavian, and the brachiocephalic.

Electrical Conduction Pathway

The heart is a rich electrical conduction relay mechanism. Specialized tissue is scattered strategically throughout the cardiac anatomy designed to relay impulses that provoke the contractile action of the pump. The sinoatrial (SA) node is known as the heart's natural pacemaker. From here, impulses travel over the conduction paths to the atrioventricular (AV) node. The impulse is then transmitted to the Bundle of His and terminate at the Purkinje fibers. Figure 9–4 illustrates the con-duction pathway.

EXERCISE 9–1

1. Name the two phases of the cardiac cycle. _____

2. Name the three layers of heart muscle. _____

3. Semilunar valves are so-named because they resemble the shape of the _____.

ICD-9-CM CODE SELECTION

- How is the code for screening cardiology examinations and testing selected?
- How is the code for combination diseases selected?
- How is the code when converting open procedures selected?
- How is the ICD-9-CM code for multiple services linked to multiple CPT codes submitted on the same claim (commonly 8–10 CPT codes per case)?

The following section presents guidelines for understanding the unique code selection for cardiology.

Official Coding Guidelines

As previously covered, the Official Coding Guidelines for ICD-9-CM are published by the NCHS, a division of DHHS, with a team from the AHA, AHIMA, and CMS. Effective April 1, 2005, this coding curriculum references the ICD-9-CM guidelines in its cardiology chapter. Codes must always reference the most current edition, as the code selection logic may change with each new update, especially when the ICD-10-CM is introduced.

Hypertension

The Hypertension Table should be reviewed with all of your clinical staff. By taking time for this simple task, you will improve upon the documentation and the proper code selection for your practice. The Hypertension Table is located in the Index, Volume 2 areas of the ICD-9-CM code book. There are extensive combination codes to be considered.

> **Essential Hypertension, Not Otherwise Specified 401.X:** The fourth digit is selected based upon the documentation indicating Malignant essential hypertension 401.0 or Benign essential hypertension 401.1.

Coding Tip *If the documentation is lacking, query the physician and request the documentation to be updated accurately. In order to select a Hypertension diagnosis code, the documentation must support the code selection per the options available. Do not simply select the 401.9 code for all cases.*

> **Hypertension with Heart Disease (An example of the combination ICD-9-CM code concept):** When the documentation in the chart:

- states "due to hypertension" *or* the due-to cause is implied, the codes are selected from 402 area instead of 425.8, 429.XX.
- does not state "due to hypertension" *or* implied, select both the Hypertension and the Heart disease codes.
- states "heart failure," select another code for the type.
- states CHF plus other systolic or diastolic failure, select additional codes.

The ICD-9-CM guidelines direct to select the ICD-9-CM code from the documentation in the medical record. If the practice uses an encounter capture form, the information must match the medical record indications for hypertension. Double checking the medical record is encouraged for accurate code selection and claim submission implementing the HIPAA rules for transaction and data sets.

Hypertensive Renal Disease with Chronic Renal Failure 403.XX: Early in the care, the physician may have a provisional diagnosis (rule out R/O, chronic renal failure versus acute renal disease, etc.).

- This logic is different from the previous Hypertension with Heart Disease concept. Here, the renal failure with hypertension <u>is</u> coded as Hypertensive renal disease.
- One code indicates both the Hypertensive renal disease and the CRF.

Hypertensive Heart and Renal Disease 404.XX: When the documentation in the chart:

- states both hypertensive renal disease and hypertensive heart disease
- states hypertension with renal disease, it <u>is</u> coded as Hypertensive heart and renal disease.
- states heart failure, select another code for the type.
- states CHF plus other systolic or diastolic failure, select additional codes.

Hypertensive Cerebrovascular Disease (Sequencing and prioritizing concept)

- Cerebrovascular disease code is first selected 430–438.XX.
- Additional code for the hypertension is selected.

Hypertension Retinopathy

- Hypertensive retinopathy is first selected 362.XX.
- Additional code for the hypertension is selected.

Hypertension, Secondary

- The underlying reason is first selected.
- Additional code for the hypertension is selected.

Hypertension, Transient: Transient means it comes and goes, not consistently found. Often this is the diagnosis early in the treatment plan.

- Elevated B/P 796.2 is selected unless diagnosed with hypertension previously.
- Pregnancy hypertension that is transient is 642.3XX. This may be indicated on the specific encounter, not necessarily on all claims.

Hypertension, Controlled: When the physician is caring for this disease and the treatment is controlling the hypertension adequately, select one code from 401–405 area.

Hypertension, Uncontrolled

- When the treatment is not effective, if the patient is noncompliant and it is affecting the hypertension, or is simply not responsive, select a code based upon the type of hypertension.
- Review of the medical record is advised for this coding.

Elevated B/P 796.2: If the physician has not yet diagnosed the patient with hypertension, select 796.2 for as many encounters as documented. It is up to the physician to diagnose the patient with the illness/disease. This determination of the definitive diagnosis may occur over an extensive period, not necessarily during one encounter or visit.

Injury and Poisoning

Code selection is a bit different for injuries with damage to blood vessels. First, the primary injury must be determined. Ask is the injury to the blood vessels or other anatomy? The code is selected based upon this primary fact.

Primary injury to the blood vessel (inferior vena cava per gunshot wound homicide), the first code is the Injury to the blood vessel 900–904. The second code may describe the incident or cause (gunshot wound), the E code describing the injury. The code selection is based upon the documentation.

Primary injury to RT thigh, and the common femoral artery, the first code is the RT thigh injury, second code is the Blood vessel 900–904, and third code is the E code describing the injury.

Classification of Factors Influencing Health Status and Contact with Health Service

History

Both the personal history of illness and the family history are commonly selected for cardiovascular disease. There are not specific codes for every possible type of medical history.

Personal history indicates the condition is past, the patient is no longer receiving treatment, there is a potential for recurrence, and continued monitoring of the care is required.

Family history codes are selected when documented, and the family history may cause a higher risk of illness for the patient.

Screening

In caring for the cardiology patient, medical tests and procedures will be frequently performed, providing the information for the physician to determine the definitive diagnosis. Screening services may be performed to review specific diagnoses, or age groups per statistical findings. Insurance plans policies may further guide the patient and/or physician to request the performance of screening services.

Services provided to rule out, confirm suspicions, or compile findings from various signs and symptoms that have presented for the patient will require codes. The codes are selected from the Ill-Defined Signs and Symptoms chapter, *not* from the screenings for the rule out purpose. Select a code for the documented sign or symptom. Do not select a code as though the patient has the illness, disease, or condition purpose.

When an office visit for other illness is performed, which includes a screening service, add the screening code in addition to the illness.

When a screening service is part of another screening, do not report two codes; for example, B/P checks when providing a routine physical.

When an illness is determined and treated during a screening visit, the screening is the first code and the finding is the second code. This is a key concept rule that is required to be implemented accurately.

Follow-Up

The follow-up codes are selected for ongoing care after the treatment has been completed and symptoms no longer exist.

Code the follow-up as the first code, with the history of _____ as the second code.

■ *Highlight*

If the illness recurs, the illness code rather than the follow-up code is used first.

Chronic illness code selection does not utilize the follow-up concept.

Donor

Cardiac transplantation donor codes are selected from the V59 area for the donor claim, not the recipient claim.

Counseling

There are many details to consider when selecting ICD-9-CM codes for counseling services, frequently presenting for the care of cardiology patients and the continuity of care. When counseling is affecting the care of the patient and/or the treatment plan, a code is selected. The codes are also reported on the patient's claim if the counseling is provided for the family or caregiver.

Nonspecific V codes

When a patient is awaiting an organ transplant, the code is V49.83.

Aftercare may be listed as the primary code for hospital admissions. The aftercare codes are not yet accepted as primary codes for outpatient or physician services and may only be listed as second or subsequent codes. The aftercare codes are covered medical benefits for many insurance plans.

Misadventures and Complications of Care Guidelines

The E870–876 codes are reported when the documentation indicates an incident occurred. Some examples of misadventures are:

- Blood vessels are "nicked" during an operative session.
- While using a power injector, [something] occurred.

When the documentation reflects scenarios of an incident, add an E code to the other diagnosis codes.

The E878–879 codes are reported when the documentation indicates an abnormal reaction or complication occurs. The devices could fail, for example, or the tissue might be rejected.

The other area of the ICD-9-CM codes that may be considered for current incidents or complications of procedures will be found in the 996 area of the code book. For example, when the physician is providing care within a postoperative time period, due to complications, the ICD-9-CM code must be linked properly. The use of 996 chapter codes will affect the reimbursement.

Diagnostic Coding and Reporting Guidelines for Outpatient Services

While sequencing of the ICD-9-CM codes are standard throughout the guidelines, there are other distinct rule variances between hospital and physician office location code selection. Most noticeable, the provisional diagnosis (work-up) that is commonly provided by physicians requires the selection of a code describing the signs and symptoms. Hospital code selection does not follow this rule.

■ *Highlight*

Have you ever heard "Never use rule out code selection"? This concept is gained from information using the Hospital location code selection criteria. The proper code selection for physician services when the documentation states rule-out versus considering multiple possible diagnoses is the Signs and Symptoms ICD-9-CM codes. It is perfectly fine for the physician to chart rule out; however, it would be improper to select the ICD-9-CM code as though the patient has the disease prior to the definitive diagnosis.

ICD-9-CM Code for the Diagnosis, Condition, Problem, or Other Reason for Encounter/Visit

First select a code for the chiefly responsible reason for the visit or encounter. The code is frequently a sign/symptom until it is confirmed by the physician.

Then, select additional codes for coexisting conditions. Remember to use the proper combination coding for cardiology when multiple organs or illnesses are present.

Chronic Diseases

The chronic illness code is selected each date of service the physician has documented treatment for that illness. Otherwise, the chronic disease ICD-9-CM code is not selected and not reported on the claim, even if the illness continues.

Coding Tip *The selection and the reporting of chronic illness ICD-9-CM code might occur when the documentation reflects the treatment of the illness or is affecting the treatment plan, per specific date of the encounter. Just because a patient has a chronic illness does not justify the need to report an ICD-9-CM code by every physician that cares for the patient. There may be pressure to revise this code selection principle.*

Code All Documented Conditions That Coexist

Other illnesses that are present at the time of the visit, with documentation that treatment occurred, would have additional codes selected. If not treated or not documented, do not select additional codes. The "History of" codes are selected as additional codes whenever associated to the care for that particular date.

Patients Receiving Diagnostic Services Only

This code rule commonly applies for cardiology services when the patient receives a diagnostic test and no additional professional care on the same date.

If the diagnostic test is immediately read (interpreted) with the written report, select the code for the definitive diagnosis located in the report. Additional pretest signs and symptoms are not selected. If the report does not indicate the definitive diagnosis and additional testing is ordered, then select the signs and symptoms.

Patients Receiving Therapeutic Services Only

Also common for cardiology is radiation therapy (nuclear cardiography) and cardiac rehabilitation encounters. These require the code selection to prioritize the sequence, first the V code for therapeutic services, followed by the reason for the care today, or illness code.

Pre-Op Evaluations Only

When the patient has a preoperative EKG, the first code is V72.8, with the second code the reason for the surgery. Then the codes are listed for the findings.

The preoperative EKG may be bundled into the admission services and not reimbursed by the insurance plan. Before performing the service, contact the insurance plan to determine the benefits and, if necessary, properly complete the ABN.

EXERCISE 9–2

echocardiogram (echo)
A noninvasive test that evaluates the interior of the heart and its major vessels by means of ultrasonic beams bouncing images off the structures and vessels in the heart via a transducer. The echoes or beams are transmitted to a monitor for the mapping of the heart's function, size, shape, blood flow, etc. Three common techniques are used: Doppler ultrasounds, color-flow mapping, and 2D/M Mode.

1. Patient is scheduled for quarterly **echocardiogram (echo)**. As per chart, she has a history of taking Phen-Phen for a weight loss program. Patient will see the physician later in the week to review the results and discuss the treatment plan.

   Echocardiogram: Normal and no change from previous test

   Select the proper ICD-9-CM codes _____

2. The patient is diagnosed with cardiac hypertrophy, largely due to the hypertension. CHF. B/P 155/85 sitting. Continued treatment plan, see again in three weeks.

   Select the proper ICD-9-CM codes _____

CPT

CPT codes are selected to describe and report the work performed in cardiology, using codes from the 30000, 70000, 90000, and Category III chapters of CPT. Many laboratory and additional diagnostic tests may be ordered, identifying the medical indication for the ordering of the study, all utilizing accurate code selection.

Evaluation and Management

The Centers for Medicare and Medicaid Services (CMS) publishes information for the federally funded programs (Medicare retirement and disability, Railroad, Medicaid, TRICARE, and Federal employee plans). The Evaluation and Management 1995 and 1997 guidelines were created in partnership between CMS and AMA for the documentation and code selection of encounters or visits. The rules state that per encounter the physician may choose to perform either the 1995 or the 1997 Evaluation and Management guidelines. Within each of the guideline sets, there is the option to provide the problem-focused to comprehensive level general multisystem examination (head-to-toe concept) or specialty examination (including cardiovascular), along with the history and medical decision-making components. The AMA CPT publication is similar to the 1995 guidelines located in the front of CPT in the Evaluation and Management Guidelines pages. It is necessary to review the E/M chapter for further guidance and clarification of the specific criteria required for the code selection.

Selection of the proper series of codes in the CPT code book starts according to place of service. For cardiology, place of service is very important and will affect the reimbursement dramatically. If services are provided at multiple locations within the same date (midnight to midnight) the guidelines for each code series will direct the coder regarding the code bundling. For example, when an E/M service is performed at the physician office location, and later on the same date the patient is admitted into the hospital, only one E/M code is selected, the Hospital admit code 99221-223, using the criteria from all locations.

Consultation encounters (whether provided at the physician office or other locations) have very detailed criteria for documentation and code selection. The criteria are:

- An opinion or advice *regarding a specific problem* is requested by another physician or professional. "Cardiology consult" is not satisfactory; the specific illness/disease or symptom needs to be documented in the request.

- A consultant may initiate diagnostic treatment at the encounter. "I'll schedule the patient for PTCA" indicates the consultant has assumed the care without the treatment transition authorized by the sending/requesting physician, and is not correct criteria.

- A consultant provides a written report to the requesting physician so that physician may manage the care for the specific problem. "For _____ (this illness/disease) my recommendations for you are _____. Let me know if I can further assist you with the care of this patient" nicely describes a consultation service.

- A consultant does not assume the management of the condition. "I'll see the patient again in three days" does not meet the consultation criteria, and suggests the consultant has assumed partial transfer of care for this illness.

The Evaluation and Management chapter guidelines in CPT provide more details regarding the true definitions of consultation and the required documentation.

Critical care services also have criteria for documentation and specific concepts. These codes are frequently selected for cardiology care.

Critical care is the direct care of the critically ill, managing vital organ system failure. High complexity decision making needs to be documented, along with the "time in and time out" per episode. The total critical care time (unit/floor time) for the date, midnight to midnight, is then added for the selection of the code. Critical care codes are *not* selected based upon the location of the service, and may be provided at any site. Management of noncritical care and no vital organ system deterioration is reported with the E/M codes, and not the critical care.

Critical care codes 99291–92 are selected based upon thirty-minute increments. For example, 105 minutes on one date is coded as:

> 99291 × 1 units
> 99292 × 2 units
> 99223–25 × 1
> 31500 Intubation, emergency

If the diagnosis codes vary per line, link them appropriately for the actual services rendered.

When critical care codes are selected and reported on the claim in addition to any other E/M services provided by the same physician, modifier -25 may be required. Any additional surgical or other procedure codes may also be reported with the exception of this list of included services:

> 93561–62 Interpretation of cardiac output measurements or Blood gases results
> 71010, 15, 20 Chest x-rays
> 94760, 61, 62 Pulse oximetry
> 99000 Diagnostic data stored in computers (EKG, BP)
> 43752, 91105 Gastric intubation
> 92953 Temporary transcutaneous pacing
> 36000, 36410, 36415, 36540, 36600 Vascular access procedures

■ Highlight

- *For the emergency placement of endotracheal tube by laryngoscopy, select only the code for the ET tube placement. The reason for the placement must be documented.*
- *Management and direction of CPR as a nonattending physician code selection is 92950. The time for this service is not included in the critical care time.*
- *Routine monitoring is part of critical care services; do not select additional monitoring codes. If significant review and monitoring is required, document the time specifically required for the service.*
- *Ventilation management and CPAP are included in critical care services.*

Prolonged physician services with direct patient contact are also likely to be selected for cardiology services. These are selected when documentation reflects the additional time for management of the history, exam, or medical decision making beyond the usual care. This series of codes is not reported for the counseling or coordination of care concepts that may also present. Again, the time in and time out needs to be documented. The code selection process is similar to the critical care, in that all time provided for the date is added together to select the code. However, unlike critical care services, for prolonged services all additional services and procedures would also be coded and reported on the claim.

> 105 minutes is coded as:
> 99354 × 1
> 99355 × 2
> 99213 (no modifiers are used)
> 36000 Vascular access

The details of accurate coding will dramatically affect the reimbursement for cardiology services. The remainder of the CPT codes within the E/M chapter is also likely to be provided by the physician caring for cardiology patients.

90000 SERIES OF CPT

Cardiography

Many diagnostic tools may be used to evaluate and assess various vessels, mitral, tricuspid, pulmonic, or semilunar valves, electrical pathways, and the heart muscle. Furthermore, some diagnostic procedures naturally progress to therapeutic intervention, as explored later.

Electrocardiograms (ECG according to CPT, or EKG) are performed by physicians of various specialties to assess the heart's electrical activity patterns. Used for monitoring and evaluating many cardiovascular diseases, ECGs are especially helpful with congenital heart disease, congestive heart failure, arrhythmias, myocardial infarctions (MI, aka heart attack), and valvular problems. In addition to performing 12-lead ECGs in the office and hospital setting, telephonic or computer transmission of rhythm strips may be performed.

The codes are selected based upon the type of ECG and whether the physician has documented the interpretation and report or simply a "tracing." A tracing is simply a strip that is generated out of the ECG machine. The ECG may be a 12-lead (wires) or less attached to the patient with an electrode patch.

When the physician monitors a patient connected to the ECG for extended time, in addition to the performance of the strip with the interpretation and report, select the Prolonged codes or Stand-by code, as applicable, plus the ECG code.

Coding Tip *When reporting the G0344 exam, select G0366 for Routine EKG, 12 leads with interpretation and report, or G0367 or 68 indicating without the report. The 93000 ECG code is not reported with the Welcome to Medicare exam, if the EKG is performed for screening purposes.*

▬ Highlight

The index does not reflect the abbreviations of EKG or ECG. The quickest use of the index is to look up the term electrocardiography.

Type of recording
Most common EKG is Evaluation

ECGs are an inherent component of another commonly performed study, the treadmill or stress test. Exercise or medications may be used to "stress" the heart while monitoring the activity. The use of medications during the testing is known as pharmacological stress testing. The medications may be administered via various routes, commonly given orally or intravenously. Maximal pushes the heart to the maximum degree of performance, and submaximal is just under the patient's potential maximum performance zone.

Drugs and/or radionuclides may be administered during the testing to provide diagnostic information for the physician. Thallium or technetium is commonly used.

Stress testing codes are also selected based upon whether the physician provides the interpretation and report or simply the tracing.

The Pulmonary function service 94621 includes the stress test. Code 93015 is not used.

■ Highlight

Stress tests include access for IV and infusion service and EKG strips. Additional HCPCSII codes are selected for the medications if purchased by the physician.

Monitoring may also include 24-hour recordings, with various levels of analyses. The codes are matched specifically to the services that are being rendered per physician.

Refer to Table 9–2 for common echocardiogram combination options involving multiple CPT codes.

Echocardiography

Using echocardiography, the ultrasonic signals bounce off of the heart structure, for the evaluation of blood flow, and directional and valvular function. The procedure has relatively minimal risk, is noninvasive, and the equipment has much better visualization as the technology has improved.
   Echocardiography is a two-dimensional (2D) or Doppler ultrasound of:

- cardiac chambers
- valves
- great vessels
- pericardium

For the transthoracic echo, a probe or wandlike device is passed over the chest area, where lotion has been applied. The transesophageal echo is a bit more complex, usually with an endoscopic instrument probe (or perhaps video camera) swallowed or intranasally introduced to evaluate the heart valves, chambers, and vessels. The codes are selected by the anatomical site and purpose, and then by the

TABLE 9–2   **Echocardiography Diagnostics.**

Type of Echocardiogram	Description
TTE echocardiogram for congenital anomalies	Echocardiogram, complete, for congenital anomalies
	Echocardiogram, limited, for congenital anomalies
TTE echocardiogram for normal structures	Echocardiogram, complete, real-time with image documentation (2D) with or without M-Mode recording
	Echocardiogram, limited, real-time with image documentation (2D) with or without M-Mode recording
TEE for normal cardiac structures	Echocardiography, transesophageal, complete, real-time with image documentation (2D) (with or without M-Mode recording); including probe placement, image acquisition, interpretation, and report
	Placement of transesophageal probe only
	Image acquisition, interpretation and report only
TEE for congenital anomalies	Echocardiography, transesophageal, for congenital cardiac anomalies; including probe placement, image acquisition, interpretation, and report
	Placement of transesophageal probe only
	Image acquisition, interpretation, and report only
Doppler echo	Doppler echocardiography, pulsed and/or continuous wave with spectral display, complete
	Doppler echocardiography, pulsed and/or continuous wave with spectral display, limited
Color-flow mapping	Doppler color-flow velocity mapping
TTE stress echocardiography	Echocardiography, real-time with image documentation (2D) with or without M-Mode recording, during rest and cardiovascular stress test using treadmill, bicycle exercise, and/or pharmacologically induced stress, with interpretation, and report

aorta
The main arterial trunk within the circulatory system. All other arteries, except the pulmonary artery, are branches off of this main channel. This vessel originates in the left ventricle of the heart and passes upward toward the neck. The carotid (major artery to the brain) and the coronary (major artery to the heart) are branches of the aorta. Blood that has been cleaned and freshly oxygenated flows through the aorta to the various body organs.

type of the echo (complete or limited). There are two anatomical sites, transthoracic (TTE) or transesophageal (TEE). The first, TTE, is topically performed recording through the chest wall and skin. The TEE is performed with an endoscopic instrument probe swallowed or intranasally introduced to capture the study. The abbreviations look very similar and may sound similar when the physician dictates and the operative notes are transcribed. If the operative procedure describes the endoscopic work, there may be a typographical error, indicating the wrong echo service. Query the physician if the notes look inaccurate.

Documentation for the 93307 Transthoracic echo (TTE) will reflect 2D and M-mode examination requirements, which are:

- All four chambers of the heart
- The aortic, mitral, and tricuspid valves
- The pericardium
- Adjacent portions of the **aorta**
- Complete functional and anatomic evaluation

- Measurements recorded or the reason not visualized
- Included as seen, pulmonary veins and arteries, pulmonic valve, and the inferior vena cava

If all of the previous components are not documented or provided, the *limited echo code* is selected. The permanent pertinent images, videotape, or digital data report and interpretation for the limited echo includes relevant findings including quantitative measurements and any recognized abnormalities.

Documentation Requirements

If the permanent recordings are not available, the echocardiography codes are not selected at all. All echos must document:

- Thorough evaluation of organ or anatomic region
- Image documentation
- Final written report of interpretation

Echocardiography may progress to obtain a Doppler pulsed or continuous wave or color-flow mapping study using the same equipment, providing additional information for diagnosis. The Doppler color-flow mapping evaluates the valvular diameters, flow volumes, and pressure gradients. Documentation for the medical necessity reason for these additional studies is required, and must link the proper ICD-9-CM code for each test. Select a code for all three tests, the echo, Doppler, and the mapping, when documentation is present.

▬ *Highlight*

If medical necessity is not indicated and the Doppler or mapping is provided for screening purposes, the advance beneficiary notice must be properly completed prior to providing the studies. The patient is financially obligated for noncovered screening services.

Additional procedures are coded when performed with an echo, such as stress testing or other radiological services. Modifier -51 for multiple procedures is attached to any codes that are not add-on (+) indicated.

A9700 Echo contrast or C9122 Perflutren lipid echo contrast material is the HCPC-SII code to select when the supplies are purchased and provided by the physician.

 Coding Tip

Look up Echocardiography
Then type TTE or TEE

Less commonly performed is the intravascular ultrasound study for diagnostic purposes. The codes for this procedure are 92978–79.

EXERCISE 9–3

1. TEE is the acronym for _____. TTE stands for _____.

2. Holter monitors are worn for at least _____ hours.

3. When coding for congenital cardiac anomalies, coders should take care that the _____ code matches and links to the appropriate CPT code category.

4. Read the following medical report for an echocardiography study, then assign the correct ICD-9-CM and CPT codes.

PATIENT: Adrian Babb

DOB: 06/11/1933

HOSPITAL #: 32116897

PHYSICIAN: Jason Finkle, DO

DATE: July 15, 1999

CLINICAL INDICATION: This is a 66-year-old female recently presenting to Memorial Hospital with congestive heart failure and new onset atrial fibrillation. She is here for assessment of mitral regurgitation after treatment with Betapace and reversion to sinus rhythm. However, the patient is now back in atrial fibrillation with moderate to fast response and is still taking Betapace and Coumadin.

STUDIES PERFORMED: Evaluation includes 2-D transthoracic echocardiography, color-flow imaging, and Doppler exam, and is technically adequate.

IMPRESSION:

1. Technically adequate study.

2. Overall left ventricular size is mildly dilated with normal wall thickness with diastolic function to assess because of atrial fibrillation. Overall systolic function appears to be at the lower limit of normal with an ejection fraction of 50% though evaluation is somewhat difficult because of the fast irregular rhythm. Segmental evaluation reveals no gross abnormality though the septum is difficult to assess in terms of its function and the posterior wall is not seen. However, other walls appear to contract normally.

3. Right ventricular size is normal with normal wall thickness and normal overall right ventricular function.

4. There is mild right atrial enlargement and moderate left atrial enlargement.

5. Valvular structures: The aortic valve is a normal structure without stenosis or regurgitation. The mitral valve is a normal structure without stenosis or prolapse and there is a 1+, mild mitral regurgitation. The tricuspid valve is a normal structure with stenosis with trace to 1+, trace to mild tricuspid regurgitation.

6. There is no pericardial effusion. No gross intracardiac mass or thrombus is appreciated; however, left atrial appendage is never completely visualized.

7. Inferior vena cava collapsibility is normal, indicating normal right atrial pressure. Pulmonary artery pressure is normal.

CONCLUSION: Echocardiography reveals the patient to be back in atrial fibrillation with overall fairly well-preserved right and left ventricular

continues

systolic function though left ventricular function is somewhat difficult to assess and mild decrease in ejection fraction cannot be excluded. Diastolic function could not be assessed. There is only mild mitral regurgitation at this time. Right-sided pressures are normal.

Hard copy data is printed.

Jason Finkle, DO

ICD-9-CM code(s) _____

CPT code(s) _____

Invasive and/or Interventional Procedures

Sometimes, the ECG, or echocardiography, services do not provide the information for the diagnosis, or the physicians may choose to perform a more aggressive interventional, therapeutic procedure. The therapy is selected based upon the specific issue or illness. For example, the electrical impulses may need **cardiogenic shock,** forcing the patient's electrical impulses back into a normal sinus rhythm, controlled pattern. This procedure may be referred to as **cardioversion** or defibrillation, depending upon the chamber of the heart that is corrected and/or the equipment or procedure rendered.

cardiogenic shock
An abnormal and often critical body state resulting in inadequate supplies of oxygen to the body's organs and tissues because of heart failure.

cardioversion
An electric shock to the heart muscle, which helps to convert an arrhythmia into a normal or sinus rhythm.

Cardiac Catheterization

When the physician is evaluating illness or disease within the coronary area (the heart), a cardiac catheterization or angiogram may be performed. These procedures begin with an access or introduction of a specialized catheter through the skin, manipulating and feeding the catheter into the heart anatomy and conducting multiple professional services while the catheter is in place. The catheterization is typically visually reviewed on a screen, may be recorded using various storage of data processes, and captures anatomical measurements while in place. The catheter may also be used to obtain blood samples or measure blood gases.

The 93501 series of CPT are for the heart (coronary, within or around the heart) catheterization procedures. The cardiac catheterization procedures often begin as a diagnostic procedure, while during the same session the care may progress to therapeutic or surgical care.

The catheterization procedures include:

- Local anesthesia of the access site
- If the CPT code has the conscious sedation symbol, then sedation is included
- Access or introduction of the catheter by percutaneous (puncture of needle or catheter) or cutdown (small incision over the vessel) method (however, not the injection services; power injectors are additionally coded)
- Positioning and repositioning of the catheter within the postoperative time
- Recording of intracardiac and intravascular pressure
- Obtaining blood samples for gases or dilution

- Measurements of cardiac outputs including electrode placement
- Routine catheter removal, simple closure of the site
- Final interpretation and report

1. Code series 93501. The access may be into the vein, artery, or both depending upon the procedure. When the documentation reflects only the **selective catheterization** service, without the cardiac catheterization procedure, only the access codes from 36011–18 are selected and reported. The uses of the 93501–566 codes include the access catheterization along with the previous recordings.

   The codes in the 93501–566 are modifier -51 exempt and most have the conscious sedation included symbol. Additional HCPCS II modifiers are applied for:

   LC left circumflex, coronary artery

   LD left anterior descending artery

   RC right coronary artery

   RT right

   LT left

   If the insurance plan does not accept describing the anatomical sites with the HCPCSII modifier codes of LC, LD, or RC, the modifier -59 with RT/LT may be required.

selective catheterization
The procedure of feeding or gently guiding and manipulating the catheter into a specific branch of the blood vessel or anatomy.

Coding Tip *The catheterization codes are selected by determining the access and the final destination of the tip of the placement of the catheter. As you read the report, make a note regarding each area and the specific services that are documented. This will guide you for the multiple code selection that is common. Watch to see if the tip is pulled back and inserted into another vessel of the exact same vascular family or another vascular family. If along the way, the physician cuts, injects, or performs additional professional services, it is possible that more codes may be considered. After you have your notes, then compare to the codes, the CPT guidelines, and finally the insurance bundling rules.*

2. After you have selected the catheterization access code, then determine if the physician also provided an injection angiography service from the 93539 series of codes. Select the code from this series only one time per cardiac catheterization.

3. After you have selected the injection angiography service, then determine if the physician also provided the supervision and interpretation for the radiology services from the 93555 series of codes for the guidance (retrograde) during the procedure. The additional codes from 93555 or 56 are used.

4. Was anything else performed or supplies provided by the physician? Radioelements placed or injections of other items? Any other procedures beyond the coronary territory?

Coding Tip *Cardiac Catheterization*

Then select a code for the anatomical site per tip of the catheter—the final destination point.

■ *Highlight*

stent

Following the dilation of an artery, usually by means of balloon angioplasty, the stent is loaded on a special catheter with an expandable balloon. Both devices are threaded into a guide catheter and threaded to the occlusion site. The cardiologist then positions and deploys the stent by expanding the balloon. The stent is composed of a meshlike material that assists in keeping the vessel open and clear of future occlusions.

NOTE: CCI concepts are substantially different from those in the CPT. Review carefully.

*Coronary artery interventions include **stent** placement, atherectomy, and balloon angioplasty. Medicare recognizes only the RC, LC, and LD with these procedures. Select one code for the most comprehensive service per coronary artery with the proper modifier. If additional services are provided in additional arteries/branches, select the add-on code. Do not indicate modifier -59 with the additional therapeutic services provided on the same artery.*

Coronary artery angioplasty, atherectomy, or stenting include the access procedure, infusion, fluroscopy, and EKG.

If an EKG is performed prior or after the cardiac cath, use modifier -59. During the case, the EKG is not coded.

Key fact: Placement of an occlusive device, angioseal, or vascular plug into the access site as a closure is coded with G0269. Do not select 75710 or G0278 in addition.

G0290 and G0291 are selected for Transcatheter placement of drug eluding intracoronary stent, each vessel.

Renal artery angiography during cardiac catheterization code selected is G0275 (instead of 75722 Angiography, renal, unilateral, selective, radiological supervision and interpretation or 75724 Angiography, renal, bilateral, selective, radiological supervision and interpretation) if no selective catheterization is performed. This is simply injecting the dye, but not advancing a catheter into the renal vessels.

If renal artery catheterization is performed, do not select G0275; see 36245 with 75722-24 instead.

For iliac artery angiography during cardiac catheterization, if no selective catheterization is performed select G0278. If iliac artery catheterization is performed, do not select G0278.

5. For each participating or accepting assignment claim, determine the bundling rules for the list of codes you are considering. As just described, the CCI rules differ from AMA/CPT for the services that are included in the catheterization procedures. Each plan may have its own policy per CPT code payment or bundling rules. The rules may outline per plan, the "included" or "select an additional" code per services, particularly for the Supervision & Interpretation and the Angiography care.

heart catheterization

A diagnostic test designed to examine the heart via a catheter placed within a major artery in the arm (brachial) or a major groin artery (femoral). The catheter passes through vessels into the heart's arterial system. Dye is injected to trace blood circulation through the heart. Obstruction in flow indicates the presence of thrombi, plaque, stenosis, or collapsed vessels. This procedure may also be called angiography or an angiogram.

Right **heart catheterization** is commonly performed with access inserted percutaneously into a large vessel, perhaps the femoral, internal jugular, or brachial or subclavian veins. The catheter is threaded over a guidewire and manipulated (positioned) into the right atrium, ventricle, **pulmonary artery,** and pulmonary capillary wedge.

Percutaneous transluminal coronary angioplasty (PTCA) remains a very common procedure. The percutaneous codes are selected per vessel and per specific anatomical site. Additional procedures may be performed during the same session, and often additional codes with modifiers are selected. Figure 9–5 provides a diagram of the instrument within the vessel.

pulmonary artery

A major blood vessel that transports blood between the heart and the lungs for oxygenation. Deoxygenated blood is carried from the right ventricle via this vessel, which forks into the right and left lungs. The pulmonary vein then carries freshly oxygenated blood into the left atrium of the heart for passage into the left ventricle and, subsequently, into systemic circulation.

INTRACARDIAC ELECTROPHYSIOLOGICAL PROCEDURES/STUDIES

From the Medicine chapter of CPT, electrophysiology (EP) is organized according to the procedure, the device, and the body site. CPT codes indicate the therapeutic interventions, EP follow-up studies, cardioverter-defibrillator assessment, and

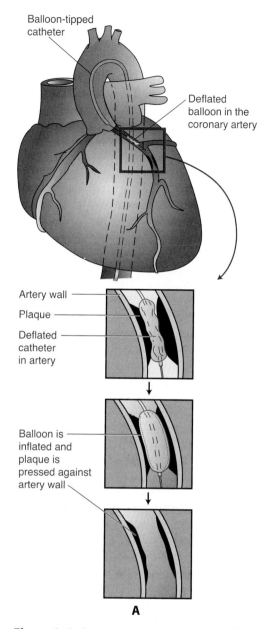

Balloon-tipped catheter

Deflated balloon in the coronary artery

Artery wall

Plaque

Deflated catheter in artery

Balloon is inflated and plaque is pressed against artery wall

A

Figure 9–5 A percutaneous transluminal coronary angioplasty (PTCA). Demonstrates the function of a balloon-tipped catheter during PTCA.

pacemaker
Electrical (battery-powered) device that helps maintain normal sinus heart rhythm by stimulating cardiac muscles to contract or pump. Pacemakers come in single or dual chamber models and are programmed to sense and correct low heart rates or abnormal rhythms. The devices can be set a fixed number of beats per minute.

intracardiac ablation of arrhythmias. Selection of CPT codes for the monitoring and analysis of **pacemaker** and/or ICD operations is based on documentation by the physician.

The 93600 code series also includes the:

- access or introduction of the electrode catheters
- repositioning
- recording of EKG prior and during the test
- analysis of information
- report

The first two components are typically diagnostic services; the third component is considered therapeutic, or for surgical correction of a problem. The physician determines the level of care to provide for each patient based upon the reactions and findings. These are:

- arrhythmia induction
- mapping
- ablation (therapeutic, not diagnostic)

All of the codes in the series are modifier -51 exempt. Select a code based upon the exact procedure that is performed, for each component, whether on the same date or different dates. Again, do not select a code for each repositioning and running test or ablation service.

OTHER VASCULAR STUDIES

The tests measure the electronic activity of the vascular system in a different method than the EKG, usually without introduction of catheters. Codes 93724–736 measure pacemaker systems in a variety of methods, where codes 93741–744 measure the cardiodefibrillator combined systems. The codes are selected based upon whether reprogramming is performed and whether single or dual chamber. The 93745 was new in 2005. This popular service indicates the set-up and programming of a wearable cardiodefibrillator, ECG with report and transmission, and instructions with the patient diary of activities.

 **Highlight**

Plethysmography, or ambulatory blood pressure monitoring, may have specific medical benefit coverage rules. The advance beneficiary notice may be required.

Outpatient cardiac rehabilitation codes are selected for the physician service, at the rehabilitation place of service, depending upon the ECG session.

NONINVASIVE VASCULAR DIAGNOSTIC STUDIES

The 93875 code series is selected to indicate various devices that analyze the flow of arteries and veins through the vessels, by scanning or Doppler. The analysis may include the cranial, extremities, or abdominal areas. The criteria for selecting a CPT code require that:

- Hard copy output is created by the machine for all data
- Bidirectional vascular flow is analyzed

If the equipment does not provide these two criteria, the vascular study is included in the E/M visits codes and not additionally coded with the 93875 series of codes.

Highlight

Handheld or other equipment may be sold at conferences, encouraging all specialty physicians to purchase the apparatus. Not all equipment that is avail-

able offers the requirements presented in this section. If the equipment does not produce hard copy output or does not analyze the bidirectional flow, it does not meet the criteria for selecting the codes from this series of CPT codes. No additional reimbursement will be received by the physician, regardless of the medical necessity for the studies.

The equipment may progress from B-scan ultrasound, to include Doppler mapping with color flow. The physician may further require additional studies such as plethysmography or pulmonary studies.

Coding Tip	*Do not look up the test name by abbreviation, such as TCD. About the only index term referenced to Doppler external studies is* *Vascular studies* *Next, look up Arterial or Venous, then the Anatomical site* *Other approaches to the index for these tests may also work.*

Visceral vascular is the anatomy of mesenteric, celiac, and renal vessels. When reporting 93975, a complete study per organ is required. With the duplex scan, an abdominal ultrasound service may also be provided and an additional code would be selected.

30000 SERIES OF CPT

Heart and Pericardium

The CPT codes for the 33010 series are performed to surgically correct an illness/disease of the heart, such as removal of fluid from the pericardium, or removal of a foreign body or tumor. The operative report should clearly indicate the exact location of the surgical services that are rendered for which the codes are specifically selected.

Pacemaker or Pacing Cardioverter-Defibrillator

Pacemakers have evolved, and often include the insertion of combination cardioverter-defibrillator pacemakers. A pacemaker may be required to regulate the heart rhythm either temporarily or permanently. A temporary pacemaker may be inserted transcutaneously, whereas the permanent pacemaker may require surgery to insert the leads and to create a "pocket" just beneath the skin, for placement of the apparatus. The work for these services includes:

- creation of the pocket for the system
- attaching the electrodes/leads to the proper site for optimal response
- programming the system (can be done intraoperatively or postoperatively)

The style of single chamber or dual chamber is determined based upon medical necessity. The dual chamber electrodes/leads are placed with one in the atrium and one in the ventricle of the heart. If an additional electrode is placed in the second ventricle, an additional code 33224 or 33225 is selected.

Formation of the pocket subcutaneously is included in the codes. If a thoracotomy is required for the placement of the epicardial electrodes, the 33243 or 33245 code series is considered.

Coding Tip | *The CPT descriptions call the removal or change of the battery, "changing the pulse generator." Select one code for the removal and another code for the insertion of a new pulse generator. For example, 33234–235 in addition to the 33212–213 code may be selected.*

Another procedure may either be repositioning the electrodes (33215 or 26) or, more commonly, changing the electrodes (33206, 208, 210–213, or 224).

Biventricular pacing is also known as resynchronization Therapy.

HCPCSII G0297–G0300 codes are selected for insertion of single, dual chamber pacing cardioverter defibrillator pulse generator, or the leads. Review these codes in lieu of the CPT codes, to select based upon the documentation.

The 33240 series of codes is selected for the implantable defibrillator system surgical care based upon the specific descriptions and the documentation of the procedure. Select additional codes from the 93000 series when applicable. If the defibrillator is removed subcutaneously and the electrode system is removed via thoracotomy, select 33241 and 33243. If the physician progresses to insert a new system, select at least two codes plus the EP 93000 series codes. Select 33241 with 33243 *or* 33244 with 33249 as applicable. When any of the procedures is discontinued, modifier -53 may be attached to the procedure.

Electrophysiologic Operative Procedures

Atrial or ventricular arrhythmogenic pathway problems may be corrected by ablation during a surgical procedure, or with a pulmonary bypass (use of heart/lung perfusion equipment) procedure. The codes in 33250–261 are selected for these specialized services.

Patient Activated Event Recorder

The 33282 and 33284 codes are for implanted event recorders. The codes include:

- Implantation
- Programming and reprogramming

A separate code 33284 is selected for the removal, using the same logic as pacemakers. The subsequent programming (not associated to the implantation service) is coded with 93727.

Wounds of the Heart and Great Vessels

The codes in the 33300 series are usually for repairs due to trauma or other maloccurrence (procedural error) purposes. The ICD-9-CM codes are very important to reflect the reason for the care.

Only if a separate incision were made into the heart (atrial or ventricular) for the removal of a coronary thrombus (blood clot) would an additional code be selected. Use of modifier -59 is required.

Cardiac Valves

Use of modifier -51 is required with many of these procedures. The codes are selected based upon the valve that is repaired and the type of the repair. The terminology for grafts is the same as with the integumentary system; homograft (porcine/pig), allograft (synthetic). Additional cardiac bypass or devices such as a ring may be placed as well.

Coding Tip

Look in the CPT index using these three steps:

Valvuloplasty (this will guide you the most directly to the cardiac valves)
Then select the specific valve: aortic, mitral, tricuspid, or pulmonary
Then select the specific with or without bypass (use of the heart/lung machine)

Select a code for each valve that is repaired or reconstructed.

Coronary Artery Anomalies

The codes in the 33500 series include the endarterectomy and/or angioplasty. The repairs are often due to congenital concerns.

Endoscopy

33508 is selected to report when the harvest of the vein is obtained endoscopically. The code is a sister code to 33510–23. Do not select 33508 if the procedure is performed without endoscope and is procured using an open surgical technique.

Venous Grafting Only for Coronary Artery Bypass

Vein Only Graft: If the operative report states venous grafts only, select 33510–516. The codes in this series include the harvest of the saphenous vein. The codes do not include the harvest of other vein segments.

Co-surgeons or assistant surgeons are likely to participate in these cases. Use modifiers to accurately report the proper person involved in the care.

Combination Arterial-Venous Grafting for Coronary Artery Bypass

Artery and Vein Graft: The 33517 code series are frequently used in caring for patients. The coding logic requires two codes, one for the combination venous graft and another for the arterial graft.

Again, the harvest of the saphenous vein and artery for grafting is included, with the exception of the harvest of upper extremity artery (35600) or upper extremity vein (35560) or 35562 femo-popliteal vein (93572). For these harvest exceptions, additional codes are selected.

Arterial Grafting for Coronary Artery

Arterial Only Graft or Combination of Arterial-Venous Grafts: Hints for the selection of these codes are the included vessels of

- internal mammary artery
- gastroepiploic artery
- epigastric artery
- radial artery
- arterial conduits procured from other sites

Again, the logic requires two codes—one for the Arterial graft (33533–536) and another for the Combination arterio-venous graft (33517–723). Again, the Upper extremity artery harvest would be additionally coded with 35600, or the Fem-popliteal vein harvest (35572).

■ *Highlight*

- *CCI initially states that when coronary artery bypass is performed, select the one code for the more comprehensive procedure. Yet, one code in the combo venous codes and one code for arterial grafting can be reported together, for those combination cases where vein and artery are used as conduits.*
- *For peripheral vascular, at any specific site of obstruction, only one type of bypass is performed, therefore multiple grafts are mutually exclusive. If different sites are treated with different bypass procedures, modifier -59 or anatomic modifiers are required.*

Coronary Endarterectomy

This open procedure is used to remove plaque from within the coronary arteries, in addition to the bypass procedure. No modifier -51 is required.

Repair of Heart and Anomalies

Services for the repair of the heart, such as septal defect, sinus of valsalva, and total anomalous pulmonary venous drainage are not specifically listed in the CPT index. They are found under:

Heart
Then Repair
Then the procedure

Heart/Lung Transplantation

These procedures are not provided at every hospital; usually large centers have been designated for this particular service. 2005 CPT revised the code structure for the services to reflect three codes for each component that is described per physician. If one physician provides all three components, three codes are reported, plus any additional therapeutic services that are performed during the case.

1. Harvest donor cadaver cardiectomy includes:
   - pneumonectomy
   - harvest of the heart
   - preservation of the heart

Additional CPT codes are selected if repair procedures are required for the donor heart. These are not included in the basic harvesting services.

2. Backbench work is the preparation of the donor heart for placement
   - dissection of the anatomy (two areas) that is to be placed
3. Recipient heart transplantation includes
   - lung transplantation
   - recipient placement care

Cardiac Assist, Ventricular Assist

Cardiac assist devices are attached to provide the circulation while the heart or lungs are not producing effectively. 33960–61 is selected based upon 24-hour segments.

33967 and 968 for the intra-aortic balloon assist device are selected based upon the access (insertion) point and include the graft of the same site.

Arteries and Veins

The procedures in this series include:

- the inflow and outflow by any procedure
- the arteriogram
- aortic procedures, including the sympathectomy

The codes are selected based upon:

- arterial or venous
- procedure performed
- anatomical site of the specific site

Endovascular Repair of Abdominal Aortic Aneurysm

Use modifier -50 when applicable for these codes. The codes in this series include:

- open femoral or iliac artery exposure (access)
- device manipulation and deployment (stents)
- closure of the arteriotomy site (access)
- balloon angioplasty within the target treatment zone
- stent deployment within the target treatment zone

When providing endovascular repairs, additional codes are often selected for:

- introduction of catheters
- extensions of 34825, 34826, and 75953 for the radiologic supervision and interpretation (S&I)
- introduction of guidewires
- extensive repair or replacement of arteries
- fluroscopic guidance (75952–75953)
- angiography
- renal transluminal angioplasty
- arterial embolization
- intravascular ultrasound
- balloon angioplasty of native arteries outside of the endoprosthesis target zone before or after the deployment of the graft
- stent of native arteries outside of the endoprosthesis target zone before or after the deployment of the graft

These procedures often require the professional services of more than one physician, or two specialists. Modifier -62 is selected for each service code that are performed together.

Endovascular Repair of Iliac Aneurysm

Use modifier -50 when applicable for 34900. This code is selected for multiple purposes repairing the iliac artery. The logic is similar to the previous Endovascular includes/excludes. The Fluroscopic guidance partner code is 75954 for the angiography of the iliac arteries.

Direct Repair of Aneurysm or Excision and Graft Insertion for Aneurysm, Pseudoaneurysm, Ruptured Aneurysm, and Associated Occlusive Disease

If the patient has a diagnosis of an abdominal aortic aneurysm and occlusive disease, and an aortobifemoral bypass to correct the aneurysm is performed, code only from this section of the CPT code book. The codes in this series are not selected if the procedure is performed via the vessel or endovascularly.

This series of codes includes preparation of artery for anastamosis including endarterectomy. Select the codes based per specific site and the type of the aneurysm.

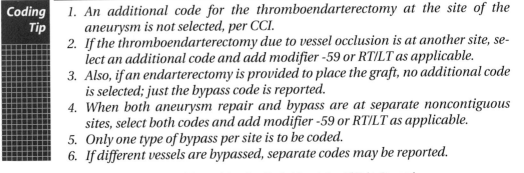

Coding Tip

1. An additional code for the thromboendarterectomy at the site of the aneurysm is not selected, per CCI.
2. If the thromboendarterectomy due to vessel occlusion is at another site, select an additional code and add modifier -59 or RT/LT as applicable.
3. Also, if an endarterectomy is provided to place the graft, no additional code is selected; just the bypass code is reported.
4. When both aneurysm repair and bypass are at separate noncontiguous sites, select both codes and add modifier -59 or RT/LT as applicable.
5. Only one type of bypass per site is to be coded.
6. If different vessels are bypassed, separate codes may be reported.

7. *If one vessel has multiple occlusions, with multiple bypass at different sites, multiple codes are selected, and add modifier -59 or RT/LT.*
8. *The most comprehensive code is selected per site, of thrombectomy, embolectomy, or endarterectomy.*
9. *If a balloon thrombectomy fails, and converts to open thromboendarterectomy, select only the code for the open, more comprehensive procedure.*

It is obvious from these examples that CPT and CCI do not have the same rules or logic.

Repair Arteriovenous Fistula

Select for the surgical repair of congenital or acquired fistulas per vessel site.

Repair Blood Vessel Other Than for Fistula, with or without Patch Angioplasty

Select for direct repair of blood vessels, often for trauma purposes.

Thromboendarterectomy

These are not selected for coronary artery sites; select per vessel. Note that 35390 is an add-on code to use with 35301, should a return trip to O.R. be required after one month. This logic is unique within the surgical codes.

angioplasty
A medical cardiology procedure in which a catheter with an inflatable balloon on the tip is passed through a vessel and inflated at the site of an obstruction within the vessel wall. As the balloon inflates, any soft plaque is flattened against the vessel wall to prevent obstruction of blood flow and to open up the vessel for blood passage.

Angioscopy

Angioscopy may be performed during another case, and if it is documented, select +35400, no modifier.

Transluminal Angioplasty, Atherectomy

Atherectomy is the removal of an atheromatous deposit that is blocking the blood flow within a vessel. The blockage may be within the coronary itself or within the vessels leading to the heart. The fatty or plaque deposits impede blood flow and prohibit adequate circulation to a body organ, thereby impeding proper function. The physician carefully cuts, or removes, the build-up either in total or in particles and pieces. If removed in one piece, it may be described as an extraction atherectomy. The procedure may be tedious, may advance to a more invasive procedure, or may be discontinued. Use modifier -53 to describe a procedure that is discontinued, after initiating. Figure 9–6 demonstrates a particular instrument that may be used by the physician, although other instruments may provide a similar service.

Select one code for the access, a second code for the angioplasty service, and another for the radiological supervision and interpretation.

The two components are often provided with another procedure; add the codes and modifiers as necessary.

If the physician provides the radiological supervision and interpretation, add the codes 75962–68, 75978. Select the code per access—either open or percutaneous, and then select a code per vessel.

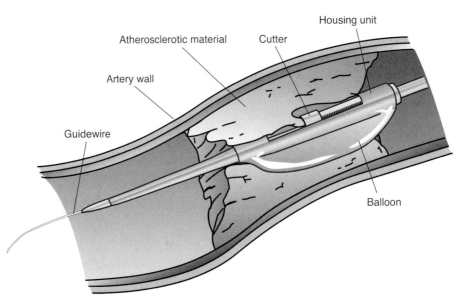

Figure 9–6 The Simpson Coronary AtheroCath cuts the atherosclerotic plaque away from the artery wall.

When selecting codes for the percutaneous services, also code for the catheter placement and the supervision and interpretation radiology services performed by the same physician.

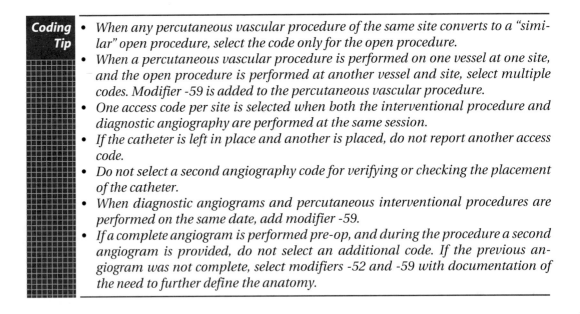

Coding Tip

- *When any percutaneous vascular procedure of the same site converts to a "similar" open procedure, select the code only for the open procedure.*
- *When a percutaneous vascular procedure is performed on one vessel at one site, and the open procedure is performed at another vessel and site, select multiple codes. Modifier -59 is added to the percutaneous vascular procedure.*
- *One access code per site is selected when both the interventional procedure and diagnostic angiography are performed at the same session.*
- *If the catheter is left in place and another is placed, do not report another access code.*
- *Do not select a second angiography code for verifying or checking the placement of the catheter.*
- *When diagnostic angiograms and percutaneous interventional procedures are performed on the same date, add modifier -59.*
- *If a complete angiogram is performed pre-op, and during the procedure a second angiogram is provided, do not select an additional code. If the previous angiogram was not complete, select modifiers -52 and -59 with documentation of the need to further define the anatomy.*

Bypass Graft Vein

While performing the bypass graft by vein, when harvesting of:

- the saphenous vein, do not select an additional code.
- an upper extremity vessel, an additional code is selected.
- a femoropopliteal (fem-pop) portion, an additional code is selected.

- a graft from two distant (not connected) sites, also select the add-on code 35682; no modifier -51; 100 percent should be reimbursed.

- A graft from three-plus distant sites, also select the add-on code 35683; no modifier -51; 100 percent should be reimbursed. The use of modifier -50 is reported when appropriate.

The bypass procedures often require multiple codes to report more than one bypass provided during one operative session. Read the entire operative report, making notes of each anatomical site of harvest, whether synthetic material is used and where the connections are made for the bypass graft. Then, consider CPT codes. Read CPT guidelines and parenthetical tips carefully, for the likely additional codes to report.

Arteries may be harvested for the venous bypass, or composite grafts. Composite grafts are multiple veins connected together for use as an arterial bypass conduit. The codes are selected when two-plus segments are harvested from the opposite (contralateral) extremity from the bypass graft extremity.

Adjuvant procedures describe synthetic patches for additional services that are occasionally necessary. Transposition and reimplantation are performed to repair aneurysms or traumatic injuries. There are specific codes for repeat procedures for the bypass services explorative work or other postoperative complications.

Determining the postoperative time period will affect the selection of modifiers, and may vary per insurance plan. This concept is critical to proper payment of claims. The standard for this determination varies per insurance plan, and may not be the published CMS policies.

Vascular Injection Procedures

The procedures in this series include:

- Local anesthesia
- Introduction of needles or catheter
- Injection (manual or power injection) of the contrast materials
- Pre and post injection care (site care)

When providing vascular injection procedures, additional codes are often selected for:

- Catheters
- Drugs (when purchased by the physician)
- Contrast media (when purchased by the physician)

vascular families
Arterial, venous, pulmonary, portal, lymphatic.

Selective catheterization includes the lesser order vessels of the same **vascular family.** If additional catheterization is performed within the same vascular family, the additional codes are selected. The families are arterial, venous, pulmonary, portal, and lymphatic. When additional first order vessels are different from a previously selective and coded family, an additional code is selected.

nonselective
Directly placed into the anatomical site, not fed into the area.

One must clearly understand selective versus nonselective access or placement of a catheter. In simple terms, selective is when the physician has to "feed" or gently guide the catheter into a specific branch of the blood vessel or anatomy. **Nonselective** is when the physician punctures directly into the main blood vessel site or anatomy (not manipulated or fed into place).

bifurcation
The point where the blood vessels split into two branches.

Per vascular family, count the **bifurcations** (branching-off points) to determine the second or third order. It is rather common to have codes for one family, at the second or third order, and also codes for another family at the first order (e.g., third order arterial, first order renal).

Codes are selected based upon the final placement of the tip. To assist in determining the order, the coder should ask, "What is the anatomical site of the final point of the catheter?" and then count the branches that have occurred along the way.

Visualizing five types of the vascular families as trees can help clarify these concepts. The arterial tree is very common. If the injection site is the femoral artery, and the catheter is fed into the abdominal aorta, that is considered the main trunk, or nonselective. The catheter progresses into a primary branch (first order might be the brachiocephalic or innominate), and then into another branch (second order might be the common carotid), and finally into a tiny branch (third order external carotid). Then, often the surgeon completes the injection for that family, pulls back and places the catheter into another tree, perhaps the renal tree. Again, the coder must ask, how far does the catheter move into the renal tree? If it enters the branch, the code considered is the first order renal tree. The catheter placement codes are not selected for the contrast or dye that runs into each area; the codes are selected for the physician placing the catheter in each anatomical site.

Nonselective placement is when the catheter (or perhaps needle) is simply placed directly into the main trunk of the family tree, or vessel. The codes describe this as introduction, rather than the selective terminology.

Flow-directed catheter (Swan-Ganz) codes are reported with 93503.

Coding Tip	• *If the patient has existing Swan-Ganz lines and a blood sample is collected, do not select an additional collection code. No additional professional service was necessary for the collection.* • *Swan-Ganz catheters are often inserted for patients in order to carefully monitor their hemodynamic status. Table 9–3 explains when to consider selecting the Swan-Ganz versus the Right heart catheterization codes.* • *Replacing a catheter may be performed to prevent further complications, infection, or illness. Although this is a common medical standard, it may not be an insurance covered benefit for the patient. Prior to replacing the cath, it is required to investigate the insurance benefits.*

Venous

The codes in this series are selected for intravenous (IV) therapy (punctures through the skin). The infusion services are coded with additional codes if provided by the physician. The codes are selected based upon the age of the patient and the type of venipuncture that is performed, whether a sample collection, transfusion, or cut-down.

In selecting the codes for the treatment of veins (e.g., telangiectasia vs. varicose) watch the plural versus singular definition. For 36468, the code is selected one time, whether single or multiple injections of multiple veins; yet, for other than spider veins, the code 36470 is used per vein.

The code for endovenous ablation treatments automatically includes supervision and interpretation, and monitoring, without having to choose additional S&I codes.

■ *Highlight*

Due to the Medicare Part D revisions, there will likely be revisions to the CCI manual after this textbook is written. It is therefore advised to review the current CCI manual, which is published each October.

TABLE 9–3   Right Heart Catheterization vs. Swan-Ganz Catheter Placement.

According to the *American College Of Cardiology's Practical Reporting of Cardiovascular Services and Procedures,* RHC is distinguished from Swan-Ganz placement by the following grid:

Context	Swan-Ganz 93503	Rt Heart Catheterization (RHC)
Typically performed in the cath lab and/or in conjunction with other cardiac catheterization procedures		X
The catheter is removed after the procedure		X
The catheter may be left in place for further monitoring/measurement purposes	X	
Typically placed in ICU	X	
Typically used for diagnostics		X
Can be placed preoperatively to monitor hemodynamic status	X	

The intravenous infusion service codes include the placement or access services. Do not select an additional code for the access service, whether IV or CVP. Selective arterial catheterization access services are additionally coded.

Central Venous Access Procedures (Placement of CVP Line)

The CVP definition is the tip ends at the subclavian, brachiocephalic (innominate) or iliac veins, superior or inferior vena cava, or the right atrium. If the CVP ends at a different site, then select from the other venous access codes and not the CVP codes.

The access may be through various vessels, the jugular, subclavian, femoral, inferior vena cava, or peripherally (extremities or head). For infants, the scalp and head are commonly selected sites. The physician may insert a subcutaneous catheter or place a subcutaneous port or pump or may directly insert it into a port or pump device. Read the report carefully for each possible service component:

- Insertion/access through a new site may or may not be tunneled under the skin.
- Repair of the device without removal. The physician may use medications or instruments to clear the device and improve the function.
- Partial replacement when only the catheter is replaced, keeping the port or pump in place.
- Complete replacement at the same site, exchanged out entirely.
- Removal of the device.
- If coding for multiple catheters from separate access sites, select the code with the quantity of two.
- When removing the old and placing a new one at a separate site, codes are selected for both procedures.

Supervision and interpretation imaging codes are selected in addition to the procedures. If the physician progresses to place medications into the port/pump, additional codes are selected.

Arterial punctures are performed to obtain arterial blood gases and perhaps culture and sensitivity testing or for infusion therapy. The arterial puncture codes are selected for simple line placement.

Hemodialysis Access, Intervascular Cannulation for Extracorporeal Circulation, or Shunt Insertion

Hemodialysis cannula has a tendency to clot and may require thrombectomy, medical injection, or revisions. Many of the codes have the description of separate procedure, which indicates perhaps the procedure is being performed as part of another procedure. Review the report for each service, then whether modifier -59 is appropriate.

The arteriovenous fistula serves as the connection port to the dialysis apparatus. If imaging services are provided, select additional codes.

Transcatheter Procedures

Transcatheter procedures are the therapeutic services that are provided through the catheter. The transcatheter procedure area of cardiology coding is rapidly improving, so watching for new codes and description changes is advised. The codes are for noncoronary services.

For most of the codes, there are typically three components for the transcatheter procedures, and one should select a code for each component that is documented:

- Catheter placement/Access
- Transcatheter therapeutic service
- Supervision and interpretation of the radiology imaging

Intravascular Ultrasound

The intravascular ultrasound services include:

- vascular access
- all transducer manipulations and repositioning within the vessel
- before and after the therapy

The intravascular ultrasound may be used during therapeutic procedures, and the procedure is sometimes included in the therapeutic procedure code. Investigate and research bundling issues per insurance plan, prior to selecting the additional intravascular ultrasound code.

The intravascular ultrasound procedures are different from many of the other CPT codes, as the access is included in the codes and not separately reported. However, they do not include other therapeutic services that may be performed via the catheter (transcatheter) or the supervision and interpretation imaging 75945, 75946 codes.

Stents

Stents are deployed to reinforce vessel walls, helping to prevent the obstruction of blood flow. The stent may be placed within the vessels leading toward the heart or other anatomical sites. If stents are placed within the heart (intracoronary), in addition to within the vessels, a separate code is selected for each. Insurance plans, including CMS, may not have specific policies published for the payment of the services. Investigation of the insurance coverage prior to the operative session is advised.

New in 2005 were the transcatheter of the intravascular stents into the carotid artery. If placed in the extracranial vertebral or the intrathoracic carotid, the Category III code 0075T or 0076T is selected. If the transcatheter is placed intravascularly into *other* than carotid, coronary, or vertebral, select the 37205 and 37206 codes. It is very important to select the code based upon the exact anatomical structure for these codes.

Ligation

Ligation, or "stripping," of veins is less commonly performed. Today, laser or radiofrequency ablation procedures are the method of choice to care for large varicose veins. The codes are not selected for phlebitis or arteriography services.

The code 37205 is commonly selected for the procedure of Angio access arteriovenous fistula removals.

EXERCISE 9–4

Name the vascular families.

1.

2.

3.

4.

5.

RADIOLOGY

Radiology services may require the modifier -59. The term "with contrast" is defined as material given intravascularly, intra-articularly (joint), or intrathecally. With cardiology, frequently contrast is used to visualize the vessels either before, during, or after various services.

Injection of intravascular contrast is part of the "with contrast" codes of CT, CTA, MRI, and MRA.

■ *Highlight*

- *If CPT does not describe the administration component, the administration of contrast code for access is not selected.*
- *For a risk prevention access line (in case of necessity during the procedure) or to administer the contrast, the access code is not selected.*
- *If performing intravenous injections on the same date, no additional code is selected for contrast administration on the same date; considered bundled.*

Radiology services require a written report, signed by the interpreting physician. The services may be provided by a radiologist or by another physician. Whoever performs the service, with proper documentation, selects and reports the proper code. The radiology specialty association suggests the content of the reports, which at a minimum should describe the anatomy markers and identify the findings.

Table 9–4 is a great tool to guide understanding of the surgical procedure with the probable radiological component services. As new procedure codes are implemented, it is wise to add them to this format.

■ *Highlight*

According to the CCI, radiology services include:

Limited historical inquiry regarding the reasons for the exam
Allergies
Informed consent
Discussion of the follow-up
Review of the medical record

If a separate, significantly identifiable E/M service is performed by the radiologist, an additional code may be selected, and may need a modifier.

Vascular Procedures

Aorta, Arteries, Veins, and Lymphatics

New in the 2005 CPT code book are guidelines describing transcatheter care with angiography services. When a diagnostic (when nothing is corrected) angiography is performed, do not select additional codes for the contrast injection, vessel measurement, or postangioplasty stent angiography. Read the description of the CPT codes carefully for accurate code selection.

When a diagnostic angiography is performed with an interventional procedure, additional codes are selected for:

No prior angiographic study is available for the surgeon
and a full study is performed
and decision to intervene is based upon the study

or

Prior study is available
and Condition has changed
or inadequate visualization of the anatomy or pathology
or clinical change during the procedure that requires a new evaluation beyond the area of intervention

If the angiography is performed at a separate session, report all codes.

TABLE 9–4   Surgical Procedure with Radiology Component with possible procedures chart.

Surgical Procedure	Radiology Component (not a complete list of radiology services)	Additional Surgical Procedures
10021–10022	76003 76360 76393 76942	
10140–10160	76095 76096 76360 76393	
19000–19001	76095 76096 76393 76942	
19030	76086 76088	
19102–19103	76095 76096 76360 76393 76942	
19290–19291	76095 76096 76942	
20206	76360 76393 76942	
20220	76003	
20225	76003 76360 76393	
20501	76080	
20553	76003 76393 76942	
20610	76003 76360 76393 76942	
21116	70332	
22520 22521 22522	76012 76013	
23350	73040	
	76003 and 73201 OR 73202	
	76003 and 73222 OR 73223	
24220	73085 OR 76003	
25246	73115	
27093 27095	73525 OR 76003	
27096	73542 OR 76005	
27370	73580 OR 76003	
27648	73615 OR 76003	
31656	71040 71060	
31708	70373 71040 71060	
32000	76003 76360 76942	
32002	76003 76360 76942	
31710 31715	71040 71060	
32019 32020	75989	

continues

TABLE 9–4 **Surgical Procedure with Radiology Component with possible procedures chart.** continued

Surgical Procedure	Radiology Component (not a complete list of radiology services)	Additional Surgical Procedures
32201	75989	
32400 32405	76003 76360 76393 76942	
33010 33011	76930	
33200–33249	71090	
34800–34808	75952	
34825 34826	75953	
34900	75954	
35205	75960	
35450–35460	75962–75968	
35474	75625	
35470–35476	75978	
35480–35495	75992–75996	
36000	75820 75822	36005 36011 36406 36410 36420 36425
36000–36012	75870 75872 75880 75860 75870 75872 75880	36100–36218
36000–36012	75831 75833 75840 75842 75889 75891 75889 75891	
36000–36013	75600 75605 75625 75710 75726 75716 75801–75822	36400–36425 36100–36200
36000–36013	75630 75722 75724 75731 75733 75736 75746	36400–36425 36100–36200 36245–36248
36000–36013	75650 75660 75662 75665 75671 75676 75680 75685 75756 75820	36400–36425 36100–36218
36000–36015	75705 75774	36400–36425 36100–36248
36000–36015	75741 75743	36400–36425
36002	76003 76360 76393 76942	
36005	75820 75822	
31710 31715	71040 71060	
36010	75825 75827	
36011	75885 75887	36012 36481

continues

TABLE 9–4   Surgical Procedure with Radiology Component with possible procedures chart. continued

Surgical Procedure	Radiology Component (not a complete list of radiology services)					Additional Surgical Procedures				
36140	75710	75790				36145	36215	36217	36245–36247	36870
36200	75716	75625	75630	75650	75680	93554				
36010–36012	75825 75842	75827 75860	75831 75901	75833 75902	75840	36100–36218				
36215–36218	75600–75790		75945	75946		93501	93508–94556			
36245	75650	75710	75722	75724						
36246	75710									
36247–36248	75710	75716	75774	75962						
36400–36510	75801–75822		75820							
36460	76941									
36481	75885	75887								
36500	75893									
36555–36590	76937	75998								
36595	75901									
36596	75902									
36597	76000									
36861	76861									
36870	75790									
37195 37200	75970	75945	75946			36100–36299	52007	48102	49180	
37200	75970					36100–36299	52007			
37201	75896									
37202	75896	75966	75968			92975	92977			
37203	75961									
37204	75894					61624	61626			
37205	75960					92980	92981			
31710 31715	71040	71060								
37206	75960									
37207 37208	75960					93980	92981	36215–36248		
37209	75900									

continues

TABLE 9–4 **Surgical Procedure with Radiology Component with possible procedures chart.** continued

Surgical Procedure	Radiology Component (not a complete list of radiology services)				Additional Surgical Procedures
37250 37251	75945				36215–36248
37250 37251	75946				
37450–37460	75962	75964	75966	75968	35470–35476
37620	75940				
38200	75810				
38505	76360	76393	76942		
38790 38792	75801–75807	78195			
42400 42405	76003	76360	76393	76942	
42550	70390				
43200–43215	74235				
43216–43226	74360				
43246	74350				
43247	74235				
43260–43272	74328	74329	74330	ercp74363	
43458	74360				
43750	74350				
43760	75984				
44015	74355				
44500	74340				
44901	75989				
45305	74360				
46000	76003	76360	76393	76942	
46001	76003	76942			
31710 31715	71040	71060			
47000–47001	76003				
47011	75989				
47370	76940				
47380 47381	76940				
47382	76362	76394	76940		

continues

TABLE 9–4   Surgical Procedure with Radiology Component with possible procedures chart. continued

Surgical Procedure	Radiology Component (not a complete list of radiology services)				Additional Surgical Procedures
47490	75989				
47500	74320				
47505	74305				
47510	74363	75980			
47511	74363	75982			
47525	75984				
47530	75984				
47555 47556	74363	75982			
47630	74327				
48102	76003	76360	76393	76942	
48400	74300–74305				
48511	75989				
49021 49041 49061	75989				
49081	76360	76942			
49180	76003	76360	76393	76942	
49400	74190				
49423	75984				
49424	76080				
49427	75809	78291			61070
50021	75989				
50081	76000	76001			
31710 31715	71040	71060			
50200	76003	76360	76393	76942	
50390	74425	74470	76003	76360	76393 76942
50392	74475	76360	76942		
50393	74480	76003	76360	76942	
50394	74425				
50395	74475	74480	74485		

continues

TABLE 9–4 **Surgical Procedure with Radiology Component with possible procedures chart.** continued

Surgical Procedure	Radiology Component (not a complete list of radiology services)	Additional Surgical Procedures
50396	74425 74475 74480	
50398	75984	
50684	74425	
50688	75984	
50690	74425	
51010	76942	
51600	74430 74455	
51605	74430	
51610	74450	
51710	75984	
52010	74440	
52320–52355	74485	
52351	74485	
53600–53665	74485	
54230	74445	
55300	74440	
55700	76942	
55859	76965	77776–77784
58340	74740 76831	
58345	74742	
58823	75989	
58970	76948	
59000	76946	
59012	76941	
59015	76945	
60001	76360 76942	
60100	76003 76360 76393 76942	
60280 60281	76536	
61055	70015 72240 72255 72265 72270	62284

continues

TABLE 9–4   **Surgical Procedure with Radiology Component with possible procedures chart.** continued

Surgical Procedure	Radiology Component (not a complete list of radiology services)	Additional Surgical Procedures
61070	75809	
61624 62626	75894	
61751	CT 70450 70460 70470	
	MRI 70551 70552 70553	
62268 62269	76003 76360 76942	
62270–62273	76005 72775	
62280–62282	76005 72775	
62287	76003	
62290 62291	72285 72295	
62310–62319	76005	
64470–64484	76005	
64620	76005	
64622–64627	76005	
65205–65265	70030 76529	
68850	70170 78660	
92975 92977	75894 75896	
92982–92984	75966 75968	
93303 93304	Fetal only 76825–76828	
93325	76825 76826 76827 76828	
Cardiac Cath	93555 93556	
93505	76932	
93508	93556	
93580 93581	93303–93317 93662	
95965	CT 70450–70470	
	MRI 70551–70553	

 Coding Tip   *Abdominal aortograms include the abdominal X-rays, and no additional codes are reported if these films and views are obtained.*
When diagnostic angiography and percutaneous intravascular interventional are performed on the same date, modifier -59 is added. The medical necessity and documentation must reflect the need for a repeat study.

HCPCSII G0288 is selected for Reconstruction, CT angiography of aorta for the decision for surgery. This is often overlooked by coders.

Transcatheter Procedures

The transcatheter procedures include the components of the contrast injection, vessel measurement, or completion angiography/venography unless the CPT description states otherwise.

Similar logic as in the previous section applies: if the need for the diagnostic test is documented, then both codes are selected. In the absence of documentation, additional codes are not selected.

Fluroscopic Guidance

Fluroscopic guidance codes are selected when the surgeon documents the fluroscopy during the operative session, identifying the anatomy that is visualized. Physicians may describe the service as C-arm or retrograde.

Coding Tip *Do not select a fluroscopy code plus the ultrasound guidance or additional fluroscopy services during one procedure. Select one code only for the highest level of service procedure.*

Ultrasonic Guidance Procedures

These services may be performed in addition to the access or therapeutic services for various imaging.

Coding Tip *If both ultrasound guidance and diagnostic echography are performed and documented, select a code for both services.*

Follow-up ultrasound study 76970 cannot be reported with echocardiograms or ultrasound guidance on the same date.

When selecting the 76986 for guidance of venous or combined arterial venous coronary artery bypass grafting, modifier -59 is to be added. Code 76986 is not selected for the guidance of the harvest component of service, according to CCI. This varies from CPT logic.

Ultrasound guidance and fluroscopy cannot be reported at the same procedural session. Select the higher service.

Nuclear Medicine

The nuclear medicine codes are selected in addition to other services. The elements or radiopharmaceuticals are also coded when the items represent a cost (purchased) by the physician practice. Various radiopharmaceuticals may be used to create the stress effect. Select an additional HCPCSII code (may or may not be a J code) when applicable.

Myocardial perfusion imaging evaluates the viability of the heart, how well the blood is circulating through the vessels, and the risks that may be present. Thallium chloride or other medications injected twice tag (mark) the red blood cells, allowing the physician to visualize the flow through the anatomical structures, via planar or spectral analysis.

Pharmacological stress may be injected during imaging procedures. Medications such as dipyridamole, dobutamine, and adenosine cause the heart to function as if it were operating under physical exercise. The cardiac stress testing codes are selected in addition to the imaging codes, when provided.

Multiple gated acquisition (MUGA) studies are provided to evaluate the cardiac phases of contraction and relaxation, identifying the Right and Left ventricular function. Gated exercise studies review the wall motion study and measurement of the blood ejection fraction or the assessment of the force of the blood passing through the ventricles. Select multiple codes for the MUGA, the stress test, and each medication for this procedure, commonly four procedure codes. Link the proper ICD-9-CM for each service, identifying the medical necessity.

Positron emission tomography (PET) evaluates the metabolic function of the heart. The medical necessity and the insurance benefits should be reviewed prior to providing the test, as this is a costly procedure and frequently is not a medical covered benefit. Select the CPT code 78459 for evaluation of the heart or 78491–92 for imaging perfusion. Historically, HCPCSII codes were to be selected for Medicare.

If the myocardial perfusion and imaging tests are provided with cardiac stress, also select the cardiac stress testing codes.

Therapeutic Radiopharmaceutical

Radiopharmaceuticals (nuclear medicine) provide the evaluation through various routes, to correct an illness/disease. If administering orally or intravenous (IV), no additional codes for the administration are selected. If administering by other means, select an access code plus the therapeutic radiopharmaceutical codes.

 *Highlight*

The access code is included in the procedure code, per CCI. No additional code for the access service is selected.

EXERCISE 9–5

Read the following medical reports and assign the correct ICD-9-CM and CPT codes.

1.

Patient:	Rudy, Carlton
DOB:	11/28/46
Hospital #:	5790873
Physician:	Walter Hill, MD
Date:	March 16, 20XX

CLINICAL INDICATIONS: The patient was found to have a severe blockage of the LAD involving a large diagonal.

continues

ICD-9-CM code(s) _____

CPT code(s) _____

METHOD: After 10,000 units of heparin were given, a 10 French system was placed. A 1 French #4 Judkins left guide was advanced to the left coronary artery. A 0.014 extra support exchange wire was advanced down the diagonal. Then, a 6 French atherocath was advanced over the wire to the diagonal. There were four cuts made in this area. We then pulled the cutter back and noted insufficient relief of the blockage; therefore, the atherocath was readvanced and three more cuts were made. Then the same wire was advanced down the LAD. A 7 French atherocath was advanced to the LAD lesion, and a series of cuts were made. At this point, the patient was having pain and it seemed to be getting worse. A 0.014 Traverse wire was advanced down the diagonal with the support wire remaining in the LAD. A 2-mm Rally balloon was advanced to the diagonal lesion, and this was inflated up to 6 atmospheres. The pain felt much better after this balloon was deflated. Then a 3.5-mm Rally balloon was advanced down into the LAD lesion. We inflated in both areas separately and then simultaneously. At this point, angiography showed successful resolution of both lesions. The procedure was then completed. The patient was returned to his room in good condition. Surgery was on standby.

SUMMARY: Successful atherectomy and angioplasty of the left anterior descending and diagonal.

Walter Hill, MD

2.

Patient: Shelton, Kevin

DOB: 09/23/55

Hospital #: 5438558709

Physician: Phyllis Kitts, MD

Date: August 24, 20XX

CLINICAL INDICATIONS: Angina, congestive heart failure, nonsustained ventricular tachycardia, atrial fibrillation, and multiple familial cardiac risk factors.

HEMODYNAMICS: The right ventricular end diastolic pressure is elevated. The pulmonary capillary wedge pressure, pulmonary artery pressure, and left ventricular end diastolic pressure are severely elevated. Severe systemic hypertension is present. There are no valvular gradients detected. The resting cardiac index is preserved.

LEFT VENTRICULOGRAPHY: Left ventriculography was performed with the patient in the right anterior oblique projection. The left ventricle is normal in size and demonstrates severe inferobasal hypokinesis. The remainder of the left ventricle contracts normally. The overall extent of contraction is mildly to moderately reduced. There is trace mitral insufficiency without prolapse.

CORONARY ARTERIOGRAPHY: Selective coronary arteriography was performed with the patient in various right and left anterior and sagittal oblique projections.

The left main coronary artery is mildly irregular but free of significant disease. The left main provides a ramus intermedius branch. The ramus

continues

intermedius bifurcates shortly after its origin. The more lateral branch is narrowed 90% at the junction between the proximal and middle thirds of the vessel.

The left anterior descending coronary artery is large in caliber and extends over the apex. The anterior descending is moderately irregular throughout its course. The anterior descending is narrowed 80% in its mid portion.

The left circumflex is nondominant. The left circumflex is narrowed 80% proximally. There are two small distal obtuse marginals that are mildly irregular.

The right coronary artery is dominant. The right coronary artery is totally occluded at the junction between the proximal and middle thirds of the vessel. The distal vessel fills extensively via left to right collateral circulation.

The native left internal mammary artery was nonselectively visualized and appears to be suitable for use as a graft.

Aortography of the distal abdominal aorta reveals severe, diffuse extasia of the distal aorta below the renal arteries. The right common iliac is occluded at its origin. The left iliac and femoral arteries are heavily calcified and with diffuse moderate disease. There are two renal arteries supplying the left kidney. The inferior artery is narrowed 80–90% proximally. The right renal artery is narrowed at least 80%.

CONCLUSIONS:

1. CAD, severe, triple vessel
2. Left ventricular dysfunction
3. Severe elevation of the left heart-filling pressure
4. Severe pulmonary hypertension
5. Elevated right heart-filling pressure
6. Mitral insufficiency, trace
7. Bilateral renal artery stenosis
8. Peripheral vascular disease with total occlusion of the right common iliac artery at its origin

ICD-9-CM code(s) _____

CPT code(s) _____

COMMENTS: This patient is with symptomatic triple vessel coronary artery disease with left ventricular dysfunction. He would benefit by CABG surgery although such surgery would be at increased risk for complications. The patient has significant bilateral renal artery stenosis and should undergo evaluation by Wilson Nesmith, DO, for possible renal arterial intervention by way of stent or balloon placement.

Phyllis Kitts, MD

EXERCISE 9–6

1. Define thrombolysis. _____

2. Define embolysis. _____

3. Pericardiocentesis withdraws fluid from what cardiac structure? _____

4. Cardiac tumors are known as _____.

5. Name the three types of atherectomy. 1) _____, 2) _____, 3) _____

6. PTCA is an acronym for _____ _____ _____ _____.

7. Read the following medical report for angioplasty and stent implantation, then assign the correct ICD-9-CM and CPT codes.

ICD-9-CM code(s) _____

CPT code(s) _____

Patient:	Yandell, Vernon
DOB:	2/14/39
Hospital #:	9674538
Physician:	Barton Sellers, MD
Date:	June 19, 20XX

CLINICAL INDICATIONS: Status post PTCA of the right coronary artery now with recurrent angina. Patient underwent cardiac cath earlier today that revealed a tight proximal mid-RCA at the site of previous angioplasty.

METHOD: Patient was brought to the cardiac cath laboratory and was prepped and draped in the usual sterile fashion. The patient had been premedicated with dextran for possible stent placement. The previously placed 5 French sheath was exchanged for an 8 French sheath over a guidewire. An 8 French right 4 hockey stick was then advanced over the guidewire and positioned in the right coronary ostium. A #1 guidewire was then advanced down to the right coronary artery across the proximal mid-RCA stenosis. A 1.5 mm Rally balloon was then advanced over the guidewire and positioned across the mid-RCA. Balloon angioplasty was performed to a peak atmospheric pressure of 6 atmospheres at one minute. The balloon was withdrawn and repeat angioplasty was performed. This time the balloon was readvanced and positioned in the proximal mid-RCA and angioplasty was performed to a peak atmospheric pressure of 12 atmospheres for 2 minutes. The balloon was withdrawn and a repeat angiogram was performed. The balloon was then exchanged for a 3 mm Cook stent balloon. This was advanced into the vasculature and positioned in the proximal mid-RCA. Balloon was inflated over 2 minutes to a peak atmospheric pressure of 6 atmospheres. The balloon was withdrawn and repeat angiogram was performed.

RESULTS: The proximal mid-RCA was successfully angioplastied from a 70% stenosis to a 0% residual with intracoronary stent placement.

RECOMMEND: Persantine, aspirin, coumadin, and heparin.

Barton Sellers, MD

EXERCISE 9–7

1. The acronym AICD describes what device? _____.

2. "EP" signifies _____.

3. What two main categories do pacemakers fall into? 1) _____,
   2) _____

4. A pacemaker "battery" is also known as a _____.

Read the following medical reports, then assign the correct ICD-9-CM and CPT codes.

5.

Patient:	Murphy, Bonnie
DOB:	02/17/50
Hospital #:	2789670
Physician:	James Reesor, MD
Date:	May 21, 20XX

CLINICAL INDICATIONS: History of ventricular fibrillation requiring DC cardioversion. This episode occurred while patient was having an episode of ischemia with STT wave changes. However, the patient did not rule in for a myocardial infarction.

METHOD: The patient was brought to the EP laboratory. He was prepped and draped in the usual sterile fashion. After local anesthesia was obtained, the right femoral vein was entered percutaneously at two separate sites. Two 6 French sheaths were advanced over guidewires and positioned into the right femoral vein. A 6 French quad catheter was then advanced into the vasculature and positioned at the high right atrium. In addition, a 6 French quadripolar catheter with a deflectable tip was advanced into the vasculature and positioned in the most proximal His-Purkinje area. Programmed electrical stimulation was performed in the high right atrium. The atrial catheter was then repositioned in the right ventricular apex, and again programmed electrical stimulation was performed. Finally, the ventricular catheter was positioned in the right ventricular outflow track, and again programmed electrical stimulation was performed. Following completion of the procedure, the sheaths were removed and hemostatis obtained with hand pressure.

ICD-9-CM code(s) _____

CPT code(s) _____

PROTOCOLS:

1. Baseline intervals were measured.

2. Programmed atrial extra stimulation was performed using a drive train of 600 msec with the introduction of two extra stimuli in order to determine the refractories.

continues

---

3. Rapid atrial pacing was performed in order to assess the point of AV node of Wenckebach.

4. Sinus node recovery times were measured using drive trains of 600, 500, and drive trains of 600, 500 and 400 msec.

5. Ventricular extra stimulation was performed using sensed and paced ventricular extra stimulation according to a Wellens Protocol. This stimulation protocol was again repeated at the right ventricular outflow track.

RESULTS:

1. Baseline intervals: the AH interval is 75 msec. The HV interval was 47 msec. The RS duration was 106 msec.

2. Sinus node: The patient has normal sinus node function. The longest corrected sinus node recovery time was 303 msec. This occurred using paced trial drive train of 500 msec.

3. AV node: The patient maintained 1:1 AV conduction to a cycle length of 350 msec. The patient developed AV node on Wenckebach at 340 msec. The AV node FRP was 410 msec. Ventricular dysrhythmias—no ventricular dysrhythmias could be induced.

CONCLUSIONS:

1. Normal sinus node function

2. Normal AV node function

3. No ventricular dysrhythmias could be induced

RECOMMENDATIONS: Would recommend continuing the patient on his anti-ischemic medication. I do not feel that anti-arrhythmic therapy or an implantable defibrillator is justified at this point since the patient's symptoms did occur with ischemia.

James Reesor, MD

ICD-9-CM code(s) _____

CPT code(s) _____

6.

Patient:	Williams, Betty
DOB:	01/20/35
Hospital #:	4507789
Physician:	Alene Walker, MD
Date:	May, 17 20XX

CLINICAL INDICATIONS: Syncope

METHOD: The patient was brought to the Head-Up Tilt lab and was placed supine for 5 minutes and was then tilted to 30 degrees for 5 minutes and finally to 60 degrees for 30 minutes.

Next, the patient again was laid supine. IV Isuprel was administered at 0.04 mcg/kg/min. The patient was then tilted to 60 degrees for 22 minutes, again with continuous ergodynamic monitoring.

RESULTS: The baseline head-up tilt test revealed normal heart rate and blood pressure response following the administration of I.V. Isuprel. The

continues

patient's heart rate fell from 127 to 71/min and blood pressure fell from 123 to 105 mmHg. The patient felt nauseated, but no syncope was elicited.

CONCLUSIONS: The patient probably does have a vasodepressor component to her syncope; however, the specificity of this test is impaired because the patient did not actually have a syncopal episode while on the table.

RECOMMENDATIONS: It would be reasonable to try a trial of low-dose beta blockade.

Alene Walker, MD

7.

Patient:	Foster, Martin
DOB:	10/24/45
Hospital #:	6398254
Physician:	Davis Abercrombie, MD
Date:	April 21, 20XX

ICD-9-CM code(s) _____

CPT code(s) _____

CLINICAL INDICATIONS: Easily inducible sustained monomorphic ventricular tachycardia in a patient with an LV aneurysm.

METHOD: The patient was brought to the EP lab and was prepped and draped in the usual sterile fashion. The left subclavian vein was entered percutaneously, and a guidewire was inserted under fluoroscopic guidance by Dr. Judson Danielson. A pacemaker pocket was then fashioned down into the area underlying the pectoralis fascia. An 11 French peel-away introducer sheath was then advanced over a guidewire. The 10 French Endotek lead was then advanced through the sheath and positioned in the right ventricular apex. Bradycardia pacing was performed followed by defibrillation threshold testing. The defibrillation testing was performed via the AICD. The AICD was programmed, positioned in the generator pocket, and the pocket was closed using three layers including a subcuticular stitch by Dr. Danielson.

AICD DATA: The AICD is a Ventak mini II, model #1763, serial #800132. The Endotek lead is a CPI, model #0125, serial #0125211359, and this is a 70 cm. length. The bradycardia pacing R wave is 12 millivolts. The threshold was 0.5 volts. The resistance at threshold was 460 ohms using a pulse width of 0.5 msec. During the defibrillation threshold testing in test #1 the patient received a one joule shock with an impedance of 30 ohms.

Defibrillation threshold test #1: The patient was induced into ventricular fibrillation using overdrive pacing via the device. A 15-joule shock was then delivered that was unsuccessful in bringing the patient back to normal sinus rhythm. A 270-joule rescue shock was administered via the device and successfully converted the patient back to a normal sinus rhythm.

Test #2—The patient was induced into ventricular fibrillation with overdrive pacing. A 20-joule shock was then administered via the device. It also was unsuccessful in converting the patient back to a normal sinus rhythm. A 28-joule rescue shock was administered via the device and successfully converted the patient back to a normal sinus rhythm.

continues

Test #3—The proximal cord was pulled back further into the IVC. The patient was induced into ventricular fibrillation using the overdrive pacing. A 20-joule shock was administered via the device and successfully converted the patient back to normal sinus rhythm. This was also with reverse polarity.

Test #4—The patient was induced into ventricular fibrillation with overdrive pacing. A 20-joule shock was administered, which successfully converted the patient back to a normal sinus rhythm. The energy was delivered via the device. This was also performed by the reverse polarity.

CONCLUSIONS: Successful AICD implantation with a defibrillation threshold of less than or equal to 20 joules using reverse polarity.

David Abercrombie, MD

ICD-9-CM code(s) _____

CPT code(s) _____

8.

Patient:	Crow, Bill
DOB:	03/22/39
Hospital #:	778414968
Physician:	Michael DuBonnet, MD
Date:	November 12, 20XX

CLINICAL INDICATION: Arrhythmia due to a pacemaker lead fracture and malfunction.

METHOD: After informed consent was obtained, the patient was brought to the operative suite in a fasting state. Conscious sedation was administered by anesthesia throughout this case. The patient's chest was prepped and draped in a sterile fashion. Sensorcaine 0.5% was infiltrated in the left pre-pectoral area over the chronic packing pocket for local anesthesia. A 4 cm incision was made over the chronic pulse generator. The old pulse generator was removed. The atrial and ventricular leads were disconnected from the pulse generator. Atrial sensing and pacing thresholds were measured and found to be excellent. Ventricular lead showed evidence for fracture, which was intermittent. A new Active fixation ventricular lead was placed via a 10 French peel-away sheath into the left subclavian venous system under fluoroscopic guidance with only modest difficulty in passing the HRA-SVC juncture. Excellent pacing system thresholds were obtained. Ten-volt output showed no extra cardiac capture. Chronaxie and rheobase measurements were obtained. The lead was affixed to underlying fascia using 0 strength Ethibond in the prescribed manner and using the provided anchoring sleeves. The pocket was then washed with antimicrobic solution. The chronic ventricular lead was capped. The new leads were attached to the chronic pulse generator and the system was placed in the left pre-pectoral pocket after revision to accommodate the new hardware. The wound was then closed in three layers using 2-0 and 3-0 Vicryl. The patient tolerated the procedure well and without apparent complication.

FINDINGS: The chronic ventricular lead was a CPI4262060500. It showed evidence for intermittent fracture and was capped. The chronic atrial lead was a CPI4269254320. The atrial sensing was 2.0 millivolts. The

continues

impedance was 440 ohms. The capture threshold was 1.1 volts at 0.5 millisecond pulse width. The new ventricular lead was a CPI426952 cm lead, serial number 288198. The sensing was unmeasurable due to lack of underlying rhythm. The impedance was 740 ohms. The capture threshold was 0.7 volts at 0.5 milliseconds pulse width. The rheobase was 0.4 volts and the chronaxie was 0.3 milliseconds. The generator was a chronic pulse generator, serial number CPI230405627.

CONCLUSIONS: Successful new ventricular lead placement, successful ventricular capping, successful pocket revision.

PLAN: Return to the patient's room, check PA and lateral chest X-ray in the morning. Continue IV antibiotics. Check rhythm without magnet EKG in the morning. Discharge tomorrow if no complications are apparent.

Michael DuBonnet, MD

USING MODIFIERS EFFECTIVELY

Modifiers are selected to indicate special circumstances surrounding the specific encounter or procedure allowing the proper reporting on the claim. The procedure or encounter should be described as a "mirror image" of the services that were provided. This will entail use of the two-digit modifiers located in the CPT code book and also the HCPCSII national modifiers that are activated per local carrier. For each insurance participation agreement, the coder is advised to obtain the rules and policies for the modifier use, as this is not standardized. Workers' compensation and automobile insurance plans may have very specific modifier requirements.

Although the intention of HIPAA transaction and data sets is to standardize the codes that are transmitted electronically, in actuality many variances still exist. HIPAA requires each practice to investigate and determine the policies of all participating insurance plans prior to submitting the claim to verify whether the plan will accept assignment.

CONSIDERING AN UNLISTED CODE? CATEGORY III

According to CPT rules (and HIPAA) a coder must choose Category III codes in lieu of an unlisted procedure code. The Category III codes are updated every January and July and can be accessed free of charge at www.ama-assn.org.

cardiomyopathy
A condition or general term describing a problem with the heart muscle.

0024T Nonsurgical septal reduction therapy for hypertrophic obstructive **cardiomyopathy;** with coronary arteriograms, with or without temporary pacemaker.
0068T+ Acoustic heart sound recording and computer analysis; with interpretation and report. (List with 93000.)
0069T+ Acoustic heart sound recording and computer analysis only. (List with 93005.)
0070T+ Interpretation and report only. (List with 93010.)
0074T Online evaluation and management services, per encounter, provided by a physician, using the internet or similar electronic communications network in response to a patient's request, *established patient.*

> **Coding Tip** *Per AMA/CPT, online evaluations are to be performed using HIPAA security standards, no examination is required, and not for every e-mail communication. The 0074T is only reported for established patients, ongoing treatment, and is not for new patients to establish professional services.*

0075T Transcatheter placement of extracranial vertebral or intrathoracic carotid artery stent(s), including radiologic supervision and interpretation, percutaneous; initial vessel

0076T+ each additional vessel. (List with 0075T.)

ipsilateral
Same side.

Per CPT, when **ipsilateral** extracranial vertebral or intrathoracic carotid arteriogram (including imaging and selective catheterization) confirms the need for stenting, then codes 0075T and 0076T should be selected. These codes include all ipsilateral extracranial vertebral or intrathoracic carotid catheterization, all diagnostic imaging for ipsilateral extracranial vertebral or intrathoracic carotid artery stenting, and all related radiologic supervision and interpretation. If stenting is not indicated, then the appropriate codes for selective catheterization and imaging should be reported in lieu of code 0075T.

Partner with 34800–34826

0078T Endovascular repair using prosthesis of abdominal aortic aneurysm, pseudoaneurysm or dissection, abdominal aorta, involving visceral branches (superior mesenteric, celiac and/or renal artery(ies)). *Implemented 7/1/05.*

Use 0078T, 0079T, 0080T, or 0081T with 35454, 37205–08 when outside of the target zone of the endoprosthesis.

Do not use 0078T with 34800–05, 35081, 35102, 35452, 35472, 37205–08.

0079T+ Placement of visceral extension prosthesis for endovascular repair of abdominal aorta, aneurysm involving visceral vessels, each visceral branch. (List with 0078T.)

0080T Endovascular repair of abdominal aortic aneurysm, pseudoaneurysm or dissection, abdominal aneurysm involving visceral vessels, using fenestrated modular bifurcated prosthesis (*two* docking limbs, radiological supervision and interpretation).

0081T+ Placement of visceral extension prosthesis for endovascular repair of abdominal aortic aneurysm involving visceral vessels, each visceral branch, radiological and supervision interpretation. (List with 0080T.)

0086T Left ventricular filling pressure indirect measurement by computerized calibration of the arterial waveform response to Valsalva maneuver.

0104T Inert gas rebreathing for cardiac output measurement; during rest. *Implemented 7/1/05.*

0105T (Same as previous) during exercise. *Implemented 7/1/05.*

CATEGORY II CODES

The codes in this series are for tracking and data collection purposes, and are optional to report on the claim. Unlike the Category III codes, they may not be selected in lieu of a Category I (regular CPT) code. The Category II codes are also updated in January and July annually. These are the Category II codes that would likely present for cardiology services.

1000F Tobacco use, smoking, assessed
1001F Tobacco use, nonsmoking, assessed
1002F Anginal symptoms and level of activity assessed
2000F Blood pressure, measured
4000F Tobacco use cessation intervention, counseling
4001F Tobacco use cessation intervention, pharmacologic therapy
4002F Statin therapy prescribed
4006F Beta-blocker therapy, prescribed
4009F Angiotensin converting enzyme inhibitor therapy, prescribed
4011F Oral antiplatelet therapy, prescribed

SUMMARY

Cardiology services progress from the early diagnostic stages, to the therapeutic and correction of illness and disease.

Understanding the anatomy and physiology terminology, the latest technology and devices, and the unique scenarios is required for accurate code selection. The professional coder will continually seek to learn as he or she gains experience in a practice.

The CPT codes are introduced two times per year, although the publication is only printed once per year. The ICD 9-CM codes may also be introduced two times per year, but are not always distributed. The HCPCSII codes are introduced throughout the year and distributed quarterly.

The patient may have financial obligations for the services that are rendered, and HIPAA requires that the practice advise the patient of each participating plan's claim coverage prior to the care.

REFERENCES

AMA CPT Assistant. (2004). Chicago: American Medical Association.

AMA current procedural terminology 2005 professional edition. (2004). Chicago: American Medical Association.

AMA principles of CPT coding. (2004). Chicago: American Medical Association.

ICD-9-CM expert for physicians volumes 1 & 2 (6th ed.). (2004). Salt Lake City, UT: Ingenix.

Kotoski, G. M. (2005). *CPT coding made easy: A technical guide.* MCMG Multimedia Publishers.

Updateable expert HCPSC Level II (16th ed.). (2005). Salt Lake City, UT: Ingenix.

Chapter 10
OB/GYN

KEY TERMS

abortion	gravidity	pelvic relaxation
antepartum	lactation	postpartum
anteverted	leiomyomas	presentation
copulation	menarche	prolapse
dilation	menopause	puerperium
echography	ovulation	retroverted
effacement	parity	trimester
gestation	parturition	

LEARNING OBJECTIVES

Upon successful completion of this module, you should be able to:

1. Recognize and define female reproductive anatomy and physiology.
2. Name the primary organs of the reproductive system.
3. Define and illustrate proper usage of OB/GYN terminology.
4. Accurately assign ICD-9-CM, CPT, and HCPCSII codes for exercises.
5. Sequence a series of codes with the most appropriate principal or primary diagnosis and procedure for claims.
6. Explain the significance of global service in the practice of obstetrics and gynecology.
7. State the differences between obstetric and gynecologic services.
8. Name diagnostics used in obstetrics and gynecology.

INTRODUCTION

This chapter introduces the many facets of obstetrics and gynecology. Physicians working within this specialty care for the healthy obstetrical patient and treat diseases of the female reproductive organs such as benign or malignant tumors, hormonal disorders, infections, and disorders related to pregnancy. Basic terms, office and hospital procedures, and diseases related to this specialty are identified and described.

This chapter discusses how to accurately assign diagnoses codes using the *International Classification of Diseases, 9th Revision, Clinical Modification, Volumes 1 and 2* (ICD-9-CM). Diagnoses are used to identify the reason for the service. Do not assign diagnostic codes for outpatient services where "suspected," "rule-out," "possible," or "probable" phrases precede the physician's impression. Instead, code the sign or symptom that prompted the visit.

This chapter also explores how to assign procedure codes relating to the specialty of obstetrics and gynecology using the *Current Procedural Terminology* (CPT) manual. Procedure codes are used to identify the service that was rendered. Great care should be taken when assigning a code, and the medical record or any other available pertinent documentation should be reviewed to identify the most appropriate and inclusive code. Only by using the most complete and detailed codes can the coder be certain that the resulting collection of data will be of use to a health care facility or other group needing information and that the assignment of codes results in the provider's maximum allowable reimbursement.

UNIQUE ASPECTS OF CODING OB/GYN

A woman's reproductive organs are a very private part of her body and many female patients discuss a variety of sensitive issues with their OB/GYN physician. Tactfulness in obtaining coding information and patient confidentiality must be observed by the coder. Female patients often feel close to their OB/GYN physicians and not only divulge delicate information, but want the physician to act as their primary care physician (PCP). This is sometimes allowed by insurance companies and managed care plans and occasionally the physician is listed as both a PCP and a specialist in the insurance directory. The coder needs to be aware if the patient is seeking treatment from a PCP or a specialist because this impacts the coding of evaluation and management services. Other physicians involved in the delivery of gynecologic and obstetric services would include family practice physicians, general practitioners, doctors of osteopathic medicine, general surgeons, and internal medicine physicians.

Often the physician's evaluation and management service turns into a counseling session and appropriate documentation and coding must be used for these situations. Because of the close proximity of the urogenital system, many OB/GYN physicians also diagnose and treat urinary problems. An understanding of urinary system CPT codes 50010 to 53899 is necessary. Other unique aspects of coding OB/GYN are mentioned throughout this chapter.

SUBSPECIALTIES OF OB/GYN

Because of the complexities of the female reproductive system, several subspecialties exist to help deliver the best medical care. Some would include fetal diagnostics, gynecologic endoscopy, gynecologic oncology, clinical geneticist, perineonatologist, premenstrual syndrome medicine, reproductive endocrinology, and urogynecology. See Table 10–1 for a complete description of these subspecialties, and Table 10–2 for abbreviations for various health care professionals.

ANATOMY AND PHYSIOLOGY OF THE FEMALE REPRODUCTIVE SYSTEM

The primary function of the female reproductive system is to produce offspring. The ovaries are the sex organs that produce eggs to be fertilized by the male sperm. The ovaries also produce hormones that control the menstrual cycle and help maintain

TABLE 10-1   Subspecialties of OB/GYN.

Subspecialty	Definition
Fetal Diagnostics	Provides antepartum diagnostic and therapeutic services including antepartum fetal heart rate testing, high resolution obstetrical ultrasound, fetal echocardiography, biophysical profile, fetal Doppler flow studies, chorion villus sampling, amniocentesis, fetal umbilical vein blood sampling, and fetal surgery.
Gynecologic Endoscopy	Specializes in the use of hysteroscopy, laparoscopy, and pelviscopy to diagnose and manage gynecologic conditions. Provides the service of laser therapy.
Gynecologic Oncology	Provides comprehensive care for women with gynecologic neoplasms, including the surgical management of patients with cancer and preinvasive disease of the female genital tract. Provides the administration of chemotherapy, immunotherapy, and the coordination of radiation treatments.
Geneticist (Clinical)	Specializes in the study of the causes and inheritance of genetic disorders including chromosomal aberrations and the transmission of genetic factors from generation to generation.
Perineonatologist	Specializes in maternal-fetal medicine and provides consultation on patients with complications of pregnancy. Services include genetic counseling, prematurity prevention, fetal echocardiography, and antenatal testing using the most current diagnostic and treatment modalities.
Premenstrual Syndrome Medicine	Provides patients with accurate diagnosis and individualized treatment for premenstrual syndrome.
Reproductive Endocrinology	Provides medical care for women suffering from problems with menstruation, symptoms of masculinization, abnormal milk production of the breast, menopause, hormone replacement, and endometriosis. Specializes in the diagnosis and treatment of infertility including diagnostic laparoscopy, ovulation induction, intrauterine insemination, in vitro insemination, intrafallopian transfer, microsurgery, and donor oocyte transfer.
Urogynecology	Provides diagnosis and treatment for women with functional disorders of the lower urinary tract such as urinary stress incontinence and problems of anatomical support of the female pelvis.

pregnancy. The sex hormones, estrogen and progesterone, play a vital role in the development and function of the reproductive organs and in sexual behavior and drive. They are also responsible for the development of secondary sex characteristics. Follicle-stimulating hormone (FSH) and luteinizing hormone (LH) are referred to as gonadotropinsi, which stimulate the production of other hormones and help produce the ovum (egg). The uterus houses the developing fetus and the vagina provides a route for delivery. The female breasts produce milk to feed the infant after birth.

The female reproductive system consists of external and internal organs. The external organs are called the external genitalia and the internal organs consist of the vagina, the uterus, fallopian tubes, and ovaries.

TABLE 10–2 **Abbreviations Relating to OB/GYN Health Care Professionals.**

Abbreviation	Position
CCE	Certified Childbirth Educator
CCS	Certified Coding Specialist
CFA	Certified First Assistant (surgical)
CMA	Certified Medical Assistant
CNM	Certified Nurse Midwife
CPC	Certified Procedure Coder
CST	Certified Surgical Technician (2nd surgical assistant)
FACOG	Fellow of the American College of Obstetricians and Gynecologists
HIM	Health Information Management
IBCLC	International Board Certified Lactation Consultant
LPN	Licensed Practical Nurse
MD	Doctor of Medicine
PA–C	Physician's Assistant–Certified
RMA	Registered Medical Assistant
RNFA	Registered Nurse First Assistant (surgical)
RNP	Registered Nurse Practitioner

External Structures

External Genitalia The external genitalia, also called the vulva, can be seen on physical examination and include the labia majora, labia minora, clitoris, urethral orifice, and mons pubis (see Figure 10–1). The labia majora (large vaginal lips) are the outer folds of the vagina and the labia minora (small vaginal lips) are the inner folds on either side of the orifice, the opening to the vagina. These serve as protective barriers. The Bartholin's glands, located on either side of the vaginal orifice and the Skene's glands, located near the meatus, which is the external opening to the urethra, secrete lubricating fluids. Occasionally these glands get blocked and a cystic formation or abscess develops, which may become large and painful needing incision and drainage. The clitoris, a very sensitive organ of erectile tissue, plays a role in sexual arousal and is the structure that corresponds to the male penis. The mons pubis is the hairy skin that surrounds the vulva. The perineum is the area located between the vaginal opening and the anus. This area is often cut during childbirth in a procedure called an episiotomy to prevent tissue from being torn.

Breasts The breasts are two mammary glands that are considered accessory organs of the female reproductive system (see Figure 10–2). Their primary function

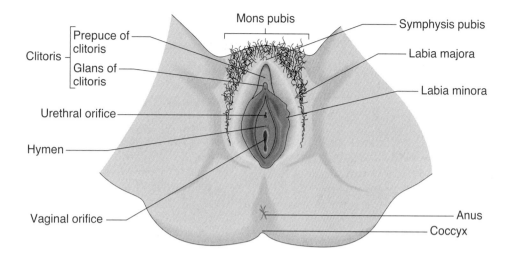

Figure 10–1 Female external genitalia.

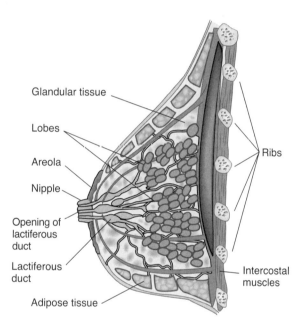

Figure 10–2 Female mammary glands (sagittal view).

parturition
Labor and delivery.

lactation
Process of secreting milk from the breasts.

is to produce milk for the nourishment of the infant. After giving birth, which is referred to as **parturition,** hormones stimulate **lactation,** which is the production of milk. These glands are divided into a number of lobes that are further subdivided and produce secretions that are channeled through ducts that culminate in the opening of the nipple. The pigmented area that surrounds each nipple is referred to as the areola.

Internal Structures

copulation
Act of sexual intercourse.

Vagina The vagina is a muscular tube that extends from the uterus to the exterior of the body (see Figures 10–3 and 10–4). This thin, elastic canal provides an entrance from the outside to the internal organs. It receives the penis (and semen) during sexual intercourse, which is referred to as **copulation,** and serves as the birth canal when it dilates, thus enlarging to provide a passageway for the delivery of the infant.

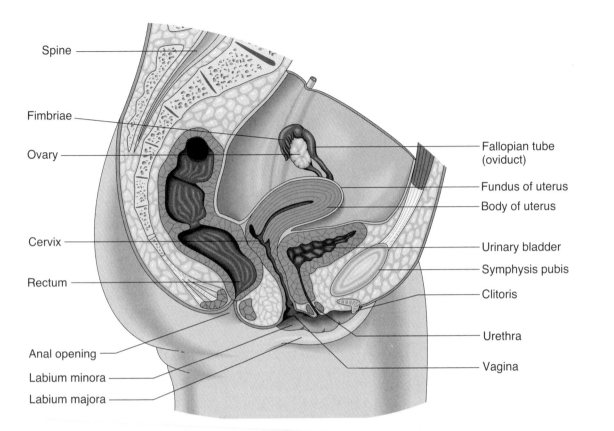

Spine

Fimbriae

Ovary

Cervix

Rectum

Anal opening

Labium minora

Labium majora

Fallopian tube
(oviduct)

Fundus of uterus

Body of uterus

Urinary bladder

Symphysis pubis

Clitoris

Urethra

Vagina

Figure 10–3 Female reproductive organs (sagittal view).

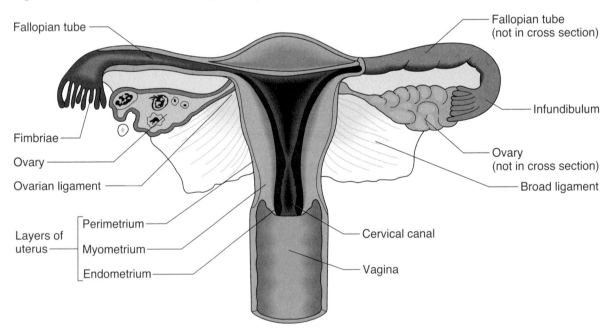

Fallopian tube

Fimbriae

Ovary

Ovarian ligament

Layers of
uterus

Perimetrium

Myometrium

Endometrium

Fallopian tube
(not in cross section)

Infundibulum

Ovary
(not in cross section)

Broad ligament

Cervical canal

Vagina

Figure 10–4 Female reproductive organs (anterior view).

menarche
Time when the first
menstruation begins.

menopause
Time when menstruation
ceases.

Ovaries The ovaries are the primary organs of the female reproductive system. They are two small almond-shaped organs that are suspended by ligaments above and on either side of the uterus (see Figure 10–4). They usually produce ova (eggs) every twenty-eight days during the reproductive years from **menarche** to **menopause.** Menarche is the beginning of the menstrual function. Menopause is the cessation, either naturally occurring or surgically caused. The ovaries also provide hormones, which serve the needs of the reproductive cell and/or developing fetus. These hormones, estrogen and progesterone, are referred to as sex hormones and are responsible for the maturation of secondary sex characteristics such as axillary and pubic hair, onset of menses, widening of the pelvis, increased fat deposits, enlargement of accessory organs, and the development of breasts. The ovum grow and develop within a small sac in the ovary, referred to as a follicle. The ovum matures under the influence of hormones and the follicle grows and finally bursts open to release the egg. This is referred to as **ovulation.**

Fallopian Tubes The fallopian tubes, sometimes called oviducts or uterine tubes, originate just below the fundus of the uterus (see Figure 10–4). The outer end of each tube curves over the top of each ovary and opens into the abdominal cavity. Although they are not connected to the ovary, the flared ends of the oviducts have fingerlike projections called fimbriae that sweep the ovum into the oviduct where fertilization occurs. The fertilized egg then travels down the tube toward the uterus.

Uterus The uterus is a pear-shaped structure situated between the urinary bladder and the rectum (see Figure 10–3). It is a muscular organ that receives the fertilized ovum and provides an appropriate environment for the developing offspring (see Figure 10–4). The wall of the uterus consists of three layers. The endometrium is the innermost glandular layer that is ever-changing with the menstrual cycle. The superficial portion of this mucous membrane pulls loose and sloughs with menstruation each month. The myometrium is the bulky middle layer, which consists of smooth muscle. This muscle plays an important role during labor as it contracts and forces the fetus out of the womb. The perimetrium is the outer, membranous tissue layer, which is continuous with the broad ligaments that suspend the uterus.

The top rounded portion of the uterus is called the fundus. As the uterus grows during pregnancy, the fundus is palpated by the obstetrician and a measurement is taken from the top of the fundus to the pubic bone to determine the size of the developing fetus (see Figure 10–5). The major portion of the uterus is referred to as the corpus or body. The lower portion, a narrow outlet that extends into the vagina, is called the cervix. The cervix is the neck of the uterus and the area from

ovulation
Release of the ovum from the ovary; usually occurs every 28 days.

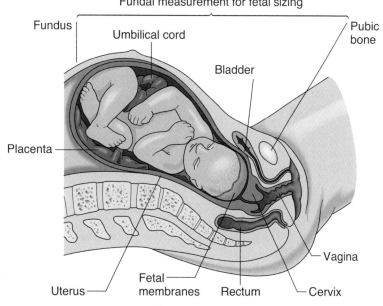

Figure 10–5 Fetus in utero at term.

which a Papanicolaou smear (Pap test) is taken. The opening in the cervix, referred to as the endocervical canal, dilates during labor to allow passage of the fetus. Four sets of ligaments hold the uterus in place and permit it to grow and move during pregnancy.

After the ovum implants in the rich blood supply offered by the endometrium, the placenta forms to serve as a transport system for blood and nutrients. The hormone, human chorionic gonadotropin (hCG) begins to secrete and is essential for the maturation and maintenance of pregnancy. This hormone can be measured in serum blood and urine and is detected in various forms of pregnancy testing.

OBSTETRICS AND GYNECOLOGY (OB/GYN)

As the name implies, obstetrics and gynecology (OB/GYN) are two specialties in one. Unlike other specialties, OB/GYN almost exclusively cares for women. For details concerning specific coding challenges, the OB/GYN specialty is divided into separate areas dealing with the pregnant and the nonpregnant patient.

ICD-9-CM Official Guidelines

The Chapter 11 codes in the ICD-9-CM guidelines associated with pregnancy have a rather unique sequencing priority. The Chapter 11 codes are placed first, with other codes following for most encounters. If the pregnancy is incidental to the encounter, code V22.2 is selected rather than the Chapter 11 codes since there is no care or treatment of the pregnancy at that particular encounter. The "not affecting the pregnancy" statement is determined by the provider and is documented.

Impending or threatened condition. Select the code with these standards:

- If the threatened condition did occur, code as confirmed diagnosis.
- If it did not occur, look under the main entry for the condition to see if there is a code option for "impending or threatened." If there are no subentry options under the main condition, code the existing underlying conditions that are present and *not* the condition that is impending or threatened.

HIV infection in pregnancy, childbirth, and the puerperium. This is the first indication of a common important rule. Chapter 15 codes are sequenced first.

If the encounter is for the purpose of an HIV-related illness, select:

- 647.6X, Other specified infectious and parasitic diseases in the mother, classified elsewhere, but complicating pregnancy.

Additional code for HIV-related illness treated at this encounter: If the encounter is for the purpose of asymptomatic HIV during pregnancy, select 647.6*X* and V08.

Additional code for HIV-related illness treated at this encounter: If the encounter is for the purpose of asymptomatic HIV during pregnancy, select 647.6*X* and V08.

An asymptomatic patient encounter for HIV testing: Select V73.89 for the HIV screening and V69.8 (Other problems related to lifestyle) if the patient is in a high-risk group for HIV. When the patient has signs or symptoms of HIV or previously confirmed HIV related disease, and is tested today; or confirmed HIV, code the signs and symptoms or the confirmed HIV related diagnosis. Counseling (V65.44) may be added to any of these encounters when performed, and may also be the exclusive code for an encounter to discuss the results.

HIV Testing encounter with coding examples are:

Asymptomatic patient normal risk	V73.89 HIV screening
Asymptomatic patient high risk	V73.89 HIV screening and V69.8 Other problems related to lifestyle
Signs and symptoms of HIV or previously confirmed HIV related disease	Signs and symptoms OR confirmed HIV related diagnosis
Counseling (additional code if documented)	V65.44 HIV counseling

Primary malignancy previously excised. If the primary malignancy has been excised from its site with no further treatment, V10 Personal history of malignancy is selected. If the diagnosed and treated malignancy metastasizes to another site, select the secondary malignancy code, followed with V10 for the primary malignancy.

Encounter for current treatment chemotherapy and radiation therapy. If surgical removal is followed by chemotherapy or radiation therapy, select the neoplasm code. If the encounter is for chemo or radiation therapy only, select V58.0 and/or V58.1. If the patient is receiving both, select both codes.

Complications of chemo/radiation therapy. For complications of chemo/radiation therapy, select the V58.0 and/or V58.1, followed by the complication illness code.

Chapter 11 (630–677). Again, when 630–677 illness is managed or treated, the illness code is the first code, followed by other codes. Chapter 11 codes are placed only on the mother's claim (not the baby's). The fifth digits are required, and can be tricky to locate. Find the code, then search *previous* to the code for the proper fifth digit.

Routine antenatal/prenatal visits. If no complications are present, select V22.*X* as the first diagnosis. If other illness is treated at the encounter, do not list V22.*X* codes in conjunction with other 630–677 codes.

Prenatal outpatient visits for high risk. Select V23.*X* for high-risk pregnancy prenatal visit as the first diagnosis. Secondary codes from 630–677 are listed when treated.

Episode with no delivery. For an encounter without the delivery, select the codes for the complications of the encounter.

Delivery. The principal diagnosis is the main circumstance for delivery. For C-sections, select a code for the main reason the C-section is performed, unless it is unrelated to the condition resulting in the delivery (e.g., auto accident). For every delivery, a V27.0–V27.9 code is indicated. Do not select these after the delivery; it is needed only on the initial service.

Fetal conditions affecting the mother. Select 655 codes only if the fetal condition is affecting the mother. If the fetal condition exists but is not harming the mother, it is not coded.

In-utero surgery. If surgery is performed on the fetus during the prenatal time, a code from 655 is selected. Do not select a code from Chapter 15 (baby's codes) for the mother's claim.

Current conditions complicating pregnancy. Select a code from 648.*X* if a current condition is affecting the pregnancy, followed by additional codes for the condition.

Diabetes in pregnancy. For pregnant women with diabetes mellitus (DM), select 648.0*X* followed by a code from the 250 describing the type of DM. Add V58.67 if current long-term use of insulin also applies, as applicable.

Gestational diabetes. Gestational diabetes often presents in those who did not have DM previously. It places greater risk for DM after pregnancy. Select 648.8*X* for the gestational DM. If treated with insulin, add V58.67.

Normal delivery 650. The 650 code is primary, and "solo." Do not select additional codes from Chapter 11; codes from other chapters may follow 650 only if not complicating the pregnancy. Add V27.0 with this code. Codes 650 and V27.0 are linked.

Postpartum. Postpartum begins at the completion of delivery and ends at six weeks. The peripartum is the last month of pregnancy, ending at five months after delivery.

Pregnancy-related complications after six weeks. The physician may diagnose a condition related to the pregnancy after the first six weeks. Select the code from Chapter 11 if this is the documentation.

Postpartum complications occurring during the same encounter as the delivery. The fifth digit of the codes describes this situation. Select the fifth digit carefully.

Encounter for routine postpartum care if delivery occurred elsewhere. If the mother delivers other than at the hospital, with normal postpartum care, no complications, select V24.0. If the delivery occurs other than at the hospital, do not select the delivery code; select postpartum conditions.

Late effect of complication pregnancy. When a sequelae (condition) is cared for after the initial complication of the pregnancy, 677 follows the condition. In other words, select a code for the condition, followed by the 677, indicating that it is due to the late effect of pregnancy.

Abortions 634–637. The fifth digit describes the specific episode of care; select the code carefully. If a complication caused the abortion, select the code from the 640–651 series. Do not select a code from the 660 with complications of abortion. Code 639 is selected for all complications following abortion. If the abortion results in a liveborn fetus, select 644.21 followed by V27, outcome of delivery. Select 634 or 635 for the encounter caring for the retained products of abortion, with fifth digit 1.

Maternal causes of perinatal morbidity. Select 760–63 for the baby claim if the maternal condition actually affects the newborn. If the mother has a condition that has not affected the baby, this is not coded.

Screening. Screening is the testing for disease in well individuals. If a patient has a sign or symptom, and testing is performed to rule out or confirm a suspected diagnosis, this test is a "diagnostic examination," and not a screening. The sign or symptom is selected as the code. This fact is of utmost importance for the Pap testing and mammography testing.

Screening may be the primary code if the purpose of the encounter is screening. If the encounter is for other reasons, list those first, followed by the screening. Do not list a screening code in addition to the routine pelvic examination, because it is inherent. Should a condition be discovered during the screening, follow the screening code with the condition codes.

Observation. If the encounter is for observation of a suspected condition that is not found, select a V code. If any signs or symptoms are present, select those codes instead of the observation code.

Aftercare. Aftercare is defined as occurring after the initial treatment was completed, and the patient has continued current care during the healing and recovery phase. There is no time frame specified. If the care is current acute disease, do not select aftercare *except* radiotherapy and/or chemotherapy. Aftercare for mastectomy service is common.

Follow-up. Follow-up differs from aftercare, in that follow-up cares for a condition that is fully treated and no longer exists. Select for continuing surveillance of a condition. Select an additional history code, V24 with V67.

Counseling. Counseling codes are selected usually as additional codes, if not part of the disease code.

Family planning or fertility planning. Select codes from the V25 or the V26 series when treated at the encounter. More discussion regarding the selection of the Pap and pelvic ICD-9-CM codes will be found later in this chapter.

OBSTETRICS (OB)

puerperium
Time after delivery that it takes for the uterus to return to its normal size; usually three to six weeks.

Obstetrics is the branch of medical science that has to do with the pregnancy process from conception to childbirth and through the **puerperium.** The puerperium is the recovery time, after delivery, that it takes for the uterus to return to normal size; usually three to six weeks. The obstetrician provides maternity care, including the delivery of the child, and postpartum care for the healthy obstetrical patient as well as the patient experiencing complications brought on by the pregnancy and conditions that complicate the pregnancy such as anatomical defects or disease. Maternity CPT codes 59000 series are used for obstetrical care including abortion. This area of medicine is especially difficult to code because of the many intricacies that may stem from a complication, generating complex details that can affect a diagnosis. If the patient were not pregnant, these conditions would be found in various chapters of ICD-9-CM; however, since the patient is pregnant, these conditions have been reclassified to the pregnancy chapter. The following main terms are used to locate various pregnancy complications in the alphabetic index of ICD-9-CM:

1. Childbirth
2. Delivery
3. Labor
4. Pregnancy
5. Puerperium

Newborn services are coded separately from the mother's services. Use V27.0–V27.9 to identify the outcome of delivery on the mother's chart.

gravidity
Term used to indicate the number of pregnancies a woman has had; gravida is used with numerals (e.g., 0, I, II).

parity
Term used to indicate the number of pregnancies in which the fetus has reached viability; approximately 22 weeks of gestation. May also be used with a series of numerals to indicate the number of full-term infants, pre-term infants, abortions, and living children (e.g. Para 0-1-0-1).

gestation
Time in which a woman is pregnant and fetal development takes place.

trimester
First, second, and third three-month period of which the pregnancy is divided.

Terms Common to OB

Gravidity and **parity** are terms used to describe a woman's history of pregnancy and childbirth. Gravidity refers to the number of pregnancies and parity refers to the number of pregnancies in which the fetus has reached viability, approximately twenty-two weeks of gestation. See Table 10–3 for a complete description of terms relating to reproductive history.

The time a woman is pregnant and fetal development takes place is referred to as **gestation.** The pregnancy is divided into three **trimesters.** The total gestation, from fertilization of the ovum to delivery of the baby, is approximately 266 days. However, the figure 280 days is used most often to calculate the estimated date of delivery (EDD) starting from the first day of the last menstrual period (LMP). The time from the LMP to the end of the twelfth week make up the first trimester. The fertilized ovum is referred to as an embryo during the first eight weeks of life. Starting from the thirteenth week of gestation to the end of the twenty-seventh week make up the second trimester. The third trimester starts at the twenty-eighth week of gestation and extends to the estimated date of confinement (EDC). When coding, it is important to understand what trimester a patient is in. The severity of a condition accompanying pregnancy can often be substantiated by the number of weeks gestation in which it occurs.

Rhythmic contractions, dilation of the cervix, and a discharge of bloody mucus from the cervix and vagina, referred to as "show," mark the start of true labor.

TABLE 10–3   Terms Relating to Reproductive History.

Term	Meaning
para	A term used with numerals to designate the number of pregnancies that have resulted in the birth of a viable offspring
nullipara (O)	No live offspring
unipara (I)	One live offspring
bipara (II)	Two live offspring
tripara (III)	Three live offspring
quadripara (IV)	Four live offspring
multipara	Two or more live offspring (also called pluripara)
para 0-2-3-2	Series of numbers used to indicate the complete reproductive history. When a series of numbers are used:
para <u>0</u>	the first number represents full term infants
para 0-<u>2</u>	the second number represents preterm infants
para 0-2-<u>3</u>	the third number represents abortions
para 0-2-3-<u>2</u>	the fourth number represents living children
gravida (G)	Pregnant woman
primigravida	First pregnancy (also called unigravida)
primipara	Delivery of one offspring regardless of whether it is alive or dead
secundigravida	Second pregnancy
multigravida	Many pregnancies (also called plurigravida)
G-2 para-1	Combination of gravidity and parity; two pregnancies with one live birth

Labor is divided into three stages. Stage 1, the dilation stage, is the time from the onset of true labor to the complete dilation of the cervix; usually reaching 10 cm in diameter. This may last from six to twenty-four hours and is the longest stage. Stage 2, the expulsion stage, is the period from full dilation to delivery of the infant. This stage usually takes about an hour for the first birth and approximately twenty minutes for subsequent births, but may take as long as two hours. Stage 3, the placental stage, is the final phase when the placenta, also called afterbirth, is delivered. This stage is usually accomplished in fifteen minutes. Failure to progress in any of the above stages of labor may constitute a complication and the possible need of a cesarean section to secure safe delivery of the fetus. Complications may include obstructed labor, abnormality of forces of labor, and long labor.

Maternity Package of CPT

antepartum
Time of pregnancy from conception to onset of delivery.

postpartum
Time after giving birth.

One of the unusual aspects of OB is the global fee that encompasses the **antepartum,** delivery, and **postpartum** period of a normal pregnancy. The initial and subsequent history, all physical examinations, recording of blood pressure, weight, fetal heart tones, routine urinalysis, and monthly visits up to twenty-eight weeks gestation are included in antepartum care. After twenty-eight weeks, biweekly visits up to thirty-six weeks gestation, and weekly visits until delivery are also covered in antepartum care. All other visits or services should be coded separately.

Delivery services include the hospital admission with history and physical, the management of uncomplicated labor, and the vaginal or cesarean delivery. Episiotomy and use of forceps are also included. Any medical problems complicating the labor and delivery management should be coded separately utilizing codes in the Evaluation and Management section and Medicine section of the CPT manual.

Normal, uncomplicated hospital and office visits for six weeks following vaginal or cesarean section (C/S) delivery are included in postpartum care.

Because of the extended length of care of the OB patient, it is not unusual for more than one physician to provide complete obstetrical care. If a physician provides part or all of the antepartum and/or postpartum care, but does not perform delivery due to referral to another physician or termination of pregnancy by abortion, the antepartum and postpartum care CPT codes 59409–59410 and 59414–59430 should be used.

Other E/M services used in OB include a new or established patient office visit to determine pregnancy, hospital observation services, office and hospital consultations, and confirmatory consultations emergency department services, possible critical care services and newborn care.

EXERCISE 10–1

Use the ICD-9-CM and CPT manuals to code the following exercises.

1. At the physician's office, the obstetrician performs an ultrasound on a pregnant patient, 16 weeks gestation, for complete fetal and maternal evaluation:

   One fetus, chorionic sac intact, measurement 20 gm, intracranial, spinal, abd, heart, cord and placenta normal.

   What CPT code would be used to bill for this service?

2. An obstetrical patient has just delivered twins. One is liveborn and one is stillborn. What ICD-9-CM code(s) would be used to show the outcome of delivery?

3. A woman was seeing her OB/GYN physician for the first and part of the second trimesters of her pregnancy until the physician moved to another city. What code would this physician select for the first five prenatal visits?

Maternity Care and Delivery of Normal Pregnancy

The vast majority of OB care is provided without complication and can be coded using CPT code 59400, routine obstetric care including antepartum care, vaginal delivery (with or without episiotomy, and/or forceps) and postpartum care. ICD-9-CM code 650, normal delivery requiring no assistance, and V27.0, indicating the outcome of delivery as a single liveborn infant, would be appropriate. For a cesarean delivery with routine obstetric care including antepartum and postpartum care CPT code 59510 is used. Occasionally patients who have had a previous C/S may successfully deliver vaginally. When this occurs, CPT codes 59610–59614 are used.

Fetal monitoring during labor by the attending physician is considered a part of the obstetrical package. If a consulting obstetrician or perinatologist performs fetal monitoring during labor with written report, CPT codes 59050 or 59051 may be reported. Fetal nonstress tests and fetal contraction stress tests may be reported separately.

Complications in and of Pregnancy

When a patient is admitted because of a condition that is complicating the pregnancy or is a complication of pregnancy, the code for the obstetric complication should be the principal diagnosis. Additional codes to add detail and specificity may be used where appropriate.

Some of the more common complications of pregnancy include anemia, gestational diabetes, and hydramnios. Anemia is a reduction, below normal in the number of erythrocytes (RBCs) in the concentration of hemoglobin, or in the volume of packed red blood cells (RBCs). These all affect the oxygen-carrying capacity of the blood and can be diagnosed by an abnormal complete blood count (CBC) or hematocrit (HCT), which are included in a routine prenatal laboratory test or obstetric panel. Gestational diabetes occurs when there is a glucose intolerance with the onset of pregnancy. This can be determined from a fasting blood sugar (FBS) test to screen for diabetes. The patient may also have to undergo a postprandial (PP) blood test or glucose tolerance test (GTT) to better determine the level of intolerance. Hydramnios refers to an excess amount of amniotic fluid that is seen on ultrasound.

Toxemia is a rarer complication that may arise in pregnancy, as is toxoplasmosis. Toxemia, a potentially life-threatening condition for the patient and fetus, occurs most frequently in primiparas (see Table 10–4) who are twelve to eighteen years old and women thirty-five years of age and older. It is rarely apparent before the twenty-fourth week of pregnancy. The toxemic patient presents with pregnancy-induced hypertension, proteinuria, and edema. This condition is also known as preeclampsia and if the patient's condition is not successfully treated, it may progress to eclampsia. As symptoms worsen, the patient may experience sudden weight gain, headaches, dizziness, spots before the eyes, nausea, vomiting, and ultimately have a seizure. If convulsions occur, they may result in abruptio placentae, which is a separation of the placenta from the uterus.

Toxoplasmosis is an acute or chronic widespread disease of animals and humans caused by the parasite Toxoplasma gondii. It is acquired by eating uncooked lamb, pork, or goat meat, and exposure to infected cat litter. It can infect a fetus transplacentally as a result of maternal infection. If the mother acquires toxoplasmosis, lesions may occur in the brain, heart, liver, lungs, and muscles. If the fetus contracts the congenital form, central nervous system lesions may occur, causing blindness, brain defects, and death.

The appropriate diagnosis code should be applied as the principal diagnosis if a pregnant patient experiences septicemia, a condition of bacteria in the blood-

TABLE 10–4   Types of Abortion.

Type	Definition
accidental	abortion that occurs spontaneously
ampullar	tubal abortion
artificial	abortion surgically induced
complete abortion	abortion in which the complete products of conception are expelled
criminal abortion	illegal abortion
early abortion	abortion within the first 12 weeks of pregnancy
elective abortion	induced abortion done at the request of the mother for other than therapeutic reasons
habitual abortion	three or more consecutive spontaneous abortions occurring within the 20th week of gestation
imminent abortion	impending abortion
incomplete abortion	abortion in which parts of the products of conception are retained in the uterus
inevitable abortion	abortion that cannot be stopped
infected abortion	abortion associated with infection from retained material in the uterus
missed abortion	abortion in which the embryo or fetus has died prior to the 20th week of gestation and the products of conception have been retained for at least 8 weeks
septic abortion	abortion in which there is an infection of the products of conception and in the endometrial lining of the uterus
spontaneous abortion (SAB)	abortion occurring before the 20th week of gestation without apparent cause
therapeutic abortion (TAB)	abortion induced for the safeguard of the mother's mental or physical health; term also used for any legal abortion
threatened abortion	signs and symptoms of uterine bleeding and cramping before the 20th week of gestation that appear to threaten the continuation of pregnancy
tubal abortion	abortion where the embryo or fetus has been expelled through the distal portion of the fallopian tube

stream, or septic shock. A pregnancy complication code should also be used to add emphasis to the patient's condition.

EXAMPLE

038.2	Pneumococcal septicemia
647.9	Infectious and parasitic conditions in the mother classifiable elsewhere, but complicating pregnancy, childbirth, or the puerperium; other specified infections and parasitic diseases

Sepsis and septic shock associated with abortion, ectopic pregnancy, and molar pregnancy are classified to codes 630 to 639 (Complications of Pregnancy, Childbirth, and the Puerperium) of ICD-9-CM, Chapter 11. See Complications Mainly Related to Pregnancy in Chapter 11, categories 640–648 for problems such as hemorrhage in pregnancy, hypertension complicating pregnancy, excessive vomiting, threatened labor, infections in the mother, and so forth.

dilation
Stretching and opening of the cervix during labor to facilitate the baby's passage through the pelvis; measured in centimeters.

effacement
Obliteration of the cervix during labor as it shortens from one or two centimeters in length to paper thin, leaving only the external os; expressed as a percentage.

Various medications may be used to rid complications of pregnancy, such as Braxton-Hicks contractions or premature **dilation.** Braxton-Hicks contractions are light, usually painless, irregular uterine contractions that gradually increase in intensity and frequency and become more rhythmic during the third trimester. They are often referred to as "false labor." Although usually harmless, if they occur with great frequency during the first or second trimester, they occasionally cause premature **effacement** and/or dilation of the cervix. Effacement is the obliteration of the cervix as it shortens from 1 or 2 centimeters in length to paper thin, leaving only the external os. Dilation is the stretching and opening of the cervix during labor to facilitate the baby's passage through the pelvis. The stages of effacement and dilation can usually let the health care staff determine how close a mother is to delivery. An oral or injectable medication, such as terbutaline sulfate, may be administered to "calm down" the Braxton-Hicks contractions and delay delivery of a premature infant. Appropriate injection codes from the Medicine section of the CPT and possible Level II HCPCS codes should be assigned to such situations. These are national codes developed for and updated by the Medicare system.

EXERCISE 10–2

Use the ICD-9-CM manual to code the following exercises.

1. Hyperemesis gravidarum (mild), 1st trimester _____

2. Threatened labor (38 weeks gestation) _____

3. An expectant woman is on her way to a friend's house for lunch. While driving there she becomes very weak and takes herself to a nearby health care clinic. Her blood sugar is checked, and it is elevated. A diagnosis of gestational diabetes is made. _____

4. A 24-week pregnant woman with current edema of the joint areas and a history of high blood pressure suddenly began to have seizure-like convulsions. Her husband called 911 and explained what was happening. An ambulance rushed her to the nearest hospital due to severe eclampsia. _____

5. At her scheduled doctor's appointment, a 32-week primigravida mentions that she has been experiencing some bleeding on occasion. She states that it has not been painful; therefore, she only thought it to be normal for this stage of pregnancy. There is usually enough blood to cause her to wear undergarment protection. She also says this has been happening for the past three days. The physician sends her to the hospital for an ultrasound and a diagnosis of antepartum hemorrhage is made. _____

Multiple Births More than one fetus may or may not present a complication depending on the number, position, and week of gestation in which delivery occurs. With the use of fertility drugs, the number of multiple births has increased significantly. When coding deliveries, always include a code for the status of the infant. These include codes V27.0–V27.9 and are found under "outcome of delivery" in Volume 2 of the ICD-9-CM. If a multiple pregnancy affects the fetus or newborn, use code 761.5.

Ectopic Pregnancy Ectopic pregnancy is a term used to indicate all forms of pregnancy in which implantation occurs outside the uterus. It is also called tubal pregnancy because 95 percent of ectopic pregnancies occur in the fallopian tube. If the embryo does not spontaneously abort, its growth may cause the tube to rupture. This becomes a life-threatening condition as hemorrhage occurs and may lead to peritonitis, an inflammation of the lining in the abdominal cavity, causing future infertility. Surgical intervention is needed and CPT codes 59120–59151 may be used in conjunction with ICD-9-CM codes from category 633.

Placental Anomalies Abnormalities in the size, shape, or function of the placenta, placental membranes and cord, and the amniotic fluid make up placental anomalies. The most common occurrences are placenta accreta, in which the placenta grows deep into the muscle tissue of the uterus. The placenta does not release at the time of birth and bleeding may occur. Placenta previa occurs with implantation anywhere in the lower segment of the uterus. It may present a partial blockage of the cervix, called partial placenta previa, or full blockage, called full placenta previa. In either case, the patient is prone to bleeding and normally delivers by cesarean section to prevent hemorrhage and interruption of the fetal oxygen supply. Placenta abruptio, as mentioned earlier, is the premature separation of the placenta from the wall of the uterus. This usually happens after the twentieth week of gestation in women over thirty-five years of age who are multigravidas. This, also, can be a life-threatening condition as hemorrhage may occur and interrupt the fetal blood supply. ICD-9-CM codes from category 641 are used for these conditions.

Postpartum Disorders Puerperal infections are those related to childbirth and occur during the postpartum period. Cleanliness and sterile techniques have improved the chances of avoiding such infections, and antibiotics have improved the chances of recovery. The treatment of most puerperal infections would fall under the global obstetrical package and not be coded separately. However, in the case of severe infection needing extended treatment, additional codes would be used.

> **EXAMPLE**
>
> | | |
> |---|---|
> | 99254 | Initial inpatient consultation |
> | 99183 | Hyperbaric oxygen therapy |
> | 11000 | Debridement of infected skin |
> | 670.04 | Puerperal cellulitis (postpartum) |

Administration of Medication for OB Complications To a coder, understanding which medications an obstetric patient received may allow for more defined and accurate coding. For instance, a patient enters the hospital for Braxton-Hicks contractions and her insurance provider is a diagnostic-related group (DRG) payor. Researching her medication administration record (MAR) and determining that she received an antibiotic could prompt the coder to further query the physician and learn that she was also treated for a pregnancy-induced kidney infection, although such was poorly documented. Since resources were used for this complication during the same episode of care, it may be coded to incorporate a complication or comorbidity (cc) into the DRG. The original reason for the patient seeking care, the premature contractions, must still be used as the principal diagnosis; however, depending upon the DRG used (cc-dependent vs. non cc-dependent), adding such a code could bring the facility greater monetary intake to help pay for that patient's stay, strengthen the case mix index, and ultimately increase overall profits.

EXERCISE 10–3

Use the ICD-9-CM and CPT manuals to code the following exercises as if billing for the obstetrician.

1. Abruptio placenta, antepartum _____

2. Echography of a 24-week pregnant female shows a multiple gestation. The physician informs her she is carrying triplets. _____ _____ _____

3. Laparoscopic surgical treatment of a tubal ectopic pregnancy requiring salpingectomy _____ _____ _____

Diagnostics in OB There are diagnostic procedures that are used in the detection of pregnancy complications. Included is amniocentesis, a percutaneous transabdominal puncture of the uterus to obtain amniotic fluid. The fluid is examined in a laboratory to determine abnormalities in the fetus. An ultrasound, also called sonogram, may be used to visualize deep structures, such as the uterus, ovaries, and a baby in utero. The use of ultrasound can determine location, position, size, and some defects of the fetus, as well as placental localization and amount of amniotic fluid.

Chorionic villus sampling, a procedure usually performed during the end of the first trimester, can be used to diagnose certain genetic disorders. Fetal tissue is aspirated by catheter through the cervical canal from the villi area of the chorion under ultrasonic guidance. The chorionic villi are branching projections on the outer layer of the developing embryo which provide exchange of oxygen and nutrients with carbon dioxide and waste products.

abortion

Termination of a pregnancy before the fetus is viable. Spontaneous abortion occurs naturally; also called miscarriage. Therapeutic abortion is induced and is a deliberate interruption of pregnancy.

Abortion The term **abortion** refers to the termination of a pregnancy before the fetus is viable. A spontaneous abortion (SAB) occurs naturally and is often referred to as a miscarriage. A therapeutic abortion (TAB) is an induced abortion, which is a deliberate interruption of the pregnancy. The term TAB originally referred to an abortion done for the physical and mental well-being of the mother; however, today it is applied to all elective abortions. Although the term abortion is used to refer to both the SAB and the TAB, care should be exercised when speaking to a patient who has experienced a miscarriage. Various terms are used to better describe specific situations when an abortion occurs. Table 10–4 offers a complete listing of these terms with definitions. CPT codes 59812 to 59870, found under Maternity Care and Delivery in the Surgery section, are used for various types of abortion. Medical treatment of spontaneous complete abortion should be coded using Evaluation and Management codes 99201–99233. Occasionally, a patient will be placed under observation in a hospital due to a spontaneous abortion. Evaluation and Management codes 99217 to 99220 should be assigned.

Anatomic Problems The manner in which the fetus appears to the examiner during delivery is referred to as the fetal **presentation.** The correct fetal position is for the head to present first in a vertex presentation. Occasionally, housed within the uterus the fetus may be stationed in an inappropriate and incorrect position for birthing. It may become necessary for the health care provider to turn the baby to the correct delivery position. This is considered to be a type of pregnancy complication. Examples of such include breech presentation, brow presentation, face presentation, shoulder presentation, and transverse presentation. See Table 10–5 for a complete listing of presentations with definitions. ICD-9-CM codes in category 652 are used for malposition and malpresentation of the fetus.

When there is a disproportionate relationship of the fetal head to the maternal pelvis, it is called cephalopelvic disproportion. Disproportions can be due to an unusually large fetus, an abnormally formed fetus, or an abnormality of the bony pelvis. ICD-9-CM codes found in category 653 are used for various disproportion problems.

Fetal Problems When a fetal condition affects the management of the mother (i.e., extra observation, in-depth diagnostic studies, or termination of pregnancy), ICD-9-CM codes from categories 655, Known or suspected fetal abnormality

presentation
Manner in which the fetus appears to the examiner during delivery (e.g., breech, cephalic, transverse, vertex).

TABLE 10–5   Birthing Presentations.

Presentation	Description
breech presentation:	feet or buttocks present first
complete breech	thighs of the fetus are flexed on the abdomen and the legs are flexed upon the thighs
frank breech	legs of the fetus are extended over the anterior surface of the body
footling breech	foot or feet present first
brow presentation	baby's head is slightly bent forward so that the forehead (brow) presents first
cephalic presentation	head of fetus presents in any position
compound presentation	limb presents alongside the presenting part
face presentation	head is sharply extended so that the face presents first
funic presentation	umbilical cord appears during labor
longitudinal presentation	long axis of fetus is parallel to long axis of mother
oblique presentation	long axis of fetus is oblique (neither perpendicular nor parallel) to that of the mother
placental presentation	placenta presents first
shoulder presentation	shoulder presents first
transverse presentation	side presents first; fetus is lying crosswise
vertex presentation	upper and back parts of fetal head present first

affecting management of mother, and 656, Other fetal and placental problems affecting the management of the mother, are assigned.

Disease Gestational trophoblastic disease (GTD) is a term used for abnormalities of the placenta that lead to tumor-like changes. Two of the more common types are hydatidiform mole and choriocarcinoma. Hydatidiform mole, also called molar pregnancy, appears as a mass of cysts resembling a bunch of grapes growing in the uterus and results from abnormal fertilization. The uterus enlarges and there are abnormally high levels of hCG, but there is no sign of fetal movement. Some moles are aborted spontaneously in mid-pregnancy; however, if the diagnosis is made early, abortion is usually performed to ensure complete removal of the abnormal cells which could give rise to malignant tumors. Choriocarcinoma is a malignant tumor made up of placental tissue which often arises from a preexisting complete mole. The tumor cells are highly invasive and secrete abnormally high levels of hCG. This type of cancer metastasizes rapidly, but fortunately it responds to chemotherapy if found early. A hydatidiform mole is classified using ICD-9-CM 630 unless it presents a malignancy, then it is classified using code 236.1. If a previous molar pregnancy affects the management of a current pregnancy, code V23.1 is used.

Rh incompatibility occurs when a mother is Rh-negative, the father is Rh-positive, and the baby is Rh-positive. The mother and baby's blood are incompatible, and, if mixed during delivery, can cause an immune response that results in a condition called erythroblastosis fetalis. In this condition, hemolysis occurs, which is the destruction of the fetal red blood cells. The medication RhoGAM, an Rh immune globulin, is given to the mother to suppress the immune reaction. This is usually administered half-way through the pregnancy and again within seventy-two hours of delivery. ABO blood typing can alert health care personnel to the possibility of this condition and amniocentesis can aid both in the detection of erythroblastosis fetalis and in the intrauterine or fetal transfusion. RhoGAM is also recommended to Rh-negative patients who have had abortion, miscarriage, and ectopic pregnancy, to protect future Rh-negative infants. HCPCS code J2790 is used to bill for RhoGAM injections.

Lactation

Obstetricians are responsible for evaluating the female breast and diagnosing breast diseases and complications due to pregnancy. Disturbances in lactation may be due to a variety of reasons including abnormalities of parts of the mammary glands, anemia, emotional disturbances, malnutrition, and inflammation of the breast, referred to as mastitis. Most procedure codes relating to the breast would be found within the integumentary system of the Surgery section in the CPT manual.

Lactation consultants are persons trained in the art of breastfeeding. If certified, they hold the title International Board Certified Lactation Consultant (IBCLC). They may be independent or employed by an obstetrician, a clinic, or lactation institute.

Maternity Care and Delivery for Complications

There are codes to select for the combination of the antepartum, delivery, and the postpartum services for the *uncomplicated* case. See CPT 54000, 59510, and 59610. However, when care is provided for complications, select either the E/M codes for complication visits, or alternative procedure codes if the complication procedure is documented. The associated ICD-9-CM for the complication from the 996 chapter must be linked properly.

The services that are included in the combination codes are:

Antepartum
- Initial and subsequent history
- Physical examinations
- Recording of weight
- Blood pressures
- Fetal heart tones
- Routine chemical urinalysis
- Monthly visits to 28 weeks, biweekly visits to 36 weeks, and weekly to delivery

Delivery
- Admission including history and physical (H&P)
- Management of *uncomplicated* delivery (including delivery of normal placenta)
- Episiotomy
- Forceps delivery

Postpartum
- Visits for uncomplicated care at the hospital and physician office

Typically, besides caring for the pregnancy, more services are performed by the obstetrician. This is a partial listing of services.

- High-risk visits, select E/M codes with the associated ICD-9-CM for the risk and treatment
- Hyperemesis, preterm labor, premature rupture of membranes, cardiac problems, diabetes, hypertension, toxemia
- Visits for primary care purposes, select E/M with the associated ICD-9-CM for the illness (cold, flu, etc.)
- Hospital visits during the pregnancy, except one visit within twenty-four hours of delivery
- Maternal **echography**
- Fetal echography
- Fetal echocardiography
- Fetal biophysical profile
- Amniocentesis
- Chorionic villus sampling
- Fetal contraction stress test
- Fetal nonstress test
- Hospital and observation care visits for premature labor (prior to 36 wks)
- Insertion of cervical dilator
- External cephalic version
- Standby for infant (select code 99360 if no procedures are performed, such as delivery)
- Insertion of transcervical or transvaginal fetal oximetry sensor
- Introduction of hypertonic solution and/or prostaglandins to initiate labor
- Tracheloplasty or hysterorrhaphy

echography
Use of ultrasound to evaluate anatomy to aid in diagnosis.

Usually, the physician does not start the IV at the hospital place of service and personally supervise oxytocin administration; therefore, the physician does not select 9078_ IV services.

■ *Highlight*

Included in the maternity package per NCCI are:

> *Fetal monitoring during labor*
> *Episiotomy*
> *Delivery of placenta*
> *Antepartum care*
> *Delivery*
> *Postpartum care*
> *Postoperative pain management provided by the same physician*
> *Venipuncture, venous intracath, IV for anesthestic agent by OB/GYN physician*

Services that are separately coded in addition to the maternity services are:

> *Ultrasound*
> *Amniocentesis*
> *Special screening tests for genetic conditions*
> *Unrelated to the pregnancy conditions*
> *High-risk illness services*

Depending upon the circumstances, a physician or same group practice may provide only the first few visits, prior to transferring the care to another physician. If three or less antepartum visits are provided, select E/M codes. If four to six visits, select the 59425 code, whereas seven or more visits select the 52426 code.

The same concept may apply for the physician who provides only the delivery or the postpartum care. The CPT describes each of the service options for vaginal delivery or C-section.

During the C-section delivery, the physician may perform a tubal ligation. The code is an add-on code, 58611 to the C-section code. If the patient has benefits for this service, it should be reimbursed at 100 percent, and not multiple surgery payment reduced.

Abortion

If a fetus dies in utero prior to twenty-two weeks, this is defined as a missed abortion or the pathology term might be documented as blighted ovum. Medical spontaneous abortion services are E/M codes (99201–233). Surgical is indicated with the 59812 series of codes.

Ectopic Pregnancy

The ectopic pregnancy may be treated surgically, either using a scope or an open procedure. Usually, the physician will attempt to preserve the female anatomy as much as possible, and work to avoid complications. Watch for the terminology of salpingostomy versus salpingectomy, and for a "maloccurrence" or complication during the surgical procedure that may occur.

Code 59150 is selected for the Laparoscopic treatment of the ectopic pregnancy, no salpinectomy or oophorectomy; the 5912X series is for the Surgical treatment of the ectopic pregnancy for the open abdominal or vaginal approach. Read the operative note carefully to determine if the treatment is through a laparoscope entering the abdominal wall through a trocar, or whether the incision is made into the abdomen, guiding to the accurate code selection.

If the ectopic pregnancy is treated medically, E/M codes plus the medication J code or 99070 are selected.

New Neonatal Procedures

Within the antepartum period, medical science is quickly evolving for the care of the neonate. Many procedures that are performed on the infant while in utero do not yet have dedicated CPT codes. The unlisted codes are frequently the only option. However, it is now proper coding procedure to review the Category III codes twice annually, in January and again in July, to see if there are new Category III codes available.

Multiple Births and Twins

The coding for multiple births can be very complex. The births may not be equal; one may be successfully performed vaginally, whereas the second may require a C-section. Next, the diagnosis codes may vary between Baby A and Baby B. The insurance plan may further have special policies for reporting the services, so inquiry prior to submitting the claim should be accomplished. Submitting each service per line item is frequently required when coding for multiple births.

Postpartum Curettage

Postpartum curettage is rather commonly performed. This is the scraping of the uterine cavity to remove pieces of retained placenta or clots, using a curette, instrument, or suction. In reviewing the operative/procedure notes, watch for the possibility of the use of the hysteroscope rather than direct visualization and scraping.

EXERCISE 10–4

Use the ICD-9-CM Volumes 1 and 2, CPT, and HCPCSII manuals to code the following exercise.

1. Chorionic villus sampling, any method _____

2. Breech presentation of fetus in womb _____

3. Amniocentesis with ultrasonic guidance _____

4. A woman 20 weeks pregnant is seen with complaints of severe abdominal cramping and no fetal movement for the past 24 hours. The physician suspects early fetal death, and, after tests, confirms a missed abortion. Surgical completion is performed. _____ _____

Assign ICD-9-CM diagnosis and procedure codes to the following as if billing in a hospital setting. *Sequence* codes as appropriate with *principal* diagnosis and procedure listed first.

5. A 35-week pregnant female comes into the hospital complaining of bleeding. An ultrasound and urinalysis are done. Placenta previa is seen and the urinalysis indicates the patient has a urinary tract infection. The physician decides that an emergency cesarean section is necessary to enable the baby to live. A low cervical C/S is performed that night, and both mother and baby do fine. _____

6. An expectant mother of 27 weeks gestation begins experiencing small contractions that are approximately five minutes apart. As the contractions become closer and stronger, she decides they are not Braxton-Hicks contractions and that she must go to the emergency room. The ER physician wants to place her on a monitor to look at the frequency and duration of the contractions. While being wheeled to an OB observation bed, she accidentally scrapes her elbow on an IV cart. The doctor applies an antibiotic ointment to the injury and gives her Brethine to stop the premature contractions. You are billing for the ER physician. _____

Gynecology (GYN)

The gynecologist treats females experiencing infertility, structural abnormalities of female organs, sexually transmitted diseases, sexual dysfunction, menstrual abnormalities, and other diseases. Female genital system CPT codes 56405 to 58999 and Laparoscopy/Hysteroscopy CPT codes 56300 to 56399 are used for most gynecological procedures including in vitro fertilization.

Evaluation and Management Services

As mentioned earlier, the OB/GYN physician can serve as a primary care physician and a specialist. The coder must be aware of the capacity in which the physician is serving the patient in order to code correctly.

When the physician's evaluation and management service turns into a counseling session, appropriate documentation and coding must be used. When counseling and/or coordination of care dominates more than 50 percent of the physician/patient face-to-face time spent in the office, or other outpatient setting (or floor/unit time in a hospital or nursing facility), then time is considered the key factor to qualify for a particular level of E/M services.

> **EXAMPLE**
>
> An established GYN patient is seen for leukorrhea (white vaginal discharge). The physician performs a problem-focused history and examination with a straightforward medical decision, diagnosis Trichomonas vaginalis. When the physician prescribes medication and instructs the patient to give one-half of the prescription to her sexual partner, the patient reveals she has multiple sexual partners. A conversation evolves in which the patient asks several questions regarding other sexually transmitted diseases, contraceptive methods, and the effects of all of this on a possible future pregnancy. The face-to-face time the physician spends in counseling the patient ends up being thirty minutes.

With this type of visit the physician typically spends ten minutes face-to-face with the patient; however, because of the patient's questions, the extended time the physician spent was more than 50 percent and becomes the controlling factor to qualify for a higher level of E/M service. This office visit typically would be coded 99212; however, because of the extra time spent face-to-face with the patient (30 minutes instead of 10 minutes), the E/M service can be upgraded to 99214. The physician must carefully document the nature of counseling in this case. The time-only factor cannot include any delays or interruptions not associated with patient counseling or coordination of care.

Preventive medicine counseling provided as a separate encounter, such as sexual practices or family problems, should be coded using individual counseling Evaluation and Management CPT codes 99401 to 99404. These codes cannot be used if the patient seeking counseling has symptoms or an established illness.

Special Service and Report Codes Special service codes commonly used in the OB/GYN practice, found in the Medicine section of the CPT manual, are as follows:

1. 99000   Handling of specimens for transfer from the physician's office to a laboratory

2. 99024   Postoperative follow-up visit normally included in global service, if E/M related to procedure

3. 99058   Office services provided on an emergency basis

4. 99070   Supplies and materials provided by the physician over and above those usually included with the office visit or other services rendered

5. 99071   Educational supplies, with cost to physician

6. 99078   Physician educational services rendered to patients in a group setting

Well Woman Examinations

Of all of the services that are provided in health care today, probably the least understood and frequently modified services, from a coding perspective, is the well woman examination. Insurance plan benefits should be checked, double-checked, and triple-checked for the well woman care due to the frequent policy changes, benefit updates, and coding revisions.

The HIPAA privacy rules regarding the care of the OB/GYN patient must be upheld. The patient trusts her privacy will be maintained. The HIPAA privacy consent form should clearly indicate with whom the patient intends to share information regarding her health. In the absence of the release with the HIPAA privacy consent, the physician should obtain a written medical release form prior to sharing information with anyone other than another health care provider for the illness/disease. In simple words, use caution when leaving voicemail messages, mailing reminders for appointments, or during any other inquiry for medical discussions.

AMA/CPT Preventive Medicine Service

The preventive examination according to the AMA/CPT is coded with the 9938X New patient and 9939X Established patient series of codes. In the E/M chapter, the guidelines for selection of the preventive codes were discussed in detail. To encourage learning for this particular subject, these concepts will be repeated here, in a specialty-specific manner. The AMA/CPT refers to the well woman exam as a Preventive Medicine Service, and describes such services as follows:

1. The services are dependent upon the age of the patient. In other words, the extent and topic of discussion, examination, and risk factor reduction for a sixteen-year-old female may vary from the extent and topic of discussion for a thirty-six-year-old female, or a seventy-eight-year-old female.

2. The comprehensive preventive services are not equal to the 99201–99350 services. In other words, the E/M guidelines describe how to determine the extent of the comprehensive illness examination: as a general multisystem exam or a complete single organ exam; the guidelines do *not* describe the examination requirements for the preventive examination.

3. The preventive services include counseling/anticipatory/risk factor reduction (e.g., contraceptive management counseling, preventive STD, age-specific screening recommendations, etc.).

4. All immunizations, ancillary studies, procedures, and additional screening tests are to be reported with a separate code. For instance, if an MMR immunization is rendered during the preventive medicine service, the MMR medication *plus* the administration code are reported; if a urinalysis dipstick is performed and documented, the additional urinalysis code is reported; if a surgical procedure is performed and documented, the additional surgical procedure code is reported. According to the AMA/CPT the preventive medicine services are not part of the radiology, pathology, medicine, or other 'package' (see Table 10–6).

5. The combination services discussion proceeds from simple to complex care.

   a. If during the preventive medicine service, the physician provides care for an "insignificant or trivial problem/abnormality" that does *not* require Additional history, Examination, and medical decision making (MDM), then no additional E/M code is selected. For example, the physician performs a general medical preventive service, including a gyn pelvic exam with Pap collection, and progresses to order a T7 lab test to check the thyroid level. If the physician does not perform an additional history, exam and MDM at this encounter specifically regarding the T7, then no additional E/M code is to be selected. Only the 9938*X* or the 9939*X* code would be reported (Figure 10–6).

   As you can see, if the combination of preventive medicine services and the illness services are performed at the same encounter, on the same date, by the same physician, it is highly possible that the claim would be multiple pages.

   b. If during the preventive medicine service (described previously), the physician provides care for an illness or disease that is significant enough to require an *additional* history, examination and medical decision making, then 9938*X* or 9939*X* followed by a 99201–99215 with modifier -25 is selected. In other words, the physician cares for the thyroid illness during this encounter, with the performance of an additional history, examination, and medical decision making. (Level of care is documented; see claim example of combination encounter Figure 10–7.)

    The physician practice is required to properly complete the advance beneficiary notice *prior* to performing the services. With this task, the practice is to inform the patient as to the financial obligations for each line

TABLE 10–6 Commonly Performed Services during a Preventive Medicine Service.

Common Preventive Medicine Services

90471 also medication code	Immunization administration; one vaccine
90472+ also medication	Immunization administration; each additional vaccine
90473 also medication code	Immunization administration; by intranasal or oral route
90474+ also medication code	Immunization administration; each additional vaccine
90780–90788 also medication	Therapeutic infusion or injection
99173	Screening test of visual acuity, quantitative, bilateral (Snellen chart)
92567	Tympanometry (Whisper test and tuning fork are part of the preventive exam and not separately coded)
81000–03	Urinalysis dipstick services
81025	Urine pregnancy test
84830	Ovulation tests, by visual color comparison methods for HLH
99000	Collection and handling
93000	EKG, 12 lead with interpretation, for screening
86580	TB skin test, intradermal
86490	Coccidiodomycosis
86485	Candida skin test
36415	Collection of venous blood by venipuncture

item. With the multiple pages and the extensive varieties in the insurance benefits, this is ever challenging. For example, many beneficiaries are not responsible for the payment of the deductible for the well woman exam, yet the deductible is applicable for all other services performed at the same encounter. Or the benefits may waive the deductible and the co-insurance for the Pap collection, yet not for the examination. Informing the patient accurately is a very difficult task.

PLEASE
DO NOT
STAPLE
IN THIS
AREA

CARRIER

| | PICA | | | | | **HEALTH INSURANCE CLAIM FORM** | | PICA | |

1. MEDICARE	MEDICAID	CHAMPUS	CHAMPVA	GROUP HEALTH PLAN	FECA BLK LUNG	OTHER	1a. INSURED'S I.D. NUMBER	(FOR PROGRAM IN ITEM 1)
(Medicare #)	(Medicaid #)	(Sponsor's SSN)	(VA File #)	(SSN or ID)	(SSN)	(ID)		

2. PATIENT'S NAME (Last Name, First Name, Middle Initial)

3. PATIENT'S BIRTH DATE MM DD YY SEX M F

4. INSURED'S NAME (Last Name, First Name, Middle Initial)

5. PATIENT'S ADDRESS (No., Street)

6. PATIENT RELATIONSHIP TO INSURED Self Spouse Child Other

7. INSURED'S ADDRESS (No., Street)

CITY   STATE

8. PATIENT STATUS Single Married Other

CITY   STATE

ZIP CODE   TELEPHONE (Include Area Code) ( )

Employed   Full-Time Student   Part-Time Student

ZIP CODE   TELEPHONE (INCLUDE AREA CODE) ( )

9. OTHER INSURED'S NAME (Last Name, First Name, Middle Initial)

10. IS PATIENT'S CONDITION RELATED TO:

11. INSURED'S POLICY GROUP OR FECA NUMBER

a. OTHER INSURED'S POLICY OR GROUP NUMBER

a. EMPLOYMENT? (CURRENT OR PREVIOUS) YES NO

a. INSURED'S DATE OF BIRTH MM DD YY SEX M F

b. OTHER INSURED'S DATE OF BIRTH MM DD YY SEX M F

b. AUTO ACCIDENT?   PLACE (State) YES NO

b. EMPLOYER'S NAME OR SCHOOL NAME

c. EMPLOYER'S NAME OR SCHOOL NAME

c. OTHER ACCIDENT? YES NO

c. INSURANCE PLAN NAME OR PROGRAM NAME

d. INSURANCE PLAN NAME OR PROGRAM NAME

10d. RESERVED FOR LOCAL USE

d. IS THERE ANOTHER HEALTH BENEFIT PLAN? YES NO **If yes**, return to and complete item 9 a-d.

READ BACK OF FORM BEFORE COMPLETING & SIGNING THIS FORM.
12. PATIENT'S OR AUTHORIZED PERSON'S SIGNATURE I authorize the release of any medical or other information necessary to process this claim. I also request payment of government benefits either to myself or to the party who accepts assignment below.

SIGNED   DATE

13. INSURED'S OR AUTHORIZED PERSON'S SIGNATURE I authorize payment of medical benefits to the undersigned physician or supplier for services described below.

SIGNED

14. DATE OF CURRENT: MM DD YY ◄ ILLNESS (First symptom) OR INJURY (Accident) OR PREGNANCY(LMP)

15. IF PATIENT HAS HAD SAME OR SIMILAR ILLNESS. GIVE FIRST DATE MM DD YY

16. DATES PATIENT UNABLE TO WORK IN CURRENT OCCUPATION MM DD YY MM DD YY FROM   TO

17. NAME OF REFERRING PHYSICIAN OR OTHER SOURCE

17a. I.D. NUMBER OF REFERRING PHYSICIAN

18. HOSPITALIZATION DATES RELATED TO CURRENT SERVICES MM DD YY MM DD YY FROM   TO

19. RESERVED FOR LOCAL USE

20. OUTSIDE LAB? YES NO $ CHARGES

21. DIAGNOSIS OR NATURE OF ILLNESS OR INJURY. (RELATE ITEMS 1,2,3 OR 4 TO ITEM 24E BY LINE)

1. V76 . 0   3. V76 . 47

2. V72 . 3   4. V77 . 3

22. MEDICAID RESUBMISSION CODE   ORIGINAL REF. NO.

23. PRIOR AUTHORIZATION NUMBER

24. A DATE(S) OF SERVICE						B Place of Service	C Type of Service	D PROCEDURES, SERVICES, OR SUPPLIES (Explain Unusual Circumstances) CPT/HCPCS MODIFIER	E DIAGNOSIS CODE	F $ CHARGES	G DAYS OR UNITS	H EPSDT Family Plan	I EMG	J COB	K RESERVED FOR LOCAL USE
From MM	DD	YY	To MM	DD	YY										
09	01	20XX				11		99386	1,2,3,4						
09	01	20XX				11		99000	1,2,3						

25. FEDERAL TAX I.D. NUMBER   SSN EIN

26. PATIENT'S ACCOUNT NO.

27. ACCEPT ASSIGNMENT? (For govt. claims, see back) YES NO

28. TOTAL CHARGE $

29. AMOUNT PAID $

30. BALANCE DUE $

31. SIGNATURE OF PHYSICIAN OR SUPPLIER INCLUDING DEGREES OR CREDENTIALS (I certify that the statements on the reverse apply to this bill and are made a part thereof.)

SIGNED   DATE

32. NAME AND ADDRESS OF FACILITY WHERE SERVICES WERE RENDERED (If other than home or office)

33. PHYSICIAN'S, SUPPLIER'S BILLING NAME, ADDRESS, ZIP CODE & PHONE #

PIN#   GRP#

PATIENT AND INSURED INFORMATION

PHYSICIAN OR SUPPLIER INFORMATION

(APPROVED BY AMA COUNCIL ON MEDICAL SERVICE 8/88) **PLEASE PRINT OR TYPE**

APPROVED OMB-0938-0008 FORM CMS-1500 (12/90), FORM RRB-1500
APPROVED OMB-1215-0055 FORM OWCP-1500, APPROVED OMB-0720-0001 (CHAMPUS)

Figure 10–6 Claim example for AMA/CPT Pap, preventive medicine with supplies.

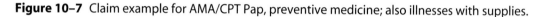

17. NAME OF REFERRING PHYSICIAN OR OTHER SOURCE					17a. I.D. NUMBER OF REFERRING PHYSICIAN			18. HOSPITALIZATION DATES RELATED TO CURRENT SERVICES

Reproduced as form:

19. RESERVED FOR LOCAL USE

20. OUTSIDE LAB? ☐ YES ☐ NO $ CHARGES

21. DIAGNOSIS OR NATURE OF ILLNESS OR INJURY. (RELATE ITEMS 1,2,3 OR 4 TO ITEM 24E BY LINE)

1. V70 . 0
2. V72 . 3
3. V76 . 47
4. 245 . 8

22. MEDICAID RESUBMISSION CODE ___ ORIGINAL REF. NO.

23. PRIOR AUTHORIZATION NUMBER

24. A DATE(S) OF SERVICE						B Place of Service	C Type of Service	D PROCEDURES, SERVICES, OR SUPPLIES (Explain Unusual Circumstances) CPT/HCPCS / MODIFIER		E DIAGNOSIS CODE	F $ CHARGES	G DAYS OR UNITS	H EPSDT Family Plan	I EMG	J COB	K RESERVED FOR LOCAL USE
From MM DD YY			To MM DD YY													
09	01	20XX				11		99386		1,2,3		1				
09	01	20XX				11		99213	25	4		1				
09	01	20XX				11		99000		1,2,3		1				

PHYSICIAN OR SUPPLIER INFORMATION

Figure 10–7 Claim example for AMA/CPT Pap, preventive medicine; also illnesses with supplies.

CMS Pap Smears

The necessity for investigating the benefits also holds true for the CMS patient. The information contained here is accurate at the time of publication, yet could easily be updated or revised in a particular geographic area or with national coverage decisions. Each benefits carrier should be checked for CPT, HCPCSII, modifier use, and ICD-9-CM codes. It is important to note that CMS divides the Pap smear into two policies: one for diagnostic Pap smears and another for screening Pap smears.

Diagnostic Pap

The diagnostic Pap is currently a local carrier policy with a separate coding policy attachment. Only certain illnesses are considered a covered benefit for the CMS patient:

- Previous cancer of the female genital tract
- Previous abnormal or suspicious Pap smear
- Abnormal or suspicious findings of female genital tract
- Neoplasm of the female genital tract
- Inflammatory disease of the female genital tract
- Abnormal bleeding
- Early onset of intercourse and multiple sexual partners are risk factors, but probably related to exposure of STD, especially human papillomavirus (HPV).

These indicators or conditions are to be documented in the medical record and the correlative ICD-9-CM code is selected. The thin prep, Bethedsa, or AutoPap may be used. Per CMS, monolayer cell prep technique is considered to be investigational with autocyte and the AutoPap.

Screening Pap Smear and Pelvic Examinations for Early Detection of Cervical or Vaginal Cancer

The screening Pap smear is a national coverage decision. A screening Pap is covered for:

1. No test in the preceding three years

   or

2. a woman of childbearing age

3. Evidence of high risk of developing cervical cancer with qualified healthcare professional recommendation for more frequent testing than every three years. High risk is (the ICD-9-CM code must be on the claim):

   Early onset of sexual activity under sixteen years of age

   Multiple sexual partners (five or more per lifetime)

   History of STD (including HIV)

   Fewer than three negative or any Pap smear within the previous seven years

   DES-exposed daughters of women who took DES during pregnancy

Screening Pelvic Examination

There are specific coverage determinations for the screening pelvic exam.

1. The screening pelvic exam may be performed by a physician, certified nurse midwife, PA, NP, or CNS if authorized by state law.

2. One exam every twenty-four months for asymptomatic patient: V76.2, V76.47 or V76.49

3. Once every twelve months if high risk: V15.89:

   Early onset of sexual activity under sixteen years of age

   Multiple sexual partners (5 or more per lifetime)

   History of STD (including HIV)

   Fewer than three negative or any Pap smear within the previous seven years

   DES-exposed daughters of women who took DES during pregnancy

4. Once every twelve months if woman of childbearing age (premenopausal), with abnormality present within the previous three years

Use code G0101 for the pelvic examination, according to CMS (as listed in the 1997 E/M Genitourinary Examination Guidelines), which must include the examination of seven or eleven anatomical sites. The examination does not include the history or risk counseling service as described by the preventive medicine services listed in the AMA/CPT 9938X series. If selecting the G0101 code, the pelvic examination that is to be performed and documented must include:

- Inspection and palpation of the breasts for masses, lumps, tenderness, symmetry, or nipple discharge
- Digital rectal exam including sphincter tone, presence of hemorrhoids, rectal masses
- External genitalia general appearance, hair distribution or lesions
- Urethral meatus size, location, lesions, or prolapse

- Urethra masses, tenderness, scarring
- Bladder fullness, masses, tenderness
- Vagina general appearance, estrogen effect, discharge lesions, pelvic support, cystocele or rectocele
- Cervix general appearance, lesions, discharge
- Uterus size contour, position, mobility, tenderness, consistency, descent, or support
- Adnexa/parametria masses tenderness, organomegaly, nodularity
- Anus and perineum

If the G0101 is a covered benefit (twenty-four months or eleven months for high risk), the patient is not obligated for a deductible for this particular service. The deductible will apply for other services listed on the same claim (see Table 10–7).

Combination E/M illness "distinct" reasons for services provided on the same date by the same physician, may be submitted on the claim with modifier -25 on the E/M, with the additional history, examination, and medical decision making documentation.

When Q0091 Screening Pap smear; obtaining, preparing, and conveyance of cervical or vaginal smear to the lab is selected in addition to the E/M service, on the same date by the same physician, again modifier -25 is placed on the E/M. The patient is obligated for the deductible (e.g., vaginitis examination with collection of the Pap smear).

Routine 99381 series combination services:

- Covered portion is billed, limiting charge/assignment rules apply.
- Beneficiary is responsible for the noncovered portion of the visit, 9938X codes, the current fee that exceeds the current established charge for the covered visit.
- The ABN is not required for the noncovered portion because routine visits are statutorily exempt.
- Beneficiary is responsible for any other noncovered routine services.

TABLE 10–7   CMS Screening Pap Smear or Pelvic Exam ICD-9-CM Chart.

Screening Pap Smear (Q0091) or Screening Pelvic Exam (G0101) ICD-9-CM	
Low-Risk Codes	*Every 24 months*
V76.2	Special screening for malignant neoplasms, cervix
V76.47	Special screening for malignant neoplasms, vagina
V76.49	Special screening for malignant neoplasm, other site (for patient without uterus or cervix)
V72.31	Routine gyn exam if full gyn exam is performed
High-Risk Code	*Every 12 months*
V15.89	Other

Coding Tip *Effective July 1, 2005, the previous diagnoses must be listed in the first pointer position on the claim, or the claim will be rejected.*

Unless medically precluded, the preventive services should be performed on a separate date than illness care for the majority of patients.

The patient requests a preventive medicine examination, the last Pap smear was 3 years ago. She has been asymptomatic during this time. The physician performs a history, preventive medicine examination to include seven of eleven anatomical sites, and obtains the screening Pap smear specimen, preps and sends this to the lab. During the examination, the physician progresses to care for the thyroid illness, documenting an additional EPF history and EPF exam.

The CMS claim processing accepts only one ICD-9-CM per line, although multiple codes actually correlate to the care and the documentation. Carefully reviewing the policies per CMS carrier guide to the ICD-9-CM code that is applicable for each of the services.

The codes shown on Figure 10–8 indicate the exact financial amount the patient is responsible for, for each of the line items, for a physician who is a participating provider with Medicare. The ABN is not required for the 99386; however, an ABN is required for all of the remaining procedures listed. If the patient has a frequency limitation for the G0101 or the Q0091, the ABN needs to be properly completed.

BC/BS and Selected Medicaid Exceptions

While the CPT preventive medicine codes reflect a thorough history, examination and risk factor reduction counseling service, the CMS and BCBS policies have partial benefit services commonly known as 'carve outs'. These partial services correspond to specific policies reflected with the HCPCSII codes. Codes G0101 and Q0091 are commonly selected for the CMS patient, whereas there is an additional S chapter for the Blue Cross/Blue Shield (BC/BS) patients. Codes S0610 Annual gyn examination for a new patient or S0612 established patient describe services

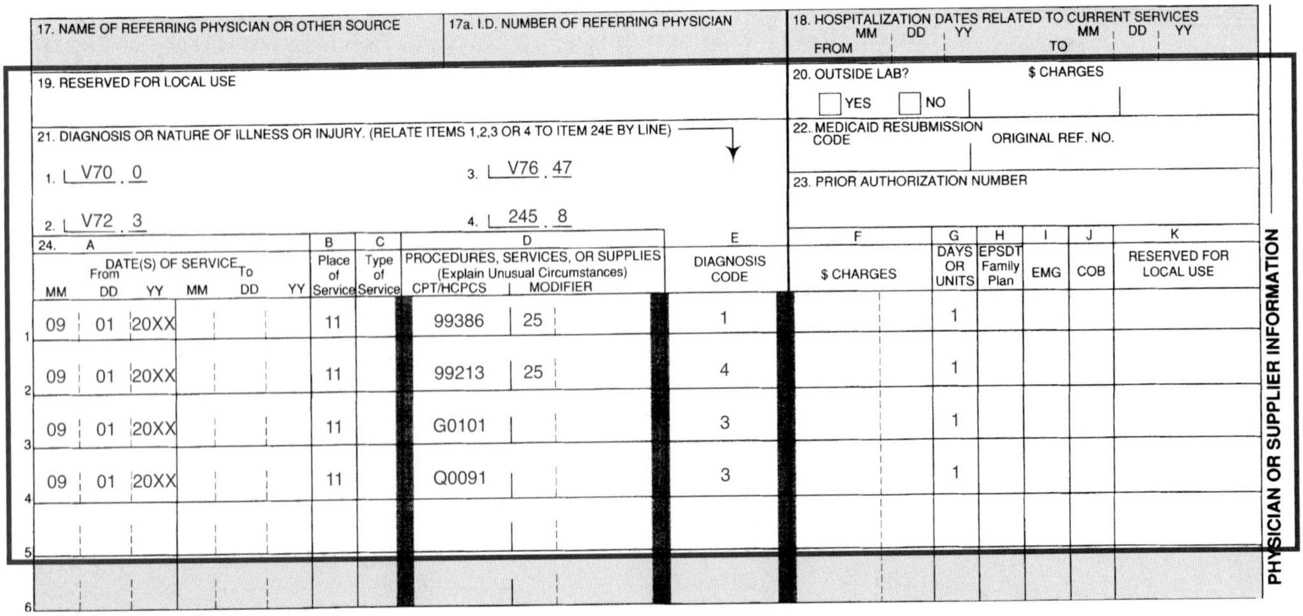
17. NAME OF REFERRING PHYSICIAN OR OTHER SOURCE | 17a. I.D. NUMBER OF REFERRING PHYSICIAN | 18. HOSPITALIZATION DATES RELATED TO CURRENT SERVICES MM DD YY FROM MM DD YY TO

19. RESERVED FOR LOCAL USE | 20. OUTSIDE LAB? YES NO $ CHARGES

21. DIAGNOSIS OR NATURE OF ILLNESS OR INJURY. (RELATE ITEMS 1,2,3 OR 4 TO ITEM 24E BY LINE) | 22. MEDICAID RESUBMISSION CODE ORIGINAL REF. NO.

1. V70 . 0 3. V76 . 47 | 23. PRIOR AUTHORIZATION NUMBER

2. V72 . 3 4. 245 . 8

24.	A DATE(S) OF SERVICE From MM DD YY	To MM DD YY	B Place of Service	C Type of Service	D PROCEDURES, SERVICES, OR SUPPLIES (Explain Unusual Circumstances) CPT/HCPCS	MODIFIER	E DIAGNOSIS CODE	F $ CHARGES	G DAYS OR UNITS	H EPSDT Family Plan	I EMG	J COB	K RESERVED FOR LOCAL USE
1	09 01 20XX		11		99386	25	1		1				
2	09 01 20XX		11		99213	25	4		1				
3	09 01 20XX		11		G0101		3		1				
4	09 01 20XX		11		Q0091		3		1				
5													
6													

PHYSICIAN OR SUPPLIER INFORMATION

Figure 10–8 Claim example for CMS Pap collection low risk breast and pelvic; also illness exam.

not equal to the CPT or the CMS descriptions. The local BC/BS maintain the policies, modifier use and bundling rules associated with the use of the S codes. For example, modifier 25 may or may not be applicable with an additional E/M illness service or the Q0091 code.

Some of the state Medicaid programs have recently chosen to activate and to implement coding policies for the S0610 and S0612 codes requiring the coder to research for the local Medicaid policies.

EXERCISE 10–5

Use the ICD-9-CM, CPT, and HCPCSII manuals to code the following exercises.

1. A 25-year-old established patient comes to the gynecologist for a routine periodic comprehensive reevaluation. _____ _____

2. Office consultation for a 30-year-old with dysfunctional uterine bleeding; blood is drawn and sent to an outside laboratory for testing. _____ _____ _____

3. A 36-year-old patient calls in a panic because she has just found a large lump in her breast. She states "the skin looks funny around it and it hurts." The physician asks the staff to work her in on an emergency basis. _____

Contraception

One of the main reasons women see their gynecologists is for recommendations and prescriptions regarding contraception. Most methods of contraception are prescribed during an evaluation and management service. Birth control pills are the most commonly used contraceptive product in the United States. The patient requires a prescription from a physician and periodic monitoring of blood pressure and other risk factors. Other physician services regarding contraception that are not included in E/M services are injections of birth control medications, implantation of birth control capsules, insertion of birth control devices, and surgery. See Table 10–8 for a complete listing of birth control methods. The procedure code for the insertion of implantable contraceptive capsules is found in the Surgery/Integumentary section of the CPT manual. Induced abortion is usually performed using the surgical procedure dilation and curettage. CPT codes 59840–59857 would apply to such services and are found in the Surgery/Maternity section.

Tubal ligation is a permanent method of birth control typically performed with a laparoscope. An incision is made in the abdomen, often in the umbilicus, and a small tube is inserted through which the ligation instrument is introduced. A cut, referred to as a transection, is made across the oviducts, and the uterine tubes are blocked so that a fertilized egg cannot pass into the uterus for implantation. Methods for blocking the tubes include fulguration (burning the ends of the tubes) or securing devices such as bands, clips, or Falope rings (which are put in place on the ends of the tubes). Various ligation procedure codes are found in the Laparoscopy/Hysteroscopy section of the CPT manual. If tubal ligation is performed at the same time as a cesarean section, code 58611 would apply.

TABLE 10–8   Female Contraceptive Methods.

Method	Description
abortion	removal of embryo from the uterus
abstinence	voluntarily refraining from sexual intercourse
birth control pill (BCP)	synthetic hormones taken orally that interrupt normal hormone secretion and prevent ovulation
cervical cap	a small cap-like device placed over the cervix prior to intercourse
chemical barriers	spermicidal creams, foams, and jellies placed deep in the vagina that create an unfavorable environment for sperm to survive
coitus interruptus	withdrawing the penis from the vagina before ejaculation
diaphragm	a rubber or plastic dome-shaped mechanical barrier placed in the vagina near the cervix that prevents sperm from entering the uterus
intrauterine device (IUD)	a small device placed in the uterus by the physician to prevent implantation of the fertilized egg
morning-after pill (MAP)	drug taken orally that contains estrogen and progesterone. When taken within 72 hours of unprotected intercourse it interrupts the fertilization and/or implantation of the egg
progesterone implant	a synthetic implant, called Norplant, placed under the skin that releases progestin over a 5-year period to prevent ovulation
progesterone injection	synthetic progesterone, called Depo-Provera, administered every three months to prevent ovulation
rhythm method	abstaining from intercourse at the time of ovulation
tubal ligation	surgical procedure in which the uterine tubes are cut and ligated (tied) or cauterized (burned) or closed off with a small ring

Office Procedures

A variety of office procedures are performed in a gynecologist's practice. During a routine gynecologic examination, a Pap smear is taken to evaluate cervical tissue for cancer. If the laboratory reports an abnormal Pap smear, a colposcopy may be performed. The colposcope is an instrument used to look into the vagina, opened with the use of a speculum, and to observe the cervix. The physician can see, under magnification provided by the colposcope, what areas of the cervix have abnormal cells. Often a sampling of cells is taken from the cervix and scrapings from the inner canal, referred to as a cervical biopsy with endocervical curettage. Procedure codes for colposcopy are found under Endoscopy in the Surgery/Female Genital System.

A common procedure performed to evaluate the endometrial lining of the uterus is an endometrial biopsy. This may be performed if the patient is experiencing dysfunctional uterine bleeding (DUB) or postmenopausal bleeding. A plastic tube is passed through the cervix into the uterine cavity and a sample of tissue is aspirated into the tube. A biopsy, using a metal instrument to collect a sample, may also be performed.

A more invasive procedure is dilation and curettage (D&C). The small cervical canal is opened or dilated to allow passage for a curette, an instrument used to scrape the lining of the endometrium. Both endometrial sampling and D&C allow for microscopic visualization of malignant cells for diagnostic purposes and are coded using CPT codes 58100–58120. When a D&C is performed with any other pelvic surgery, it may be viewed by some third-party payers as an integral part of the pelvic surgery and therefore not reimbursed.

Other office procedures include laser treatment for the destruction of vaginal warts and cryosurgery, performed on the cervix to freeze abnormal dysplastic tissue and allow normal tissue to grow in its place. These procedure codes would be found in the Surgical/Integumentary section. Incision, destruction, and excision of lesions and areas of the external genitalia are listed in the Surgery/Female Genital System section under codes 56405 to 56810. Important definitions describing a simple procedure, radical procedure, partial procedure, and complete procedure are found preceding this section.

Exploratory Laparotomy

When a patient presents with pelvic pain of unknown etiology, and the preliminary diagnostic tests do not review a specific finding, a common procedure is the exploratory laparotomy. This simply describes the procedure to open the abdomen and assess the anatomy. More often than not, while assessing the anatomy, the physician determines the cause of the pelvic pain and progresses to treat the problem. The problem may be appendicitis, endometriosis, endometritis, ovarian cysts or tumors, leiomyomata (fibroid tumors), or other tumors. For the rare case where the exploratory laparotomy only is performed, 49000 is selected. If the care progresses, since 49000 has "separate procedure" within the description, it is considered part of the treatment procedure of the same incisional site. A rather common procedure is the 49200 for the open intra-abdominal excision of endometriomas, where the 49000 is not also selected. Report only the 49200 even if the physician performed the 49000 en route to the procedure.

▬ *Highlight*

When a pelvic exam is performed in conjunction with a gyn procedure, either as a necessary part of the procedure or confirmatory, the exam is not separately reported. A diagnostic pelvic exam may be performed for the purpose of deciding to perform a procedure; however, this is included in the E/M service at the time the decision for surgery is made.

Laparoscopy

The laparoscopy describes the placement of the trocar and scope into the abdomen to assess various anatomical sites of abdomen, peritoneum, and the omentum. The first procedure is often for the purpose of diagnosing and evaluating the anatomical sites. If the procedure does not progress through this same laparoscopy, select the 49320. Again, however, through the same scope, the physician may choose to treat a concern. For laparoscopy with aspiration of a right ovarian cyst, select only the surgical laparoscopic code 49322-RT without the additional code for the diagnostic laparoscopy (49320).

EXERCISE 10–6

Read the following operative report and select the applicable CPT, ICD-9-CM, and HCPCSII codes.

PREOPERATIVE DIAGNOSIS: 1. Cyclic right lower quadrant pain, occurring at time of menses

2. Suspected endometriosis

POSTOPERATIVE DIAGNOSIS: 1. Stage II endometriosis

2. Pelvic adhesions

3. Left ovarian cyst

PROCEDURES: 1. Operative laparoscopy with right salpino-oophorectomy

2. Lysis of adhesions

3. Ablation of endometriosis

4. Drainage left ovarian cyst

ANESTHESIA: General Anesthesia

IV FLUID: 800 ml of lactated ringers

ESTIMATED BLOOD LOSS: Minimal

COMPLICATIONS: None

INDICATIONS: The patient is a 49 yr old gravida 6, para 5, white female, who has noted severe pain in the right lower quadrant every time she has a period. The pain is sharp, constant, and remits when her menses end. This has been occurring every month and has been worsening over time. A pelvic ultrasound was normal with the exception of a 1.4 cm isoechoic lesion on the right ovary, questionably a complex cyst. Endometriosis was suspected and the patient wished definitive diagnosis and therapy with a laparoscopy.

FINDINGS: Diagnostic laparoscopy revealed a normal uterus with normal tubes bilaterally. There were endometriotic implants on both ovaries and peritoneal blebbing in the cul-de-sac. There were also foci of endometriosis in both ovarian fossae. The right ovary was densely adherent to the right pelvic sidewall. There was a filmy adhesion from the sigmoid colon to the left pelvic sidewall and another filmy adhesion of the right colon to the anterior abdominal wall. All adhesions were lysed and the right tube and ovary were removed.

PATHOLOGY: Right tube and ovary.

PROCEDURE: The patient was taken to the operative room and placed in the dorsal supine position. General endotracheal anesthesia was administered, and the patient placed in the modified dorsal lithotomy position via the Allen stirrups. An examination under anesthesia revealed a small, mobile, anteverted uterus without adnexal masses. The patient was then prepped, sterile draped, and her bladder emptied. A bivalve speculum was placed into the vagina and the anterior cervical lip grasped with a tenaculum. A Hulka clamp was gently placed into the uterus without difficulty for uterine manipulation and all other instruments were then removed from the vagina.

continues

The infraumbilical and periumbilical areas were infiltrated with 0.25% Marcaine and the umbilicus was elevated with towel clips. A curvilinear incision was made in the inferior umbilicus and a Veress needle placed without difficulty. Correct positioning was confirmed with a hanging drop test. Four liters of carbon dioxide gas were insufflated until adequate pneumoperitoneum was obtained. The Veress was removed and a 7-mm trocar advanced. The video laparoscope was placed through the trocar sleeve and no trauma was noted at the insertion site.

The patient was placed in Trendelenburg and a 5-mm suprapubic port was placed under direct visualization. The pelvis was then inspected with the findings as noted above. Attention was paid to the right ovary which had multiple endometriotic implants and was struck down to the right pelvic sidewall. I felt this ovary was the cause of the pain, and she would benefit from removal. Another 5-mm trocar was placed in the left lower quadrant. The right tube was held on traction and the infundibulopelvic ligament cauterized and cut using the Everest bipolar forceps which were set at 30 watts. Hemostasis was assured.

I had to mobilize the ovary off the pelvic sidewall and this was done by gently pulling the ovary upward. Using rather firm traction, the adhesions were bluntly lysed and the ovary was freed from the pelvic sidewall. The broad ligament beneath the utero-ovarian ligament was then cauterized and lysed. Next, the Everest forceps were used to cauterize the tube 1-cm lateral to the cornual area. This was cut. We were left with the utero-ovarian ligament which was cauterized and cut and in this way the tube and ovary were freed. Selected areas of bleeding on the uterus were made hemostatic and the operative site was inspected, hemostatis assured.

The 7-mm umbilical trocar was removed and replaced with a 10-mm port. A 5-mm laparoscope was placed through the suprapubic site and the Endocatch placed through the umbilical port. The tube and ovary were placed in the Endocatch bag. The bag was cinched tightly and brought up to the umbilical incision. The trocar was removed and the tube and ovary within the bag were easily removed through the umbilical incision. This was handed off to pathology. The 10-mm trocar was then replaced and the 10-mm scope placed through the umbilical port.

The filmy adhesions from the sigmoid mesocolon were then held on traction and the adhesions easily taken down with the laparoscopic EndoShears. Hemostasis was assured. The filmy adhesions from the ascending colon to the anterior abdominal wall were taken down as well. We then turned our attention to the left ovary. The left tube was grasped and the underside of the ovary visualized. There were several foci of endometriosis as well as a 3-cm simple-appearing cyst on the lateral pole. Using a needle-tip Bovi, the endometriotic implants were all cauterized and the cyst opened. Serous fluid was drained. The cyst wall was then extensively cauterized using a combination of the Everest bipolar forceps, the laparoscopic EndoShears and finally Kleppinger bipolar forceps with ultimately excellent hemostasis achieved and the cyst wall completely cauterized to decrease the risk of future cyst formation. The ovarian capsule looked clean and no more endometriosis was noted.

The entire pelvis was then copiously irrigated and suctioned. Small foci of endometriosis in the cul-de-sac were all cauterized with the needle-tip Bovie. The site of the left ovarian cystectomy was inspected. Hemostasis assured. The RSO operative site was inspected and hemostasis assured. The procedure was terminated. All instruments removed from the abdomen, and pneumoperitomeum released. The umbilical fascia was reapproximated using a figure-of-eight sutre of 0 Vicrayl on the UR-6

continues

needle. The umbilical incision was reapproximated using subcuticular suture of 4-0 Monocryl. Interrupted sutures of 4-0 Monocryl were place in the 5-mm ports. The Hulka clamp was removed from the uterus. She awoke from anesthesia and was taken to the recovery room in stable condition. The patient tolerated the procedure well. Sponge, lap, needle, and instrument counts were correct x2. One gram Ancef was given preoperatively.

CPT codes _____

ICD-9-CM codes _____

HCPCSII codes _____

Vulva, Perineum, and Introitus

Incision and drainage (I&D) are anatomically described. If the anatomy is not documented clearly, consider selecting 10040, 1006X in lieu of the I&D for the vulva.

Destruction is the use of laser, cryo (portable or large) chemical, or electrosurgery to remove lesions. Select the code 56501 if the documentation states vulva or external genitalia. The extensive term is not clarified by CPT and is the physician's judgement.

Biopsy of the vulva or perineum may be performed as part of another excision. Select 56605 and 56606 per lesion, if only biopsy(ies) are performed. If the biopsy is not of the vulva or perineum, consider 11420–426, 11620–626.

Vulvectomy codes are often described by the specific anatomical area of excision. The 56633 is rarely performed. The CPT code vulvectomy descriptions are very specific for the external genitalia area. In order to select the proper code, careful review of documentation with these descriptions is key. Physician documentation may vary from these terms, for example extensive removal. Making accurate distinctions between the following terms is not difficult when the coder is aware of their separate, specific meanings:

- *Simple* is the removal of skin and superficial tissues.
- *Radical* is the removal of skin and deep superficial tissues.
- *Partial* is removal of less than 80 percent of the entire vulvar area.
- *Complete* is the removal of greater than 80 percent of the vulvar area.

Repair of the genitalia may use codes from various areas of the CPT code book. If coding for these services, it is necessary to review the parenthetical tips near the 56810. Whether or not the repair is due to obstetrical reasons will determine the code selection.

EXERCISE 10–7

Read the following operative report and select CPT, modifiers, ICD-9-CM, and HCPCSII codes.

PREOPERATIVE DIAGNOSIS: 1. Right Bartholin cyst 6 cm

2. Left labial cyst 4 cm

POSTOPERATIVE DIAGNOSIS: 1. Right Bartholin cyst 6 cm

2. Left labial cyst 4 cm

OPERATION PERFORMED: Marsupialization Bartholin right cyst

I&D left labial cyst

FINDINGS: Right labial Bartholin cyst about 6 cm, left labial cyst about 4 cm.

PROCEDURE: The patient was taken to the OR. After general anesthetic was administered, sterilely cleaned and draped. First the right Bartholin site was identified and an incision made at the vaginal and vulvar junction for 3 cm. Purulent discharge was drained. Incision was exteriorized by a baseball stitch and marsupialization of the cyst wall was done without any complications.

Left labial cyst was identified again and drained on the inner side of the labia minora. Cyst wall was marsupialized. The patient tolerated the procedure well. Suture, sponge, instrument, and needle count was correct. Complete hemostasis achieved, triple antibiotic cream applied, and left the OR in stable condition.

CPT codes _____

Modifiers _____

ICD-9-CM codes _____

HCPCSII codes _____

Vagina

Again, whether the procedure is obstetrical or nonobstetrical will affect the code selection, as will the terminology suffix describing the procedure: —*otomy* is cutting into, —*entesis* is aspiration. The destruction of vaginal are internal lesions; if external, select the vulva codes.

Fitting and insertion of a tandem or pessary codes are selected from the 57155 series. Notice the insertion of radioelements for radiation therapy are codes from the 77XXX codes. The radiation therapy remains a popular treatment today.

Vaginal packing procedure is sometimes required, and if nonobstetrical, is code 57180.

The repair of the vagina is usually performed in conjunction with another procedure, either urethral suspension work, or other vaginal wall repair. The most common procedure is the 57260, Anterior and posterior colporrhaphy, or the A&P repair. In reviewing operative notes, observe for the additional repair of the enterocele or other anatomical repairs. Also, determine if the approach for the repair is open, abdominal, or vaginal.

The paravaginal defect repairs the urethra, bladder, and the vaginal prolapse.

Colposcopy is the evaluation of the vagina using an endoscope. Frequently, the physician will obtain one biopsy or multiple tissue samples. 57421 is quantity of one, when multiple tissue samples are obtained. If the physician uses the colposcope also to visualize the vulva or external genitalia, select additional codes from the 56820 series; if visualizing the cervix, select 57452 series. A very common procedure is the colposcopy with loop electrode of the cervix (LEEP). However, if the physician also performs the colposcopy with endocervical curettage, this service is not coded additionally when the LEEP is performed.

■ *Highlight*

If the colposcopy is performed as a scout for another procedure, the colposcopy is not coded. If a diagnostic colposcopy is performed resulting in the decision to perform a noncolposcopy *procedure, select coloposcopy with the –58 modifier.*

Cervix

The excision cervix 57500 series of services is selected when the procedure performed is directly visualized, without the use of a colposcopy or other scope apparatus. The codes in this series are described by the type of the equipment that is used to treat the illness/disease. For example, the 57522 LEEP, without the use of the colposcopy, is a common procedure.

The radical trachelectomy, with extensive removal of the pelvic anatomy, is often performed with multiple physicians. The -62 modifier is frequently selected with this service due to the complexity of the case. Most of the additional procedures that are also performed during these extensive cases are also coded; for example, the hysterectomy codes.

Uterus

The 58100 series contains very popular codes, describing many cases. It will be necessary to read the descriptions carefully and to review the parenthetical tips in the CPT code bank to accurately select the codes. Multiple coding is likely, with the common use of either -51 or -59 modifier as appropriate.

Endometrial and endocervical biopsy is one code, if biopsies were obtained and sent for pathology. Not every case includes a biopsy. If the physician only excises (curettage), do not select the 58100 code.

Myomectomy is an open abdominal approach or vaginal approach, and the services describe the number of tumors and the total weight of the tumors. This information is documented on the pathology report, although it may also be described in the operative report by the surgeon. The depth of the tumor is also described by the codes, with either surface or intramural level. This depth should be described in the operative notes clearly, guiding to the accurate code selection.

Hysterectomy is the removal of the uterus. There are multiple codes for the open hysterectomy services, either through the abdomen or incision through the vagina. To code for the hysterectomy, the coder needs to read the operative report for these details:

- What is the approach? Abdomen is 58150–58240, vaginal open is 58260–58294.
- What tissue is removed: Corpus uterus plus cervix, salpingectomy and/or oophorectomy, (unilateral or bilateral)? If more anatomy is removed, there may be a combination code that should be selected.
- Did the physician repair other anatomy during the case?

An intrauterine device is inserted into the uterus, using an instrument that guides it directly through the vagina into the cervix and places it in the uterus. There are various types of IUDs manufactured. A code is selected for the professional service to place the IUD into the uterus and another HCPCSII code or 99070 for the IUD item, if purchased by the physician for the patient.

The artificial insemination procedures are typically performed by infertility specialists, but may be performed by any physician. The sperm washing procedure is commonly performed by many OB/GYN physicians assisting in the early diagnosis.

Hysterosalpingography and chromatubation of the oviduct are usually performed using radiology procedures. The operative notes or radiology report for the additional 768XX procedures with the use of -26 modifier for the professional component must be reviewed. The physician may also guide a catheter to evaluate the patency of the fallopian tube (salping) from the uterus orifice to the ovary or fimbria area.

A relatively new code is the endometrial cryoablation with endometrial curettage, using ultrasound guidance 58356. This code includes the 76XXX codes.

Laparoscopy/Hysteroscopy

Again, as with other anatomical sites, the surgical scope services include the diagnostic scope services. This coding can become complex.

When the peritoneoscopy (abdominal through the peritoneum) diagnostic scope is performed, select 49320. When the diagnostic hysteroscopy is performed, select 58555. Notice that two areas of the CPT code book may be involved in selecting the codes, depending upon the anatomical sites that are entered. Both of these services are for *diagnostic* only care, and do not describe the surgical or therapeutic correction services.

Coding Tip	*Laparo = abdominal; wall directly visualizes the abdominal wall and anatomical structures*
	Hystero = uterus; directly visualizes the canal and the cavity of the uterus

Modifier -50 is not usually necessary with this series, as most descriptions include bilateral sites.

The 58545 series describe the scope entering through the abdomen, for the surgical removal of various areas. The weight of the uterus is again a necessary fact for selecting the code. According to the CPT assistant, selecting 58550 indicates "most work is via the laparoscope, with a posterior cut into the vagina."

The 58558 series of codes describe the scope entering through the canal and the cavity of the uterus, for the surgical removal of the various area. There are more code selections using this approach.

And, especially for this area of coding, the physicians are choosing to use different types of scopes to perform unique procedures, removing anatomy that is not currently described by a code. The 58578 or 58579 unlisted codes are likely to be selected when these situations are found documented in the operative report. And, as science advances, the Category III codes must be at least semiannually reviewed in order to stay current with new procedures and devices.

EXERCISE 10–8

Read the following operative report and select the proper CPT, modifiers, ICD-9-CM and HCPCSII codes.

PREOPERATIVE DIAGNOSIS(ES): 1. Dysfunctional uterine bleeding

2. Endometrial polyp

POSTOPERATIVE DIAGNOSIS(ES): 1. Normal appearing endometrial cavity

2. Small endometrial polyp arising from the posterior body of the uterus

PROCEDURE PERFORMED: 1. Endometrial ablation

ANESTHESIA: General

PROCEDURE: The patient was taken to the operating room after general anesthetic was administered. Sterilely cleaned and draped. Bladder was not catheterized. Bimanual exam revealed the uterus to be multiparous size, anteverted. Adnexa not palpable. Posterior vaginal wall retracted with a weighted speculum. Anterior lip of the cervix held with a tenaculum. Internal cervical os was dilated up to 7 mm without any complications. Hysteroscope was introduced along with light source. There was correct placement ascertained. Bilateral tubal ostia appeared normal. Endometrial cavity appeared normal. There was a small polyp posteriorly on the endometrial cavity. Hysteroscope was removed. Curettage was done and specimens sent for pathology. This was followed by further dilating the cervical canal to 8 mm, followed by introduction of a NovaSure instrument. After placing this NovaSure, ascertaining the position, the cavity assessment test was not passed in spite of two attempts. The procedure was abandoned. Instruments were removed. Hysteroscope reinserted. Cavity appears normal. There is no obvious pathology noted. Hysteroscope removed.

The patient tolerated the procedure well. There was a small tear on the anterior lip of the cervix, repaired with 2-0 Vicryl. Suture, sponge, instrument, and needle count correct. Left the operating room in stable condition.

CPT codes _____

Modifiers _____

ICD-9-CM codes _____

HCPCSII codes _____

Oviduct

The first codes in the 58600 series describe the open approach. As with all areas of the CPT, it is improper to select open codes if the procedure approach was laparoscopically or hysteroscopically performed.

Laparoscopy of the Ovary and Tubes

It is likely the codes from the 493XX series will be used either in combination with the series of codes in the 5866X or in lieu of these codes. Read carefully to determine the exact anatomy and then compare to the description of the codes.

> **EXAMPLE**
>
> 58662 Laparoscopy, surgical; with fulguration or excision of lesions of the ovary (one), pelvic viscera or peritoneal surface by any method
>
> vs.
>
> 49222 Laparoscopy, surgical; with aspiration of cavity or cyst (ovarian cyst) single or multiple
>
> Notice how similar the descriptions of these procedures are, both of the anatomical site ovary. Code 58662 describes the ablation or the excision, whereas 49222 describes the aspiration.

Adhesions

Lysis of adhesions per CPT is clarified in the CPT Assistant with two examples. However, the operative note will need to describe the lysis of adhesions from the exact anatomical sites before a code can be selected. Were they removed from the intestine, adnexa, ovary, salping, uterus? Where the adhesions are connected and removed is key in selecting codes. Next, is lysis performed during an open approach or laparoscopically?

The January 1996 CPT Assistant states that lysis of adhesions codes are selected when the adhesions are multiple in number, dense in nature, cover the primary field to preclude visualization, with "considerable" additional time and effort (documented) beyond the usual procedure, and increased risk to the patient. The operative note should clearly include these details when a code for lysis of adhesions is selected. The code may be a separate code if the anatomical area has a code describing lysis, or modifier -22 may be added to the primary procedure code describing the additional, unusual professional work effort.

March 2003 CPT Assistant states 58660 may be reported in addition to the primary procedure if dense, extensive adhesions require additional work. If the documentation is clear, add modifier -59 to the 58660 when performed in addition to another primary procedure. Certainly, AMA has guided the requirement for specific documentation for the lysis of adhesions services.

■ *Highlight*

The National Correct Coding Initiative (NCCI) concept surrounding lysis of adhesions varies from the AMA/CPT definition.

Lysis of adhesions is not to be separately coded when performed with other surgical laparoscopic procedures.

Ovary

Ovarian cysts may be treated by aspiration with a laparoscope (49XXX) or open. The codes in the series 58800 are for open approach, not using the scope, and describe the drainage rather than simple aspiration procedure.

The excisional ovarian services describe either the open removal of the cyst or of the entire ovary. Most codes describe unilateral or bilateral within the description, so the use of the -50 modifier is not required. The 58943 series may be performed by multiple physicians, often with the -62 modifier.

Operating Microscope

Occasionally, the surgeon requires the use of the operating room microscope to aid in the visualization of the procedure. This code is not selected for small microscopic equipment, such as the loupes or glasses, nor is it selected for the listed codes. The code is selected in addition to most gynecologic services, and most often would be used for either the perineonatologist services or the ovarian and salping work. Code 69990 is an add-on code, no modifier -51 is applied, and it should be paid without the multiple surgical payment reductions.

Other Anatomical Sites

It is not uncommon for the OB/GYN physician to encounter additional illness or disease while performing their services, whether in conjunction with E/M visits or surgical procedures. It is therefore to be expected that the OB/GYN coder will have to become familiar with more than just the OB/GYN section of the code book. The surgeon may repair intestines, encounter vascular concerns or metastases or perform an appendectomy, to name a few examples. Reading the operative note and inquiring more details from the physician becomes a necessity for the OB/GYN services.

Payment

For the OB/GYN services, investigating insurance benefits *prior* to the performance of the service is paramount. The benefits (or limitations) may vary, even during a nine-month pregnancy. Or, for the hysterectomy services, there is a high probability of certain quality indicators that must be provided before the case is scheduled for surgery, perhaps including a second opinion. Lacking these steps, the services are likely denied in full, with no payment to the physician for the excellent care that was rendered.

EXERCISE 10–9

Use the ICD-9-CM and CPT manuals to code the following exercises.

1. Laparoscopic tubal ligation using Falope ring. _____ _____

2. Colposcopy with cervical biopsy and endocervical curettage for cervical dysplasia performed during a comprehensive initial consultation involving high complexity of medical decision making. _____ _____ _____

3. Endometrial biopsy for postmenopausal bleeding on a new patient. _____ _____

4. Laser treatment for the destruction of ten vaginal warts (molluscum contagiosum) on an established patient. _____ _____

Hospital Procedures

The gynecologist is a specialized surgeon in the area of female reproductive organs. The CPT code 57410, Pelvic examination under anesthesia is included in routine evaluation of the surgical field in all major and many minor gynecological procedures and is not to be reported separately.

Infertility

When a woman comes to the gynecologist for infertility, often the husband is included in the initial workup. Since most couples do not know where the problem lies, a simple semen analysis can rule out most male-related problems. Female problems are more plentiful and complicated to explore. Some common problems include incompatible vaginal secretions or cervical mucus, anovulation, implantation problems, and blockage of the fallopian tubes. Following are a few of the tests and procedures performed on infertility patients with a brief description of each. A postcoital test (PCT) is an inspection of the mucus from the vagina after intercourse to detect the motility and viability of the sperm as it appears in the cervical mucus. Semen washing, using a chemical, is performed to produce better sperm motility. Hormone blood levels may be drawn at a specific time of the menstrual cycle to determine if the patient is ovulating. Hysteroscopy may be performed to visualize the lining of the uterus. Laparoscopy is used to visualize the outside of the uterus, the ovaries, and fallopian tubes. In a procedure called hysterosalpingogram, frequently done with laparoscopy, dye is inserted via the cervix and forced up through the uterus and fallopian tubes. If it easily spills into the abdominal cavity it is an indication that the uterine tubes are free from blockage. If it does not spill, or requires much force to spill, it is an indication that there is a blockage. A catheter may also be inserted into the fallopian tube for diagnostic purposes or to help free the tube from obstruction.

Various forms of artificial insemination, intracervical or intrauterine, may be performed on the infertile woman. CPT codes 58321 and 58322 are used for such procedures. CPT codes 58970, 58974, and 58976 are used for in vitro fertilization procedures.

EXERCISE 10–10

Use the ICD-9-CM and CPT manuals to code the following exercises.

1. Sperm washing for artificial insemination. _____ _____

2. A woman has tried to conceive for over a year. After a thorough physical examination and other diagnostic tests, she learns that her cervix is considered incompetent. _____ _____

3. Repair of enterocele (vaginal approach) and rectocele with posterior colporrhaphy. _____

4. Hysterosalpingogram done on an infertility patient for tubal occlusion. _____ _____

5. Surgical assist for abdominal hysterectomy with bilateral salpingectomy, removal of right ovary, and lysis of adhesions. _____

Structural Abnormalities of the Female Organs

The normal position of the uterus is tipped slightly forward and referred to as **anteverted.** A **retroverted** uterus is tipped backward. With aging, trauma, or excessive stretching from the act of childbirth, the supporting ligaments of the uterus and bladder may become weakened and **pelvic relaxation** occurs. The displacement of the uterus, bladder, vagina, and rectum may cause significant discomfort and a variety of symptoms that may necessitate surgical correction.

Uterine **prolapse** occurs as pelvic muscles and ligaments become overstretched or weakened and allow the uterus to fall downward into the vaginal canal. A cystocele is the prolapse of the urinary bladder into the vagina causing pressure, urinary frequency, urgency, and incontinence with coughing, sneezing, laughing, or activity, referred to as urinary stress incontinence. A uterine suspension and anterior vaginal colporrhaphy may need to be performed to bring the bladder to its normal position and repair the stretched vagina. A vaginocele, also known as a colpocele, is a prolapse or falling of the vagina, or hernia protruding into the vagina. A rectocele is the prolapse of the rectum into the vagina. This causes constipation, a bearing down feeling, and possibly incontinence of gas and feces.

Sexually Transmitted Diseases (STDs)

Sexually transmitted diseases (STDs), also called venereal diseases, are among the most common contagious diseases in the United States. Transmission occurs through body fluids such as blood, semen, and vaginal secretions during vaginal, anal, or oral sex. Occasionally they are spread by contact with infected skin. The physician is often able to make a diagnosis from visual examination. Serum blood tests and vaginal cultures are used to confirm the disease. Most treatment includes medication; often it is the administration of oral or injectable antibiotics. Lesions are removed using chemical or surgical methods. Patient education and counseling are often involved to ensure patients do not spread the disease. See Table 10–9 for a listing and description of sexually transmitted diseases.

Cancer of the Female Reproductive Tract

Tumors of the reproductive tract are found in women of reproductive age and are most common in postmenopausal women. Various forms of benign and malignant neoplasms occur in all areas of the female reproductive tract. Malignant lesions account for 10 percent of all cancer deaths in women. See Table 10–10 for a listing and description of the most common forms of female cancer.

Other Diseases of the Female Reproductive Tract

Endometriosis is a condition that occurs when endometrial tissue migrates outside of the uterus into the pelvic or abdominal cavity. This tissue implants on other organs and responds to hormonal signals as if it were within the uterus. The misplaced tissue fills with blood and sloughs causing severe pain. Although benign and self-limiting, it is a cause of infertility. Laparoscopy may confirm the diagnosis of endometriosis and is used to remove the endometrial implants.

Uterine fibroid tumors are the most common tumors of the female reproductive tract. They occur in 50 percent of all women who reach age fifty. They are nonma-

TABLE 10–9   Sexually Transmitted Diseases.

Name	Definition
AIDS	Acquired immunodeficiency syndrome is caused by human immunodeficiency virus (HIV). The virus attacks and destroys the immune system leaving the body vulnerable to invasion by other microorganisms.
chancroid	A bacterial infection, also called soft chancre, that causes ulceration and enlargement of the lymph glands (lymphadenopathy). It is usually contacted through sexual intercourse and can spread to other areas of the body.
chlamydia	An infection that is caused by the bacteria *Chlamydia trachomatis,* which invades the vagina and cervix. It is the leading cause of infertility and pelvic inflammatory disease.
condylomata acuminata	An infection that causes genital warts, which may itch or burn. It is spread by direct skin-to-skin contact during sexual intercourse.
gonorrhea	A contagious inflammation of the genital mucous membrane transmitted chiefly by sexual intercourse and caused by the bacteria Neisseria gonorrhoeae. It often spreads unknowingly and can cause infertility, eye and throat infections, and pelvic inflammatory disease.
hepatitis B	An inflammation of the liver, also called serum hepatitis, that results in liver cell destruction. As it travels throughout the body the patient feels ill and may have fever, weight loss, jaundice, fatigue, abdominal pain, and digestive disturbances.
herpes genitalis	Herpes simplex virus (HSV), type 2 is spread by direct skin-to-skin contact and causes a local infection that produces ulcerations on the skin and mucosa of the genitals.
syphilis	The spirochete bacterium causes a chronic infection that sometimes appears as a chancre sore in the primary stage. In the second stage, as the organism spreads, it may involve any organ or tissue. During this time numerous symptoms can be present as it becomes systemic. A latent period usually follows which may last from one to forty years when the patient is asymptomatic. Later, widespread invasion may take place resulting in disabling or life-threatening conditions.
trichomoniasis	Infection of the genitourinary tract caused by Protozoa trichomonas. It can cause urethritis (inflammation of the urethra) with dysuria (painful urination) and itching.

leiomyomas
Myoma or tumor of muscular tissue involving the non-striated muscle fibers, also known as fibroid tumors.

lignant tumors, also called **leiomyomas,** which are made up of smooth muscle that grows within the myometrium of the uterus. The patient may be asymptomatic, or experience pelvic pain, constipation, urinary frequency, and heavy or prolonged periods. Leiomyomas may be treated surgically with myomectomy, a shelling out of the myometrium with preservation of the rest of the uterus. In younger women of childbearing age, myomectomy would be the recommended surgical treatment. In cases where there are multiple tumors or tumors large in size, or the woman is not concerned with childbearing, a hysterectomy may be performed. Refer to Table 10–11 for a listing of hysterectomies.

A collection of different types of cysts may occur on the ovaries. Occasionally they become large and cause discomfort or menstrual irregularities. If they rupture and bleed into the pelvic cavity they may require surgical intervention. Mittelschmerz is abdominal pain that occurs at the time of ovulation, midway between menstrual periods.

TABLE 10–10 **Female Reproductive Cancer.**

Type	Description
cervical	One of the most common forms of gynecologic cancer. An ulceration of the cervix occurs causing vaginal discharge and spotting. A Pap smear usually detects this slow-growing cancer in early stages. Cryotherapy, laser ablation, electrocautery, surgical resection (referred to as conization), and hysterectomy are all treatment options.
endometrial	The most common cancer of the female reproductive tract where ulcerations of the endometrium develop causing vaginal bleeding accompanied by a white or yellow vaginal discharge (leukorrhea). Most commonly occurs in postmenopausal women who have never had children. Diagnosis is made by endometrial biopsy or dilation and curettage. Complete hysterectomy with bilateral salpingo-oophorectomy is usually performed.
ovarian	The leading cause of female reproductive cancer deaths in women. Abnormal tissue development occurs leading to ovarian cancer which is the most difficult of all female cancers to detect. A pelvic mass may be palpated on physical examination, however this is usually at a later stage. The patient may experience lower abdominal pain, weight loss, and general poor health. A total abdominal hysterectomy with bilateral salpingo-oophorectomy is usually performed as well as excision of nearby lymph glands. If found in later stages, a complete exenteration of the abdomen and pelvic organs may be necessary.
uterine	Several types of endometrial carcinoma arise from the endometrial lining and may invade the uterine wall. Found most commonly in nullipara women between the ages of 50 and 60 years old, this form of cancer may metastasize to the ovaries, fallopian tubes, and other organs. Symptoms include menorrhagia, metrorrhagia, watery or thick, foul-smelling discharge, and postmenopausal bleeding. Depending on the stage and age of the woman, a hysterectomy and bilateral salpingo-oophorectomy may need to be performed.
Vaginal	A rare form of cancer exhibiting symptoms of leukorrhea and bloody vaginal discharge. Treatment usually involves surgical excision of the tumor.
Vulvar	Squamous cell carcinoma of the vulva accounts for 3 percent of all gynecologic cancers. It occurs mainly in postmenopausal women. A small hard lump develops and grows into an ulcer. It may weep and bleed and if not treated, will metastasize to other areas.

Locate the main term(s) in the Alphabetic Index, Volume 2 first. Review any subterms under the main term and follow any cross-reference instructions. Always verify the code that has been selected from the Index in the Tabular List, Volume 1. Refer to any instructional notations and assign the code to the highest level of specificity. Code the diagnosis until all elements are completely identified.

EXAMPLE

A patient has a hysterectomy for intramural leiomyoma of uterus.

ICD-9-CM code 218.1

Although the diagnosis uterine leiomyoma is listed under code 218, this three-digit code cannot be used because there are four selections below it which are described further, all having four digits. You must choose from one of the four-digit codes, 218.0, 218.1, 218.2, or 218.9. In this case, code 218.1 describes the diagnosis

TABLE 10–11   Types of Hysterectomies.

Procedure	Definition
Hysterectomy	Surgical removal of the uterus
Supracervical hysterectomy	Surgical removal of the fundus and corpus portions of the uterus (leaving the cervix)
Total abdominal hysterectomy (TAH)	Complete surgical removal of the entire uterus using an abdominal approach
Vaginal hysterectomy (Vag Hyst)	Surgical removal of the uterus using a vaginal approach
Oophorectomy	Surgical removal of the ovary
Salpingectomy	Surgical removal of the fallopian tube
Salpingo-oophorectomy	Surgical removal of both the fallopian tube and the ovary (unilateral/one; bilateral/two)
Hysterosalpingo-oophorectomy	Surgical removal of the uterus, fallopian tube, and ovary
Total abdominal hysterectomy with bilateral salpingo-oophorectomy	Surgical removal of uterus, both tubes and both ovaries

exactly. There are no five-digit codes listed under this category, so the highest level of specificity is a four-digit code. Always sequence the primary diagnosis first. The primary diagnosis is listed by the use of the ICD-9-CM code that represents the diagnosis, condition, problem, or other reason for the encounter/visit shown in the medical record to be chiefly responsible for the outpatient services provided during the encounter/visit. Second, list all additional codes that describe any coexisting conditions that affect patient care or management.

Menstrual Abnormalities

The beginning of menstruation is called menarche. As mentioned earlier, this occurs at puberty with the secretion of the female sex hormones estrogen and progesterone. Menstrual disorders are often triggered by hormonal abnormalities that control the menstrual cycle. The normal menstrual cycle is twenty-eight days with an average length of blood flow lasting five days. The first day of any blood loss is considered the first day of the menstrual cycle whether it is spotting or a regular flow. This day is important in the calculation and determination of what may be happening to cause an abnormal cycle. A woman typically menstruates throughout her reproductive years until the onset of menopause, which is the cessation of menses. If a patient does not have a menstrual flow it is called amenorrhea. Painful or difficult menstruation is referred to as dysmenorrhea. Excessive menstrual flow or too frequent menstruation is called abnormal uterine bleeding. See Table 10–12 for a list of common terms relating to the menstrual cycle.

TABLE 10–12 Terms Relating to Menstruation.

Term	Definition
amenorrhea	Without menses.
dysmenorrhea	Painful menstruation.
menarche	Beginning of menstrual function at time of puberty.
menometrorrhagia	Excessive uterine bleeding at and between menstrual periods.
menopause	Cessation of hormone production and menstruation.
menorrhalgia	Painful menses.
menorrhagia	Excessive uterine bleeding at time of menstruation.
menorrhea	Discharge at time of menses.
menostaxis	Prolonged menstrual period.
menses	The regular recurring uterine bleeding from the shedding of the endometrium.
metrorrhagia	Uterine bleeding occurring at irregular intervals.
oligomenorrhea	Scanty or infrequent menstruation.
postmenopause	The period of life after menopause.
premenstrual	Occurring before regular menstruation.

Inflammatory Conditions

Inflammatory conditions of the female genital tract may be localized or involve other genital organs and adjacent structures. The suffix *-itis* on the end of a word indicates an inflammation. The beginning of the term indicates the organ involved. Some conditions are cervicitis (cervix), endometritis (endometrium), oophoritis (ovaries), salpingitis (uterine tubes), vaginitis (vagina), vulvitis (vulva), and vulvovaginitis (vulva and vagina). There are many reasons for female genital inflammation. A spermicide, tampon, or the act of intercourse could cause a local inflammation. The fungal infection *Candida albicans,* also known as Monilia or yeast infection, can cause vulvovaginitis. Bacterial and viral infections, such as those found in venereal disease, are common causes of inflammation, genital tract infections, and pelvic inflammatory disease (PID). PID is an inflammation of the entire female reproductive tract, the most common cause of which is STD. As these organisms travel up the fallopian tubes into the abdominal cavity the body fights to rid them. PID symptoms include fever, chills, backache, a foul-smelling vaginal discharge, and a painful, tender abdomen. During this process adhesions may form attaching organs to other organs and blocking the lumen (opening) of the fallopian tube. This is the most common cause of infertility. In severe cases, the peritoneum, a membrane that covers the abdominal wall, becomes inflamed and a condition called peritonitis may result. If the infection gets into the bloodstream, septicemia and even death may occur.

The Female Breast

Gynecologists evaluate the female breast and diagnose breast disease. Most procedure codes for these services would be found within the integumentary system of the surgery section in the CPT manual. A common benign condition of the breast in which small sacs of tissue and fluid develop is fibrocystic breast disease. In this disease cystic lumps or nodules are noticed in the breast and may be accompanied by premenstrual tenderness. A mammogram confirms this diagnosis.

A fibroadenoma is a common benign neoplasm of the breast derived from glandular tissue. Following the coding instructions of a neoplasm in Chapter 1, first research the main term fibroadenoma in the alphabetic index. The subclassifications are referenced to M codes, which are used primarily in cancer registries. Refer to the Neoplasm table, breast, benign, to assign the code 217.

The American Cancer Society statistics show breast cancer to be the most commonly occurring malignant disease in women and is the second leading cause of cancer death in American women (lung cancer is the first). A majority of breast lumps are discovered by women on self-examination. Others are found by the gynecologist who performs a breast examination as part of the routine gynecologic examination, or by mammography, a radiographic examination of the breasts for the detection of cancer. Some signals include skin changes, puckering, or leakage from the nipple. Most women needing lumpectomy or mastectomy for the removal of malignant tumors and breast tissue are referred to general surgeons.

■ *Highlight*

While breast cancer occurs mostly in women, it does occur in men. ICD-9-CM does contain specific codes for male breast as well as female breast.

EXERCISE 10–11

Use the ICD-9-CM manual to code the following exercises.

1. Endometriosis of the broad ligament. _____

2. Chlamydial vulvovaginitis. _____

3. Fibrocystic breast disease. _____

4. Mittelschmerz. _____

5. Carcinoma in situ of the cervical canal. _____

Use the ICD-9-CM, CPT, and HCPCSII manuals to code the following exercises.

6. Uterine suspension with anterior colporrhaphy for uterine prolapse with cystocele. _____ _____

7. I&D of Bartholin's gland abscess complicating pregnancy. _____ _____

8. Resection of ovarian malignancy with bilateral salpingo-oophorectomy and omentectomy. _____ _____

9. A new patient, gravida 5 para 0-0-5-0 appears in the gynecologist's office with acute urethritis, leukorrhea, and severe pelvic pain. The patient is a habitual aborter with a history of irregular menses. She confides in the doctor about her drug use and sexual promiscuity. The physician performs a comprehensive examination and takes a vaginal culture to rule out gonorrhea. The culture is sent to an outside laboratory along with a blood sample for a CBC and sed rate technician obtained by venipuncture. A urine pregnancy test and urinalysis (automated with microscopy) are performed in the office. The pregnancy test is negative and the UA indicates a mild nonspecific UTI. The physician orders an intramuscular injection of antibiotic and the patient is advised to schedule a follow-up appointment in three days. _____ _____ _____ _____ _____ _____ _____ _____ _____

Use the ICD-9-CM, CPT, and HCPCSII manuals to code the following exercise sequencing the principal diagnosis with the appropriate procedure.

10. A 19-year-old sexually active teenager is seen as a new patient complaining of pain with intercourse. She states that there has been no hemorrhaging other than her normal monthly menses and that she does not have any nausea, dizziness, or vomiting. As part of the routine exam, the physician performs a quantitative hCG serum pregnancy test, which is negative. A pelvic examination is done with Pap smear and the physician palpates several abnormal masses along the patient's abdominal wall. The patient flinches in pain when this area is touched. The physician performs a complete pelvic ultrasound to rule out leiomyoma and malignant neoplasm. The results are essentially negative, so a vaginal hysteroscopy is recommended. The patient wants to proceed immediately. Endometrial polyps are seen covering the lower one-third of the woman's endometrium. The physician then removes the polyps by ablation at the same episode of care. _____ _____ _____ _____ _____ _____ _____

SUMMARY

The practice of obstetrics and gynecology are two-specialties-in-one serving the needs of pregnant and nonpregnant women.

The reproductive organs consist of the external genitalia, the vagina, uterus, fallopian tubes, and ovaries. The primary purpose of the reproductive organs is to produce offspring.

Obstetrics is the branch of medical science that has to do with the pregnancy process from conception to childbirth and through the puerperium. A global package concept is used to code and bill for obstetrical services, which includes normal uncomplicated antepartum, delivery, and postpartum care.

A pregnancy is divided into three trimesters and labor is divided into three stages. Complications in and of pregnancy are numerous and include abortion, anatomic problems, anemia, ectopic pregnancy, fetal problems, gestational diabetes, hydramnios, placental anomalies, malpresentations, multiple births, postpartum disorders, and Rh incompatibility.

A gynecologist is a physician and surgeon who treats females experiencing infertility, structural abnormalities of female organs, sexually transmitted diseases, sexual dysfunction, menstrual abnormalities, inflammatory conditions, breast disease, female cancer, and other diseases. OB/GYN physicians perform preventative services including contraceptive counseling, screening Pap smears, breast examinations, and complete physical examinations. Unique aspects of coding OB/GYN include the dual role of the physician serving the pregnant and nonpregnant patient, and acting as primary care physician and specialist. Many sensitive issues surrounding OB/GYN services and the complexities of the complications of and in pregnancy add to the difficulty in coding this specialty.

REFERENCES

Chabner, D-E. (2004). *The language of medicine* (7th ed.) Philadelphia: Elsevier.

Dorland's illustrated medical dictionary (30th ed.) (2003). Philadelphia: Elsevier.

Fordney, M. T. (2004). *Insurance handbook for the medical office* (8th ed.) Philadelphia: Elsevier.

Huffman, E. K. (1994). *Health information management* (10th ed.) Berwyn, IL: Physicians; Record Company.

Miller-Keane, (2005). *Encyclopedia & Dictionary of Medicine, Nursing, & Allied Health* (7th ed.) Philadelphia: Elsevier.

St. Anthony's Medicare unbundling guidebook. (1998). Salt Lake City: Ingenix, UT.

Taber's cyclopedic medical dictionary (20th ed.) (2005). Philadelphia: Davis.

UCLA Medical Center/Medical Group. (1996–1997). *Physician's handbook for patient referral.* Los Angeles: UCLA Medical Center.

Chapter 11
Radiology, Pathology, and Laboratory

KEY TERMS

automated
brachytherapy
computerized axial
    tomography (CAT scan)
hyperthermia

intracavitary
magnetic resonance imaging (MRI)
manual
qualitative
quantitative

radiation absorbed dose (RAD)
ribbons
sources

LEARNING OBJECTIVES

Upon successful completion of this module, you should be able to:

1. Identify subsections of the radiological section.
2. Code the various types of radiological procedures.
3. Identify the different types of laboratory procedures.
4. Explain the difference between qualitative and quantitative.
5. Code the different procedures related to the radiology and laboratory sections.

INTRODUCTION

This chapter introduces learners to specialty coding in the areas of radiology and laboratory and pathology. The chapter focuses mainly on CPT coding, with relevant examples from ICD-9-CM integrated where appropriate. The first half of this chapter covers the specialty of radiology and includes nuclear medicine and diagnostic ultrasound. The second half of this chapter discusses pathology and laboratory guidelines. Learners should have a copy of the CPT code book nearby as they begin studying this chapter.

RADIOLOGY

Radiology is a medical specialty that involves the use of radioactive substances such as X-rays and radioactive isotopes in the prevention, detection, diagnosis, and treatment of disease. The field of radiology includes many specialty areas, including radiation therapy, nuclear medicine, ultrasound, computed tomography, magnetic resonance imaging, and special procedures such as angiography. A radiographer is a specialist who produces images (or radiographs) of parts of the human body. Depending on their level of training and experience, radiographers may also perform more complicated tests such as preparing contrast media for patients to drink and operating special equipment used for computerized tomography, magnetic resonance imaging, and ultrasound. Radiation therapists prepare cancer patients for treatment, and administer prescribed radiation doses to parts of the body. A radiologist is a physician who interprets the images prepared by the radiographer and makes patient treatment recommendations.

CPT—RADIOLOGY

The radiology section of the CPT code book includes four subsections:

1. Diagnostic Radiology (Diagnostic Imaging)
2. Diagnostic Ultrasound
3. Radiation Oncology
4. Nuclear Medicine

The coder should become familiar with the differences between these subsections and not code based on the area of the body being treated because each subsection covers details of the area of the anatomy being treated. For example, diagnostic procedures on the spine and pelvis, such as a radiologic examination of the spine, are included within the Diagnostic Radiology subsection. Ultrasound procedures such as echography of the spinal canal are included within the Diagnostic Ultrasound subsection. "Notes" are provided at the beginning of, as well as within other parts of the subsections that explain terminology, such as A-mode, M-mode, or B scan ultrasound.

Physician Billing

Most physician offices do not have radiologic equipment in their offices and, therefore, refer patients to hospitals or radiologic outpatient facilities. In these cases, the coders for these physicians would not be assigning radiology codes unless the physician provides radiological supervision and interpretation.

Radiological Supervision and Interpretation

Many codes in the Radiology section of CPT include the following phrase in the description—"radiological supervision and interpretation." These codes are used to describe the radiological portion of a procedure that two physicians perform. In situations where the physician provides the supervision, interpretation, and the performance of the procedure, two codes are reported: a radiological code and a code from the surgery section. This is often referred to as a "complete procedure."

> **EXAMPLE**
> Percutaneous placement of IVC filter—complete procedure. The physician submits the following codes: 75940 and 37620. Code 75940 identifies the radiologic procedure—including interpretation of the results—and code 37620 identifies the procedure.

 *Highlight*

The radiological supervision and interpretation codes do not apply to the radiation oncology subsection.

RADIOLOGY MODIFIERS

It is often necessary to modify procedures or services codes. This section introduces the common radiology modifiers and provides examples of how each might be used.

-22 (09922) Unusual Procedural Services

This modifier is intended for use when the service provided is greater than that usually required for the listed procedure. Modifier -22 may be used with **computerized axial tomography (CAT scan)** codes when additional slices are required or more detailed examination is necessary.

computerized axial tomography (CAT scan) This type of radiological procedure is used to scan any part of the body; most useful in scanning brain, lung, mediastinum, retroperitoneum, and liver.

-26 (09926) Professional Component

The professional component includes supervision of the procedure, reading and interpreting the results, and documenting the interpretation in a report. This service can be done by the physician who ordered the radiologic procedure or by the radiologist on staff at the hospital or outpatient center. The technical component includes performing the actual procedures and expenses of the supplies and equipment. This service is usually provided by the technician at a hospital or an outpatient facility. The physician would report a professional component by attaching the modifier -26 to the appropriate radiologic procedure. The outpatient facility would report the technical component modifier -tc (technical component) to the same procedure. Modifier -tc is a Level II HCPCS modifier.

> **EXAMPLE**
>
> 73550—Radiological examination of femur. The physician should report the following: 73550-26. The clinic should report the following: 73550-tc.

Coding Tip *When reporting a code describing "radiological supervision and interpretation," do not report modifier -26 along with the procedure. The "radiologic supervision and interpretation" code already describes the professional component.*

> **EXAMPLE**
>
> Peritoneogram with the physician providing only the supervision and interpretation of this procedure. The physician should report the following: 74190- peritoneogram, radiologic supervision and interpretation.

In this example, modifier -26 would not be appropriate because the descriptor code 74190 already indicated that the physician provided only the supervision and interpretation for the procedure. Reporting that would cause the claim to be denied.

> **EXAMPLE**
>
> 74329—Endoscopic catheterization of the pancreatic ductal system, radiological supervision and interpretation.

-51 (09951) Multiple Modifiers

Modifier -51 may be reported to identify that multiple radiologic procedures were performed on the same day or during the same episode. Adding 09951 on the CMS 1500 claim form justifies a multiple procedure.

-52 (09952) Reduced Services

Modifier -52 may be reported to identify that a radiologic procedure is partially reduced or eliminated at the discretion of the physician.

-53 (09953) Discontinued Procedure

Modifier -53 is used when the physician elected to discontinue or terminate a diagnostic procedure usually because of risk to the patient.

-59 (09959) Distinct Procedural Service

Modifier -59 may be used to identify that procedure or service was distinct or independent from other services provided on the same day.

-RT and -LT Modifiers

Modifiers -RT and -LT are HCPCS Level II modifiers that should be used when bilateral procedures are performed. To report these modifiers to reflect a bilateral radiological procedure, code the procedure twice and attach -RT to one of the codes and -LT to the other.

> **EXAMPLE**
> 73520-RT and 73520-LT-radiologic examination, hips, minimum two views each hip, bilateral.

■ *Highlight*

Modifiers -RT and -LT apply to Medicare claims, and their use varies according to reporting requirements of medical programs and other third party payers.

EXERCISE 11–1

Assign the appropriate CPT codes for the following procedure(s); include modifiers and HCPCS Level II modifiers when applicable.

1. Radiologic examination, temporomandibular joint, open and closed mouth; unilateral _____

2. Radiologic examination, chest, two views, frontal and lateral; professional component only _____

3. Radiologic examination, knee, arthrography, radiological supervision and interpretation _____

4. Barium enema with KUB _____

5. Hysterosalpingography, radiological supervision and interpretation _____

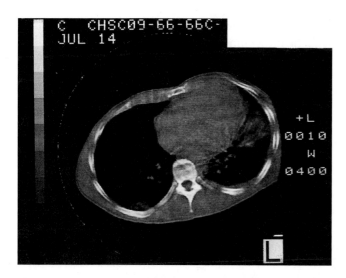

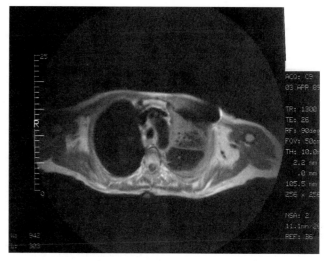

Figure 11–1 An example of a computerized tomography: a CT scan of a chest showing pleural effusion.

Figure 11–2 An example of magnetic resonance imaging: an MRI of a chest.

DIAGNOSTIC RADIOLOGY (DIAGNOSTIC IMAGING)

The production of a picture, image, or shadow that represents the object being investigated is diagnostic radiology. The classic technique for imaging is the x-ray.

Codes 70010–76499 describe diagnostic radiology services. They are further subdivided by anatomic site and then by specific type of procedure performed: CAT scan, MRI, x-ray, and MRA scan. These radiology procedures may be found in the alphabetic index of the CPT manual by referring to the main term "x-ray," "CAT scan," **"magnetic resonance imaging (MRI),"** and "magnetic resonance angiography."

> **magnetic resonance imaging (MRI)**
> This type of radiological procedure is used to scan brain, spinal cord, soft tissues, and adrenal and renal masses. More superior scan than the CAT.

CPT provides separate codes for radiologic procedures using contrast media. Contrast media is a term used to describe chemical substances that are introduced into the body to enable the soft tissue vessels and organs (for example, the liver) to be seen with x-rays. The contrast medium is administered either orally or intravenously. Examples of some contrast media are barium, iohexol, and renografin. Common x-ray procedures using contrast material include barium enema, endoscopic retrograde cholangiopancreatogram, fistulogram, intravenous pyelogram, and hysterosalpingogram.

CAT scans may also be performed with or without contrast material (see Figure 11–1). This radiological procedure is helpful in evaluating the brain, lung, mediastinum, retroperitoneum, and the liver.

In most instances, MRI scans are almost equal to CAT scans, but MRIs are superior in evaluating the brain, spinal cord, soft tissues, adrenal and renal masses (see Figure 11–2). For patients who have metallic objects, such as pacemakers, metallic fragments, and vascular clips in the central nervous system, this procedure is contraindicated. Contrast material may also be used when performing MRI scans; the most common is gadolinium (gadipentetate dimeglumine).

DIAGNOSTIC ULTRASOUND

Diagnostic ultrasound is considered a subsection that lists codes 76506–76999. Similar to diagnostic radiology, it is also further subdivided by anatomical sites. These codes may be found in the index by referring to "ultrasound" or "echography." Diagnostic ultrasound involves the use of high frequency waves to visualize internal structures of the body. Ultrasounds are commonly performed for evaluation of the abdomen, pelvis, and ear, and for gynecologic and obstetrical diagnoses. Figure 11–3 shows some examples of diagnostic ultrasound equipment.

Four types of diagnostic ultrasound are recognized:

A-mode A one-dimensional ultrasonic measurement procedure.

M-mode A one-dimensional ultrasonic measurement procedure with movement of the trace (delayed time for the sound to hit the specimen being scanned and then back to screen) to record amplitude and velocity of moving echo-producing structures. This mode is used for the heart and vessels using color flow.

B-scan A two-dimensional ultrasonic scanning procedure with a two-dimensional display. This scan is the same as A-mode, except with two display dimensional.

Real-time scan A two-dimensional ultrasonic scanning procedure with display of both two-dimensional structure and motion with time. "Real time" means that the image can be visualized as it is being produced.

■ *Highlight*

The medicine chapter in the CPT manual also includes ultrasound involving the following areas:

Arterial Studies of the Extremities (93922–93931)
Venous Studies of the Extremities (93965–93971)
Cerebrovascular Arterial Studies (93875–93893)
Visceral and Penile Vascular Studies (93975–93981)
Ultrasound of the Heart—Echocardiography (93303–93350)

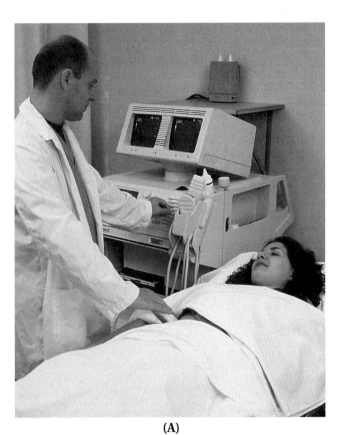

(A)

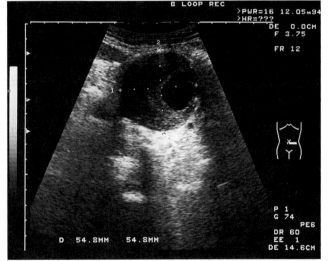

(B)

Figure 11–3 (A) Ultrasonic equipment. (B) A diagnostic ultrasound.

EXERCISE 11–2

Assign the appropriate CPT codes for the following procedure(s); include CPT modifiers and Level II modifiers, when applicable.

1. Echography, pregnant uterus, B-scan and/or real time with image documentation; complete first trimester _____

2. Echography, transvaginal nonobstetrical _____

3. Ultrasonic guidance for pericardiocentesis, radiological supervision and interpretation _____

4. Ultrasonic guidance for interstitial radioelement application _____

5. Gastrointestinal endoscopic ultrasound, radiological supervision and interpretation _____

RADIATION ONCOLOGY

The radiation oncology codes (77261–77999) describe therapeutic use of radiation to treat diseases, especially neoplastic tumors. Radiation therapy is used as a primary therapy to treat certain types of malignancies, such as leukemia. The most common type of radiation used in treatment is electromagnetic radiation with x-rays and gamma rays.

X-rays are photons generated inside a machine, while gamma rays are photons emitted from a radioactive source. Radiation is measured in units known as the **rad (radiation absorbed doses)** or the gray, which is equal to 100 rad.

radiation absorbed dose (RAD)
A unit of measure in radiation.

The delivery of radiation may be external or internal. External radiation therapy involves the delivery of a beam of ionizing radiation from an external source through the patient's skin toward the tumor region. Internal radiation therapy, also known as brachytherapy, involves applying a radioactive material inside the patient or in close proximity. This material may be contained in various types of devices such as tubes, needles, wires, seeds, and other small containers (see Figure 11–4). Common radioactive materials used in brachytherapy include radium-226, cobalt-60, cesium-137 and iodine-125. The three types of brachytherapy are interstitial (into the tissues), intracavitary (implanted into body cavities), and surface applications. Interstitial brachytherapy involves the use of radiation sources placed in special devices and then implanted in body cavities. Surface application brachytherapy uses radioactive material that is contained on the surface of a plaque or mold and applied directly or close to the surface of the patient.

Radiation Treatment Delivery

The series of codes 77401–77418 describes the technical component of delivering the radiation treatment, as well as the various energy levels administered. To assign these codes, the appropriate information is needed:

1. The number of treatment areas involved.
2. The number of ports, parts, or devices that are surgically implanted (for easy removal of blood, for example).

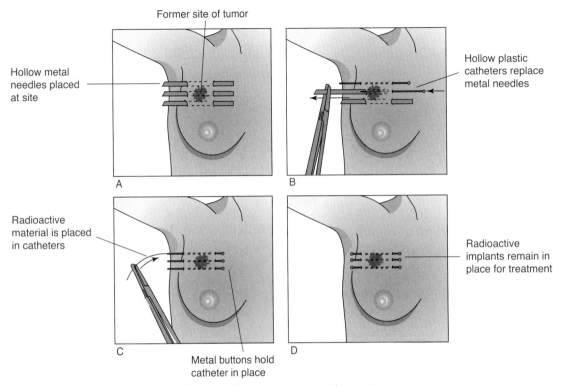

Former site of tumor

Hollow metal needles placed at site

Hollow plastic catheters replace metal needles

A

B

Radioactive material is placed in catheters

Radioactive implants remain in place for treatment

C

D

Metal buttons hold catheter in place

Figure 11–4 Brachytherapy is often used in the treatment of breast cancer.

3. The number of shielding blocks, or shields, used to protect parts of the body from radiation.

4. The total million electron volts (MEV) administered.

Hyperthermia

hyperthermia
This procedure uses heat to raise the temperature of a specific area of the body to try to increase cell metabolism and increase the destruction of cancer cells.

intracavitary
Within a cavity.

Hyperthermia involves using heat to raise the temperature of a specific area of the body to try to increase cell metabolism and, consequently, increase the destruction of cancer cells. Hyperthermia is usually performed as an adjunct to radiation therapy or chemotherapy. The hyperthermia codes (77600–77615) in the CPT book include external, interstitial, and **intracavitary** treatment. If administered at the same time, radiation therapy should be reported separately.

Clinical Brachytherapy

brachytherapy
A natural or manmade radioactive element that is applied in or around a particular treatment field.

sources
Intracavitary placement or permanent interstitial placement in clinical brachytherapy.

ribbons
Temporary interstitial placement in clinical brachytherapy.

Clinical **brachytherapy** uses natural or manmade radioactive elements that are applied in or around a particular treatment field. A therapeutic radiologist provides supervision of radioactive elements and interpretation of appropriate dosages. When the services of a surgeon are needed, a modifier -66 (surgical team) or -62 (two surgeons) may be reported to ensure that both physicians are reimbursed. Codes 77750–77799 include the admission to the hospital and daily visits provided by the physician. The codes differentiate between interstitial and intracavitary brachytherapy and are further subdivided to identify the number of **sources/ribbons** applied: simple (1–4 source ribbons), intermediate (5–10 source ribbons), or complex (>10 ribbons). CPT defines sources as intracavity placement or permanent interstitial placement. Ribbons refer to temporary interstitial placement.

■ *Highlight*

Surgeons are required for this type of therapy because this procedure is done internally on a patient. If any type of complication occurs invasively, a surgeon might need to assist the radiologist.

EXERCISE 11–3

Assign the appropriate CPT codes for the following procedure(s); include modifiers and Level II modifiers when applicable.

1. Teletherapy isodose plan (hand); simple (one or two) parallel opposed unmodified ports directed to a single area of interest _____

2. Radiation treatment delivery, two separate treatment areas three or more ports on a single treatment area, use of multiple blocks, 15 MEV _____

3. Hyperthermia, externally generated; superficial heating degree is 8 cm _____

4. Intracavitary radioelement application; complex _____

5. Supervision, handling, loading of radioelement _____

NUCLEAR MEDICINE

Nuclear medicine involves the administration of radioisotopes (radioactive elements that assist in the diagnosis of disease). The radioactive isotope deteriorates spontaneously and emits gamma rays from inside the body that enable the physician to view internal abnormalities. Some radioisotopes are selectively absorbed by tumors or by specific organs in the body and thus make them visible on the scan. This subsection (78000–79999) includes nuclear medicine procedures according to body systems, such as cardiovascular. Some of the more common diagnostic nuclear medicine scans include bone, cardiac, lung, renal, and thyroid scans, as well as thallium 201, technetium 99m pyrophosphate, technetium 99m ventriculogram, and the multigated acquisition scans.

Bone Scans

Bone scans are performed as part of metastatic workups, to identify infections such as osteomyelitis; to evaluate the hip with a prosthetic device; to distinguish pathologic fractures from traumatic fractures; and to evaluate delayed union of fractures.

Cardiac Scans

Cardiac scans are performed for diagnosis of myocardial infarction, stress testing, measurement of cardiac output, and diagnosis of ventricular aneurysms.

Thallium 201 Scan

The thallium 201 scan examines myocardial perfusion, with normal myocardium appearing as "hot," and ischemic or infarcted areas appearing as "cold."

Technetium 99m Pyrophosphate Scan

The technetium 99m pyrophosphate scan identifies recently damaged myocardial tissue, and it is most sensitive twenty-four to seventy-two hours after an acute myocardial infarction.

Technetium 99m Ventriculogram Scan

The technetium 99m ventriculogram scan identifies abnormal wall motion, cardiac shunts, size and function of heart chambers, cardiac output, and ejection fraction.

Multigated Acquisition Scan

The multigated acquisition scan is another form of this type of study.

 Coding Tip *When these tests are performed during exercise and or pharmacologic stress, the appropriate stress testing code from the 93015–93018 range should be reported in addition to the appropriate code from the nuclear medicine subsection.*

Lung Scans

Lung scans ventilation-perfusion [V/Q] can reveal pulmonary disease, chronic obstructive pulmonary disease, and emphysema. When performed along with chest x-rays, these scans are important tools in evaluating pulmonary emboli.

Renal and Thyroid Scans

Renal scans are performed to evaluate the overall functions of the kidneys. Thyroid scans are most commonly performed with technetium 99m pertechnetate, and they are useful in detecting nodules.

EXERCISE 11–4

Assign the appropriate CPT code for the following procedure(s). Include modifiers and HCPCS Level II modifiers when applicable.

1. Thyroid imaging, with uptake; single determination _____

2. Liver and spleen imaging; static only _____

3. Cardiac shunt detection _____

4. Whole body scan _____

5. Renal scan with vascular flow and function study _____

Read the following report, then assign the correct ICD-9-CM and CPT codes for physician billing.

RADIOLOGY REPORT

Patient Name: Jan Clure   **Admitting Physician:** Ken Shallow, M.D.
Hospital No.: 11049   **Procedure:** Intraoperative cholangiogram.
X-ray No.: 98-1504   **Date:** 03/12/----

Findings: Intraoperative cholangiogram was performed. Contrast was injected through the cystic duct remnant. There was mild dilatation of the common duct with free flow of contrast into the duodenum. However, there was a 6-mm filling defect in the proximal common duct that probably represents a stone.

Impression: Evidence of a common duct stone. Mild dilatation of the common bile duct.

_____
Ann Jones, M.D.

AJ:xx
D:03/13/----
T:03/13/----

C: Bernard Kester, M.D.

ICD-9-CM code(s) _____   CPT code(s) _____   _____

Read the following report, then assign the correct ICD-9-CM and CPT codes for physician billing.

RADIOLOGY REPORT

Patient Name: Sam Chandler   **Admitting Physician:** Lisa Andrews, M.D.
Hospital No.: 11503   **Procedure:** Chest, PA only.
X-ray No.: 98-29050   **Date:** 12/13/----

When films are compared to previous radiographs, there is interval increase of the right subcutaneous emphysema. There is interval demonstration of very small pneumothorax along the right lower chest. There is some interval change in the position of the right lower chest catheter, the tip of which is seen at a lower level than in the previous exam. There is no interval change in the position of the second catheter. Heart and lungs appear unremarkable without any active process; unchanged since previous exam.

Impression: 1. Increase in right subcutaneous emphysema.
                    2. Recurrent right pneumothorax, small.

_____
Larry Erwin, M.D.

LE:xx
D:12/13/----
T:12/13/----

ICD-9-CM code(s) _____   CPT code(s) _____

Read the following report, then assign the correct ICD-9-CM and CPT codes for physician billing.

RADIOLOGY REPORT

Patient Name: Ellen Parker   **Admitting Physician:** Sara Loyola, M.D.

Hospital No.: 11259   **Procedure:** Right hip and pelvis.

X-ray No.: 98-2823   **Date:** 09/25/----

Right Hip

There is a fracture through the right femoral neck. There is also evidence of intertrochanteric fracture of the right hip. No other joint or soft tissue abnormalities.

Impression: Intertrochanteric fracture of the right hip. There also appears to be a fracture of the right femoral neck.

Pelvis

A bipolar left hip prosthesis is noted in place. There is an intertrochanteric fracture of the right hip. There also appears to be a nondisplaced fracture through the right femoral neck. No other joint or soft tissue abnormalities.

Impression: Intertrochanteric fracture of the right hip. There is also evidence of a nondisplaced fracture through the right femoral neck.

Paula Robins, M.D.

PR:xx
D:09/25/----
T:09/25/----

ICD-9-CM code(s) _____   CPT code(s) _____

Read the following chart notes and radiology report and assign the correct ICD-9-CM and CPT codes for physician billing.

Patient Name: Grahm, Craig   **Date:** 6/28/----

This is a new patient in the office today complaining of an injury to the right foot. This morning he accidentally smashed his RT foot into a kitchen cabinet and has noticed pain, swelling, and ache on ambulation since then.

Examination: V.S.: W-191.5, BP-110/80 (sitting), P-64 & reg, R-16, T-96. His LT FOOT is quiescent. His RT FOOT has an enlarging hematoma on the dorsum with warmth and flexion deformities of the PIP's as before with tenderness over the entire FOREFOOT region.

Impression: Trauma RT foot

Plan: We will check an x-ray of the RT foot to R/O fracture. If there is none, he will treat with rest, ice, mild compression from a sock and elevation and after a day or 2 if he feels well may then proceed to prn heat.

Addendum: Because of the results of the x-ray the 2nd and 3rd toe were taped with paper tape to help in immobilization.

Lowery Johnson, M.D.

ICD-9-CM code(s) _____   CPT code(s) _____

RADIOLOGY REPORT

Patient Name: Craig Grahm   **Physician:** Lowery Johnson, M.D.

Hospital No.: 11259989-998   **Procedure:** AP & lateral of RT foot

X-Ray No.: 88-7784511   **Date:** 06/28/----

Views of the **RT foot** reveal a faint line of translucency in the proximal shaft in the 2nd toe about 1/3 proximal to PIP. There is also soft tissue swelling.

Impression: 1. A small nondisplaced fracture of the shaft of the 2nd proximal phalanx.

Carole Kincaid, M.D.
Radiologist

ICD-9-CM code(s) _____   CPT code(s) _____

Read the following chart notes and radiology report and assign the correct ICD-9-CM and CPT codes for physician billing.

Patient Name: Highgrove, Lynn   **Date:** 10/18/----

She is again about the same as on her last visit. She has had no stomatitis, dermatitis, pruritis, GI upset, or increase in bruisability.

Examination: V.S.: W-178.5, BP-130/80 (sitting), P-64 & reg, R-16, T-96.4 SKIN, MOUTH & NOSE are clear (she has a rather chronic malar flush). I believe that there is more synovial thickening of PIP 5 and especially 4 on the RT which is becoming more cystic. Thickening of MCP's 2 & 3, RT greater than LT, remains a problem. Her WRISTS, ELBOWS, & SHOULDERS are unremarkable. HIPS & TROCHANTERS are essentially normal. KNEES show cool soft tissue hypertrophy with crepitation. Her ANKLES are puffy. Her FEET are quintessence with bony hypertrophy.

Impression: RA

Plan: Call in Rx for MTX 2.5 mg #16 with no refills. Continue 10 mg q week. Continue Prednisone 7.5 mg q.o.d., calcium and vitamin D and the folic acid. I will monitor her CBC and because of the meds a liver profile and SMA. We will now evaluate x-rays of her hands to compare with those taken in 1995 to see the extent of joint damage and/or progression. We will also arrange for a DEXA bone density over the next month or two because of the chronic Prednisone dosage. She will RTO in 4 weeks but call sooner if needed.

Lowery Johnson, M.D.

ICD-9-CM code(s) _____   CPT code(s) _____

RADIOLOGY REPORT

Patient Name: Lynn Highgrove
Hospital No.: 225987
X-Ray No.: 99-55894778

Physician: Lowery Johnson, M.D.
Procedure: Bilateral Hands, AP and lateral
Date: 10/18/----

Multiple views of the HANDS reveal juxta-articular osteoporosis. There is some degenerative change at each 2nd and 3rd DIP and each 1st IP joint in the LT 1st MCP. There is significant erosive and cystic change in the 3rd LT PIP with joint space narrowing, soft tissue swelling and ulnar deviation of the middle phalange. There is loss of cartilage space in the 2nd LT, 2nd 3rd RT MCP's with erosive change at MCP 2 on the RT and possibly 3. These films were compared to ones taken on June 5th, 20—. They show definite progression of erosive change and cartilage loss at the 3rd LT PIP and some increase in cartilage loss at the 2nd LT MCP. On the RT there is no significant change and degenerative change with spur formation is also noted from both sets of films at the 2nd RT PIP.

Impression: 1. Rheumatoid arthritis of the hands with erosions and some progression particularly in the LT 3rd PIP since 20XX.

_____
Carole Kincaid, M.D.
Radiologist

ICD-9-CM code(s) _____   CPT code(s) _____

Read the following chart notes and radiology report and assign the correct ICD-9-CM and CPT codes for physician billing.

Patient Name: Thomas, Daniel   **Date:** 11/12/----

He was doing well until 4 to 5 weeks ago when he noted the onset of pain again in his LT shoulder and upper arm. It is often worse after bed and definitely worse on motion of the LT shoulder. This happened after he began gardening but he does not particularly remember traumatizing it. He also had pain and swelling in his RT 2nd PIP which is starting to feel slightly better. He has had no stomatitis, dermatitis, GI upset, chest pain or increase in fatigue.

Examination: V.S.: W-170, BP-166/76 (sitting), P-68 & reg, R-16, T-96.4 He is in some distress from LT SHOULDER pain on motion. His HANDS show bony hypertrophy but there is definite thickening, slight erythema, warmth, tenderness and pain on flexion of the RT 2nd PIP. In addition the PIP's again show some restriction of flexion due to a rather chronic tenosynovitis. His MPC's & DIP's are otherwise unremarkable. There is decrease in extension of the LT ELBOW, which is not tender or inflamed. The RT ELBOW and each WRIST are normal. There is significant limitation of abduction of the LT SHOULDER by almost 60 degrees with pain on abduction, external and internal rotation; rotation is also limited. His RT SHOULDER shows restriction of abduction by about 30 degrees with some stiffness on rotation. There is limitation of rotation and lateral tilt of the CERVICAL SPINE. THORACIC SPINE is unremarkable. He has straightening of the LUMBOSACRAL SPINE with decrease in extension and flexion but denies pain or tenderness. There is decrease in external rotation of each HIP by 40 degrees on the RT, 60 on the LT with some ache in the LT. His KNEES & ANKLES are unremarkable. His FEET show some bony hypertrophy.

Impression: Arthritis, SLE vs. RA. He also has LT shoulder capsulitis.

Plan: I will continue to monitor his UA, SMA-7 and liver profile because of the NSAID and also check a sed rate again to R/O traumatic arthropathy. We will check an x-ray of his LT shoulder today. In addition he will receive 80 mg of DepoMedrol IM and begin the use of Darvocet-N-100 q 6 h prn pain. Given Rx for #60 with 3 refills. He may increase the Naprolan to 500 mg t.i.d., p.c. for 10 days. He was then reminded again about ROM exercises for his LT shoulder including wall, crawl, pendulum exercises and isometric rotator cuff strengthening. If he is not better over the next 10 days he will call and injection may be warranted. Otherwise RTO in about 6 months but call sooner if needed.

_____
Lowery Johnson, M.D.

ICD-9-CM code(s) _____   CPT code(s) _____

RADIOLOGY REPORT

Patient Name: Daniel Thomas   **Physician:** Lowery Johnson, M.D.

Hospital No.: 11503   **Procedure:** Left Shoulder, AP and Lateral

X-ray No.: 98-2922560   **Date:** 11/12/----

Views of the LT SHOULDER reveal large cystic areas in the humeral head. There is a considerable amount of calcification around the bicipital groove and in the subacromial space with corticated erosions on the superior surface of the humeral head near the bicipital groove and another erosive lesion on the inferomedial aspect of the humerus. A small spur is also seen near the superior border of the glenoid fossa and at the medial inferior border of the head of humerus at the medial aspect of the erosion. The acromioclavicular joint is well maintained. The glenohumeral articulation appears normal.

Impression: 1. Erosive arthropathy of the LT humeral head with degenerative osteoarthritis.
                   2. Calcific subacromial bursitis.

_____

Carole Kincaid, M.D.
Radiologist

ICD-9-CM code(s) _____   CPT code(s) _____

CPT—PATHOLOGY AND LABORATORY

Similar to radiology, clinical laboratory testing is critical to the detection, diagnosis, and treatment of disease. Under physicians' orders, medical technologists, technicians, or other qualified laboratory personnel perform a range of specialized tests by examining body fluids, such as urine, blood, tissues, and cells. Laboratory personnel prepare patient specimens for examination and interpret tests, looking for microorganisms, such as parasites, analyzing the chemical contents of body fluids, and matching blood types. All test results are then reported to the physician who initially ordered the test.

The pathology and laboratory section of CPT includes services by a physician or by technologists under the responsible supervision of a physician. This section includes codes for such services and procedures as organ or disease panel tests, urinalysis, hematologic and immunologic studies, and surgical and anatomic pathologic examinations.

These are the specific subsections in this chapter of the CPT code book:

Organ or Disease Oriented Panels	80048–80076
Drug Testing	80100–80103
Therapeutic Drug Assays	80150–80299
Evocative/Suppression Testing	80400–80440
Consultations (Clinical Pathology)	80500–80502
Urinalysis	81000–81099
Chemistry	82000–84999
Hematology and Coagulation	85002–85999
Immunology	86000–86849
Transfusion Medicine	86850–86999
Microbiology	87001–87999
Anatomic Pathology	88000–88099
Cytopathology	88104–88199
Cytogenetic Studies	88230–88299
Surgical Pathology	88300–88399
Transcutaneous Procedures	88400
Other Procedures	89050–89240
Reproductive Medicine Procedures	89250–89356

Physician Billing

When reporting laboratory services provided by the physician, the coder must determine whether the physician performed the complete procedure or only a component of it. Some physician offices maintain sophisticated laboratory equipment on their premises so they are able to provide complete lab testing. A complete test would include obtaining the sample/specimen (blood or urine), handling the specimen, performing the actual procedure/test, and analyzing and interpreting the results. Most physicians will send their blood to an outside lab or a hospital lab for testing. In these cases the physician may only report the collection and handling of the specimen.

EXAMPLE

Biopsy of the ovary performed by Dr. Smith and the specimen was sent to a pathologist for review and interpretation. Dr. Smith uses the code 58900 for the actual biopsy of the ovary. The pathologist reports 88305 for the review and interpretation of the specimen.

■ *Highlight*

Reminder: When blood is drawn in the physician's office and is sent out for testing, the physician's office can bill only for the venipuncture. The laboratory or source performing the tests requested will bill the patient for services rendered.

CLIA '88

The Clinical Laboratory Improvement Amendments (CLIA 1988) was passed by Congress in 1988 and enacted in 1992 to improve the quality of laboratory tests performed on specimens taken from the human body and used in diagnosis, prevention, and treatment of disease. All laboratories must register with CLIA '88 and comply with its requirements to be certified by the U.S. Department of Health and Human Services (DHHS). A few laboratories, such as those that perform only forensic tests, those certified by the National Institute on Drug Abuse to perform urine testing, those that perform research unrelated to patient treatment, and those that are with licensure are exempt from CLIA '88 regulations.

CLIA '88 designated four levels of testing based on complexity: waived tests, physician-performed microscopy tests (also waived tests), moderate complexity tests, and high complexity tests. Waived tests and physician-performed microscopy tests are of low complexity (see Table 11–1). To perform these tests a laboratory must obtain a certificate of waiver. Approximately 75 percent of all tests performed in the United States are of moderate complexity and include tests such as throat cultures, white blood counts, Gram staining, and urine cultures. High complexity tests involve specialized procedures in cytogenetics, histocompatability, histopathology, and cytology. Laboratories performing moderate- and high-complexity tests go through a series of CMS certifications and are inspected by the DHHS every two years.

quantitative
Expresses specific numerical amounts of an analyte.

qualitative
Tests that detect a particular analyte.

Quantitative and Qualitative Studies

The laboratory and pathology section includes codes that will state whether the procedure is **quantitative** or **qualitative** in nature. Qualitative screening refers to tests that detect the presence of a particular analyte (substance), constituent,

TABLE 11–1   Waived Tests.

Dipstick or tablet reagent urinalysis for the following:

- Bilirubin
- Glucose
- Hemoglobin
- Ketone
- Leukocytes
- Nitrite
- pH
- Protein
- Specific gravity
- Urobilinogen

Fecal occult blood

Spun microhematocrit

Microscopic examination of the following:

- Urine sediment
- Pinworm preparation
- Vaginal wet mount preparation

Ovulation tests: visual color tests for human luteinizing hormone

Whole blood clotting time

Urine pregnancy tests

Slide card agglutination tests to screen for the following:

- Antistreptolysin O (ASO)
- C reactive protein (CRP)
- Rheumatoid factor
- Infectious mononucleosis

Gram stain (on discharges and exudates)

Potassium hydroxide (KOH) preparation on cutaneous scrapings

Erythrocyte sedimentation rate

Sickle cell screening: methods other than electrophoresis

Glucose screen whole blood dipstick method: visual color comparison determination

Semen analysis

Automated hemoglobin by single analyte instruments

or condition. Typically, qualitative studies are performed first to determine if a particular substance is present in the sample being evaluated. In contrast, quantitative studies provide results expressing specific numerical amounts of an analyte in a sample. These tests are usually performed after a qualitative study and identify the specific amount of a particular substance in the sample.

EXAMPLE

Human Gonadotropin chorionic (hCG) quantitative code 84702 represents a pregnancy test. When this test comes back from the lab it will have a titer or number that represents how many weeks the patient is pregnant. Gonadotropin chorionic (hCG) qualitative code 84703 represents a pregnancy test with a negative or positive reading.

Pathology and Laboratory Modifiers

These are some of the most commonly used modifiers in the pathology and laboratory section.

-22 Unusual Procedural Services: This modifier is intended for use when the service provided is greater than the one usually required for the listed procedure.

-26 Professional Component: In circumstances where a laboratory or pathologic procedure includes both a physician (professional) component and a technical component, modifier -26 can be reported to identify the physician (professional) component.

-32 Mandated Services: Modifier -32 may be reported when groups such as a third party payer or peer review organization mandates a service.

-52 Reduced Services: Modifier -52 may be reported to indicate that a laboratory or pathologic procedure is partially reduced or eliminated at the discretion of the physician.

-53 Discontinued Procedure: Modifier -53 may be reported to indicate that the physician elected to terminate a procedure due to circumstances that puts the patient at risk.

-59 Distinct Procedural Service: Modifier -59 may be used to identify that a procedure or service was distinct or independent from other services provided on the same day. This modifier may be used when procedures are performed together because of a specific circumstance, though they usually are not.

-90 Reference (Outside) Laboratory: Modifier -90 may be reported to indicate that another party besides the reporting physician performed the actual laboratory procedure.

-91 Repeat Clinical Diagnostic Laboratory Test: Modifier -91 may be reported when it is necessary to repeat the same laboratory test on the same day on the same patient to obtain subsequent (multiple) results.

EXAMPLE

Dr. Smith performed a venipuncture to obtain a blood sample for an obstetrical panel. He prepared the sample for transport and it was sent to an outside lab for testing. Dr. Smith should report 80055-90 to describe the laboratory test with the interpretation and analysis being performed at an offsite lab, along with a code for the venipuncture, 36415.

ORGAN OR DISEASE ORIENTED PANELS

The series of codes 80048–80076 describe laboratory procedures known as panels or profiles in which more than one procedure is typically performed from one blood sample. Some of the panels in this series include the basic metabolic panel, the general health panel, and the electrolyte panel. For example, the basic metabolic panel includes all of the following:

- Calcium
- Carbon Dioxide
- Chloride
- Creatinine
- Glucose
- Potassium
- Sodium
- Urea Nitrogen (Bun)

These panel components are not intended to limit the performance of other tests. If one performs tests specifically indicated for a particular panel, those tests should be reported separately in addition to the panel.

EVOCATIVE/SUPPRESSION TESTING

These tests (code range 80400–80440) allow the physician to determine a baseline of the chemical and the effects on the body after evocative (materials that a patient must take because the body does not produce them naturally) or suppressive agents are administered. In reviewing the codes in this series, note that the description for each panel identifies the type of test included in that panel, as well as the number of times a specific test must be performed.

> EXAMPLE
>
> 80422 Glucagon tolerance panel, for insulinoma. This panel must include the following:
>
> > Glucose (82947 x 3)
> > Insulin (83525 x 3)

 Coding Tip *Attendance and monitoring by the physician during the test should be reported with the appropriate code as well as the prolonged physician care codes if they apply.*

CHEMISTRY

This series of codes (82000–84999) is used to report individual chemistry tests. Examination of these specimens is quantitative unless specified. Clinical information derived from the results of laboratory data that is mathematically calculated (final calculations after all specimens have been analyzed through a machine) is considered part of the test procedure and therefore is not a separately reportable service.

EXAMPLE

Free thyroxine index (T7)

HEMATOLOGY AND COAGULATION

This series of codes in range 85002–85999 is used to report such procedures as complete blood counts (CBC) and bone marrow aspiration and biopsy, and coagulation procedures such as a partial thromboplastin time (PTT). A complete blood count includes:

white blood cell count (WBC)	mean corpuscular volume (MCV)
red blood cell count (RBC)	differential screen (WBC)
hemoglobin (HGB)	platelet count
hematocrit (HCT)	mean corpuscular hemoglobin (MCH)
mean corpuscular hemoglobin concentration (MCHC)	

Coding Tip *When coding the different types of procedures in the hematology and coagulation section, the coder should understand the difference between automated and manual testing.* **Automated** *testing is the use of clinical laboratory instruments that assay large numbers of samples (blood, urine, etc.) mechanically, and* **manual** *testing is performed by or with hands.*

automated
Laboratories that assay large numbers of samples mechanically.

manual
Performing something by hand or with the hands.

IMMUNOLOGY

This series of codes (86000–86849) is used to report components of the immune system and their functions. Different procedures that are done in this section are HIV testing and testing for infectious agents/antigens.

EXAMPLE

86592 Syphilis test qualitative

86803 Hepatitis C antibody

TRANSFUSION MEDICINE

This series of codes (86850–86999) is used to report blood typing, transfusion, and antibody identification.

MICROBIOLOGY

This series of codes (87001–87999) is used to report identification and classification of different types of bacteria identification methods. For example, separate codes exist for different types of cultures, such as stool, throat, or urine. This section also covers mycology, parasitology, and virology.

ANATOMIC PATHOLOGY

This series of codes (88000–88099) is used to report autopsies. These codes represent physician services only. Use modifier -90 for outside laboratory services.

CYTOPATHOLOGY

This series of codes (88104–88299) is used to report Pap smears (Figure 11–5), needle aspirations, and chromosomal testing.

EXAMPLE

A patient is seen in the office for a routine annual Pap smear and pelvic examination. The cervical smear obtained at the time of the visit is sent to a cytopathology laboratory for screening and interpretation. The physician uses the preventive medicine service code from the Evaluation and Management section of the CPT to bill for the encounter with the patient and the collection of the specimen. The cytopathologist reports from codes 88141–88155, 88164–88167, or 88174–88175 for the screening and interpretation, depending on the type of screening/evaluation performed.

SURGICAL PATHOLOGY

This series of codes (88300–88399) is used to report specimens removed during surgical procedures known as a unit of service. CPT defines a specimen as "tissue or tissues that is/are submitted for individual and separate attention, requiring examination and pathologic diagnosis."

Services 88300–88309 include accession, examination, and reporting of the specimen. Service codes 88304–88309 describe all other specimens requiring gross and microscopic examination, and represent additional ascending levels of physician work.

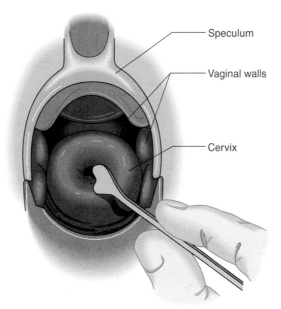

Speculum

Vaginal walls

Cervix

Figure 11–5 Pap smear, codes 88104–88299.

Level I	88300	Surgical pathology diagnosed by gross examination only, without microscopic examination. Example: Gross examination of renal calculi
Level II	88302	Gross and microscopic to confirm identification and the absence of disease. Example: Foreskin, newborn
Levels III–VI	88304–88309	All other specimens requiring gross and microscopic examination, and represent additional ascending levels of physician work.

Examples :

Level III	88304	Tonsil and/or adenoids
Level IV	88305	Kidney biopsy; colorectal biopsy
Level V	88307	Non-traumatic extremity amputation
Level VI	88309	Total resection of colon

When submitting two or more specimens, separate codes should be used to identify the appropriate level for each.

EXAMPLE

Gross and microscopic examination of two separate fallopian tube biopsies. The pathologist reports the codes 88305 and 88305 to identify the examination of two separate specimens.

■ *Highlight*

Codes 88300–88309 include the accession, examination, and reporting of a specimen. When performed by the pathologist, services identified in codes 88311–88365 and 88399 may be reported.

EXERCISE 11–5

Code the pathology and laboratory procedures; use two-digit modifiers when applicable.

1. Sedimentation rate. _____

2. Urine pregnancy test, by visual color comparisons. _____

3. General health panel. _____

4. Cytopathology smears, automated thin prep, automated screening up to three with definitive hormonal evaluation. _____

5. Vitamin K. _____

6. Confirmatory test for HIV-1 antibody. _____

7. Folic acid; serum. _____

8. Chlamydia, IgM. _____

9. Ova and parasites, direct smears concentration and identification.
   _____

10. Hemogram and platelet count automated and manual differential count.
    _____

11. Urinalysis non-automated without the microscope. _____

12. Histamine. _____

13. Basic metabolic panel. _____

14. Prothrombin time. _____

15. Syphilis test qualitative. _____

SUMMARY

As doctors and scientists learn about the causes of various types of diseases, coders will continue to learn each and every year more and more codes with higher levels of specificity. Each year as the American Medical Association looks at the changes in the health field, we will continue to see new and better technology.

In dealing with Radiology and Pathology/Laboratory, technology will always be advancing and will give opportunity for more coding of very exciting procedures.

REFERENCES

Cowling, C. (1998). *Delmar's radiographic positioning and procedures* (Vol. II). Clifton Park, NY: Thomson Delmar Learning.

Lindh, W. Q. (2000). *Delmar's comprehensive medical assisting: Administrative and clinical competencies.* Clifton Park, NY: Thomson Delmar Learning.

Pfeiffer, M. (1997). *Basic radiology.* (Self-published manual).

Stepp, C., & Woods, M. A. (1998). *Laboratory procedures for medical office personnel.* Philadelphia: Saunders.

Chapter 12
Medicine

KEY TERMS

administration	infusion	toxoids
immune globulin	injections	vaccine

LEARNING OBJECTIVES

Upon successful completion of this chapter, you should be able to:

1. Select a code for both the administration and the vaccine.
2. Identify the variety of service categories in the CPT Medicine chapter.
3. Understand the modifier use or exemptions rules for the codes in these series.

INTRODUCTION

The Medicine chapter is unusual in comparison to the other chapters within CPT. Specifically, it includes a wide array of various services and procedures for various anatomy and purposes.

MEDICINE GUIDELINES

It is common in this chapter for multiple codes to be selected when performed on the same date by the same physician. The use of modifiers may not be necessary, as many of the codes are modifier exempt, add-on codes, or have special instructional guidelines. Read very carefully for the specific codes prior to selecting the modifiers.

 Coding Tip *It is also important to verify the insurance plan policies and code selection rules when selecting the Medicine codes. The insurance plan may have specific requirements for the use of modifier -25, modifier -51, or modifier -59, all common for procedures and services in the Medicine chapter.*

The categories contained in the CPT Medicine chapter are shown in Table 12–1.

TABLE 12–1   Medicine Chapter Categories in CPT.

Medicine Chapter Categories

Immune globulins (the medication component)

Immunization (vaccine/toxoid) administration (the administration "giving" component)

Vaccines and toxoids (the medication component)

Infusions (the administration "giving" component) not used for chemotherapy

Injections (the administration "giving" component)

Psychiatry services

Biofeedback

Dialysis

Gastroenterology

Ophthalmology

Otorhinolaryngologic

Cardiovascular

Noninvasive vascular

Allergy and clinical immunology

Endocrinology

Neurology

Central nervous system test

Health and behavior assessment

Chemotherapy administration (the administration "giving" component)

Photodynamic therapy

Dermatological procedures

Physical medicine

Medical nutrition therapy

Acupuncture

continues

TABLE 12–1   Medicine Chapter Categories in CPT—continued

Medicine Chapter Categories
Osteopathic manipulative treatment
Chiropractic treatment
Special procedures
Qualifying circumstances for anesthesia
Conscious sedation
Other services
Home health by nonphysicians

IMMUNE GLOBULINS

immune globulin
Animal protein with similar antibody activity.

The Medicine chapter begins with a listing of medications, known as **immune globulins.** These medications are commonly rendered to prevent illness, often after the patient has been exposed to the illness. The CPT guides the selection of an *additional* code for the administration. Also, as we discussed earlier, all of the codes in this series are modifier -51 exempt. This concept is relatively new, and may be overlooked by coders. Figure 12–1 reflects a typical claim for the administration of hepatitis IG IM.

IMMUNIZATION ADMINISTRATION

administration
The professional service of giving or rendering, often associated with medications or solutions.

injections
A parenteral route of administration during which a needle penetrates the skin or muscle; subcutaneous injection; intramuscular injection.

In the CPT 2005, two new codes were added to select when the physician performs counseling with the patient and family at the time of the encounter for the child immunization. The codes in this series are very specific for the type of **administration** and the volume of **injections** that are given. It is important to understand that some immunizations are "combination," where multiple medications are within one vial or bottle and are administered in one method (for example, intramuscularly). Other medications are not supplied in combination form, yet may be drawn up into one syringe and administered in one injection. Yet again, some medications are not to be mixed together at all, and must be administered in individual sites, causing the need for multiple injections of each medication. The physician orders the medication and the administration according to the pharmaceutical recommendations.

If the physician does not provide counseling at the encounter, the administration of the vaccine is reported with 90471 series of codes. An additional code from the vaccines and toxoids series is selected.

PLEASE
DO NOT
STAPLE
IN THIS
AREA

| | | | | PICA | | | | | **HEALTH INSURANCE CLAIM FORM** | | | PICA | |

| PICA | | | | | | | | | | **HEALTH INSURANCE CLAIM FORM** | | PICA | |

1. MEDICARE   MEDICAID   CHAMPUS   CHAMPVA   GROUP HEALTH PLAN   FECA BLK LUNG   OTHER
(Medicare #)   (Medicaid #)   (Sponsor's SSN)   (VA File #)   (SSN or ID)   (SSN)   (ID)

1a. INSURED'S I.D. NUMBER   (FOR PROGRAM IN ITEM 1)

2. PATIENT'S NAME (Last Name, First Name, Middle Initial)

3. PATIENT'S BIRTH DATE   MM   DD   YY   SEX   M   F

4. INSURED'S NAME (Last Name, First Name, Middle Initial)

5. PATIENT'S ADDRESS (No., Street)

6. PATIENT RELATIONSHIP TO INSURED   Self   Spouse   Child   Other

7. INSURED'S ADDRESS (No., Street)

CITY   STATE

8. PATIENT STATUS   Single   Married   Other
Employed   Full-Time Student   Part-Time Student

CITY   STATE

ZIP CODE   TELEPHONE (Include Area Code)   (   )

ZIP CODE   TELEPHONE (INCLUDE AREA CODE)   (   )

9. OTHER INSURED'S NAME (Last Name, First Name, Middle Initial)

10. IS PATIENT'S CONDITION RELATED TO:

11. INSURED'S POLICY GROUP OR FECA NUMBER

a. OTHER INSURED'S POLICY OR GROUP NUMBER

a. EMPLOYMENT? (CURRENT OR PREVIOUS)   YES   NO

a. INSURED'S DATE OF BIRTH   MM   DD   YY   SEX   M   F

b. OTHER INSURED'S DATE OF BIRTH   MM   DD   YY   SEX   M   F

b. AUTO ACCIDENT?   PLACE (State)   YES   NO

b. EMPLOYER'S NAME OR SCHOOL NAME

c. EMPLOYER'S NAME OR SCHOOL NAME

c. OTHER ACCIDENT?   YES   NO

c. INSURANCE PLAN NAME OR PROGRAM NAME

d. INSURANCE PLAN NAME OR PROGRAM NAME

10d. RESERVED FOR LOCAL USE

d. IS THERE ANOTHER HEALTH BENEFIT PLAN?   YES   NO   If yes, return to and complete item 9 a-d.

READ BACK OF FORM BEFORE COMPLETING & SIGNING THIS FORM.
12. PATIENT'S OR AUTHORIZED PERSON'S SIGNATURE I authorize the release of any medical or other information necessary to process this claim. I also request payment of government benefits either to myself or to the party who accepts assignment below.

SIGNED ___   DATE ___

13. INSURED'S OR AUTHORIZED PERSON'S SIGNATURE I authorize payment of medical benefits to the undersigned physician or supplier for services described below.

SIGNED ___

14. DATE OF CURRENT: MM   DD   YY   ILLNESS (First symptom) OR INJURY (Accident) OR PREGNANCY(LMP)

15. IF PATIENT HAS HAD SAME OR SIMILAR ILLNESS. GIVE FIRST DATE   MM   DD   YY

16. DATES PATIENT UNABLE TO WORK IN CURRENT OCCUPATION   MM   DD   YY   FROM   TO   MM   DD   YY

17. NAME OF REFERRING PHYSICIAN OR OTHER SOURCE

17a. I.D. NUMBER OF REFERRING PHYSICIAN

18. HOSPITALIZATION DATES RELATED TO CURRENT SERVICES   MM   DD   YY   FROM   TO   MM   DD   YY

19. RESERVED FOR LOCAL USE

20. OUTSIDE LAB? $ CHARGES   YES   NO

21. DIAGNOSIS OR NATURE OF ILLNESS OR INJURY. (RELATE ITEMS 1,2,3 OR 4 TO ITEM 24E BY LINE)

1. 401 . 1   3. L___ . ___

2. V01 . 79   4. L___ . ___

22. MEDICAID RESUBMISSION CODE   ORIGINAL REF. NO.

23. PRIOR AUTHORIZATION NUMBER

24. A. DATE(S) OF SERVICE						B. Place of Service	C. Type of Service	D. PROCEDURES, SERVICES, OR SUPPLIES (Explain Unusual Circumstances) CPT/HCPCS	MODIFIER	E. DIAGNOSIS CODE	F. $ CHARGES	G. DAYS OR UNITS	H. EPSDT Family Plan	I. EMG	J. COB	K. RESERVED FOR LOCAL USE
From MM	DD	YY	To MM	DD	YY											
07	01	20XX				11		90371		2		1				
07	01	20XX				11		90782		2		1				
07	01	20XX				11		99213	25	1,2		1				

25. FEDERAL TAX I.D. NUMBER   SSN EIN

26. PATIENT'S ACCOUNT NO.

27. ACCEPT ASSIGNMENT? (For govt. claims, see back)   YES   NO

28. TOTAL CHARGE $

29. AMOUNT PAID $

30. BALANCE DUE $

31. SIGNATURE OF PHYSICIAN OR SUPPLIER INCLUDING DEGREES OR CREDENTIALS (I certify that the statements on the reverse apply to this bill and are made a part thereof.)

SIGNED ___   DATE ___

32. NAME AND ADDRESS OF FACILITY WHERE SERVICES WERE RENDERED (If other than home or office)

33. PHYSICIAN'S, SUPPLIER'S BILLING NAME, ADDRESS, ZIP CODE & PHONE #

PIN#   GRP#

(APPROVED BY AMA COUNCIL ON MEDICAL SERVICE 8/88)   **PLEASE PRINT OR TYPE**   APPROVED OMB-0938-0008 FORM CMS-1500 (12/90),   FORM RRB-1500
APPROVED OMB-1215-0055 FORM OWCP-1500, APPROVED OMB-0720-0001 (CHAMPUS)

CARRIER

PATIENT AND INSURED INFORMATION

PHYSICIAN OR SUPPLIER INFORMATION

Figure 12–1 Claim for administration of hepatitis IG IM.

VACCINES AND TOXOIDS

vaccine
A suspension of microorganisms that are administered to prevent illness.

toxoids
Toxins that are treated and revised, given to stimulate antibody production.

The **vaccines** and **toxoids** codes are found in the CPT code book. Most of the other medications will be found in the HCPCSII code book. Notice all of the codes in this series are also modifier -51 exempt. It is common upon review of the medical record to find multiple vaccines during one encounter or session. An additional code for the administrations of each injection, orally or intranasally rendered, is selected.

THERAPEUTIC INFUSIONS

infusion
Introduction of a solution into tissue or an organ.

Infusions are intravenous therapy where a bag or bottle of solution infuses into the patient over a course of time. Select 90780 for the infusion of the first 60 minutes, then add 90781 for additional time. The prolonged service codes and modifiers are not used in addition to the codes in this series; however, an additional physician encounter may occur. If the additional history, exam, and medical decision making or critical care services are documented, select additional E/M codes and use modifier -25. Code 90780 is not selected for "IV push" or other immediately rendered medications that are not infused over time.

Additional HCPCSII codes are selected for the medication or solutions that are given. If no HCPCSII code exists, then the unlisted HCPCSII codes or the CPT supply code as applicable per insurance plan are to be selected.

INJECTIONS

The injection administration codes are selected in addition to the vaccine/toxoid or other medication codes. The codes are described by the type of injection and also by the item that is rendered. The intramuscular injection, for example, may be either 90782 for medications other than antibiotics or 90788 if an antibiotic is given. If an allergy or chemotherapy medication is given, codes from that area of the CPT code book instead are to be selected.

PSYCHIATRY

The guidelines for the Psychiatry series of codes describe the services between the office and the hospital facility. The psychiatry series has a few codes that describe a combination of E/M with additional therapy. The physician may provide an E/M service only, the combination service, or simply the therapy. The medical record will document these options, and the code is then selected.

The psychiatric diagnostic interview examination components are:

- History
- Mental Status
- Disposition
- Optional discussion with family or others
- Ordering of diagnostic studies

Different techniques may be employed, by working with others for information or use of interactive means, seeking to determine the symptoms and response to treatments initiated.

PSYCHIATRIC THERAPEUTIC CARE

Psychotherapy is the treatment of mental illness and behavioral disturbances by the professional through definitive communication, attempts to alleviate emotional disturbances, reverse or change patterns of behavior, and encourage growth. This description is often misinterpreted and leads to inaccurate code selection.

Interactive therapy is involved, often the use of toys or items encouraging the patient to demonstrate actions. Examples of insight oriented therapy include affective listening, discussion of reality, or combination of supportive techniques.

Codes are selected by the exact description for the type of therapy, the location for the care, the total time professionally documented, and the E/M history, exam, and medical decision making services.

If the psychiatric care includes procedures or additional treatment, such as electroconvulsive therapy or hypnotherapy, additional codes are selected.

Coding Tip *Psychiatric services are usually considered mental health benefits for most insurance plans. The patient may or may not have coverage for this care. Contact the insurance plan prior to the care, and offer the advance beneficiary notice if the patient is able to make his or her own financial decisions. Otherwise, discuss with the family members prior to the care.*

BIOFEEDBACK

The codes in this series are very specialized and selectively used; very few physicians are performing this service. The service may be in addition to other therapies and is additionally coded. It is again recommended that insurance coverage be investigated for this therapy prior to rendering the care and properly completing the ABN.

DIALYSIS

The kidney functions to remove wastes and urea from the body. The build-up of waste in the bloodstream causes additional medical concerns, causing the heart and other organs also to function inefficiently. When the kidney organ fails to perform partially or entirely, physicians order the use of mechanical equipment to remove the urea. The equipment is connected to the patient by introducing a vascular access device or catheters.

End Stage Renal Disease (ESRD) describes the chronic illness. The CPT codes are divided into categories for the care of ESRD and other dialysis patient care. The ESRD dialysis code is selected one time for the entire month (thirty days) of dialysis services. The ESRD code includes:

- Establishment of the dialysis cycle
- Evaluation and management outpatient care for dialysis
- Telephone calls and patient management during the dialysis

If the patient is admitted, additional E/M codes are selected, and the dialysis at the hospital is reported with different codes than the outpatient ESRD codes. When significant additional E/M services not related to dialysis are documented with an additional history, exam, and medical decision making, an additional E/M code and modifier -25 are selected.

The patient may require dialysis without the entire month of ESRD dialysis. For this, the CPT code series 90922 are selected to indicate the services per day, rather than a full month.

Another category series of codes beginning with 90935 is available to select for the acute, non-ESRD dialysis care.

The final category series of codes are selected for the performance of dialysis other than through the arteriovenous access, such as peritoneal dialysis. These are selected per date of service. In this area of codes, there are also teaching codes per course of training.

GASTROENTEROLOGY

The majority of the codes in the gastroenterology section are selected when diagnostic services are performed on the esophagus or gastric (stomach) area, defining the functions or disease. After a small amount of topical anesthetic gel, the patient assists by swallowing upon command, while the tube is inserted to the site. Measurements may be obtained during the procedure, providing the results to assist the physician in determining a definitive diagnosis. Washings and other specimens are often obtained and submitted to the laboratory.

There is a Breath hydrogen test, 91065 for the detection of lactase deficiency. Do not confuse this code with the very common study, H. pylori breath test analysis. Code 91065 is not selected for H. pylori.

A few codes are for tubes and tests that are inserted rectally.

OPHTHALMOLOGY

Ophthalmologist and other physicians perform diagnostic testing services, frequently in addition to the surgical treatment. The ophthalmological services may be performed with three options: ophthalmological services alone, ophthalmological services in combination with an E/M, or E/M service using the 1995 or 1997 E/M guidelines with an additional code for the Special ophthalmological services. There are CPT codes that combine the E/M and the ophthalmoscopy service that may be considered, depending upon the level of documentation and the care that was actually provided. The combination codes have two levels, intermediate and comprehensive. New patient or established patient, according to the standard AMA/CPT definitions, also categorizes the CPT codes. The routine ophthalmoscopy is part of the general and special ophthalmologic services.

The intermediate service includes:

- The evaluation of a new or existing illness *with* a new diagnostic or management problem that is not related to the primary diagnosis
- History, general medical observation
- External ocular and adnexal examination
- Other diagnostic procedures as indicated
- Use of mydriasis
- Slit lamp examination, keratometry, *routine* ophthalmoscopy, retinoscopy, tonometry, or motor evaluation
- Routine ophthalmoscopy

The comprehensive service includes the following descriptors:

- A general medical evaluation of the complete visual system
- May be at more than one session
- History, general medical observation
- External and ophthalmoscopic examinations
- Gross visual fields
- Basic sensorimotor examination
- Biomicroscopy
- Exam with cycloplegia or mydrisis
- Tonometry
- Initiation of diagnostic and treatment programs such as prescription of medication, arranging for diagnostic services, consultations, or radiology and laboratory procedures
- Slit lamp examination, keratometry, *routine* ophthalmoscopy, retinoscopy, tonometry, or motor evaluation
- Routine ophthalmoscopy

When special ophthalmological services are performed, an additional code is selected. Special ophthalmological service is the evaluation:

- Beyond the services of general ophthalmological service

    or

- Special treatment is rendered

The Interpretation and Report are included in the special ophthalmological services, which varies from the Radiology chapter of codes. Special ophthalmological services include only the *routine* ophthalmoscopy. If the indication were non-routine, the codes would be selected in addition to other services.

The next important aspect for ophthalmology is to carefully review the description per CPT code and determine whether to apply modifier -50 to the code. Also, modifier -52 may or may not be applicable, depending upon the specific description of the CPT code.

The insurance plans may have a different policy for the use of modifier -50 or modifier -52 per CPT code. It is necessary to investigate the insurance benefits prior to performing the care, and properly complete the advance beneficiary notice when applicable. The Medicare Fee Schedule is published by CMS annually, which further depicts multiple concepts for bilateral indicators. This publication can be modified quarterly. HCPCSII codes may describe services for glaucoma screening or S codes for BC/BS patients that may be selected in lieu of the CPT codes.

Contact Lens Services

Physicians may also provide care for contact lens patients, such as fitting, instructions, training, and incidental revisions. Additional codes are selected for the prescription of the optical and physical characteristics. Occasionally, patients will have a follow-up appointment with no need for additional fitting. This contact lens service is included in the general ophthalmological service; no additional code is selected for the contact lens care in this scenario.

Ocular Prosthetics

Artificial eye codes are unilaterally described, and typically only one is fitted. The use of modifiers RT/LT are required to properly report the eye.

Spectacle Services

The CPT codes in the 92340 series are selected when the physician fits the patient for eyeglasses (spectacles), with the measurement of anatomical facial characteristics, lab specification order, and final fitting. The codes do not include the actual eyeglasses that are typically purchased by the patient. Simply writing a prescription for the spectacle is included with the refraction code.

OTORHINOLARYNGOLOGIC SERVICES

The codes in the 92502 series are selected when otorhinolaryngologic diagnostic and treatment services beyond the usual are provided, or when no E/M services are performed. The codes are categorized by the type of testing that is performed, often depicting the function testing.

It is very important with each of these services to investigate the insurance coverage prior to performing the service. It is possible the patient may not have coverage, or may have limited coverage per diagnosis or indication, or limited frequency of the testing. The advance beneficiary notice is to be properly completed prior to the service being performed.

Cochlear implants and devices are improving rapidly, therefore increasing the potential for new Category III codes in the future. New Category III codes must be reviewed every January and June for the most current information.

CARDIOLOGY

Refer to Chapter 9—Cardiology and the Cardiovascular System—for an in-depth discussion of this area of the CPT code book.

PULMONARY

Unique to other areas of the CPT code book, the codes in this area *include* the laboratory procedure, with the interpretation and the results. The codes do not include the medications that are used during the procedures. The medication codes are typically selected from the HCPCSII codes. The codes do not include the access for venous or arterial services, either obtaining samples or catheterization procedures.

When the documentation reflects an E/M service, with a history, examination, and medical decision making, the additional E/M code with modifier -25 is selected.

The AMA/CPT Assistant and the CPT parenthetical tips are abundant for this series of codes, often describing details for the specific components or if additional services are performed on the same date.

ALLERGY AND CLINICAL IMMUNOLOGY

Sensitivity services (e.g., the scratch tests) using clinical judgment of the physician are the:

- History, exam, and observation of the patient
- Selective cutaneous and mucous membrane tests

Immunotherapy is the treatment using extracts given at intervals. These are commonly known as allergy injections, which may be administered by the allergy specialist physician or other physicians. The quantity of the injections is determined by the individual venoms, and requires careful reading of the medical record in comparison with the CPT codes. It is also recommended that the coder review the actual payment of the claim for accuracy, often necessitating appeal process implementation.

Allergy therapy is expanding, based upon clinical trials and improvements. There are a few codes for the environmental concepts.

Creating or mixing allergens is called the "provision of allergen extracts." The administration of the allergen may occur at the same office/practice where the allergen extract is prepared, or the bottle may be given to another physician office for the administration services. There are categories for the various combinations of services, depending upon the scenario.

Coding Tip	*CPT describes the allergen dose as the amount of antigen administered in a single injection from a multiple dose vial. A single dose vial contains a single dose of antigen administered in one injection.*

ENDOCRINOLOGY

There is only one glucose monitoring long-term code, which includes the entire professional component of endocrinology services; however, if an E/M service is documented, an additional code using modifier -25 must be selected.

Sleep Testing

The CPT guidelines prior to 95805 state the facility requirements and six hours or more of testing. If under six hours are recorded, modifier -52 is attached to the code. Most procedures require an attendant technologist. Polysomnography must record sleep and staging, including an EEG, EOG, and EMG.

Extra parameters are:

- ECG
- Airflow
- Ventilation and respiratory effort
- Gas exchange by oximetry, transcutaneous monitoring, or end tidal gas analysis
- Extremity muscle activity, motor activity/movement
- Extended EEG monitoring
- Penile tumescence
- Gastroesophageal reflux
- Continuous blood pressure monitoring

- Snoring
- Body positions

NEUROLOGY AND NEUROMUSCULAR PROCEDURES

The EEG, muscle range of motion testing, and EMG tests are rather straightforward procedures. The extended EEG is beyond forty minutes, documented. The CPT code is matched to the documentation.

Intraoperative Neurophysiology

Code 95920 is an add-on, typically selected quantity of one per hour, during neurosurgical procedures. It depicts the activities of the brain while the surgery is underway and is very helpful for treatment and optimal therapeutic results.

Neurostimulator Analysis-Programming

The neurostimulators are inserted using surgical codes, from the 61885 area of the CPT code book. The codes in the 95970 series are selected for the professional service to program the devices, and/or analyze the responses. The devices may also be filled with medications, either chemotherapy or other medications for continuous internal drug delivery.

Motion Analysis

In order to select the codes in the 96000 series, the laboratory facility components and the inclusion of the 3-D kinetics are required. It is likely the codes are selected by quantity of one unit per date per patient.

CENTRAL NERVOUS SYSTEM ASSESSMENTS/TESTS

The testing includes visual motor responses and abstractive abilities with a written report. Many are developmental tests or neurobehavioral examination. If less than the described full hour of service is performed, modifier -52 is applied to the main code.

Coding Tip *A common service is the "Mini-mental exam." This service is not justified for the selection of the CNS testing. Mini-mental exams are part of the E/M services and not additionally coded.*

HEALTH AND BEHAVIOR ASSESSMENT

 Coding Tip *The codes in this series are selected when other than a physician performs the service. If a physician performs the services, an E/M or preventive code, and not the Health Assessment codes, must be selected.*

The codes in the 96150 series are specifically selected for the health care depicted in the guidelines just prior to the code. The codes are very similar to either the psychiatric service or counseling rule for E/M. The codes are not preventive services.

The assessment is for the intervention of biopsychosocial factors for physical health, designed to correct specific disease. An illness or disease has been diagnosed, but not mental health. If the patient has both psychiatric, E/M, preventive, individual counseling or group counseling, *and* health assessment, only one code is selected for the predominant service. Both codes are not selected for the same date of service, even if one is earlier in the day and the other service later the same day.

CHEMOTHERAPY ADMINISTRATION

Chemotherapy codes are selected for the administration of the medications, using various techniques. The access or catheterization services are additionally coded.

If the E/M history, examination, and decision making are documented in addition to the description of the chemotherapy services, a code is selected for both, and modifier -25 is added to the E/M.

Preparation of the chemotherapy is included in the administration. If preparation is extensive, modifiers should be selected.

A separate code is selected for each method of administration and each medication.

PHOTODYNAMIC THERAPY AND DERMATOLOGICAL PROCEDURES

Photodynamic therapy and dermatological procedures are often performed by dermatology practices, correcting skin illnesses. Additional E/M services are often documented and codes are selected.

PHYSICAL MEDICINE AND REHABILITATION

The codes in the 97001 series are selected for physical therapist and occupational therapist services. A code is selected for each service that is documented, per date. The codes are not flagged with a modifier -51 exemption, yet for all of the codes in this series, do not use modifier -51.

Modalities

Modalities are to be applied by qualified health care professionals, not necessarily the physician. However, the scope of practice in each state may designate what persons can or cannot perform the services. Investigation is required prior to selecting the codes.

There are two categories, supervised and constant attendance. For the supervised services, the provider direct contact is not required, whereas for the constant attendance services the provider performs the care directly.

Therapeutic Procedures

These are services for the application of skills or services to improve function, directly performed by the physician or therapist. The services are at various locations and describe a variety of specific techniques or training. Many of the descriptions state each 15 minutes of time; therefore the medical record documentation should also describe the time in increments of 15 minutes. The quantity documented in the medical record is counted for each 15-minute segment, and reported on the claim.

Active Wound Care Management

The CPT 95597 series descriptions are very detailed and lengthy. The services include the removal of tissue, assessment of the wound, and instructions. Nonselective methods removal of tissue is defined as the use of wet-to-dry dressing removal, enzyme removal, or abrasion. Selective methods of removal are the use of scissors or sharps, scalpel, forceps, or other instruments. The active wound care service is directly performed by the provider, again within the professional licensure scope of practice per state. Active wound care is to:

- Remove devitalized and/or necrotic tissue
- Promote healing

This care includes the 11040–11044 debridement CPT code services within the description; therefore, it is not proper to select the debridement codes along with the active wound care codes.

The codes are selected based upon the documentation per session of the total square centimeters of surface area. In the Integumentary chapter of this book, the surface area definition is conveniently listed. It is possible that more than one session per date of service would be medically necessary for these codes.

MEDICAL NUTRITION THERAPY

The codes in the 97802 series describe specific medical nutrition therapy and intervention provided by the professional *other than the physician*. When a physician provides medical nutrition therapy, the E/M code or other specific treatment service (tube placement) is selected. The medical nutrition therapy codes are per 15-minute increments for either individual care or group sessions, and again as documented in the medical record.

ACUPUNCTURE

The 97810 series of codes is selected for the professional service in 15-minute intervals of time; however, the time for the needles to remain inserted is not captured (counted). The time is described as the first 15 minutes, then the additional time or reinsertion of the needles. Frequently, the professional service is accomplished within the first 15 minutes, and additional time or reinsertion is not required.

The descriptions for the code selection have two categories: without electrical stimulation or with electrical stimulation. One or the other of these two categories may be selected per session, not both. In other words, it is not proper to first select a code from the nonelectrical and then select an additional code upon attaching to the electrical during the same session.

When the documentation reflects an additional E/M history, exam, and medical decision making, select an additional E/M code and attach modifier -25.

OSTEOPATHIC MANIPULATION

Osteopathic manipulation is a manual treatment performed by the physician for the care of somatic dysfunction and other disorders. The service is abbreviated as OMT, and has specific body region descriptions of:

- Head
- Cervical
- Thoracic
- Lumbar
- Sacral
- Pelvic
- Lower extremities
- Upper extremities
- Rib cage
- Abdomen and viscera region

Note these regions are not described the same as the body areas in the E/M chapter and guidelines. When an E/M history, exam, and medical decision making service is documented in addition to the OMT service, select an additional E/M code and add modifier -25. Different diagnoses are not required; however, additional E/M charting is required.

CHIROPRACTIC MANIPULATIVE TREATMENT

The 98940 series is abbreviated as CMT, meaning manual treatment to influence joint function. The codes are selected based upon medical necessity for the documentation of whether the spinal or extraspinal regions are treated (refer to Table 12–2).

When an E/M history, exam, and medical decision making service is documented in addition to the CMT service, select an additional E/M code and add modifier -25. Different diagnoses are not required, but additional E/M charting is required. The advance beneficiary notice is frequently required for these services. Investigation to determine the coverage policies is required prior to providing the care.

SPECIAL SERVICES

This area of services describes a variety of care provided. Many of the codes are the five-digit modifiers, with slightly different descriptions from the two-digit modifiers. If the insurance plan does not accept the two-digit modifiers, investigate to determine if the codes in this area of CPT are applicable.

TABLE 12–2   CMT Regions.

CMT Spinal Regions	CMT Extraspinal Regions
98940, 98941, or 98942	**98943**
Cervical region including the atlanto-occipital joint	Head region including temporomandibular joint, excluding the atlanto-occipital joint
Thoracic region including the costovertebral and costotransverse joint	Lower extremities
Lumbar region	Upper extremities
Sacral region	Rib cage excluding costotransverse and costovertebral joints
Pelvic region	Abdomen

In addition, there are codes for handling of specimens, on-call services that are required by the hospital, after-hour patient care, educational items, and so forth.

Coding Tip

Several times throughout this book we have said "just because there is a CPT code does not mean the service will be paid." This concept is of utmost importance for the codes in the 99000 series. There are CPT codes and descriptions for many services that the insurance plan may have determined to be bundled into another CPT code. Investigation with each insurance plan is required prior to selecting the codes and reporting on the claims.

QUALIFYING CIRCUMSTANCES FOR ANESTHESIA

All of the 99100 series of codes are add-on codes, according to CPT. They may be selected in addition to a variety of anesthesia codes, located in the Anesthesia chapter of CPT. Not all insurance plans accept the qualifying circumstances codes; therefore, it is necessary to investigate prior to selecting the codes.

Sedation with or without Analgesia

This is commonly known as conscious sedation, correlating to the CPT symbol. CPT defines the service performed by the same physician as the procedure "to achieve a medically controlled state of depressed consciousness while maintaining the patient's airway, protective reflexes, and ability to respond to stimulation or verbal commands." An independently trained observer is required to monitor the patient. If another physician performs the conscious sedation, that physician would select the codes from the Anesthesia chapter of CPT, and not use the conscious sedation codes. The codes describe the method of analgesia administration, which needs to be documented.

Other Services

The codes in the Other Services area of the CPT code book are very often overlooked. When documented, the code should be selected, and the insurance plan should be investigated to determine the coverage recommended prior to submitting the claim. For example, code 99173 is the Screening eye test very frequently performed with preventive examinations for all ages of patients. Many insurance plans do cover this CPT service, in addition to the preventive exam.

Code 99175 Phlebotomy is described as "therapeutic." This is the removal of blood from the patient as the medical treatment, not for the purposes of obtaining a sample of blood for pathology testing.

HOME HEALTH PROCEDURES

The 99500 series of codes are *not* for physician services. These are selected when nonphysician professionals provide home health care, and describe the therapeutic service rendered.

Right after these are the home infusing services, selected for the administration of drugs by infusion at the home setting.

SUMMARY

The Medicine chapter includes a wide array of medications and services. Modifier selection is likely to vary greatly depending upon each insurance plan's policies and procedures. Multiple CPT codes are likely to be selected in reporting the services that are performed.

REFERENCES

AMA CPT assistant. (2004). Chicago: American Medical Association.
AMA current procedural terminology 2005 professional edition. (2004). Chicago: American Medical Association.

Chapter 13
Billing and Collections

LEARNING OBJECTIVES

Upon successful completion of this module, you should be able to:

1. Explain the importance of billing and collection practices in the outpatient setting.
2. Demonstrate the patient registration process.
3. Compare the advantages and disadvantages between cycle billing and monthly billing.
4. List the advantages and disadvantages of a computerized billing system.
5. Explain the accounts receivable process.
6. Explain account aging and the purpose of an age analysis.

INTRODUCTION

Previous chapters have discussed coding rules including specialty area guidelines. This chapter gives instruction in proper billing techniques and the collection of payment in the ambulatory care setting.

It is estimated that 94 percent of patients have some type of insurance coverage or third party payer involvement. This requires the following responsibilities of front office personnel:

- new patient registration and established patient recheck
- interpretation of insurance contracts
- preparation of the encounter form
- posting financial transactions to the patient account

A major objective of accurately coding diagnoses and procedures and submitting claims with correct information is to receive reimbursement for services rendered. This leads to another vital function in any facility—the billing and collections process. Obtaining information for billing occurs the first time the patient comes into the office, clinic, or hospital and completes the registration form. This information is then checked with the patient on each return to the facility in order to maintain updated patient records, both medical and financial.

PATIENT REGISTRATION

Patient registration forms vary from practice to practice but all should contain the following information (Figure 13–1):

- patient name, address, birth date, Social Security number, marital status
- telephone numbers where patient can be reached: home, work, and cell phone
- insurance information—carrier's name, name of insured, plan name/identification number, group and/or policy numbers
- name of responsible party (spouse, parent, guardian)
- address, phone number, social security number of responsible party and the relationship to the patient
- a photocopy of the patient's driver's license if permitted by state law

▰ *Highlight*

It is important to always request the insurance card(s) and photocopy both the front and back sides to keep in the patient file as indicated in Figure 13–2.

Fee Schedules

Before the process of billing and the collection of payment is discussed, it is essential to understand that patient fees are based on three commodities the physician provides: time, judgment, and services.

Individual medical practices determine fees that will be charged for those services and procedures performed in the office. This fee schedule may be based upon several factors:

- The economic level of the community
- The physician's experience
- The medical specialty of the practice
- Charges of other physicians in the area
- The cost of the service or supply

Lowery B. Johnson, M.D.
Hwy 311 Suite A31
Sellersburg, IN 47172
812-246-1234

Please complete this form.

NAME: _____

STREET ADDRESS: _____ APT: _____

CITY: _____ STATE: _____ ZIP: _____

HOME PHONE (& area code) _____

WORK PHONE: (& area code) _____

CELL PHONE: (& area code) _____

SOCIAL SECURITY NUMBER: _____

SEX: Male _____ Female _____ Age _____ Date of Birth _____

MARITAL STATUS: Married _____ Single _____ Separated _____ Divorced _____ Widowed _____

PERSON TO CONTACT IN EMERGENCY: _____ PHONE: _____

EMPLOYED: Full Time _____ Part Time _____ Retired _____ Not Employed _____

EMPLOYER: Company Name: _____ Phone:_____

        Address: _____

        Location/Department Where You Work: _____

STUDENT STATUS: Full-time Student _____ School _____

        Part-time Student _____ School _____

INSURANCE COMPANY: _____

    Policy Number: _____ Group Number: _____

    Name of Insured:_____ Relationship to You: _____

    Address: _____

    Deductible: _____ Percent of Coverage: _____

OTHER INSURANCE COMPANY: _____

    Policy Number: _____ Group Number: _____

    Name of Insured:_____ Relationship to You: _____

    Address: _____

    Deductible: _____ Percent of Coverage: _____

WHAT BRINGS YOU TO SEE THE DOCTOR? _____

_____

IS YOUR CONDITION RELATED TO:

    AUTO ACCIDENT: _____ DATE: _____ STATE WHERE OCCURRED: _____

    OTHER ACCIDENT: _____DATE: _____ STATE WHERE OCCURRED: _____

    YOUR EMPLOYMENT: _____

ARE YOU ALLERGIC TO ANY MEDICATIONS: _____

REFERRED TO US BY: _____

CHECK HERE IF REFERRED BY PHYSICIAN: _____

Figure 13–1 Patient registration form.

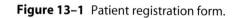

Figure 13–2 Insurance card (front and back).

EXERCISE 13–1

1. List the three commodities a physician has to sell when setting fees for the medical office.

    a. _____

    b. _____

    c. _____

2. What is the purpose of copying the patient's insurance card and retaining it in the patient's medical chart?

The maximum amount the insurance carrier or government program will cover for specified services is called the allowable charge or allowed amount. The difference between the physician charge and the allowable charge is called a nonallowed charge. Allowable charges are often based on **usual, customary, and reasonable (UCR) fees**.

> **usual, customary, and reasonable (UCR) fees**
> A method used to average fee profiles to determine what is allowable for reimbursement.
> **usual** = a physician's average fee for a service or procedure;
> **customary** = the average fee for the service or procedure based on national trends rather than regional or local customs;
> **reasonable** = a fee that is acceptable for a service that is unusually difficult or complicated, requiring more time and effort to preform.

Usual—The physician's average fee for a service or procedure

Customary—The average fee for that service or procedure within an area, based on national trends rather than regional or local customs

Reasonable—A fee that is generally accepted for a service or procedure that is extraordinarily difficult or complicated, requiring more time or effort for the physician to perform

EXAMPLE

Dr. Johnson charges $150 for a new patient office visit including a complete history and physical examination. The usual fee charged for this same service of other physicians in the same community with similar training and experience ranges from $125 to $200. Dr. Johnson's fee of $150 is within the customary range and would be paid under an insurance plan's usual and customary basis.

EXERCISE 13-2

1. Dr. Dogood, a gastroenterologist, performs flexible diagnostic sigmoidoscopies in the office. His charge for this procedure is $195. The usual fee charged for this procedure by other gastroenterologists in this city is from $190 to $210.

Is Dr. Dogood's fee within the usual and customary range for insurance payment?

---

resource-based relative value system (RBRVS)
A method of predetermining values for physician services for Medicare established in 1992, calculating units based on services performed, practice expenses, and professional liability insurance.

Medicare physician fee schedule (PFS)
A listing of allowable charges for services rendered to Medicare patients.

relative value unit (RVU)
Payment component based on physician work, practice expense, and malpractice expense.

limiting charge
A percentage limitation on fees that nonparticipating physicians are allowed to bill Medicare patients above the fee schedule amount.

nonparticipating physician (nonPAR)
A health care provider who has not signed a contract with an insurance company (also known as an out-of-network provider).

participating physician (PAR)
A health care provider who has signed a contract with an insurance company to provide medical services to subscribers in the contract plan (also known as an in-network provider).

Physicians who participate in federally funded medical insurance programs, such as Medicaid, CHAMPUS/TRICARE and CHAMPVA, must accept the UCR fee as payment in full. The patient cannot be billed the difference between their fee and the UCR fee. The amount would be adjusted on the patient's account. Most private insurance carriers utilize UCR fees but are not regulated under federal law. Therefore, the patient with a private insurance company can be billed the difference.

Before 1989, Medicare Part B used customary, prevailing, and reasonable charges in a fee-for-service payment system. In 1989, the **resource-based relative value system (RBRVS)** was passed to reform Medicare payments to physicians. In January 1992, implementation of the RBRVS took place with the new payment system of **Medicare physician fee schedule (PFS).** All physicians' services are listed on the PFS with reimbursement made at 80 percent of the fee schedule amount. The Medicare physician fee schedule is the method of payment for physicians' services, outpatient physical and occupational therapy services, radiology services, and diagnostic tests. This fee schedule is updated annually on April 15.

RBRVS assigns a CPT code, which has an associated **relative value unit (RVU).** Therefore, each medical service reflects the physician's skill, judgment, and time required to perform the service, professional liability expenses related to that service, and overhead costs associated with the service.

The relative value units are converted to dollar amounts based on the code assignments, which form the basis of the RBRVS fee schedule. This schedule, in turn, creates uniform payments with adjustments made for geographic differences. Thus, the growth rate of spending for physicians' services, procedures, and supplies has been significantly reduced for Medicare Part B patients since the 1992 implementation of RBRVS.

A **limiting charge** is percentage limitation on fees that **nonparticipating physicians (nonPARs)** are allowed to bill Medicare patients above the fee schedule amount. The limiting charge applies to every service listed in the Medicare physician's fee schedule that is performed by a nonparticipating (nonPAR) physician, including global, professional, and technical services. Different prices are listed for each CPT code. The fee schedule amount is determined by multiplying the relative value unit (RVU) weight by the geographic index and the conversion factor. The **participating physician (PAR)** receives the fee schedule amount. For the nonparticipating physician, the fee schedule amount of the allowable payment is slightly less than the participating physician's payment. Chapter 14 further explains nonPAR versus PAR requirements.

The limiting amount is a percentage over the allowable 115 percent times the allowable amount. The limiting charge is important because that is the maximum amount a Medicare patient can be billed for a service. Medicare usually pays 80 percent of the allowable amount for covered services. The patient can then be billed the difference between the Medicare payment and the limiting charge. The patient is notified of the limiting charge for each service on the Medicare Remittance Advice.

AMBULATORY PATIENT GROUPS

Hospital inpatient prospective payment system (IPPS), hospital outpatient prospective system (OPPS), and ambulatory payment classifications (APCs) are covered in Chapter 16, Inpatient Coding.

Diagnosis-related groups (DRGs) is a classification system grouping inpatients in relation to diagnosis and treatment of the reason for hospitalization. This results in a fixed-fee payment to the hospital based on the diagnosis rather than fee-for-service.

DRG classifications were derived from more than ten thousand ICD-9-CM codes divided into twenty-five major diagnostic categories. These diagnoses were assigned a DRG number and a specific value relating to geographic area, type of hospital, teaching status of the hospital, and other specifications. DRG classifications are based on:

- principal diagnosis
- secondary diagnosis
- surgical procedure(s)
- age and sex of the patient
- comorbidity and complications
- discharge status

DRGs are discussed further in Chapter 16.

PAYMENT & BILLING PROCESSES

Payment at Time of Service

Communication lines must be open between the patient and the medical office to maintain effective collection practices. Patients should know up-front the provider's billing policies and collection procedures. Use the patient's initial contact with the office as the first point of control for collections. When making the appointment for the new patient, take a few minutes to discuss payment policies. Get insurance information at this time to check provider participation agreement and verify if your physician(s) is participating with the patient's insurance plan. This saves both the staff and the patient valuable time. When appointments are scheduled for established patients, they can be reminded of an outstanding balance and asked to make a payment when they come in.

A patient brochure is an effective method to explain the office's payment and collection policies established by the physician employers and managers of the practice as indicated in Figure 13–3. The brochure can be mailed to the new patient prior to the first appointment. Patients appreciate knowing their payment responsibilities. If the patient anticipates a problem in meeting the outlined payment policy, a payment schedule can be worked out that is agreeable to both the patient and the office.

Displaying a notice in the office stating that payment at time of service is required has the following advantages:

Figure 13–3 Billing and insurance excerpts from a patient brochure.

- It ensures prompt collection of fees.
- It eliminates further bookkeeping work.
- It reduces the cost of preparing and mailing a statement to the patient.
- It increases cash flow for the practice.

Many offices encourage payment at time of service by accepting cash, personal checks, and major credit and debit cards.

When a patient pays in cash, carefully count the cash before placing it in the cash drawer. Always prepare a receipt to give to the patient as a record of cash payment as shown in Figure 13–4.

When a patient pays by check, review the check to see that it is properly written:

- The date is current.
- The amount of the check is the correct amount.
- The name of the physician or practice is spelled properly.
- The person whose name is imprinted on the check signs the check.
- Never accept a check for more than the amount due.
- If a patient is new or unfamiliar, identification can be requested.

An example is shown in Figure 13–5.

Immediately endorse the check and place in the cash drawer for the bank deposit to be made that day.

Credit cards are now becoming an accepted method of payment in the medical office. Patients find credit cards convenient, especially when the bill is large. To accept credit cards in the medical office, the credit card company must be contacted to establish the account. There is a service charge to accept credit cards that is deducted from payment issued to the office. For example, if a patient charges services totaling $50 on a credit card, the office will receive between $45 and $49.

The American Medical Association (AMA) condones the acceptance of credit cards in the medical office but advises not to use this as an advertising lure for the practice. Also, patients paying by credit card should not be charged higher fees to recover the service charge by the credit card company to the practice.

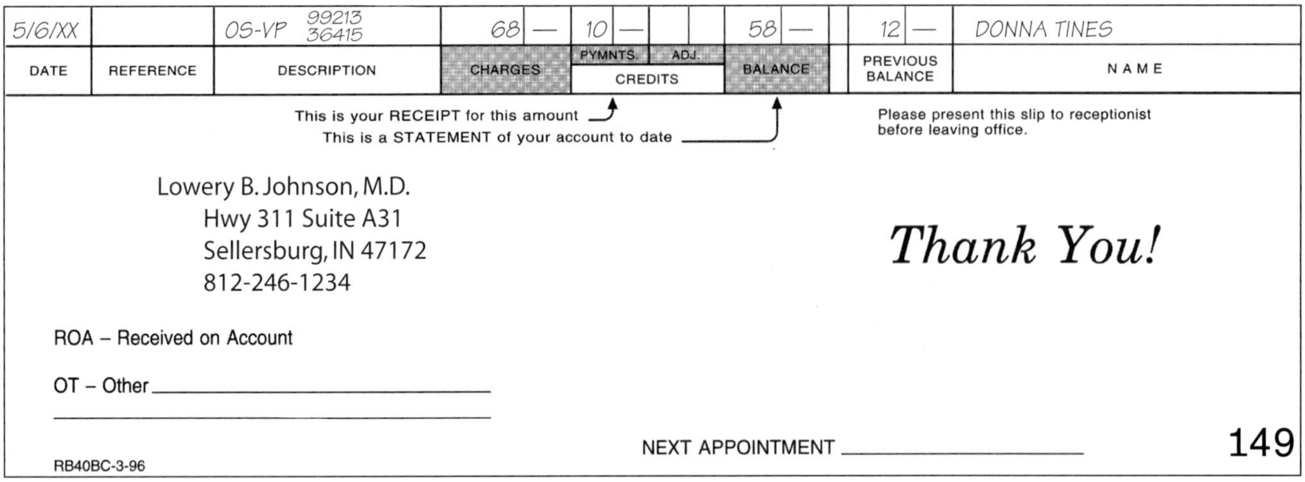

5/6/XX		OS-VP 99213 36415	68 —	10 —		58 —	12 —	DONNA TINES
DATE	REFERENCE	DESCRIPTION	CHARGES	PYMNTS.	ADJ.	BALANCE	PREVIOUS BALANCE	NAME
				CREDITS				

This is your RECEIPT for this amount
This is a STATEMENT of your account to date

Please present this slip to receptionist before leaving office.

Lowery B. Johnson, M.D.
Hwy 311 Suite A31
Sellersburg, IN 47172
812-246-1234

Thank You!

ROA – Received on Account

OT – Other ____________

NEXT APPOINTMENT ____________ 149

RB40BC-3-96

Figure 13–4 Receipt for payment given to a patient, especially cash payments.

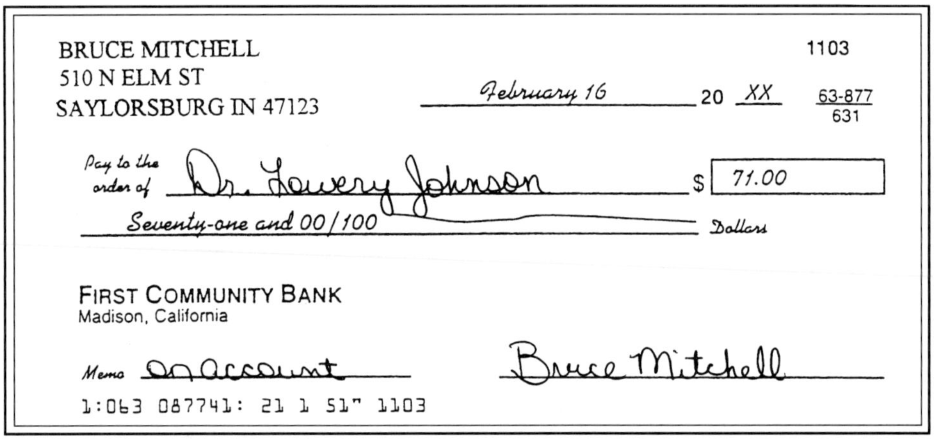

BRUCE MITCHELL
510 N ELM ST
SAYLORSBURG IN 47123

1103

February 16 20 XX 63-877/631

Pay to the order of Dr. Lowery Johnson $ 71.00

Seventy-one and 00/100 Dollars

FIRST COMMUNITY BANK
Madison, California

Memo on account Bruce Mitchell

1:063 087741: 21 1 51" 1103

Figure 13–5 Payment by check.

Credit and Payment Policy

Payment at time of service is not always possible for all patients and for many practices. Therefore, it is important to have a formal credit and collection policy established. Following are some questions to address in setting up this policy:

- When will payment be due from the patient?
- What kind of payment arrangements can be made?
- How and when will patients be reminded of overdue accounts?
- When is the bill considered delinquent?
- When exceptions are made to the policy, who makes them?
- Will a collection agency be utilized?

A written, straightforward credit and collection policy will eliminate confusion and serve as a guide to both the patient and the billing personnel.

In some situations, a payment schedule is arranged with determination of a down payment, whether interest is to be charged, and scheduling of installment payments scheduled. When there is a bilateral agreement between the physician and the patient to pay for a procedure in more than four installments, the physi-

Truth in Lending Act
A consumer protection act requiring a written statement when there is a bilateral agreement between the physician and patient to pay for a procedure in more than four installments, disclosing finance charges, if any.

cian must disclose finance charges in writing. The **Truth in Lending Act** (also known as Regulation Z of the Consumer Protection Act of 1969) requires providers of installment credit to clearly state the charge in writing and express the interest as an annual rate. Even if no finance charges are made, the form must be completed and must contain the following conditions:

- fees for services
- amount of any down payment
- the date each payment is due
- the date of the final payment
- the amount of each payment
- any interest charges to be made

The AMA rules that it is appropriate to assess finance or late charges on past due accounts, if the patient is given advance notice. This can be done by:

- displaying a notice at the reception desk.
- publishing the notice in the patient brochure.
- including the notice on the patient statement.

Figure 13–6 gives an example of notice of late charges on the patient registration form.

The patient signs the agreement and is given a copy. A copy is retained with the patient's record. If a patient decides to pay a certain amount on a bill monthly, with the office billing monthly for the full amount, and there are no interest charges applied, the Truth In Lending Act does not apply. Figure 13–7 gives an example of this agreement.

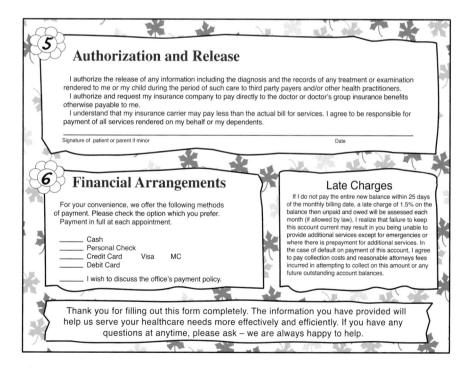

Figure 13–6 A patient registration form explaining late charges.

Lowery B. Johnson, M.D.
Hwy 311 Suite A31
Sellersburg, IN 47172
812-241-1234

TRUTH-IN-LENDING PAYMENT AGREEMENT

Patient ___Autumn Leaf___

Address ___10586 Payment Place #2 E___

___Sellersburg, IN 47178___

I agree to pay **$ 200.00** per ~~week~~/month on my account balance of $ ___1000.00___.

Payments are due by the ___5th___ of each ___Month___ and will begin ___May 5, 20XX___
                                (week/month)   (date)

Interest will/will not be charged on the outstanding balance (see Truth-In-Lending form below for rate of interest).

I agree that if payments are not made in the full amount stated above or if payments are not received on time, the entire account balance will be considered delinquent and will be due and payable immediately.

I agree to be responsible for any reasonable collection costs or attorney fees incurred in collecting a delinquent account.

_____   _____
Date   Signature

This disclosure is in compliance with the Truth-In-Lending Act.

_____   _____
Responsible Party if other than patient   City, State Zip Code

1. Cash Price (Medical and/or Surgical Fee) $___1200.00___
   Less cash down payment (Advance) $___200.00___
2. Unpaid Balance of Cash Price $___1000.00___
3. Amount Financed $___1000.00___
4. FINANCE CHARGE $___– 0 –___
5. Total of Payments (3+4) $___1000.00___
6. Deferred Payment Price (1+4) $___1200.00___
7. ANNUAL PERCENTAGE RATE   ___– 0 –___

The "Total of Payments" shown above is payable to Lowery B. Johnson, M.D., at the address shown above in ___5___ monthly installments of $ ___200.00___, the first installment being payable ___May 5th___ ,___20XX___, and all subsequent installments are due on the same day of each consecutive month until paid in full.

_____   _____
Date   Signature

Figure 13–7 Truth In Lending Agreement.

BILLING

Patient billing can range from a simple process to a more complicated procedure. It must be done efficiently and accurately and in an organized manner. Receiving payment for services rendered is the income of the practice and necessary for it to succeed. Billing can be handled internally by the medical office staff, or, for a fee, by an outside billing agency. The type of billing done within the medical facility depends on the size of the practice, the patient load, and financial goals.

Payment at time of service is the expected norm in today's medical offices and is the best opportunity to collect fees, especially copayments and existing balances. The **charge slip, superbill,** or **encounter form,** as indicated in Figure 13–8, is given to the patient at the checkout desk, serving as the first statement.

charge slip, superbill, encounter form
A three-part form with a record of account information for services performed including charges and payment; can also serve as an insurance reporting form.

The Complete Statement

Statements to patients must be professional looking, legible, accurate, and include all services and charges. They should contain not only the information for the patient but information needed to process medical insurance claims:

- patient's name and address
- patient's insurance identification number
- insurance carrier
- date of service
- description of service
- accurate procedure (CPT) and diagnosis (ICD-9-CM) codes for insurance processing
- itemization of fees for services performed with charges totalled
- provider's name, address, and telephone number

Figure 13–9A and 13–9B are examples of a complete statement.

Not all patients are able to pay at time of service and not all practices can accommodate this type of payment method. Sending a statement in the mail can be accomplished by:

- mailing a special statement form or copy of the ledger card, which can be typed or printed.
- mailing a computer-generated statement resulting in a more professional looking statement.

■ *Highlight*

In mailing any statement, always enclose a self-addressed return envelope to make payment convenient for the patient.

Use return envelopes of another color to assist in prompting patients to pay. A green envelope attracts more attention than a white envelope. It may prompt a patient to take a second look at what it is and who it is from.

Ledger Card or Special Statement Form

A special statement form is another way to bill the patient. It is typed or printed and also mailed in a window envelope. The statement lists the date of service, description of service, charges, payments, and balance since the last statement mailed.

Lowery B. Johnson, M.D.
Hwy 311 Suite A31
Sellersburg, IN 47172
812-246-1234

ID.# 237485319
Provider # 19368

ABN ☐   GC ☐

OFFICE VISITS	CPT	FEE	OFF. PROC. CONT'D	CPT	FEE	LABS CONT'D	CPT	FEE	INJECTIONS	CPT	FEE
NEW PATIENT			Biopsy Lesion 1st Lesion	11100		PSA Total	84153		Allergy Shot X1	95115	
Level 1	99201		Each add'l Lesion	11101		Rapid Strep Test	87880		Allergy Shot X2	95117	
Level 2	99202		Skin Tag Removal up to 15	11200		Sed Rate, Nonauto	85651		B-12 Injection	J3420	
Level 3	99203		Destruction 1 Lesion	17000		SGOT (AST)	84450		Demerol 100 MG	J2175	
Level 4	99204		Destruction 2-14 Lesions, each	17003		Special Handling	99000		Demerol & Phenergan Combined	J2180	
Level 5	99205		Ear Lavage	69210		SGPT (ALT)	84460		Depomedrol 80 MG	J1040	
ESTABLISHED PATIENT			EKG	93000		T4	84436		Depoprovera 150	J1055	
Level 1	99211		Foreign Body Removal-Ear	69200		TSH	84443		Depo-estradiol to 5 MG	J1000	
Level 2	99212		Foreign Body Removal-Eye	65205		Uric Acid	84550		Depo-testadiol to 1 ML	J1060	
Level 3	99213		Holter Monitor	93225		Urine Pregnancy Test	81025		Kenalog Per 10 MG	J3301	
Level 4	99214		Medicare Prostate Exam	G0102		Urinalysis/dipstick w/ micro	81000		Phenergan	J2550	
Level 5	99215		Nebulizer Treatment	94640		Urinalysis/dipstick w/o micro	81002		Testesterone, 1cc, 200 mg	J1080	
PREVENTIVE MEDICINE NEW PATIENT			Pap Smear	Q0091		Urinalysis, auto w/ micro	81001		Toradol per 15 mg	J1885	
Age 1-4 Yrs	99382		PELVIC/BREAST	G0101		Urinalysis, auto w/o micro	81003				
Age 5-11 Yrs	99383		Spirometry	94010		Urinalysis, auto w/o micro	81003				
Age 12-17 Yrs	99384		Spirometry/Pre & Post	94060		Wet Mount	87210				
Age 18-39 Yrs	99385		Vision Screen	99173							
Age 40-64 Yrs	99386		Vision, Auto	99172							
Age 65 & Older	99387										

						IMMUNIZATIONS			**X-RAYS**		
PREVENTIVE MEDICINE ESTABLISHED PT			**LABS**			ADMIN. FEE	90782		Abdomen (AP)	74000	
Age 1-4 Yrs	99392		Fingerstick Medicare	36416		ADMIN FEE-ATB (antibiotic)	90788		Ankle 2V/3V	73600/73610	
Age 5-11 Yrs	99393		Venipuncture	G0001/36415		ADMIN. FEE - IMMUN	90471		Cervical 2V/3V	72040	
Age 12-17 Yrs	99394		Bun	84520		ADMIN. FEE IMMUN - EACH ADD	90472		Chest 1V/ Chest 2V	71010/71020	
Age 18-39 Yrs	99395		CBC	85025		DPT	90701		DEXA scan (Spine)	76075	
Age 40-64 Yrs	99396		Creatinine Blood	82565		DtaP	90700		Finger(s) Min. 2V	73140	
Age 65 & Older	99397		DNA Probe-Chlamydia	87490		Polio	90712		Foot 2V	73620	
			DNA Probe-Gonorrhea	87590		MMR	90707		Lumbar Spins 2V/3V	72100	
PROLONGED SERVICES			Glucose, Serum	82947		HIB	90645		Mammogram-Diagnostic Bilat.	76091TC	
One Hour	99354		Glucose Finger	82948		Hepatitis B - 0-17 Yrs/18 & Up	90744/90746		Mammogram-Screening	76092TC	
Add'l 30 Min	99355		Hemoglobin Glyc	83036		18 & Up / Medicare	90746/G0010		Mammogram-Unilateral Diag.	76090TC	
CONSULTATION			Hepatic Function Panel	80076		Influenza/Medicare	90658/G0008		Wrist 2V	73100	
Level 1, Problem Focused	99241		KOH	87220		Varicella	90716				
Level 2, Expanded	99242		LDL, Direct	83721		Pneumovax/Medicare	90732/G0009				
Level 3, Detailed Low,	99243		Lipid Panel	80061		Hepatitis A - 2 Dose 0-17 Yrs/18 & Up	90633/90632				
Level 4, Compre/Mod	99244		Metabolic Panel, Basic	80048		TD	90718				
Level 5, Compre/High	99245		Metabolic Panel, Comp	80053		Tetanus	90703				
OFFICE PROCEDURES			Occult Blood	82270		Rocephin Per 250 MG	J0696				
Aspiration, Puncture Hematoma	10160		PPD	86580		LA Bicillin 1,200,000 U	J0570				
Audiometry (Air Only)	92552		Protime	85610							

Diagnosis: (1) _____

(2) _____

(3) _____

(4) _____

DATE	TIME	PATIENT		REASON	PRIOR BALANCE

TICKET NO.	DR.#	DOCTOR	LOCATION	D.O.B.	TODAY'S CHARGE

PATIENT NO.	RESPONSIBLE PARTY	PH #	REFERRING DR.	ADJUSTMENTS

Return Appointment: _____

SEX M F	ADDRESS	CITY/STATE	ZIP CODE

Other: _____

RECAP	OVER 90	OVER 60	OVER 30	CURRENT	TOTAL DUE	PT	BC	CS	PAY CHOICE	TODAY'S PAYMENTS

INSURANCE COMPANY	BA	SCT	POLICY I.D.	RELATIONSHIP TO INSURED	BALANCE DUE

SELF SPOUSE CHILD OTHER

Figure 13–8 Superbill, encounter form, charge slip.

DATE	TRANSACTION TYPE	AMOUNT	TRANSACTION DESCRIPTION	RESPONSIBLE PARTY	ITEM BALANCE
03/11/20XX	Charg	80.00	OFFICE VISIT, NEW PATIENT - LEVEL 3 Insur Filed on 03/30/98 to Payer-A	Patient	46.95
04/03/20XX	Charg	1157.79	FISTULECTOMY SUBMUSCULAR Insur Filed on 04/21/98 to Payer-A	Payer-A	1157.79
04/13/20XX	Paymt	−26.55	From Payer-A, for 03/11/20XX		
04/13/20XX	Adjmt	−6.50	From Payer-A, for 03/11/20XX PER EOB PT RESP DEDUCT/COPAY 4-13-XX		

ACCOUNT NO.	0–30 DAYS	31–60 DAYS	61–90 DAYS	91–120 DAYS	OVER 120 DAYS	PATIENT DUE
17665	46.95	0.00	0.00	0.00	0.00	$46.95

ACORDIA OF CENTRAL IND (461)   ID: XPN406761759   PRI   <-- Payer-A

INS. PENDING
$1157.79

4723

Figure 13–9A Two examples of patient statements showing procedure, charge, payment, adjustment. Figure 13–9A gives an aging of the bill, the amount currently due, and the amount pending insurance.

Computerized Statement

electronic medical record (EMR)
Computer-based medical record or patient chart.

Today's information technology has allowed physicians' practices to invest in **electronic medical record (EMR)** systems to enter and document patient office and hospital notes, test results, medications, as well as the integration of patient billing and the accounts receivable process in the office.

Electronic medical records call for not only the confidentiality of a patient's record but security of that record. HIPAA Security Rule mandates regulations to protect electronic information to provide safeguards pertaining to storage, transmission, and access to protected health care information.

One security measure is the use of passwords to individuals requiring access to various computer files. A computer program can also track individual access to files to trace accessibility of information.

ANESTHESIOLOGY ASSOCIATES OF CLARK COUNTY, INC.

PLEASE INDICATE CHANGES IN THIS INFORMATION ON THE REVERSE SIDE

ACCOUNT NO.

129438-00   406761759

BALANCE DUE

$40.00

AMOUNT PAID

TO INSURE PROPER CREDIT PLEASE REMOVE AND RETURN THIS PORTION WITH YOUR PAYMENT

DATE OF SERVICE	DESCRIPTION OF SERVICE	AMOUNT
4/03/20XX	FOR ANESTHETIC CARE	$400.00
	DIAGNOSIS CODE 565.0 PROCEDURE CODE 46270	
	TIME 8:30 TO 9:15	
6/15/20XX	BLUE SHIELD PAYMENT	$360.00-
	***CURRENT BALANCE	$40.00
	YOUR INSURANCE HAS PAID ITS PORTION.	
	THE BALANCE IS YOUR RESPONSIBILITY.	

TAX ID# - 35-1273296

DATE	PATIENT NAME	ACCOUNT NO.	PLEASE PAY THIS AMOUNT	
6/17/20XX		129438-00		$40.00

▲ PAYMENTS RECEIVED AFTER THIS DATE WILL APPEAR ON NEXT STATEMENT

IMPORTANT MESSAGE REGARDING YOUR ACCOUNT

PLEASE MAKE CHECK PAYABLE TO: ANESTHESIOLOGY ASSOCIATES OF CLARK COUNTY, INC.

Figure 13–9B The statement shows the amount due after the insurance has paid the practice.

HIPAA transaction and code sets
Any set of codes used for encoding data elements, such as tables of terms, medical concepts, diagnosis and procedure codes.

HIPAA transaction and code sets standards have been implemented to provide standardized electronic format for providers and payers to send and receive transactions. These include:

- Health Care Eligibility Benefit Inquiry and Response—Information about a patient's health plan, covered treatments and procedures, and any coordination of benefits (Figures 13–10A and 13–10B)
- Health Care Claim or Encounter Information—For billing, diagnosis and procedure codes, and payment requests a provider sends to a payer

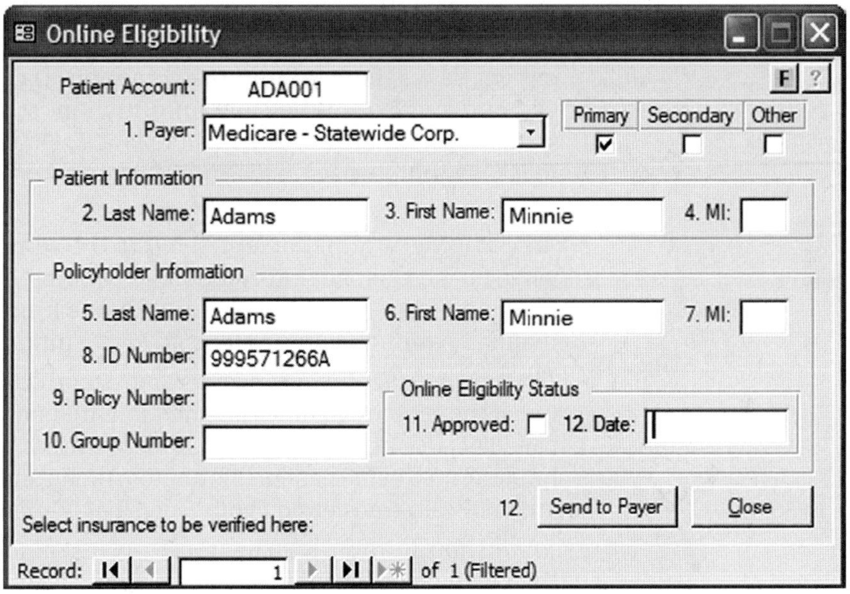

Figure 13–10A On-line eligibility window prior to transmission.

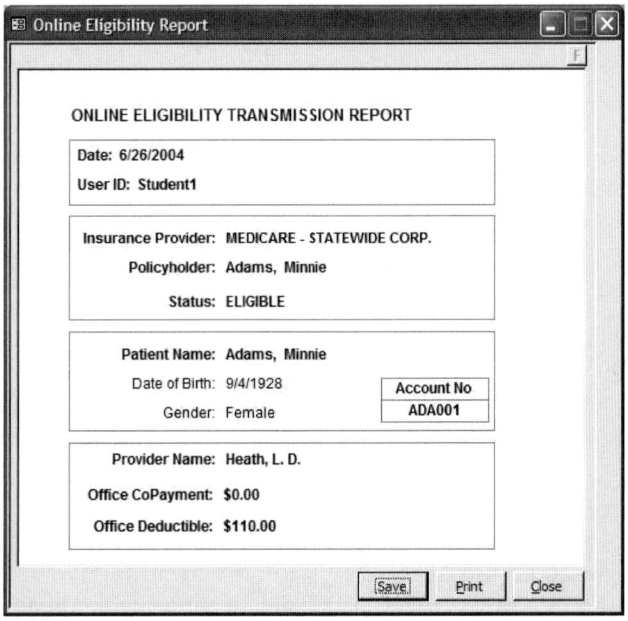

Figure 13–10B On-line eligibility transmission report.

- Health Care Claim Status Request—To check status of a claim submitted for reimbursement
- Health Care Services Review—Request for precertification and referral
- Claims Payment and Remittance Advice—Payment and remittance advice via electronic funds transfer (EFT) to the provider's designated bank account

Prior to implementing a computerized system, consideration must be given to changes in the way administrative procedures are performed.

Computerizing the medical office has disadvantages as well as advantages. It is important to recognize these and to make adequate preparation for any disruption to the efficiency of office functions during the transition to computerization. Training in basic computer functions and terminology is essential.

The advantages of a computerized medical office include:

- *Efficiency.* Repetitive tasks can be performed in a variety of formats. Once initial patient data is entered into the computer, it can be used in different formats without re-entering the same information, such as insurance forms, patient statements, superbills, and mailing labels. Office computers can be networked to allow multiple users access to files in the computer database at various work stations.
- *Accessibility.* Information entered into the computer is much easier to retrieve when needed. Patient information, once entered, can be retrieved and displayed on the monitor (screen) with a few simple functions, without having to search manually through filing systems to locate information needed.
- *Updates and corrections.* Updating and/or correcting patient files can be performed much more quickly and easily than in a manual system where changes/updates would need to be made in several different areas. Changing a patient's address can be performed in the patient information menu and once changes are made they are automatically transferred to other data fields existing in the program.
- *Production.* Computers can process a large amount of information much faster than using manual methods. Compiling information for statistical or research purposes can be performed with very few keystrokes using a computerized system. Patient files can be searched to generate reports requesting information such as past due accounts.
- *Reduced Costs.* After the initial cost of purchasing the computer system and software, operating costs are decreased due to the reduction of time required in performing administrative procedures.

Many offices will attest that the advantages of a computerized billing system outweigh the disadvantages. Some of the disadvantages are:

- *Initial cost.* There is an initial investment for the purchase of the computer and peripherals such as a printer and the programs (software) the office has selected for setting up a computer system. Medical management software costs will vary from vendor to vendor. Hardware expense will depend on the number of computer terminals and the type and number of printers required for the practice. Determining the computer requirements that meet the needs of the medical office is important before purchasing the computer system. It is also financially beneficial to shop around and negotiate the best deal that meets the specific needs of the practice.
- *Initial investment of time.* It takes considerable time to learn how to operate a computer and the billing program. Many software vendors will provide staff training as well as technical support when problems are encountered. Converting from a manual to a computerized system can take six months to a year and

frustration can occur in the conversion process. Once the conversion process is completed, the outcome is positive. Proper training of all personnel will help overcome some of the frustration that may occur.

- *Transition Process.* There is data that must be entered before complete conversion to computerization can occur. For example, patient registration records must be set up by entering demographic information on each patient. Diagnosis and procedure codes most frequently used in the medical office will also need to be entered. There are software programs available with codes already included so that only a few codes may need to be entered. Coding software is also available for purchase. While this data is being entered, front office procedures are still being performed manually. Once all information is entered, and the computer system is operational, additional information can be entered without being a time-consuming task.

- *Malfunctions.* Even the best computer system and software can and will occasionally fail due to operator error, malfunction of the hardware, or a "bug" in the system.

■ *Highlight*

When a patient presents a new insurance card, it is copied front and back for the medical record. Ensure that the information is entered into the computer database for accurate claim form submission to the correct insurance carrier. Entering data incorrectly or not updating data such as address and changes in insurance coverage will result in insurance filing and billing errors.

It is important when purchasing a medical management program to look closely at the administrative needs of the office and what type of features or options will allow the office to perform tasks easily and efficiently. These programs are available through software vendors. Systems of specialization in a medical management computer program are:

1. file maintenance
2. appointment scheduling
3. patient registration
4. posting transactions
5. insurance billing
6. reports

File Maintenance. Before the office can perform administrative procedures, there are a number of tasks that must be performed in the file maintenance system so that the program will operate properly. These tasks include entering the practice and provider information, diagnosis and procedure codes, insurance carriers, and referring physicians into the database and assigning passwords. In addition, any personal physician identification and group numbers assigned to the participating physician or medical practice by the insurance carrier should be entered.

Scheduling Appointments. Computerized appointment scheduling allows front office staff to schedule, cancel, reschedule, and locate an appointment rapidly. In addition, a daily appointment list can be printed, as well as a cancellation log and patient reminder card.

Patient Registration. Once the patient has completed the patient registration form, an account can be established. This is done by entering the demographic

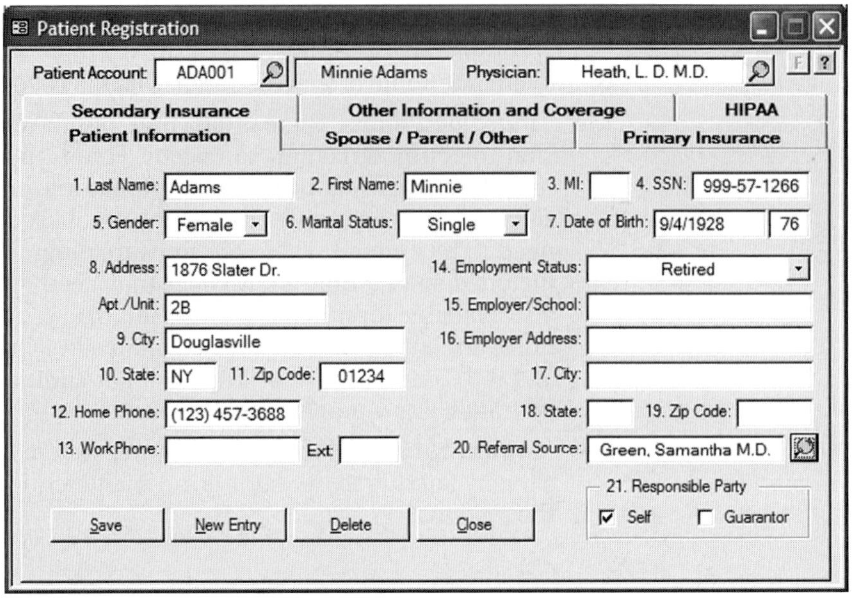

Figure 13–11A Patient demographic information in the patient registration record.

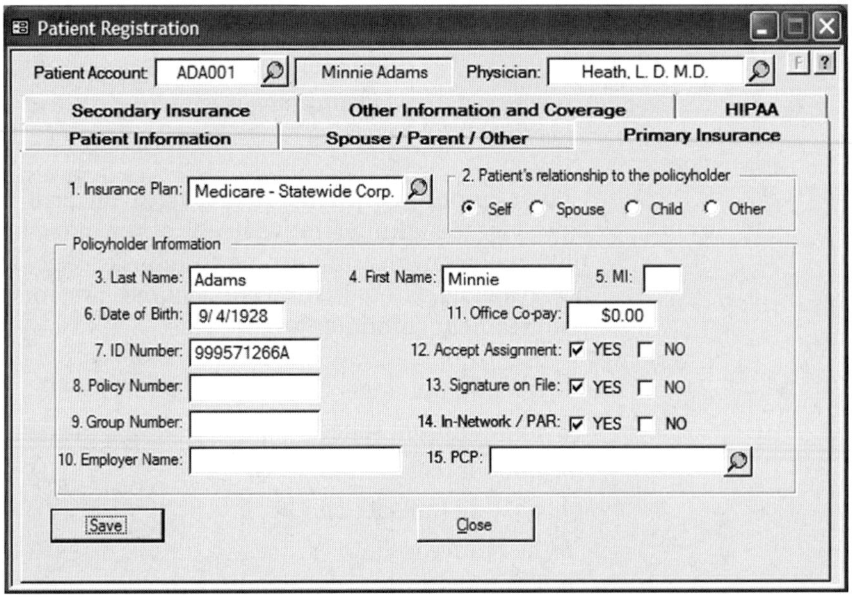

Figure 13–11B Primary Insurance information in the patient registration record.

and insurance data into the database. The patient's chart can also be prepared at this time (Figures 13–11A and 13–11B).

Posting Transactions. Charges for procedures and services performed by the provider can be entered as well as payments made by the patient or third party payer to generate a current balance. A hard copy can be printed for the patient as a receipt, patient statement, or insurance claim (Figure 13–12).

Patient Billing. When charges and payments are posted to the patient's account, the information is stored in the database and is available for patient billing. The management program can search the database to retrieve information necessary to generate statements for patients with outstanding balances. After the statements are printed, they are folded and mailed in window envelopes, or a self-mailer can be used.

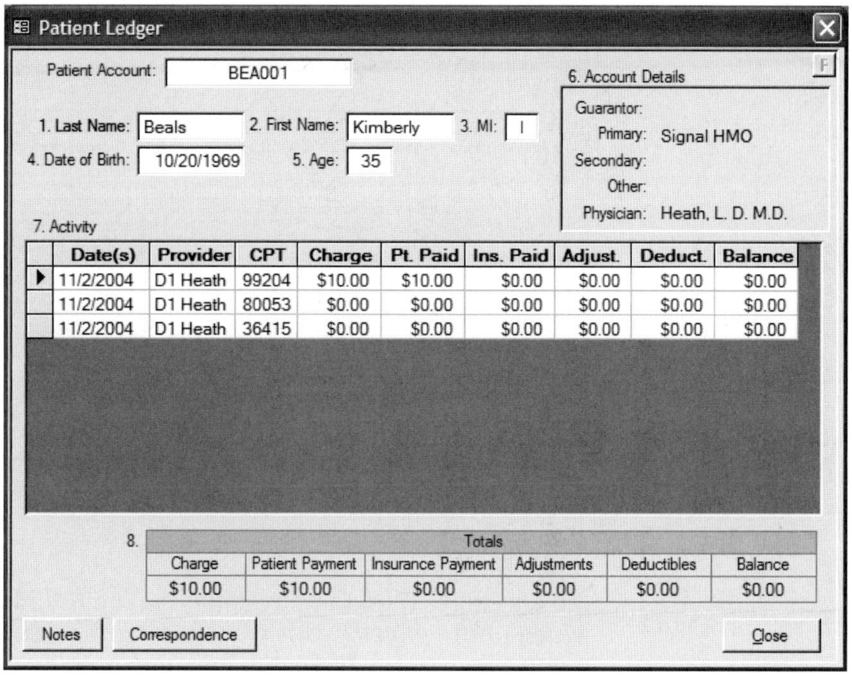

Figure 13–12 Patient's ledger open on the computer screen shows transactions posted with patient co-payment.

Insurance Billing. When posting charges to a patient account, procedure and diagnosis codes are also entered. This information is stored in the database and is later used to complete the insurance claim form.

Reports. This system can generate a variety of reports to allow the physician to review practice and business activities. For example, information can be obtained to track volume and type of procedures performed in the office.

Generating the Computerized Statement

To generate statements, the correct software application will need to be selected. All financial accounts in the practice database with a balance due will be processed. In preparing the bills, the computer will select the accounts that meet the criteria that have been selected for processing, such as accounts that are thirty days past due with a finance charge applied. Another example for this process is to omit statement preparation for Medicaid patients. When this preparation process is complete, the statement will be printed. The order in which statements are printed can also be selected to meet the needs of the office and/or postal regulations for presort rates. This could be by alphabetical order for office needs or by zip code for lower presort rates.

Medical office management software can be purchased with options that include messages to be placed on the statement such as overdue payment reminders and status of insurance filing or even the patient's next appointment date (Figure 13–13). Other options include mailing labels for statements generated and a summary report listing patients billed that include account numbers and the total amount of the statement. In addition, a grand total of all statements can also be printed.

Patient statements are now ready to be mailed and there are options for this process. Standard envelopes may be used with the printed labels attached to

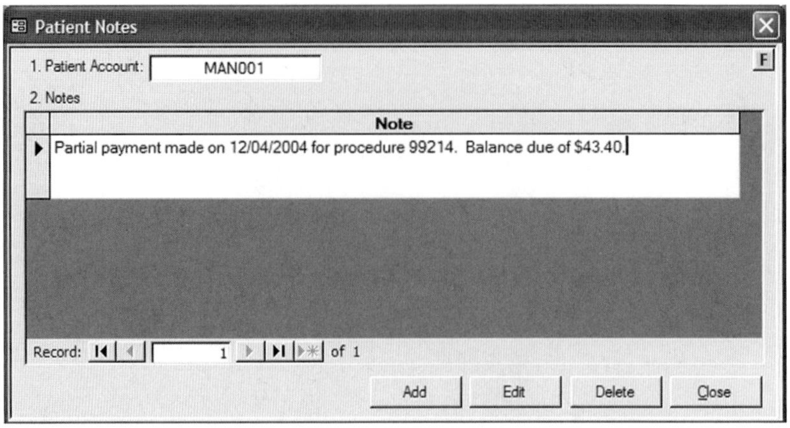

Figure 13–13 Example of a notation made for patient billing.

the envelopes. Window envelopes can be used with statements inserted along with a return envelope for payment. A time-saving method is the mailer statement, which prints the patient statement and a return envelope in continuous form with perforation for separation, also called a self-mailer, as seen in Figure 13–14.

Many payments are received daily in the mail, particularly insurance payments. These payments are posted in the same manner (Figures 13–15A and 13–15B). No receipt is required unless specifically requested by the patient. Physician charges for visits, surgeries, and other services performed in a hospital, nursing home, or other facility are also posted.

In addition to charges added to an account and payments credited to an account, adjustments can also be applied to an account (Figure 13–16).

Adjustments, also known as "write-offs," are changes made in a patient's account not related to charges incurred or payments received. Some examples of adjustments are adding a late charge or a bank fee for a returned check, or a participating provider's deduction per contract agreement.

Figure 13–17 shows a Blue Shield discount on a hospital charge.

Adjusting the account keeps the account current and the accounts receivable figure up to date.

Bookkeeping Tips

Bookkeeping is the recording of daily business transactions. The physician's office is a business, and complete, correct, and current financial records are important for:

- prompt billing and collection procedures.
- accurate reporting of income to federal and state agencies.
- financial planning of the practice.

Bookkeeping errors such as duplicate billing and incorrect charge totals can result in lost income as well as patients for the practice.

Some suggestions for bookkeeping accuracy are:

1. Pay attention to detail.
2. Write clearly and legibly, using the same type of pen, preferably black ink.

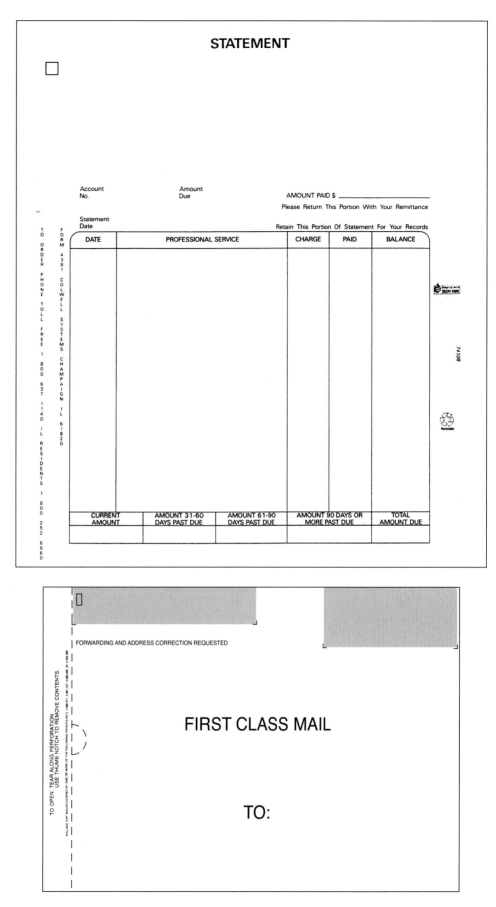

Figure 13–14 Computerized statement with self-mailer.

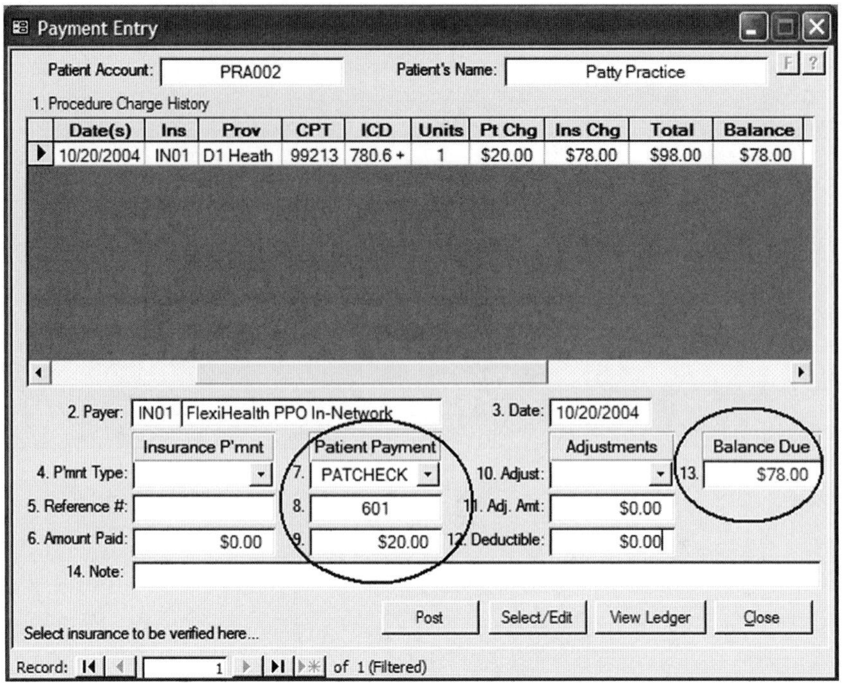

Figure 13–15A Example of payment entry transaction.

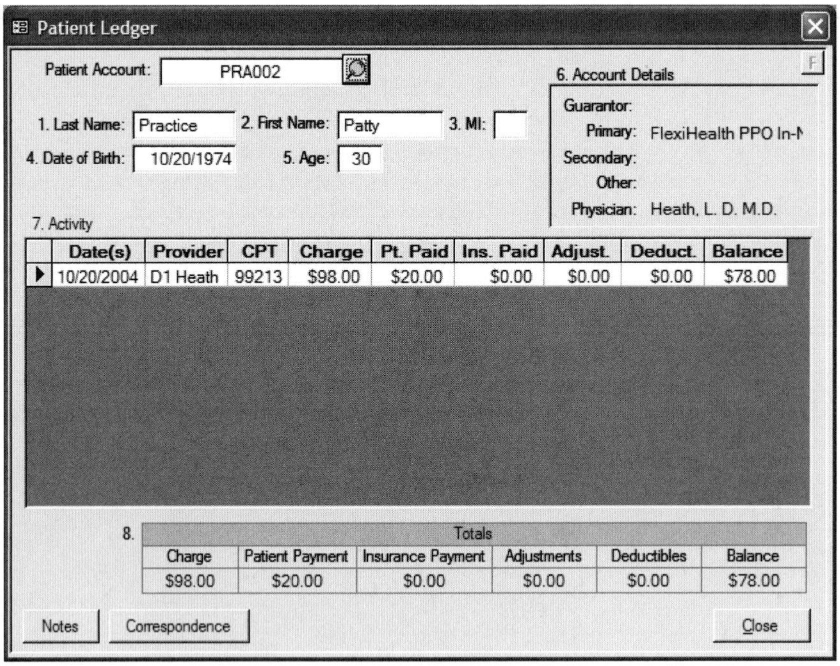

Figure 13–15B Example of computerized patient ledger.

3. Do not erase, write-over, or mark out a figure. Do not use correction fluid. A single line can be drawn through the incorrect figure with the correct figure written above it.

4. Keep columns of figures aligned.

5. Double check columns of figures by adding twice. Financial records cannot be almost correct. Bookkeeping is either right or wrong—there is no in-between.

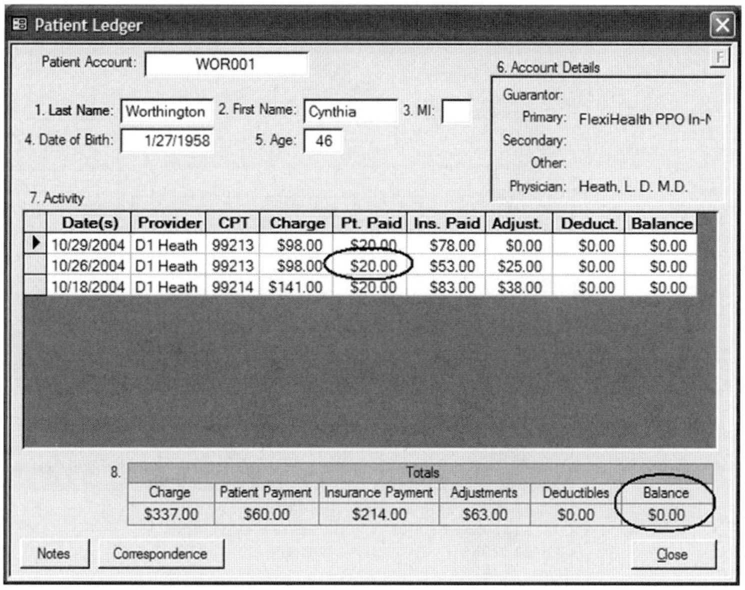

Figure 13–16 Example of patient payment, insurance payment, and adjustments.

External Billing

An outside or external billing service can be contracted to manage patient accounts. The service maintains the ledger cards and posts charges and payments from copies of superbills provided by the medical office. The service prepares monthly statements with instructions that payments be returned to them. It deposits payments directly to the medical office's bank account and submits a report of all transactions.

This billing method works well in practices with limited clerical staff or those with a large patient load. There should be one employee responsible for coordinating activities between the office and the billing service.

THE BILLING PROCESS

When to mail out statements to patients is often determined by the size of the medical practice and the economic status of the community. Smaller offices may find the monthly billing cycle to be the most efficient. Large practices may prefer cycle billing as it allows flexibility in the billing schedule.

Monthly Billing

monthly billing
Billing patients at one designated time of the month.

Monthly billing is just what the name states: billing all patients at a designated time of the month. Typically, statements should leave the office on the 25th of the month to be received by the first day of the following month. A major disadvantage of monthly billing is other duties may be neglected during this time-consuming period.

Cycle Billing

cycle billing
Accounts divided alphabetically into groups with each group billed at a different time.

In **cycle billing,** all accounts are divided alphabetically into groups with each group billed at a different time. Statements are prepared in the same schedule each month. In a large practice with numerous statements to process monthly,

Clark Memorial Hospital
Jewish Hospital Health Network Partner

P.O. Box CS10
Jeffersonville, IN 47131-7010
812-283-2389

STATEMENT

STATEMENT DATE	PAY THIS AMOUNT	ACCOUNT NUMBER
5/16/20XX	243.27	1025411

DATE OF SERVICE 4/03/20XX — SHOW AMOUNT PAID HERE $

PATIENT NAME

PLEASE DETACH AND RETURN TOP PORTION WITH YOUR PAYMENT

DATE	DESCRIPTION	PAYMENTS	BALANCE
4/23/20XX	FINAL BILL AMOUNT		4,025.75
05/11/20XX	BLUE CROSS OF IN DISCOUNT	1,520.52CR	
05/11/20XX	PAYMENT—BLUE CROSS 13	2,261.96CR	

TOTAL AMOUNT DUE**** 243.27

PLEASE NOTE

YOUR INSURANCE COMPANY HAS PAID ITS SHARE OF YOUR BILL.
THE ABOVE BALANCE IS NOW DUE FROM YOU.
**QUESTIONS CONCERNING YOUR ACCOUNT CALL

Your Insurance has been billed. This copy of your bill is for your records.

Figure 13–17 Insurance payment and adjustment of a hospital statement.

this is a more efficient method of billing. The statements can be mailed as they are completed or mailed at one time. A typical cycle billing schedule is shown in Table 13–1. This can be varied to accommodate the needs of the individual practice. The major advantage of cycle billing is that it provides a steady flow of funds throughout the month.

Past Due Accounts

No matter how efficient and effective the billing process may be, there will still be collections on some accounts. The most common reasons for a past due account are:

- Inability to pay—simply not having the money to pay the bill. Medical bills have last priority.
- Negligence or forgetfulness, or misplacing the statement.

- Unwillingness to pay. When a patient complains about a charge or refuses to pay, it may have nothing to do with finances. There could be dissatisfaction with the care or treatment received. The physician or office manager should be made aware of those situations for immediate attention.

TABLE 13–1   Typical Schedule for Cycle Billing System.

To Cycle Bill Patient Accounts:

1.	Divide the alphabet into four sections: A–F, G–L, M–R, S–Z.
2.	Prepare statements for patients whose last names begin with A through F on Wednesday and mail them on Thursday of the first week of the month. (Week 1)
3.	Prepare statements for patients whose last names begin with G through L on Wednesday and mail them on Thursday of Week 2.
4.	Prepare statements for patients whose last names begin with M through R on Wednesday and mail them on Thursday of Week 3.
5.	Prepare statements for patients whose last names begin with S through Z on Wednesday and mail them on Thursday of Week 4.

EXERCISE 13–3

1. Name the three most common reasons an account may become past due.

a. _____

b. _____

c. _____

2. Name the two types of billing.

THE COLLECTIONS PROCESS

Collection of delinquent accounts begins with determining how much has been owed for what length of time.

accounts receivable (A/R)
The amount of money owed to the medical practice by its patients.

account aging
A method of identifying how long an account is overdue by the length of time it has been unpaid.

Accounts receivable (A/R) is the amount of money owed to the medical practice by its patients. **Account aging** is a method of identifying how long an account is overdue by the length of time it has been unpaid. The accounts are aged into the following categories:

Current—0 to 30 Days
31 to 60 Days
61 to 90 Days
91 to 120 Days
120 Days and over

Aging of an account determines how long charges have remained unpaid from one billing date to another. Aging can begin the date the statement is sent to a patient or based on the aging parameters within a billing system. Any unpaid amount ages by the thirty-day time period shown above each time statements are sent and remains unpaid.

Medical office management computer systems can automatically calculate and age the balance due on individual overdue accounts to indicate the length of time the account has been overdue.

The classification of past due accounts and the account aging process is necessary to review and determine which accounts need follow-up. An age analysis is a summary that lists all patient account balances, when the charges were made, the most recent payment received, and any special notes concerning the account, as shown in Figure 13–18.

Management consultants recommend fees to be collected at the time of service, and a collection ratio of at least 90 percent should be maintained. A collection ratio is a method used to gauge the effectiveness of the ambulatory care setting's billing practices. This is calculated by dividing the total collections by the net charges (gross charges minus adjustments). This yields a percentage, which is the collection ratio, as explained in Table 13–2.

Another important factor is the accounts receivable ratio, which measures the speed with which outstanding accounts are paid, which is generally two months.

04/04/20XX									Page 1
SUMMARY AGING REPORT BY ACCOUNT BASED ON DATE PATIENT BILLED (Pat. Only)									
All Accounts Aging Category: 1–5 DOL Pay <= 04/04/20XX									
Acc #	Name	Phone No.	DOL Pay	Unapplied	Current	31–60	61–90	120+	Total
114	Rawles, Deb	812-246-1256	03/20/2000		102.50				102.50
25	Leaf, Autumn	812-246-7789	12/02/1999					250.00	250.00
110	Martin, Kathy	502-585-1134	02/14/2000			115.00			115.00
214	Burton, Craig	502-585-1459	03/15/2000		53.75				53.75
REPORT TOTALS					156.25	115.00		250.00	521.25

Figure 13–18 Summary of account aging.

TABLE 13–2   Collection Ratio.

Total Receipts	=	$40,000
Managed Care Adjustments	+	$ 3,000
Medicare Adjustments	+	$ 2,000
Total Received	=	$45,000
Total Charges	÷	$52,000
Collection Ratio after adjustments	=	**86.5%**

The accounts receivable ratio is figured by dividing the current A/R balance by the average monthly gross charges. The A/R ratio provides a picture of the state of collections and probable loss within the practice. The longer an account is past due, the less the likelihood of successfully collecting the account.

COLLECTION TECHNIQUES

An effective approach to the collection of past due accounts in the medical office is a combination of letters and telephone calls. It is preferable to first call the patient concerning the delinquent account. The patient may have misplaced or forgotten the bill, and a telephone call can often resolve the situation quickly and inexpensively. When making telephone collection calls, there are ethical issues to remember:

- Be tactful, courteous, and diplomatic.
- Treat patients respectfully.
- Do not threaten or antagonize.

Fair Debt Collection Practices Act
A consumer protection policy against abusive collection practices by debt collectors.

The **Fair Debt Collection Practices Act** is designed to protect consumers against abusive practices by debt collectors. This act mandates that when making collection calls, personnel cannot:

- Call before 8 A.M. or after 9 P.M. or make excessive calls.
- Use abusive language or make threats to coerce a consumer into making a payment.
- Publish a list of consumers who allegedly refuse to pay debts, except to report to a credit reporting agency.
- Threaten to notify an employer that a consumer has not paid bills.
- Advertise or publicize the debt to embarrass a consumer into paying.
- Send misleading letters that appear to be from a government agency or court.
- Try to collect more than is owed.

■ *Highlight*

Check state laws regarding guidelines for times to make collection calls. Be aware of the different time zones within state boundaries and nationwide to avoid an abusive telephone collection practice.

In addition to the Fair Debt Collection Practices Act and the Truth In Lending Act discussed earlier, other laws governing collection practices that health care employees must be familiar with are:

- *Fair Credit Reporting Act of 1971.* Provides guidelines for the reporting and collecting of credit background information to businesses to use in evaluation of an individual's application for credit, insurance, or employment. It allows consumers to learn the nature and substance of information collected about them by credit reporting agencies, and to correct and update information.
- *Guide Against Debt Collection Deception (Federal Trade Commission).* Provides guidelines for creditors in their collection efforts, and provides the consumer with protection from fraudulent and deceptive tactics.
- *Notice on Use of Telephone for Debt Collecting (Federal Communications Commission).* Outlines specific times calls can be made, and prohibits threatening

phone calls and other harassment. States and localities may also have additional statutes concerning the use of the telephone for debt collection.

- *Equal Credit Opportunity Act of 1975.* Prohibits discrimination in the granting of credit on the basis of sex, race, age, marital status, religion, or nationality.
- *Fair Credit Billing Act.* States a sixty-day time limit for patients who have a complaint with a bill to inquire about the error. The complaint must be acknowledged and documented within thirty days of receipt of the complaint. The provider has a maximum of ninety days or two billing cycles to correct the error. In the event no error is detected, an explanation of the bill and its accuracy must be explained to the patient.

■ *Highlight*

Keep accurate records in telephone collections. Document what was said, any amount of a promised payment, and date of the promised payment. If nothing is received at that time, follow-up will be necessary.

Collection Letters

The most effective approach to collections combines telephone calls and letters on past due accounts. Collection letters are sent to encourage patients to pay past due balances after regular statements have been mailed. Lack of payment is usually not considered serious until after sixty days. When there has been no response to telephone calls and statements, a series of collection letters begins. Collection experts recommend the steps shown in Table 13–3:

TABLE 13–3   Collection Time Line.

Payment at time of service	Payment is received at time of the service or visit; payment and insurance information is obtained and discussed.
30 days after service rendered	First billing statement is sent.
60 days past due	Second billing statement is sent with reminder of past-due balance; letter or telephone call to discuss payment arrangements; get commitment in writing (Figure 13–19).
90 days past due	Third billing statement is sent with strong reminder of past-due balance. No payment or other contact to result in collection action (Figure 13–20).
120 days past due	Final notice is sent requesting payment. Specify time frame for payment; no payment will result in collection agency (Figure 13–21).
Final action	No payment or other correspondence results in turnover to collection agency. Notice of termination letter is sent certified mail, return receipt requested (Figure 13–22).

The final notice letter should be exactly that: a final demand for payment. If you continue to send letters after the final notice, the patient will doubt your attempts at collecting the account. The final notice letter should be sent certified mail, return receipt requested. This provides documentation the letter was mailed and received by the patient. If the letter is undeliverable, it will be returned to the billing office marked accordingly.

When all collection attempts by the medical office have been unsuccessful, many practices seek the assistance of an outside collection agency. At this point, many practices will terminate medical services to the patient. An example of this Notice of Termination of Medical Services Letter is seen in Figure 13–22. This letter is also mailed to the patient by certified mail, return receipt requested for legal purposes for documentation of delivery and receipt. If undeliverable, it will be returned to the billing office, marked accordingly.

■ *Highlight*

Never place a past due notice on the mailing envelope of the statement, or use a postcard to communicate financial or collection information. This is an invasion of privacy.

Lowery B. Johnson, M.D.
Hwy 311 Suite A31
Sellersburg, IN 47172
812-246-1234

May 3, 20XX

Autumn Leaf
10586 Payment Place #2E
Sellersburg, IN 47178

Dear Ms Leaf:

As we discussed in our telephone conversation today, we will expect a payment from you in the amount of $125.00 on May 15 and the balance of $125 on June 15, 20XX.

Please notify our billing office immediately if any problem should occur to prevent payment of this past due account.

Sincerely,

Susan B. Dunn
Office Manager

Figure 13–19 Telephone follow-up letter.

Lowery B. Johnson, M.D.
Hwy 311 Suite A31
Sellersburg, IN 47172
812-246-1234

July 5, 20XX

Autumn Leaf
10586 Payment Place #2E
Sellersburg, IN 47178

Dear Ms. Leaf:

We have not received payments from you as promised in the telephone call with you on May 3, 20XX.

Your account remains unpaid with a balance of $250.00, which is 90 days past due. Mastercard and Visa are accepted for your convenience in paying this bill, as well as cash and checks.

Please call me at 555-2244 if you have a question about your account. Otherwise we expect your payment immediately.

Sincerely,

Susan B. Dunn
Office Manager

Figure 13–20 Collection letter ninety days.

Collection Agencies

When choosing a collection agency, ask for referrals from other physicians, ambulatory care centers, and hospitals. Many agencies deal specifically with health care facilities and will work compatibly with the medical office's philosophy of ethics in patient care. Ask what the agency's approach is for collection methods and request sample letters and notices.

When a collection agency has been selected, the following patient information must be supplied:

- Full name and last known address
- Name of employer and business address
- Name of spouse, if applicable
- Total debt
- Date of last payment or charge on the account
- Method taken by the office to collect the debt
- Any response to collection attempts

Lowery B. Johnson, M.D.
Hwy 311 Suite A31
Sellersburg, IN 47172
812-246-1234

August 9, 20XX

Autumn Leaf
10586 Payment Place #2E
Sellersburg, IN 47178

Dear Ms. Leaf:

Your account with our office remains unpaid after several telephone calls and letters. Your account is seriously past due at 120 days.

Unless we receive your payment within the next ten (10) days, we will have no alternative but to turn this account over to a collection agency.

Please send us our payment or call this office before August 19, 20XX. This is our final attempt to collect this past due account.

Sincerely,

Susan B. Dunn
Office Manager

Figure 13–21 Collection letter 120 days—final notice requesting payment.

Once the account has been turned over to the collection agency, the medical office should follow these guidelines:

1. Note on the patient's account that it has been given to the collection agency.
2. Discontinue sending statements.
3. Refer the patient to the collection agency if he or she contacts the office about the account.
4. Promptly report any payments received by the office to the agency, as a percentage of this payment is due them.
5. Contact the agency if new information is obtained that could help in collecting the debt.

The collection agency will retain a portion of payment recovered, usually 40–60 percent.

Lowery B. Johnson, M.D.
Hwy 311 Suite A31
Sellersburg, IN 47172
812-246-1234

August 19, 20XX

Autumn Leaf
10586 Payment Place #2E
Sellersburg, IN 47178

Dear Ms. Leaf:

Since we have received no response from you regarding your past due account, this has now been turned over to the Goody Medical Collections Bureau. Further attempts at collecting this debt using whatever legal action necessary will come from this agency.

Because of the unsatisfactory manner in which you have handled your financial obligations to Dr. Johnson, we find it necessary to terminate further medical care from this office.

We will remain available for your medical care for the next 30 days from the date you receive this letter. This will give you sufficient time to choose a physician for your continued medical care. With your signed consent, your medical records will be made available to the physician you designate.

In the event you require medical services from this office in the next 30 days, payment in full will be required at the time of service.

Sincerely,

Susan B. Dunn
Office Manager

Figure 13–22 Notice of termination letter.

Small Claims Court

In certain circumstances, consideration may be given to bringing a delinquent case to small claims court. Small claims courts typically:

- Handle cases that involve only a limited amount of debt (which varies from state to state)
- Do not permit representation by an attorney or collection agency
- Are efficient in their proceedings and less expensive to utilize

A key factor when using small claims court: the court only determines if the charge or account is valid. If the court rules in favor of the medical office, the office still must collect the money from the defendant.

Special Collection Situations

Bankruptcy

Bankruptcy is defined as a legal declaration of an individual's inability to pay debts owed. The number of individual bankruptcies filed in the United States continues to rise. This is especially true as the elderly population increases and the number of noninsured individuals and families in need of medical procedures and services climbs as jobs are lost and benefits are decreased.

This increase has a significant impact on health care providers whose bills often make up a large portion of the debts discharged in the bankruptcy court. Because the physician's fee is an unsecured debt, it is one of the last to be paid. (U.S. Bankruptcy Court).

bankruptcy
A legal declaration of an individual's inability to pay debts.

Bankruptcy is governed under the Bankruptcy Act of 1978 and the Bankruptcy Amendment Act of 1984. There are different types or chapters of bankruptcy, usually determined by legal advice that can be voluntary or involuntary. The main objectives of a bankruptcy proceeding are the collection and distribution of a debtor's assets and the discharge of the debtor from obligations. The decree terminating the bankruptcy proceeding is called a "discharge," which releases the debtor from the debt. What should you do in the medical office when a patient files bankruptcy? When verbal or written notice is received that a debtor has filed bankruptcy, immediately discontinue all collection attempts. The U.S. Bankruptcy Court is now involved, and it will make the decision about who will receive any assets that are available. Any further contact with the debtor may constitute a violation of the protection of the bankruptcy court. If you have questions, contact your office attorney or the debtor's attorney. If an account has been turned over to a collection agency and you receive notice of a bankruptcy proceeding, contact the agency immediately. Copies of any bankruptcy notices received from the bankruptcy court should be sent to the agency so that appropriate action may be taken on the account.

Figures 13–23 and 13–24 are examples of notices from bankruptcy court.

Billing Minors

Statements for services performed to minors must be addressed to a parent or guardian.

A statement addressed to a child, or patient under the legal age declared in that state, may prove difficult to collect payment if the parents take the attitude that they are not responsible because the statement is not addressed directly to them. If the parents are separated or divorced, the parent who brings the child to the office for medical services may be responsible for payment. Financial agreements in these circumstances exist between the parents and should not involve the medical staff.

birthday rule
Guideline for determination of the primary insurance policy when dependents are covered on two or more policies.

In some circumstances, a child may be covered under two insurance policies. The **birthday rule** determines which policy is primary and which is secondary. The birthday rule states that the primary policy is the one taken out by the policyholder with the earliest birthday occurring in the calendar year.

EXAMPLE

Tom Brown is a dependent child carried on both parents' policies. His father's policy is through his employment at General Motors. His mother's policy is a group policy through her employer, Good Samaritan Hospital.

The father's birth date is June 6, 1950.
The mother's birth date is February 1, 1955.

February 1 is the earliest birth date in the year, and would be the primary policy for Tom, with his father's policy secondary.

FORM B10 (Official Form 10) (04/04)

UNITED STATES BANKRUPTCY COURT _____ DISTRICT OF _____		PROOF OF CLAIM
Name of Debtor	Case Number	

NOTE: This form should not be used to make a claim for an administrative expense arising after the commencement of the case. A "request" for payment of an administrative expense may be filed pursuant to 11 U.S.C. § 503.

Name of Creditor (The person or other entity to whom the debtor owes money or property):

☐ Check box if you are aware that anyone else has filed a proof of claim relating to your claim. Attach copy of statement giving particulars.

Name and address where notices should be sent:

☐ Check box if you have never received any notices from the bankruptcy court in this case.

☐ Check box if the address differs from the address on the envelope sent to you by the court.

Telephone number:

THIS SPACE IS FOR COURT USE ONLY

Account or other number by which creditor identifies debtor:

Check here ☐ replaces   a previously filed claim, dated:_____
if this claim ☐ amends

1. Basis for Claim
- ☐ Goods sold
- ☐ Services performed
- ☐ Money loaned
- ☐ Personal injury/wrongful death
- ☐ Taxes
- ☐ Other _____

- ☐ Retiree benefits as defined in 11 U.S.C. § 1114(a)
- ☐ Wages, salaries, and compensation (fill out below)
  Last four digits of SS #: _____
  Unpaid compensation for services performed
  from _____ to _____
  (date)   (date)

2. Date debt was incurred:

3. If court judgment, date obtained:

4. Total Amount of Claim at Time Case Filed: $ _____ _____ _____ _____
(unsecured)   (secured)   (priority)   (Total)

If all or part of your claim is secured or entitled to priority, also complete Item 5 or 7 below.

☐ Check this box if claim includes interest or other charges in addition to the principal amount of the claim. Attach itemized statement of all interest or additional charges.

5. Secured Claim.
☐ Check this box if your claim is secured by collateral (including a right of setoff).

Brief Description of Collateral:
☐ Real Estate   ☐ Motor Vehicle
☐ Other _____

Value of Collateral: $_____

Amount of arrearage and other charges at time case filed included in secured claim, if any: $_____

6. Unsecured Nonpriority Claim $_____

☐ Check this box if: a) there is no collateral or lien securing your claim, or b) your claim exceeds the value of the property securing it, or if c) none or only part of your claim is entitled to priority.

7. Unsecured Priority Claim.
☐ Check this box if you have an unsecured priority claim

Amount entitled to priority $_____
Specify the priority of the claim:
☐ Wages, salaries, or commissions (up to $4,925),* earned within 90 days before filing of the bankruptcy petition or cessation of the debtor's business, whichever is earlier - 11 U.S.C. § 507(a)(3).
☐ Contributions to an employee benefit plan - 11 U.S.C. § 507(a)(4).
☐ Up to $2,225* of deposits toward purchase, lease, or rental of property or services for personal, family, or household use - 11 U.S.C. § 507(a)(6).
☐ Alimony, maintenance, or support owed to a spouse, former spouse, or child - 11 U.S.C. § 507(a)(7).
☐ Taxes or penalties owed to governmental units-11 U.S.C. § 507(a)(8).
☐ Other - Specify applicable paragraph of 11 U.S.C. § 507(a)(___).
*Amounts are subject to adjustment on 4/1/07 and every 3 years thereafter with respect to cases commenced on or after the date of adjustment.

8. Credits: The amount of all payments on this claim has been credited and deducted for the purpose of making this proof of claim.

9. Supporting Documents: *Attach copies of supporting documents,* such as promissory notes, purchase orders, invoices, itemized statements of running accounts, contracts, court judgments, mortgages, security agreements, and evidence of perfection of lien. DO NOT SEND ORIGINAL DOCUMENTS. If the documents are not available, explain. If the documents are voluminous, attach a summary.

10. Date-Stamped Copy: To receive an acknowledgment of the filing of your claim, enclose a stamped, self-addressed envelope and copy of this proof of claim

THIS SPACE IS FOR COURT USE ONLY

Date	Sign and print the name and title, if any, of the creditor or other person authorized to file this claim (attach copy of power of attorney, if any):

Penalty for presenting fraudulent claim: Fine of up to $500,000 or imprisonment for up to 5 years, or both. 18 U.S.C. §§ 152 and 3571.

FIGURE 13–23 Notice of bankruptcy.

FORM B9A (Chapter 7 Individual or Joint Debtor No Asset Case (12/03)

UNITED STATES BANKRUPTCY COURT _____ **District of** _____

Notice of
Chapter 7 Bankruptcy Case, Meeting of Creditors, & Deadlines

[A chapter 7 bankruptcy case concerning the debtor(s) listed below was filed on _____ (date).]
or [A bankruptcy case concerning the debtor(s) listed below was originally filed under chapter _____ on _____ (date) and was converted to a case under chapter 7 on_____.]

You may be a creditor of the debtor. **This notice lists important deadlines.** You may want to consult an attorney to protect your rights. All documents filed in the case may be inspected at the bankruptcy clerk's office at the address listed below. NOTE: The staff of the bankruptcy clerk's office cannot give legal advice.

See Reverse Side For Important Explanations.

Debtor(s) (name(s) and address):	Case Number:
	Last four digits of Soc. Sec. No./Complete EIN or other Taxpayer I.D.No.:
All Other Names used by the Debtor(s) in the last 6 years (include married, maiden, and trade names):	Bankruptcy Trustee (name and address):
Attorney for Debtor(s) (name and address):	Telephone number:
Telephone number:	

Meeting of Creditors:

Date: /   /   Time: (   ) A.M.   Location:
                                      (   ) P.M.

Deadlines: Papers must be *received* by the bankruptcy clerk's office by the following deadlines:

Deadline to File a Complaint Objecting to Discharge of the Debtor *or* to Determine Dischargeability of Certain Debts:

Deadline to Object to Exemptions: Thirty (30) days after the *conclusion* of the meeting of creditors.

Creditors May Not Take Certain Actions

The filing of the bankruptcy case automatically stays certain collection and other actions against the debtor and the debtor's property. If you attempt to collect a debt or take other action in violation of the Bankruptcy Code, you may be penalized.

Please Do Not File A Proof of Claim Unless You Receive a Notice To Do So.

Address of the Bankruptcy Clerk's Office:	For the Court:
	Clerk of the Bankruptcy Court:
Telephone number:	
Hours Open:	Date:

Figure 13–24A Bankruptcy court notice of discharge of debtor(s) including explanations.   (continues)

EXPLANATIONS **FORM B9A (9/97)**

Filing of Chapter 7 Bankruptcy Case	A bankruptcy case under chapter 7 of the Bankruptcy Code (title 11, United States Code) has been filed in this court by or against the debtor(s) listed on the front side, and an order for relief has been entered.
Creditors May Not Take Certain Actions	Prohibited collection actions are listed in Bankruptcy Code § 362. Common examples of prohibited actions include contacting the debtor by telephone, mail or otherwise to demand repayment; taking actions to collect money or obtain property from the debtor; repossessing the debtor's property; starting or continuing lawsuits or foreclosures; and garnishing or deducting from the debtor's wages.
Meeting of Creditors	A meeting of creditors is scheduled for the date, time and location listed on the front side. *The debtor (both spouses in a joint case) must be present at the meeting to be questioned under oath by the trustee and by creditors.* Creditors are welcome to attend, but are not required to do so. The meeting may be continued and concluded at a later date without further notice.
Do Not File a Proof of Claim at This Time	There does not appear to be any property available to the trustee to pay creditors. *You therefore should not file a proof of claim at this time.* If it later appears that assets are available to pay creditors, you will be sent another notice telling you that you may file a proof of claim, and telling you the deadline for filing your proof of claim.
Discharge of Debts	The debtor is seeking a discharge of most debts, which may include your debt. A discharge means that you may never try to collect the debt from the debtor. If you believe that the debtor is not entitled to receive a discharge under Bankruptcy Code § 727(a) *or* that a debt owed to you is not dischargeable under Bankruptcy Code § 523(a)(2), (4), (6), or (15), you must start a lawsuit by filing a complaint in the bankruptcy clerk's office by the "Deadline to File a Complaint Objecting to Discharge of the Debtor or to Determine Dischargeability of Certain Debts" listed on the front side. The bankruptcy clerk's office must receive the complaint and the required filing fee by that Deadline.
Exempt Property	The debtor is permitted by law to keep certain property as exempt. Exempt property will not be sold and distributed to creditors. The debtor must file a list of all property claimed as exempt. You may inspect that list at the bankruptcy clerk's office. If you believe that an exemption claimed by the debtor is not authorized by law, you may file an objection to that exemption. The bankruptcy clerk's office must receive the objection by the "Deadline to Object to Exemptions" listed on the front side.
Bankruptcy Clerk's Office	Any paper that you file in this bankruptcy case should be filed at the bankruptcy clerk's office at the address listed on the front side. You may inspect all papers filed, including the list of the debtor's property and debts and the list of the property claimed as exempt, at the bankruptcy clerk's office.
Legal Advice	The staff of the bankruptcy clerk's office cannot give legal advice. You may want to consult an attorney to protect your rights.

—Refer To Other Side For Important Deadlines and Notices—

Figure 13–24B Continued

If both policyholders have the same birth dates, the primary policy is the policy in effect the longest. The *year* of birth is not considered in the birthday rule.

Emancipated Minors

Minors cannot be held responsible for payment of a bill unless they are emancipated.

An **emancipated minor** is a person under the age of majority, usually eighteen or twenty-one years old, as defined by state statute, who is one of the following:

emancipated minor
A person under the age of majority, usually 18 to 21 years of age as defined by state statute, who is self-supporting, married, serving in the armed forces, and/or living separate from parents.

- married
- self-supporting
- serving in the armed forces
- living separately from parents or a legal guardian

An emancipated minor who comes to the medical facility requesting treatment is responsible for the charges incurred.

EXERCISE 13–4

1. Explain the correct procedure to follow in billing a minor.

2. Define emancipated minor.

3. Applying the birthday rule to the following scenario, which policy is primary?

   Jennifer Catz is a nine-year-old child carried on both her parents' health care policies. Her father's policy is through his employment at General Foods.

   Jennifer's mother is employed at National American Life Insurance Company with medical insurance coverage through her employer.

   Jennifer's father's birth date is September 2, 1960.

   Jennifer's mother's birth date is September 28, 1956.

Tracing Skips

skip
A person who has apparently moved without leaving a forwarding address.

A "**skip**" is a person who has apparently moved, leaving no forwarding address. If a statement is returned to your office "No Forwarding Address," or "Undeliverable," determine first if there are any errors made in addressing the envelope. Compare the address on the envelope with the one on the patient registration form in the chart. If the address is correct, the billing office may try to call the patient. The copy of the driver's license obtained during the patient registration process can be used as a tracking device to locate the patient. If all these efforts fail, a decision should be made on whether to pursue the debt. This usually depends on office policy and the amount that is owed. The unpaid account at this time could be turned over to a collection agency.

EXERCISE 13–5

1. Explain the *first* thing to do when a statement is returned to the office, "Moved—No Forwarding Address."

Billing for a Deceased Patient

accept assignment
To accept payment received for a claim as full payment after copayment and/or coinsurance amounts have been collected.

Health care providers sometimes write off accounts of deceased patients simply due to lack of information on whom to bill and how to bill.

When the patient has Medicare, submit the claim with the physician accepting assignment by marking "X" in "Yes" box in Block 27. **Accept assignment** means the physician or provider will accept what Medicare pays and not bill the difference between the cost of the service and the Medicare payment. For example, Medicare is billed for a service that cost $150. The Medicare payment is in the amount of $98. When the provider accepts assignment, the payment of $98 is accepted as payment in full. The remaining balance or difference of $52 is adjusted or written off. No signature is required by a family member. In Block 12 where the patient's signature is required, type in "Patient Died (date)".

If the physician does not accept assignment on a Medicare patient, the balance on the account will remain unpaid until the estate is settled. Individuals filing to receive benefits on behalf of a deceased beneficiary are encouraged to submit documentation to establish their entitlement, such as a letter of appointment, proof of executorship, and copies of receipted funeral bills.

When you receive word that a patient has died, show courtesy by not sending a statement in the first week or so after the death. Address the statement to "Estate of (name of patient)" and mail to the patient's last known address. If your office had a long-term relationship with the deceased, the surviving spouse or family member usually will notify the billing office if there is an estate and who is the executor or administrator.

A call to the probate court in the county clerk's office where the estate was entered can verify that the estate has been or will be probated. If there is a special form for the billing provider to complete, such as proof of claim, the clerk of the probate court, the executor, or the administrator will assist you in filing your claim.

PROFESSIONAL COURTESY

professional courtesy
Medical treatment free of charge or at a reduced rate, or accepting what insurance pays as full payment to physicians and their families, office employees and their families, and other health care professionals, such as dentists, pharmacists and clergy, as determined by office policy.

The Centers for Medicare and Medicaid services (CMS) defines **professional courtesy** as providing health care services on a free or discount basis to a physician, his/her immediate family members, and office staff. The Stark II/Phase II of CMS have set criteria for exceptions: Professional courtesy is offered to all physicians on the entity's bona fide medical staff or in the local community without regard to the volume or value of referrals or other business generated between the parties.

Health care services provided are typically routinely provided by the entity. The professional courtesy policy is in a written format and meets approval of the governing body of the health care provider.

When professional courtesy is extended due to a financial hardship, the insurer should be informed in writing of any reduction or adjustment so the insurer is aware of the arrangement. It is recommended any co-pays, co-insurance, and deductibles be collected as contracted under the insurance plan.

EXERCISE 13–6

Match the term with its definition, placing the correct letter in the space provided.

_____ 1. bankruptcy

_____ 2. birthday rule

_____ 3. receipt

_____ 4. charge slip/encounter form

_____ 5. posting

_____ 6. transaction

_____ 7. account

_____ 8. accounts receivable

_____ 9. cycle billing

_____ 10. skip

a. the patient's financial record

b. a record of payment received

c. the amount of money owed to a business

d. legal declaration of inability to pay debts

e. accounts grouped to bill at different times throughout the month

f. transferring information from one record to another

g. form providing account information, charges, payments, CPT and ICD-9-CM codes

h. the occurrence of a financial activity to be recorded

i. determination of primary and secondary policy of a child

j. One who avoids paying bills

SUMMARY

Initial patient contact usually starts with a telephone call inquiring about the practice and scheduling the appointment. The initial face-to-face contact starts at the reception window with patient registration for preparation of the patient record. There must be an understanding of the patient registration process for both new and established patients. There must be a working knowledge of insurance regulations, especially those contracts with which the physician participates such as HMOs and federal programs.

Billing procedures, including deductibles, co-payments, and referrals, as well as the actual billing process, must be accurately performed. The collection policy and how to handle various collection problems must be managed by understanding federal and state regulations mandating this process.

Continuing education is required to keep up-to-date and current in changes relative to administrative skills. This is accomplished by attending seminars and reading newsletters, manuals, and bulletins. Today's technology allows patients to communicate and interact with health care providers through e-mail and web sites. Many physicians can answer basic questions or concerns by e-mail. As this communication mode increases, insurance carriers will need to consider a reimbursement format for services rendered using these nontraditional methods.

REFERENCES

Correa, C. (2005) *Getting started in the computerized medical office.* Clifton Park, NY: Thomson Delmar Learning.

Fordney, M., French, L., & Follis, J. (2004). *Administrative medical assisting* (5th ed.). Clifton Park, New York: Thomson Delmar Learning.

Green, M., & Rowell, J. (2006). *Understanding health insurance: A guide to billing and reimbursement* (8th ed.). Clifton Park, NY: Thomson Delmar Learning.

United States Bankruptcy Court. Retrieved August 31, 2005, from www.uscourts.gov/bankruptcycourts.html.

Chapter 14
Filing the Claim Form

LEARNING OBJECTIVES

Upon successful completion of this chapter, you should be able to :

1. Abstract information from the patient medical record to complete the CMS-1500 claim form.
2. Complete the CMS-1500 for commercial and government carriers.
3. Recognize common guidelines to complete the CMS-1500 claim form.
4. Differentiate between a participating (PAR) physician and a nonparticipating physician (nonPAR).
5. Define and explain the two parts of Medicare.
6. Define Medicaid and the regulations mandated for provider participation.
7. Define the regulations mandated for Workers' Compensation coverage.
8. Explain the functions of the health maintenance organization (HMO).
9. Define TRICARE/CHAMPVA.
10. Identify various Blue Cross/Blue Shield policies and their benefits.

INTRODUCTION

Approximately 94 percent of patients seeking health care have some type of insurance coverage. This means completion of a claim form, an intricate part of the billing process, is necessary.

Each insurance program such as Medicare and Medicaid has terms pertinent to its particular program. The terminology that is common to all programs is discussed before each program is introduced.

What is really meant when the question is asked, "What kind of insurance do you have?" In the medical office, we are referring to health insurance. Health insurance is defined as a contract between the insured and an insurance company or government program designed to reimburse a portion of the cost of medically necessary treatment to those who are sick or injured, or preventive services as a means of preventing illness or injury, or to seek early diagnosis and treatment. Medical care and treatment can be rendered in many settings: physician's offices, clinics, hospitals, ambulatory care centers, and nursing homes, just to name a few. More and more medical care today is performed in the outpatient setting as a means of reducing medical costs.

Medical practices today see patients with a variety of health insurance plans:

- Employer sponsored private plans
- Insurance plans
- Health maintenance organizations
- Medicare
- Medicaid
- Individual policies
- TRICARE/CHAMPVA
- Worker's Compensation

Third-party payers involved in the reimbursement proceedings in the medical practice may be insurance companies and employers. A third-party payer is an individual or company that makes a payment on a debt, but is not a party involved in the creation of the debt. In the physician/patient contract, the first party is the patient who is seeking medical care; the second party is the physician or provider of the service or supply.

Due to the variety of health insurance plans, there will be various methods of reimbursement.

- *Fee-for-service* reimbursement is the traditional method of reimbursement. Each service performed has a price that is charged to the patient's account.
- *Capitation* is the reimbursement method used by some HMOs and other managed care plans. This method pays the health care provider a fixed amount per person enrolled for a period of time regardless of whether expenses are incurred or not, rather than by the type or number of services performed.
- *Episode-of-care* reimbursement is a payment method of issuing one lump sum for services rendered to a patient for a specific illness. Global surgical fee payment is an example of this reimbursement method for physicians who perform major surgeries. The global surgical fee payment includes the preoperative visit, the surgery, and the postoperative visit. Any surgical complications are usually paid on a fee-for-service basis.

coordination of benefits
Coordination of payment of services submitted on the claim form when a patient is covered by two or more primary medical insurance policies.

When a policyholder has two or more medical insurance policies, **coordination of benefits** determines the plan of payment. Coordination of benefits (COB) is a ruling in an insurance policy or state law requiring insurance companies to coordinate reimbursement of benefits when a policyholder has two or more medical insurance policies. This is a legal attempt so that the benefits from the combined policies do not exceed 100 percent of the covered benefits of the combined policies for all medical expenses submitted.

EXERCISE 14–1

1. Define health insurance.

2. Name four types of health insurance plans presented to the health care facility.

    1. _____

    2. _____

    3. _____

    4. _____

3. Name four health care settings in which medical treatment can be given.

1. _____

2. _____

3. _____

4. _____

THE HEALTH INSURANCE CLAIM FORM

Claim forms can be submitted to the carrier electronically or on paper. In April 1975 the American Medical Association (AMA) approved a universal claim form called the health insurance claim form or HCFA-1500. This was a standardized form that could be used to submit both group and individual claims for physician services. In 1990, the HCFA-1500 was revised and printed in red so claims could be optically scanned using optical character recognition (OCR) by the insurance carriers. The current form, CMS-1500, is under revision with transition to the new form scheduled for October 2006, with the finalized form mandatory in February 2007.

The National Uniform Claim Committee (NUCC), American Medical Association and Centers for Medicare and Medicaid Services have worked together to revise the 12/90 version of the CMS-1500 form to accommodate the addition of the National Provider Identifier (NPI) number on the claim form and to ensure its function prior to the May 23, 2007 deadline for reporting the NPI.

The NUCC has recommended the following timeline for this transition:

- October 1, 2006: Health plans, clearinghouses, and other information support vendors should be ready to handle and accept the revised 1500 claim form (08/05).
- October 1, 2006–February 1, 2007: Providers can use eigher the current (12/90) version or the revised (08/05) version of the 1500 claim form.
- February 1, 2007: The current (12/90) version of the 1500 claim form is discontinued; only the revised (08/05) form is to be used.

In addition, the UB-92 used in hospitals is being revised to the UB-04 to begin in March 2007.

A test version of the revised (08/05) form can be viewed at www.nucc.org.

This universal claim form is now accepted by Medicare, Medicaid, CHAMPUS, and private companies, although electronic claims submission is preferred to reduce the costs and expedite reimbursement. An example is shown in Figure 14–1.

The following guidelines are recommended in the preparation of claims for OCR:

- Claim forms should be typed. Any handwritten data, with the exception of blocks requiring signatures, will have to be manually processed resulting in a delay in payment of the claim.
- Claim forms must be typed on the original red printed form. Photocopies of claims cannot be optically scanned.
- Proper printer alignment of claim forms is necessary.
- Do not interchange a zero with the alpha character O.
- Use pica type (10 characters per inch) and type all alpha characters in uppercase or capital letters.

Figure 14–1 CMS-1500 Universal Claim Form.

- Leave one blank space between the patient/policyholder's last name, first name, and middle initial.
- Do not use punctuation in the patient/policyholder's name, except for a hyphen in a compound name.
- Do not use titles such as Sr., Jr., unless they appear on the patient's insurance ID card.
- Do not add dollar signs, decimals, or commas in any dollar field.
- Do not add the decimal in the diagnostic code number as it is imprinted on the form.
- List only one procedure per line.
- Do not add a dash in front of a procedure code modifier.
- Do not add parentheses when designating the area code of the telephone number as they are imprinted on the form.
- *Do* use two zeros in the cent column when the fee is listed in whole dollars.
- All dates should be typed using eight-digit dates representing month, day, and year, taking care to remain within the vertical dividers within the block.

    EXAMPLE: 01/01/2008
- Do not type anything in the upper left-hand corner of the claim form as indicated on the form, "Do Not Write In This Space."

The name and address of the insurance company to receive a paper claim can be typed in the upper right-hand corner of the form.

Completing the CMS-1500

The patient information required to complete the top portion of the CMS-1500 is retrieved from the patient's registration form found in the chart. Verify the patient has signed the release of medical information statement either by signing the claim form or a special form unique to the practice and retained in the patient's chart. This special form authorizes the processing of the claim form without the patient's signature on each form submitted. In Block 12 of each claim form filed for that patient, **"signature on file"** must be typed or stamped, as in Figure 14–2.

Figure 14–3 shows an example of a special statement form adopted for use by a particular medical office.

This dated, signed statement to release information is generally considered to be valid for one year from the signature date. However, most offices update medical records yearly, including the statement to release medical information. Undated signed forms are assumed to be valid until revoked by the patient or guardian. CMS allows government programs to accept both dated and undated authorizations.

There are exceptions to the need for a signed authorization for release of information. These exceptions are patients covered by Medicaid and those covered by Workers' Compensation. The federal government has mandated in these programs that the patient is a third-party beneficiary in a contract between the health care provider and the governmental agency that sponsors these programs. When the provider agrees to treat Medicaid patients or a Workers' Compensation

signature on file
A statement typed or stamped on the claim form for authorization purposes, indicating the patient has signed a release of medical information retained in the patient's chart.

READ BACK OF FORM BEFORE COMPLETING & SIGNING THIS FORM.

12. PATIENT'S OR AUTHORIZED PERSON'S SIGNATURE I authorize the release of any medical or other information necessary to process this claim. I also request payment of government benefits either to myself or to the party who accepts assignment below.

SIGNED SIGNATURE ON FILE   DATE

13. INSURED'S OR AUTHORIZED PERSON'S SIGNATURE I authorize payment of medical benefits to the undersigned physician or supplier for services described below.

SIGNED

Figure 14–2 "Signature on File."

Lowery B. Johnson, M.D.
Hwy 311 Suite A31
Sellersburg, IN 47172
812-246-1234

ASSIGNMENT OF BENEFITS

I instruct my insurance company to pay benefits directly to Dr. Lowery Johnson for services rendered and that such payment should be mailed to this physician's office. A photocopy of this assignment shall be as valid as the original.

I also authorize this office to release such medical information as may be required to process my claim with the insurance company.

_____
Signature

_____
Date

Figure 14–3 Special form for authorization and assignment of benefits.

patient, they agree to accept the program's payment as payment in full for covered procedures performed to those patients. The patient can only be billed for services that are not covered, or when the insurance carrier determines the patient was ineligible for benefits on the dates of services reported.

If the patient is physically or mentally unable to sign, the person representing the patient may sign for the patient. This is accomplished by indicating the patient's name on the signature line, followed by the representative's name, address, relationship to the patient, and the reason the patient cannot sign. Medicare and Medigap carriers accept this authorization indefinitely unless the patient or the patient's representative revokes this arrangement.

If the patient is illiterate or physically handicapped and unable to sign the authorization, an "X" can be made on the signature line. A witness must sign his/her name and address next to the "X."

Another exception to the signed authorization is when filing claims for medical services provided by a physician to patients seen at a hospital that are not expected to be seen in that physician's office for follow-up care. These patients are required to sign an authorization for treatment and release of medical information at the hospital before being seen by the health care provider. If the hospital's release form is written to include the release of information from the hospital and the physician's service in treating the patient, claims submitted by the physician's office for his/her charges do not require a separate release of medical information form from the patient. "Signature on file" can be typed or stamped in Block 12. The hospital can provide a copy of the signed authorization if it is needed at a later date for verification purposes.

Block 13 of the CMS-1500 is the assignment of benefits authorization. The patient's signature here allows the insurance company to pay claim benefits directly to the physician or provider rather than to the patient. Obtaining this authorization can also be accomplished by an assignment of benefits to the physician statement as demonstrated in Figure 14–4.

READ BACK OF FORM BEFORE COMPLETING & SIGNING THIS FORM.	13. INSURED'S OR AUTHORIZED PERSON'S SIGNATURE I authorize payment of medical benefits to the undersigned physician or supplier for services described below.
12. PATIENT'S OR AUTHORIZED PERSON'S SIGNATURE I authorize the release of any medical or other information necessary to process this claim. I also request payment of government benefits either to myself or to the party who accepts assignment below.	
SIGNED ___SIGNATURE ON FILE___ DATE ____	SIGNED ___SIGNATURE ON FILE___

Figure 14–4 Payment authorization.

EXERCISE 14–2

1. What is the purpose of obtaining a signature on file form?

2. What are the two exceptions to the need for release of information?

3. What is the recommended procedure to obtain the signature for release of medical information when the patient is treated in the hospital and not expected to be seen for follow-up in the office?

The lower portion of the CMS-1500 contains information abstracted from the patient's medical record.

The following instructions are generally recognized for filing commercial and health maintenance organization (HMO) fee-for-service claims. Some regional carriers may require information in special blocks based on local requirements; typically those blocks are marked "Reserved for Local Use."

Patient and Policy Identification

Block 1 (Figure 14–5)—**Program Destination Boxes**—Place "X" in the box of program for which you are submitting the claim form.

Block 1A—Insured's Identification Number—Enter the insurance identification number as it appears on the policyholder insurance card.

1. MEDICARE MEDICAID CHAMPUS CHAMPVA GROUP HEALTH PLAN FECA BLK LUNG OTHER	1a. INSURED'S I.D. NUMBER (FOR PROGRAM IN ITEM 1)
(Medicare #) (Medicaid #) (Sponsor's SSN) (VA File #) (SSN or ID) (SSN) (ID)	
2. PATIENT'S NAME (Last Name, First Name, Middle Initial)	3. PATIENT'S BIRTH DATE MM DD YY SEX M ☐ F ☐	4. INSURED'S NAME (Last Name, First Name, Middle Initial)

Figure 14–5 CMS-1500 Blocks 1–1A.

Block 2—Patient's Name (Figure 14–6)—Enter the full name, last name first, followed by first name and middle initial, of the patient. Incorrect format of name or nicknames could cause rejection of the claim.

Figure 14–6 CMS-1500 Blocks 2, 3, 4.

Block 3—Patient's Birth Date—Enter birth month, date, and year, using eight-digit dates. Place dates in between parallel lines.

EXAMPLE

01/01/1950

Block 4—Insured's Name—If insured is same as patient, enter "SAME." If different than patient, enter last name first, followed by first name, then middle initial as it appears on the insurance card.

Block 5—Patient's Address (Figure 14–7)—Enter patient's complete mailing address on line 1, city and two-letter initials of state on line 2, zip code, area code, and telephone number on line 3.

Block 6—Patient Relationship to Insured—Place "X" in the appropriate box for patient's relationship to insured.

Block 7—Insured's Address—If the insured's address is the same as the patient's address listed in Block 5, enter the word "SAME." If different, type in the mailing address of the insured.

Block 8—Patient Status—Place "X" in the appropriate boxes pertaining to the patient.

> **Note**
> If the patient is between the ages of nineteen and twenty-three, is dependent on a family policy, and is a full-time student, the claim will not be paid unless the patient proves full-time student status at the time of the medical encounter. Written acknowledgment of the student's status from the school, college, or university should be filed with the first claim of each semester.

Figure 14–7 CMS-1500 Blocks 5, 6, 7, 8.

Block 9—Other Insured's Name (Figure 14–8)—If none, *leave blank.* If there is secondary or supplemental health care coverage, the insured's name of the secondary policy is entered, last name, first name, middle initial. In 9a, enter the policy number or group number of the secondary policy; 9b, date of birth and sex, employer of the insured, if the coverage is an employer-sponsored group policy or an organization/union as identified on the patient's identification card.

Figure 14–8 CMS-1500 Block 9.

Block 10—Is Patient's Condition Related to (Figure 14–9).

Block 10a—Employment (Current or Previous)—In most cases mark "X" in "No" box. "YES" indicates the services reported in Block 24d are related to an on-the-job injury and the previously filed Workers' Compensation claim has been rejected. To file claim with commercial carrier in these circumstances, a copy of the Workers' Compensation Explanation of Benefits and/or letter indicating rejection of the claim must be attached to the commercial claim.

Block 10b—Auto Accident—Mark "X" in the appropriate box. "YES" indicates possible third-party liability. The commercial health insurance claim carrier will return the claim until the issue of third-party liability coverage is settled.

Block 10c—Other Injury—Mark "X" in the appropriate box. "YES" indicates possible third-party liability. If this is not the case, enter one or more E codes in Block 21 in addition to the code(s) for the type of injury to indicate cause of injury and its place of occurrence.

Block 10d—Reserved for Local Use—Leave blank. Many states use this block for medicaid information

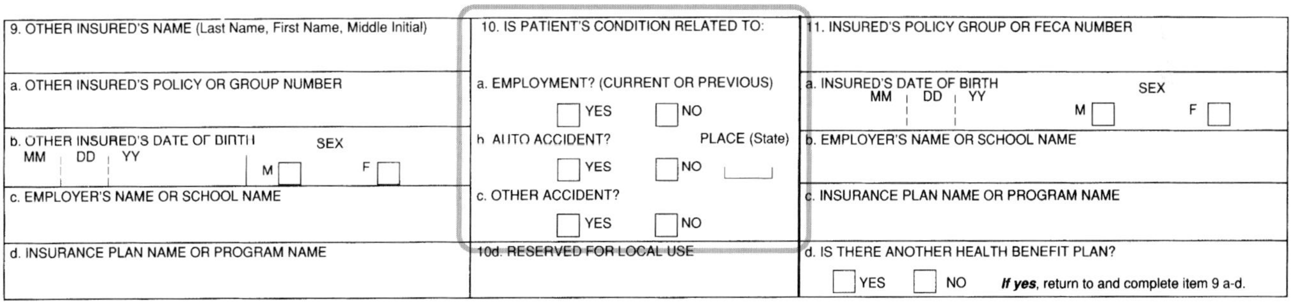

Figure 14–9 CMS-1500 Block 10.

Block 11—Insured's Policy Group or FECA Number (Figure 14–10)—Enter the policy or group number if one is indicated on the card. Not all policies have FECA numbers. FECA (Federal Employees' Compensation Act) provides Workers' Compensation coverage to federal and postal workers, including wage replacement, medical and vocational rehabilitation benefits for work-related injury and occupational illness. For example, coal miners afflicted with black lung disease and the federal workers injured in the 1995 Oklahoma City bombing tragedy are covered under FECA.

Block 11a—Insured's Date of Birth and Sex—Enter the birth date (using the eight-digit date) and sex of the insured, other than patient, named in Block 4.

Block 11b—Employer's Name or School Name—Enter the name of the employer if the coverage is an employer-sponsored group policy or an organization/union/school name, if one is identified on the patient's identification card.

Block 11c—Insurance Plan Name or Program Name—Enter the name of the carrier for the patient's policy.

Block 11d—Is There Another Health Benefit Plan?—Mark "X" in "NO" box if patient is covered by only one insurance. If "YES" is marked, complete Block 9a–d to indicate a secondary policy.

9. OTHER INSURED'S NAME (Last Name, First Name, Middle Initial)	10. IS PATIENT'S CONDITION RELATED TO:	11. INSURED'S POLICY GROUP OR FECA NUMBER
a. OTHER INSURED'S POLICY OR GROUP NUMBER	a. EMPLOYMENT? (CURRENT OR PREVIOUS) ☐ YES ☐ NO	a. INSURED'S DATE OF BIRTH MM DD YY SEX M ☐ F ☐
b. OTHER INSURED'S DATE OF BIRTH MM DD YY SEX M ☐ F ☐	b. AUTO ACCIDENT? PLACE (State) ☐ YES ☐ NO	b. EMPLOYER'S NAME OR SCHOOL NAME
c. EMPLOYER'S NAME OR SCHOOL NAME	c. OTHER ACCIDENT? ☐ YES ☐ NO	c. INSURANCE PLAN NAME OR PROGRAM NAME
d. INSURANCE PLAN NAME OR PROGRAM NAME	10d. RESERVED FOR LOCAL USE	d. IS THERE ANOTHER HEALTH BENEFIT PLAN? ☐ YES ☐ NO **If yes**, return to and complete item 9 a-d.

Figure 14–10 CMS-1500 Block 11.

Block 12—Authorization for Release of Information (Figure 14–11)—Patient's signature is entered here, or "Signature on file" and/or a computer generated signature is entered. This signature authorizes release of medical information necessary to process the claim. It also authorizes payment of benefits to the provider of the service or supplier when the provider or supplier accepts assignment on the claim.

Block 13—Authorization for Payment of Benefits to the Provider—The patient's signature authorizes direct payment to the physician for the benefits due the patient. "Signature on file" is acceptable if an assignment statement has been previously signed and is on file.

READ BACK OF FORM BEFORE COMPLETING & SIGNING THIS FORM. 12. PATIENT'S OR AUTHORIZED PERSON'S SIGNATURE I authorize the release of any medical or other information necessary to process this claim. I also request payment of government benefits either to myself or to the party who accepts assignment below.	13. INSURED'S OR AUTHORIZED PERSON'S SIGNATURE I authorize payment of medical benefits to the undersigned physician or supplier for services described below.
SIGNED _____ DATE _____	SIGNED _____

Figure 14–11 CMS-1500 Blocks 12, 13.

Diagnostic and Treatment Data

Block 14—Date of Illness, First Symptom, Injury, Pregnancy, LMP (last menstrual period) (Figure 14–12)—Enter data from the patient's medical record, if it is available. In cases where the history does not give the first date but does give an approximation, count back to the approximated date and enter it on the claim form.

EXAMPLE

Today's date 1/9/2000, record states, "injured 2 months ago." The date typed would be 11/09/1999.

Block 15—If Patient Has Had Same or Similar Illness, Give First Date—Enter the data if applicable.

Block 16—Dates Patient Unable To Work in Current Occupation—Enter data if applicable.

14. DATE OF CURRENT: MM DD YY ILLNESS (First symptom) OR INJURY (Accident) OR PREGNANCY(LMP)	15. IF PATIENT HAS HAD SAME OR SIMILAR ILLNESS. GIVE FIRST DATE MM DD YY	16. DATES PATIENT UNABLE TO WORK IN CURRENT OCCUPATION MM DD YY MM DD YY FROM TO

Figure 14–12 CMS-1500 Blocks 14, 15, 16.

Block 17—Name of Referring Physician or Other Source (Figure 14–13)—Enter the name of the referring/ordering physician(s) or other health care provider, if any of the following services are listed in Block 24d:

consultation, surgery, diagnostic testing, physical or occupational therapy, home health care, or durable medical equipment

A referring or ordering physician is a physician or nonphysician practitioner who requests an item or service for the beneficiary, such as consultation, surgery, diagnostic testing, physical or occupational therapy, home health care, durable medical equipment, or pharmaceutical services for the patient. For Assistant Surgeon claims, enter the name of the attending surgeon.

Block 17a—ID Number of Referring Physician—Enter the referring or ordering physician's unique provider identification number (UPIN) as assigned by Medicare. If there is no referring provider, leave blank.

The revised (08/05) CMS-1500 form will add block 17b to accommodate the NPI of the referring physician required in 2007.

Block 18—Hospitalization Dates Related to Current Services—Enter the admission date and the discharge date using eight-digit date, if any procedure/service is provided to a patient who is admitted to the hospital as an inpatient.

Block 19—Reserved for Local Use—Information to be entered is determined by regional carriers. Consult appropriate billing manual or the carrier to determine if any information is required for this block. This area is usually reserved for physical or occupational therapists, chiropractor services, or unlisted procedure code or a claim for a drug that is not otherwise classified.

Block 20—Outside Lab—Mark "X" in NO box if all laboratory procedures included on this claim form were performed in the provider's office.

Mark "X" in YES box if laboratory procedures listed on the claim form were performed by an outside laboratory and billed to the referring health care provider. If YES is marked, enter the total amount charged for all tests performed by the outside laboratory. The charge for each test should be entered as a separate line in Block 24f and the name and address of the outside laboratory included in Block 32.

■ *Highlight*

Some local carriers may have other specific instructions for completing Block 20.

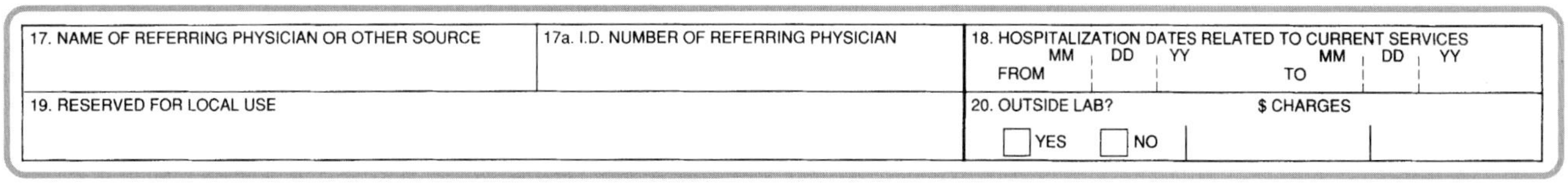

17. NAME OF REFERRING PHYSICIAN OR OTHER SOURCE	17a. I.D. NUMBER OF REFERRING PHYSICIAN	18. HOSPITALIZATION DATES RELATED TO CURRENT SERVICES MM | DD | YY MM | DD | YY FROM TO
19. RESERVED FOR LOCAL USE		20. OUTSIDE LAB? $ CHARGES ☐ YES ☐ NO

Figure 14–13 CMS-1500 Blocks 17, 17a, 18, 19, 20.

Block 21—Diagnosis or Nature of Illness or Injury (Figure 14–14)—Enter the ICD-9-CM code(s) for the diagnosis of conditions treated on this claim in this space. Four codes can be submitted per claim form, listing the primary diagnosis code first, followed by any secondary diagnostic codes. To link the correct ICD-9-CM code with the CPT code in Block 24D, use the indicators 1, 2, 3, or 4 in Block 24E. All diagnoses and procedures must be supported by documentation in the medical record. If the patient's encounter to the medical facility has no formal diagnosis, enter the code for the patient's complaints or symptoms.

The number of indicators in Block 24E can vary per insurance carrier. Many accept only one indicator per service or procedure; others will accept up to four indicators per ICD-9-CM code. Unless there are concurrent conditions related to the encounter, it is recommended to list only one illness or injury, procedure, and treatment per claim.

Block 22—Medicaid Resubmission Code—Leave blank. Used for Medicaid claims only.

Block 23—Prior Authorization Number—Enter the assigned prior authorization number when the patient's insurance plan requires specific services to be authorized by the patient's primary physician or the carrier's managed care department before the procedure is performed. Some carriers may require written authorization to be attached to the claim form.

19. RESERVED FOR LOCAL USE					20. OUTSIDE LAB? $ CHARGES				
					☐ YES ☐ NO				
21. DIAGNOSIS OR NATURE OF ILLNESS OR INJURY. (RELATE ITEMS 1,2,3 OR 4 TO ITEM 24E BY LINE)					22. MEDICAID RESUBMISSION CODE ORIGINAL REF. NO.				
1. └──.──		3. └──.──			23. PRIOR AUTHORIZATION NUMBER				
2. └──.──		4. └──.──							

24. A DATE(S) OF SERVICE From MM DD YY To MM DD YY	B Place of Service	C Type of Service	D PROCEDURES, SERVICES, OR SUPPLIES (Explain Unusual Circumstances) CPT/HCPCS | MODIFIER	E DIAGNOSIS CODE	F $ CHARGES	G DAYS OR UNITS	H EPSDT Family Plan	I EMG	J COB	K RESERVED FOR LOCAL USE

Figure 14–14 CMS-1500 Blocks 21, 22, 23.

Block 24A—Date(s) of Service (Figure 14–15)—Enter the date the procedure was performed in the "FROM" column. Do not fill in the "TO" column for a single procedure entry. To list similar procedures with same procedure codes and charges performed on consecutive dates, indicate the last day the procedure was performed in the "TO" column. In Block 24G, enter the number of consecutive days or units in the "days/units column." Do not submit charges for services or procedures performed in different years on the same claim form. Doing so may result in deductible and eligibility factors that could result in a pending or rejected claim, therefore delaying payment.

Block 24B—Place of Service (POS)—Enter the correct POS code number from the following list of codes.

School	03
Homeless Shelter	04
Indian Health Service Freestanding Facility	05
Indian Health Provider-Based Facility	06
Tribal 638 Freestanding Facility	07
Tribal 638 Provider-Based Facility	08
Provider's Office	11
Patient's Home	12
Assisted Living Facility	13
Group Home	14
Mobile Unit	15
Urgent Care Facility	20
Inpatient Hospital	21
Outpatient Hospital	22
Emergency Room–Hospital	23
Ambulatory Surgical Center	24
Birthing Center	25
Military/Uniformed Services Treatment Facility	26
Skilled Nursing Facility	31
Nursing Facility	32
Custodial Care Facility	33
Hospice	34

Ambulance–Land	41
Ambulance–Air or Water	42
Independent Clinic	49
Federally Qualified Health Center	50
Inpatient Psychiatric Facility	51
Psychiatric Facility–Partial Hospitalization	52
Community Mental Health Center	53
Intermediate Care Facility/Mentally Retarded	54
Residential Substance Abuse Treatment Facility	55
Psychiatric Residential Treatment Center	56
Nonresidential Substance Abuse Treatment Facility	57
Mass Immunization Center	60
Comprehensive Inpatient Rehabilitation Facility	61
Comprehensive Outpatient Rehabilitation Facility	62
End-Stage Renal Disease Treatment Facility	63
Public Health Center	71
Rural Health Center	72
Independent Laboratory	81
Other place of service not identified above	99

CMS has updated this list to accommodate new facilities available to render patient care. The Centers for Medicare and Medicaid Services' web site posinfo@cms.hhs.gov gives a description for each place of service code. Any codes not listed are classified as "unassigned" codes reserved for future use.

Block 24C—Type of Service Codes (TOS)—Enter the correct TOS code from the following list of codes. NOTE: Not all carriers use TOS codes.

Medical Care	1
Surgery	2
Consultation	3
Diagnostic X-ray	4
Diagnostic Laboratory	5
Radiation Therapy	6
Anesthesia	7
Assistant Surgeon	8
Other medical services	9
Pneumococcal Vaccine	V
Second surgical opinion	Y

Block 24D—Procedures, Services, or Supply Codes—Enter the correct five-digit CPT code or HCPCS Level II/III code number and any required modifiers for the procedure being reported in this block. No more than six procedures/services can be listed per claim.

Block 24E—Diagnosis Code—Enter the reference number (1 through 4) for the ICD-9-CM code listed in Block 21 that most closely justifies the medical necessity for each procedure listed in Block 24d.

■ *Highlight*

Some carriers will accept more than one reference number on each line. If more than one reference number is used, the first number stated must represent the primary diagnosis that justifies the medical necessity for performing the procedures on that line. Do not use commas, dashes, or slashes to separate multiple reference numbers.

Block 24F—Charges—Enter the fee for the procedure charged to the patient's account. If identical, consecutive procedures are reported on this line, enter the TOTAL fee charged for the combined procedures.

Block 24G—Days or Units—Enter the number of days/units or services reported on each line. This block is most commonly used for multiple visits, units of supplies, anesthesia minutes, or oxygen volume. If only one service is performed, the number 1 must be entered.

Block 24H—EPSDT (Early and Periodic Screening for Diagnosis and Treatment)—Leave blank. This block is used for identifying all services that are provided under the special Medicaid EPSDT program.

Block 24I—EMG (Emergency Treatment)—Check this box when the health care provider determines that a medical emergency existed and a delay in treatment would be injurious to the patient. This is especially important in a managed care situation and no prior authorization was obtained before the start of emergency treatment.

The NPI will be entered in this block on the revised (08/05) CMS-1500 form effective 2007.

Block 24J—COB (Coordination of Benefits)—Leave blank.

Block 24K—Reserved for Local Use—Some areas may require the physician performing or providing a service to enter a PIN/NPI here for each line of service. If required, this number is typically the physician's state license number.

Figure 14–15 CMS-1500 Blocks 24.

Provider/Billing Entity Identification

Block 25—Federal Tax ID Number (Figure 14–16)—Every physician, whether in a solo practice or group practice, is issued an individual federal tax identification number referred to as an employer identification number (EIN). This number is issued by the Internal Revenue Service for income tax purposes. Every physician also has a social security number (SSN) for personal use. A physician in a solo practice may be issued a tax identification number (TIN) which is their social security number. Enter the appropriate number and check the appropriate box. Enter the provider's Employer Tax Identification Number (EIN) and check the appropriate box.

Block 26—Patient Account Number—If a numerical identification is assigned to identify the patient's account or ledger card, enter that number here. Leave blank if the practice files patient accounts by patient name rather than number.

Block 27—Accept Assignment—Mark "X" when appropriate for Medicare claims. Participating physicians MUST accept assignment. Nonparticipating physicians may accept on a case-by-case basis. Assignment must be accepted for Medicare/Medicaid patients. Accepting assignment means the physician or provider will accept what Medicare pays and not bill the difference between the cost of the service and the Medicare payment. The difference is adjusted or written off.

The following providers or suppliers must file claims accepting assignment:

- Clinical diagnostic laboratory services
- Physician services to Medicare/Medicaid beneficiaries
- Participating physician/supplier services
- Services of physician assistants, nurse practitioners, clinical nurse specialists, nurse midwives, certified registered nurse anesthetists, clinical psychologists, and clinical social workers
- Ambulatory surgical center services for covered procedures
- Home dialysis supplies and equipment
- Ambulance services

Block 28—Total Charge—Add up all charges on this claim form and enter the total in this block. If multiple claims for one patient are completed because there are more than six services/procedures reported, the total charge recorded on each claim form must represent the total of the items on each separate claim form submitted.

Block 29—Amount Paid—Enter the amount the patient has paid toward the required annual deductible, or any co-payments collected from the patient for the procedures listed on this claim form.

Block 30—Balance Due—Enter the amount subtracted from the figure in Block 29 from the figure in Block 28.

Figure 14–16 CMS-1500 Blocks 25, 26, 27, 28, 29, 30.

Block 31—Signature of Physician or Supplier (Figure 14–17)—If arrangements have not been made with major health insurance carriers to permit either a signature stamp or a typed name and professional title, the provider must sign each claim. When transmitting claims electronically to an insurance company, a certification letter must be filed with the insurance company to replace the signature usually required in this space.

Block 32—Name and Address of Facility Where Services Rendered—Complete when the services listed on the claim form were performed at a site other than the patient's home.

If the "YES" box in Block 20 is checked, enter the name and address of the laboratory that performed the laboratory procedures.

When filing durable medical equipment, orthotic, and prosthetic claims, enter the name, address, or location where the order was placed.

When billing for purchased diagnostic tests performed outside the physician's office but billed by the physician, enter the facility's name, address, and CMS-assigned NPI where the test was performed.

Block 33—Physician's Supplier's Billing Name, Mailing Address, Phone Number, Provider's Identification Number (PIN), and Group Number (GRP)—Type in the official name of the practice/clinic and the full mailing address on the next three lines. Do not put the zip code in the last line of this block where the words "PIN# GRP#" appear. The phone number, including the area code, are typed to the right of the phrase "& PHONE #." It may overlap into the above printing. Enter any carrier-assigned participating identification number (PIN) and/or group practice identification number (GRP) in the appropriate space. Providers who charge Medicare patients a fee for durable medical equipment (DME) must list a DME number in this block.

The revised (08/05) CMS-1500 will add a field in blocks 32 and 33 to enter the NPI.

25. FEDERAL TAX I.D. NUMBER SSN EIN	26. PATIENT'S ACCOUNT NO.	27. ACCEPT ASSIGNMENT? (For govt. claims, see back) YES NO	28. TOTAL CHARGE $	29. AMOUNT PAID $	30. BALANCE DUE $
31. SIGNATURE OF PHYSICIAN OR SUPPLIER INCLUDING DEGREES OR CREDENTIALS (I certify that the statements on the reverse apply to this bill and are made a part thereof.) SIGNED DATE	32. NAME AND ADDRESS OF FACILITY WHERE SERVICES WERE RENDERED (If other than home or office)		33. PHYSICIAN'S, SUPPLIER'S BILLING NAME, ADDRESS, ZIP CODE & PHONE # PIN# GRP#		

Figure 14-17 CMS-1500 Blocks 31, 32, 33.

 **Highlight**

When filing insurance claims for a medical practice, it is critical to obtain and read updated billing manuals, newsletters and brochures that contain changes, as they become effective.

Figure 14–18 is an example of a completed CMS-1500 form.

Common Errors That Delay Claims Processing

After checking the claim form for errors, retain a copy of the claim for office files, post the date of the claim filing on the patient's account/ledger, and mail to the insurance carrier. Some common errors that delay processing of the claim, or result in rejection of the claim are:

- Incorrect patient insurance identification number
- Incorrect CPT code with failure to use modifier when valid
- Incorrect ICD-9-CM code with failure to use fourth or fifth digits when required
- ICD-9-CM code does not correspond with CPT code as a service performed or treatment provided by the physician to validate procedure was medically necessary
- Failure to identify referring physician and the identification number
- Incorrect charges and total amounts that do not equal total charges
- Missing place-of-service code required for Medicare, Medicaid, and CHAMPVA and TRICARE, and most commercial carriers

PLEASE
DO NOT
STAPLE
IN THIS
AREA

PICA		**HEALTH INSURANCE CLAIM FORM**	PICA

1. MEDICARE (Medicare #) **MEDICAID** (Medicaid #) **CHAMPUS** (Sponsor's SSN) **CHAMPVA** (VA File #) **GROUP HEALTH PLAN** (SSN or ID) [X] **FECA BLK LUNG** (SSN) **OTHER** (ID) | **1a. INSURED'S I.D. NUMBER** (FOR PROGRAM IN ITEM 1)
403082214

2. PATIENT'S NAME (Last Name, First Name, Middle Initial)
PEARL OPAL J

3. PATIENT'S BIRTH DATE MM DD YY 12 24 1968 **SEX** M [ ] F [X]

4. INSURED'S NAME (Last Name, First Name, Middle Initial)
PEARL BRUCE J

5. PATIENT'S ADDRESS (No., Street)
7775 SMITH RD

6. PATIENT RELATIONSHIP TO INSURED
Self [ ] Spouse [X] Child [ ] Other [ ]

7. INSURED'S ADDRESS (No., Street)
SAME

CITY SMITHFIELD **STATE** IN

8. PATIENT STATUS
Single [ ] Married [X] Other [ ]
Employed [ ] Full-Time Student [ ] Part-Time Student [ ]

CITY **STATE**

ZIP CODE 47222 **TELEPHONE (Include Area Code)** (513) 222-4773

ZIP CODE **TELEPHONE (INCLUDE AREA CODE)** ( )

9. OTHER INSURED'S NAME (Last Name, First Name, Middle Initial)

10. IS PATIENT'S CONDITION RELATED TO:

11. INSURED'S POLICY GROUP OR FECA NUMBER
EPN500

a. OTHER INSURED'S POLICY OR GROUP NUMBER

a. EMPLOYMENT? (CURRENT OR PREVIOUS) [ ] YES [X] NO

a. INSURED'S DATE OF BIRTH MM DD YY 07 07 1967 **SEX** M [X] F [ ]

b. OTHER INSURED'S DATE OF BIRTH MM DD YY **SEX** M [ ] F [ ]

b. AUTO ACCIDENT? [ ] YES [X] NO **PLACE (State)**

b. EMPLOYER'S NAME OR SCHOOL NAME
SMITHFIELD ELECTRICAL CO

c. EMPLOYER'S NAME OR SCHOOL NAME

c. OTHER ACCIDENT? [ ] YES [X] NO

c. INSURANCE PLAN NAME OR PROGRAM NAME
CIGNA

d. INSURANCE PLAN NAME OR PROGRAM NAME

10d. RESERVED FOR LOCAL USE

d. IS THERE ANOTHER HEALTH BENEFIT PLAN?
[ ] YES [ ] NO *If yes*, return to and complete item 9 a-d.

READ BACK OF FORM BEFORE COMPLETING & SIGNING THIS FORM.
12. PATIENT'S OR AUTHORIZED PERSON'S SIGNATURE I authorize the release of any medical or other information necessary to process this claim. I also request payment of government benefits either to myself or to the party who accepts assignment below.

SIGNED SIGNATURE ON FILE DATE

13. INSURED'S OR AUTHORIZED PERSON'S SIGNATURE I authorize payment of medical benefits to the undersigned physician or supplier for services described below.

SIGNED

14. DATE OF CURRENT: MM DD YY 05 01 20XX ILLNESS (First symptom) OR INJURY (Accident) OR PREGNANCY(LMP)

15. IF PATIENT HAS HAD SAME OR SIMILAR ILLNESS. GIVE FIRST DATE MM DD YY

16. DATES PATIENT UNABLE TO WORK IN CURRENT OCCUPATION MM DD YY FROM TO

17. NAME OF REFERRING PHYSICIAN OR OTHER SOURCE

17a. I.D. NUMBER OF REFERRING PHYSICIAN

18. HOSPITALIZATION DATES RELATED TO CURRENT SERVICES MM DD YY FROM TO

19. RESERVED FOR LOCAL USE

20. OUTSIDE LAB? [ ] YES [ ] NO **$ CHARGES**

21. DIAGNOSIS OR NATURE OF ILLNESS OR INJURY. (RELATE ITEMS 1,2,3 OR 4 TO ITEM 24E BY LINE)
1. 599.0
2.
3.
4.

22. MEDICAID RESUBMISSION CODE **ORIGINAL REF. NO.**

23. PRIOR AUTHORIZATION NUMBER

24. A DATE(S) OF SERVICE From MM DD YY — To MM DD YY	B Place of Service	C Type of Service	D PROCEDURES, SERVICES, OR SUPPLIES (Explain Unusual Circumstances) CPT/HCPCS | MODIFIER	E DIAGNOSIS CODE	F $ CHARGES	G DAYS OR UNITS	H EPSDT Family Plan	I EMG	J COB	K RESERVED FOR LOCAL USE
05 01 20xx	11		90213	1	46 00	1				
05 01 20xx	11		81000	1	18 00	1				

25. FEDERAL TAX I.D. NUMBER 75-2166173 SSN [ ] EIN [X]

26. PATIENT'S ACCOUNT NO.

27. ACCEPT ASSIGNMENT? (For govt. claims, see back) [ ] YES [ ] NO

28. TOTAL CHARGE $ 64 00

29. AMOUNT PAID $ 10 00

30. BALANCE DUE $ 54 00

31. SIGNATURE OF PHYSICIAN OR SUPPLIER INCLUDING DEGREES OR CREDENTIALS (I certify that the statements on the reverse apply to this bill and are made a part thereof.)

SIGNED *Lowery Johnson MD* DATE 5/1/20XX

32. NAME AND ADDRESS OF FACILITY WHERE SERVICES WERE RENDERED (If other than home or office)
LOWERY JOHNSON MD
HWY 311 SUITE A31
SELLERSBURG IN 47172

33. PHYSICIAN'S, SUPPLIER'S BILLING NAME, ADDRESS, ZIP CODE & PHONE #
LOWERY JOHNSON MD
HWY 311 SUITE A31
SELLERSBURG IN 47172
PIN# 1948 GRP# (822) 752-9118

(APPROVED BY AMA COUNCIL ON MEDICAL SERVICE 8/88) *PLEASE PRINT OR TYPE* FORM HCFA-1500 (U2) (12-90) FORM OWCP-1500 FORM RRB-1500

Figure 14–18 CMS-1500 completed for a commercial insurance carrier.

- Missing type-of-service code required for CHAMPVA and TRICARE and some commercial carriers
- Incorrect, missing, or duplicate dates of service
- Incomplete provider information such as name, address, identification numbers

When the insurance company receives the insurance claim form, the computer first scans the claim form for patient and policy identification to match with subscriber name. CPT codes are checked with services determined as covered procedures contained in the policy. CPT codes are cross-matched with ICD-9-CM codes to certify the medical necessity of the claim. A **preexisting condition** clause may be checked in the policy. This is a medical condition under active treatment at the time application is made for an insurance policy. This could result in the disease or condition to be listed as an uncovered service not reimbursable in an insurance policy.

Claims can be classified as to their status for submission to an insurance carrier as clean, dirty, pending, rejected, or incomplete. A clean claim indicates the claim form contains all information necessary for processing, patient information is complete and current, and the claim is submitted in a timely fashion. A clean claim has no deficiencies, has not been folded or stapled, and passes all electronic requirements for submission.

Another term used to identify the status of a claim is a dirty claim. This is a claim that is submitted with errors and requires manual processing. Many of these claims result in payment rejection.

A claim that is pending means it is being reviewed, or additional information is required.

A rejected claim is one that has questions and needs additional information, requiring resubmission of the claim by the provider.

An incomplete claim is one with missing information and requires correction and resubmission by the provider.

Software is now available to assist in the coding and billing process. Claim scrubber software reviews the claim for errors in the claim format as well as coding problems or inconsistencies. Encoder software is primarily used to assign appropriate codes for services and procedures, but it also aids in eliminating bundled services and recognizing appropriate modifiers and CPT/ICD-9-CM agreement for services. Many billing software packages contain a prebilling process that reviews claims electronically or by paper before submission to allow for immediate correction and resubmission.

The common data file is checked to determine if the patient is receiving concurrent care for the same condition by more than one physician.

Charges submitted on the claim form are verified with the allowed charges of the policy. Determination is made of the patient's annual deductible obligation. The **deductible** is the total amount the patient must pay for covered services before insurance benefits are payable. Co-payment requirement is then determined. **Co-payment** is a specified dollar amount the patient must pay the provider for each visit or service. **Coinsurance** is a specified percentage of the insurance-determined allowed fee, for each service the patient must pay the health care provider.

The **explanation of benefits (EOB)** is a summary explaining how the insurance company determines its reimbursement, containing the following information:

- A list of all procedures and charges submitted on the claim form
- A list of procedures submitted on the claim form but not covered by the policy
- A list of all allowed charges for each covered procedure
- The amount of the deductible, if any, subtracted from the total allowed charges

preexisting condition
A medical condition under active treatment at the time application is made for an insurance policy, possibly resulting in an exclusion of that disease or illness.

deductible
A specified amount of covered medical expense that must be paid by the insured to a health care provider before benefits will be reimbursed by the insurance company.

co-payment
A specified dollar amount a patient or policyholder must pay to the health care provider for each medical service or procedure received, as determined in the insurance contract.

coinsurance
A specified amount of insurance determined for each service the patient must pay the health care provider.

explanation of benefits (EOB)
A summary explaining an insurance company's determination for reimbursements of benefits; for Medicare claims, this is referred to as a remittance advice (RA).

- The patient's financial responsibility for the claim, such as the co-payment
- The total amount payable on this claim by the insurance company
- Direct payment means the physician receives the insurance check and the EOB
  Direct payment occurs when:
  1. The physician participates with an insurance carrier in a contract agreement.
  2. The patient signs Block 13 on the CMS-1500 authorization of benefits statement to pay benefits directly to the physician.
  3. Box 27 on the CMS-1500 is marked "Yes" to accept assignment.

An example of carrier's EOB is shown in Figure 14–19.

HEALTH CARE CLAIM SUMMARY

This summary shows claims processed for the insured of   SANDRA L JOHNSON   ID NUMBER   406–7
Any payments shown were made during the period of   JUN 01, 20XX   through   JUN 08, 20XX

TOTAL CHARGES PROCESSED	$400.00

TOTAL PAID TO YOU	$.00		TOTAL PAID TO PROVIDER	$360.00

TOTAL AMOUNT NOT PAID	$40.00

This amount is the sum of the LESS DEDUCTIBLE column plus the AMOUNT NOT PAID column

PLEASE REFER TO THE CODES IN THE EXPL COLUMN AND THEIR EXPLANATIONS.

CLAIM NUMBER	PATIENT	PROVIDER (PROV)	TYPE OF SERVICE	SERVICE DATES FROM	TO	TOTAL CHARGES	BASIC PAYS YOU OR PROVIDER	ELIGIBLE CHARGES	MAJOR MEDICAL LESS DEDUCT-IBLE	PAYS YOU OR PROVIDER	AMOUNT NOT PAID
8138064538	SANDRA	GINGER Q MAGUIRE	ANESTHESIA	040398	040398	400.00		400.00		360.00PROV	40.00
						400.00	.00PROV	400.00	.00	360.00PROV	40.00

IF YOUR BENEFIT SUMMARY INCLUDES CHARGES YOU DON'T RECOGNIZE, IT COULD BE THE RESULT OF A MISHANDLED OR FRAUDULENT CLAIM. PLEASE NOTIFY YOUR CUSTOMER SERVICE REPRESENTATIVE.

EXPLANATION:
872 THIS AMOUNT IS THE COINSURANCE (SHARE) THAT IS YOUR RESPONSIBILITY UNDER YOUR POLICY

THIS IS NOT A BILL

FOR CUSTOMER ASSISTANCE CALL TOLL FREE 1-800-553-2084
SEND WRITTEN INQUIRIES TO: ANTHEM INSURANCE COMPANIES, INC, PO BOX 590, GREENWOOD IN 46142-0590

DEAR INSURED: This summary of claims received on behalf of you and any other persons covered under your policy. We are providing it to you to help you better understand how your coverage is working to protect you.

CONTACT US AT THE PHONE OR ADDRESS SHOWN ABOVE:
IF YOU HAVE MOVED; we will correct your address.
IF YOUR IDENTIFICATION CARD HAS BEEN LOST OR STOLEN; we will replace it.
IF YOU HAVE ANY QUESTIONS ABOUT THIS CLAIM SUMMARY OR YOUR COVERAGE; we will be glad to answer them.

ADDITIONAL REMINDERS:
· WE CANNOT RETURN ANY PAPERS YOU SEND US. If you need to send us this summary or any other papers, please make photocopies beforehand. You may need them for income tax purposes.
· YOU HAVE THE RIGHT TO APPEAL ANY CLAIM WE DON'T PAY OR PAY ONLY IN PART. Mail us a request to review your claim within sixty (60) days of the date you received this summary.

Figure 14–19 One carrier's Explanation of Benefits.

EXERCISE 14–3

Match the term with its definition, placing the letter of the correct answer in the space provided.

_____ **1.** Explanation of benefits

_____ **2.** Preexisting condition

_____ **3.** Deductible

_____ **4.** Co-payment

_____ **5.** Coinsurance

a. A specified dollar amount the patient must pay the provider for each visit or service

b. A summary outlining the insurance company's determination of reimbursement

c. A medical condition under active treatment at the time application is made for an insurance policy

d. The total amount the patient must pay for covered services before insurance benefits are payable

e. A specific percentage of the insurance-determined allowed fee for each service the patient must pay the health care provider

MEDICAID

Medicaid
A jointly sponsored federal and state government medical assistance program to provide medical care for persons with incomes below the national poverty level.

In 1965, Congress passed Title 19 of the Social Security Act establishing a jointly sponsored federal and state government medical assistance program to provide medical care for persons with incomes below the national poverty level. This assistance program is known as **Medicaid.** Individual states may have local names for their program, such as Medi-Cal in California. Coverage and benefits vary greatly from state to state since each state mandates its own program following federal guidelines. The current qualifications for Medicaid eligibility are as follows:

• Medically indigent low-income individuals and families
• Aged and disabled persons covered by Supplemental Security Income (SSI) and Qualified Medicare Beneficiaries (QMBs)
• Persons covered by Aid to Families with Dependent Children (AFDC) funds. AFDC covers:
  1. Children and qualified family members who meet specific income eligibility requirements
  2. Pregnant women who meet the income requirements and would qualify if their babies were already born
• Other pregnant women not covered by AFDC
• Persons receiving institutional or other long-term care in nursing and intermediate care facilities

Other programs and benefits sponsored by Medicaid are as follows:

• Early and Periodic Screening, Diagnostic, and Treatment (EPSDT) provides preventive services such as physical examinations, immunizations, dental, vision, and hearing examinations to children under the age of twenty-one years.

- Maternal and Child Health Programs (MCHPs) is a state and federal program for children under the age of twenty-one years that have special health care needs. Some of these conditions are cerebral palsy, cystic fibrosis, mental retardation, epilepsy, and rheumatic and congenital heart disease. MCHP assists families in providing access to health assessments and preventive and primary care services. Assistance is also available for prenatal, delivery, and postpartum care for at-risk pregnant women who cannot afford this care.

- Medicaid also works with Medicare to provide beneficiaries with low income and qualify for financial assistance. One of these programs is the Medicaid Qualified Medicare Beneficiary (QMB). These recipients must be aged, disabled, qualify for Medicare benefits, have limited financial resources, and have incomes below the federal poverty level.

- Some states now have managed care plans in their Medicaid program. This works much the same way as other managed care plans as the patient will have a primary care physician and must utilize physicians, clinics, and hospitals that participate in their plan.

Many of these plans have a co-payment requirement or a share of the cost paid each month for Medicaid eligibility. In some states this is referred to as spend down or liability.

The patient must present a valid Medicaid identification card on each visit. Eligibility should be confirmed for each visit, since eligibility could fluctuate from month to month. Failure to check eligibility could result in a denial of payment.

■ *Highlight*

Medicaid is the payer of last resort. If there is other medical coverage or liability, this must be billed first.

Any provider who accepts a Medicaid patient must accept the Medicaid-determined payment as payment in full. It is against the law for a provider to bill a Medicaid patient for Medicaid-covered services. Some states require providers to sign formal Medicaid participation contracts; other states do not require contracts. However, because most Medicaid patients have income below the poverty level, collection of fees for uncovered services is difficult.

CMS-1500 is the claim form used in most states to submit a provider's fees. Some states do use a state-developed special optical scanning form. The local Medicaid office can supply this information if there is uncertainty about what claim form to use.

The following instructions are for filing Medicaid claims using the CMS-1500 form only.

Block 1	Check Medicaid.
Block 1a	Enter patient's Medicaid ID number.
Block 2	Enter patient's name (last name, first name, middle initial).
Block 3	Patient's date of birth (entering eight-digit dates).
Block 4	Enter "same" or leave blank.
Block 5	Enter patient's address.
Block 6	Check "self."
Block 7	Enter "same" or leave blank.
Block 8	Check appropriate marital status.
Block 9–9d	Leave blank.
Block 10–10d	Leave blank. 10d is regionally determined. In some states, the share of cost (SOC) is indicated in this block by entering SOC and the dollar amount paid.

Block 11a–d	Leave blank.
Block 12	Patient's signature is not required on Medicaid claims.
Block 13–16	Leave blank.
Block 17	Enter the complete name and degree of referring, requesting, ordering or prescribing provider, if appropriate.
Block 17a	Enter the Medicaid ID number of the provider.
Block 18	Enter dates, if appropriate.
Block 19	Enter the Medicaid provider number of the practice rendering the service.
Block 20	Check "No" box. A Medicaid provider cannot bill for services performed by another provider.
Block 21	Enter ICD-9-CM code(s).
Block 22	Leave blank.
Block 23	Enter the prior authorization number if applicable. If written authorization was obtained, attach a copy to the claim.
Block 24a	Enter the date service was rendered using eight-digit dates.
Block 24b	Enter the appropriate CMS Place of Service (POS) code listed.
Block 24c	Enter the appropriate Type of Service (TOS) code listed below, if applicable.
Block 24d	Enter CPT code(s) and modifiers as appropriate.
Block 24e	Enter the diagnosis reference number from Block 21 that best proves the medical necessity for this service on this line.
Block 24f	Enter charge for service rendered.
Block 24g	Enter the number of units for service reported on this line.
Block 24h	Enter "E" if the service is rendered under the Early and Periodic Screening, Diagnosis, and Treatment program. Enter "F" if the service is for Family Planning. Otherwise, leave blank.
Block 24i	Enter "X" if the service was for a medical emergency and performed in an Emergency Room.
Block 24j	Leave blank.
Block 24K	Leave blank. Use if regionally determined.
Block 25	Enter provider's Federal Tax Employment Number. Check the "EIN" box.
Block 26	If applicable, enter the patient account number. This number will then be listed on the EOB, making it easier to identify when files are indexed numerically rather than alphabetically.
Block 27	Check "Yes" box. Providers treating Medicaid patients *must* accept assignment.
Block 28	Enter total charges.
Block 29	Leave blank.
Block 30	Enter total charges.
Block 31	The provider's signature or signature stamp is used.
Block 32	Enter the name, address, and Medicaid provider number of the facility where services were rendered, *if other than the provider's office or patient's home.*
Block 33	Enter the provider's billing name, address, and phone number. Next to "PIN" enter the Medicaid provider number.

Figure 14–20 is an example of a completed CMS-1500 for a Medicaid patient.

PLEASE DO NOT STAPLE IN THIS AREA

HEALTH INSURANCE CLAIM FORM

CARRIER

PICA | | | | PICA

1. MEDICARE (Medicare #) | **MEDICAID** [X] (Medicaid #) | **CHAMPUS** (Sponsor's SSN) | **CHAMPVA** (VA File #) | **GROUP HEALTH PLAN** (SSN or ID) | **FECA BLK LUNG** (SSN) | **OTHER** (ID) | **1a. INSURED'S I.D. NUMBER** (FOR PROGRAM IN ITEM 1)
257885301

2. PATIENT'S NAME (Last Name, First Name, Middle Initial)
JONES BONNIE L

3. PATIENT'S BIRTH DATE MM DD YY
10 10 1990 M [ ] **SEX** F [X]

4. INSURED'S NAME (Last Name, First Name, Middle Initial)
SAME

5. PATIENT'S ADDRESS (No., Street)
7611 MORTON ST

6. PATIENT RELATIONSHIP TO INSURED
Self [X] Spouse [ ] Child [ ] Other [ ]

7. INSURED'S ADDRESS (No., Street)
SAME

CITY TEMPLE **STATE** IN

8. PATIENT STATUS
Single [X] Married [ ] Other [ ]

CITY **STATE**

ZIP CODE 47555 **TELEPHONE (Include Area Code)** (822) 361-5678

Employed [ ] Full-Time Student [ ] Part-Time Student [ ]

ZIP CODE **TELEPHONE (INCLUDE AREA CODE)** ( )

9. OTHER INSURED'S NAME (Last Name, First Name, Middle Initial)

10. IS PATIENT'S CONDITION RELATED TO:

11. INSURED'S POLICY GROUP OR FECA NUMBER

a. OTHER INSURED'S POLICY OR GROUP NUMBER

a. EMPLOYMENT? (CURRENT OR PREVIOUS)
[ ] YES [ ] NO

a. INSURED'S DATE OF BIRTH MM DD YY **SEX** M [ ] F [ ]

b. OTHER INSURED'S DATE OF BIRTH MM DD YY **SEX** M [ ] F [ ]

b. AUTO ACCIDENT? PLACE (State)
[ ] YES [ ] NO

b. EMPLOYER'S NAME OR SCHOOL NAME

c. EMPLOYER'S NAME OR SCHOOL NAME

c. OTHER ACCIDENT?
[ ] YES [ ] NO

c. INSURANCE PLAN NAME OR PROGRAM NAME
MEDICAID

d. INSURANCE PLAN NAME OR PROGRAM NAME

10d. RESERVED FOR LOCAL USE

d. IS THERE ANOTHER HEALTH BENEFIT PLAN?
[ ] YES [X] NO *If yes,* return to and complete item 9 a-d.

READ BACK OF FORM BEFORE COMPLETING & SIGNING THIS FORM.
12. PATIENT'S OR AUTHORIZED PERSON'S SIGNATURE I authorize the release of any medical or other information necessary to process this claim. I also request payment of government benefits either to myself or to the party who accepts assignment below.

SIGNED _____ DATE _____

13. INSURED'S OR AUTHORIZED PERSON'S SIGNATURE I authorize payment of medical benefits to the undersigned physician or supplier for services described below.

SIGNED _____

14. DATE OF CURRENT: MM DD YY
06 25 20XX
ILLNESS (First symptom) OR INJURY (Accident) OR PREGNANCY(LMP)

15. IF PATIENT HAS HAD SAME OR SIMILAR ILLNESS. GIVE FIRST DATE MM DD YY

16. DATES PATIENT UNABLE TO WORK IN CURRENT OCCUPATION MM DD YY
FROM ___ TO ___

17. NAME OF REFERRING PHYSICIAN OR OTHER SOURCE

17a. I.D. NUMBER OF REFERRING PHYSICIAN

18. HOSPITALIZATION DATES RELATED TO CURRENT SERVICES MM DD YY
FROM ___ TO ___

19. RESERVED FOR LOCAL USE

20. OUTSIDE LAB? $ CHARGES
[ ] YES [ ] NO

21. DIAGNOSIS OR NATURE OF ILLNESS OR INJURY. (RELATE ITEMS 1,2,3 OR 4 TO ITEM 24E BY LINE)
1. 782.1
2. ___
3. ___
4. ___

22. MEDICAID RESUBMISSION CODE ORIGINAL REF. NO.

23. PRIOR AUTHORIZATION NUMBER

24. A DATE(S) OF SERVICE From MM DD YY	To MM DD YY	B Place of Service	C Type of Service	D PROCEDURES, SERVICES, OR SUPPLIES (Explain Unusual Circumstances) CPT/HCPCS MODIFIER	E DIAGNOSIS CODE	F $ CHARGES	G DAYS OR UNITS	H EPSDT Family Plan	I EMG	J COB	K RESERVED FOR LOCAL USE
06 25 20XX		11		90212	1	46 00	1				

25. FEDERAL TAX I.D. NUMBER SSN EIN
75-2166173 [ ] [X]

26. PATIENT'S ACCOUNT NO.

27. ACCEPT ASSIGNMENT? (For govt. claims, see back)
[X] YES [ ] NO

28. TOTAL CHARGE $ 46 00

29. AMOUNT PAID $

30. BALANCE DUE $ 46 00

31. SIGNATURE OF PHYSICIAN OR SUPPLIER INCLUDING DEGREES OR CREDENTIALS (I certify that the statements on the reverse apply to this bill and are made a part thereof.)
SIGNED *Lowery Johnson MD* DATE 6/25/20XX

32. NAME AND ADDRESS OF FACILITY WHERE SERVICES WERE RENDERED (If other than home or office)
LOWERY JOHNSON MD
HWY 311 SUITE A31
SELLERSBURG IN 47172

33. PHYSICIAN'S, SUPPLIER'S BILLING NAME, ADDRESS, ZIP CODE & PHONE #
LOWERY JOHNSON MD
HWY 311 SUITE A31
SELLERSBURG IN 47172
PIN# 1948 GRP# (822) 752-9118

(APPROVED BY AMA COUNCIL ON MEDICAL SERVICE 8/88)

PLEASE PRINT OR TYPE

FORM HCFA-1500 (U2) (12-90)
FORM OWCP-1500 FORM RRB-1500

Figure 14–20 Completed CMS-1500 for Medicaid.

crossover claim
An electronic transfer of information submitted on a Medicare claim to Medicaid or the patient's Medigap carrier.

The deadline for submitting Medicaid claims varies from state to state. Claims should be filed as soon as possible. With Medicare/Medicaid crossover claims, the deadline follows Medicare Guidelines of December 31 of the year following the date of service. A **crossover claim** occurs when the Medicare carrier will electronically transfer the information submitted on the Medicare claim form to Medicaid or Medigap carrier. Medicare will also process the patient's Medicare deductible and coinsurance responsibilities and any information regarding a noncovered service or procedure by Medicare.

MEDICARE

Medicare
A federal health insurance program for persons over 65 years of age, retired, on social security benefits, receiving social security disability benefits, or end-stage renal disease coverage.

Medicare is a federal health insurance program authorized by Congress and managed by CMS. Created in 1965 as Title 18 of the Social Security Act, it is the largest single medical program in the United States offering benefits in all fifty states.

Persons eligible for Medicare benefits include:

- People age sixty-five and over, retired, on Social Security Administration (SSA) benefits, railroad retirement, or civil service retirement.
- People who have received Social Security Disability Insurance (SSDI) benefits for two years.
- People with end-stage renal disease (ESRD).

Local Social Security Administration offices take applications for Medicare benefits. All persons who meet the eligibility requirements receive Medicare Part A Benefits (Hospital Insurance). Medicare Part A covers inpatient, institutional services, hospice, and home health care.

Those persons eligible for full medical benefits may choose to take Medicare Part B (Medical Insurance), by paying an annual premium to the Social Security Administration or having the premium automatically deducted from the monthly social security check.

As previously discussed in Chapter 12, it is important to always check the patient's insurance card or cards and retain a photocopy in the patient's medical record. This is especially important with a Medicare patient as the card indicates whether the patient has both Medicare Parts A and B, and the effective dates. It will also verify the correct Medicare claim or identification number. A replica of a Medicare card is shown in Figure 14–21.

This is the patient's health insurance claim number. It must be shown on all Medicare claims exactly as it is shown on the card—*including the letter at the end.*

This shows hospital insurance coverage.

This shows medical insurance coverage.

The date the insurance starts is shown here.

Figure 14–21 Example of a Medicare card, showing patient has Parts A and B.

When a husband and wife both have Medicare, they receive separate cards and claim numbers. A patient whose Medicare claim number ends in "A" will have the same social security number and claim number. A patient whose Medicare claim number ends in "B" or "D" will have different social security and Medicare claim numbers.

Table 14–1 designates what some of the letters following a Medicare claim number represent.

A distinction from this Medicare format is Railroad Retirement Medicare. This Medicare claim number has one to three letters before the numbers, as shown in Figure 14–22. Railroad retirement beneficiaries have the same benefits and deductibles under Parts A and B as other Medicare recipients.

This chapter will focus on Medicare Part B, which is the part designed to cover such outpatient services as:

- Physician office services
- Physical therapy
- Diagnostic lab testing
- Radiology
- Periodic pap smears and mammograms
- Influenza, pneumonococcal and hepatitis B vaccines
- Drugs that are not self-administered

TABLE 14–1   Explanation of some of the letters following a Medicare Claim Number.

Code	Description
A	Wage earner
B	Husband's number when wife is 62 years or older
D	Widow
HAD	Disabled adult
C	Disabled child
J, J1, or K1	Special monthly benefits; Never worked under Social Security

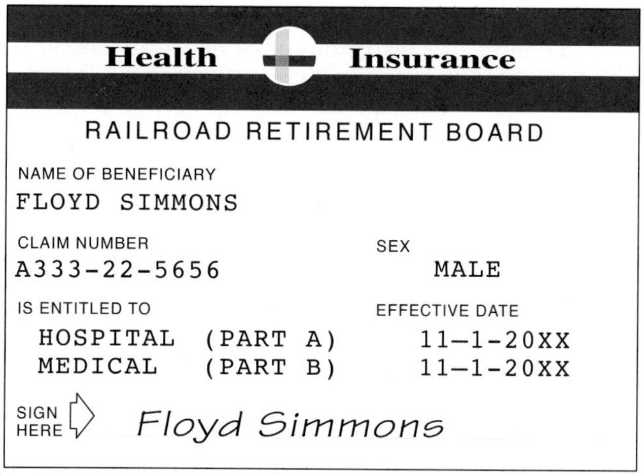

Figure 14–22 Example of a Railroad Medicare card, showing patient has Parts A and B.

Current Procedural Terminology (CPT) © 2005 American Medical Association. All Rights Reserved.

- Ambulance services
- Durable medical equipment and supplies used in the home certified by a physician

Today the majority of physicians contract to be a Medicare participating physician (PAR). Incentives to increase the number of health care providers to sign PAR agreements include:

- Direct payment of all claims
- Faster processing of claims resulting in quicker reimbursement
- A five percent higher fee schedule
- Annual PAR directories available to Medicare patients
- All unassigned remittance advice (RA), formerly known as explanation of benefits (EOB) forms, to patients include a message making them aware of the reduced out-of-pocket expenses if they use a PAR

Under the PAR agreement, the physician accepts assignment on all claims, agreeing to eighty percent of the allowable payment from Medicare plus the remaining twenty percent of reasonable charges after the deductible has been met.

Physicians electing not to participate as a contracted Medicare Provider (nonparticipating physician or NonPAR) can accept assignment on a claim-by-claim basis, but there are restrictions.

- All Medicare claims must be filed by the provider.
- Fees are restricted to charging no more than the limiting fee charge on non-assigned claims, or no more than fifteen percent above the NonPAR Medicare fee schedule, which is 5 percent below the PAR fee schedule.
- Collections are restricted to only the deductible and coinsurance due at the time of service on assigned claims.
- NonPARs *must* accept assignment on clinical laboratory charges.

Table 14–2 gives an example of a NonPAR fee and payment rate.

Table 14–3 is an example of a PAR fee and payment rate.

NonPARs who accept assignment are not restricted to billing the limited fee. However, the Medicare payment will only be at the NonPAR approved rate. NonPARs submitting an assigned claim may collect any unpaid deductible and the 20 percent coinsurance of the Medicare schedule at the time the service is rendered. If the full fee is collected at the time of service, the assigned status of the claim becomes void.

Federal law requires all physicians and suppliers to submit claims to Medicare if they provide a Medicare-covered service to a patient enrolled in Medicare Part B. The CMS-1500 is the form used to submit those claims.

Federal law also mandates accepting assignment on all clinical laboratory charges when the patient has lab services and other medical or surgical services. The NonPAR physician accepts assignment on only the lab services. In such a case two claim forms will need to be submitted, one for the lab procedures with Block 27 checked "Yes" to accept assignment, and one for other services.

Assignment must be accepted on all services performed by nurse practitioners, midwives, certified nurse anesthetists, and physician assistants, as well as psychologists, clinical psychologists, and clinical social workers.

Medicare is only required to pay for services and supplies that are considered to be reasonable and medically necessary for the diagnosis stated on the claim form. Medicare will not cover procedures considered experimental or still under investigation or being tested. To be considered medically reasonable and necessary, the supply or service must:

- Be consistent with the symptoms or diagnosis of the illness or injury under treatment

TABLE 14–2   Example of NonPAR Fee and Payment Rate.

NonPAR Charges Limiting Fee or Charge	$85.00
NonPAR Approved Rate	$70.00
The difference between Limiting Fee or Charge & NonPAR Rate	$15.00
Plus (+) 20% of NonPAR approved Rate $70.00	$14.00
Patient Owes	$29.00

TABLE 14–3   Example of PAR Fee and Payment Rate.

PAR charges usual fee	$100.00
PAR Medicare approved rate	$75.00
PAR adjusted difference between the usual charge and approved rate	$25.00
Patient pays PAR 20% of approved rate	$15.00

- Be necessary and consistent with generally accepted professional medical standards
- Not be furnished primarily for the convenience of the patient, attending physician, or other physician or supplier

An advance beneficiary notice (ABN) is a payment rule that allows physicians and clinics to bill patients with Medicare benefits for services that could be determined not medically necessary by Medicare. When a medical service or procedure that is governed by frequency limitations or may possibly be considered not medically necessary, the ABN allows the patient to be financially responsible. The routine billing of services or procedures considered not medically necessary may result in civil monetary penalties for the facility. An ABN policy can increase revenue since the ABN must indicate reason for possible Medicare denial and requires the patient's signature acknowledging financial responsibility.

In cases where the provider feels the treatments or services are justified, the options are explained to the patient with an agreement in writing to pay the full cost of the uncovered procedure. This advanced beneficiary notice (ABN) agreement is signed by the patient prior to receiving the medical service. This advance notice must state a reason why the physician believes Medicare is likely to deny the claim. The notice must contain accurate information so the patient can make an informed decision on whether or not to receive the service and pay for it without Medicare reimbursement.

An acceptable advance notice as determined by CMS must include the following:

- Date of service
- A narrative of the particular service
- A statement that the physician/supplier believes Medicare is likely to deny payment for the particular service
- An accurate reason why the physician/supplier believes Medicare is likely to deny payment
- The beneficiary's signed and dated agreement to pay, obtained *before* the service is performed

Failure to obtain this advanced beneficiary notice Medicare for services not reasonable and necessary will result in the following:

- Nonparticipating physicians who do not accept assignment must refund to the patient any amounts collected that have been denied by Medicare as considered not reasonable and necessary.

- The participating physician or nonparticipating physician accepting assignment may be held liable for services considered by Medicare to be not reasonable and necessary. If payment has been collected from the beneficiary for such services, the provider is required to refund the amount collected from the patient within thirty days of receiving Medicare's notice.

To avoid delay of claim processing, a copy of this notice may be submitted with the claim. An example of a CMS-approved is outlined in Figure 14–23.

Medicare can be primary insurance coverage or a secondary payer or supplemental policy. It is important to know the Medicare status in order to correctly submit the claim form.

Circumstances under which Medicare may be secondary to other insurance include:

- Group health plan coverage such as the person who continues working after the age of sixty-five
- Liability coverage such as automobile accidents
- Work-related illness and injury that falls under Workers' Compensation, veterans benefits, or black lung disease

When Medicare is primary, additional insurance is often purchased to supplement the Medicare program by covering the patient's deductible and coinsurance obligations. This additional coverage can be:

1. Medigap
2. Employer Sponsored Medicare Supplemental Plan

Medigap
A private, commercial insurance plan purchased by a patient as a supplementary plan to Medicare coverage.

A **Medigap** policy is a private, commercial insurance plan with the premiums paid directly by the patient, which is offered to persons entitled to Medicare benefits to supplement those benefits. It is designed to "fill in the gaps" in Medicare coverage by providing payment for some of the charges for which Medicare does not have responsibility due to deductibles, coinsurance amounts, or other Medicare-imposed limitations. These policies must meet federal government standards for Medigap coverage. These claims are handled in one of two ways:

1. PAR—Medicare is filed first, then the Medicare carrier can electronically transfer claim information completed in Blocks 9 through 9D to the Medigap carrier.

2. NonPAR providers are not required to include Medigap information on the claim form, although many offices will file the Medigap claim for the patient. To do this, the patient must provide a copy of the Medicare **remittance advice (RA)** with the Medigap claim.

remittance advice (RA)
A summary explaining the insurance company's determination for reimbursement of benefits; also referred to as Explanation of Benefits.

An employer-sponsored plan is a plan available to employees at the time of their retirement from the company. These plans are not regulated by the federal government but follow the guidelines established in the employer's regular health insurance plan. Premiums are paid to the insurance carrier via the employer. Health care providers are not required to file claims through employer-sponsored retirement plans, although many do, or the patient can file for benefits after the Medicare RA is received.

Lowery B. Johnson, M.D.
Hwy 311 Suite A31
Sellersburg, IN 47172
812-246-1234

ADVANCE BENEFICIARY NOTICE

Medicare will only pay for services that it determines to be "reasonable and necessary" under Section 1662 (a) (1) of the Medicare law. If Medicare determines that a particular service, although it would otherwise be covered, is not "reasonable and necessary" under Medicare program standards, Medicare will deny payment for that service. I believe that in your case, Medicare is likely to deny payment for:

1. _____

2. _____

for the reason(s) checked below:

Medicare does not usually pay for this:

_____ number of visits or treatments

_____ service or this number of services within this period of time

_____ injection or this number of injections

_____ because it is a treatment that is yet to be proved effective

_____ office visit unless it was needed because of an emergency

_____ same services by more than one doctor during the same time period

_____ equipment

_____ laboratory test

_____ visit since it is more than one visit per day

_____ extensive procedure

_____ same service by more than one doctor of the same specialty

_____ nursing home visit since only one is allowed per month

Medicare Beneficiary Agreement

I have been notified by my physician that he/she believes that, in my case, Medicare is likely to deny payment for the services identified above, for the reasons checked. If Medicare denies payment, I agree to be personally and fully responsible for payment.

_____   _____
Date   Beneficiary Signature

Figure 14–23 Advance beneficiary notice (ABN).

The following outlines step by step how to complete the CMS-1500 for a primary Medicare claim, with Medigap supplemental policy.

Block 1	Enter "X" in Medicare box.
Block 1a	Enter Medicare ID number including alpha suffix for traditional Medicare, alpha prefix for Railroad Medicare.
Block 2	Enter last name, first name, and middle initial as they appear on the Medicare card. Use no punctuation.

Block 3	Enter patient's date of birth using eight-digit dates. (01/01/1929) Mark appropriate gender of the patient.
Block 4	Enter "Same" or leave blank.
Block 5	Enter patient's address and telephone number.
Block 6	Mark "Self" or leave blank.
Block 7	Enter "Same" or leave blank.
Block 8	Mark appropriate marital and employment status boxes. Mark "Single" if widowed or divorced.
Block 9	Enter last name, first name, middle initial to indicate Medigap Policy *if different* from patient's name in Block 2. If patient and insured are the same, enter "Same."
Block 9a	Enter "Medigap," followed by the policy and/or group number.
Block 9b	Enter the eight-digit date of birth of Medigap insured if different from patient.
Block 9c	If Medigap PAYERID is known and entered in block 9d leave blank. This is identified by the numbers "99" in the seventh and eighth positions of the nine-digit ID number. If the PAYERID is not known, enter abbreviated mailing address of the Medigap carrier as listed on the insured's identification card.

EXAMPLE

231 Cannon Street

Talltown, IN 12345

Is entered as: "231 Cannon St IN 12345"

Block 9d	Enter **Medigap PAYERID nine-digit number**. If no number is available, enter the Medigap Plan name.

▬ *Highlight*

Information in Blocks 9, 9a, 9b, and 9d must be complete and accurate in order to transfer or cross over claim information to the Medigap insured.

Blocks 10a–10c	Mark "No." If any are checked "Yes," the third-party liability or Workers' Compensation would be primary and filed first; Medicare would be secondary.
Block 11	Enter "None" or leave blank.
Block 11a–11c	Leave blank.
Block 11d	Leave blank. Not required by Medicare.
Block 12	Patient signature required or patient can sign a separate authorization for release of medical information retained in the patient's chart. If authorization is on file, enter "Signature on File."
Block 13	PAR Providers—Enter "Patient Signature on File" if the patient has a signed Medigap authorization on file.
Block 14	Enter date of the beginning of the illness reported on this claim, or date accident or injury occurred.
Block 15	Leave blank.
Block 16	If the patient is employed and unable to work in current occupation, enter the eight-digit dates. This entry may indicate employment-related insurance coverage.
Blocks 17&17a	Enter name of referring, requesting, ordering or supervising physician, and the Unique Provider Identification number (UPIN) of this physician.

The list below groups provider services differentiating referring, requesting, ordering, and supervising physician:

Group 1—Physician Services

- Consultation
- Surgery
- Independent diagnostic radiology provider
- Independent diagnostic laboratory provider

All referrals need the name of the referring provider. Both the referring and the ordering physician's name must be included if the consultant personally orders and performs diagnostic testing on a patient.

Group 2—Nonphysician Services

- Physical therapy
- Audiology
- Occupational therapy
- Durable medical equipment (DME)
- Prosthesis
- Orthotic devices
- Parenteral and enteral nutrition
- Immunosuppressive drug claims
- Portable X-ray services

All claims need the name of the ordering physician.

Group 3—Physician Extender/Limited License Practitioners

- Physician Assistants
- Nurse Practitioners
- Other Limited License Practitioners referring patients for consultation services

All claims need the name of the supervising physician.

Blocks 17&17a	Leave blank if the physician reporting all the services is the attending physician.
Block 18	Enter Dates of Admission and Discharge when services relate to hospitalization.
Block 19	Required for the following:

- Chiropractor Claims: Enter eight-digit date required x-ray was taken.
- Global Surgery Claims: Two physicians sharing postop care. Enter appropriate eight-digit date care was assumed or relinquished.
- Unlisted CPT codes in Block 24d: Enter a description of the actual service. If the description does not fit, attach the narrative to the claim.
- Modifier "99" in Block 24d. Enter all modifiers covered in Block 24d by multiple modifiers "99." Enter the line number being reported followed by an equal sign listing all modifiers that apply to that line.

  EXAMPLE

  1 = 25   58   80

- Independent Physical or Occupational Therapist and all podiatrist claims: Enter eight-digit date patient was last seen by the referring or ordering physician and the UPIN of attending physician.

- CPT Code for "Not Otherwise Classified Drug" in Block 24d: Enter Name of the drug.
- Independent Laboratory Claim: When a portable EKG is performed or lab specimens are obtained from a patient at home or an institution enter "Homebound."

Block 20	"Yes" indicates an outside lab performed a diagnostic test listed on this claim form. The provider billing this claim form was billed for the test, and the provider is billing the patient.
Block 21	Enter ICD-9-CM code, primary code first. Up to four codes may be entered.
Block 22	Leave blank.
Block 23	Enter prior authorization number if required for procedure listed.
Block 24a	Enter date of service in "To" column. "From" is used only if billing for same service, same CPT code, on consecutive days. For consecutive dates, first date of service is in "To" block, last date of service in "From" block.
Block 24b	Enter appropriate Place of Service (POS) code. (Refer to page 380 for complete listing.)
Block 24c	Leave blank. Not required for Medicare.
Block 24d	Enter CPT or HCPCS code of service performed and any appropriate modifier. If more than two modifiers are required, use modifier "99" and follow instructions for Block 19 for multiple modifiers.
Block 24e	Enter the ICD-9-CM code from Block 21 that best proves medical necessity for this service.
Block 24f	Enter the amount charged for service performed. For consecutive services reported on one line, enter the charge for a single service, indicating number of units in 24g.
Block 24g	Enter number of units reported on this line.
Block 24h–24j	Leave blank.
Block 24k	Solo practices leave blank. Group practices enter PIN of the provider performing the service.
Block 25	Enter physician's federal tax employer ID number, marking the "EIN" box.
Block 26	If applicable, enter the patient account number. This number will then be listed on the RA for numerical identification of an account.
Block 27	"Yes" or "No" option must be marked. "Yes" must be marked for all PAR claims. NonPARs may mark either box. Assignment *must* be accepted on the following claims:

- Medicare/Medicaid crossover claims
- All clinical diagnostic laboratory services
- Services performed by physician assistants, nurse practitioners, midwives, nurse anesthesiologists, clinical psychologists, and social workers
- Ambulatory surgical center claims

Block 28	Enter total charges submitted on this claim.
Block 29	Enter payments made by patients for covered services reported on this claim.

Block 30	Leave blank.
Block 31	Enter provider's name and credentials, either signature or signature stamp, and date claim was prepared.
Block 32	Enter the name and address of the facility where services are *if other than patient's home.*
Block 33	Enter the official name of the practice, mailing address and phone number.
	Solo providers enter PIN number to the right of "PIN." Providers in group practices enter group PIN number to the right of "GRP."

Clarification Of PIN, UPIN, NPI, and PAYERID

State license number is required for each physician in order to practice medicine within a state. This number is sometimes also used as a provider number (Block 24k of CMS-1500).

Employer identification number (EIN) is assigned by the Internal Revenue Services to each individual physician for income tax purposes (Block 25 of CMS-1500).

Social security number (SSN) is issued to each physician. This is also referred to as a tax identification number (TIN) (Block 25 of the CMS-1500).

Group provider number (GRP) is used for the physician performing a service in a group practice that submits claims to an insurance carrier using the group name instead of the individual physician's name (Block 33 of CMS-1500).

Durable medical equipment number (DME) is used for Medicare providers who supply and charge for items such as wheelchairs, surgical dressings, urinary catheters, etc. (Block 33 of CMS-1500).

Facility provider number is issued to hospitals, laboratories, skilled nursing facilities, and radiology centers to be used by the performing physician to report services performed at that location (Block 32 of CMS-1500).

PIN is the provider identification number assigned to a health care provider by an insurance company to be used on all claims filed by the provider.

UPIN is the unique provider identification number assigned by CMS to a physician to be used as identification on Medicare claim forms.

NPI is the National Provider Identifier, assigned by CMS as an identification number for Medicare claim forms, bills, and correspondence. The NPI is an eight-digit number to identify the provider with a two-digit location identifier. The objective of the NPI number is to develop a uniform system to standardize and simplify the use of provider identification number process. It will assist in detecting and tracing fraudulent and abusive submission of claim forms. When using the NPI, it is entered in Blocks 24J and K.

PAYERID is the payer identification number assigned to identify all third party payers of health care claims.

Figure 14–24 shows a completed claim form for a patient with Medicare Part B and Medigap coverage.

Medicare/Medicaid (Medi-Medi)

Medicare patients whose incomes are below the federal poverty level are also eligible for Medicaid, referred to as Medi-Medi. When a patient has both Medicare and Medicaid, the claim can be filed by "crossover" method. This means once the billing office has submitted the claim to Medicare, Medicare will automatically electronically transfer the Medicare claim and payment information to Medicaid for payment of any service that is covered by Medicaid but not Medicare.

PLEASE
DO NOT
STAPLE
IN THIS
AREA

CARRIER

HEALTH INSURANCE CLAIM FORM

| | PICA | | | | | | | | PICA | |

1. MEDICARE	MEDICAID	CHAMPUS	CHAMPVA	GROUP HEALTH PLAN (SSN or ID)	FECA BLK LUNG (SSN)	OTHER (ID)	1a. INSURED'S I.D. NUMBER (FOR PROGRAM IN ITEM 1)
[X] (Medicare #)	(Medicaid #)	(Sponsor's SSN)	(VA File #)				322758721B

2. PATIENT'S NAME (Last Name, First Name, Middle Initial)
SANDERS ELIZABETH D

3. PATIENT'S BIRTH DATE MM DD YY
03 15 1930 M   F [X] SEX

4. INSURED'S NAME (Last Name, First Name, Middle Initial)
SAME

5. PATIENT'S ADDRESS (No., Street)
8900 TIN ROOF CT

6. PATIENT RELATIONSHIP TO INSURED
Self [X] Spouse   Child   Other

7. INSURED'S ADDRESS (No., Street)
SAME

CITY
SELLERSBURG   STATE IN

8. PATIENT STATUS
Single [X]   Married   Other
Employed   Full-Time Student   Part-Time Student

CITY   STATE

ZIP CODE 47172   TELEPHONE (Include Area Code) (822) 752-1111

ZIP CODE   TELEPHONE (INCLUDE AREA CODE) (   )

9. OTHER INSURED'S NAME (Last Name, First Name, Middle Initial)
SAME

10. IS PATIENT'S CONDITION RELATED TO:

11. INSURED'S POLICY GROUP OR FECA NUMBER

a. OTHER INSURED'S POLICY OR GROUP NUMBER
MEDIGAP 23110

a. EMPLOYMENT? (CURRENT OR PREVIOUS)
YES [X] NO

a. INSURED'S DATE OF BIRTH MM DD YY   SEX M   F

b. OTHER INSURED'S DATE OF BIRTH MM DD YY   SEX M   F

b. AUTO ACCIDENT?   PLACE (State)
YES [X] NO

b. EMPLOYER'S NAME OR SCHOOL NAME

c. EMPLOYER'S NAME OR SCHOOL NAME
RETIRED – SCOTT CO SCHOOL DIST

c. OTHER ACCIDENT?
YES [X] NO

c. INSURANCE PLAN NAME OR PROGRAM NAME
MEDICARE

d. INSURANCE PLAN NAME OR PROGRAM NAME
WESTCO

10d. RESERVED FOR LOCAL USE

d. IS THERE ANOTHER HEALTH BENEFIT PLAN?
[X] YES   NO   If yes, return to and complete item 9 a-d.

READ BACK OF FORM BEFORE COMPLETING & SIGNING THIS FORM.

12. PATIENT'S OR AUTHORIZED PERSON'S SIGNATURE I authorize the release of any medical or other information necessary to process this claim. I also request payment of government benefits either to myself or to the party who accepts assignment below.

SIGNED SIGNATURE ON FILE   DATE _____

13. INSURED'S OR AUTHORIZED PERSON'S SIGNATURE I authorize payment of medical benefits to the undersigned physician or supplier for services described below.

SIGNED _____

PATIENT AND INSURED INFORMATION

14. DATE OF CURRENT: MM DD YY
06 18 20xx
ILLNESS (First symptom) OR INJURY (Accident) OR PREGNANCY(LMP)

15. IF PATIENT HAS HAD SAME OR SIMILAR ILLNESS. GIVE FIRST DATE MM DD YY

16. DATES PATIENT UNABLE TO WORK IN CURRENT OCCUPATION MM DD YY   MM DD YY
FROM   TO

17. NAME OF REFERRING PHYSICIAN OR OTHER SOURCE
THOMAS DUDLEY MD

17a. I.D. NUMBER OF REFERRING PHYSICIAN
12089

18. HOSPITALIZATION DATES RELATED TO CURRENT SERVICES MM DD YY   MM DD YY
FROM   TO

19. RESERVED FOR LOCAL USE

20. OUTSIDE LAB? $ CHARGES
YES   NO

21. DIAGNOSIS OR NATURE OF ILLNESS OR INJURY. (RELATE ITEMS 1,2,3 OR 4 TO ITEM 24E BY LINE)
1. 726.10
3. __.__
2. __.__
4. __.__

22. MEDICAID RESUBMISSION CODE   ORIGINAL REF. NO.

23. PRIOR AUTHORIZATION NUMBER

24. A DATE(S) OF SERVICE		B Place of Service	C Type of Service	D PROCEDURES, SERVICES, OR SUPPLIES (Explain Unusual Circumstances) CPT/HCPCS MODIFIER	E DIAGNOSIS CODE	F $ CHARGES	G DAYS OR UNITS	H EPSDT Family Plan	I EMG	J COB	K RESERVED FOR LOCAL USE
From MM DD YY	To MM DD YY										
06 18 20XX		11		99242	1	105 00	1				
06 18 20XX		11		20610	1	55 00	1				

PHYSICIAN OR SUPPLIER INFORMATION

25. FEDERAL TAX I.D. NUMBER   SSN EIN
75-2166173   [X]

26. PATIENT'S ACCOUNT NO.

27. ACCEPT ASSIGNMENT? (For govt. claims, see back)
[X] YES   NO

28. TOTAL CHARGE
$ 160 00

29. AMOUNT PAID
$

30. BALANCE DUE
$ 160 00

31. SIGNATURE OF PHYSICIAN OR SUPPLIER INCLUDING DEGREES OR CREDENTIALS (I certify that the statements on the reverse apply to this bill and are made a part thereof.)

SIGNED 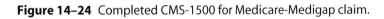Lowery Johnson MD   DATE 6/20/20XX

32. NAME AND ADDRESS OF FACILITY WHERE SERVICES WERE RENDERED (If other than home or office)
LOWERY JOHNSON MD
HWY 311 SUITE A31
SELLERSBURG IN 47172

33. PHYSICIAN'S, SUPPLIER'S BILLING NAME, ADDRESS, ZIP CODE & PHONE #
LOWERY JOHNSON MD
HWY 311 SUITE A31
SELLERSBURG IN 47172
PIN# 1948   GRP# (822) 752-9118

(APPROVED BY AMA COUNCIL ON MEDICAL SERVICE 8/88)   **PLEASE PRINT OR TYPE**

FORM HCFA-1500 (U2) (12-90)
FORM OWCP-1500   FORM RRB-1500

Figure 14–24 Completed CMS-1500 for Medicare-Medigap claim.

It is important to remember that assignment must be accepted on Medi-Medi claims. Payment should be received by the billing office two to four weeks after the Medicare payment has been received. If assignment is not taken, both Medicare and Medicaid payments may be sent to the patient, and a collection problem could exist due to state policy of not billing the patient for covered services.

A completed CMS-1500 for Medicare-Medicaid services is shown in Figure 14–25. Note in Block 27, assignment *must* be accepted by marking the "Yes" box.

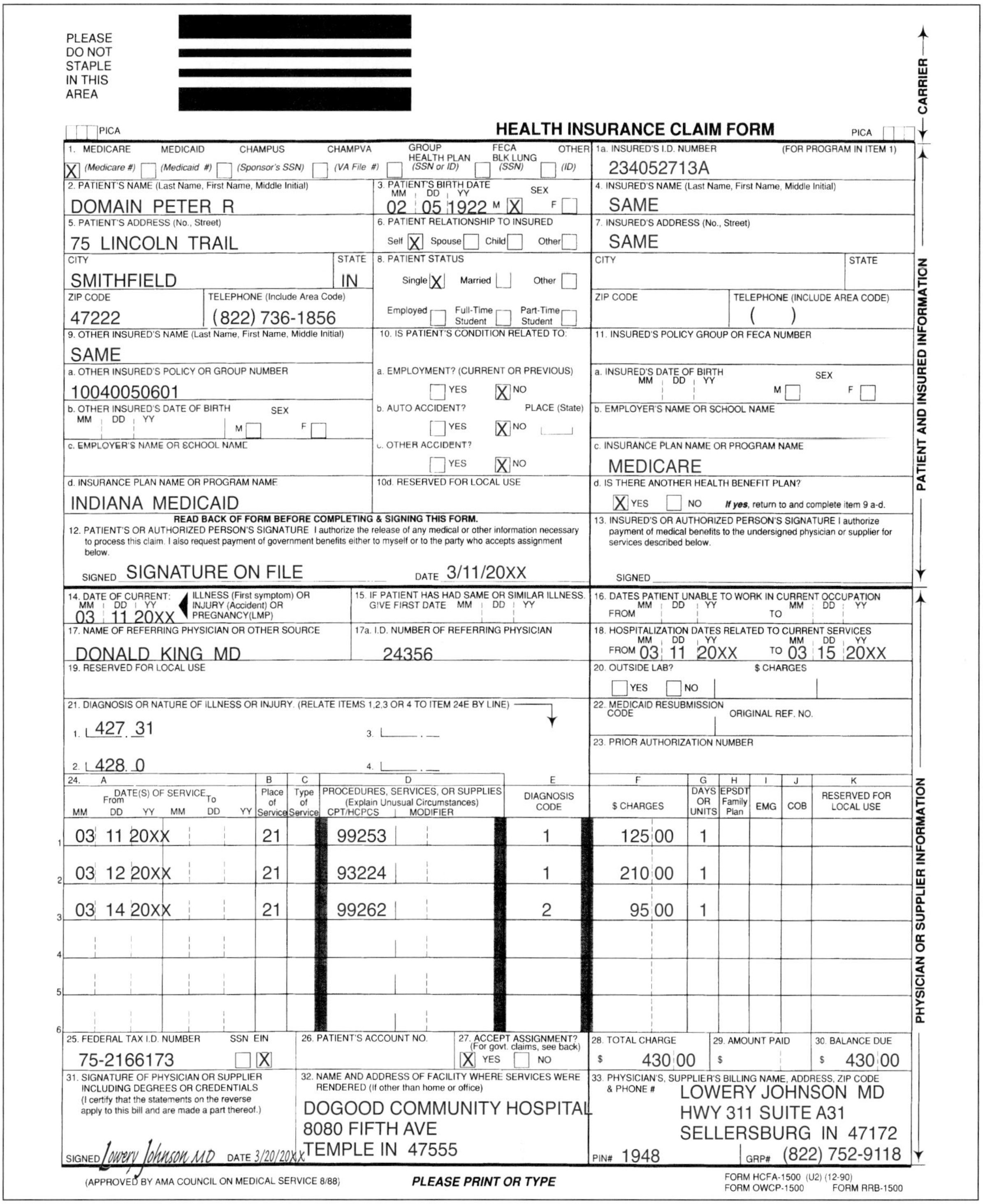

Figure 14–25 Completed CMS-1500 for Medicare-Medicaid (Medi-Medi) claim.

Extra-coverage plans are insurance plans that cover a specific disease or special hospital indemnity policies. The specified disease plans pay only upon documentation and physician certification of the disease, such as cancer or AIDS. Special hospital indemnity plans are advertised as policies paying a specified amount for every day the patient is hospitalized. Payment for these claims is made directly to the patient and is not reportable to Medicare or any other primary health insurance plan.

MEDICARE AS SECONDARY PAYER

Medicare is a secondary payer when the patient is eligible for Medicare and also covered by one or more of the following plans:

- An employer-sponsored group health plan with more than twenty covered employees
- Disability coverage through an employer-sponsored group health plan with more than 100 covered employees
- A third-party liability policy if treatment is for an injury covered by automobile insurance and self-insured liability plans
- Workers' Compensation injury or illness
- End-stage renal disease covered by an employer-sponsored group health plan of any size during the first eighteen months of the patient's eligibility for Medicare
- A Veterans Affairs (VA) preauthorized service for a beneficiary eligible for both VA benefits and Medicare
- Black lung disease

All primary plans are filed first. Medicare is filed after the RA from the primary plan has been received. A copy of the RA must be attached to the Medicare claim when submitted. Providers are not required to file Medicare secondary claims unless the patient specifically requests it.

For clarification purposes of primary and secondary plans, when a Medicare patient is seen in the medical office, a Medicare secondary payer form can also be completed by the Medicare beneficiary. An example of this form is shown in Figure 14–26.

The deadline for filing Medicare claims is December 31 of the year following the date of service. However, all claims should be filed promptly to avoid potential problems with billing and collections.

SUBMITTING A CLAIM FOR A DECEASED PATIENT

To submit a claim for a patient who has died, the following rules apply:

1. Participating physician—Assignment is accepted in Block 27 of the CMS-1500. In Block 12, any previous Signature On File is now invalid. Enter the statement "Patient died on (date)."
2. Nonparticipating physician—Assignment may be accepted as above. If the physician does not accept assignment, the following must be submitted:
   a. The person representing the estate of the deceased or the person responsible for the bill signs Block 12 of the CMS-1500.
   b. Include the name and address of the responsible party or the person representing the estate.
   c. Block 27 of the CMS-1500 is marked "No."

Practon Medical Group, Inc.
4567 Broad Avenue
Woodland Hills, XY 12345
Telephone 013/486-9002

LIFETIME BENEFICIARY CLAIM AUTHORIZATION AND INFORMATION RELEASE

Patient's
Name___Busaba McDermott___Medicare I.D. Number_329-98-6745__

I request that payment of authorized Medicare benefits be made either to me or on my behalf to (name of physician/supplier) for any services furnished me by that physician/supplier. I authorize any holder of medical information about me to release to the Centers for Medicare and Medicaid Services and its agents any information needed to determine these benefits or the benefits payable to related services.

I understand my signature requests that payment be made and authorizes release of medical information necessary to pay the claim. If other health insurance is indicated in Item 9 of the CMS-1500 claim form or elsewhere on other approved claim forms or electronically submitted claims, my signature authorizes releasing of the information to the insurer or agency shown. In Medicare assigned cases, the physician or supplier agrees to accept the charge determination of the Medicare carrier as the full charge, and the patient is responsible only for the deductible, coinsurance, and noncovered services. Coinsurance and the deductile are based upon the charge determination of the Medicare carrier.

Busaba McDermott	May 15, 20XX
Patient's Signature	Date

Figure 14–26 Medicare special authorization and assignment form.

A facility or provider not familiar with the deceased patient or unsure of the responsible party or a representative of the estate can call the probate court in the county clerk's office for verification of an estate to be probated.

Any balance remaining on the account of the deceased patient will remain open until the estate is settled. If any portion of the bill has previously been paid by the patient's family, this person must complete a CMS-1660 form for reimbursement. This form can be obtained from the CMS web site.

HEALTH MAINTENANCE ORGANIZATIONS (HMOS)

Many physicians today are enrolled as participating physicians in health maintenance organizations, more commonly referred to as HMOs.

The term managed care is derived from the HMO concept of medical care. They manage, negotiate, and contract for health care at the same time, keeping health care costs down. The goal of HMOs is to promote wellness and preventive medical care, covering the cost of annual examinations, routine x-rays, laboratory procedures, Pap smears, and mammograms. This encourages patients to undergo routine annual checkups, which can save costs by diagnosing medical problems before they become critical, therefore helping to lower medical costs.

To participate in an HMO plan, members and dependents must enroll in the plan. Most HMOs charge their members a co-payment (specified dollar amount) for office visits, emergency room visits, and other services. Most insurance cards for HMO patients indicate these co-pay amounts on the card. The patient is responsible for this fee and it should be collected at the time of the visit. If it is not paid, the patient is billed directly for the co-pay amount. Physicians participating in an HMO are listed in a directory published by the HMO that is distributed to its members. The member chooses a physician from the list as a primary care physician (PCP), also referred to as a gatekeeper, to manage the health care of the member. This management requires the patient to contact the PCP for referrals to hospitals, emergency rooms and specialists.

The following example illustrates of how the PCP manages the health care of an HMO patient:

EXAMPLE

A patient makes an appointment with the primary care physician to discuss symptoms possibly related to allergies: headaches, nasal drainage, cough. Oral medications alleviate the symptoms but side effects from the medications occur: daytime drowsiness, insomnia at night, dry mouth. The PCP refers the patient to an allergist for consultation and allergy testing. The referral form states how many visits may be required (consultation, allergy testing, and allergy vaccine if indicated).

Prior authorization or preapproval is required by HMOs for hospital admissions and surgeries.

CHAMPUS/TRICARE/CHAMPVA

TRICARE
Health care program for active duty members of the military and their dependents. (Previously known as CHAMPUS.)

CHAMPVA
Health care program for dependents of disabled veterans or those who died as a result of conditions related to their armed service.

CHAMPUS/**TRICARE/CHAMPVA** are federal government programs that provide health care benefits to families of personnel currently serving in the uniformed services, retired military personnel, and veterans of the armed forces.

CHAMPUS is the acronym for Civilian Health And Medical Programs of the Uniformed Services. It was originally founded to assist individuals in the military with medical expenses by their families. CHAMPUS then expanded and has been renamed TRICARE in an attempt to standardize benefits and control increasing health care costs.

TRICARE is a health benefits program for dependents of those serving in the military with the following eligibility:

- Spouse and unmarried children up to age twenty-one (age twenty-three if a full-time student) of military members who are in active duty, the United States Coast Guard, Public Health Service, or the National Oceanic and Atmospheric Administration (NOAA)
- Disabled children over age twenty-one
- Military retirees and eligible family members
- Spouse and unmarried children of deceased, active, or retired service members as long as the spouse has not remarried
- Former spouses of military personnel who meet length-of-marriage criteria and other requirements

- Outpatient services for spouse and children of North Atlantic Treaty Organization (NATO) nation representative
- Beneficiaries that are disabled and less than sixty-five years of age who have Medicare Parts A and B
- Spouses, former spouses, or dependent children of military personnel who have been physically or emotionally abused with the person found guilty and discharged for the offense

Individuals not eligible for TRICARE are:

- CHAMPVA beneficiaries
- Those eligible for Medicare age sixty-five and over not enrolled in Medicare Part B
- Military personnel parents
- Those eligible for medical care and treatment at a military facility or from a civilian provider

Those serving in active duty in the military services and those dependents eligible for TRICARE mainly receive health care services from a military treatment facility or hospital. When the service is not available at such a facility, a nonavailability statement (NAS) is required for the following:

- nonemergency inpatient services
- transfer of a beneficiary to another hospital
- maternity care (valid from entry into the prenatal program until forty-two days postpartum)
- referral to a civilian provider for care not available at a military facility

An NAS certification is valid for thirty days and could result in nonpayment for medical services if not obtained. No advance authorization is required in an emergency.

The definition of a medical emergency, as stated in *CHAMPUS News No 95-17,* is a "sudden and unexpected onset of a medical condition, or the acute worsening of a chronic condition, that is treating of life, limb or sight, and which required immediate medical treatment or which required treatment to relieve suffering from painful symptoms. Pregnancy-related medical emergencies must involve a sudden and unexpected medical complication that puts the mother, the baby, or both at risk."

An urgent medical problem is defined also in the same *CHAMPUS News* article as a "medical situation that isn't life threatening, but you need medical care." Preauthorization is required for treatment by a civilian medical facility or provider for urgent medical problems.

The Defense Enrollment Eligibility Reporting System (DEERS) is a computerized database that providers can use to check eligibility of a TRICARE patient. TRICARE provides three choices of health care benefits:

1. TRICARE Prime operates as a managed care program of a full service health maintenance organization (HMO) with a point-of-service option. Benefits go beyond the Extra and Standard plans to provide additional coverage for preventive and primary care services, such as immunizations and physical examinations.
2. TRICARE Extra is a network of physicians operating as a preferred provider organization (PPO).

3. TRICARE Standard is the standard CHAMPUS coverage available to all beneficiaries seeking care from a military treatment facility or civilian provider or facility.

TRICARE does utilize a network of physicians and participating physicians. These providers file claims and are reimbursed directly from TRICARE. Some plans require co-pays, coinsurance, and deductibles.

A nonparticipating physician may provide medical services to a patient with TRICARE. Usually these beneficiaries file their own claims with TRICARE reimbursing the beneficiary directly. In this case, the nonparticipating health care provider cannot bill more than 115 percent of the TRICARE allowable charge. The physician can accept assignment on a case-by-case basis.

CHAMPVA is the acronym for Civilian Health And Medical Program of the Veterans Affairs. CHAMPVA covers the expenses of dependent spouses and children of veterans with total, permanent, service-connected disabilities. It also covers surviving spouses and dependent children of veterans who have died in the line of duty or as a result of disabilities connected to the uniformed service.

CHAMPVA beneficiaries are allowed to choose civilian health care providers.

In the civilian medical facility treating the CHAMPUS/TRICARE/CHAMPVA patient, follow these guidelines to process a CMS-1500 claim for services rendered:

1. Check the patient's identification card for name, ID number, issue date, effective date and expiration date. Make a copy of the front and back of the card.

■ *Highlight*

TRICARE/CHAMPVA uses the term "sponsor" instead of insured or subscriber. The sponsor is the service person—active duty, retired, deceased—whose relationship to the patient provides eligibility for the program.

In Block 1a, enter the following:

TRICARE:	Sponsor's social security number.
CHAMPVA:	Patient's veterans affairs file number.
NOAA/NATO:	Type "NOAA" or "NATO" and sponsor's ID number.
Block 7:	Active duty sponsor: Sponsor's duty station address.
Blocks 17–17a:	Name of referring physician and EIN or SSN. If patient is referred from a military treatment facility, enter name of facility and attach form DD 2161 "Referral for civilian medical care."
Block 27:	Mark appropriate box. NonPARs may elect to accept assignment on a case-by-case basis.

2. If a patient has other insurance, including Workers' Compensation and liability policies, TRICARE/CHAMPVA are secondary payers.
3. TRICARE is primary when the other insurance is Medicaid or a supplemental policy to TRICARE.

The deadline for filing TRICARE/CHAMPVA claims is one year from date of service.
Figure 14–27 is an example of a completed CMS-1500 claim form for a Tricare patient.

PLEASE DO NOT STAPLE IN THIS AREA

↑ CARRIER →

[ ] PICA

HEALTH INSURANCE CLAIM FORM

PICA [ ] [ ]

1. MEDICARE	MEDICAID	CHAMPUS	CHAMPVA	GROUP HEALTH PLAN (SSN or ID)	FECA BLK LUNG (SSN)	OTHER	1a. INSURED'S I.D. NUMBER (FOR PROGRAM IN ITEM 1)
(Medicare #) [ ]	(Medicaid #) [ ]	(Sponsor's SSN) [X]	(VA File #) [ ]	(SSN or ID) [ ]	(SSN) [ ]	(ID) [ ]	300543030

2. PATIENT'S NAME (Last Name, First Name, Middle Initial)
DUCHANE PATRICIA S

3. PATIENT'S BIRTH DATE MM 07 | DD 01 | YY 1992   SEX M [ ] F [X]

4. INSURED'S NAME (Last Name, First Name, Middle Initial)
DUCHANE WILLIAM T

5. PATIENT'S ADDRESS (No., Street)
2510 NORTH ST APT 21B

6. PATIENT RELATIONSHIP TO INSURED
Self [X] Spouse [ ] Child [ ] Other [ ]

7. INSURED'S ADDRESS (No., Street)
ZION AIR FORCE BASE

CITY DUVALL   STATE IN

8. PATIENT STATUS
Single [X] Married [ ] Other [ ]
Employed [ ] Full-Time Student [ ] Part-Time Student [ ]

CITY APPLACHIA   STATE NY

ZIP CODE 47232   TELEPHONE (Include Area Code) (511) 293-2190

ZIP CODE 22330   TELEPHONE (INCLUDE AREA CODE) ( )

9. OTHER INSURED'S NAME (Last Name, First Name, Middle Initial)

10. IS PATIENT'S CONDITION RELATED TO:

11. INSURED'S POLICY GROUP OR FECA NUMBER
NONE

a. OTHER INSURED'S POLICY OR GROUP NUMBER

a. EMPLOYMENT? (CURRENT OR PREVIOUS) YES [ ] NO [X]

a. INSURED'S DATE OF BIRTH MM | DD | YY   SEX M [ ] F [ ]

b. OTHER INSURED'S DATE OF BIRTH MM | DD | YY SEX M [ ] F [ ]

b. AUTO ACCIDENT? PLACE (State) YES [ ] NO [X]

b. EMPLOYER'S NAME OR SCHOOL NAME

c. EMPLOYER'S NAME OR SCHOOL NAME

c. OTHER ACCIDENT? YES [ ] NO [X]

c. INSURANCE PLAN NAME OR PROGRAM NAME

d. INSURANCE PLAN NAME OR PROGRAM NAME

10d. RESERVED FOR LOCAL USE

d. IS THERE ANOTHER HEALTH BENEFIT PLAN?
YES [ ] NO [X] **If yes**, return to and complete item 9 a-d.

READ BACK OF FORM BEFORE COMPLETING & SIGNING THIS FORM.
12. PATIENT'S OR AUTHORIZED PERSON'S SIGNATURE I authorize the release of any medical or other information necessary to process this claim. I also request payment of government benefits either to myself or to the party who accepts assignment below.
SIGNED SIGNATURE ON FILE   DATE 6/25/20XX

13. INSURED'S OR AUTHORIZED PERSON'S SIGNATURE I authorize payment of medical benefits to the undersigned physician or supplier for services described below.
SIGNED SIGNATURE ON FILE

14. DATE OF CURRENT: MM 06 | DD 25 | YY 20XX ILLNESS (First symptom) OR INJURY (Accident) OR PREGNANCY(LMP)

15. IF PATIENT HAS HAD SAME OR SIMILAR ILLNESS. GIVE FIRST DATE MM | DD | YY

16. DATES PATIENT UNABLE TO WORK IN CURRENT OCCUPATION
FROM MM | DD | YY TO MM | DD | YY

17. NAME OF REFERRING PHYSICIAN OR OTHER SOURCE

17a. I.D. NUMBER OF REFERRING PHYSICIAN

18. HOSPITALIZATION DATES RELATED TO CURRENT SERVICES
FROM MM 03 | DD 11 | YY 20XX TO MM 03 | DD 15 | YY 20XX

19. RESERVED FOR LOCAL USE

20. OUTSIDE LAB? YES [ ] NO [ ] $ CHARGES

21. DIAGNOSIS OR NATURE OF ILLNESS OR INJURY. (RELATE ITEMS 1,2,3 OR 4 TO ITEM 24E BY LINE)
1. 870 . 0
2. E884 . 0
3. ___ . ___
4. ___ . ___

22. MEDICAID RESUBMISSION CODE   ORIGINAL REF. NO.

23. PRIOR AUTHORIZATION NUMBER

24. A DATE(S) OF SERVICE From MM DD YY	To MM DD YY	B Place of Service	C Type of Service	D PROCEDURES, SERVICES, OR SUPPLIES (Explain Unusual Circumstances) CPT/HCPCS	MODIFIER	E DIAGNOSIS CODE	F $ CHARGES	G DAYS OR UNITS	H EPSDT Family Plan	I EMG	J COB	K RESERVED FOR LOCAL USE
1	06 25 20XX		23	1	99282		1	185 00	1				
2	06 25 20XX		23	2	12051		1	110 00	1				
3													
4													
5													
6													

25. FEDERAL TAX I.D. NUMBER SSN [ ] EIN [X]
75-2166173

26. PATIENT'S ACCOUNT NO.

27. ACCEPT ASSIGNMENT? (For govt. claims, see back) YES [ ] NO [X]

28. TOTAL CHARGE $ 295 00

29. AMOUNT PAID $

30. BALANCE DUE $ 295 00

31. SIGNATURE OF PHYSICIAN OR SUPPLIER INCLUDING DEGREES OR CREDENTIALS (I certify that the statements on the reverse apply to this bill and are made a part thereof.)
SIGNED Lowery Johnson MD DATE 6/25/20XX

32. NAME AND ADDRESS OF FACILITY WHERE SERVICES WERE RENDERED (If other than home or office)
DOGOOD COMMUNITY HOSPITAL
8080 FIFTH AVE
TEMPLE IN 47555

33. PHYSICIAN'S, SUPPLIER'S BILLING NAME, ADDRESS, ZIP CODE & PHONE #
LOWERY JOHNSON MD
HWY 311 SUITE A31
SELLERSBURG IN 47172
PIN# 1948   GRP# (822) 752-9118

(APPROVED BY AMA COUNCIL ON MEDICAL SERVICE 8/88)   **PLEASE PRINT OR TYPE**

FORM HCFA-1500 (U2) (12-90)
FORM OWCP-1500   FORM RRB-1500

↓ PATIENT AND INSURED INFORMATION   PHYSICIAN OR SUPPLIER INFORMATION →

Figure 11–27 Completed CMS-1500 for CHAMPUS claim.

WORKERS' COMPENSATION

Workers' Compensation is a program covering on-the-job accidents and injuries or illness related to employment. This program is mandated by federal and state governments. Premiums are paid by employers to a statewide fund to cover medical expenses and a portion of lost wages directly related to the employee's injury or illness. This premium is determined by the number of employees and the degree of risk posed by the job.

Workers' Compensation benefits vary from state to state. Five principal types of benefits may be available:

1. Medical treatment—Hospitals, physician and medical services, medications, and supplies are covered for treatment that is reasonable and medically necessary for the injured or ill worker.
2. Temporary disability indemnity—The ill or injured person receives wage compensation benefits.
3. Permanent disability indemnity—Monetary compensation may be cash payments or a lump sum based on a rating system used to determine the percentage of the disability that is deemed permanent.
4. Vocational rehabilitation benefits—Many times an injured worker may not be able to return to the job previously held at time of injury but is a candidate for education and/or training for other employment.
5. Death benefits—The dependents of a worker who has died because of an accident or illness may receive compensation for their loss.

There are three types of Workers' Compensation claims that may be submitted:

1. Nondisability claim—This is when an employee receives a minor injury seen and treated by a physician but does not require missing work for recovery.
2. Temporary disability claim—This is a total or partial disability that occurs when an employee cannot perform work duties from the date of the injury until the employee returns to full work duties or limited duty, or is medically determined to be permanently disabled.
3. Permanent disability—This is when an employee is injured resulting in impairment of normal function of a body part, such as loss of a body part, that is expected to continue through the lifetime. A case manager will evaluate the severity of the injury, the age of the injured person, and the occupation of the injured. Most often temporary disability is granted to see if the person can improve or be eligible for rehabilitation before reaching the final determination of permanent disability.

Most states have an Employer's Report of Occupational Injury or Illness that must be completed for documentation and reporting of a work-related injury or illness. The physician rendering treatment to an injured employee must also complete a report of occupational injury or illness form. This form documents details of the accident or illness in the patient's own words with the patient's complaints and symptoms. The physician enters objective findings from the examination and all x-ray and laboratory results and a full description of the treatment and the treatment plan. Information must be submitted as to the patient's ability to return to work and an estimated date to return to regular or limited duty and any job restrictions. This form must be signed and dated in ink by the physician. This report is not a form submitted for reimbursement. This may be a CMS-1500 form or other form as required by the state Workers' Compensation fund. The injured worker receives no bills, pays no deductible or coinsurance, and is covered 100 percent for medical expenses related specifically to that injury or illness.

In most states information in the patient's medical record is accessible to the injured patient's employer and the insurance claims adjuster. Understand that the only information accessible is what has been provided for the Workers' Compensation case only. It does not include other information in the medical record unrelated to the injury or illness currently being treated. All other information in the record is confidential and requires an authorization to be released to a third party.

Figure 14–28 is a sample Workers' Compensation claim form.

INSTRUCTIONS

1. Type answers to All questions and file original with the Workers' Compensation Commission within 72 hours after first treatment.
2. DO NOT FAIL to forward to the Workers' Compensation Commission PROGRESS REPORTS and FINAL REPORT upon discharge of patient.

DO NOT WRITE IN THIS SPACE
WCC CLAIM #
EMPLOYER'S REPORT Yes ☐ No ☐

WORKERS' COMPENSATION COMMISSION

This is First Report ☐   Progress Report ☐   Final Report ☐

EVERY QUESTION MUST BE ANSWERED AND FORM SIGNED

1. Name of Injured Person: Maureen A. Santega | Soc. Sec. No. 610-98-7432 | D.O.B. 7/19/69 | Sex M ☐ F ☑

2. Address: (No. and Street) 905 Raymond Lane | (City or Town) Atlanta | (State) GA | (Zip Code) 30385-8893

3. Name and Address of Employer: Majors Concrete Company, 238 Leaf Lane, Atlanta, GA 30342-3329

4. Date of Accident or Onset of Disease: 4/9/XX | Hour: A.M. ☑ P.M. ☐ | 5. Date Disability Began: 4/9/XX

6. Patient's Description of Accident or Cause of Disease: Concrete truck struck and backed over patient's foot while she was pouring concrete at job site

7. Medical description of Injury or Disease: Massive bruising to left foot, no broken bones, great deal of pain associated with bruises

8. Will injury result in:
(a) Permanent defect? Yes ☐ No ☑ If so, what? | (b) Disfigurement Yes ☐ No ☑

9. Causes, other than injury, contributing to patients condition: None

10. Is patient suffering from any disease of the heart, lungs, brain, kidneys, blood, vascular system or any other disabling condition not due to this accident? Give particulars: No

11. Is there any history or evidence present of previous accident or disease? Give particulars: No

12. Has normal recovery been delayed for any reason? Give particulars: No

13. Date of first treatment: 4/10/XX | Who engaged your services? patient

14. Describe treatment given by you: Darvon, 100 mg q4h prn for pain

15. Were X-Rays taken? Yes ☑ No ☐ | By whom? — (Name and Address) Edwin Gordon, M.D. 802 Manor Lane, Atlanta 30303 | Date 4/10/XX

16. X-Ray Diagnosis: No broken bones

17. Was patient treated by anyone else? Yes ☐ No ☑ | By whom? — (Name and Address) | Date

18. Was patient hospitalized? Yes ☐ No ☑ | Name and Address of Hospital | Date of Admission: Date of Discharge:

19. Is further treatment needed? Yes ☐ No ☑ | For how long? | 20. Patient was ☑ will be ☐ able to resume regular work on: 4/14
Patient was ☐ will be ☐ able to resume light work on:

21. If death ensued give date: | 22. Remarks: (Give any information of value not included above)

23. I am a qualified specialist in: orthopedics | I am a duly licensed Physician in the State of: Maryland | I was graduated from Medical School (Name) Johns Hopkins | Year 1967

Date of this report: 6/21/XX | (Signed) *John N. Sparks, M.D.*

Address: 8504 Capricorn Drive Atlanta GA 30312 | Phone: (404) 544-0078 | (This report must be signed PERSONALLY by Physician)

Figure 14–28 An example of a Workers' Compensation claim form.

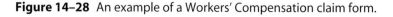

BLUE CROSS/BLUE SHIELD

Blue Cross/Blue Shield (BC/BS)
One of the oldest and largest insurance providers providing health benefits nationwide.

Blue Cross/Blue Shield (BC/BS) is a nationwide corporation providing health care benefits such as hospital expenses, outpatient care, dental and vision benefits, and home care to its members. Typically Blue Cross covers hospital expenses; Blue Shield covers physician services.

Coverage plans vary under BC/BS coverage. Two basic types of policies are offered: service benefit and indemnity benefit. A service benefit policy may have higher premiums but lower out-of-pocket expenses for the patient. An indemnity benefit policy may feature lower premiums with a deductible and coinsurance amount payable by the subscriber.

Some patients may present a Blue Shield card that has a double-headed arrow with an "N" and a three-digit number signifying membership in a permanent reciprocity plan (see Figure 14–29). The plan allows the insured to be treated anywhere in the United States with treatment expenses covered, whether the treatment is an emergency or not. The "N" and three-digit number must be entered on the claim form when filing for services rendered.

Many BlueCross/BlueShield plans have converted to a for-profit status operating as any other private insurance carrier. This allows a variety of plans with deductibles, co-payments, and specific coverage benefits differing from patient to patient. Because of the different plans, reimbursement will depend upon the specific plan. For example, the patient may pay the physician directly with a Blue Shield claim filed for reimbursement. A physician's office may file a claim and bill the patient for the difference between the payment and fee charged. The payment is usually sent to the insured for services provided by nonparticipating physicians. Participating physicians are paid directly. Various methods are used by BC/BS to determine payment:

- Primary method of payment is usual, customary, and reasonable (UCR) fees.
- Relative Value Scale (RVS). A five-digit number and a unit value are assigned to each procedure based on the procedure's relative value compared to that of other common procedures. A conversion factor is applied to the unit value to determine payment.
- Diagnosis Related Groups (DRGs). This pays a fixed fee based on the patient's diagnosis rather than actual services performed.

As with many other health insurance companies, Blue Shield negotiates participating contracts with providers. A Blue Shield PAR must submit claims for its patients, and adjust the difference between the amount charged and the approved

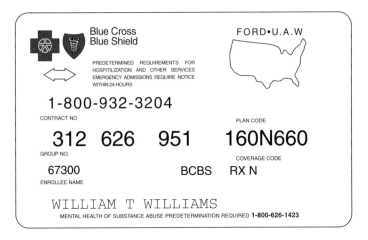

Figure 14–29 Example of a Blue Cross/Blue Shield card showing reciprocity.

fee on all covered services included in a policy written by the local corporation. Blue Shield agrees to make direct payments to PARs, and provide assistance and educational means.

Providers who have not signed a participating contract (nonPAR) can bill the entire amount of the fee charged for services performed. The claim can be filed by the billing office or the patient. In either case, the payment will be sent directly to the patient.

BC/BS has unique features that set them apart from other commercial health insurance groups:

- A patient's policy cannot be cancelled by BC/BS due to poor health or greater-than-average benefit payments.
- Any rate increase and/or benefit changes must get approval from the state insurance commissioner.
- BC/BS plans can be converted from group to individual coverage and can be transferred from state to state.
- In negotiating contracts with health care providers, Blue Shield agrees to make prompt, direct payment of claims, provide assistance with claim filing, and provide training seminars, manuals, and newsletters to keep personnel current and up-to-date in billing and claim filing.

In some states BC/BS assists in the administration of government programs such as Medicaid, Medicare, and TRICARE. Many patients have BC/BS as supplemental coverage to Medicare. One of the largest national plans is the Federal Employee Health Benefit Program (FEP) serving federal government employees. These cards will have the words "Government-Wide Service Benefit Plan," and the identification number begins with an "R" followed by eight digits. On the front of the card is a three-digit enrollment code. There are four enrollment options the government employee can select when applying for the program:

    101 Individual, high option plan
    102 Family, high option plan
    103 Individual standard, (low) option plan
    104 Family standard, (low) option plan

Figure 14–30 shows the FEP Blue Shield card. The FEP is primary when a patient also has TRICARE or MEDICAID. It coordinates benefits with Medicare Parts A and B, and any other employer group policy.

The deadline for filing Blue Shield claims is one year from the date of service.

Figure 14–31 is an example of a Blue Shield claim form.

Figure 14–30 Example of a Blue Cross/Blue Shield Federal Employee Plan (FEP) card.

HEALTH INSURANCE CLAIM FORM

PLEASE DO NOT STAPLE IN THIS AREA

CARRIER

| PICA | | PICA |

1. MEDICARE (Medicare #) **MEDICAID** (Medicaid #) **CHAMPUS** (Sponsor's SSN) **CHAMPVA** (VA File #) **GROUP HEALTH PLAN** (SSN or ID) **FECA BLK LUNG** (SSN) **OTHER** [X] (ID)

1a. INSURED'S I.D. NUMBER (FOR PROGRAM IN ITEM 1)
404883124 XEP

2. PATIENT'S NAME (Last Name, First Name, Middle Initial)
ANTON JEREMY D

3. PATIENT'S BIRTH DATE MM DD YY: 12 24 1955 **SEX** M [X] F

4. INSURED'S NAME (Last Name, First Name, Middle Initial)
SAME

5. PATIENT'S ADDRESS (No., Street)
6702 MOUNTAINTOP RD

6. PATIENT RELATIONSHIP TO INSURED
Self [X] Spouse Child Other

7. INSURED'S ADDRESS (No., Street)
SAME

CITY SMITHFIELD **STATE** IN

8. PATIENT STATUS
Single Married [X] Other

CITY **STATE**

ZIP CODE 47222 **TELEPHONE (Include Area Code)** (822) 273-0880

Employed Full-Time Student Part-Time Student

ZIP CODE **TELEPHONE (INCLUDE AREA CODE)** ( )

9. OTHER INSURED'S NAME (Last Name, First Name, Middle Initial)

10. IS PATIENT'S CONDITION RELATED TO:

11. INSURED'S POLICY GROUP OR FECA NUMBER
PPD8021

a. OTHER INSURED'S POLICY OR GROUP NUMBER

a. EMPLOYMENT? (CURRENT OR PREVIOUS) YES [X] NO

a. INSURED'S DATE OF BIRTH MM DD YY **SEX** M F

b. OTHER INSURED'S DATE OF BIRTH MM DD YY **SEX** M F

b. AUTO ACCIDENT? YES [X] NO **PLACE (State)**

b. EMPLOYER'S NAME OR SCHOOL NAME
TIPTON SUPPLY CO

c. EMPLOYER'S NAME OR SCHOOL NAME

c. OTHER ACCIDENT? YES [X] NO

c. INSURANCE PLAN NAME OR PROGRAM NAME
BLUE SHIELD

d. INSURANCE PLAN NAME OR PROGRAM NAME

10d. RESERVED FOR LOCAL USE

d. IS THERE ANOTHER HEALTH BENEFIT PLAN? YES NO [X] *If yes*, return to and complete item 9 a-d.

READ BACK OF FORM BEFORE COMPLETING & SIGNING THIS FORM.
12. PATIENT'S OR AUTHORIZED PERSON'S SIGNATURE I authorize the release of any medical or other information necessary to process this claim. I also request payment of government benefits either to myself or to the party who accepts assignment below.
SIGNED SIGNATURE ON FILE DATE

13. INSURED'S OR AUTHORIZED PERSON'S SIGNATURE I authorize payment of medical benefits to the undersigned physician or supplier for services described below.
SIGNED

PATIENT AND INSURED INFORMATION

14. DATE OF CURRENT: ILLNESS (First symptom) OR INJURY (Accident) OR PREGNANCY(LMP) MM DD YY 06 25 20XX

15. IF PATIENT HAS HAD SAME OR SIMILAR ILLNESS. GIVE FIRST DATE MM DD YY

16. DATES PATIENT UNABLE TO WORK IN CURRENT OCCUPATION MM DD YY FROM TO MM DD YY

17. NAME OF REFERRING PHYSICIAN OR OTHER SOURCE

17a. I.D. NUMBER OF REFERRING PHYSICIAN

18. HOSPITALIZATION DATES RELATED TO CURRENT SERVICES MM DD YY FROM TO MM DD YY

19. RESERVED FOR LOCAL USE

20. OUTSIDE LAB? YES NO **$ CHARGES**

21. DIAGNOSIS OR NATURE OF ILLNESS OR INJURY. (RELATE ITEMS 1,2,3 OR 4 TO ITEM 24E BY LINE)
1. 870 0
2. E884 0
3.
4.

22. MEDICAID RESUBMISSION CODE **ORIGINAL REF. NO.**

23. PRIOR AUTHORIZATION NUMBER
1239011−1

24. A DATE(S) OF SERVICE From MM DD YY	To MM DD YY	B Place of Service	C Type of Service	D PROCEDURES, SERVICES, OR SUPPLIES (Explain Unusual Circumstances) CPT/HCPCS MODIFIER	E DIAGNOSIS CODE	F $ CHARGES	G DAYS OR UNITS	H EPSDT Family Plan	I EMG	J COB	K RESERVED FOR LOCAL USE
1	03 11 20XX		11		99242	1	65 00	1				
2	04 03 20XX		23		46060 80	2	287 50	1				
3												
4												
5												
6												

25. FEDERAL TAX I.D. NUMBER SSN EIN
75-2166173 [X]

26. PATIENT'S ACCOUNT NO.

27. ACCEPT ASSIGNMENT? (For govt. claims, see back) YES [X] NO

28. TOTAL CHARGE $ 352 50

29. AMOUNT PAID $

30. BALANCE DUE $ 352 50

31. SIGNATURE OF PHYSICIAN OR SUPPLIER INCLUDING DEGREES OR CREDENTIALS (I certify that the statements on the reverse apply to this bill and are made a part thereof.)
SIGNED *Lowery Johnson MD* DATE 4/3/20XX

32. NAME AND ADDRESS OF FACILITY WHERE SERVICES WERE RENDERED (If other than home or office)
DOGOOD SURGICAL CENTER
8080 FIFTH AVE
TEMPLE IN 47555

33. PHYSICIAN'S, SUPPLIER'S BILLING NAME, ADDRESS, ZIP CODE & PHONE #
LOWERY JOHNSON MD
HWY 311 SUITE A31
SELLERSBURG IN 47172
PIN# 12001 GRP# (822) 752-9118

PHYSICIAN OR SUPPLIER INFORMATION

(APPROVED BY AMA COUNCIL ON MEDICAL SERVICE 8/88)
PLEASE PRINT OR TYPE
FORM HCFA-1500 (U2) (12-90)
FORM OWCP-1500 FORM RRB-1500

Figure 14–31 Completed CMS-1500 for Blue Shield claim.

EXERCISE 14-4

Match the term with its definition, placing the letter of the correct answer in the space provided.

_____ **1.** Workers' Compensation

_____ **2.** Medicaid

_____ **3.** BlueCross/BlueShield

_____ **4.** Medicare Part A

_____ **5.** Medicare Part B

_____ **6.** TRICARE/CHAMPVA

a. A nationwide federation of local nonprofit service organizations providing health care to all its subscribers

b. Hospital insurance for persons age 65 and over, disabled, or with end-stage renal disease

c. Federal program providing health care benefits to families of armed forces and retired military personnel and veterans

d. An assistance program to provide medical care for persons with incomes below the national poverty level

e. Medical coverage optional for persons age 65 and over, disabled, or with end-stage renal disease

f. Coverage for work related illness or injury

ELECTRONIC CLAIM PROCESSING

One function of a computerized office system is the preparation and generation of insurance claims. Transmitting claims electronically can reduce costs and expedite reimbursement, as payment may be processed within approximately seven to fourteen days after the insurance carrier has received the claim. The billing program scans the medical practice database to obtain the information necessary to complete each block on the claim form. Claim forms can then be transmitted electronically directly to the insurance carrier. A paper claim can be printed to send to an insurance carrier or retain in the office files.

The Health Insurance Portability and Accountability Act (HIPAA) of 1996 legislated health insurance reform and administrative simplification. One provision of the administrative simplification directs the federal government to provide electronic standards for electronic transfer of healthcare data between healthcare providers and payers. This standardizes the format for electronic claim submission. The HIPAA code set standards allows a healthcare provider to check patient eligibility and deductibles, request prior authorization, submit claims electronically, send attachments, check status of claims, and receive remittance advice/explanation of benefits summaries. Fee schedules, limiting charges, and codes can be accessed. Carrier manuals and other information can be obtained from individual web sites such as Centers for Medicare and Medicaid Services.

Electronic claims can be submitted using a carrier-direct system. This requires entering the claim form data and transmits via the modem over the telephone line directly to an insurance carrier. A distinct advantage of the carrier-direct system is the error-edit process. If an error is made during the electronic filing process, the error is identified and can be corrected immediately.

Physicians can also use the National Electronic Information Corporation (NEIC), which provides a national network to receive, process, edit, sort, and transmit claims by using one version of software. A clearinghouse, also known as third-party administrator, can be used to receive insurance claims, separate by carrier, edit each claim for errors, and forward claims electronically to the designated carrier. A clearinghouse can also process manual claims to carriers that do not have electronic claim file systems in place. All claims are checked for completeness and accuracy before being processed for reimbursement. Claims that are incorrect are manually reviewed. Rejected claims are returned to the medical practice.

The submission of electronic claims has many advantages when compared to the manual process. One of the biggest advantages is improved cash flow as payment from electronically submitted claims is received in two weeks or less, as compared to four to eight weeks when completed manually. Electronic claim submission leaves an audit trail of chronologically submitted data. A software program can be installed to edit claims to ensure correct coding and billing practices. An error can be corrected immediately to avoid further delay in the submission of a claim.

It is important to update billing and claim submission software as ICD-9-CM and CPT codes are added, deleted, or changed annually. Failure to do so can result in rejected claims.

INSURANCE CLAIMS FOLLOW-UP

A system must be developed in order to follow up insurance claims. A tickler file can be set up as a manual system or in a computer system as a reminder to telephone or send inquiries to insurance carriers about unpaid claims. A copy of the claim form can be filed in the tickler file then retrieved when the remittance advice (RA) or explanation of benefits (EOB) and check are received. Review the RA or EOB and compare with the claim form. A copy of the RA or EOB is attached to the claim form copy and filed in a folder for paid claims. Copies of claim forms remaining in the tickler file past the time limit for processing of payment denial can be resubmitted to the insurance carrier, indicating on the copy that this is a second request.

An insurance claims register can also be used to follow status of claim forms. This can be a three-ring binder using indexes identifying various insurance companies. A copy of the claim form can be filed under the index of the insurance carrier and the submission information is recorded in the insurance claims register. The register as demonstrated in Figure 14–32 contains columns to note the date the claim was submitted, the amount of the claim, and the date payment was received. When payment is received and posted to the patient's account, the copy of the claim is removed from the binder and placed in the patient's chart or a separate file maintained for audit purposes. A line is drawn through the information on the register to indicate claim status is complete.

Problem Claims

No matter how accurate, complete, and efficient the medical office may be, there will still be problem claims that require some type of action. Some of these prob-

INSURANCE CLAIM REGISTRY						
Date Filed	Patient Name	ID Number	Insurance Company	Amount Filed	Amount Paid	Follow-up Date
05/11/20XX	Opal Pearl	403-08-2214	CIGNA	$ 54.00		06/30/20XX
06/25/20XX	Patricia Duchane	300-54-3030	CHAMPUS	$ 295.00	$ 236.00	

Figure 14–32 An insurance claim registry can be used to follow status of claim forms.

lems are claims that are denied, rejected, or lost, incorrect payment, down coding, and pending claims.

When claims are delinquent or pending, this means payment is overdue due to the claim being reviewed or additional information required or an error has been made. An insurance tracer form can be used to follow up these problem claims as indicated in Figure 14–33.

State laws require insurance companies to notify the insured when a claim is denied and the reason for the denial. Federal laws require Medicare to issue an explanation for each denied service.

Claim forms are stamped the date received by the insurance carrier. A claim number is assigned and logged into the payer system. If the claim has not been received and logged in or has been lost, a copy of the original claim can be resubmitted indicating this is a copy of the original claim submitted on (date).

Earlier in this module the most common reasons why claim forms are rejected were listed. When claim forms are rejected, make the necessary corrections or provide additional information, and resubmit the claim for regular processing. Do not send a corrected claim for review or appeal.

When a claim is denied, it is usually denied due to medical coverage policy or program issues. These issues may be:

- The procedure was not a covered service in the policy.
- Treatment submitted was for a preexisting condition.
- Patient was no longer covered by policy when service was rendered, or service was performed before coverage was in effect.
- Service was not medically necessary.

When notice of denial is received, notify the patient by telephone or mail so he/she is aware of the denial. An appeal is then made with a request for a review in writing. Figure 14–34 is an example of a Request for Review of Part B Medicare Claim Form CMS-1964.

Occasionally claims are processed by an insurance carrier resulting in lowered reimbursement due to down coding. Down coding occurs in the following situations:

- Insufficient diagnostic information submitted on the claim form.
- Conversion of a CPT or ICD-9-CM code submitted on a claim form by the insurance carrier.
- Routine use of unspecified ICD-9-CM codes with the number "9" as the fourth or fifth digit.

The impact of down coding is lowered reimbursement. Review the EOBs and RAs to identify reasons a claim may be down coded. Use appropriate codes,

INSURANCE COMPANY_____ DATE _____

ADDRESS:_ _____

PATIENT NAME_____ NAME OF INSURED_____

IDENTIFICATION NUMBER_____

EMPLOYER NAME & ADDRESS_____

DATE CLAIM FILED_____ CLAIM AMOUNT_____

Attached is a copy of the original claim submitted to you on _____. We have not yet received a request for additional information and still await payment of this claim. Please review the attached duplicate and process for payment.

If there are any questions regarding this claim, please answer the following and return this letter to our office.

IF CLAIM HAS BEEN PAID:

        Date of payment   _____

        Amount of payment   _____

        Payment made to: _____

IF CLAIM HAS BEEN DENIED:

        Reason for denial   _____

                      _____

        Has the patient been notified: ☐ Yes   ☐ No

IF CLAIM IS STILL PENDING:

        Please state reason why?

        _____

        _____

Please return this insurance claim tracer in the enclosed envelope or you may fax to (222) 663-2211.

Thank you in this request.

Sincerely,

Judy Jolly, CMA
Insurance Specialist

Figure 14–33 An example of an insurance claim tracer used to follow up delinquent claims.

DEPARTMENT OF HEALTH AND HUMAN SERVICES
CENTERS FOR MEDICARE & MEDICAID SERVICES

FORM APPROVED
OMB NO. 0938-0033

REQUEST FOR REVIEW OF PART B MEDICARE CLAIM
Medical Insurance Benefits – Social Security Act

NOTICE – Anyone who misrepresents or falsifies essential information requested by this form may upon conviction be subject to fine and imprisonment under Federal Law.

1. Carrier's Name and Address	2. Name of Patient
	3. Health Insurance Claim Number

4. I do not agree with the determination you made on my claim as described on my Explanation of Medicare Benefits dated:

5. MY REASONS ARE: (Attach a copy of the Explanation of Medicare Benefits, or describe the service, date of service, and physician's name. NOTE: If the date on the Explanation of Medicare Benefits mentioned in Item 4 is more than 120 days ago, include your reason for not making this request earlier.)

6. Describe illness or injury:

7. ☐ I have additional evidence to submit. (Attach such evidence to this form.)
   ☐ I do not have additional evidence.

COMPLETE ALL OF THE INFORMATION REQUESTED. SIGN AND RETURN THE FIRST COPY AND ANY ATTACHMENTS TO THE CARRIER NAMED ABOVE. IF YOU NEED HELP, TAKE THIS AND YOUR NOTICE FROM THE CARRIER TO A SOCIAL SECURITY OFFICE, OR TO THE CARRIER. KEEP THE DUPLICATE COPY OF THIS FORM FOR YOUR RECORDS.

8. SIGNATURE OF *EITHER* THE CLAIMANT *OR* HIS REPRESENTATIVE

Claimant	Representative	
Address	Address	
City, State and ZIP Code	City, State and ZIP Code	
Telephone Number	Date	Telephone Number	Date

Form CMS-1964 (09/91)

Figure 14–34 Request for Review of Part B Medicare Claim can be used to request a review of a submitted claim.

indicate the medical necessity of the ICD-9-CM and CPT codes, and code to the highest level of specificity. Chapter 15 gives detailed steps in the review and appeals process.

Figure 14–35 is a summary linking the cycle that occurs from the patient visit to payment.

INSURANCE CLAIM FORM SUMMARY

Charge Slip/Superbill

1. Charge slip or superbill is attached to the outside of the patient's chart.

2. Physician sees patient, completes charge slip/superbill by marking service and diagnosis, signs charge slip/superbill, and indicates if patient needs an appointment to return.

3. Patient "checks out" at reception desk, makes return appointment if indicated by physician, and pays co-pay or other charges.

Ledger Card/Account

4. Charge slip/superbill is used to post services, charges and payments to the patient's account.

Insurance Claim Form

5. Claim form is completed and submitted to insurance carrier.

Insurance Claims Register

6. Copy of claim form is filed in pending file. Date of submission is posted on ledger card/account and recorded in the insurance claims register.

Payment

7. Payment is received and posted to patient's ledger card/account. Check is endorsed and recorded on bank deposit slip.

Patient Statement

8. Bill the patient for any balance due.

Patient or Paid File

9. Claim form copy is retrieved from the pending file and attached to the EOB and filed in patient's chart or paid file for audit.

Figure 14–35 An Insurance Claim Form Summary shows the billing and claim form cycle from the time the patient is first seen in the office until the claim is paid.

EXERCISE 14–5

Match the term with its definition, placing the correct answer in the space provided.

_____ **1.** Capitation

_____ **2.** Workers' Compensation

_____ **3.** Medicaid

_____ **4.** Medicare Part A

_____ **5.** Medicare Part B

_____ **6.** Co-payment

_____ **7.** Deductible

_____ **8.** Third-party payer

_____ **9.** Assignment of benefits

_____ **10.** TRICARE/CHAMPVA

a. Authorization to pay benefits directly to the physician

b. Federal program providing health care benefits to families of armed forces and retired military personnel and veterans

c. An individual or company making a payment on a debt

d. A reimbursement method that pays a fixed amount per person

e. Hospital insurance for persons age 65 and over, disabled, or have end-stage renal disease

f. Medical insurance optional for persons age 65 and over, disabled, or have end-stage renal disease

g. The total amount the patient must pay for covered services before benefits are payable

h. A specified dollar amount a patient must pay for each service or procedure

i. Coverage for work-related illness or injury

j. An assistance program to provide medical care for persons with incomes below national poverty level

EXERCISE 14–6

In the following exercises, complete a CMS-1500 claim form for each patient's insurance plan as indicated on the patient registration form.
Remember to:

• Refer to the patient registration form for patient information.

• Refer to the patient's medical record to complete the medical information.

• Refer to the patient's ledger card to complete charges.

PROVIDER BILLING INFORMATION

Physician: Lowery Johnson, M.D.
Internal Medicine

Address: Hwy 311 Suite A31
Sellersburg, IN 47172

Phone: (822) 752-9118

Employer ID Number: 75-2166173

PIN: 1948

Provider is a PAR with Medicare.

Hospital services performed at: Dogood Community Hospital
8080 Fifth Avenue
Temple, IN 47555

Case #1—Phila G. Badd

Welcome

Thank you for selecting our healthcare team! We will strive to provide you with the best possible healthcare. To help us meet all your healthcare needs, please fill out this form completely in ink. If you have any questions or need assistance, please ask us – we will be happy to help.

① Personal Information

Date _____ 8/2/20XX _____

Birth date _____ 9/10/1932 _____ Soc. Sec. # _____ 406-26-8683 _____

Name _____ Phila G. Badd _____ Wishes to be called _____

☐ Male ☒ Female ☐ Minor ☐ Single ☐ Married ☐ Divorced ☒ Widowed ☐ Separated

Address _____ 4515 Wildwood Circle _____

City, State, Zip _____ Sellersburg, IN 47172 _____

Employer _____ Retired _____ Occupation _____ Social Worker _____

Referred by _____ Dr. Jeff Roe _____

② Responsible Party

Who is responsible for the account? _____

Name _____ Phila G. Badd _____

Relationship to patient _____ Self _____

Birth date _____ 9/10/1932 _____ Driver's License _____ R406-26-8683001 _____

Soc. Sec. # _____ 406-26-8683 _____

Address _____ 4515 Wildwood Circle _____

City, State, Zip _____ Sellersberg, IN 47172 _____

Employer _____ Retired – Magna Services _____

Occupation _____ Social Worker _____

Work Phone _____ None _____ Ext # _____

Home Phone _____ (822) 266-5403 _____

③ Telephone

Home Phone _____ (822) 266-5403 _____

Work Phone _____ N/A _____ Ext # _____

Car Phone _____

Where do you prefer to receive calls ☒ Home ☐ Work ☐ Car

When is the best time to reach you? Time _____ Any _____ Days _____ Any _____

In the event of emergency, who should we contact?

Name _____ Ellen Sipps _____ Relationship _____ Daughter _____ Work # _____ – _____ Home # _____ 322-8121 _____

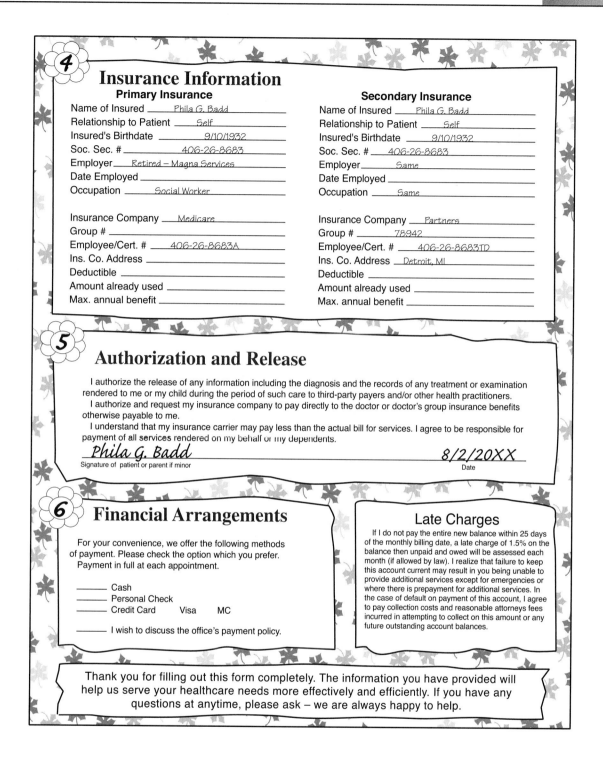

4

Insurance Information

Primary Insurance

Name of Insured _____ Phila G. Badd _____
Relationship to Patient _____ Self _____
Insured's Birthdate _____ 9/10/1932 _____
Soc. Sec. # _____ 406-26-8683 _____
Employer _____ Retired – Magna Services _____
Date Employed _____
Occupation _____ Social Worker _____

Insurance Company _____ Medicare _____
Group # _____
Employee/Cert. # _____ 406-26-8683A _____
Ins. Co. Address _____
Deductible _____
Amount already used _____
Max. annual benefit _____

Secondary Insurance

Name of Insured _____ Phila G. Badd _____
Relationship to Patient _____ Self _____
Insured's Birthdate _____ 9/10/1932 _____
Soc. Sec. # _____ 406-26-8683 _____
Employer _____ Same _____
Date Employed _____
Occupation _____ Same _____

Insurance Company _____ Partners _____
Group # _____ 78942 _____
Employee/Cert. # _____ 406-26-8683TD _____
Ins. Co. Address _____ Detroit, MI _____
Deductible _____
Amount already used _____
Max. annual benefit _____

5

Authorization and Release

I authorize the release of any information including the diagnosis and the records of any treatment or examination rendered to me or my child during the period of such care to third-party payers and/or other health practitioners.

I authorize and request my insurance company to pay directly to the doctor or doctor's group insurance benefits otherwise payable to me.

I understand that my insurance carrier may pay less than the actual bill for services. I agree to be responsible for payment of all services rendered on my behalf or my dependents.

Phila G. Badd   8/2/20XX

Signature of patient or parent if minor   Date

6

Financial Arrangements

For your convenience, we offer the following methods of payment. Please check the option which you prefer. Payment in full at each appointment.

_____ Cash
_____ Personal Check
_____ Credit Card   Visa   MC

_____ I wish to discuss the office's payment policy.

Late Charges

If I do not pay the entire new balance within 25 days of the monthly billing date, a late charge of 1.5% on the balance then unpaid and owed will be assessed each month (if allowed by law). I realize that failure to keep this account current may result in you being unable to provide additional services except for emergencies or where there is prepayment for additional services. In the case of default on payment of this account, I agree to pay collection costs and reasonable attorneys fees incurred in attempting to collect on this amount or any future outstanding account balances.

Thank you for filling out this form completely. The information you have provided will help us serve your healthcare needs more effectively and efficiently. If you have any questions at anytime, please ask – we are always happy to help.

PROGRESS NOTES		

NAME PHILA G. BADD	DATE OF BIRTH 09/10/1932 AGE 74	PAGE NO. 1

DATE	HISTORY & PHYSICAL
4/4/20XX	Weight 133–1/3 lbs. Blood pressure 180/92.
	CC: Lump in right breast
	Established patient is in the office today stating she has found a
	"lump" in her right breast. Breast exam today reveals a 1.5 x 2 cm
	nodule in the right breast around 1 o'clock. It is movable and
	nontender. Patient is referred to Dogood Community Hospital for
	bilateral mammograms tomorrow morning. She will call later
	tomorrow for results and further orders. *Lowery B. Johnson, M.D.*
4/5/20XX	Telephone Call with patient today: The bilateral mammograms done
	this morning confirm the presence of a nodule in the right breast
	as noted on breast exam yesterday, 4/4/20XX. Patient will return to
	the office tomorrow for a breast biopsy and referral to Dr. Steven
	Jones for surgical consultation. *Lowery B. Johnson, M.D.*
4/6/20XX	Office visit: Patient has returned today for biopsy of the nodule
	in the right breast. Blood pressure continues to be elevated –
	today it is 192/98 in the left arm; 190/96 in right arm.
	RECOMMENDATIONS: 1. Increase Norvasc to 10 mg each day for
	hypertension. *Lowery B. Johnson, M.D.*
4/7/20XX	The breast biopsy obtained yesterday, 4/6/20XX, reveals breast
	carcinoma. She is referred to Dr. Steven Jones for surgical
	consultation. *Lowery B. Johnson, M.D.*

STATEMENT

Lowery B. Johnson, M.D.
Hwy 311 Suite A31
Sellersburg, IN 47172
812-246-1234

PHILA G BADD
4515 WILDWOOD CIRCLE
SELLERSBURG IN 47172

| DATE | REFERENCE | DESCRIPTION | CHARGES | CREDITS | | BALANCE |
				PYMNTS.	ADJ.	
		BALANCE FORWARD ⟶				
4/4/20XX		OS – EPF	42 00			42 00
4/6/20XX		OS – DETAILED	58 00			100 00
4/6/20XX		NEEDLE BIOPSY – BREAST	155 00			255 00

RB40BC-2-96

PLEASE PAY LAST AMOUNT IN BALANCE COLUMN ⟶

THIS IS A COPY OF YOUR ACCOUNT AS IT APPEARS ON OUR RECORDS

PLEASE
DO NOT
STAPLE
IN THIS
AREA

HEALTH INSURANCE CLAIM FORM

PICA | | | | PICA | |

CARRIER

1. MEDICARE   MEDICAID   CHAMPUS   CHAMPVA   GROUP HEALTH PLAN   FECA BLK LUNG   OTHER
(Medicare #)   (Medicaid #)   (Sponsor's SSN)   (VA File #)   (SSN or ID)   (SSN)   (ID)

1a. INSURED'S I.D. NUMBER   (FOR PROGRAM IN ITEM 1)

2. PATIENT'S NAME (Last Name, First Name, Middle Initial)

3. PATIENT'S BIRTH DATE   MM   DD   YY   SEX   M   F

4. INSURED'S NAME (Last Name, First Name, Middle Initial)

5. PATIENT'S ADDRESS (No., Street)

6. PATIENT RELATIONSHIP TO INSURED
Self   Spouse   Child   Other

7. INSURED'S ADDRESS (No., Street)

CITY   STATE

8. PATIENT STATUS
Single   Married   Other
Employed   Full-Time Student   Part-Time Student

CITY   STATE

ZIP CODE   TELEPHONE (Include Area Code)
( )

ZIP CODE   TELEPHONE (INCLUDE AREA CODE)
( )

9. OTHER INSURED'S NAME (Last Name, First Name, Middle Initial)

10. IS PATIENT'S CONDITION RELATED TO:

11. INSURED'S POLICY GROUP OR FECA NUMBER

a. OTHER INSURED'S POLICY OR GROUP NUMBER

a. EMPLOYMENT? (CURRENT OR PREVIOUS)
YES   NO

a. INSURED'S DATE OF BIRTH   MM   DD   YY   SEX   M   F

b. OTHER INSURED'S DATE OF BIRTH   MM   DD   YY   SEX   M   F

b. AUTO ACCIDENT?   PLACE (State)
YES   NO

b. EMPLOYER'S NAME OR SCHOOL NAME

c. EMPLOYER'S NAME OR SCHOOL NAME

c. OTHER ACCIDENT?
YES   NO

c. INSURANCE PLAN NAME OR PROGRAM NAME

d. INSURANCE PLAN NAME OR PROGRAM NAME

10d. RESERVED FOR LOCAL USE

d. IS THERE ANOTHER HEALTH BENEFIT PLAN?
YES   NO   **If yes,** return to and complete item 9 a-d.

READ BACK OF FORM BEFORE COMPLETING & SIGNING THIS FORM.
12. PATIENT'S OR AUTHORIZED PERSON'S SIGNATURE I authorize the release of any medical or other information necessary to process this claim. I also request payment of government benefits either to myself or to the party who accepts assignment below.

SIGNED _____ DATE _____

13. INSURED'S OR AUTHORIZED PERSON'S SIGNATURE I authorize payment of medical benefits to the undersigned physician or supplier for services described below.

SIGNED _____

PATIENT AND INSURED INFORMATION

14. DATE OF CURRENT: MM   DD   YY   ILLNESS (First symptom) OR INJURY (Accident) OR PREGNANCY(LMP)

15. IF PATIENT HAS HAD SAME OR SIMILAR ILLNESS. GIVE FIRST DATE   MM   DD   YY

16. DATES PATIENT UNABLE TO WORK IN CURRENT OCCUPATION
FROM   MM   DD   YY   TO   MM   DD   YY

17. NAME OF REFERRING PHYSICIAN OR OTHER SOURCE

17a. I.D. NUMBER OF REFERRING PHYSICIAN

18. HOSPITALIZATION DATES RELATED TO CURRENT SERVICES
FROM   MM   DD   YY   TO   MM   DD   YY

19. RESERVED FOR LOCAL USE

20. OUTSIDE LAB? $ CHARGES
YES   NO

21. DIAGNOSIS OR NATURE OF ILLNESS OR INJURY. (RELATE ITEMS 1,2,3 OR 4 TO ITEM 24E BY LINE)

1. └___.___   3. └___.___
2. └___.___   4. └___.___

22. MEDICAID RESUBMISSION CODE   ORIGINAL REF. NO.

23. PRIOR AUTHORIZATION NUMBER

24. A DATE(S) OF SERVICE From MM DD YY To MM DD YY	B Place of Service	C Type of Service	D PROCEDURES, SERVICES, OR SUPPLIES (Explain Unusual Circumstances) CPT/HCPCS MODIFIER	E DIAGNOSIS CODE	F $ CHARGES	G DAYS OR UNITS	H EPSDT Family Plan	I EMG	J COB	K RESERVED FOR LOCAL USE
1										
2										
3										
4										
5										
6										

25. FEDERAL TAX I.D. NUMBER   SSN   EIN

26. PATIENT'S ACCOUNT NO.

27. ACCEPT ASSIGNMENT? (For govt. claims, see back)
YES   NO

28. TOTAL CHARGE
$

29. AMOUNT PAID
$

30. BALANCE DUE
$

31. SIGNATURE OF PHYSICIAN OR SUPPLIER INCLUDING DEGREES OR CREDENTIALS (I certify that the statements on the reverse apply to this bill and are made a part thereof.)

SIGNED _____ DATE _____

32. NAME AND ADDRESS OF FACILITY WHERE SERVICES WERE RENDERED (If other than home or office)

33. PHYSICIAN'S, SUPPLIER'S BILLING NAME, ADDRESS, ZIP CODE & PHONE #

PIN#   GRP#

PHYSICIAN OR SUPPLIER INFORMATION

(APPROVED BY AMA COUNCIL ON MEDICAL SERVICE 8/88)   **PLEASE PRINT OR TYPE**   APPROVED OMB-0938-0008 FORM CMS-1500 (12/90), FORM RRB-1500
APPROVED OMB-1215-0055 FORM OWCP-1500, APPROVED OMB-0720-0001 (CHAMPUS)

Case #2—Katrina C. Burton

Welcome To Our Office NEW PATIENT INFORMATION DATE _JUNE 10, 20XX_

PATIENT'S NAME (PLEASE PRINT)	S.S. #	MARITAL STATUS	SEX	BIRTH DATE	AGE	RELIGION (OPTIONAL)
KATRINA C. BURTON	302-15-4478	(S) M W D SEP	M (F)	1/3/1988	18	

STREET ADDRESS PERMANENT TEMPORARY	CITY AND STATE	ZIP CODE	HOME PHONE #
1005 MAIN ST.	TEMPLE IN	47555	NONE

PATIENT'S OR PARENT'S EMPLOYER	OCCUPATION (INDICATE IF STUDENT)	HOW LONG EMPLOYED	BUS. PHONE # EXT. #
NONE	NONE		

EMPLOYER'S STREET ADDRESS	CITY AND STATE		ZIP CODE

DRUG ALLERGIES, IF ANY
PENICILLIN

SPOUSE OR PARENT'S NAME	S.S. #	BIRTHDATE
ANNA BURTON	404-32-7719	01/20/1954

SPOUSE OR PARENT'S EMPLOYER	OCCUPATION (INDICATE IF STUDENT)	HOW LONG EMPLOYED	BUS. PHONE #
NONE	NONE		

EMPLOYER'S STREET ADDRESS	CITY AND STATE		ZIP CODE

*SPOUSE'S STREET ADDRESS, IF DIVORCED OR SEPARATED	CITY AND STATE	ZIP CODE	HOME PHONE #

PLEASE READ: ALL CHARGES ARE DUE AT THE TIME OF SERVICES. IF HOSPITALIZATION IS INDICATED, THE PATIENT IS RESPONSIBLE FOR FURNISHING INSURANCE CLAIM FORMS TO THE OFFICE PRIOR TO HOSPITALIZATION.

PERSON RESPONSIBLE FOR PAYMENT, IF NOT ABOVE	STREET ADDRESS, CITY, STATE	ZIP CODE	HOME PHONE #

BLUE SHIELD (GIVE NAME OF POLICYHOLDER) ☐	EFFECTIVE DATE	CERTIFICATE #	GROUP #	COVERAGE CODE

OTHER (WRITE IN NAME OF INSURANCE COMPANY) ☐	EFFECTIVE DATE	POLICY #

OTHER (WRITE IN NAME OF INSURANCE COMPANY) ☐	EFFECTIVE DATE	POLICY #

MEDICARE # ☐	RAILROAD RETIREMENT # ☐	☐ VISA or ☐ MASTERCARD #	EXP. DATE /

MEDICAID ☒ 100100536201	EFFECTIVE DATE 4/1/2004	PROGRAM #	COUNTY #	CASE #	ACCOUNT #

INDUSTRIAL ☐	WERE YOU INJURED ON THE JOB? ☐ YES ☐ NO	DATE OF INJURY	INDUSTRIAL CLAIM #

ACCIDENT ☐	WAS AN AUTOMOBILE INVOLVED? ☐ YES ☐ NO	DATE OF ACCIDENT	NAME OF ATTORNEY

WERE X-RAYS TAKEN OF THIS INJURY OR PROBLEM? ☐ YES ☐ NO	IF YES, WHERE WERE X-RAYS TAKEN? (HOSPITAL, ETC.)	DATE X-RAYS TAKEN

HAS ANY MEMBER OF YOUR IMMEDIATE FAMILY BEEN TREATED BY OUR PHYSICIAN(S) BEFORE? INCLUDE NAME OF PHYSICIAN AND FAMILY MEMBER.
MOTHER, ANNA BURTON, HAS SEEN DR. JOHNSON

REFERRED BY	STREET ADDRESS, CITY, STATE	ZIP CODE	PHONE #

ALL PROFESSIONAL SERVICES RENDERED ARE CHARGED TO THE PATIENT. NECESSARY FORMS WILL BE COMPLETED TO HELP EXPEDITE INSURANCE CARRIER PAYMENTS. HOWEVER, THE PATIENT IS RESPONSIBLE FOR ALL FEES, REGARDLESS OF INSURANCE COVERAGE. IT IS ALSO CUSTOMARY TO PAY FOR SERVICES WHEN RENDERED UNLESS OTHER ARRANGEMENTS HAVE BEEN MADE IN ADVANCE WITH OUR OFFICE BOOKKEEPER.

INSURANCE AUTHORIZATION AND ASSIGNMENT

Name of Policy Holder _____ HIC Number _____

I request that payment of authorized Medicare/Other Insurance company benefits be made either to me or on my behalf to _____
for any services furnished me by that party who accepts assignment/physician. Regulations pertaining to Medicare assignment of benefits apply.

I authorize any holder of medical or other information about me to release to the Social Security Administration and Health Care Financing Administration or its intermediaries or carriers any information needed for this or a related Medicare claim/other Insurance Company claim. I permit a copy of this authorization to be used in place of the original, and request payment of medical insurance benefits either to myself or to the party who accepts assignment. I understand it is mandatory to notify the health care provider of any other party who may be responsible for paying for my treatment. (Section 1128B of the Social Security Act and 31 U.S.C. 3801-3812 provides penalties for withholding this information).

Signature _Katrina Burton_____   Date _6/10/20XX_____

NEW PATIENT INFORMATION

F200-1 Rev. 12/94 Professional Filing Systems, Inc. To Order Call 1-800-477-7374, In Atlanta 770/396-4994

| PROGRESS NOTES | | |

NAME Katrina C. Burton   DATE OF BIRTH 01/03/1988 AGE 18   PAGE NO. 1

DATE	HISTORY & PHYSICAL
6/10/20XX	Office Service: Weight 125–3/4 lbs. B/P 102/70 T 100F. R 18.
	She was seen in the ER on 6/8/9X with symptoms of chest congestion,
	dyspnea, hemoptysis, with a T at that time of 102F. Chest x-ray
	in the ER demonstrated bronchopneumonia right lung field.
	Today in the office she continues to complain of cough productive of
	yellow-green sputum with some blood streaks. Chest x-ray in the
	office today shows patchy consolidation right lung field representative
	of bronchopneumonia. CBC reveals an elevated WBC of 18.5.
	DIAGNOSIS: Bronchopneumonia.
	RECOMMENDATIONS: 1. Keflex 250 mg q.i.d. x 2 weeks.
	2. Aspirin for temp. elevation q 4 hrs.
	She is to return one week for recheck and repeat chest x-ray.
	Lowery B. Johnson, M.D.
6/17/20XX	Office Service–Recheck: Patient continues to be quite ill with
	T 100F or greater. Continues to have productive cough with some
	blood occurring mostly at night and early a.m. She has remained on
	the Keflex as prescribed on 6/10/20XX.
	RECOMMENDATIONS: 1. Outpatient admission to Dogood Community
	Hospital for 24-hour observation, repeat chest x-ray, bronchoscopy,
	collection of sputum x 2 for acid fast stains and cultures.
	Lowery B. Johnson, M.D.
6/17/20XX	Admission to hospital observation bed, 24-hour. *P/A 42003698–1*
6/22/20XX	Office Service–Follow-up: Patient is in today for follow-up after
	24-hour observation 6/17/20XX. She has improved. Temp. today is
	99F. Lab/x-ray studies on 6/17/20XX revealed the bronchopneumonia;
	no underlying disease or neoplasm. Repeat chest x-ray today shows
	pneumonia resolving. She will continue Keflex one more week and
	then discontinue. Repeat chest x-ray will be made at that time.
	Lowery B. Johnson, M.D.

STATEMENT

Lowery B. Johnson, M.D.
Hwy 311 Suite A31
Sellersburg, IN 47172
812-246-1234

ANNA BURTON
1005 MAIN ST
TEMPLE IN 47555

RE: Katrina C. Burton

DATE	REFERENCE	DESCRIPTION	CHARGES	CREDITS		BALANCE
				PYMNTS.	ADJ.	
		BALANCE FORWARD ⟶				
6/10/20XX		OS – Comp. – NP	55 00			55 00
6/10/20XX		CBC (AUTO)	22 00			77 00
6/10/20XX		CHEST X-RAY (2 VIEWS)	118 00			195 00
6/17/20XX		OS	N/C			195 00
6/17/20XX		OBSV – INITIAL – DET	125 00			320 00
6/22/20XX		OS – P.F.	46 00			366 00
6/22/20XX		CHEST X-RAY (2 VIEWS)	118 00			484 00

PLEASE PAY LAST AMOUNT IN BALANCE COLUMN ⟶

CBC—Complete Blood Count   INJ—Injection
OS—Office Service   UA—Urinalysis
OBSV—Observation Bed   EKG—Electrocardiogram

THIS IS A COPY OF YOUR ACCOUNT AS IT APPEARS ON OUR RECORDS

PLEASE
DO NOT
STAPLE
IN THIS
AREA

CARRIER →

| | PICA | | | | | | | | | **HEALTH INSURANCE CLAIM FORM** | | PICA | |

1. MEDICARE　　MEDICAID　　CHAMPUS　　CHAMPVA　　GROUP HEALTH PLAN　　FECA BLK LUNG　　OTHER
☐ (Medicare #)　☐ (Medicaid #)　☐ (Sponsor's SSN)　☐ (VA File #)　☐ (SSN or ID)　☐ (SSN)　☐ (ID)

1a. INSURED'S I.D. NUMBER (FOR PROGRAM IN ITEM 1)

2. PATIENT'S NAME (Last Name, First Name, Middle Initial)

3. PATIENT'S BIRTH DATE MM | DD | YY　　SEX　M ☐　F ☐

4. INSURED'S NAME (Last Name, First Name, Middle Initial)

5. PATIENT'S ADDRESS (No., Street)

6. PATIENT RELATIONSHIP TO INSURED
Self ☐　Spouse ☐　Child ☐　Other ☐

7. INSURED'S ADDRESS (No., Street)

CITY　　STATE

8. PATIENT STATUS
Single ☐　Married ☐　Other ☐
Employed ☐　Full-Time Student ☐　Part-Time Student ☐

CITY　　STATE

ZIP CODE　　TELEPHONE (Include Area Code) ( )

ZIP CODE　　TELEPHONE (INCLUDE AREA CODE) ( )

9. OTHER INSURED'S NAME (Last Name, First Name, Middle Initial)

10. IS PATIENT'S CONDITION RELATED TO:

11. INSURED'S POLICY GROUP OR FECA NUMBER

a. OTHER INSURED'S POLICY OR GROUP NUMBER

a. EMPLOYMENT? (CURRENT OR PREVIOUS)
☐ YES　☐ NO

a. INSURED'S DATE OF BIRTH MM | DD | YY　SEX　M ☐　F ☐

b. OTHER INSURED'S DATE OF BIRTH MM | DD | YY　SEX　M ☐　F ☐

b. AUTO ACCIDENT?　PLACE (State)
☐ YES　☐ NO

b. EMPLOYER'S NAME OR SCHOOL NAME

c. EMPLOYER'S NAME OR SCHOOL NAME

c. OTHER ACCIDENT?
☐ YES　☐ NO

c. INSURANCE PLAN NAME OR PROGRAM NAME

d. INSURANCE PLAN NAME OR PROGRAM NAME

10d. RESERVED FOR LOCAL USE

d. IS THERE ANOTHER HEALTH BENEFIT PLAN?
☐ YES　☐ NO　**If yes**, return to and complete item 9 a-d.

READ BACK OF FORM BEFORE COMPLETING & SIGNING THIS FORM.
12. PATIENT'S OR AUTHORIZED PERSON'S SIGNATURE I authorize the release of any medical or other information necessary to process this claim. I also request payment of government benefits either to myself or to the party who accepts assignment below.

SIGNED　　DATE

13. INSURED'S OR AUTHORIZED PERSON'S SIGNATURE I authorize payment of medical benefits to the undersigned physician or supplier for services described below.

SIGNED

← PATIENT AND INSURED INFORMATION →

14. DATE OF CURRENT: MM | DD | YY　ILLNESS (First symptom) OR INJURY (Accident) OR PREGNANCY(LMP)

15. IF PATIENT HAS HAD SAME OR SIMILAR ILLNESS. GIVE FIRST DATE MM | DD | YY

16. DATES PATIENT UNABLE TO WORK IN CURRENT OCCUPATION MM | DD | YY　FROM　TO MM | DD | YY

17. NAME OF REFERRING PHYSICIAN OR OTHER SOURCE

17a. I.D. NUMBER OF REFERRING PHYSICIAN

18. HOSPITALIZATION DATES RELATED TO CURRENT SERVICES MM | DD | YY　FROM　TO MM | DD | YY

19. RESERVED FOR LOCAL USE

20. OUTSIDE LAB?　$ CHARGES
☐ YES　☐ NO

21. DIAGNOSIS OR NATURE OF ILLNESS OR INJURY. (RELATE ITEMS 1,2,3 OR 4 TO ITEM 24E BY LINE)

1. ⌊___ . ___⌋　　3. ⌊___ . ___⌋

2. ⌊___ . ___⌋　　4. ⌊___ . ___⌋

22. MEDICAID RESUBMISSION CODE　ORIGINAL REF. NO.

23. PRIOR AUTHORIZATION NUMBER

24. A DATE(S) OF SERVICE						B Place of Service	C Type of Service	D PROCEDURES, SERVICES, OR SUPPLIES (Explain Unusual Circumstances) CPT/HCPCS	MODIFIER	E DIAGNOSIS CODE	F $ CHARGES	G DAYS OR UNITS	H EPSDT Family Plan	I EMG	J COB	K RESERVED FOR LOCAL USE
From MM	DD	YY	To MM	DD	YY											
1																
2																
3																
4																
5																
6																

25. FEDERAL TAX I.D. NUMBER　SSN ☐ EIN ☐

26. PATIENT'S ACCOUNT NO.

27. ACCEPT ASSIGNMENT? (For govt. claims, see back)　☐ YES　☐ NO

28. TOTAL CHARGE $

29. AMOUNT PAID $

30. BALANCE DUE $

31. SIGNATURE OF PHYSICIAN OR SUPPLIER INCLUDING DEGREES OR CREDENTIALS (I certify that the statements on the reverse apply to this bill and are made a part thereof.)

SIGNED　　DATE

32. NAME AND ADDRESS OF FACILITY WHERE SERVICES WERE RENDERED (If other than home or office)

33. PHYSICIAN'S, SUPPLIER'S BILLING NAME, ADDRESS, ZIP CODE & PHONE #

PIN#　　GRP#

← PHYSICIAN OR SUPPLIER INFORMATION →

(APPROVED BY AMA COUNCIL ON MEDICAL SERVICE 8/88)　**PLEASE PRINT OR TYPE**

APPROVED OMB-0938-0008 FORM CMS-1500 (12/90), FORM RRB-1500
APPROVED OMB-1215-0055 FORM OWCP-1500, APPROVED OMB-0720-0001 (CHAMPUS)

SUMMARY

Today's insurance specialists, medical billers and coders, and medical assistants must have current knowledge of deductibles, co-payments, and referrals. Skill is required for CPT and ICD-9-CM coding and the medical necessity documented for reimbursement. There must be an understanding of the CMS-1500 claim form and the filing process in the practice, whether it is paper or electronic. There must be a working knowledge of Medicaid, Medicare and its secondary payers, as well as all participating provider agreements, and what information is required to submit claim forms.

In addition to understanding what amounts can be billed to the patient, coders must also know when amounts are to be adjusted. When claims are rejected, denied, or payment is not received, it is important to know how to request a review of the claim or pursue an appeal. It is essential to remain current in the profession by attending training and continuing education seminars and reading newsletters and bulletins published by the insurance carriers as proposed changes become implemented: ICD-10-CM, APGs and E/M documentation guidelines.

REFERENCES

AdminaStar Federal, Inc. *Medicare B special bulletin.* SB97-08, August 1997. Indianapolis, IN.

CMS-1500 completion instructions. Upstate Medicaid Division—B. Retrieved August 15, 2005, from www.umd.nycpic.com

Fordney, M. (2003). *Insurance handbook for the medical office* (6th ed.). Philadelphia: Elsevier.

Fordney, M., & French, L. (2003). *Medical insurance billing and coding: An essentials worktext.* Philadelphia: Elsevier.

Green, M. & Rowell, J. (2006). *Understanding health insurance: A guide to billing and reimbursement* (8th ed.). Clifton Park, NY: Thomson Delmar Learning.

HIPAA standard code set. U.S. Department of Health and Social Services. Retrieved August 30, 2005 from *www.aspe.hhs.gov*

Lindh, W., Pooler, M., Tamparo, C., & Dahl, B. (2006). *Comprehensive medical assisting: Administrative and clinical competencies* (3rd ed.). Clifton Park, NY: Thomson Delmar Learning.

Chapter 15

Payment for Professional Health Care Services, Auditing, and Appeals

KEY TERMS

advance beneficiary notice (ABN)
audit
Balanced Budget Act
capitation
covered service
down coding
False Claims Act

medical necessity
Medicare Modernization Act
nonparticipating provider
(nonPAR)
Office of Inspector General (OIG)
overpayment
participating provider (PAR)

point of service (POS)
preferred provider organization
(PPO)
reimbursement
unbundling
upcoding
withhold

LEARNING OBJECTIVES

Upon successful completion of this chapter, you should be able to:

1. Recognize the payment cycle steps.
2. Explain the components for payment, calculation, and payment strategy.
3. Describe participating, nonparticipating, and deactivation status with Medicare.
4. Recognize internal and external obstacles to accurate and timely payment.
5. Pinpoint discrepancies in billing and documentation.
6. Identify **audit** flags, targets, and compliance concepts.

audit
An evaluation of the billing practices within a medical office. Medical billing and insurance records are abstracted and compared to investigate proper billing, coding, and documentation technique and practices.

INTRODUCTION

This chapter discusses the typical payment cycle for physician office services, defining the multiple processes that affect the financial results. The payment cycle components will be reviewed in detail, from the initial phase through the appeal and potential audit phase. Table 15–1 introduces a few of the common acronyms and abbreviations that are frequently referred to by the insurance world.

TABLE 15-1   Health Insurance Claim Prefixes.

A	Annuitant
MA	Spouse
WA	Widow of retired husband
WCA	With dependent children (husband retired)
WD	Widow (husband died prior to retirement)
WCD	Widow with dependent children (husband died prior to retirement)
PA	Parent of annuitant
PD	Parent (annuitant died prior to retirement)
JA	Joint annuitant
H	Retired husband
MH	Spouse
WH	Widow
WCH	Widow and child

PAYMENT CYCLE

Every cog in the wheel must turn properly in order for the payment cycle to efficiently produce revenue and cash flow. The importance of these steps—and the potential sanctions for those who choose to purposefully bypass the rules—are presented in this chapter.

Historically, the health care service was rendered, and the patient paid directly to the medical professionals. Although this may still occur, it is much less frequent today. Now, much more commonly, the professionals and facilities are paid long after the care was provided. This retroactive payment concept is termed **reimbursement.** Unfortunately, it is becoming increasingly difficult for physicians and the health care organizations to obtain payment for the professional services that are provided.

The majority of patients expect their insurance plan will cover the health care services entirely. In reality, most patients' insurance plan coverage has limitations, typically established by the employer when setting up the benefit package. Employers make difficult decisions when selecting the health insurance benefit plans for their employees, and rising costs of health insurance premiums cause employers to continually reconsider the benefit package. There are very few insurance plans (other than a "celebrity style" Lloyds of London policy) that cover any and all health care situations.

Many patients expect that their insurance plan will pay for any and all health care services the physician and/or hospital deems appropriate. Unfortunately, the patient's awareness of the limitations of his or her insurance benefits is often not understood prior to accessing the health care system. For example, most patients

reimbursement
The act of being paid back or payment in exchange for goods or services.

would not realize the financial obligation for the co-payment and/or the deductible amount upon using emergency room care. Nor are most patients knowledgeable regarding the definition of emergency versus urgent, or other definitions that apply to their particular insurance. The first time many patients learn of their insurance plan's limitations and of their financial obligations for services rendered is upon their arrival for care at the emergency room.

This same learning curve is common for many types of patient care, including diagnostic testing (e.g., PET scans), mental health care, physical and occupational therapy, preventive services, and increasingly, drug coverage benefits. Patients begin to understand their insurance benefits and limitations only when they access the care.

More commonly the patient presents his or her insurance card at the time of receiving health care, and the patient only pays the applicable co-payment and deductible at the time of the service. The claim is sent to the insurance plan to obtain the remainder of the payment (or partial payment). Each state legislates rules for the timely payment of claims. Typical insurance payments may occur as early as 10 days or as long as 2 years after the treatment.

Appointment

For most physician offices and hospital outpatient planned care, the payment cycle begins when the appointment is scheduled for the patient. For hospital inpatient care, commonly the patient will arrive at the emergency room for care, without a scheduled appointment.

Excellent verbal and customer service skills demonstrated by staff members while setting up the appointments are perhaps the most valuable marketing and patient retention asset that a practice or organization may have. The public will often select their care providers based upon this first impression.

Obtaining Patient Demographic Information

Obtaining patient demographic information is one of the most important aspects affecting the payment for health care services today. *Accuracy is paramount, and verification of eligibility and benefit coverage for each encounter and service is required.* This is essential to the cash flow of the organization. Every detail that is captured at this early stage will dramatically affect the financial processes for the physician practice or hospital system.

Details of importance are:

- Patient's last name—changed name due to marriage or other legal name changes
- New social security number—now required for the newborn child very soon after the birth
- Date of birth for both the patient and the spouse—determines which insurance plan has the obligation for the payment
- Does the patient intend to submit an insurance claim for the services today? Sometimes the patient may choose to personally pay for care, and not submit to the insurance plan.
- Insurance card information—a copy of the front and back of the insurance card *per encounter* is required. The insurance ID or group numbers, where to send the claim, who to call to determine if the patient is insured, and the benefits listed in the card often change. The co-payment and deductible amounts may or may not be stated on the card.

- Employer information—the employer information frequently changes
- Patient status—single, married, divorced, custody, student—obtain a copy of the decree or other document as soon as possible.
- Is the care related to employment or an accident? Obtain the exact Workers' Compensation or accident information immediately.

Medicare insurance cards indicate a suffix as described by the Social Security Administration (SSA). In order to correct or revise the suffix, a correction form must be completed with the SSA. Table 15–2 lists these suffixes.

Contacting the Insurance Plan

The patient's insurance plan may require that many policies and procedures be followed prior to providing the care. The first step required for each encounter or visit is to verify the patient is insured with that particular insurance plan. The process for verifying eligibility may be to call or check electronically. This may sound like a simple requirement, but in reality may be very challenging. Examples include determining if a patient is insured soon after he or she is hired by a new employer, determining if a child patient is insured after a divorce is final, and determining if an underage patient who is pregnant and not dependent upon her parents is insured. This is known as checking the eligibility of the insured.

The next step is to the check the insurance benefits coverage and policies for the planned care, services, or items. Depending upon the type of the insurance, checking on coverage may require a separate telephone call or electronic site which may vary from the previous encounter verification for eligibility (eg: diagnostic testing vs. surgical procedure).

Determining the policies and procedures for the claim submission for the planned service is recommended. In many cases, the insurance plan may require that certain quality steps be taken prior to payment for the care. Knowing the current policies prior to the care will increase the potential for payment and will certainly improve the time required for payment. This is especially true for new technology, new scientific items, expensive medical care, and cosmetic or other radical surgical cases.

If the insurance plan describes the planned care as not a covered benefit, the patient is to be informed of the plan's limitations and must sign an **advance beneficiary notice (ABN)** (Figure 15–1). Since inception of the HIPAA rules, the ABN procedure is required for all health insurance plans that the physician (or facility) is contracted with as a **participating provider (PAR).** The ABN may or may not be required for accident patient care, as the HIPAA rules do not apply for Workers' Compensation or auto plans. More information regarding the ABN procedure will be discussed later in the chapter; at this point, understanding that obtaining the ABN will dramatically affect the payment cycle is sufficient.

Care Begins

During the time the care is being rendered, all too often the patient will ask for additional care or the physician will deem it necessary to provide more services than planned. A very smooth procedure is required that causes the care to be postponed for a moment in order to complete the ABN process. The instruction and signatures on the ABN may be obtained by the front staff, administrator, back office staff, or personally by the physician. The key is to provide the instruction accurately, properly complete the form, and obtain the patient's signature *prior* to performing the care.

advance beneficiary notice (ABN)
Notice to health insurance beneficiaries that the program will probably not pay for a service. The patient assumes financial responsibility for paying the provider directly for the service.

participating provider (PAR)
Physician who contracts to accept assignment (receives payment directly) from the health insurance program.

TABLE 15–2   **Medicare Health Insurance Claim Number Suffix Descriptions**

A	Wage Earner (Retired)
B	Wife
B1	Husband
B2	Young Wife
C1–C9	Child (including disabled or student)
D	Aged Widow
D1	Widower
D6	Surviving Divorced Wife
E	Widowed Mother
E1	Surviving Divorced Mother
E4	Widowed Father
E5	Surviving Divorced Father
F1	Father
F2	Mother
F3	Stepfather
F4	Stepmother
F5	Adopting Father
F6	Adopting Mother
G	Claimant of Lump-Sum Death Benefits
HA	Wage earner (disability)
HB	Wife of disabled wage earner
HB1	Husband of disabled wage earner
HC	Child of disabled wage earner
M	Uninsured Premium Health Insurance Benefits (Part A)
M1	Uninsured Qualified for but refused HIB (Part A)
T	Uninsured- Entitled to HIB (Part A) under deemed or renal provisions
W	Disabled Widow
W1	Disabled Widower
W6	Disabled Surviving Divorced Wife

Patient's Name: _____   Medicare # (HICN): _____

ADVANCE BENEFICIARY NOTICE (ABN)

NOTE: You need to make a choice about receiving these health care items or services.

We expect that Medicare will not pay for the item(s) or service(s) that are described below. Medicare does not pay for all of your health care costs. Medicare only pays for covered items and services when Medicare rules are met. The fact that Medicare may not pay for a particular item or service does not mean that you should not receive it. There may be a good reason your doctor recommended it. Right now, in your case, **Medicare probably will not pay for –**

Items or Services:
Because:

The purpose of this form is to help you make an informed choice about whether or not you want to receive these items or services, knowing that you might have to pay for them yourself. Before you make a decision about your options, you should **read this entire notice carefully.**
- Ask us to explain, if you don't understand why Medicare probably won't pay.
- Ask us how much these items or services will cost you (**Estimated Cost: $_____**), in case you have to pay for them yourself or through other insurance.

PLEASE CHOOSE **ONE** OPTION. CHECK **ONE** BOX.   **SIGN & DATE** YOUR CHOICE.

☐ **Option 1. YES.**   **I want to receive these items or services.**

I understand that Medicare will not decide whether to pay unless I receive these items or services. Please submit my claim to Medicare. I understand that you may bill me for items or services and that I may have to pay the bill while Medicare is making its decision. If Medicare does pay, you will refund to me any payments I made to you that are due to me. If Medicare denies payment, I agree to be personally and fully responsible for payment. That is, I will pay personally, either out of pocket or through any other insurance that I have. I understand I can appeal Medicare's decision.

☐ **Option 2. NO.**   **I have decided not to receive these items or services.**

I will not receive these items or services. I understand that you will not be able to submit a claim to Medicare and that I will not be able to appeal your opinion that Medicare won't pay.

_____   _____
Date   **Signature of patient or person acting on patient's behalf**

NOTE: Your health information will be kept confidential. Any information that we collect about you on this form will be kept confidential in our offices. If a claim is submitted to Medicare, your health information on this form may be shared with Medicare. Your health information which Medicare sees will be kept confidential by Medicare.

OMB Approval No. 0938-0566   Form No. CMS-R-131-G   (June 2002)

Figure 15–1 HIPAA requires that patients sign an advance beneficiary notice for participating health Insurance care.

ENCOUNTER FORMS, SUPERBILLS, FEE SLIPS, OR CHARGE TICKETS

Upon audit it is frequently discovered that the encounter form does not accurately correlate to the medical record. Upon interviewing staff members, it is not uncommon to hear something like "the form didn't have that as an option." This seems to be particularly true for accurately linking ICD-9-CM codes to each and every service that is performed and also for the specific dose and route of medications given. Updating the encounter form now requires a quarterly update; therefore, most offices print fewer forms at a time than they used to.

Next, the style of the physician encounter is very important. Table 15–3 depicts the recommended concepts for the physician office location. Additional forms may be beneficial for procedures or hospital inpatient physician services. The encounter form descriptions need to match CPT codes, guiding toward accurate selection. Renaming the visits (Level 4, for example) can be risky. Each checked or circled CPT service needs to clearly indicate the ICD-9-CM codes that correlate to each service clearly documented in the medical record. All too often, the encounter formats do not provide a simple approach to this valuable data.

Encounters and services that are performed by the physician at facilities outside of the physician office are also key to submitting accurate claims. A simple index card has been popular for many years, yet depending upon the specialty may not adequately allow for communication between the physician and the biller/coder. For example, the form needs to encourage clear indication for time, when required by the code. A common finding upon audit is a claim submission for a discharge from the hospital, lacking a description of the minutes if over thirty minutes; or the time in and time out for each procedure while performing critical care services; or the care of a patient in multiple settings during one date, midnight to midnight. Depending upon the specialty, the hospital services may describe 100 percent of the practice, certainly requiring frequent and detailed information to be transmitted or shared with the coder. Some physicians are beginning to carry the tools such as personal digital assistants (PDAs) or other electronic wireless apparati to assist in tracking the services provided. Additionally, some hospitals allow direct access to the medical record system from the physician office locations. The physician office can then print the necessary operative reports, pathology or radiology results, inpatient progress notes, etc.

Within the physician office location, there may be separate encounter forms for various individuals or diagnostic testing services. For example, an encounter form may be printed on a special color paper to clearly indicate that a nurse practitioner (NP) performed the encounter while there was no physician on site, and not to send the claim in using the physician provider number, also known as the physician "incident to" concepts. In other words, the claim would be submitted using the NP's provider number. Another popular form is an encounter form for the x-ray technician within an orthopedic practice setting; or a laboratory form for the lab technician within an internal medicine practice. As automation is implemented, all of these details need to be considered very carefully, encouraging accurate selection of the codes for the exact services that are rendered.

TABLE 15–3   Example of an Encounter Form.

CPT	Description of Service	ICD-9-CM	ICD-9-CM	ICD-9-CM
99201	Office visit 3 of 3 PF Hx, PF exam, Straightforward decision making	————	————	————

Current Procedural Terminology (CPT) © 2005 American Medical Association. All Rights Reserved.

Coding Tip	*The term 'incident to' refers to the care or services provided by someone other than the physician, yet submission of the claim using the physician provider number. When this is done, it is highly recommended to obtain the written policies and procedures from the insurance plan as the rules vary per insurance plan.*

For CMS, the 'incident to' policies are strictly enforced, therefore one should exactly follow every detail of the policies. For example, physicians must be present at the time of the encounter and must document their integral involvement for the care, specifically the medical decision making. The 'incident to' policies have limitations (ie: do not apply for all services, at all locations, performed by all staff levels of licensure). Each insurance plan tends to have policies, not necessarily equal to the strict CMS policy. The scope of practice of health care professionals does not necessarily correlate to the insurance payment policies. This typically causes many questions and confusion in the field, that requires detailed investigation and education for the coder.

As electronic medical records become more available and utilized in the industry, it is anticipated that fewer encounter/charge tickets will be in use. The capture will be automated by following the patient through the practice electronically rather than with paper.

Hospital facilities also meet with challenges of documentation and capturing data for the chargemaster. The working diagnosis is often not documented, since the ICD-9-CM codes are selected with a different set of guidelines from the outpatient guidelines. It is advantageous for the hospital for the physician to list the symptoms or preliminary diagnoses leading to the Diagnosis Related Group (DRG). Another challenging area is the documentation of complications or comorbidities that may arise during care. This is a huge revenue factor for hospital facilities. Focused education for this alone would dramatically affect reimbursements for hospitals. The chargemaster encounter format should be frequently reviewed and will affect hospital facility financial reimbursements.

Cheat Sheets

The most common cheat sheets tend to be either the documentation format for the E/M encounter (the AMA/CPT or 1995 Guidelines and/or the 1997 Guidelines) or the listing of the ICD-9-CM codes. Any of these popular styles can lead to very extensive sanctions and, if utilized, should be very closely monitored for accuracy.

At a recent national conference, four prominent attorneys that defend fraud cases within their practices were asked their opinions regarding the risks associated with the use of "cloned" vs. template E/M medical records. Two of the attorneys strongly opposed the use of cloned records, while two attorneys voiced less concern. The cloned record is one that includes the usual history, physical findings and/or medical decision making, whereas a template simply lists the E/M guideline components that need to be completed.

As the industry enters into the use of electronic medical records, the use of templates is becoming even more popular. The risk of abuse or fraud escalates if the formats for collecting information are not properly implemented to accurately reflect a "mirror image" of the encounter performed.

The second common cheat sheet is a specialty ICD-9-CM listing. Shortcomings of these quick references include not listing all of the digits (fifth digit lacking) or, more importantly, an incomplete description. Unfortunately, an alarming number of staff members utilize the specialty "cheat sheets" because they believe these are the only codes that are available for selection, perhaps in the absence of ever seeing an ICD-9-CM code book. Clearly, there are many more code options and there are also requirements in the ICD-9-CM guidelines when multiple code selections are necessary. The ICD-9-CM codes are updated annually October 1, whereas the cheat sheets may be years outdated. If the code is entered into a claim, this is considered to be fraudulent by the person that caused the concern (perhaps the medical staff member indicating the ICD-9-CM code on the encounter form). When updating cheat sheets, place the date and the person that created the cheat sheet on the form. When distributing a new cheat sheet, collect and file the old sheet according to the person who utilized it.

It is strongly advised to cease using all cheat sheets, and instead encourage the use of the ICD-9-CM code book. The book includes the ICD-9-CM guidelines, also helpful in determining the multiple codes that may be required to accurately describe the encounter. Finding the accurate code to indicate the reason for ordering a test, for example, is nearly an impossible task without referring to the entire book.

Finally, it is wise to begin training personnel in the basics of using the ICD-9-CM index—locating, sequencing, recognizing common abbreviations and indicators—prior to the inception of ICD-10-CM. Cheat sheets will likely be impossible with the ICD-10-CM concepts.

Collection of Payment at the Time of Service

If the patient chose to personally pay for the service, simply collect the entire amount for all care at the cashier window. Most practices have set up mechanisms to accept many forms of payment such as cash or checks, debit or credit cards.

If the patient owes for previous care, collect this fee as well, according to financial policies in place.

Charge Entry

Once the payment has been given to the practice or facility, it should be entered into some sort of an accounting system. Most physician offices use an automated practice management system to enter the payment into the patient's account, reconciling the ticket for the encounter, and balancing the date. Hospital facilities may handle payments in various methods, due to the volume of patients and personnel. The cash and daily balancing should be managed effectively, to avoid possible embezzlement risks. Again, depending upon the size of the organization, this process may vary; however, incorporating strong security and efficiency principles in overseeing the financial processes is recommended for all organizations.

Submit the Claim

Depending upon the practice management system, the claim preparation may begin at the cashier desk or may actually be submitted at this point. Smaller practices tend to implement streamlined processes, actually completing the CPT and ICD-9-CM codes and remaining details concurrently with the cashiering process. Other organizations may use a worksheet (encounter capture form) and enter partial details at the time of the visit, and then another person verifies the details of the information prior to submitting the claim. Verification at this point may include review of pathology or radiology reports, surgical operative notes, hospital visit or critical care notes, etc.

Regardless, it is imperative and required by law that the claim be transmitted with accurate information in each field, including the CPT, ICD-9-CM, and HCPCSII codes and their modifier use.

TABLE 15–4 **List of New Required Data Elements.**

Part A 837 X12 N837I	■ X12 837I transaction overhead information (ST, BHT, transmission type REF, HLs, and SE segments, along with numerous qualifiers) ■ Submitter identifier (837 overhead info) ■ Receiver name and ID ■ Billing provider tax ID number or social security number (one of the following: 1) attending physician tax ID number or social security number; 2) operating physician tax ID number or social security number; or 3) other provider tax ID number or social security number) ■ Payer identifier ■ Explanation of benefits indicator ■ Provider or supplier signature indicator
Part B 837 X12 837P	■ X12 837P transaction overhead information (ST, BHT, transmission type REF, HLs, and SE segments, along with numerous qualifiers) ■ Receiver name and ID ■ Submitter name ■ Submitter phone number ■ Billing provider tax ID number or social security number ■ Pay-to provider tax ID number or social security number ■ Rendering provider tax ID number or social security number

The CMS-1500 (previously the HCFA-1500) claim form is anticipated in the future to transition to the electronic format known as the X12N 837P for (Part B) physician services or the X12N 837I for institutional (Part A) facilities. See Table 15–4 for data elements that were not required on the previous formats. Many practice management systems are seamlessly converting the data into this new format for the physician practice. In the meantime, the data must be completed as described by the carrier or insurance plan newsletters. If submitting a paper claim rather than an electronic transmitted claim, most insurance plans, including the majority of the CMS carriers, require the use of the standard CMS-1500 red ink form imprinted with black ink data, allowing optical scanning upon receipt.

The top errors for this *new* electronic format are:

- The provider number and UPIN are incorrect or placed in the wrong fields.
- Submitter and receiver codes are not valid.
- Contractor codes are omitted.
- ISA data elements are invalid lengths.
- Taxonomy codes, if placed on the claim, are not valid.
- Character set is not valid.
- Subscriber date of birth or gender are incorrect.
- Street address and city, state, and zipcode are submitted in the wrong format.
- Phone number is missing.
- Billing provider and the rendering provider, if the same, are not both indicated.
- Dates are in the wrong format.

STEP-BY-STEP COMPLETION OF A PAPER CMS-1500 FORM

The term mandatory indicates for Medicare that the claim cannot be processed unless the information is accurately depicted in these fields. The term optional does *not* necessarily indicate the field should be left blank. It simply has not been identified as an automatic rejection field for the CMS-1500 form. If the field describes the encounter, then it should be completed as accurately as possible. Refer to Figure 15–2 with highlighted fields as you review the following list of steps.

Mandatory Box 1: Place an "X" in the Medicare, Medicaid, CHAMPUS (TRICARE), Group Health Plan, FECA, Other.

Mandatory Box 1a: Enter the insured's ID number exactly as on the current card that has been verified for eligibility.

Mandatory Box 2: Enter patient's last name, first name, middle initial.

Mandatory Box 3: Enter patient's date of birth, using 6 digits. Place an "X" in the proper M/F option.

Box 4, optional: If Medicare is secondary payer, enter the policy holder's name. If the patient is the policy-holder, enter "Same."

Mandatory Box 5 Line 1: Enter patient's address number and street. Line 2: Enter city and state. Line 3: Enter Zip code and telephone with area code.

Box 6, optional: If the patient is the insured, leave blank. If not, enter the relationship to the insured.

Box 7, optional: If the insured's address is other than the patient's, enter the insurance address.

Box 8, optional: Enter single, widowed, divorced, employed, student status

Box 9, optional: If the patient is the policy holder, enter "Same." If policyholder name is different than the Box 2 patient name, enter the policyholder's name in Box 9. If no benefits, leave blank. If Medigap enter plan name.

Box 9a, optional: Enter Medigap (highly recommended) policy number or group number per card.

Box 9b, optional: Enter if policyholder is different than patient, and enter that person's date of birth, and sex.

Box 9c, optional: Claim address of Medigap insurer. (If the unique identifier is entered in 9d, you do not need to type it in again.)

Box 9d, optional: Enter Medigap name and carrier unique identifier.

Box 10a–c, optional: Check all accurately: employment, auto accident, other accident.

Box 10d, optional: Often used to indicate MCD and the Medicaid number.

Mandatory Box 11: Insured policy group or FECA number. If patient has no insurance primary to Medicare enter "None." If recently retired, enter "None." If Medicare is *secondary*, complete the policy/group number.

Box 11a, optional: Enter insured's date of birth, six digits, and sex if other than the patient.

Box 11b, optional: If the insured just retired, enter "retired," and the date of retirement. Enter the employer.

Box 11c, optional: Enter primary insurance plan or program name.

Box 11d, optional: Leave blank.

Mandatory Box 12: "Signature on File" or one-time authorization rules may be used.

Box 13, optional: Signature authorizes Medigap payment to the participating physician.

Box 14, optional: Enter date of current illness, injury, or pregnancy.

Box 15, optional: Leave blank.

Box 16, optional: Enter if Workers' Compensation or other accident cause.

Box 17, optional: Enter referring/ordering physician name.

Box 17a, optional: Enter UPIN of referring/ordering physician, must match the name in Box 17. This is the UPIN of the physician submitting the claim.

Box 18, optional: Enter admit/discharge dates, six digits, if applicable.

Box 19, optional: Leave blank, unless insurance plan notifies of special use.

Box 20, optional: If an outside lab is used, enter "Yes" and enter the purchase price and the name of the lab performing the test in Box 32. If no outside lab services are purchased, enter "No."

Mandatory Box 21: Enter up to four diagnosis codes (do not enter the descriptions of the ICD-9-CM). This box is optional for Ambulance Provider claims.

Box 22, optional: Leave blank.

Box 23, optional: Enter professional or peer review organization ten-digit prior authorization number.

Mandatory Box 24a: Enter the month, day, and year, six digits for each procedure, service, or supply in 24d. If for one date of service, just enter the "from" date. If a consecutive range of dates, enter the "from" date and the "to" date. Use a separate line for each month.

Box 24b, optional: Enter two-digit place-of-service codes.

Box 24c, optional: Leave blank.

Mandatory Box 24d: Enter up to six lines of five-digit procedure codes, each with up to two modifiers.

Mandatory Box 24e: Link one diagnosis code pointer per line item for Medicare. For most other insurance plans, enter a comma between each diagnosis pointer, up to the Box 21 codes. Do not enter the codes, just the 1, 2, 3, or 4 pointing to the code.

Mandatory Box 24f: Enter the charge/fee.

Mandatory Box 24g: Enter the units or days.

Box 24h, optional: Leave blank.

Box 24i, optional: Leave blank.

Box 24j, optional: Leave blank.

Box 24k, optional: Enter rendering provider number if billing the claim as group provider number.

Box 25, optional: Enter federal tax ID number and check either SSN or EIN box.

Box 26, optional: Enter patient account number.

Mandatory Box 27: Enter to accept assignment or not to accept assignment. Participating must mark accept box. If the box is not indicated, it will default to accept assignment.

Mandatory Box 28: Enter total of all charges.

Box 29, optional: Enter any patient payments. Attach EOBs for secondary claim form completions.

Box 30, optional: Enter balance due after patient payment; enter 0 if patient paid the total charges.

Mandatory Box 31: Enter signature of physician or representative and date signed.

Mandatory 32: Enter hospital or facility name or source of purchased tests. If the same entity as Box 33, enter "Same." Not required for home locations.

Mandatory Box 33: Enter physician address and provider number. *Do not place UPIN* here.

PLEASE
DO NOT
STAPLE
IN THIS
AREA

▮▮▮▮▮▮▮▮▮▮
▮▮▮▮▮▮▮▮▮▮
▮▮▮▮▮▮▮▮▮▮
▮▮▮▮▮▮▮▮▮▮

☐ PICA

HEALTH INSURANCE CLAIM FORM

PICA ☐

1. MEDICARE	MEDICAID	CHAMPUS	CHAMPVA	GROUP HEALTH PLAN	FECA BLK LUNG	OTHER	1a. INSURED'S I.D. NUMBER (FOR PROGRAM IN ITEM 1)
☐ (Medicare #)	☐ (Medicaid #)	☐ (Sponsor's SSN)	☐ (VA File #)	☐ (SSN or ID)	☐ (SSN)	☐ (ID)	

2. PATIENT'S NAME (Last Name, First Name, Middle Initial)

3. PATIENT'S BIRTH DATE MM DD YY   SEX M ☐ F ☐

4. INSURED'S NAME (Last Name, First Name, Middle Initial)

5. PATIENT'S ADDRESS (No., Street)

6. PATIENT RELATIONSHIP TO INSURED
Self ☐ Spouse ☐ Child ☐ Other ☐

7. INSURED'S ADDRESS (No., Street)

CITY | STATE

8. PATIENT STATUS
Single ☐ Married ☐ Other ☐
Employed ☐ Full-Time Student ☐ Part-Time Student ☐

CITY | STATE

ZIP CODE | TELEPHONE (Include Area Code) ( )

ZIP CODE | TELEPHONE (INCLUDE AREA CODE) ( )

9. OTHER INSURED'S NAME (Last Name, First Name, Middle Initial)

10. IS PATIENT'S CONDITION RELATED TO:

11. INSURED'S POLICY GROUP OR FECA NUMBER

a. OTHER INSURED'S POLICY OR GROUP NUMBER

a. EMPLOYMENT? (CURRENT OR PREVIOUS) ☐ YES ☐ NO

a. INSURED'S DATE OF BIRTH MM DD YY   SEX M ☐ F ☐

b. OTHER INSURED'S DATE OF BIRTH MM DD YY   SEX M ☐ F ☐

b. AUTO ACCIDENT?   PLACE (State) ☐ YES ☐ NO

b. EMPLOYER'S NAME OR SCHOOL NAME

c. EMPLOYER'S NAME OR SCHOOL NAME

c. OTHER ACCIDENT? ☐ YES ☐ NO

c. INSURANCE PLAN NAME OR PROGRAM NAME

d. INSURANCE PLAN NAME OR PROGRAM NAME

10d. RESERVED FOR LOCAL USE

d. IS THERE ANOTHER HEALTH BENEFIT PLAN?
☐ YES ☐ NO   **If yes**, return to and complete item 9 a-d.

READ BACK OF FORM BEFORE COMPLETING & SIGNING THIS FORM.
12. PATIENT'S OR AUTHORIZED PERSON'S SIGNATURE I authorize the release of any medical or other information necessary to process this claim. I also request payment of government benefits either to myself or to the party who accepts assignment below.

SIGNED _____ DATE _____

13. INSURED'S OR AUTHORIZED PERSON'S SIGNATURE I authorize payment of medical benefits to the undersigned physician or supplier for services described below.

SIGNED _____

14. DATE OF CURRENT: MM DD YY ILLNESS (First symptom) OR INJURY (Accident) OR PREGNANCY(LMP)

15. IF PATIENT HAS HAD SAME OR SIMILAR ILLNESS. GIVE FIRST DATE MM DD YY

16. DATES PATIENT UNABLE TO WORK IN CURRENT OCCUPATION MM DD YY FROM   TO MM DD YY

17. NAME OF REFERRING PHYSICIAN OR OTHER SOURCE

17a. I.D. NUMBER OF REFERRING PHYSICIAN

18. HOSPITALIZATION DATES RELATED TO CURRENT SERVICES MM DD YY FROM   TO MM DD YY

19. RESERVED FOR LOCAL USE

20. OUTSIDE LAB? $ CHARGES
☐ YES ☐ NO

21. DIAGNOSIS OR NATURE OF ILLNESS OR INJURY. (RELATE ITEMS 1,2,3 OR 4 TO ITEM 24E BY LINE)

1. |___|.|___| 3. |___|.|___|

2. |___|.|___| 4. |___|.|___|

22. MEDICAID RESUBMISSION CODE   ORIGINAL REF. NO.

23. PRIOR AUTHORIZATION NUMBER

24. A DATE(S) OF SERVICE						B Place of Service	C Type of Service	D PROCEDURES, SERVICES, OR SUPPLIES (Explain Unusual Circumstances) CPT/HCPCS MODIFIER	E DIAGNOSIS CODE	F $ CHARGES	G DAYS OR UNITS	H EPSDT Family Plan	I EMG	J COB	K RESERVED FOR LOCAL USE
From MM	DD	YY	To MM	DD	YY										
1															
2															
3															
4															
5															
6															

25. FEDERAL TAX I.D. NUMBER SSN ☐ EIN ☐

26. PATIENT'S ACCOUNT NO.

27. ACCEPT ASSIGNMENT? (For govt. claims, see back) ☐ YES ☐ NO

28. TOTAL CHARGE $

29. AMOUNT PAID $

30. BALANCE DUE $

31. SIGNATURE OF PHYSICIAN OR SUPPLIER INCLUDING DEGREES OR CREDENTIALS (I certify that the statements on the reverse apply to this bill and are made a part thereof.)

SIGNED _____ DATE _____

32. NAME AND ADDRESS OF FACILITY WHERE SERVICES WERE RENDERED (If other than home or office)

33. PHYSICIAN'S, SUPPLIER'S BILLING NAME, ADDRESS, ZIP CODE & PHONE #

PIN# _____ GRP# _____

(APPROVED BY AMA COUNCIL ON MEDICAL SERVICE 8/88)   **PLEASE PRINT OR TYPE**   APPROVED OMB-0938-0008 FORM CMS-1500 (12/90), FORM RRB-1500
APPROVED OMB-1215-0055 FORM OWCP-1500, APPROVED OMB-0720-0001 (CHAMPUS)

CARRIER / *PATIENT AND INSURED INFORMATION* / *PHYSICIAN OR SUPPLIER INFORMATION*

Figure 15–2 Example of CMS-1500 form with mandatory fields highlighted.

The value of a practice management system that accurately guides for completion of each of these 33 fields cannot be underestimated. Small practices that have under ten employees, who choose to submit paper claims, have no small undertaking in submitting claims according to the requirements.

PAYER RECEIPT OF THE CLAIM

Some practice management systems provide an alert system, indicating aspects of the claim that may be erroneous and require immediate attention prior to transmitting directly to the insurance plan, or upon receipt at the insurance plan.

The insurance plan will typically receive the claim through a clearinghouse, or hub. The clearinghouse then forwards the claim to the insurance plans. At the time of this publication, electronic fields are being updated from the CMS-1500 paper claim process, to a new, streamlined HIPAA transaction and data sets electronic field capability. This translation of information may not occur smoothly and deems evaluation if rejections are noticed.

Some insurance plans allow tracking of the claim upon receipt by the insurance plan through the various departments. If available, resubmission or sending corrected information may expedite the claim payment. Otherwise, the claim may be rejected with a standard notice.

Resubmission of claims has limitations per insurance plan, especially the time limit from the date of the service to the initial claim date. This time limit is likely to vary from insurance plan to insurance plan and also from state to state, depending upon the timely payment rules per state.

FOLLOW-UP

The beginning of this chapter stressed that the collection of information from the patient is a key factor for payment. The next most important factor is claim follow-up. One very capable coder/biller recently stated she must spend 50 percent of her time researching nonpayment, resubmitting, sending additional information, or sending in an appeal for the claim. In general, the actual transmission of the claim is a very small portion of the payment cycle.

ACCURACY OF PAYMENT ON ARRIVAL

The payment may be sent to the organization in an electronic format, with a separate report to review or by a check. Then, the practice management system may automatically post the payment to the account or this feature may not be offered, depending upon the system. The small practice may post all payments manually. Regardless, reconciliation of the payment to the accounting system must be accurate.

When the payment arrives, each line item (service or supply) must be reconciled per patient and per insurance plan agreement. When payment is not received, the cause must be investigated. Did the practice overlook a process of the payment cycle? Were improper codes selected? Was a modifier inappropriately indicated for this insurance plan or omitted?

If the payment is received, is the payment amount correct according to the contract with the insurance plan? Next, clearly evaluate the patient's financial obligation per the explanation of benefits (EOB). Perhaps the deductible was not collected at the time of the service, or the co-payment or coinsurance was not as described during the verification procedure, or was not known at the time of the encounter. Enter the patient's obligation into the practice management system, and send an invoice to the patient for the portion that is due. Do not waive the co-payments and deductibles for the patient obligation, nor for professional courtesy purposes.

HIPAA is requiring the insurance payers to use standard rejection codes and definitions. This transition has not yet been fully implemented, therefore various rejection codes and definitions are indicated on the EOBs. Determining the reason the insurance plan rejected the claim is an early step toward correcting the payment problem. CMS has published on the web site www.cms.hhs.gov the standard listing of rejection codes and their definitions.

APPEALING THE CLAIM

The claim may have been partially paid per line item, or paid fully on selective line items, or unfortunately, not paid at all.

It is important to identify the root cause for the issue, the extent of the problem, and who is accountable. The decision tree may include many people for the true improvement for the claim denials. Upon investigation, communication with the state medical society, the specialty societies, or AMA may be required. Insurance legislative actions are more and more often required to resolve issues of nonpayment. Timely payment rules vary tremendously and are frequently updated by state legislation.

Upon receiving the rejection, there are two recommended steps to accomplish prior to submitting an appeal. First, obtain a second opinion, preferably in writing, regarding the coding from a Certified Professional Coder. Review these findings with the physician, and determine the proper coding for all services, including the CPT, HCPCSII, ICD-9-CM, and all potential modifier use. Second, obtain the written policies and procedures for the services from the insurance plan. Insurance plans are increasingly allowing access to their policies on the Internet, for their participating (contracted) physicians/organizations. If a physician is nonparticipating, only the patient can request the policy. The policies may guide toward various edits (either bundling or **medical necessity** ICD-9-CM), correlating to the insurance benefits.

medical necessity
The justification for an action or service based on the patient's condition, problem, or illness.

Some claims may be simply resubmitted, with the correction entered on the second claim. Particularly if data are missing, enter the lacking data and resend. Not all claims nor all insurance plans will allow resubmissions. If the rejection is for "truncated ICD-9-CM, lacking specificity" for example, CMS notified physicians in 1995 that if the fifth digit ICD-9-CM code is not entered, the claim may be rejected by the carrier and the carrier does not have to accept the corrected resubmitted claim. The physician is required to submit the claim with the highest level specificity ICD-9-CM code on the initial claim as early as October 2 each year, or potentially face the loss of revenue entirely, depending upon the CMS carrier decision.

Telephone appeals may correct the issue, without the need for a formal appeal procedure. Contact the provider hotline or other appeal line first, to attempt to correct the issue. Kindly ask to speak with a supervisor for repeated or trend issues.

August 30, 20XX

(physician name)
(physician address)

Dear Dr. _____:

RE: *(Enter the reason for the appeal, medical policy, edit, computer issue, new scientific procedure etc)*

Beneficiary/Patient Name:
Insured ID#_____Group ID#_____
Authorization#_____*(if applicable)*
Claim#_____
Date of Service_____

I am writing to respectfully request medical review for the care that was provided for *(patient name)*. The professional services performed for this case were: *(state the complications, beyond the usual, unique requirements, exceptional professional care etc)*
1)
2)
3)

The HIPAA transaction and data set standards for CPT, HCPCSII, ICD9-CM and modifiers were selected according to: *(reference specifically)*

• AMA/CPT page _____, CPT Assisant Article _____, CPT Changes _____ year, CPT Principles
• HCPCSII page _____, Coding Policy # _____ per our carrier, Coding Policy newsletter from _____
• ICD9-CM Guidelines of _____, Coding Clinic article _____
• Modifier use per (CCI, or insurance policy edits)

Attached please find the written response from (CPC or professional coding resource) regarding the accuracy of the code selection with a copy of the medical documentation including the radiology, pathology and other reports. Also, attached please find the professional publications for the scientific value, articles from JAMA, New England Journal describing the standard of care.

Thank you for your prompt response.

Sincerely,

(physician name)

Figure 15–3 Sample appeal letter.

The supervisor may have the ability to override the system and pay the claim, or may have awareness of a computer or other technical issue.

The formal appeal process will be outlined in the participating insurance contract or policies of the insurance plan. For nonparticipating physicians, the usual appeal will be a formal letter from the physician depicting the specific reason the physician believes the care should be paid, including the special report components listed in the AMA/CPT code book. In this correspondence, describe the circumstances beyond the routine or normal that occurred for this particular patient, with equal circumstances documented in the medical record. Scientific data, presentations, or other documents for accepted community standard of care may assist in the acceptance by the review hearing.

The claim appeal may be rejected, and the next step may be a hearing. Some insurance plans allow only the physician to attend the hearing. If possible, a certified coder, the administrator, and possibly an attorney, should attend the hearing with the physician, depending upon the circumstances and the level of revenue.

Figure 15–3 shows a sample appeal letter, which would need to be revised based upon the specific care and procedure. Some dictation tips are to list the patient safety, quality of care indicators, complications and comorbidity, unique scenario for this particular patient, impossibility to provide alternative medical care and why, etc. Avoid descriptions that simply request an increase payment amount, unless the contract clearly indicates the fee schedule was inappropriately paid. The appeal process is not typically the venue used to request an increase in the contractual allowances or fee schedule.

Medicare Redetermination Request Form

CMS has a form for the formal redetermination process. This form is CMS-20027 (revised 5/05) and must be submitted with any correspondence (Figure 15–4).

Medicare Request for Hearing

If the carrier determination is not satisfactory or if greater issues need to be addressed, the next step is to submit the CMS 20034 A/B U3 (revised 8/05), which is usually completed by an attorney, attaching all previous correspondence. This form is two pages (Figure 15–5).

EXERCISE 15–1

1. When is the advance beneficiary notice completed and signed?

2. List the steps for the payment cycle in the correct order.

3. What are two very important factors for the payment cycle?

DEPARTMENT OF HEALTH AND HUMAN SERVICES
CENTERS FOR MEDICARE & MEDICAID SERVICES

MEDICARE REDETERMINATION REQUEST FORM

1. Beneficiary's Name: ____________________

2. Medicare Number: ____________________

3. Description of Item or Service in Question: ____________________

4. Date the Service or Item was Received: ____________________

5. I do not agree with the determination of my claim. MY REASONS ARE:

____

____

____

6. Date of the initial determination notice ____________________

(If you received your initial determination notice more than 120 days ago, include your reason for not making this request earlier.)

____

____

____

7. Additional Information Medicare Should Consider: ____________________

____

____

____

8. Requester's Name: ____________________

9. Requester's Relationship to the Beneficiary: ____________________

10. Requester's Address: ____________________

____

11. Requester's Telephone Number: ____________________

12. Requester's Signature: ____________________

13. Date Signed: ____________________

14. ❑ I have evidence to submit. (Attach such evidence to this form.)
❑ I do not have evidence to submit.

NOTICE: Anyone who misrepresents or falsifies essential information requested by this form may upon conviction be subject to fine or imprisonment under Federal Law.

Form CMS-20027 (05/05) EF 05/2005

Figure 15–4 CMS-20027 form for formal redetermination.

DEPARTMENT OF HEALTH AND HUMAN SERVICES
OFFICE OF MEDICARE HEARINGS AND APPEALS

REQUEST FOR MEDICARE HEARING BY AN ADMINISTRATIVE LAW JUDGE   ❏ Part A   ❏ Part B

Effective July 1, 2005. For use by party to a reconsideration determination issued by a Qualified Independent Contractor (QIC)
(Amount in controversy must be $100 or more.)

Send copies of this completed form to:
Original — *Office of Medicare Hearings and Appeals Field Office specified in the QIC Reconsideration Notice*
  Copy — *Appellant*   ***Copy*** — *All other parties*
Failure to send a copy of this completed request to the other parties to the appeal will delay the start date of your appeal.
Did you send all required copies?   ❏ Yes ❏ No

Appellant *(The party appealing the reconsideration determination)*

Beneficiary *(Leave blank if same as the appellant.)*	Provider or Supplier *(Leave blank if same as the appellant.)*
Address	Address
City State Zip Code	City State Zip Code
Area Code/Telephone Number E-mail Address	Area Code/Telephone Number E-mail Address
Health Insurance (Medicare) Claim Number	Document control number assigned by the QIC

QIC that made the reconsideration determination	Dates of Service From To

I DISAGREE WITH THE DETERMINATION MADE ON MY APPEAL BECAUSE:

You have a right to be represented at the hearing. If you are not represented but would like to be, your Office of Medicare Hearings and Appeals Field Office will give you a list of legal referral and service organizations. *(If you are represented and have not already done so, complete form CMS-1696.)*

Check **Only One** Statement:	❏ I **wish** to have a hearing. ❏ I **do not wish** to have a hearing and I request that a decision be made on the basis of the evidence in my case. *(Complete form HHS-723, "Waiver of Right to an ALJ Hearing.")*	Check **Only One** Statement:	❏ I **have** additional evidence to submit. ❏ I **have no** additional evidence to submit. If you have additional evidence to submit, please attach the evidence or attach a statement explaining what you intend to submit and when you intend to submit it. If you are a provider, supplier, or beneficiary represented by a provider or supplier, the evidence must be accompanied by a good cause statement explaining why the evidence is being submitted for the first time at the ALJ level.

The appellant should complete No. 1 and the representative, if any, should complete No. 2. If a representative is not present to sign, print his or her name in No. 2. Where applicable, check to indicate if appellant will accompany the representative at the hearing. ❏ Yes ❏ No

1. (Appellant's Signature) Date	2. (Representative's Signature/Name) Date
Address	Address ❏ Attorney ❏ Non-Attorney
City State Zip Code	City State Zip Code
Area Code/Telephone Number E-mail Address	Area Code/Telephone Number E-mail Address

Answer the following questions that apply:
  A) Does request involve multiple claims? (If yes, a list of all the claims must be attached.)   ❏ Yes ❏ No
  B) Does request involve multiple beneficiaries? (If yes, a list of beneficiaries, their HICNs and the dates of service.)   ❏ Yes ❏ No
  C) Did the beneficiary assign his or her appeal rights to you as the provider/supplier?   ❏ Yes ❏ No
    (If yes, you must complete and attach form CMS-20031. Failure to do so will prevent approval of the assignment.)

Must be completed by the provider/supplier if representing the beneficiary:

I waive my rights to charge and collect a fee for representing _____ before the Office of
Medicare Hearings and Appeals.   *(Beneficiary name)*

Signature of provider/supplier representing beneficiary	Date

CMS-20034 A/B U3 (08/05) EF 08/2005   ATTACH A COPY OF THE RECONSIDERATION DETERMINATION
                                           (IF AVAILABLE) TO THIS COPY.

Figure 15–5 CMS 20034 A/B U3 to request a Medicare hearing.—continues

Must be completed by the provider/supplier if representing the beneficiary, they furnished the item(s) or services(s) at issue, and the appeal involves a question of liability under section 1879(a)(2) of the Social Security Act:

I waive my right to collect payment from the beneficiary for the furnished items or services at issue involving 1879(a)(2) of the Social Security Act.

Signature of provider/supplier representing beneficiary	Date

TO BE COMPLETED BY THE OFFICE OF MEDICARE HEARINGS AND APPEALS

Is this request filed timely? ❏ Yes ❏ No

If no, attach appellant's explanation for delay. If there is no explanation, send a Notice of Late Filing of Request for ALJ Hearing to the appellant and representative, if applicable, to request such an explanation.

Request received on	Field Office	Employee
Assigned on	Assigned by	Assigned to

Special response case?   ❏ Yes ❏ No

If yes, explain why and state the targeted adjudication deadline.

_____

_____

Interpreter/translator needed (including sign language)   ❏ Yes ❏ No

If yes, type needed:

_____

_____

If appellant not represented, has a list of legal referral and service organizations been provided.   ❏ Yes ❏ No

PRIVACY ACT STATEMENT

The legal authority for the collection of information on this form is authorized by the Social Security Act (section 1155 of Title XI and sections 1852(g)(5), 1860D-4(h)(1), 1869(b)(1), and 1876 of Title XVIII). The information provided will be used to further document your appeal. Submission of the information requested on this form is voluntary, but failure to provide all or any part of the requested information may affect the determination of your appeal. Information you furnish on this form may be disclosed by the Office of Medicare Hearings and Appeals to another person or governmental agency only with respect to the Medicare Program and to comply with Federal laws requiring the disclosure of information or the exchange of information between the Department of Health and Human Services and other agencies.

CMS-20034 A/B U3 (08/05) EF 08/2005

Figure 15–5 CMS 20034 A/B U3 to request a Medicare hearing.—continued

INSURANCE PARTICIPATION AGREEMENTS (CONTRACTS)

Health Insurance Agreements

In reality, the practice of medicine is now a business, requiring effective business skills that are not typically part of medical school training. Usually, for the purpose of increasing business, physicians and health care organizations choose to review and potentially execute (sign) insurance participation agreements (contracts). When the employers in the community select insurance for their employees, they will need various physicians and health care providers. If the patients choose to see a participating physician or facility, they are motivated in some manner, typically financially. Often, patients will have a less costly co-payment or deductible or in some instances will have no coverage if they do not see a participating care organization. The participating physician anticipates a more productive schedule and more patient volume when the insurance plan publishes the listing of participating physicians. In return, the physician typically agrees to a decreased payment amount from the insurance plan and other limitations. Within the contract language, many additional terms are likely, binding to many other policies and procedures created by the insurance plan. Every participation agreement contract should be negotiated in detail with a corporate attorney prior to signing and should be renegotiated as necessary.

The contracts may include these structured plans or modifications of:

point of service (POS)
The insurance plan encourages the patient to seek healthcare at a specific location or facility, typically where a contract for less cost has been negotiated.

- HMO–Health Maintenance Organizations
- **POS–Point of Service**
- **PPO–Preferred Provider Organization**

When a physician or health care organization decides not to participate with the health insurance plans, alternative means of advertising, marketing, and business development are usually required. One new term for this concept of practicing is "boutique." The practice may have a contractual relationship with patients, describing a package of services or items.

preferred provider organization (PPO)
The healthcare provider signs a contract to join a group, usually an insurance plan. The physician name is then published in a listing, the listing may be resold, or the patients may receive incentives and discounts when choosing to have the care with a PPO provider.

Workers' Compensation and Auto Insurance Agreements

Unlike health insurance plans, there are only a few insurance networks offering agreements for the care of Workers' Compensation and/or automobile insurance care. These agreements are likely governed by state laws; hence, the use of an attorney to negotiate is even more important. HIPAA rules and regulations do not bind these, however.

Government Payment

Medicare Modernization Act
Federal law upgrading, streamlining, and revising the Centers for Medicare and Medicaid Services.

The government is by far the largest purchaser of health care services in the United States, well into billions of dollars annually. Since it is the largest, as with any business, certain expectations are outlined by the purchaser. The complexity is increased with bureaucracy and politics and the system becomes convoluted and challenging for everyone. Reform of the system is needed in order to adequately provide health care for beneficiaries in the future. The process of reform has begun, with the implementation of the **Medicare Modernization Act,** yet much more reform will be necessary.

As stated in previous chapters, government payers include:

- Medicare
- Medicare for Disabilities (any age)
- Railroad Retirement
- Medicaid
- Federal Employees (U.S. Postal workers for example)
- TRICARE/CHAMPVA
- Indian Health Services may adopt choose to adopt CMS policies

Therefore, a choice to provide or not to provide care for government patients may dramatically affect the volume of patients and the potential income of a physician or facility.

History of Medicare

Medicare began under President Lyndon B. Johnson in 1965, as a portion of the Social Security Act. The basic intention was to provide a level of health care for every senior citizen. Over the course of time, Congress has recommended various services and has created guidelines for the budget and spending. In 1991, the resource-based relative value system (RBRVS) set the physician fee schedule at a specific rate, determined by a complex calculation. Today, the RBRVS is in need of dramatic reform to adequately pay for health care services yet provide quality of care for citizens.

covered service
A contracted benefit from the insurer to the provider and patient. For example, while infertility treatment may not be a covered service, testing and treatment until infertility is diagnosed may be a covered service with the insurer.

Balanced Budget Act
Legislation designed to balance the federal budget enacted during the Clinton administration.

The RBRVS system, under the COBRA/OBRA rules, requires a balanced budget annually. In simplistic terms, as more CPT codes services and items are approved for covered benefits, additional funds are not available from Congress. The total money pool is to be divided between all of the **covered services,** determined by CMS. The **Balanced Budget Act** of 1997 also added a few screening and prevention services to the covered benefits for the first time.

Each year, the planned fee schedule is introduced as proposed rules in the *Federal Register.* The Physician Fee Schedule, Outpatient Prospective Payment System, and Hospital Payment Schedule are the most popular documents for most health organizations. The proposed rules allow for formal comments, usually for sixty days, then are republished in the *Federal Register* as law, indicating the effective dates. If Congress is inclined, the final rules may be revised, again with a proposed set of rules and the final rules typically published. In general, many details of the government system are found in the *Federal Register* documents.

Also annually, the patient's deductible amount and the contribution amount per CPT or HCPCSII code are published in the *Federal Register.* The patient obligation fees have slowly increased over the years.

The Department of Health and Human Services oversees the Centers for Medicare and Medicaid Services. The secretary of HHS serves on the presidential cabinet.

Enrollment with Medicare

In 2007, the new National Provider Indicator (NPI) numbers per provider are to be assigned. The application form to enroll for this new number and format began in the spring of 2005. The NPI number is proposed to replace the multiple provider numbers that are required for each insurance contract.

When planning to care for CMS patients, the physician is expected to enroll prior to caring for patients. The CMS system has three major forms to complete when enrolling to provide Medicare services. The forms are the CMS-855B, CMS-855I, and CMS-855R. Upon careful completion, the lengthy forms are sent to the CMS carrier. The processing of the enrollment forms is typically three to six months, yet depending upon certain issues, may be extended. Early enrollment is recommended. Upon completion of the enrollment, the provider number is assigned, whether an individual or a group of physicians. After the provider number is assigned, the unique provider identifier number (UPIN) is assigned. The UPIN stays constant, and follows the physician whenever relocating to another carrier service area. The UPIN is typically assigned within one month after the provider enrollment is completed.

After enrolled at the local CMS carrier, each provider chooses whether to participate or nonparticipate by completing and submitting an additional form to the local carrier. The physician fee schedule lists the fees per CPT or HCPCSII in three columns: the participation fee, the nonparticipation fee, and the limiting charge.

Participating Providers

The participating providers agree to abide by the CMS policies and procedures, medical coverage determinations, and claim submission processes. In return, the payment as published in the physician fee schedule is made to the physician; therefore, the physician collects the deductible and coinsurance amount from the patient. Remember that the physician will not be paid the usual and customary fee of the practice; the CMS portion of the payment will be based upon the CMS participation fee schedule. The patient is obligated for 20 percent of each service plus the deductible amount, and this portion may be paid either by the patient personally or by a second Medicare supplement insurance plan.

Nonparticipating Providers

nonparticipating provider (nonPAR)
Providers not contracting (participating) with the insurance plan. Medicare nonPAR physicians must not exceed the limiting charge when billing beneficiaries.

The **nonparticipating provider (nonPAR)** may choose per patient whether to submit the claim as accepting assignment, which is to agree to the CMS policies and procedures, medical coverage determinations, and claim submission processes, or not. However, the claim and the fee charged to the patient are completely fixed, as the limiting charge listed in the fee schedule. In other words, the amount charged per CPT code is limited, and it is improper to collect more than that amount from the patient at any time, whether participating or nonparticipating. The CMS will pay nonparticipating claims at a 5 percent lesser rate and the payment will be sent directly to the patient. The physician then collects the CMS payment from the patient, the 20 percent for each service plus the deductible amount at the time of the care.

For participating and nonparticipating providers, the patient is obligated to pay his or her portion of the fee, and the physician or health care organization is obligated to collect the fee. It is illegal and a high risk for investigation to waive any deductibles or coinsurance amounts due. In the past, this was referred to as a professional courtesy. Once the patient has chosen to have the claim submitted, the patient has a financial obligation for the care. The only exception to this concept is if the patient is indigent, in which case the provider may choose to waive the fees. For the physician office, proof of indigence is not required and no forms are necessary. For the hospital setting, a form is completed, stating financial need.

Nonparticipating providers have less customer service and Internet access at the carrier offices than do participating providers. When investigating the policies, this can increase frustrations for both the physician and the patient.

Again, the fees are limited to the published amounts annually for nonparticipating physicians. An additional amount may not be collected from the patient.

The physician is obligated to submit the claim for the patient to the CMS carrier, whether participating or nonparticipating. Beneficiaries do not submit claims for the care.

Opt Out

The opt out concept is rather new to the CMS system. This is the private contracting concept. The physician chooses to notify the CMS carrier of the decision to opt out of CMS for two years. If the physician changes his or her mind within the first ninety days, a written affidavit may reverse the choice; otherwise, the two-year period is implemented. If at the end of the two years the physician chooses to reactivate as PAR or non-PAR, the enrollment system is implemented, which again could take time. The opt out invitation is sent on a specific date each year, allowing the physician to re-enter CMS at a specific time. Therefore, the total time out of the system may be a bit longer than the two years.

While an opt-out physician, the patient and the physician agree to the service and the payment amount. The published Medicare fee schedule, rules, and policies do not apply, and usual claims are not submitted to CMS at all. The financial processes are between the patient and the physician directly.

While an opt-out physician, emergency care may be provided and claims submitted for the emergency services.

Deactivate

The physician may choose to deactivate entirely, no longer submitting any claims to CMS at any time. Deactivation does not have a two-year limit for this process; however re-enrollment is required when re-entering the system as PAR, non-PAR or opt out. At the time of this publication, deactivation is not a typical choice; however as CMS policies and coverage rules increase while the physician payment amounts decrease, it is likely more physicians will move to deactivate in the future.

Medicare Resources

Each state is assigned to various carriers who have contracted to manage the Medicare beneficiaries. The Medicare Modernization Act plans to streamline the number of carriers. The carriers have multiple responsibilities surrounding the coverage, processing of claims, and managing appeals, each with at least one physician serving as the medical director. The carriers also implement the rules and regulations as disseminated by the National CMS department, and now policies are increasingly national coverage determinations rather than local carrier determinations.

The carriers allow Web access, where the information and coverage policies are available for anyone—no login process is required. There is also an index of all the carriers per topic, available at the CMS Web site. The CMS Web site is *www.cms.hhs.gov.* Either the search window or the links and tabs will guide to coverage details, payment processes, or laws and investigation processes per topic.

In this book, we do not have the ability to publish the multiple rules and regulations that surround the care for Medicare patients, and simply suggest prior to rendering the care and submitting the claim, the physician is required to implement all policies and procedures according to the CMS concepts. This may entail many laws, such as fraud and abuse, antitrust, Stark Amendments, and **False Claims Act,** which carry immensely expensive fines, and potential recoupment or forfeiture of future claim payments or jail.

False Claims Act
Federal legislation that prohibits submission of claims for services not rendered or for any services considered fraudulent upon investigation.

Another very important topic briefly discussed earlier in this chapter is the Incident to Physician Service rules, which are very detailed. It is advised to review the policies for this rule frequently, in detail, and implement carefully.

Advance Beneficiary Notice

One of the most important policies that was created for Medicare beneficiaries, and now under HIPAA is required for all health insurance plans, is the advance beneficiary notice (ABN) form.

The forms and procedures for completing the ABN are slightly different between physician/outpatient facilities and inpatient facilities. The physician and outpatient facility procedures will be described first.

Effective March 2001, the CMS-R-131 forms were implemented; one for physician, provider, and service items, and another for laboratory purposes. These forms standardized the language, the size of the print font, and the procedure for obtaining the signatures. Refer back to Figure 15–1 for the CMS-R-131-G form, the physician services standard form. Obtain the additional laboratory form from www.cms.hhs.gov.

Steps for ABN:

1. Notification is given to the patient if the physician believes charges may not be paid by Medicare because the service is considered nonmedically necessary according to Medicare (either local carrier or national policy).

2. A written notice is given to the patient *before* the service is rendered.

3. The patient is notified of the exact CPT code(s) for the services and the total financial obligation the patient will be responsible for. Determining this financial obligation fact may entail detailed investigation by contacting the secondary insurance Medicare supplement plan, and investigating the deductible payment amounts to date, prevention coverage carve outs, medication payment options, etc.

4. The ABN is required per visit. The ABN is offered if genuine doubt of payment, as evidenced by stated reasons.

5. The ABN is not required for statutorily excluded services or items. Unfortunately, most Medicare patients do not have any awareness of the statutory limitations, hence effective communication and education is often required. For example, routine care is not covered under Medicare. Routine may include tetanus injections, and many preventive services and medications.

6. The beneficiary agrees to pay for the service by signing the form.

7. Alterations to the format are not acceptable by CMS. The form may not be reprinted in a different format for CMS patients. The practice logo is placed on the CMS-R-131 form, clearly reflecting that it was from a particular office.

8. The ABN must give the patient the reason CMS will deny the charges, in detail. Terms such as "medically unnecessary" and "Medicare will not pay" are not acceptable. The physician must provide an informed reason to the patient. Terms such as the following should be used:
   - Medicare Part B usually does not pay for this many visits or treatments (frequency limitations).
   - Medicare Part B usually does not pay for this service.
   - Medicare Part B usually does not pay for such an extensive service.
   - Medicare Part B usually does not pay for this equipment
   - Medicare Part B usually does not pay for this lab test.

9. Two criteria must be met—1) the patient must receive the notice with the details previously described, and 2) the patient must comprehend the information. For this reason, simple terminology is necessary on the ABN forms.

10. For any encounters, the ABN must be personally offered, face to face.

11. Timely response to questions regarding the form are required, further explaining the reason for CMS anticipated nonpayment.

12. The ABN must be given in advance of the procedure, with time for the patient to rationally decide.

13. If the patient or authorized representative refuses to sign after being clearly educated, the circumstances must be charted and details added to the ABN form. The physician then determines whether to provide the care free of charge, accept partial payment, or refuse care entirely for the patient.

When the ABN is properly completed, the patient is financially obligated for the total fee amount charged by the physician, per CPT code, and is not associated to the Medicare Physician Fee Schedule Limiting Charges. This is collected at the time of the service.

The examples in real life become very challenging and complex for patients to understand. Therefore, at least for the majority of patients, it is no longer advised to routinely provide combination encounter services of preventive and other Balanced Budget Act of 1997 screening services, or statutorily exempt care on the same date as disease/illness care. The vast majority of patients do not have insurance coverage for all recommended medical care, as the physician has been trained. Communicating the benefits to the patient, the areas of noncoverage, and the exact patient financial obligation is the responsibility of the participating/contracting physician *prior* to the care. Unless medically precluded, illness care should be provided on an alternative date from the preventive or screening services or statutorily exempt care (e.g., cosmetic). For example, a disease-oriented E/M visit should not be provided on the same date as minor cosmetic surgery. This complicates the financial aspects for payment and educating the patient effectively as far as completing the ABN. Clarity is more likely if another date is scheduled for the cosmetic surgery, plus the claim for the E/M illness visit will be promptly paid. This concept is true for all health insurance participating/contracting services (not simply CMS).

Managed Care Payments

Health maintenance organization (HMO), point of service (POS), and preferred provider organization (PPO) agreements identify the various payment methodologies. The payment structure may include payments other than paying for the specific line item of service listed on the claim. The entire payment or a portion of the payment may be an incentive payment, based upon criteria developed by the insurance plan. The criteria may be either profit based or quality based. A profit-based incentive is often described with the term **withhold.** Per CPT code, an amount is put aside by the insurance plan. One example of the criteria for the withhold would be: if the entire network of physicians in the community area provide cost-effective care, a portion of the withhold amount may be distributed to the participating physicians the following year. The parties that share in the withhold and the percentage of withholding and distribution vary per contract.

Another common method of payment is **capitation.** The physician is paid a flat fee, usually monthly, to manage the health care for a group of assigned patients, whether or not a particular patient receives any encounter or visits during the

withhold
A percentage held out by the managed care organization as an incentive to keep costs, admissions, and referrals low each year. If the provider follows the plan strategy, the withhold percentage is returned with interest at a predetermined time.

capitation
Represents a common managed care payment strategy by which providers are paid according to the number of patients choosing a physician as primary caregiver. The capitation payment is made for a predetermined amount at a predetermined time each quarter or year.

month. The capitation payments are usually distributed to the primary care physicians and certain specialists of the network. The capitation payment may also include certain other frequently used services, such as a venipuncture for lab tests, etc. The capitation payments are entered into the practice management system, according to the policies of the practice. Capitation payments often describe risk pools. Risk pool criteria are established by the insurance plan, usually associated to the network providing the health care, the health of the patients within the network, and other details. The risk pool may or may not have incentive payout distributions to the health care providers.

Modifications of the HMO agreements are evolving. Common examples include when the patient is limited to the location for the care (must use a certain hospital or emergency room), the physician is limited to the medications allowed on the formulary (or only generic medications are covered), the patient needs second opinions prior to a surgical procedure, or the patient has specific medical procedures required prior to surgical options.

Payments are expected to correlate to the agreements in the contract. The contract is likely to state the period of time after the care within which the claim is to be submitted, the terms for selection of codes and their definitions, the appeal process, etc. The contract may dramatically affect the profit for the practice depending upon the volume of patients per insurance plan. Understanding the policies prior to signing the agreement is very wise and will affect the bottom line.

In most of the agreements, the patient is obligated only for the co-payment or coinsurance and the deductible for any covered service. As with Medicare, the physician is obligated under HIPAA to offer the advance beneficiary notice for all insurance plans in which the physician has agreed to participate.

Traditional Indemnity Plans

Traditional indemnity plans are commonly referred to as 80 percent/20 percent commercial insurance plans. The physician is paid 80 percent of the physician practice usual, customary, and reasonable (UCR) fee schedule, and the patient is obligated for 20 percent. A UCR fee schedule is when the individual physician determines the price per a particular service, basically creating his or her own charges for the services. When the physician agrees to participate, the physician agrees to accept the discounted fee schedule presented by the insurance plan rather than the UCR rate, and then accept 80 percent of that new insurance plan fee schedule. The patient is obligated to pay 20 percent. If the patient chooses to visit a nonparticipating physician with an nonassigned claim, the patient may have 100 percent financial obligation or may be responsible for 80 percent of the physician's UCR fees. Contracts today often bundle various insurance programs into one master agreement. In other words, if the physician agrees to the HMO contract, the physician also agrees to the traditional indemnity plan contract at the same fee schedule rate and other rules and policies. Selecting to participate among various plans within one company is becoming less available as an option for the physician.

Third Party Administrator

Some insurance plans choose to have the claims processed by an outside organization, rather than performing the task within their organization. These outside firms are known as third party administrators (TPAs). Claims are processed according to the policies of the insurance plan, implementing the edits as instructed. Appeals may or may not be managed by the TPA organization.

EXERCISE 15–2

1. What are the four physician options for contracting with CMS?

2. What is the name of the ABN form that is required to be used for CMS patients?

3. The ABN is necessary for only CMS patients. True or False?

DENIALS AND REJECTIONS

Frequently, upon receipt of the claim at the insurance plan, the claim is reviewed using an edit software system. When the factors and details for the edit are published, this is considered an open system, similar to the National Correct Coding Initiative (NCCI). The NCCI consists of three parts: 1) a manual of text describing rules and expectations for the code selections, 2) a list of mutually exclusive CPT codes pairs, and 3) a list of CPT bundling matches. The ICD-9-CM edits for CMS are published within the policies of either the National Coverage Determinations (NCD) or the Local Coverage Determinations (LCD), and are not listed within the NCCI. NCD are created by CMS for use by all carriers in the United States. Local carriers create LCD with various coverage and payment policies per state. More NCDs are anticipated in the future. The CPT manual is updated each October, whereas the listings for Column 1 and Column 2, and the mutually exclusive pair listings, are updated at midnight each quarter.

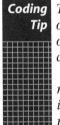

Coding Tip *The NCCI is free to download from www.cms.hhs.gov web site, available on the date of implementation. For accuracy and ease, download this on the first business date of each quarter, directly to your desktop. That way it will be at your fingertips for the claims that are transmitted or reviewed per quarter.*

Not all insurance plans ascribe to this sharing of information. The practice of not disclosing edits to physicians is commonly known as "black box edits." When this is the case, the physician learns what may or may not be a payable service or the appropriate pairing of CPT to ICD-9-CM only through the process of trial and error.

The importance of the key factors of the payment cycle covered at the beginning of the chapter should now be evident. Receipt of payment of the claim is dependent on accurate data. Other causes for denials for the submission of paper or electronic claims are:

- Patient demographic data is incorrect.
- Spouse data are incorrect.
- ID numbers are wrong.
- Patient is not eligible for the insurance plan.
- CPT codes are incorrect.
- Modifier use is incorrect.
- ICD-9-CM linkage is incorrect.
- Gender for the service listed is incorrect.

- Claim is a duplicate of a service already submitted.
- Service is noncovered per this insurance plan.
- Additional information is requested (e.g., operative note, pathology report, etc.).

Practices and organizations often miss charges for services that are rendered; this is known as lost charges, or noncaptured charges. Most often, this occurs due to inadequate communication from the physician to the coding personnel. However, other factors such as assumptions, hearsay, or prior rules may also affect the charge entry process. Effective preventive action includes managing all of the worksheets/tickets to make certain every patient that was seen for the date of service has been charged. Another step is to double check that all care that is rendered has been accurately indicated, as well as the exact medical necessity for the specific care. Updating the worksheets at least quarterly and encouraging discussion for all services that are rendered at the physician office will improve the likelihood of charge capture.

Medications that are rendered at the physician office are to be entered on the worksheet/ticket encounter form. When a different medication brand, dose, or item is purchased, as discussed in Chapter 3, the code will likely be different. This too affects reimbursement dramatically.

Electronic medical record systems are entering the medical profession and may include an automated charge capture component. The accuracy of the code selection remains paramount, and the risk of fraud for erroneous code selection lies with the person entering the data. For the practices that continue using paper charting, the typical form for capturing charges may be called the encounter form, ticket, or worksheet. Whether electronic or paper capture forms are used, the information for options and the updating of the processes should be done at least quarterly. New codes, new policies, and new concepts are evolving and need to be implemented effectively.

Today, with the updating of the CMS-1500 format to a new electronic XP format, insurance plans and clearinghouses may cause the rejection of a claim due to improper field data sets. Staying on top of the rejections and getting to the bottom of what caused them will best improve the processes that will yield dramatic financial affects.

Another frequent cause for rejections is upgrade or revision of the practice management system. The system upgrade may not correlate to the clearinghouse properly, and again the data sets may be erroneous.

Additionally, rejections and denials are typically abundant annually at the time the code sets are updated. ICD-9-CM codes are implemented for health insurance plans every October 1, while the HCPCSII and CPT codes are activated every January 1. Workers' Compensation and automobile insurers may not activate new codes on these same dates. It is obvious for financial and legal reasons that each practice *must* purchase all of the code books and implement the new codes in a timely manner or face enormous losses.

HIPAA requires health insurance plans and clearinghouses to use standard rejection codes and descriptions. This and the requirements for data sets have been challenging for the insurance plans to meet.

APPEALS

It is becoming increasingly difficult to transmit a claim indicating the services performed, documented, and coded according to the standard methodology, frequently due to the edit systems that are implemented by the insurance plans. When multiple services are reported on a claim, the probability for a rejection of at least one service is high.

The rejection codes are to be standardized, according to the HIPAA rules. In reality, the rejection codes are not yet equally indicated by all insurance plans. If, after reviewing the policies and procedures of the insurance plan (if participating), the physician believes the claim should have been paid, an appeal process may begin. This usually entails a copy of the medical record, a letter outlining the evidence to support the reason payment should occur, and any other information that the medical director or review officer might take under consideration when reviewing the claim. CMS carriers offer telephone appeals as a first-step option. A telephone appeal is not necessarily an option with all insurance plans, where only written appeals are accepted.

MIRRORED IMAGE OF THE DOCUMENTATION

The term mirrored image of the medical documentation justifying to codes selected and the information reported on the health insurance claim must be provided. Remember, the rules are not exclusively enforced for government payers, and since the inception of HIPAA, the rules apply for all electronic health insurance claims. Medical necessity is justified by the medical record component, in which the physician has indicated the reasons for the care and the reason each service is provided. When the ICD-9-CM code is listed on the claim, the reason for it must be clearly documented in the medical record. The same expectations apply to CPT and HCPCSII concepts. Each service or item is to be coded, listing the medical necessity for the service on the medical record, directly mirroring the claim.

In the absence of the mirrored image concept, the risk for investigation and potential fraud and abuse sanctions are high. The sanctions and penalty fines are given to the individual who knowingly performed the error. Sanctions are not exclusive to the physician or owner of the organization. Abuse, briefly, is whenever an error occurs. On the other hand, fraud is when purposeful intent to obtain gain is made. All persons who are involved with the transmission of the claim or capturing medical record information share in the risk of investigation and fines, if they intentionally choose not to abide by the laws.

The primary emphasis throughout this book has been on accurate documentation of the care provided. A related emphasis on adhering to the law is equally important. A final review of each claim should be made to assure the following:

- Are the codes selected on the claim accurately documented in the chart?
- Are the records legible and consistent?
- Do all entries include the date, health care professional name, and signature?
- Are test recordings properly depicted?
- Are the abbreviations standard and clear?

Health care professionals can augment the medical record, adding a note after the date/time of the initial date. It is improper to alter the medical record or revise previous information. If this action is done, it is sure to be detected during an investigation. This is an investigation for a felony, and the FBI will be seeking to find the facts and evidence. Do not purposely alter the medical record.

RISKY BEHAVIOR

down coding
The selection of a lower level code (CPT or HCPCSII) than the supporting documentation.

Down coding. For some reason, many physicians and their staff have the misguided understanding that if a lower level code is selected, it is "safer." The term for this is down coding—it is certainly not true and may in fact trigger an investigation.

The selection of the CPT, HCPCSII, and ICD-9-CM codes and their modifiers are required to be accurately reported based upon the documentation. Data are compared per geographic area, per specialty per CPT codes, commonly known as bell-curve data. If one physician (per unique physician identifier number) consistently submits claims with lower level E/M codes, the data will alert the investigation department. Down-coding sanctions, fines, and investigation processes are equal to all other false claim activities.

upcoding
The action of selecting a higher level of service or procedure code than the documentation or diagnoses support for the purpose of receiving higher reimbursement.

unbundling
Practice of billing multiple procedure codes for a group of procedures that are covered by a single comprehensive CPT code.

Upcoding. The definition of upcoding is the selection of a code higher than supported by the documentation. Locations of caution, as were discussed in the E/M chapter, are the emergency department or the consultation codes that have higher key component requirements than some of the other sites.

Unbundling. Unbundling refers to reporting multiple codes in a variety of methods, rather than selecting one specific code that describes the entire service. The accuracy of this can be challenging for nonparticipating providers who do not have access to the policies and procedures of the insurance plan, yet have chosen to accept assignment on the claim.

Frequency. Services may have a frequency limitation associated with the care. Seeking methods to report frequency in alternative means is not acceptable.

Professional courtesy. The reasons professional courtesy should not be offered include:

- It is defined as all or partial fee waived.
- If the recipient of professional courtesy is the reason for past or future referrals, this may be deemed as a kickback.
- The waiving of co-payment, coinsurance, or deductible may be perceived as an inducement.

EXERCISE 15–3

1. List five common risky behaviors that are considered fraudulent activity.

2. Is down coding safer than upcoding?

3. What is the name of the edit system that is used by CMS?

4. When is the NCCI updated?

5. What does the term "mirrored image" documentation mean?

AUDITING

The first step prior to implementing an audit may be to contact the attorney. If an audit is sought by the attorney in preparation for professional advice or guidance, the audit and the findings are confidential. The importance of this may become extremely valuable should an investigation ensue, because the auditor would not likely be called to testify against the practice, as the information derived at the audit would now be considered protected under attorney–client

overpayment
Excess amount paid in error by the insurer for codes or documentation used to support the claim for payment.

privilege. Alternatively, if a practice hires an auditor directly and then contacts an attorney, the information derived at the audit and the auditor may be called to testify against the practice. Practical wisdom consists of knowing that there are times when the attorney should be the very first call, for compliance and audit processes.

Another purpose of initiating the audit by contacting the attorney is that should the auditor discover a major **overpayment,** the attorney will guide to the process of refunding the money, entirely or prorated, depending upon the extended time and the discussions/negotiations with the health plan. Regardless, the policies and procedures are followed in accordance with participation agreements.

If underpayments are discovered, depending upon the claim filing limits per insurance plan or per state, it is possible that a revised claim or an appeal may be submitted.

Internal audits are when the practice or organization evaluates its own policies, procedures, documentation, and claims information. The audit may be for compliance or for financial purposes and should be a basis for improving quality. Conducting an internal audit within the first three to six months of the implementation of a compliance plan. There are multiple forms available and a few software options to assist in the auditing process. It is important to keep track of the progress (or lack of progress) for each audit. Figure 15–6 shows one style, yet not all audits are necessarily performed with all twenty-one steps.

External audits are when an outside, nonemployee of the organization evaluates the documentation, claims, or data. If possible, at the conclusion of the audit, the auditor should be scheduled for an educational review meeting. This meeting can prove to be invaluable because specific examples aid rapid learning of coding concepts. An external audit performed for compliance purposes should be:

- requested by the corporate attorney
- performed prospectively on data prior to the claim submission

Payer audits are those performed by the insurance plan for various purposes. They may be requested as outlined in the participation agreement and may be prospective or retrospective audits, for quality or for financial purposes. Usually, the payer audits also allow for an appeal process, although the process could be very physician time consuming. Payer audits may also hire outside corporations to perform the services, as demonstrated by the CMS Comprehensive Error Rate Testing (CERT). CERT recommends improvements of the CMS system after reviewing claims and processing.

An audit may be triggered by data per the physician, depicting outliers from the "bell curve" of other similar physicians either per specialty or per service area. A physician submitting more volume per CPT code may alert the audit department at the insurance plan. Or the audit may be triggered by a goal of the organization, such as reviewing all of one service or diagnosis (this especially applies for inpatient facilities for specific top diagnosis related groups (DRGs). Regardless, many payer audits result in a cost to the physician or organization either in the form of fines, sanctions, jail, or recoupment of future claim payments. Recoupments or sanctions are typically from $5,000 to $100,000 per physician.

Overpayment requests have become more common. A letter requesting an overpayment is received at the practice. An overpayment is usually just the refund per patient, and not a recoupment of money refunded or to be collected on future services for many patients. Prior to returning overpayments, state law must be reviewed, as there are specialized time factors to be considered.

While the majority of practices perform many E/M services, the audit of a practice should review services beyond strictly E/M codes for effective compliance. Refer to Figure 15–7 for compliance terminology.

Many hospitals and other facilities conduct financial audits, which may be performed for a variety of purposes. The financial audit may review the chargemaster

PERFORMING AN ON-SITE AUDIT
A 21-Step Work Plan

1. Randomly select five evaluation and management encounters (both inpatient and outpatient) for review of each physician audited.

2. Is the medical record complete and legible?

3. Attempt to locate the following:

    A. Reason for encounter (medical necessity issues)

    B. Relevant history

    C. Examination findings

    D. Prior diagnostic findings (if applicable)

    E. Assessment of the patient

    F. Clinical impression or diagnosis(es)

    G. Plan of care, treatment or further disposition of the patient

    H. Date and legible identity of performing provider

4. If not documented, is the rationale for ordering further diagnostics or workup implied?

5. Are past and present diagnoses accessible to the treating or consulting physician?

6. Are appropriate health risk factors identified/stated?

7. Is there documentation regarding the patient's progress, response to and/or changes in treatment, and/or revision of diagnosis(es)?

8. Are billing services/procedures and diagnoses supported within the medical record?

9. Compare billed procedures to performed date of service. Are these dates consistent?

10. Compare billed diagnosis(es) to documented diagnosis(es). Are these consistent?

11. Are the billing and performing provider the same?

12. Analyze and evaluate documentation by reviewing required components for each billed service.

13. Score documentation according to audit tools provided.

14. Complete audit analysis sheet on each service level reviewed:

    A. Tally points scored and compare to billed services

    B. Show discrepancies, insufficiencies, omissions, etc.

    C. Make needed recommendations

    D. Make constructive suggestions and appropriate comments

    E. Illustrate missing components for satisfaction of service level requirements

15. Sign and date each analysis sheet with name and title of reviewer/auditor as well as the date of the review.

16. Analyze level-of-service patterns billed by each physician.

17. Compare/contrast individual physician billing patterns within the practice.

18. Consult with the managing partner before presenting findings to determine whether results should be presented to the group or individually to the specific physician.

19. Furnish each physician with his/her individual results.

20. Prepare a summary of findings both on an individual and group basis. Furnish this summary to each physician reviewed along with individual findings and results.

21. Retain an indexed file or binder (per provider) labeled with date of review, reviewer's name and title, practice name (at the time of the review).

Figure 15–6 Performing an on-site audit: a 21-step work plan.

GLOSSARY OF COMPLIANCE TERMINOLOGY

BBA—Balanced Budget Act of 1997. A bipartisan agreement adding new penalties for combating fraud while providing budget neutral modifications to the RBRVS for subsequent years. This act added preventive screening to the SSA for the first time.

Corporate integrity agreement—A governmentally mandated compliance program between a healthcare corporation and the government in the settlement of a fraud and abuse investigation.

DHHS/HHS—The Department of Health and Human Services or HHS. CMS is part of this department of the federal government.

FCA—False Claims Act. This act prohibits "knowingly" submitting false or fraudulent claims to government payers and/or submission of false records or statements to conceal, avoid, or decrease an obligation to pay money or property to the government. "Knowingly" is defined by this act as having actual knowledge of false information, acting in deliberate ignorance of the truth and/or falsity of information, and/or acting in reckless disregard of the truth or falsity of information.

Healthcare compliance—Ensuring that a healthcare provider or facility is providing and billing for services according to the laws, regulations and guidelines governing that organization.

HIPAA—Health Insurance Portability and Accountability Act. Legislation designed to fight healthcare fraud by a broader expansion of HHS-OIG jurisdiction for all health insurance payers along with substantial increases in the investigative resources available to the OIG and FBI for healthcare enforcement. This law also clarifies and increases the number of healthcare fraud and abuse offenses while significantly increasing administrative and criminal penalties.

OIG—Office of the Inspector General. An enforcement division for the DHHS, responsible for investigation and enforcement of fraud and abuse cases and legislation.

Qui tam action—A lawsuit usually brought by an employee (often referred to as a "whistleblower") in regard to specific employer activities that employee believes to be fraudulent or abusive.

Figure 15–7 Glossary of compliance terminology.

efficiency, correlation to the UB-92 claim, average length of stay days, DRG assessment, taxation, or for other investment purposes.

Hospitals tend to analyze the total days in accounts receivable (A/R), whereas physicians typically view total income or revenue as the main factor. A more complete monthly financial review may better guide to the specific areas that need improvement. The revenue/payment cycle may have indicators that suggest additional evaluation for the organization such as:

- What is the ratio of A/R days to the total outstanding amount?

- What is the collection ratio? Is there a decrease in the cash collection (a cashier issue or a change in the practice/services), a particular insurance plan (possible bankruptcy or other tactics), billing, or practice?

- Is there a management system revision (biller not posting, electronic payments not transmitting, etc.), change in turning over to collection company process?

- Are the patients complaining?
- Is there an increased volume of rejections? (Did something change at the largest insurance plan, or in the process?)

THE OFFICE OF INSPECTOR GENERAL

Office of Inspector General (OIG)
The office that enforces the rules of CMS and federal agencies.

CMS hires the **Office of Inspector General (OIG),** working with FBI staff members. The web site *www.oig.hhs.gov* offers candid information, advisory opinions, and information regarding many specific situations. The easiest way to use this site is to simply browse or search a topic.

Typically, evidence is collected over a course of time, commonly on claims that have been previously adjudicated. The collection of evidence may extend over a long or short period of time. One of the greatest fallacies is that "if the claim is paid, it must be OK and not considered fraudulent activity." Quite to the contrary, the claim may be paid purposefully by CMS and the activity reported to the Benefit Integrity Unit Office of Inspector General (OIG) for further review.

STEPS TO TAKE WHEN AN INVESTIGATOR ARRIVES

Usually, after gathering evidence, an investigation begins. Correspondence requesting copies of the medical records, claims, and/or refund request may preface a site investigation. Alternatively, depending upon the issue, no previous notice and an immediate visit is possible. The visit may be quiet and discreet, or it may entail the local sheriff, with other criminal enforcement staff.

When an investigation occurs, it is based upon federal law, with federal investigation processes. Upon arrival, the investigator must show his or her credentials, and the practice should verify the accuracy of the credentials prior to releasing information. Next, the practice should contact its attorney immediately, and share information if advised by the attorney. During the entire time of investigation, staff should remain professional, courteous, and kind.

Depending upon the level of concern for the specific organization and issues involved, an investigation is likely to entail some or all of the following:

- Interviewing of current and past staff members
- Possible private interviews with beneficiaries regarding the exact care that was rendered
- Request for copies of medical records or search and seize warrant for the entire removal of medical records (may have a contractor hired to remove immediately from the site)
- Confiscation of computers, servers, laptops, and any other equipment
- Copies of billing records, encounter forms, or other worksheets

The individuals who are found guilty of committing the act of fraud will be prosecuted. Criminal, civil monetary penalty, or administrative sanctions are possible. Examples of some of the fines that have been imposed and related negative consequences are:

- Full page advertisement in the local newspaper describing what the practice or organization or person did
- Fines and sanctions per provider number per CPT code per claim per time period identified in the case (could be years)

- Exclusion from all federally funded programs
- Licensure impact (following may be reviewed by licensing board)
- Additional health plans cease contracts
- Required educational and corporate integrity agreements (CIA) with follow up visit for 1–3 years) to verify improvements
- Hospital staff privileges cease
- Jail time

Work Plan

The OIG annually publishes the Work Plan, depicting the areas that will be reviewed for accuracy. This document guides all practice compliance officers to the specific areas to evaluate for potential risk. If a practice implements the procedures properly, it is highly unlikely an investigation would occur.

The OIG has also published Compliance Plan Guidelines for various organizations, outlining the steps that must be included to create an effective compliance plan. There is a straightforward outline for the creation of a Physician Practice Compliance Plan, with seven required components of:

- What is your code of conduct for the organization? Written policies are required.
- What are the compliance monitoring efforts? Who is responsible?
- What is the training and education for practice ethics, policies and procedures, coding and documentation?
- What is the internal auditing process?
- What are the lines of communication?
- What is the disciplinary action plan?
- What is the response to detected violations through the investigation or disclosure of incidents?

If an effective compliance plan is in place, it may be considered during the investigation, and *may* decrease the potential sanctions. A compliance plan, however, is not likely to fully negate the risk for fines, sanctions, or recoupments. It is expected only that the plan will guide toward good policies and procedures in the management of the claims processes.

It is wise to conduct an audit, initiated by an attorney, prior to implementing the compliance plan. This baseline audit will serve as the benchmark, demonstrating the improvements that have been achieved upon implementation of the compliance plan. Figure 15–8 identifies procedures that should be implemented.

All facilities and types of claims are subject to review for accuracy. The current Work Plan has identified the following broad range of main topics:

- Medicare and Medicaid Hospitals
- Medicare Home Health
- Medicare Nursing Homes and Medicaid Long-Term and Community Care
- Medicare Physicians and Other Health Professionals
- Medicaid Mental Health Services
- Medicare Equipment and Supplies
- Medicare Drug Reimbursement
- Other Medicare Services (lab during inpatient, IDTF, therapy, and CORF)
- Medicare Managed Care Programs

CODING AND BILLING COMPLIANCE POINTS

■ Procedures and policies governing coding and billing should be written.

■ Actively seek education for all staff directly or indirectly involved with coding, documentation and/or billing, and claims submission.

■ Require and clearly communicate minimum competency level for all staff.

■ Establish non-punitive mechanisms for reporting violations.

■ Involve (as needed or appropriate) outside legal counsel.

Figure 15–8 Coding and billing compliance points.

- Medicare Contractor Operations (claims operations)

  Within the Work Plan, an example of a Medicare physician area of review is:

  Use of Modifiers with National Correct Coding Initiative Edits

  We will determine whether claims were paid appropriately when modifiers were used to bypass the National Correct Coding Initiative edits. The initiative, one of CMS's tools for detecting and correcting improper billing, is designed to provide Medicare Part B carriers with code pair edits for use in reviewing claims. A provider may include a modifier to allow payment for both services within the code pair under certain circumstances. In 2001, Medicare paid $565 million to providers who included the modifier with code pairs within the National Correct Coding Initiative. We will determine whether modifiers were used appropriately. *(OEI; 03-02-00771; expected issue date: FY 2005; work in progress)*

Notice the description of the intent to review the selection of the modifiers, with the validation of the cost to the system. The information in final parentheses describes the year the rule begins and the expected work timetable.

For hospitals, there are more than twenty tasks in the 2005 Work Plan, while for physicians there are more than fifteen task areas. Coders and health care professionals are strongly advised to review the Work Plan annually, preparing for the specific OIG investigation plans.

FRAUD RISK PREVENTION

- Consistently review and implement policies and procedures for each participating health insurance plan.
- Set the tone for integrity, honesty, and compliance with the law at all times.
- Before hiring an employee, check the "List of Excluded Individuals" posted on the OIG web site. A complete background check is recommended for employees.
- Purchase enough code books and reference materials to meet the needs of the organization, and implement the codes on proper dates (e.g., ICD-9-CM is October 1).
- Clearly outline Expectations, including conduct, in job descriptions.

- Allow and encourage employees and physicians to attend seminars that help them increase learning of coding and documentation.
- Schedule communication routinely for the billing and coding staff to share information, in a nonjudgmental setting. This simple yet very important step will assist with learning, process improvements, contractual renegotiations, the collection of fees, etc.

PENALTIES

Fines were increased in the HIPAA rules, which now state:

> $5,500 minimum to $11,000 FOR EACH FALSE HEALTH INSURANCE CLAIM, per line item on the claim, with an inflation factor to increase the penalty amount every 4 yr. So, effective 2000, and in future years, an additional 10% increase to the penalties were implemented. This does not take into consideration of recoupments, refund requests, or other financial determinations under an outcome of the investigation.

HEALTH INSURANCE PORTABILITY AND ACCOUNTABILITY ACT (HIPAA)

HIPAA statutes are extensive, and the range of topics much wider than just those associated with health care facilities and organizations. This section offers a brief explanation in hopes of conveying a succinct and simplistic understanding of HIPAA. There is a plethora of misinformation and misimplementation of the rules, particularly with the privacy standards. When obtaining professional coding advice, ask for guidance in writing.

Transaction and Data Sets (Code Sets)

The first deadline in 2000 pertained to the standardization of storage and transmission of electronic data from one point to another. In October 2002 the same formats and code sets were to be used: For outpatient claims, for example, ICD-9-CM Volumes 1 and 2 for outpatient claims, CPT for the procedures plus modifiers, and HCPCSII codes as appropriate. The dates for implementation of the code sets annually became standardized, such as ICD-9-CM on October 1, and CPT and HCPC-SII on January 1. Physicians and medical facilities are required to accurately select the code set in reporting on the claims.

The new claim format is ANSIX12. Mandatory fields must be completed by the practice management or facility software accurately, and there are also optional field formats.

Clearinghouses, software vendors, and health care plans are all required to implement these challenging revisions according to the HIPAA rules, by the stated deadlines.

HIPAA Security

The security rules are site specific, scalable, and in general, customized for each location. The majority of the rules focus on the security of the electronic protected health data, such as the physical storage, transmission, and access to nonemployees.

HIPAA Privacy

The HIPAA privacy rules have posed an extensive challenge for the health care industry, mostly due to the requirement for patients to be educated and involved in the process. Definitions of some of the terms used in the HIPAA privacy rules include:

Covered entities: Organizations that transmit and share electronic health information.

Protected health information (PHI): Any individually identifiable health information.

Privacy consent: The patient signs a form per organization that outlines the automatic release of PHI and the options the patient may have. Most consent forms state the organizations/physicians may release information for care, payment, and for health care operation purposes *without* a written medical release form from the patient.

Coding Tip *Patients do not need to sign a medical release form for the transmission of PHI for caring for the patient, payment, or health care operations. This is one of the most misunderstood areas of the HIPAA privacy rules. There are a few exceptions to the concept, such as specialized state laws that supercede the federal HIPAA rules, or for specific care issues such as mental health, sexually transmitted disease data, etc.*

Below are other terms to be familiar with:

- A *privacy officer* is the person who develops and oversees the policies and procedures at the organization.

- *Business associates* are individuals or companies that are given access to PHI at the organization, and have agreed to abide by all policies and procedures per the site. Common business associates are independent medical transcriptionists, for example.

- *Minimum necessary release* means that an organization is expected to release only the information required for the specific purpose; for example, only payment information may be disclosed in payment discussions.

- *Inspection of medical records* means that patients may request a copy of the medical record or to review the information contained in the record. Physicians may choose to release or not, based upon the medical care and potential harm to the patient. Physicians may charge for the medical record and for the labor to monitor the medical record. The patient may not alter the medical record in any way, and is not to have a writing instrument while reviewing the chart.

- Patients may request an *amendment* to correct an error in the medical record, and physicians may choose to deny this request with a written notification.

- The Office of Civil Rights is responsible for the *enforcement* of the HIPAA privacy rules, with an overall expectation to educate toward compliance as the first step, and then enforcement levels will be elevated as appropriate. Fines may be $100 per incident, up to $25,000 per year for accidental release. For purposeful distribution of PHI, the fines escalate to $250,000 and potential ten-year imprisonment.

Typical Steps for the HIPAA Privacy Process

The privacy rules require covered entities to manage protected health information using proper techniques. If the patient is presenting for non-emergency care, usually they are advised to sign the privacy consent form. If the patient has any questions, either they are quickly advised or the privacy officer is contacted for further clarification. The care is provided, the claim is transmitted, the medical transcription is prepared, and the privacy is maintained. On occasion, the patient or authorized representative requests to amend, review, or have a copy of the medical record. These decisions are typically determined by either the privacy officer, or personally by the physician in smaller offices, and the patient request is either honored or denied in writing, specifying the anticipated costs associated with the request.

In comparison with the enormous volume of medical records that are managed throughout the United States, in general, the accidental or the purposeful release of PHI has been minimal since the implementation of HIPAA rules.

EXERCISE 15–4

1. What are the three parts of HIPAA that affect most physician offices?

2. For HIPAA privacy, can you release a medical record to another health care professional that is caring for the patient without obtaining a written medical release form?

3. What is the enforcement agency for the HIPAA privacy rules?

SUMMARY

The payment cycle includes a team of personnel focusing on the proper payment for professional services. Completion of the advance beneficiary notice is required for all health insurance plans, and must be properly completed. Rules for completion of the claim form are under reform, and as the policies evolve, the reforms will need to be implemented.

Physicians and organizations have various contracting options, and these contracts affect the operations, policies, and cash flow, as well as the volume of patients. Avoiding fraud and abuse requires diligent, consistent work effort by the practice/organization.

REFERENCES

AMA Current Procedural Terminology 2005 Professional Edition. (2004). Chicago: American Medical Association.

ICD-9-CM expert for physicians Volumes 1 and 2 (6th ed.). (2004). Salt Lake City, UT: Ingenix.

OIG Work Plan for 2005. Retrieved August 15, 2005, from www.oig.cms.hhs.gov

Updateable expert HCPSC Level II (16th ed.). (2005). Salt Lake City, UT: Ingenix.

Chapter 16

Inpatient Coding

LEARNING OBJECTIVES

At the conclusion of this chapter, you should be able to:

1. Identify hospital payment systems.
2. Explain the importance of Uniform Hospital Discharge Data Set (UHDDS).
3. Differentiate between signs and symptoms.
4. Determine a principal diagnosis.
5. Determine a principal procedure.
6. Differentiate between comorbidities and complications.
7. Discuss the DRG payment system.
8. Discuss the impact of HIPAA on inpatient hospital coding.
9. Assign ICD-9-CM codes for an inpatient hospital scenario in the correct sequence.

inpatient
Refers to an acute care setting.

prospective payment system (PPS)
Also referred to as inpatient prospective payment system (IPPS); relates to inpatient or hospital-based coding. Several areas of patient care, including severity of illness, prognosis, and treatment difficulty are key to the IPPS system.

acute care facility
Inpatient hospital facility where a patient stays at least overnight for medical care.

INTRODUCTION

This chapter provides an overview of **inpatient** hospital-based coding. The focus will be to develop a comprehension of key definitions and important guidelines. The impact of **prospective payment systems (PPSs)** on **acute care facilities** and the current reimbursement environment will be discussed. Acute care facilities or inpatient facilities are those health care institutions that provide medical service with an average length of stay less than forty-five days. In most acute care facilities the mean length of stay for a patient is less than five days. Acute care facilities offer a wide range of medical services.

Hospital-based or inpatient coders utilize health record documentation to ensure that the facility is receiving the correct reimbursement based on clinical medical information. Inpatient coders, like their counterparts in the outpatient area, follow ICD-9-CM coding guidelines. One major difference between inpatient and outpatient coding is the amount of information available to the coder. Inpatient hospital stays generate physician documentation, nursing documentation, and ancillary staff documentation (for example, physical therapy, radiography, etc.). This documentation is used to determine the correct ICD-9-CM codes that are to be reported and the correct sequencing or ordering of the codes. The sequence of codes in the inpatient setting is vital because it impacts reimbursement especially for patients that have Medicare as their primary insurance carrier.

The cooperating parties responsible for the annual updates to ICD-9-CM include the Centers for Medicare and Medicaid Services (CMS), American Hospital Association (AHA), National Center for Health Statistics (NCHS), and the American Health Information Management Association (AHIMA). Updates to ICD-9-CM are published annually and are effective October 1 of each year. For a listing of recent ICD-9-CM code updates, changes, and revisions, access www.cms.gov.

HOSPITAL BASED ICD-9-CM CODING

uniform hospital discharge data set (UHDDS)
A data set used in inpatient coding to define principal diagnosis and principal procedure.

The reporting of hospital inpatient coded data is defined by the **uniform hospital discharge data set (UHDDS).** This is a unique data set that includes delineation on data elements (birth date, hospital number, gender of patient, etc.). However, UHDDS also includes important term definitions that are a foundation for hospital inpatient coding.

These terms are:

- principal diagnosis
- other reportable diagnosis
- principal procedure
- significant procedure

The Centers for Medicare and Medicaid Services (CMS) require that UHDDS guidelines are followed when reporting data on its subscribers. This is for the purpose of standardization of data reporting to ensure that statistics and reimbursement methodologies like DRGs can be calculated correctly. More information on the DRG system is discussed later in this chapter.

Principal Diagnosis

The UHDDS defines principal diagnosis as the condition established after study to be chiefly responsible for the admission of a specific patient to the hospital for care. The key part of this definition are the words "after study," as this directs the coder to take into consideration the entire episode of medical care and treatment to determine what was the main clinical reason for this patient seeking care. The principal diagnosis then translates into an ICD-9-CM code. This code will be the first code reported under the UHDDS requirement. It is important for the hospital

admission diagnosis
Sign, symptom, complaint documented in the health record reported from the patient as main reason for seeking medical care.

sign
An objective medical complaint.

symptom
A subjective medical complaint.

coder to understand the difference between **admission diagnosis** and principal diagnosis. An admission diagnosis is assigned at registration when the patient presents to the hospital for treatment. This is often reported to the registration or nursing staff as signs and/or symptoms. A **sign** is an objective medical complaint that is a condition that can be observed by another person, typically a medical professional. A **symptom** is a subjective medical complaint reported by the patient that cannot be observed. Often admission diagnosis and sign/symptoms reported will not be the principal diagnosis.

EXAMPLE

A patient presents to the emergency department of her local hospital. She complains of a nosebleed and a severe headache. The triage nurse observes blood trickling from the patient nares. The nurse also notes that the patient seems to be in pain from a headache. The patient is noted to have a blood pressure of 176/100. This patient is admitted to the emergency department. Admission diagnosis: Nosebleed.

discharge diagnosis
Found in a discharge summary, this is a list of diagnoses that can include conditions treated during this inpatient admission, other reportable diagnoses, and medical history information.

The patient is seen by the emergency department physician, given antihypertensive medications and admitted to the medical floor for observation. The patient responds to IV medication and is discharged after two days in an improved condition. **Discharge diagnoses** listed by the physician on the health record are: hypertension, severe epistaxis, and headache.

Sign—Nosebleed

Symptom—headache

Admission diagnosis—Nosebleed

Principal diagnosis—Hypertension

In the previous example the sign and symptom would not be reported since they are part of the disease process of hypertension for this patient. Signs and symptoms are often documented but not reported by the inpatient coder if they are common or known parts of an established diagnosis. It is important for a hospital coder to have a complete knowledge of human anatomy, physiology, and disease processes (pathophysiology).

Other Diagnoses

other reportable diagnosis
Other diagnoses in addition to the discharge diagnosis that directly relate to the current episode of care.

V codes
Codes that identify important patient history or reason for a patient seeking medical care when no diagnosis, symptoms, or signs present to be reported.

Other diagnoses are reportable if they directly relate to the current episode of care. A patient's past medical history may be relevant based on related care and/or treatment he or she receives during a specific hospital stay. **Other reportable diagnosis** can be reported as current conditions or as **V codes.** V codes identify important patient history or reason for a patient seeking medical care when no diagnosis, symptoms, or signs present to be reported.

EXAMPLE

A patient presents to the hospital complaining of chest pain. He is admitted to the emergency department, evaluated, and sent to the intensive care unit (ICU). Patient's history includes a previous coronary artery bypass graft (CABG) five years ago. The patient is under treatment for hypertension and high cholesterol. He receives treatment and is found to be suffering from gastroesophageal reflux disease. He is discharged after one day in the ICU.

Principal diagnosis—Gastroesophageal Reflux Disease

Additional diagnoses—Hypertension and High Cholesterol

V code—History of CABG

V codes can also be reported as principal diagnosis codes when no medical condition is found. For example, if a patient is admitted for observation following a multiple vehicle accident (MVA) to rule out a concussion and no concussion is found. If the patient reports no signs or symptoms, a V code would be reported as the principal diagnosis code for this admission (V71.4 Observation following other accident).

When coding newborn charts, a V code is always reported as the principal diagnosis to reflect that the chart is that of a new baby. The code category for reporting on newborn health records is V30, Liveborn infants according to type of birth. The code range for newborns is V30 to V39 (Table 16–1). This code category requires the addition of both a fourth and fifth digit.

When coding newborn health records, the principal diagnosis code will always be a code from the V30 to V39 category. These V codes reflect that this is a newborn record and the status of the birth. Additional ICD-9-CM codes can be used after the V30 category to report any congenital conditions, perinatal conditions, or other reportable diagnoses that are present for that newborn on the birth health record. If the newborn is transferred to another health care facility for medical treatment, the V30 code would not be reported on that subsequent health record.

TABLE 16–1   Coding Newborn Charts.

V30.XX	Single liveborn
V31.XX	Twin, mate liveborn
V32. XX	Twin, mate stillborn
V33.XX	Twin, unspecified
V34.XX	Other multiple, mates all liveborn
V35.XX	Other multiple, mates all stillborn
V36.XX	Other multiple, mates live and stillborn
V37.XX	Other multiple, unspecified
V39.XX	Unspecified
Fourth digit for this category is:	
.0	Born in hospital
.1	Born before admission to hospital
.2	Born outside hospital and not hospitalized
Fifth digits for this category are:	
0	delivered without mention of cesarean delivery
1	delivered by cesarean delivery

EXAMPLE

Baby boy Jacobs is born at Hospital A. He is a live single birth delivered vaginally in the hospital by Dr. Mitchell. This baby is noted to have a fractured clavicle due to his travel through the birth canal. He is also found to have a ventricular septal defect of his heart. Baby Jacobs is transferred out of Hospital A to Hospital B for further medical treatment. For Hospital A, the principal diagnosis would be V30.00. The fractured clavicle and ventricular septal defect (767.2, 745.4) would also be coded on Hospital A health record. For the Hospital B record, only the fractured clavicle and the ventricular septal defect would be coded.

Another coding application of V codes is to represent relevant patient medical history. V codes can be used to provide information on a patient's past medical history that could impact current medical care or treatment. Not all of a patient's past medical history is correctly reported as V codes. Only relevant medical history should be reported.

EXAMPLE

A patient is admitted via the emergency department (ED) with an admission diagnosis of severe abdominal pain and chest pain. The patient's past medical history includes: a broken femur with surgical reduction following a MVA (this injury occurred 5 years ago), arteriosclerosis for which the patient had a three-vessel coronary artery bypass graft (CABG) seven years ago; hypertension for which the patient is currently taking medication; and a history of migraines. The patient has not had a migraine in six months since doing relaxation exercises and taking vitamins. After admission to an inpatient floor and evaluation, it is determined that the patient has an abdominal aneurysm that will require surgical repair. The patient is scheduled for surgery. After surgery the patient is transferred to the intensive care unit (ICU) for observation and nursing care. While in the ICU, antihypertensive medications are added to the patient's postoperative orders. After three days in the ICU the patient is discharged in an improved condition. No further chest pain is reported by the patient after surgical repair of aneurysm. Discharge diagnoses: abdominal aneurysm, chest pain, history of CABG, history of ORIF, history of migraines, and hypertension.

    Principal diagnosis—Abdominal aneurysm

    Other reportable diagnosis—Hypertension, chest pain, history of CABG

    Principal procedure—Repair of abdominal aneurysm

In the previous example, the history of femur fracture and migraines, while documented by the physician in his exam, were not treated or relevant during this specific inpatient admission. The patient's medical history of hypertension is relevant and important given the current problem, abdominal aneurysm, and the fact that the patient was treated during this admission with antihypertensive medications given by the nursing staff.

principal procedure
The definitive procedure most often related to the principal diagnosis.

significant procedure
A procedure that is surgical in nature, carries an anesthetic risk, carries a procedural risk, and requires a skilled clinician to perform.

Principal Procedure and Significant Procedure

Principal procedure is defined as the definitive procedure most often related to the principal diagnosis. Commonly, the principal procedure is the surgical event that addressed the principal diagnosis that is being reported. For a procedure to be principal, it must first be significant. UHDDS outlines 4 specific conditions for a procedure to be deemed significant. For a hospital to report a **significant procedure** the event should be 1) surgical in nature, 2) have an anesthetic risk, 3) a procedural risk, and 4) require the skill of a trained clinician. Additional procedures done during a hospital stay are also reported, which can be for additional medical problems that are other reportable diagnoses.

EXAMPLE

A patient is admitted for a laparoscopic cholecystectomy. This surgery is done for chronic cholecystitis with cholelithiasis. The patient is also found to have an axillary abscess on the first postoperative day. This abscess is incised and drained on the second postoperative day. The patient is discharged on the third postoperative day.

Principal procedure—Laparoscopic cholecystectomy

Significant (reportable) procedure—Incision & Drainage (I&D) of axillary abscess

UNCONFIRMED CONDITIONS

unconfirmed conditions
Diseases or diagnosis(ies) identified by a physician in the health record documentation as possible, probable, or likely but not confirmed as a final diagnosis(ies).

An additional area that a hospital-based coder must be aware of is **unconfirmed conditions.** In an inpatient setting conditions identified as "rule out," "probable," "possible," or "likely" are coded as if confirmed. For example, possible gastritis would be coded as gastritis, 535.00. Conditions identified as "ruled out" are not coded. This concept can often directly relate to medical necessity. If a medical condition is believed to be present and after diagnostic study it is determined if that specific condition is not present, the question may be raised as to the need for a hospital admission. This condition has been "ruled out" often based on diagnostic testing. This concept is also important because of the potential impact on hospital reimbursement and reporting a ruled out condition would be a violation of the False Claims Act (FCA).

Highlights

Medicare program integrity (PI)
Developed under HIPAA to provide strategies for the federal government to use to ensure that medical claims are paid properly.

*HIPAA legislation includes a provision establishing the **Medicare program integrity (PI)**. The main goal of this program is to pay claims correctly. CMS has established four strategies to achieve this goal.*

- *Preventing fraud*
- *Early detention through claims review and claim analysis*
- *Coordination with contractors and law enforcement agencies*
- *Fair enforcement policies*

Coding errors or billing errors are not considered fraud. CMS recognizes that errors can occur; however, repetitive submission of claims determined to be in violation of CMS regulations will be investigated under the PI and could be deemed as fraud or abuse.

For more information on Medicare's program integrity reference, go to the CMS web site, www.cms.hhs.gov.

In an inpatient setting there are occasions when a diagnosis or disease is documented as "probable," "likely," "suspected," or "rule out" as a final notation upon the patient's discharge from the hospital. In these cases, the condition is coded and reported as if it were a definitive diagnosis. If a condition that is identified as "probable" is not coded, the impact may be seen in the reduction of the amount the hospital is reimbursed. This would happen under the PPS system if the hospital is reported for a patient using the DRG methodology. This "probable" condition was worked up and required the utilization of resources (radiology, laboratory, etc.). If the condition is not coded on an inpatient record, the funds reimbursed to the hospital may be significantly reduced. Further information on the DRG system is included later in this chapter.

EXERCISE 16–1

Select the correct answers.

1. A patient presents to emergency department (ED) of his local hospital complaining of severe facial pain and headache. After radiographic studies it is determined that the patient has pansinusitis. The patient is admitted for treatment with intravenous (IV) antibiotics. The principal diagnosis for this admission is _____ (headache, facial pain, severe facial pain, pansinusitis).

2. Joseph Roberts is admitted to a local hospital following a multiple vehicle accident (MVA) with the complaint of chest pain, abdominal pain, and pain of the forearm. After workup and evaluation, Mr. Roberts is diagnosed with a blocked heart artery, abdominal aneurysm, and an open wound of his forearm. The patient has an abdominal MRI and an arterial radiographic study. One day after admission, the patient has a coronary artery bypass graft (CABG) to correct the blocked artery. Medication is used to treat his abdominal aneurysm. The open wound of the forearm is cleaned and sutured at the bedside by the surgical resident. The principal procedure for this admission is _____ (treatment of the abdominal aneurysm, CABG, suturing of forearm open wound, radiographic studies).

EXERCISE 16–2

Select the correct answers.

Susan Wilcox is admitted to her physician's office with a chief complaint (CC) of hematuria and pyuria. The pyuria was confirmed on an office urine test. Ms. Wilcox is admitted for further workup and treatment. A kidney, ureter, bladder (KUB) x-ray is taken and further urine and blood testing is done. The patient also reports the additional symptom of nausea after she is admitted. The nursing staff notes a fever of 101 on the patient's chart. The patient is treated with IV antibiotics for twenty-four hours and then switched to oral (PO) medications. She is discharged on the second day after admission in an improved condition. Discharge diagnoses are listed on the discharge summary as: gross hematuria, pyelonephritis due to E. coli, fever.

1. The diagnoses of "gross hematuria" is considered a _____ (sign, symptom, principal diagnosis, past medical history).

2. The pyuria reported is classified as a _____ (sign, symptom, principal diagnosis, past medical history).

3. The principal diagnosis reported for Ms. Wilcox is _____ (pyuria, hemturia, pyelonephritis, fever and nausea).

EXERCISE 16–3

Select the correct answers.

A patient presents to the local emergency department (ED) of a local hospital at 8:15 P.M. with a complaint of stomach pain. The patient also has a history of congestive heart failure (CHF) for which he has been treated for the past five years. On examination in the ED it is noted that the patient has a lower leg infection from a small cut suffered two days prior to the ED visit. The patient's leg wound is cleaned and topical antibiotics are applied. PO antibiotics are also started in the ED for the cellulitis. After workup in the ED the patient is admitted for further testing. This testing includes a cholecystography. One day after admission the patient is diagnosed with obstructive cholelithiasis and has a laparoscopic cholecystectomy. Her discharge diagnoses are severe abdominal pain, obstructive cholelithiasis, CHF, and leg cellulitis.

1. This patient's principal diagnosis is _____ (severe abdominal pain and CHF, cellulitis, obstructive cholelithiasis, laparoscopic cholecystectomy).

2. _____ (Wound cleansing, Antibiotic treatment, Laparoscopic cholecystectomy, Cholecystography) is the principal procedure in this case.

3. The patient's CHF is classified as a _____ (complication, comorbity, principal diagnosis, principal procedure).

EXERCISE 16–4

Select the correct answers.

1. A forty-five-year-old female is admitted with a chief complaint of a "headache that will not go away." Patient has a history of benign breast nodule that was removed five years prior to this admission. She is admitted for further inpatient workup and treatment. She receives several diagnostic tests, including CT scan of her brain. No diagnosis or disease is found and she is treated with analgesics for pain and discharged to follow-up with the Headache Center as an outpatient. Discharge diagnosis listed by the attending physician is cerebral aneurysm ruled out. The diagnosis to be coded on this inpatient health record is _____ (no diagnoses, nothing was found; history of benign breast disease; cerebral aneurysm; headache).

2. Mrs. Mae Garfield is a seventy-year-old female who has been treated for progressive increasing pain in her back by her personal physician. She is to the point that she is unable to move. She is brought to the ER and admitted after x-ray showed severe compression fractures of the lumbar vertebrae due to her senile osteoporosis. An injection of anesthetic was done into the spinal canal. Mrs. Garfield also suffers from non-insulin dependent diabetes (NIDDM) and degenerative joint disease (DJD) of her hands and right hip. What would be the principal diagnosis code for Mrs. Garfield's chart?
   a. 805.4, 733.13
   b. 805.4
   c. 724.5, 733.00
   d. 733.13

CODE ASSIGNMENT

Inpatient coding utilizes ICD-9-CM Volumes 1, 2, and 3 for code assignment. Volume 1 and Volume 2 are used for diagnostic codes, while Volume 3 is used for procedural coding. Acute care facilities are required to use ICD-9-CM Volume 3 codes for the reporting of procedures. Facility policies and procedures for coding will vary and often hospitals will code inpatient health records with codes from Volume 3 of ICD-9-CM and codes from Healthcare Common Procedure Coding System (HCPCS)/Current Procedural Terminology (CPT). This can be for reimbursement purposes or for facility statistical purposes. The coding of HCPCS or CPT codes on inpatient health records also may be dependent on the relationship of the provider to the facility. If the physician is employed by the hospital, the billing department of the hospital would be facilitating the physician billing to the insurance provider, therefore requiring the use of HCPCS/CPT codes. Physician reporting of procedures and services requires the use of HCPCS/CPT codes. Hospitals are required to use ICD-9-CM for the reporting of diagnoses and procedures.

■ *Highlight*

UB-92
Uniform Bill 1992 version, a form used by hospitals for claim submission.

National Uniform Billing Committee (NUBC)
Formed in 1975, this committee develops the UB-92 form in conjunction with the AHA.

discharge summary
A document that provides a detailed account of the patient's hospital course, specifically outlining treatment and patient response.

face sheet
The cover sheet of an inpatient health record, which lists demographic and financial information for the patient.

comorbidities
Chronic conditions that existed before inpatient admission.

complications
Conditions that occur after a patient is admitted to the hospital; may be the result or side effect of care rendered.

Hospitals utilize the **UB-92** *form, universal billing form, for reporting of codes to providers. The UB-92 form was designed by the* **National Uniform Billing Committee (NUBC).** *Outpatient utilizes the CMS-1500 billing form to report diagnoses and procedures.*

HIPAA legislation has approved specific code sets that are used in the inpatient and outpatient arenas of medical reimbursement. For inpatient hospital reporting, ICD-9-CM is the required code set. For outpatient reporting, ICD-9-CM is required to report diagnoses code or codes, and the HCPCS code set is required to report supplies, procedures, and services. HCPCS includes the coding classification of CPT. There are two levels of recognized HCPCS codes: level one is CPT, and level two is HCPCS. HCPCS codes reflect various supplies and equipment, while CPT codes are used to report physician-performed services and procedures. There are other HIPAA approved code sets for other types of medical facilities. Further information on other code sets can be found at www.aspe.hhs.gov/admnsimp.faqcode.html.

The source document for code assignment in an inpatient setting is the health record. The starting point for inpatient coding is often the **discharge summary.** This document should provide a detailed account of the patient's hospital course, specifically outlining treatment and patient response. At the conclusion of the discharge summary, medical diagnoses and procedures are listed. This is often under the heading of discharge diagnoses. This list of diagnoses can include conditions treated during this inpatient admission, other reportable diagnoses, and medical history information. The sequence may or may not be correct for the inpatient coding process. The inpatient coder must determine the principal diagnosis. Physicians often list discharge diagnoses and procedures on the **face sheet** of the health record. The face sheet is the cover sheet of an inpatient health record and also lists demographic and financial information for that patient. Again, the sequencing of the diagnoses and or procedures may not be correct based on UHDDS guidelines.

Other reportable diagnoses that are relevant to that specific episode of care can be **comorbidities** and/or **complications.** Chronic conditions, which the patient had before this specific admission, are comorbidities. Complications are those conditions that occur after a patient is admitted to the hospital and may be the result or side effect of care rendered.

EXAMPLE 1:

The following diagnoses are listed on a discharge summary of patient G. Wilcox, a thirty-six-year-old male.

- Respiratory insufficiency
- Acute exacerbation of asthma
- History of left femur fracture from MVA

After review of the chart, the inpatient coder determines that asthma is the principal diagnosis. The documentation of respiratory insufficiency is noting medical necessity, and the documentation of the history of femur fracture has no relevance to the current admission. Diagnosis coded is 493.90 (Asthma).

EXAMPLE 2:

The following diagnoses are listed on a discharge summary of patient J. Fielding, a seventy-five-year-old patient.

- Shortness of breath
- Pneumonia due to influenza
- Type II diabetes mellitus
- Degenerative joint disease (DJD) of the hands

After reviewing the chart, the inpatient coder designates Pneumonia due to influenza (487.0) as the principal diagnosis; Type II Diabetes Mellitus (250.00), and DJD (715.94) are also coded as comorbidities. Shortness of breath is not coded separately, since it is a symptom of the patient's pneumonia.

CMS publishes a list of recognized complications and comorbidities. A current listing can be found at www.provider.ipro.org. Table 16–2 is a partial listing of some complications and comorbidities. Some of the reportable comorbidities are also signs that could be part of a patient's health record documentation.

TABLE 16–2   Recognized Complications and Comorbidities.

Alcoholism	Anemia
Atrial fibrillation	Atrial flutter
Atelectasis	Cardiogenic shock
Cellulitis	Congestive heart failure (CHF)
Decubitus ulcer	Dehydration
Type I diabetes mellitus	Hematuria
Malnutrition	Melena
Respiratory failure	Urinary tract infection (UTI)

abnormal findings
Information documented in a health record typically on a radiograph report or a lab report that identifies an anomaly in the test that was given.

Abnormal Findings

ICD-9-CM has a specific guideline that addresses the coding of **abnormal findings** that are documented on laboratory or other types of ancillary reports. These abnormal findings are not linked to a specific disease process or medical disorder.

The findings may be addressed with medical treatment; however, they may not be noted on a discharge summary or a face sheet. While the inclusion of the findings is important for a complete health record, inpatient coders do not automatically assign codes based solely on abnormal lab or x-ray findings. If the abnormal finding is treated with further testing or the administration of drugs, it is appropriate for the coder to query the physician to determine if the abnormal finding is significant and if it should be coded and reported.

■ *Highlight*

Refer to the ICD-9-CM Official Guidelines, Section III, B for abnormal findings guidelines.

EXERCISE 16–5

1. A patient is admitted with a diagnosis of profuse menstrual bleeding. She is admitted for a dilation and curettage (D&C). The D&C is performed and the patient is admitted for inpatient overnight stay. The patient is discharged one day after her admission to follow-up with her physician. In what volume of ICD-9-CM would the coder find the correct code for the D&C?

   _____

2. An inpatient hospital coder is helping out her colleagues by coding outpatient surgery charts. These particular groups of charts are patients that were only seen in the ambulatory surgical unit (ASU) and were not admitted to an inpatient hospital floor. What code set(s) or code classification(s) would the coder use to code these ASU charts?

   _____

EXERCISE 16–6

Select the correct answers.

Sally Jones, an eighty-five-year-old patient, is admitted for treatment from her residence at Living Waters Nursing Home Community. Mrs. Jones is admitted for surgical debridement of a decubitus ulcer. Mrs. Jones is also complaining of blood in her urine when she is admitted. This patient has a medical history of hypertension, type II diabetes mellitus, and congestive heart failure (CHF), all of which she is under current medical treatment for by her primary physician. Also, Mrs. Jones is a breast cancer survivor for the past fifteen years. Her complaint of hematuria is evaluated. Two days after admission for the surgery, Mrs. Jones is noted to have dyspnea. A chest x-ray is taken and a diagnosis of pneumonia is made. A urine test confirms that she has a UTI. She is treated for the pneumonia and UTI with antibiotics. She also receives oxygen for the pneumonia.

1. Which of the following diagnoses would be comorbidities for this patient? _____ (decubitus ulcer, pneumonia, breast cancer, CHF).

2. The principal diagnosis for Mrs. Jones's health record is
_____ (UTI, pneumonia, hypertension, decubitus ulcer).

3. The principal procedure for Mrs. Jones's health record is:
_____ (urine test, surgical debridement, antibiotic
therapy, oxygen therapy).

4. Mrs. Jones's diagnosis of pneumonia would be classified as a
_____ (complication, principal diagnosis,
history, comorbidity).

EXERCISE 16–7

Select the correct answer.

A patient, Carol Caulfield, is admitted after suffering a fall from a ladder at her
home. Carol has a confirmed Colles' fracture of the right wrist, an ulna shaft fracture of the left forearm, a laceration of the shoulder, and multiple contusions. She
is admitted for surgical treatment and reduction of her fractures. Her lacerated
shoulder is repaired with sutures in the ED. Two days after surgery Carol has a postoperative wound infection of the surgical site of her ulnar fracture that had resulted
at the location where she had an open reduction with internal fixation (ORIF). This
postoperative infection would be classified as a _____
(comorbidity, complication, principal diagnosis, principal procedure).

EXERCISE 16–8

Select the correct answers.

Sally Childs, a seven-year-old, is seen in the ED of a local hospital. Sally fell from a
jungle gym thirty-six hours previously and now presents with the complaint of
lower leg pain. She is noted to have an open wound of the lower right leg and multiple contusions of her face, legs, and forearms. She is also noted to have a laceration of her left ear. Her lacerated ear is repaired with sutures in the emergency
department. The nursing staff in the ED cleans and bandages her contusions. Sally
is determined to have a cellulitis of her leg wound. She is admitted for surgical debridement. The surgical debridement is performed on the first admission day.
Twelve hours after surgery Sally begins to complain of throat pain. She is examined
and found to have tonsillitis. This is the fifth time in twelve months that Sally has
had tonsillitis. A consultation with an ears, nose, and throat (ENT) specialist is
done and it is determined that a tonsillectomy is needed for this patient. The tonsillectomy is performed on her third date of admission.

1. The principal diagnosis in this case is _____ (multiple
contusions, fall from jungle gym, cellulitis, tonsillitis).

2. The principal procedure for the Sally Childs case is _____
(debridement, tonsillectomy, suture repair, cleaning and bandaging of
contusions).

Conventions

conventions
Unique components of ICD-9-CM classification system that provide direction and/or additional information to individuals using classification. Example: inclusion notes, exclusion notes, NEC, NOS, use additional code, code first underlying code.

ICD-9-CM coding **conventions** should be identified and followed when doing hospital coding. These conventions include

- Not otherwise specified (NOS)
- Not elsewhere classified (NEC)
- Punctuation conventions
- Inclusion notes
- Exclusion notes
- Unspecified codes
- Code first
- Use additional code

NEC
Not elsewhere classified.

NOS
Not otherwise specified.

NEC is defined as "not elsewhere classified." This convention relates to the situation where the health record documentation is very specific but when the coder refers to the ICD-9-CM coding manual, no specific code is found to meet the documentation. **NOS** is defined as "not otherwise specified." This convention relates to the situation where the health record documentation is not very specific; however, there are codes in ICD-9-CM that identify specific disease components.

Punctuation conventions include brackets and parentheses. These punctuations are used in Volume 1 in the tabular list, and Volume 2 in the alphabetic index. In the tabular list, brackets are used to enclose synonyms, or alternative words. In the alphabetic index, brackets are used to identify manifestation codes and identify required codes. Parentheses are used in both sections as a way to provide supplementary words, which may or may not be present in the health record documentation.

Inclusion notes identify conditions, diseases, and disorders that are included under a specific code. Exclusion notes identify those conditions, diseases, and disorders that are not to be coded with that specific ICD-9-CM code. Unspecified codes are those usually with a 9 or 0 and the last digit. An inpatient coder should limit the usage of unspecified codes. A complete health record should provide clinical information that would warrant the assignment of a more specific code. "Code first" relates to the pathophysiology of specific disorders. This convention directs the code to identify this situation by using multiple codes. This concept extends to "use additional code" and "in diseases classified elsewhere."

EXAMPLE 1:

The health record documentation on a patient identifies "acute otitis media." The physician does not document if this is due to allergies or another cause. The coder assigns 382.9, Acute otitis media, NOS.

EXAMPLE 2:

The health record documentation on a patient identifies "right forearm fracture." There is no documentation of an x-ray report and no further information is in the chart on the exact location of the fracture. The coder assigns 813.80, Closed fracture of forearm, NEC.

▬ *Highlignt*

Refer to the official ICD-9-CM guidelines for further information on the conventions of this classification. The conventions are found under Section I of the guidelines.

CODING GUIDELINES

coding guidelines
Published in the ICD-9-CM coding manual, these provide a framework for the reporting of diagnoses and procedural codes.

ICD-9-CM lists multiple **coding guidelines.** Coding guidelines are published in the ICD-9-CM coding manual and can also be obtained from the American Hospital Association (AHA). Coding guidelines provide a framework for the reporting of diagnoses and procedural codes. ICD-9-CM has general coding guidelines and chapter-specific guidelines. Chapter-specific guidelines are focused on a body system or disease process. **Specificity,** using both the alphabetic index and tabular list, and sign and symptom coding are important general coding guidelines used in hospital-based coding.

specificity
The concept of identifying the most detailed code based on ICD-9-CM classification system, its guidelines, and the documentation in the health record.

The correct method for finding an ICD-9-CM diagnosis code is to find the code first using the alphabetic index and then refer to the tabular listing. It is vital to check the tabular listing for inclusion and exclusion notes. Also, the tabular listing is where direction is often given on fourth and fifth digit requirements. The inclusion of fourth and fifth digits is important to ensure that invalid codes are not being used. ICD-9-CM codes should be as specific as possible, based on the clinical information that is being used as the source document for coding. Specificity is defined as: "the state of being specific; having a relation to a definite result or to a particular cause." If a health record documents a specific disease process or a specific location of a disease, it is vital that this information is reflected in the ICD-9-CM code chosen.

In general, signs and symptoms are not coded in an inpatient setting when they are the common elements of a definitive disease as identified in the health record. For example, the common sign of pneumonia is shortness of breath. If both shortness of breath and pneumonia were documented as diagnoses in the inpatient health record, only pneumonia would be the condition coded.

Chapter-Specific Guidelines

There are many diagnostic-specific ICD-9-CM guidelines. An inpatient coder should be very familiar with all of the guidelines and conventions that govern ICD-9-CM. Below is a listing of several important diagnostic or chapter-specific coding guidelines that can directly impact inpatient coding. They are:

- Human immunodeficiency virus (HIV)
- Hypertensive heart disease
- Hypertensive heart and renal disease
- Hypertensive renal disease
- Septicemia

HIV can be coded only when it is confirmed in the health record documentation. This is a specific guideline for this disease. If an HIV-identified patient is admitted with a commonly seen HIV-related diagnosis, 042 HIV is coded as the principal diagnosis. If an HIV-identified patient is admitted with an unrelated condition, the concept of principal diagnosis is applied.

EXAMPLE

A patient with HIV is admitted with severe shortness of breath. After admission and workup, it is determined that the patient has pneumocystis carinii pneumonia (PCP). The codes for this admission would be 042 HIV and 136.3 PCP pneumonia.

combination code category
Allows codes to reflect two conditions with one ICD-9-CM code; usually used in the area of hypertensive heart disease.

Hypertensive heart disease is coded to **combination code category** 402. This is done when the health record documentation states a "causal" relationship between the patient having hypertension and heart disease. A causal relationship can be documented with the terms "due to," or using the word "hypertensive" can imply it. When a patient is found to have both hypertensive heart and hypertensive renal disease, this is coded to the combination code category of 404. Combination code categories are used in the area of hypertensive heart disease. These combination categories allow the coder to reflect two conditions with one ICD-9-CM code.

When a patient is documented to have chronic renal failure (CRF) and hypertension (HTN), the coder can assume that these conditions are related and therefore code them to the combination category of 403. The relationship of CRF and HTN does not have to be documented with the terms "due to" or "caused by." This is due to the underlying pathophysiology of patients who have CRF.

Septicemia is coded with a code from category 038 Septicemia and 995.9 Systemic inflammatory response syndrome. Under category 995.9 there is a "code first" notation that directs the coder to code first the underlying systemic infection. For example, if a patient is documented to have sepsis due to streptococcal organism, the correct codes in the correct sequence would be 038.0 and 995.91.

Hospital-based coders should follow all chapter-specific coding guidelines. These guidelines relate to major disease types. Given the variety of medical conditions that are treated in acute care facilities, a hospital coder must be knowledgeable of all diseases and how they are to be coded based on ICD-9-CM guidelines. Clarification of coding issues can be found in a publication of the American Hospital Association (AHA) entitled the *ICD-9-CM Coding Clinic*. The publication provides information and clarification on specific coding questions and/or scenarios based on actual questions submitted by coders working in the field. The AHA publishes the coding clinic quarterly and it is available via subscription.

■ *Highlight*

A listing of official ICD-9-CM coding guidelines is available on the National Center for Health Statistic's web site, www.cdc.nchs.gov. Remember that ICD-9-CM is updated annually. New codes are added, codes are deleted, and codes are revised to this classification system. The ICD-9-CM coding clinic is available for purchase from the AHA at www.ahaonlinestore.com.

per diem
Method of reimbursement based on a per-day charge for services.

contract rate
Predetermined rate based on negotiations with the facilities within the network.

diagnosis related group (DRG)
A predetermined reimbursement rate based on several components; all Medicare recipients are required to be billed using the DRG system when claims are submitted to CMS.

inpatient prospective payment system (IPPS)
Relates to inpatient or hospital-based coding. Several areas of patient care, including severity of illness, prognosis, and treatment difficulty are key to the IPPS system.

HOSPITAL REIMBURSEMENT ENVIRONMENT

Hospitals are reimbursed for services provided in several ways, **per diem, contract rate,** or **diagnosis related group (DRG).** Per diem reimbursement is based on a per day charge for services. This method of payment is also known as retrospective payment since it is determined after the patient has left the hospital facility and the charges have been sent to the third-party payer. Contract rate refers to the managed care environment that is a predetermined rate based on negotiations with the facilities within the network. Contract rates are often used by managed care providers such as a PPO.

Diagnosis Related Group (DRG)

One major influence on hospital based coding and reimbursement has been the creation of the **inpatient prospective payment system (IPPS).** This reimbursement methodology was required to be applied to all Medicare patients in the mid 1980s. The IPPS was developed by Yale University researchers and was based on the concept of patient case mix complexity. Several key areas of patient care were designated as vital to the IPPS system. These included severity of illness, prognosis, and treatment difficulty. Today the IPPS system used is built upon the researchers at Yale that devised the current diagnosis related groups (DRGs).

 Highlight

major diagnostic category (MDC)
Part of the hierarchy of Diagnostic Related Groups (DRGs). First a disease or condition is grouped to a MDC which is either a body system or medical specialty. Currently there are 25 MDCs in the DRG system. Example: MDC 1 is for diseases or disorders of the nervous system.

hospital base rate
Set by CMS and determined by the type of hospital, type of services provided, and location of the hospital.

relative weight
Value assigned by Center for Medicare and Medicaid Services (CMS) for each DRG. This value is reported in the Federal Register and can be used to calculate a reimbursement amount for a facility.

grouper
Refers to software that allows for the automation of the DRG assignment process.

disposition
The location the patient is discharged to at the end of the hospital inpatient admission.

IPPS can also be referred to as PPS or prospective payment systems. IPPS relates to inpatient- or hospital-based coding. There are also outpatient prospective payment systems, or OPPS. The most common one that is used today is APC (ambulatory payment classification). APCs are focused on CPT codes that are reported by physicians and other outpatient or ambulatory facilities.

DRGs are built upon a group of **major diagnostic categories (MDCs).** MDCs are typically grouped by body system. For example MDC 1 is for the nervous system, while MDC 3 is for ears, nose, and throat (ENT). There are twenty-five separate MDCs under this PPS. These groups are broad categories, which are further broken down into over 500 DRGs. A DRG is defined as "classification of diagnoses in which patients demonstrate similar resource consumption and length-of-stay patterns." DRGs are also based on **hospital base rate** and **relative weight.** DRGs are a predetermined reimbursement rate based on the components listed above. All Medicare recipients are required to be billed using the DRG system when claims are submitted to CMS. The dollar amount for a specific hospital is determined by CMS in advance of any patient claim being processed. CMS publishes annual updated information on relative weight and length of stay in the *Federal Register.* This information can determine a specific hospital reimbursement amount based on the hospital base rate. Base rate is set by CMS and is determined by the type of hospital, type of services provided, and region of the country the hospital is in.

DRGs are identified as three-digit numbers that are often assigned by **grouper** software. The software allows for the automation of the DRG assignment process. Flowcharts can also be used to determine a specific DRG. DRGs are driven by the principal diagnosis, age of the patient, and the **disposition** of the patient. The disposition of a patient is the location the patient is discharged to at the end of the hospital inpatient admission. Under the DRG system, code sequencing is important. The sequence of ICD-9-CM codes influences the DRG assigned. The incorrect identification of a code as the principal diagnosis could lower or raise the amount reimbursed to a hospital. If the principal diagnosis is incorrectly assigned, this could be a case of HIPAA violation for the facility.

■ Highlight

length of stay (LOS)
The amount of full days a patient is admitted to an acute care facility.

DRGs are updated annually; these changes include relative weight changes, reclassifications for specific DRGs, and addition of new ICD-9-CM codes into a DRG. These updates are incorporated into the encoder grouping software that is commonly utilized by hospitals to determine a DRG assignment.

DRG are used to gather information on Medicare patients treated in a hospital environment. This information in the form of statistics is used for reimbursement but can be used to identify quality of care issues. The UHDDS guidelines discussed earlier also require the reporting of **length of stay (LOS)** for all inpatient admissions. Length of stay is the number of full days a patient is admitted to an acute care facility. The statistics gathered from LOS can be used to determine if specific groups of patients are on average receiving medical care and being discharged in a time frame that is consistent with national standards. DRGs allow hospitals and Medicare the ability to gather data based on disease categories.

UB-92

UB-92 or Uniform Bill 1992 version is used by hospitals for claim submission (Figure 16–1). This form is also known as the HCFA-1450. This billing form is one of two standardized billing forms used in the United States. The other form, CMS-1500, is used to report ambulatory and/or professional services. The UB-92 form (Figure 16–1) was developed by the National Uniform Billing Committee (NUBC) in cooperation with the American Hospital Association (AHA). This committee was formed in 1975 and has released several versions of this standardized form that have been approved and used since then. The monitoring and updating of this billing form to meet HIPAA legislation is one of the functions of the NUBC. In May 2005, the NUBC announced that it has updated the UB-92 form with a 2004 version. This will be known as the UB-04. This revised form will be mandated for use beginning March 1, 2007. This revised standardized billing form will follow the latest HIPAA standards for electronic claims submission. Approximately 80 percent of all inpatient admissions are currently being submitted in an electronic format directly to the payer.

Case Mix

case mix index (CMI)
Provides information on the type of patients treated by third-party payer.

A hospital's **case mix index (CMI)** provides information on the type of patients treated by third-party payer. The information from a CMI can be used to identify various populations of patients and determine if the hospital is serving a specific group more than another. This information can also help the facility to determine if a particular payer is responsible for a larger portion of the hospital total reimbursement dollars. CMI information can be analyzed and measured using computerized software.

HIPAA

HIPAA legislation that relates to inpatient hospital-based coding directly addresses required code sets for reporting. This was discussed earlier in the chapter. Another area of HIPAA that can impact hospital coding is when remote coding is performed by hospital employees. Given the current shortage of qualified and experience hospital coders, employers are using various methods to attract and keep excellent coders. One method is to allow for remote or home-based coding. When this is done, HIPAA regulations on privacy and security must be followed. Various steps must be taken to ensure that HIPAA guidelines are met. An important point is for the facility/employer to ensure that all coders, including those that are working from home are educated on HIPAA requirements. This requirement details that the coding staff is updated on changes and/or clarification to HIPAA regulations. Per HIPAA guidelines, employers are responsible to train their employees on privacy regulations.

■ *Highlight*

> *The Department of Health and Human Services released a fact sheet on HIPAA, "Protecting the Privacy of Patients' Health Information," which can be viewed at www.hhs.gov/news/facts/privacy.html.*

A concern when discussing remote coding is the physical environment that the coder will be working in. Are the health records secure if they are located in the employee's home? Does the employee have adequate electronic devices to ensure data security if the information is being accessed via computer? Is the employee access controlled when he or she is using remote devices to gain entry into hospital computer systems? Does the employee understand how to control and prevent the access of health record information by family and friends that may be present

ST11843 1PLY UB-92

APPROVED OMB NO. 0938-0279

1

2

3 PATIENT CONTROL NO.

4 TYPE OF BILL

5 FED. TAX NO.

6 STATEMENT COVERS PERIOD FROM THROUGH

7 COV D. 8 N-C D. 9 C-I D. 10 L-R D. 11

12 PATIENT NAME

13 PATIENT ADDRESS

14 BIRTHDATE 15 SEX 16 MS ADMISSION 17 DATE 18 HR 19 TYPE 20 SRC 21 D HR 22 STAT 23 MEDICAL RECORD NO.

CONDITION CODES 24 25 26 27 28 29 30 31

32 OCCURRENCE CODE DATE 33 OCCURRENCE CODE DATE 34 OCCURRENCE CODE DATE 35 OCCURRENCE CODE DATE 36 OCCURRENCE SPAN CODE FROM THROUGH 37 A B C

a b

38

39 VALUE CODES CODE AMOUNT 40 VALUE CODES CODE AMOUNT 41 VALUE CODES CODE AMOUNT

a b c d

42 REV. CD. 43 DESCRIPTION 44 HCPCS / RATES 45 SERV. DATE 46 SERV. UNITS 47 TOTAL CHARGES 48 NON-COVERED CHARGES 49

1 2 3 4 5 6 7 8 9 10 11 12 13 14 15 16 17 18 19 20 21 22 23

50 PAYER 51 PROVIDER NO. 52 REL INFO 53 ASG BEN 54 PRIOR PAYMENTS 55 EST. AMOUNT DUE 56

A B C

57 DUE FROM PATIENT ▶

58 INSURED'S NAME 59 P. REL 60 CERT. - SSN - HIC. - ID NO. 61 GROUP NAME 62 INSURANCE GROUP NO.

A B C

63 TREATMENT AUTHORIZATION CODES 64 ESC 65 EMPLOYER NAME 66 EMPLOYER LOCATION

A B C

67 PRIN. DIAG. CD. 68 CODE 69 CODE 70 CODE 71 CODE 72 CODE 73 CODE 74 CODE 75 CODE 76 ADM. DIAG. CD. 77 E-CODE 78

79 P.C. 80 PRINCIPAL PROCEDURE CODE DATE 81 OTHER PROCEDURE CODE DATE A OTHER PROCEDURE CODE DATE B 82 ATTENDING PHYS. ID

OTHER PROCEDURE CODE DATE C OTHER PROCEDURE CODE DATE D OTHER PROCEDURE CODE DATE E 83 OTHER PHYS. ID A a b

84 REMARKS a b c d

OTHER PHYS. ID B a b

85 PROVIDER REPRESENTATIVE X 86 DATE

UB-92 HCFA-1450 OCR/ORIGINAL I CERTIFY THE CERTIFICATIONS ON THE REVERSE APPLY TO THIS BILL AND ARE MADE A PART HEREOF.

Figure 16–1 UB-92 form.

in the home? These are all important questions that must be addressed and answered before beginning remote coding. Some experts in the field suggest that a home visit by the coding supervisor or health information manager should take place, especially if the coder will be using paper-based health records for home-based coding. HIPAA security regulations specifically address the requirements for electronic data. However, securing paper-based documents is an issue of patient confidentially and should not be overlooked when dealing with remote coding.

EXERCISE 16–9

Select the appropriate answer.

DRGs are a type of PPS that is driven by the concept of _____ _____ (406 MDCs and used for outpatient services; additional diagnoses codes and additional surgical codes; mandate by federal government to be used on all insurance carrier types; principal diagnosis and patient disposition).

EXERCISE 16–10

Select the appropriate answer.

1. An HIV patient is admitted following a motor vehicle crash (MVC). The patient has an open femur fracture, which is treated with an open reduction with internal fixation. The patient continues HIV antiviral medication while he is in the hospital for the femur fracture. What would be the correct sequence for the diagnostic codes in this case?
_____ (042 HIV and 821.10 Open femur fracture; 821.10 Open femur fracture and 042 HIV).

2. A patient is admitted with the chief complaint of chest pain. The patient is admitted for further workup and study. After admission it is determined that the patient had an acute myocardial infarction (AMI) of the anterolateral wall of his heart. The patient is under treatment for hypertension on an outpatient basis. The patient also has a history of bladder cancer, which was treated six years prior. The patient is admitted for treatment to the intensive care unit (ICU). While in ICU the patient develops pneumonia due to Escherichia coli. The patient receives antihypertensive medication by mouth while in the ICU. The patient also receives IV antibiotics for his pneumonia. After three days in the ICU he is transferred to a medical unit bed for two days. On the medical floor, antihypertensives and antibiotics are given to the patient by the nursing staff. On the sixth hospital day, the patient is discharged in an improved condition.

   a. What would be the diagnoses reported in this case?
   _____ _____ _____

   b. What would be the ICD-9-CM codes that match these diagnoses? Remember to put them in the correct sequence.
   _____ _____ _____

EXERCISE 16–11

Circle the correct answer after each case study.

1. A patient is admitted for an appendectomy. After surgery it is noted in the health record that the patient has an extremely low potassium level. This is documented on a laboratory report. In examining the physician's orders, the coder notes that the attending physician ordered intravenous potassium for this patient. This was administered, a repeat lab test was done, and the patient's potassium level was in the acceptable normal range. The discharge diagnosis listed on this patient's discharge summary is a ruptured appendix. The procedure listed on the face sheet is appendectomy. What should the coder do about the finding of an abnormal potassium level?

   a. Code it as an abnormal lab finding.
   b. Query the physician if this is a disease/diagnosis that is clinically significant.
   c. Not code it since it was not documented on either the face sheet or the discharge summary.
   d. Check with the coding supervisor if the facility has a policy regarding coding lab test results.

2. An eighty-year-old female patient, Sarah Richardson, was admitted with fever, malaise, and left flank pain. A urinalysis laboratory test was performed on the first admission day that showed bacteria more than 100,000/ml. This was followed by a culture, showing E. coli growth as the cause of the UTI. Mrs. Richardson is also on current medication therapy for hypertension, arteriosclerotic heart disease (ASHD), and chronic obstructive pulmonary disease (COPD). The codes that are assigned for this inpatient visit are:

   a. 599.0, 041.4, 496, 414.01, 401.9
   b. 599.0, 780.6, 789.00, 496, 414.01, 401.9
   c. 041.4, 496, 414.01, 401.9
   d. 599.0, 041.4, V12.59, 401.9

3. Mr. Fielding, a sixty-seven-year-old patient presents with an admission diagnosis of gross hematuria. Mr. Fielding has Medicare A and B as his primary insurance provider. He is admitted for further workup and treatment. It is determined after study that this patient has severe benign prostatic hyperplasia (BPH). On the third hospital day, Mr. Fielding has a transurethral prostatectomy performed. He is discharged on the fourth hospital day in an improved condition. Which of the below set of codes is the correct one for this inpatient admission?

   a. 600; 60.2
   b. 600.0; 60.21
   c. 600.00, 599.7; 60.29
   d. 600.0, 599.7; 60.21

4. Mary Snow presented to the ED of her local hospital with severe abdominal pain and amenorrhea. Serum hCG was lower than normal. There were also endometrial and uterine changes. She was diagnosed with a tubal pregnancy. A unilateral salpingectomy with removal of tubal

pregnancy was performed. Which of the following sets of codes is the correct code assignment?

a. 633.80, 66.62
b. 633.10, 66.62
c. 633.10, 66.4
d. 633.10, 66.02

EXERCISE 16–12

Circle the correct answer after each case study.

1. Mary Alice, a newborn female infant, was delivered spontaneously at term. She was noticed to be jaundiced on the initial screening labs. Her total bilirubin was increased and she was started on phototherapy under bilirubin lights. She progressed rapidly and was discharged to home with her mother. Diagnoses listed on face sheet are Newborn jaundice, healthy newborn. Provide the ICD-9-CM codes that would be reported for Mary Alice: _____

EXERCISE 16–13

Circle the correct answer after each case study.

1. The following was documented in the History & Physical (H&P) of Mr. Jackson:
   This patient was admitted with a diagnosis of acute myocardial infarction (AMI). He was hospitalized for pneumonia last year and two years ago had surgery for a bleeding gastric ulcer. Additional history is that he was diagnosed five years ago with Parkinson's disease, which is getting progressively worse. He is being treated with Levodopa. Mr. Jackson's medical history also notes emphysema being treated with bronchodilators and corticosteroids. These medications are continued while Mr. Jackson is receiving inpatient treatment.
   Discharge Summary: The discharge summary repeats the information in the H&P, and adds the following information: *during the hospital stay, patient developed CHF, which is confirmed by x-ray. CHF treated with lasix and oxygen therapy. Discharge diagnoses: AMI, Parkinson's disease, CHF, emphysema, history of pneumonia and bleeding gastric ulcer.*
   What are the diagnoses that are reportable for Mr. Jackson?

   a. AMI, CHF, Parkinson's disease, emphysema
   b. AMI, CHF
   c. AMI, CHF, Parkinson's disease, emphysema, pneumonia, bleeding ulcer
   d. AMI, pneumonia, CHF, emphysema

2. Charles Tripp, a forty-five-year-old male, is admitted with the complaint of groin pain. He is admitted for further workup and treatment. Mr. Tripp is found to have an inguinal hernia. He is scheduled for hernia repair on the second day of admission. The hernia repair is successful, but postoperative blood work shows that Mr. Tripp has an elevated blood sugar level and is complaining of numbness of his hands and feet. An endocrinologist is consulted on the case and diagnoses Mr. Tripp with type II diabetes mellitus. He is given nutrition education from the hospital registered dietitian. Mr. Tripp also has a history of high cholesterol, cigarette smoking, and chronic bronchitis. How would Mr. Tripp's diagnosis of a inguinal hernia be classified?

   a. Principal procedure
   b. Comorbidity
   c. Complication
   d. Principal diagnosis

SUMMARY

UHDDS is a data set used in inpatient coding to define principal diagnosis and principal procedure. Admission diagnosis is defined as the sign/symptom/disease identified at registration to the hospital before being evaluated by a physician. Principal diagnosis is defined as the condition after study to be the cause for admission of the patient to the hospital. Principal procedure most often relates to the principal diagnosis. Significant procedure is defined by UHDDS as a procedure that is surgical in nature, carries an anesthetic risk, carries a procedural risk, and requires a skilled clinician to perform. Other reportable diagnoses are coded and reported that are related to the specific inpatient hospital stay. V codes can be coded as principal diagnosis codes or as supplemental diagnoses codes.

A sign is an objective medical complaint; a symptom is a subjective medical complaint. Signs and symptoms are not coded when they are documented and a definitive diagnosis is also documented. Only the definitive diagnosis would be coded. Level of specificity is important when assigning ICD-9-CM codes in a hospital setting.

Comorbidities are chronic conditions that are present in a patient during an inpatient hospital stay. Complications are those conditions that arise after a patient is admitted to the hospital. Comorbidities and complications should be coded when documented on an inpatient health record.

DRG is a type of prospective payment system used in an inpatient setting and required for Medicare recipients. Coding conventions, like NEC and NOS, are important components of the ICD-9-CM classification system. Combination code categories are used per chapter-specific coding guidelines.

REFERENCES

AHIMA Staff. (2004). *HIPAA in practice: The health information manager's perspective.* American Health Information Management Association. Chicago.

Brown, F. (2005). *ICD-9-CM coding handbook.* American Hospital Association Press.

Department of Health and Human Services. *Protecting the privacy of patients' health information.* Retrieved July 15, 2005, from www.hhs.gov/news/facts/privacy.html

DRG Expert: A comprehensive guidebook to the DRG classification systems. (2005) Salt Lake City, UT: Ingenix.

Green, M., & Bowie, M. (2005). *Essentials of health information management: Principles and practices.* Clifton Park, NY: Thomson Delmar Learning.

National Center for Health Statistics. *ICD-9-CM official coding guidelines.* Retrieved August 1, 2005, from www.cdc.gov/nchs/data/icd9/icdguide.pdf

Taber's Cyclopedic Medical Dictionary (20th ed.) (2005). Philadelphia: Davis.

Glossary

abnormal findings   Information documented in a health record typically on a radiograph report or a lab report that identifies an anomaly in the test that was given.

abortion   Termination of a pregnancy before the fetus is viable. Spontaneous abortion occurs naturally; also called miscarriage. Therapeutic abortion is induced and is a deliberate interruption of pregnancy.

abscess   Skin or cutaneous abscesses are collections of pus caused by a bacterial infection. This is usually caused when a minor skin injury allows skin bacteria to penetrate and cause an infection.

accept assignment   To accept payment received for a claim as full payment after copayment and/or coinsurance amounts ahve been collected.

account aging   A method of identifying how long an account is overdue by the length of time it has been unpaid.

accounts receivable (A/R)   The amount of money owed to the medical practice by its patients.

achalasia   The inability of muscles to relax.

acute care facility   Inpatient hospital facility where a patient stays at least overnight for medical care.

administration   The professional service of giving or rendering, often associated with medications or solutions.

admission diagnosis   Sign, symptom, complaint documented in the health record reported from the patient as main reason for seeking medical care.

advance beneficiary notice (ABN)   Notice to health insurance beneficiaries that the program will probably not pay for a service. The patient assumes financial responsibility for paying the provider directly for the service.

alphabetic index   Volume 2 of ICD-9-CM, the alphabetic listing of diagnoses.

American Academy of Professional Coders (AAPC)   The professional association for medical coders providing ongoing education, certification, networking and recognition, with certifications for coders in physicians' offices and hospital outpatient facilities.

American Health Information Management Association (AHIMA)   One of the four cooperating parties for ICD-9-CM. Professional association for over 38,000 Health Information Management Professionals throughout the country.

American Hospital Association (AHA)   American Hospital Association, one of the four cooperating parties for ICD-9-CM.

anesthesia   The pharmacological suppression of nerve function.

anesthesiologist   A physician specializing in the evaluation and preparation of a patient for surgery, the introduction of the anesthesia for the procedure, the maintenance phase and the emergence and postoperative phase.

angioplasty A medical cardiology procedure in which a catheter with an inflatable balloon on the tip is passed through a vessel and inflated at the site of an obstruction within the vessel wall. As the balloon inflates, any soft plaque is flattened against the vessel wall to prevent obstruction of blood flow and to open up the vessel for blood passage.

antepartum Time of pregnancy from conception to onset of delivery.

anteverted Tipped forward; in gynecology, this term is used to describe the normal position of the uterus.

aorta The main arterial trunk within the circulatory system. All other arteries, except the pulmonary artery, are branches off of this main channel. This vessel originates in the left ventricle of the heart and passes upward toward the neck. The carotid (major artery to the brain) and the coronary (major artery to the heart) are branches of the aorta. Blood that has been cleaned and freshly oxygenated flows through the aorta to the various body organs.

aphakia Absence of the crystalline lens of the eye.

arthropathy A vague, general term meaning pathology affecting a joint.

audit An evaluation of the billing practices within a medical office. Medical billing and insurance records are abstracted and compared to investigate proper billing, coding, and documentation technique and practices.

automated Laboratories that assay large numbers of samples mechanically.

Balanced Budget Act Legislation designed to balance the federal budget enacted during the Clinton administration.

bankruptcy A legal declaration of an individual's inability to pay debts.

benign lesions A noncancerous injury, wound, or infected patch of skin.

bifurcation The point where the blood vessels split into two branches.

biopsy Tissue or organ removal for study or examination.

birthday rule Guideline for determination of the primary insurance policy when dependents are covered on two or more policies.

Blue Cross/Blue Shield (BC/BS) One of the oldest and largest insurance providers providing health benefits nationwide.

Board of Advanced Medical Coding (BAMC) An organization of coders, clinicians, and compliance professionals dedicated to the evaluation, recognition, and career advancement of professional medical coders within physician practices, facility and post-acute settings.

brachytherapy A natural or manmade radioactive element that is applied in or around a particular treatment field.

burns A burn is an injury to tissue resulting from heat, chemicals, or electricity. The depth or degree of burns is identified as first degree, second degree, and third degree.

capitation Represents a common managed care payment strategy by which providers are paid according to the number of patients choosing a physician as primary caregiver. The capitation payment is made for a predetermined amount at a predetermined time each quarter or year.

cardiogenic shock An abnormal and often critical body state resulting in inadequate supplies of oxygen to the body's organs and tissues because of heart failure.

cardiomyopathy A condition or general term describing a problem with the heart muscle.

cardioversion An electric shock to the heart muscle, which helps to convert an arrhythmia into a normal or sinus rhythm.

case mix index (CMI) Provides information on the type of patients treated by third-party payer.

Category II Optional alphanumeric codes for statistical data research and development purposes.

Category III Required alphanumeric codes for emerging technology instead of unlisted codes.

category Categories are three-digit representations of a single disease or group of similar conditions, such as category 250, Diabetes Mellitus. Many categories are divided further into subcategories and subclassifications.

catheter A tubular, flexible instrument for withdrawal of fluids from, or introduction of fluids into, a body cavity.

Centers for Medicare & Medicaid Services (CMS) An administrative agency within the Department of Health and Human Services (DHHS) that oversees Medicare, Medicaid, and other government programs. Formerly known as the Health Care Financing Administration (HCFA).

CHAMPVA Health care program for dependents of disabled veterans or those who died as a rsult of conditions related to their armed service.

charge slip, superbill, encounter form A three-part form with a record of account information for services performed including charges and payment; can also serve as an insurance reporting form.

chief complaint (CC) A subjective statement made by a patient describing his or her most significant or serious symptoms or signs of illness or dysfunction.

circumflex artery A branch of the LCA (left coronary artery), this artery supplies the left atrium of the heart, the rear surfaces of the left ventricle and the rear portion of the heart's dividing wall or septum.

closed fracture One in which the fracture site does not communicate with the outside environment.

co-payment A specified dollar amount a patient or policyholder must pay to the health care provider for each medical service or procedure received, as determined in the insurance contract.

coding guidelines Published in the ICD-9-CM coding manual, these provide a framework for the reporting of diagnoses and procedural codes.

coinsurance A specified amount of insurance determined for each service the patient must pay the health care provider.

combination code category Allows codes to reflect two conditions with one ICD-9-CM code; usually used in the area of hypertensive heart disease.

comorbidities Chronic conditions that existed before inpatient admission.

complications Conditions that occur after a patient is admitted to the hospital; may be the result or side effect of care rendered.

computerized axial tomography (CAT scan) This type of radiological procedure is used to scan any part of the body; most useful in scanning brain, lung, mediastinum, retroperitoneum, and liver.

conscious sedation A decreased level of consciousness during a procedure without being put completely to sleep. The patient is able to respond to verbal instructions and stimulation.

consultation A type of service provided by a physician (usually a specialist) whose opinion or advice regarding evaluation and management of a specific problem is requested by another physician or other appropriate source.

contract rate Predetermined rate based on negotiations with the facilities within the network.

contralateral The opposite side.

conventions Unique components of ICD-9-CM classification system that provide direction and/or additional information to individuals using classification. Example: inclusion notes, exclusion notes, NEC, NOS, use additional code, code first underlying code.

cooperating parties Four agencies who share responsibility for maintaining and updating ICD-9-CM.

coordination of benefits Coordination of payment of services submitted on the claim form when a patient is covered by two or more primary medical insurance policies.

coordination of care The arrangement and/or organization of patient care to include all health care providers.

copulation Act of sexual intercourse.

counseling The act of providing advice and guidance to a patient and his or her family.

covered service A contracted benefit from the insurer to the provider and patient. For example, while infertility treatment may not be a covered service, testing and treatment until infertility is diagnosed may be a covered service with the insurer.

crossover claim An electronic transfer of information submitted on a Medicare claim to Medicaid or the patient's Medigap carrier.

cycle billing Accounts divided alphabetically into groups with each group billed at a different time.

debridement A procedure where foreign material and contaminated or devitalized tissue are removed from a traumatic or infected lesion or wound until the surrounding healthy tissue is exposed.

deductible A specified amount of covered medical expense that must be paid by the insured to a health care provider before benefits will be reimbursed by the insurance company.

definitive diagnosis Diagnosis based upon physician findings; the determination of the illness or disease is made by the physician.

dermatitis An inflammation of the upper layers of the skin (eczema). Drugs taken internally can also cause skin reactions, which are considered adverse reactions. Sunburn is classified as dermatitis in ICD-9-CM.

dermis The middle layer of the integument, or skin.

diagnosis related group (DRG) A predetermined reimbursement rate based on several components; all Medicare recipients are required to be billed using the DRG system when claims are submitted to CMS.

dilation Stretching and opening of the cervix during labor to facilitate the baby's passage through the pelvis; measured in centimeters.

discharge diagnosis Found in a discharge summary, this is a list of diagnoses that can include conditions treated during this inpatient admission, other reportable diagnoses, and medical history information.

discharge summary A document that provides a detailed account of the patient's hospital course, specifically outlining treatment and patient response.

dislocation A disarrangement of two or more bones from their articular processes.

disposition The location the patient is discharged to at the end of the hospital inpatient admission.

down coding The selection of a lower level code (CPT or HCPCSII) than the supporting documentation.

DRG Diagnosis Related Groups, method of prospective payment used by Medicare and other third-party payers for hospital inpatients.

echocardiogram (echo)   A noninvasive test that evaluates the interior of the heart and its major vessels by means of ultrasonic beams bouncing images off the structures and vessels in the heart via a transducer. The echoes or beams are transmitted to a monitor for the mapping of the heart's function, size, shape, blood flow, etc. Three common techniques are used: Doppler ultrasounds, color-flow mapping, and 2D/M Mode.

echography   Use of ultrasound to evaluate anatomy to aid in diagnosis.

effacement   Obliteration of the cervix during labor as it shortens from one or two centimeters in length to paper thin, leaving only the external os; expressed as a percentage.

electronic medical record (EMR)   Computer-based medical record or patient chart.

emancipated minor   A person under the age of majority, usually 18 to 21 years of age as defined by state statute, who is self-supporting, married, serving in the armed forces, and/or living separate from parents.

endoscopy   Inspection of organs or cavities by use of a tube through a natural body opening or through a small incision.

enteral   The patient receives feeding or medication into the intestine.

epidermis   The outer layer of the integument, or skin.

epidural   Located over or upon the dural.

eponym   A disease, disorder, or procedure named after the person who researched, identified, or developed a particular procedure, disease, or disorder.

etiology   Cause of the disease or illness.

evaluation and management section codes (E/M)   The first section of the CPT coding manual that describes office visits, hospital visits, nursing facility visits, and consultations.

examination   A critical inspection and investigation, usually following a particular method, performed for diagnostic or investigational purposes.

excision   Remove by cutting out.

explanation of benefits (EOB)   A summary explaining an insurance company's determination for reimbursements of benefits; for Medicare claims, this is referred to as a remittance advice (RA).

face sheet   The cover sheet of an inpatient health record, which lists demographic and financial information for the patient.

Fair Debt Collection Practices Act   A consumer protection policy against abusive collection practices by debt collectors.

False Claims Act   Federal legislation that prohibits submission of claims for services not rendered or for any services considered fraudulent upon investigation.

fascia   The tissue that connects muscles.

fasciocutaneous flap   The fasciocutaneous is fibrous tissue beneath the skin; it also encloses muscles and groups of muscles, and separates their several layers or groups. The flap is the placement of portion of tissue or skin and may or not include the fascio. Pedicle, local or distant are all commonly used flap terms.

fissure   A groove, split, or natural division.

fistula   An abnormal tubelike passage from a normal cavity to another cavity or surface.

general anesthesia   A state of unconsciousness, produced by anesthetic agents, with absence of pain sensation over the entire body.

gestation   Time in which a woman is pregnant and fetal development takes place.

gravidity Term used to indicate the number of pregnancies a woman has had; gravida is used with numerals (e.g., 0, I, II).

grouper Refers to software that allows for the automation of the DRG assignment process.

guidelines Within the CPT code book, the guidelines are the pages or paragraphs prior to a series of codes. There are also 1995 or 1997 E/M guidelines that were separately distributed by CMS.

Health Insurance Association of America (HIAA) An agency providing statistics and resources for public health information which includes diseases, pregnancies, aging, and mortality.

Health Insurance Portability and Accountability Act (HIPAA) Mandates regulations that govern privacy, security, and electronic transactions standards for health care information.

Healthcare Common Procedure Coding System (HCPCS) Coding system that consists of CPT and national codes (level II), used to identify procedures, supplies, medications (except vaccines), and equipment.

Healthcare Common Procedure Coding System Level II (HCPCSII) The second level of the coding system created by CMS for reporting of procedures, supplies, medications, equipment, and items.

heart catheterization A diagnostic test designed to examine the heart via a catheter placed within a major artery in the arm (brachial) or a major groin artery (femoral). The catheter passes through vessels into the heart's arterial system. Dye is injected to trace blood circulation through the heart. Obstruction in flow indicates the presence of thrombi, plaque, stenosis, or collapsed vessels. This procedure may also be called angiograpy or an angiogram.

HIPAA transaction and code sets Any set of codes used for encoding data elements, such as tables of terms, medical concepts, diagnosis and procedure codes.

history of present illness (HPI) Inquiry from the first sign or symptom through today of the patient's experiences that associate to the chief complaint and reason for the visit. Specific documentation is required for the HPI.

history A record of past events; a systematic account of the medical, emotional, and psychosocial occurrences in a patient's life and of factors in the family, ancestors, and environment that may have a bearing on the patient's condition.

hospital base rate Set by CMS and determined by the type of hospital, type of services provided, and location of the hospital.

hyperthermia This procedure uses heat to raise the temperature of a specific area of the body to try to increase cell metabolism and increase the destruction of cancer cells.

ICD-10-CM International Classification of Diseases, 10th Revision, Clinical Modification.

ICD-10-PCS International Classification of Diseases, 10th Revision, Procedure Classification System.

immune globulin Animal protein with similar antibody activity.

incision Cut into.

infusion Introduction of a solution into tissue or an organ.

inhaled solution (INH) The patient inhales the medication, may use respiratory equipment commonly known as the Intermittent Positive Pressure Breathing treatment.

injection not otherwise specified (INJ) The patient receives an injection other than the options listed, such as intradermal or an injection directly into anatomy.

injections   A parenteral route of administration during which a needle penetrates the skin or muscle; subcutaneous injection; intramuscular injection.

inpatient prospective payment system (IPPS)   Relates to inpatient or hospital-based coding. Several areas of patient care, including severity of illness, prognosis, and treatment difficulty are key to the IPPS system.

inpatient   Refers to an acute care setting.

insurance abuse   Inconsistent activities considered unacceptable business practice.

insurance fraud   Intentional, deliberate misrepresentation of information for profit or to gain some unfair or dishonest advantage.

internal derangement   A range of injuries of the joint involving the soft tissues such as the synovium, cartilage, and ligaments.

International Classification of Diseases, 9th Revision, Clinical Modification (ICD-9-CM)   Coding system used to report diagnoses, diseases, and symptoms and reason for encounters for insurance claims.

intra-arterial (IA)   The patient receives through the artery system.

intracavitary   Within a cavity.

intramuscular (IM)   The patient receives an injection into the muscular system. This is the most common method of administration.

intrathecal (IT)   The patient receives through the membrane.

intravenous (IV)   The patient receives through the venous system.

ipsilateral   Same side.

lactation   Process of secreting milk from the breasts.

leiomyomas   Myoma or tumor of muscular tissue involving the non-striated muscle fibers, also known as fibroid tumors.

length of stay (LOS)   The amount of full days a patient is admitted to an acute care facility.

limiting charge   A percentage limitation on fees that nonparticipating physicians are allowed to bill Medicare patients above the fee schedule amount.

local anesthesia   Anesthesia confined to one part of the body.

magnetic resonance imaging (MRI)   This type of radiological procedure is used to scan brain, spinal cord, soft tissues, and adrenal and renal masses. More superior scan than the CAT.

main term   The patient's illness or disease. In ICD-9-CM the main term is the primary way to locate the disease in the alphabetic index. Main terms are printed in boldface type, even with the left margin on each page.

major diagnostic category (MDC)   Part of the hierarchy of Diagnostic Related Groups (DRGs). First a disease or condition is grouped to a MDC which is either a body system or medical specialty. Currently there are 25 MDCs in the DRG system. Example: MDC 1 is for diseases or disorders of the nervous system.

malignant lesion   Having the properties of nearby invasive and destructive tumor growth and metastasis; changes in the tissues.

manual   Performing something by hand or with the hands.

mastectomy   Excision of the breast.

Medicaid   A jointly sponsored federal and state government medical assistance program to provide medical care for persons with incomes below the national poverty level.

medical decision making   The complexity of establishing a diagnosis and/or selecting a management option.

medical necessity The justification for an action or service based on the patient's condition, problem, or illness.

Medicare Modernization Act Federal law upgrading, streamlining, and revising the Centers for Medicare and Medicaid Services.

Medicare physician fee schedule (PFS) A listing of allowable charges for services rendered to Medicare patients.

Medicare program integrity (PI) Developed under HIPAA to provide strategies for the federal government to use to ensure that medical claims are paid properly.

Medicare A federal health insurance program for persons over 65 years of age, retired, on social security benefits, receiving social security disability benefits, or end-stage renal disease coverage.

Medigap A private, commercial insurance plan purchased by a patient as a supplementary plan to Medicare coverage.

menarche Time when the first menstruation begins.

menopause Time when menstruation ceases.

mitral valve A two-leafed or cusped valve shaped like a bishop's miter (head covering), this valve is located between the left atrium and left ventricle. Considered an atrioventricular valve, the mitral opens when the atria contract and sends blood into the ventricles. When the ventricles contract, pressure is exerted on the leaflets causing them to balloon upward toward the atria.

modifier A two-digit number placed after the usual procedure number, separated by a hyphen, which represents a particular explanation to further describe the procedure or circumstances involved with the procedure.

monthly billing Billing patients at one designated time of the month.

multiple gated acquisition (MUGA) Cardiac blood pool imaging; nuclear and multigated ventriculogram is referred to as a MUGA. This diagnostic tool evaluates left ventricular function, ventricular aneurysms, intracardiac shunting or other wall motion abnormalities. Technetium radioisotopes "tag" the blood's red cells or serum albumin. With the uptake of the radioactive isotope, a scintillation camera records the radioactivity on its primary left ventricular pass. The second pass includes an EKG and a gated camera used while the patient is manipulated to view all segments of the ventricle. Additional views may be obtained and observed after administration of sublingual (under the tongue) nitroglycerin or initiation of physical exercise.

muscle flap A layer of muscle is dissected and moved to a new site.

myelopathy Pathology of the spinal cord due to the arthritic changes of the vertebrae. Paresthesia, loss of sensation, and loss of sphincter control are the most common forms of myelopathy.

myocutaneous flap A muscle flap that contains overlying skin.

National Center for Health Statistics (NCHS) A health statistics agency that collects data from birth and death records, medical records, interview surveys, and through direct physical exams and laboratory testing that provides information to help identify and address health issues.

National Uniform Billing Committee (NUBC) Formed in 1975, this committee develops the UB-92 form in conjunction with the AHA.

NEC Not elsewhere classified.

nonparticipating physician (nonPAR) A health care provider who has not signed a contract with an insurance company (also known as an out-of-network provider).

nonparticipating provider (nonPAR) Providers not contracting (participating) with the insurance plan. Medicare nonPAR physicians must not exceed the limiting charge when billing beneficiaries.

nonselective Directly placed into the anatomical site, not fed into the area.

NOS Not otherwise specified.

occlusion Blockage or obstruction by thrombus or plaque deposits within a blood vessel or passageway.

Office of Inspector General (OIG) The office that enforces the rules of CMS and federal agencies.

Omnibus Budget Reconciliation Act (OBRA) A federal law outlining numerous areas of healthcare, establishing guidelines and penalties.

open fracture One in which the fracture site communicates with the outside environment.

orally (ORAL) The patient receives medication through the mouth (orally).

orthopedics A medical specialty concerned with the prevention, investigation, diagnosis and treatment of diseases, disorders, and injuries of the musculoskeletal system.

osteomyelitis Infection or inflammation of the bone or bone marrow. It may be acute, subacute, or chronic.

other (OTH) The patient receives any other method not listed.

other reportable diagnosis Other diagnoses in addition to the discharge diagnosis that directly relate to the current episode of care.

overpayment Excess amount paid in error by the insurer for codes or documentation used to support the claim for payment.

ovulation Release of the ovum from the ovary; usually occurs every 28 days.

pacemaker Electrical (battery-powered) device that helps maintain normal sinus heart rhythm by stimulating cardiac muscles to contract or pump. Pacemakers come in single or dual chamber models and are programmed to sense and correct low heart rates or abnormal rhythms. The devices can be set a fixed number of beats per minute.

parenteral The patient receives feeding or medication into the alimentary canal.

parity Term used to indicate the number of pregnancies in which the fetus has reached viability; approximately 22 weeks of gestation. May also be used with a series of numerals to indicate the number of full-term infants, pre-term infants, abortions, and living children (e.g. Para 0-1-0-1).

participating physician (PAR) A health care provider who has signed a contract with an insurance company to provide medical services to subscribers in the contract plan (also known as an in-network provider).

participating provider (PAR) Physician who contracts to accept assignment (receives payment directly) from the health insurance program.

parturition Labor and delivery.

past family and social history (PFSH) Pertinent inquiry of the patient's history of the illness, family history and social history with specific documentation required.

pedicle flap A flap of skin that is lifted from a healthy site, a portion of which is grafted to a new site but remains attached to its blood supply.

pedicle In skin grafting, it is the stem that attaches to a new growth.

pelvic relaxation Weakened condition of supporting ligaments of the uterus and bladder; caused by aging, trauma, or excessive stretching from the act of childbirth.

per diem Method of reimbursement based on a per-day charge for services.

pericardium Sac surrounding the heart.

physical status modifier A two-digit amendment to the anesthesia CPT codes that describes the physical status of the patient who is receiving anesthesia.

Physicians' Current Procedural Terminology (CPT)   Numeric codes and descriptors for services and procedures performed by providers, published by the American Medical Association.

plaque   Soft deposits of fatty substances that harden with time and produce rock-like obstructions within vessels. Plaque production occurs due to high-fat dietary intake, sedentary lifestyles, and hereditary tendencies in patients with progressive atherosclerosis.

point of service (POS)   The insurance plan encourages the patient to seek healthcare at a specific location or facility, typically where a contract for less cost has been negotiated.

postpartum   Time after giving birth.

preexisting condition   A medical condition under active treatment at the time application is made for an insurance policy, possibly resulting in an exclusion of that disease or illness.

preferred provider organization (PPO)   The healthcare provider signs a contract to join a group, usually an insurance plan. The physician name is then published in a listing, the listing may be resold, or the patients may receive incentives and discounts when choosing to have the care with a PPO provider.

presentation   Manner in which the fetus appears to the examiner during delivery (e.g., breech, cephalic, transverse, vertex).

primary (first) diagnosis   In the outpatient setting, the primary diagnosis is the main reason for the visit. It is usually the diagnosis taking the majority of resources for the visit.

principal diagnosis   The reason, after study, which caused the patient to be admitted to the hospital.

principal procedure   The definitive procedure most often related to the principal diagnosis.

professional courtesy   Medical treatment free of charge or at a reduced rate, or accepting what insurance pays as full payment to physicians and their families, office employees and their families, and other health care professionals, such as dentists, pharmacists and clergy, as determined by office policy.

prolapse   Falling or dropping down of an organ from its normal position or location such as the uterus, bladder, vagina, or rectum.

prospective payment system (PPS)   Also referred to as inpatient prospective payment system (IPPS); relates to inpatient or hospital-based coding. Several areas of patient care, including severity of illness, prognosis, and treatment difficulty are key to the IPPS system.

provisional diagnosis   Preliminary diagnosis, including the present signs and symptoms

puerperium   Time after delivery that it takes for the uterus to return to its normal size; usually three to six weeks.

pulmonary artery   A major blood vessel that transports blood between the heart and the lungs for oxygenation. Deoxygenated blood is carried from the right ventricle via this vessel, which forks into the right and left lungs. The pulmonary vein then carries freshly oxygenated blood into the left atrium of the heart for passage into the left ventricle and, subsequently, into systemic circulation.

pulmonic valve   A three-leaflet valve, the pulmonic is another semilunar valve. It is situated between the right ventricle and the pulmonary artery. During heart contractions, internal pressure forces this valve to open. Loss of pressure during diastole (heart relaxation) allows the valve to close.

qualitative   Tests that detect a particular analyte.

quantitative   Expresses specific numerical amounts of an analyte.

radiation absorbed dose (RAD)   A unit of measure in radiation.

radiculopathy   Disease of the spinal nerve roots.

regional anesthesia   The production of insensibility of a part by interrupting the sensory nerve conductivity from that region of the body.

reimbursement   The act of being paid back or payment in exchange for goods or services.

relative value unit (RVU)   Payment component based on physician work, practice expense, and malpractice expense.

relative weight   Value assigned by Center for Medicare and Medicaid Services (CMS) for each DRG. This value is reported in the Federal Register and can be used to calculate a reimbursement amount for a facility.

remittance advice (RA)   A summary explaining the insurance company's determination for reimbursement of benefits; also referred to as Explanation of Benefits.

removal   Removal of lesions can be by excision, destruction, shaving, or ligation. A biopsy only removes a portion of a lesion.

repair   Repair of open wounds or lacerations is classified as simple, intermediate, or complex.

resource-based relative value system (RBRVS)   A method of predetermining values for physician services for Medicare established in 1992, calculating units based on services performed, practice expenses, and professional liability insurance.

retroverted   Tipped back; in gynecology, this term is used to describe the backward displacement of the uterus.

review of systems (ROS)   Inquiry of the signs or symptoms that define the problem, affecting the body systems. Specific documentation is required for the ROS.

ribbons   Temporary interstitial placement in clinical brachytherapy.

selective catheterization   The procedure of feeding or gently guiding and manipulating the catheter into a specific branch of the blood vessel or anatomy.

semilunar valve   Named for its resemblance to the shape of the moon, the pulmonic and aortic valves are semilunar in shape.

sequencing   Arranging codes in the proper order according to the definitions of principal or primary diagnosis.

signature on file   A statement typed or stamped on the claim form for authorization purposes, indicating the patient has signed a release of medical information retained in the patient's chart.

significant procedure   A procedure that is surgical in nature, carries an anesthetic risk, carries a procedural risk, and requires a skilled clinician to perform.

sign   An objective medical complaint.

skin tag   Small, soft, flesh-colored skin flap that appear mostly on the neck, armpits, or groin.

skip   A person who has apparently moved without leaving a forwarding address.

sources   Intracavitary placement or permanent interstitial placement in clinical brachytherapy.

specificity   The concept of identifying the most detailed code based on ICD-9-CM classification system, its guidelines, and the documentation in the health record.

sphincter   Muscles that constrict an orifice.

stent   Following the dilation of an artery, usually by means of balloon angioplasty, the stent is loaded on a special catheter with an expandable balloon. Both devices are threaded into a guide catheter and threaded to the occlusion site. The cardiologist then positions and deploys the stent by expanding the balloon. The stent is composed of a meshlike material that assists in keeping the vessel open and clear of future occlusions.

subcategory   Four-digit subcategories are subdivisions of categories to provide greater specificity regarding etiology, site, or manifestations.

subclassification   Fifth-digit subclassifications are subdivisions of subcategories to provide even greater specificity regarding etiology, site, or manifestation of the illness or disease.

subcutaneous (SC)   The patient receives an injection into the subcutaneous tissue.

symptom   A subjective medical complaint.

Table of Drugs   The listing of alphabetical generic and brand name medications with the associated dose, common route, and the code.

tabular list   Volume One of ICD-9-CM is a tabular listing (numerical order) of diseases.

toxoids   Toxins that are treated and revised, given to stimulate antibody production.

transient   Short-term or disappearing after a short amount of time.

TRICARE   Health care program for active duty members of the military and their dependents. (Previously dnown as CHAMPUS.)

tricuspid valve   Diametrically larger and thinner than the mitral valve, three separate leaflets or cusps are found in this critical valve. The anterior, posterior and septal leaflets are competent only if the right ventricle's lateral wall functions correctly. The septal leaflet is attached to the interventricular septum and is in close proximity to the AV node.

trimester   First, second, and third three- month period of which the pregnancy is divided.

Truth in Lending Act   A consumer protection act requiring a written statement when there is a bilateral agreement between the physician and patient to pay for a procedure in more than four installments, disclosing finance charges, if any.

UB-92   Uniform Bill 1992 version, a form used by hospitals for claim submission.

ulcer   Loss of a portion of the skin, penetrating the dermis. Gangrene can be associated with skin ulcers. These are usually due to a vascular disease, as in diabetes. Decubitus ulcers are also known as bedsores or pressure sore. These result from a lack of blood flow and irritation to the skin over a bony projection. As the name indicates, decubiti occur in bedridden or wheelchair-bound patients or from a cast or splint.

unbundling   Practice of billing multiple procedure codes for a group of procedures that are covered by a single comprehensive CPT code.

unconfirmed conditions   Diseases or diagnosis(ies) identified by a physician in the health record documentation as possible, probable, or likely but not confirmed as a final diagnosis(ies).

uniform hospital discharge data set (UHDDS)   A data set used in inpatient coding to define principal diagnosis and principal procedure.

upcoding   The action of selecting a higher level of service or procedure code than the documentation or diagnoses support for the purpose of receiving higher reimbursement.

usual, customary, and reasonable (UCR) fees   A method used to average fee profiles to determine what is allowable for reimbursement. usual 5 a physician's average fee for a service or procedure; customary 5 the average fee for the service or procedure based on national trends rather than regional or local customs; reasonable 5 a fee that is acceptable for a service that is unusually difficult or complicated, requiring more time and effort to preform.

V codes   Codes that identify important patient history or reason for a patient seeking medical care when no diagnosis, symptoms, or signs present to be reported.

vaccine   A suspension of microorganisms that are administered to prevent illness.

various (VAR)   The patient receives the medication using various, often multiple means.

vascular families   Arterial, venous, pulmonary, portal, lymphatic.

ventricles   The two lower chambers of the heart are called the ventricles. The right ventricle is two to three times thinner in muscle tissue than the left ventricle. The greater thickness and muscle mass of the left chamber is necessary to exert enough pressure and force to propel blood into systemic circulation.

withhold   A percentage held out by the managed care organization as an incentive to keep costs, admissions, and referrals low each year. If the provider follows the plan strategy, the withhold percentage is returned with interest at a predetermined time.

Index

IMPORTANT! READ CAREFULLY: This End User License Agreement ("Agreement") sets forth the conditions by which Delmar Cengage Learning, a division of Cengage Learning Inc. ("Cengage") will make electronic access to the Delmar Cengage Learning-owned licensed content and associated media, software, documentation, printed materials, and electronic documentation contained in this package and/or made available to you via this product (the "Licensed Content"), available to you (the "End User"). BY CLICKING THE "I ACCEPT" BUTTON AND/OR OPENING THIS PACKAGE, YOU ACKNOWLEDGE THAT YOU HAVE READ ALL OF THE TERMS AND CONDITIONS, AND THAT YOU AGREE TO BE BOUND BY ITS TERMS, CONDITIONS, AND ALL APPLICABLE LAWS AND REGULATIONS GOVERNING THE USE OF THE LICENSED CONTENT.

1.0   SCOPE OF LICENSE

1.1   Licensed Content. The Licensed Content may contain portions of modifiable content ("Modifiable Content") and content which may not be modified or otherwise altered by the End User ("Non-Modifiable Content"). For purposes of this Agreement, Modifiable Content and Non-Modifiable Content may be collectively referred to herein as the "Licensed Content." All Licensed Content shall be considered Non-Modifiable Content, unless such Licensed Content is presented to the End User in a modifiable format and it is clearly indicated that modification of the Licensed Content is permitted.

1.2   Subject to the End User's compliance with the terms and conditions of this Agreement, Delmar Cengage Learning hereby grants the End User, a nontransferable, nonexclusive, limited right to access and view a single copy of the Licensed Content on a single personal computer system for noncommercial, internal, personal use only. The End User shall not (i) reproduce, copy, modify (except in the case of Modifiable Content), distribute, display, transfer, sublicense, prepare derivative work(s) based on, sell, exchange, barter or transfer, rent, lease, loan, resell, or in any other manner exploit the Licensed Content; (ii) remove, obscure, or alter any notice of Delmar Cengage Learning's intellectual property rights present on or in the Licensed Content, including, but not limited to, copyright, trademark, and/or patent notices; or (iii) disassemble, decompile, translate, reverse engineer, or otherwise reduce the Licensed Content.

2.0   TERMINATION

2.1   Delmar Cengage Learning may at any time (without prejudice to its other rights or remedies) immediately terminate this Agreement and/or suspend access to some or all of the Licensed Content, in the event that the End User does not comply with any of the terms and conditions of this Agreement. In the event of such termination by Delmar Cengage Learning, the End User shall immediately return any and all copies of the Licensed Content to Delmar Cengage Learning.

3.0   PROPRIETARY RIGHTS

3.1   The End User acknowledges that Delmar Cengage Learning owns all rights, title and interest, including, but not limited to all copyright rights therein, in and to the Licensed Content, and that the End User shall not take any action inconsistent with such ownership. The Licensed Content is protected by U.S., Canadian and other applicable copyright laws and by international treaties, including the Berne Convention and the Universal Copyright Convention. Nothing contained in this Agreement shall be construed as granting the End User any ownership rights in or to the Licensed Content.

3.2   Delmar Cengage Learning reserves the right at any time to withdraw from the Licensed Content any item or part of an item for which it no longer retains the right to publish, or which it has reasonable grounds to believe infringes copyright or is defamatory, unlawful, or otherwise objectionable.

4.0   PROTECTION AND SECURITY

4.1   The End User shall use its best efforts and take all reasonable steps to safeguard its copy of the Licensed Content to ensure that no unauthorized reproduction, publication, disclosure, modification, or distribution of the Licensed Content, in whole or in part, is made. To the extent that the End User becomes aware of any such unauthorized use of the Licensed Content, the End User shall immediately notify Delmar Cengage Learning. Notification of such violations may be made by sending an e-mail to delmar.help@cengage.com.

5.0   MISUSE OF THE LICENSED PRODUCT

5.1   In the event that the End User uses the Licensed Content in violation of this Agreement, Delmar Cengage Learning shall have the option of electing liquidated damages, which shall include all profits generated by the End User's use of the Licensed Content plus interest computed at the maximum rate permitted by law and all legal fees and other expenses incurred by Delmar Cengage Learning in enforcing its rights, plus penalties.

6.0   FEDERAL GOVERNMENT CLIENTS

6.1   Except as expressly authorized by Delmar Cengage Learning, Federal Government clients obtain only the rights specified in this Agreement and no other rights. The Government acknowledges that (i) all software and related documentation incorporated in the Licensed Content is existing commercial computer software within the meaning of FAR 27.405(b)(2); and (2) all other data delivered in whatever form, is limited rights data within the meaning of FAR 27.401. The restrictions in this section are acceptable as consistent with the Government's need for software and other data under this Agreement.

7.0   DISCLAIMER OF WARRANTIES AND LIABILITIES

7.1   Although Delmar Cengage Learning believes the Licensed Content to be reliable, Delmar Cengage Learning does not guarantee or warrant (i) any information or materials contained in or produced by the Licensed Content, (ii) the accuracy, completeness or reliability of the Licensed Content, or (iii) that the Licensed Content is free from errors or other material defects. THE LICENSED PRODUCT IS PROVIDED "AS IS," WITHOUT ANY WARRANTY OF ANY KIND AND DELMAR CENGAGE LEARNING DISCLAIMS ANY AND ALL WARRANTIES, EXPRESSED OR IMPLIED, INCLUDING, WITHOUT LIMITATION, WARRANTIES OF MERCHANTABILITY OR FITNESS OR A PARTICULAR PURPOSE. IN NO EVENT SHALL DELMAR CENGAGE LEARNING BE LIABLE FOR: INDIRECT, SPECIAL, PUNITIVE OR CONSEQUENTIAL DAMAGES INCLUDING FOR LOST PROFITS, LOST DATA, OR OTHERWISE. IN NO EVENT SHALL DELMAR CENGAGE LEARNING'S AGGREGATE LIABILITY HEREUNDER, WHETHER ARISING IN CONTRACT, TORT, STRICT LIABILITY OR OTHERWISE, EXCEED THE AMOUNT OF FEES PAID BY THE END USER HEREUNDER FOR THE LICENSE OF THE LICENSED CONTENT.

8.0   GENERAL

8.1   Entire Agreement. This Agreement shall constitute the entire Agreement between the Parties and supercedes all prior Agreements and understandings oral or written relating to the subject matter hereof.

8.2   Enhancements/Modifications of Licensed Content. From time to time, and in Delmar Cengage Learning's sole discretion, Delmar Cengage Learning may advise the End User of updates, upgrades, enhancements and/or improvements to the Licensed Content, and may permit the End User to access and use, subject to the terms and conditions of this Agreement, such modifications, upon payment of prices as may be established by Delmar Cengage Learning.

8.3   No Export. The End User shall use the Licensed Content solely in the United States and shall not transfer or export, directly or indirectly, the Licensed Content outside the United States.

8.4   Severability. If any provision of this Agreement is invalid, illegal, or unenforceable under any applicable statute or rule of law, the provision shall be deemed omitted to the extent that it is invalid, illegal, or unenforceable. In such a case, the remainder of the Agreement shall be construed in a manner as to give greatest effect to the original intention of the parties hereto.

8.5   Waiver. The waiver of any right or failure of either party to exercise in any respect any right provided in this Agreement in any instance shall not be deemed to be a waiver of such right in the future or a waiver of any other right under this Agreement.

8.6   Choice of Law/Venue. This Agreement shall be interpreted, construed, and governed by and in accordance with the laws of the State of New York, applicable to contracts executed and to be wholly preformed therein, without regard to its principles governing conflicts of law. Each party agrees that any proceeding arising out of or relating to this Agreement or the breach or threatened breach of this Agreement may be commenced and prosecuted in a court in the State and County of New York. Each party consents and submits to the nonexclusive personal jurisdiction of any court in the State and County of New York in respect of any such proceeding.

8.7   Acknowledgment. By opening this package and/or by accessing the Licensed Content on this Web site, THE END USER ACKNOWLEDGES THAT IT HAS READ THIS AGREEMENT, UNDERSTANDS IT, AND AGREES TO BE BOUND BY ITS TERMS AND CONDITIONS. IF YOU DO NOT ACCEPT THESE TERMS AND CONDITIONS, YOU MUST NOT ACCESS THE LICENSED CONTENT AND RETURN THE LICENSED PRODUCT TO DELMAR CENGAGE LEARNING (WITHIN 30 CALENDAR DAYS OF THE END USER'S PURCHASE) WITH PROOF OF PAYMENT ACCEPTABLE TO DELMAR CENGAGE LEARNING, FOR A CREDIT OR A REFUND. Should the End User have any questions/comments regarding this Agreement, please contact Delmar Cengage Learning at delmar.help@cengage.com.

StudyWare™ to Accompany Understanding Medical Coding: A Comprehensive Guide Second Edition

Minimum System Requirements

- Operating System: Microsoft Windows 98 SE, Windows 2000 or Windows XP
- Processor: Pentium PC 500 MHz or higher (750 MHz recommended)
- Memory: 64 MB of RAM (128 MB recommended)
- Screen Resolution: 800 x 600 pixels
- Color Depth: 16-bit color (thousands of colors)
- Macromedia Flash Player V7.x. The Macromedia Flash Player is free, and can be downloaded from http://www.macromedia.com

Installation Instructions

1. Insert disc into CD-ROM drive. The StudyWare™ installation program should start automatically. If it does not, go to step 2.
2. From My Computer, double-click the icon for the CD drive.
3. Double click the setup.exe file to start the program.

Technical Support

Telephone: 1-800-477-3692, 8:30 A.M.-5:30 P.M. Eastern Time
Fax: 1-518-881-1247
E-mail: delmar.help@cengage.com

StudyWare™ is a trademark used herein under license.

Microsoft® and Windows® are registered trademarks of the Microsoft Corporation.

Pentium® is a registered trademark of the Intel® Corporation.